Microsoft®

Win32™

Programmer's
Reference

VOLUME 5

Messages,
Structures,
and Macros

Microsoft
PRESS

PUBLISHED BY
Microsoft Press
A Division of Microsoft Corporation
One Microsoft Way
Redmond, Washington 98052-6399

Library of Congress Cataloging-in-Publication Data
Microsoft Win32 programmer's reference / Microsoft Corporation.
  p.   cm.
    Includes indexes.
    Contents: v. 1. Window management and graphics device interface --
v. · 2. System services, multimedia, extensions, and application
notes -- v. 3. Functions, A–G -- v. 4. Functions, H–Z -- v.
5. Messages, structures, and macros. ISBN 1-55615-515-8 (v. 1) --
ISBN 1-55615-516-6 (v. 2) -- ISBN 1-55615-517-4 (v. 3) --
ISBN 1-55615-518-2 (v. 4) -- ISBN 1-55615-519-0 (v. 5)
    1. Windows NT. 2. Computer software--Development. 3. Microsoft
Win 32. I. Microsoft Corporation.
QA76.76.O63M524 1993
005.4'469--dc20   93-15990
                                                            CIP

Printed and bound in the United States of America.

1 2 3 4 5 6 7 8 9 AG-M 8 7 6 5 4 3

Distributed to the book trade in Canada by Macmillan of Canada, a division of Canada Publishing Corporation.

Distributed to the book trade outside the United States and Canada by Penguin Books Ltd.

Penguin Books Ltd., Harmondsworth, Middlesex, England
Penguin Books Australia Ltd., Ringwood, Victoria, Australia
Penguin Books N.Z. Ltd., 182-190 Wairau Road, Auckland 10, New Zealand

British Cataloging-in-Publication Data available.

U.S. Patent No. 4974159

Document No. PC52824-0593

Contents

Introduction

The Microsoft ® Win32 ™ application programming interface (API) allows applications to exploit the power of 32-bits on the Microsoft® Windows™ family of operating systems. Applications written to the Win32 API are scalable on single and multiprocessor systems, and portable to RISC architectures. These manuals document the complete Win32 API including window management, graphics, file I/O, threading, memory management, security and networking.

Organization of This Manual

Following are brief descriptions of the chapters and appendixes in this manual.

- Chapter 1, "Data Types," describes the keywords that define the size and meaning of parameter and return values associated with the Win32 API.
- Chapter 2, "Messages," describes formatted window messages, through which Windows communicates with applications, and notification messages, which notify a control's parent window of actions that occur within the control.
- Chapter 3, "Structures," defines the structures associated with the functions that are part of the Win32 API.
- Chapter 4, "Macros," describes the purpose and defines the parameters of macros used to help manipulate data in Windows-based applications.
- Chapter 5, "Dynamic Data Exchange Transactions," describes the transactions sent by the Dynamic Data Exchange Management Library (DDEML) to an application's dynamic data exchange (DDE) callback function. The transactions notify the application of DDE activity that affects the application.

Document Conventions

The following conventions are used throughout this manual to define syntax.

Convention	Meaning
Bold text	Denotes a term or character to be typed literally, such as a predefined data type or function name (**HWND** or **CreateWindowEx**), a command, or a command-line option (**/x**). You must type these terms exactly as shown.
Italic text	Denotes a placeholder or variable: You must provide the actual value. For example, the statement **SetCursorPos**(X, Y) requires you to substitute values for the X and Y parameters.
[ ]	Enclose optional parameters.
|	Separates an either/or choice.
...	Specifies that the preceding item may be repeated.
.	Represents an omitted portion of a sample application.

In addition, certain text conventions are used to help you understand this material.

Convention	Meaning
SMALL CAPITALS	Indicate the names of keys, key sequences, and key combinations—for example, ALT+SPACEBAR.
FULL CAPITALS	Indicate filenames and paths, most type and structure names (which are also bold), and constants.
monospace	Sets off code examples and shows syntax spacing.

C H A P T E R   1

Data Types

1.1 Data Types

Data types are keywords that define the size and meaning of parameters, return values, and members associated with the functions, messages, and structures of Microsoft Windows. The following table contains character, integer, and Boolean types; pointer types; and handles. The character, integer, and Boolean types are common to most C compilers. Most of the pointer-type names begin with a prefix of **P** or **LP**. A Windows-based application uses a handle to refer to a resource that has been loaded into memory. Windows provides access to these resources through internally maintained tables that contain individual entries for each handle. Each entry in the handle table contains the address of the resource and a means of identifying the resource type.

Type	Definition
ATOM	Atom (a reference to a character string in an atom table)
BOOL	Boolean variable (should be TRUE or FALSE)
BOOLEAN	Boolean variable (should be TRUE or FALSE)
BYTE	Byte (8 bits)
CCHAR	Windows character
CHAR	Windows character
COLORREF	Red, green, blue (RGB) color value (32 bits)
const	Variable whose value is to remain constant during execution
CRITICAL_SECTION	Critical-section object
CTRYID	Country identifier
DLGPROC	Pointer to a dialog box procedure
DWORD	Doubleword (32 bits)
ENHMFENUMPROC	Pointer to an application-defined callback function that enumerates enhanced-metafile records
ENUMRESLANGPROC	Pointer to an application-defined callback function that enumerates resource languages
ENUMRESNAMEPROC	Pointer to an application-defined callback function that enumerates resource names
ENUMRESTYPEPROC	Pointer to an application-defined callback function that enumerates resource types
FARPROC	Pointer to a callback function
FLOAT	Floating-point variable
FMORDER	Array of 32-bit font-mapper values

FONTENUMPROC	Pointer to an application-defined callback function that enumerates fonts
GOBJENUMPROC	Pointer to an application-defined callback function that enumerates graphics device interface (GDI) objects
GRAYSTRINGPROC	Pointer to an application-defined callback function that draws gray text
HACCEL	Handle of an accelerator table
HANDLE	Handle of an object
HBITMAP	Handle of a bitmap
HBRUSH	Handle of a brush
HCONV	Handle of a dynamic data exchange (DDE) conversation
HCONVLIST	Handle of a DDE conversation list
HCURSOR	Handle of a cursor
HDC	Handle of a device context (DC)
HDDEDATA	Handle of DDE data
HDLG	Handle of a dialog box
HDWP	Handle of a deferred window position structure
HENHMETAFILE	Handle of an enhanced metafile
HFILE	Handle of a file
HFONT	Handle of a font
HGDIOBJ	Handle of a GDI object
HGLOBAL	Handle of a global memory block
HHOOK	Handle of a hook
HICON	Handle of an icon
HINSTANCE	Handle of an instance
HKEY	Handle of a registry key
HLOCAL	Handle of a local memory block
HMENU	Handle of a menu
HMETAFILE	Handle of a metafile
HMIDIIN	Handle of a Musical Instrument Digital Interface (MIDI) input file
HMIDIOUT	Handle of a MIDI output file
HMMIO	Handle of a file
HOOKPROC	Pointer to an application-defined hook function
HPALETTE	Handle of a palette
HPEN	Handle of a pen

HRGN	Handle of a region
HRSRC	Handle of a resource
HSZ	Handle of a DDE string
HWAVEIN	Handle of a waveform input file
HWAVEOUT	Handle of a waveform output file
HWINSTA	Handle of a workstation
HWND	Handle of a window
INT	Signed integer
LANGID	Language identifier
LCID	Locale identifier
LCTYPE	Locale type
LINEDDAPROC	Pointer to a callback function that processes line coordinates
LONG	32-bit signed value
LP	Pointer to a null-terminated Unicode ™ string
LPARAM	32-bit message parameter
LPBOOL	Pointer to a Boolean variable
LPBYTE	Pointer to a byte
LPCCH	Pointer to a constant Windows character
LPCCHOOKPROC	Pointer to an application-defined hook function
LPCFHOOKPROC	Pointer to an application-defined hook function
LPCH	Pointer to a Windows character
LPCOLORREF	Pointer to a **COLORREF** value
LPCRITICAL_SECTION	Pointer to a critical-section object
LPCSTR	Pointer to a constant null-terminated Windows character string
LPCTSTR	Pointer to a constant null-terminated Unicode or Windows character string
LPCWCH	Pointer to a constant null-terminated Unicode character
LPCWSTR	Pointer to a constant null-terminated Unicode character string
LPDWORD	Pointer to an unsigned doubleword (32 bits)
LPFRHOOKPROC	Pointer to an application-defined hook function
LPHANDLE	Pointer to a handle
LPHANDLER_FUNCTION	Pointer to a handler function
LPHWAVEIN	Pointer to a handle to a waveform input file
LPHWAVEOUT	Pointer to a handle to a waveform output file

LPINT	Pointer to a signed integer
LPLONG	Pointer to a signed long (32 bits)
LPOFNHOOKPROC	Pointer to an application-defined hook function
LPPRINTHOOKPROC	Pointer to an application-defined hook function
LPSETUPHOOKPROC	Pointer to an application-defined hook function
LPSTR	Pointer to a null-terminated Windows character string
LPTCH	Pointer to a Unicode character or a Windows character
LPTSTR	Pointer to a null-terminated Windows or Unicode character string
LRESULT	Signed result of message processing
LPVOID	Pointer to any type
LPWCH	Pointer to a Unicode character
LPWORD	Pointer to an unsigned word (16 bits)
LPWSTR	Pointer to a null-terminated Unicode character string
LUID	Locally unique identifier
MCIDEVICEID	Media control interface (MCI) device identifier
MFENUMPROC	Pointer to an application-defined callback function that enumerates metafile records
MMRESULT	Result of multimedia message processing
NPSTR	Pointer to a null-terminated Windows character string
NWPSTR	Pointer to a null-terminated Unicode string
PBOOL	Pointer to a Boolean variable
PBOOLEAN	Pointer to a Boolean variable
PBYTE	Pointer to a byte
PCCH	Pointer to a constant Windows character
PCH	Pointer to a Windows character
PCHAR	Pointer to a Windows character
PCRITICAL_SECTION	Pointer to a critical-section object
PCSTR	Pointer to a constant null-terminated Windows character string
PCWCH	Pointer to a constant Unicode character
PCWSTR	Pointer to a constant null-terminated Unicode character string
PDWORD	Pointer to an unsigned doubleword (32 bits)

PFLOAT	Pointer to a floating-point variable
PFNCALLBACK	Pointer to a callback function
PHANDLE	Pointer to a handle
PHANDLER_ROUTINE	Pointer to a handler routine
PHKEY	Pointer to a registry key
PINT	Pointer to a signed integer
PLONG	Pointer to a signed long (32 bits)
PLUID	Pointer to a locally unique identifier (LUID)
PROPENUMPROC	Pointer to an application-defined callback function that enumerates window properties
PSHORT	Pointer to a signed short (16 bits)
PSID	Pointer to a security identifier (SID)
PSTR	Pointer to a null-terminated Windows character string
PSZ	Pointer to a null-terminated Windows character string
PTCH	Pointer to a Windows or Unicode character
PTCHAR	Pointer to a Windows or Unicode character
PTSTR	Pointer to a null-terminated Windows or Unicode character string
PUCHAR	Pointer to an unsigned Windows character
PUINT	Pointer to an unsigned integer
PULONG	Pointer to an unsigned long (32 bits)
PUSHORT	Pointer to an unsigned short (16 bits)
PVOID	Pointer to any type
PWCH	Pointer to a Unicode character
PWCHAR	Pointer to a Unicode character
PWORD	Pointer to an unsigned word (16 bits)
PWSTR	Pointer to a null-terminated Unicode character string
REGSAM	Security access mask for registry key
SC_HANDLE	Handle of a service
SERVICE_STATUS_HANDLE	Handle of a service status value
SHORT	Short integer
SPHANDLE	Pointer to a handle
TCHAR	Unicode character or Windows character
TIMERPROC	Pointer to an application-defined timer callback function

UCHAR	Unsigned Windows character
UINT	Unsigned integer
ULONG	Unsigned long integer (32 bits)
USHORT	Unsigned short integer (16 bits)
VOID	Any type
WCHAR	Unicode character
WNDENUMPROC	Pointer to an application-defined callback function that enumerates windows
WNDPROC	Pointer to an application-defined window procedure
WORD	Unsigned word (16 bits)
WPARAM	32-bit message parameter
YIELDPROC	Pointer to a yield callback function

CHAPTER 2

Messages

BM_GETCHECK

```
BM_GETCHECK
wParam = 0;     /* not used, must be zero */
lParam = 0;     /* not used, must be zero */
```

An application sends a BM_GETCHECK message to retrieve the check state of a radio button or check box.

Parameters

This message has no parameters.

Return Value

The return value from a button created with the BS_AUTOCHECKBOX, BS_AUTORADIOBUTTON, BS_AUTO3STATE, BS_CHECKBOX, BS_RADIOBUTTON, or BS_3STATE style can be one of the following:

Value	Meaning
0	Button state is unchecked.
1	Button state is checked.
2	Button state is indeterminate (applies only if the button has the BS_3STATE or BS_AUTO3STATE style).

If the button has any other style, the return value is 0.

See Also

BM_GETSTATE, BM_SETCHECK

BM_GETSTATE

```
BM_GETSTATE
wParam = 0;     /* not used, must be zero */
lParam = 0;     /* not used, must be zero */
```

An application sends a BM_GETSTATE message to determine the state of a button or check box.

Parameters

This message has no parameters.

Return Value

The return value specifies the current state of the button. You can use the following bitmasks to extract information about the state:

Value	Meaning
0x0003	Specifies the check state (radio buttons and check boxes only). A value of 0 indicates the button is unchecked. A value of 1 indicates the button is checked. A radio button is checked when it contains a dot; a check box is checked when it contains an X. A value of 2 indicates the check state is indeterminate (three-state check boxes only). The state of a three-state check box is indeterminate when it is grayed.
0x0004	Specifies the highlight state. A nonzero value indicates that the button is highlighted. A button is highlighted when the user presses and holds the left mouse button. The highlighting is removed when the user releases the mouse button.
0x0008	Specifies the focus state. A nonzero value indicates that the button has the keyboard focus.

See Also   BM_GETCHECK, BM_SETSTATE

BM_SETCHECK

```
BM_SETCHECK
wParam = (WPARAM) fCheck; /* check state           */
lParam = 0;               /* not used, must be zero */
```

An application sends a BM_SETCHECK message to set the check state of a radio button or check box.

Parameters

fCheck
Value of *wParam*. Specifies the check state. This parameter can be one of the following values:

Value	Meaning
0	Set the button state to unchecked.
1	Set the button state to checked.
2	Set the button state to grayed. This value can be used only if the button has the BS_3STATE or BS_AUTO3STATE style.

Return Value   This message always returns zero.

Comments   The BM_SETCHECK message has no effect on push buttons.

See Also   BM_GETCHECK, BM_GETSTATE, BM_SETSTATE

BM_SETSTATE

```
BM_SETSTATE
wParam = (WPARAM) fState;    /* highlight state        */
lParam = 0;                  /* not used, must be zero */
```

An application sends a BM_SETSTATE message to change the highlight state of a button.

Parameters   *fState*
Value of *wParam*. Specifies whether the button is to be highlighted. A value of TRUE highlights the button. A value of FALSE removes any highlighting.

Return Value   This message always returns zero.

Comments   Highlighting affects the exterior of a button. It has no effect on the check state of a radio button or check box.

A button is automatically highlighted when the user positions the cursor over it and presses and holds the left mouse button. The highlighting is removed when the user releases the mouse button.

See Also   BM_GETSTATE, BM_SETCHECK

BM_SETSTYLE

```
BM_SETSTYLE
wParam = (WPARAM) LOWORD(dwStyle); /* style       */
lParam = MAKELPARAM(fRedraw, 0);   /* redraw flag */
```

An application sends a BM_SETSTYLE message to change the style of a button.

Parameters   *dwStyle*
Value of *wParam*. Specifies the button style. For an explanation of button styles, see the Comments section.

fRedraw
Value of the low-order word of *lParam*. Specifies whether the button is to be redrawn. A value of TRUE redraws the button. A value of FALSE does not redraw the button.

Return Value   This message always returns zero.

Comments   Following are the available button styles:

Style	Meaning
BS_3STATE	Creates a button that is the same as a check box, except that the box can be grayed as well as checked. Use the grayed state to show that the state of the check box is not determined.
BS_AUTO3STATE	Creates a button that is the same as a three-state check box, except that the box changes its state when the user selects it. The state cycles through checked, grayed, and normal.
BS_AUTOCHECKBOX	Creates a button that is the same as a check box, except that an X appears in the check box when the user selects the box; the X disappears the next time the user selects the box.
BS_AUTORADIOBUTTON	Creates a button that is the same as a radio button, except that when the user selects it, the button automatically highlights itself and removes the selection from any other buttons in the same group.
BS_CHECKBOX	Creates a small empty square, with text displayed to its right, unless this style is combined with the BS_LEFTTEXT style.
BS_DEFPUSHBUTTON	Creates a button that has a heavy black border. The user can select this button by pressing the ENTER key. This style is useful for enabling the user to quickly select the most likely (default) option.
BS_GROUPBOX	Creates a rectangle in which other controls can be grouped. Any text associated with this style is displayed in the rectangle's upper left corner.
BS_LEFTTEXT	Places text on the left side of the radio button or check box when combined with a radio button or check box style.
BS_OWNERDRAW	Creates an owner-drawn button. The owner window receives a WM_MEASUREITEM message when the button is created and a WM_DRAWITEM message when a visual aspect of the button has changed. Do not combine the BS_OWNERDRAW style with any other button styles.
BS_PUSHBOX	Unsupported. Applications should use BS_PUSHBUTTON instead.
BS_PUSHBUTTON	Creates a push button that posts a WM_COMMAND message to the owner window when the user selects the button.
BS_RADIOBUTTON	Creates a small circle that has text displayed to its right, unless this style is combined with the BS_LEFTTEXT style. Use radio buttons for groups of related but mutually exclusive choices.

BS_USERBUTTON   Obsolete. Applications should use
                                       BS_OWNERDRAW instead.

BN_CLICKED

```
BN_CLICKED
idButton = (int) LOWORD(wParam);    /* identifier of button */
hwndButton = (HWND) lParam;         /* handle of button     */
```

The BN_CLICKED notification message is sent when the user clicks a mouse
button. The parent window of the button receives this notification message
through the WM_COMMAND message. Unlike the other button notification
messages, this message is intended for applications written for any version of
Windows.

Comments   A disabled button does not send a BN_CLICKED notification message to its
                      parent window.

See Also   WM_COMMAND

BN_DISABLE

```
BN_DISABLE
```

The BN_DISABLE notification message is sent when a button is disabled. The
parent window of the button receives this notification message through the
WM_COMMAND message. This notification is provided for compatibility with
applications written for versions of Windows earlier than version 3.0. New
applications should use the BS_OWNERDRAW button style and the
DRAWITEMSTRUCT structure for this task.

See Also   WM_COMMAND, WM_DRAWITEM

BN_DOUBLECLICKED

BN_DOUBLECLICKED

The BN_DOUBLECLICKED notification message is sent when the user double-clicks a mouse button. The parent window of the button receives this notification message through the WM_COMMAND message. This notification is provided for compatibility with applications written for versions of Windows earlier than version 3.0. New applications should use the BS_OWNERDRAW button style and the **DRAWITEMSTRUCT** structure for this task.

Comments   This notification message applies only to buttons with the BS_RADIOBUTTON and BS_OWNERDRAW styles.

See Also   WM_COMMAND, WM_DRAWITEM

BN_HILITE

BN_HILITE

The BN_HILITE notification message is sent when the user highlights a button. The parent window of the button receives this notification message through the WM_COMMAND message. This notification is provided for compatibility with applications written for versions of Windows earlier than version 3.0. New applications should use the BS_OWNERDRAW button style and the **DRAWITEMSTRUCT** structure for this task.

See Also   BN_UNHILITE WM_COMMAND, WM_DRAWITEM

BN_PAINT

BN_PAINT

The BN_PAINT notification message is sent when a button should be painted. The parent window of the button receives this notification message through the WM_COMMAND message. This notification is provided for compatibility with applications written for versions of Windows earlier than version 3.0. New applications should use the BS_OWNERDRAW button style and the **DRAWITEMSTRUCT** structure for this task.

See Also   WM_COMMAND, WM_DRAWITEM

BN_UNHILITE

BN_HILITE

The BN_UNHILITE notification message is sent when the highlight should be removed from a button. The parent window of the button receives this notification message through the WM_COMMAND message. This notification is provided for compatibility with applications written for versions of Windows earlier than version 3.0. New applications should use the BS_OWNERDRAW button style and the **DRAWITEMSTRUCT** structure for this task.

See Also   BN_HILITE, WM_COMMAND, WM_DRAWITEM

CB_ADDSTRING   `Unicode`

```
CB_ADDSTRING
wParam = 0;                              /* not used, must be zero   */
lParam = (LPARAM) (LPCSTR) lpsz;         /* address of string to add */
```

An application sends a CB_ADDSTRING message to add a string to the list box of a combo box. If the combo box does not have the CBS_SORT style, the string is added to the end of the list. Otherwise, the string is inserted into the list, and the list is sorted.

Parameters   *lpsz*
                      Value of *lParam*. Points to the null-terminated string to be added. If you create the combo box with an owner-drawn style but without the CBS_HASSTRINGS style, the value of the *lpsz* parameter is stored rather than the string it would otherwise point to.

Return Value   The return value is the zero-based index to the string in the list box of the combo box. If an error occurs, the return value is CB_ERR. If insufficient space is available to store the new string, it is CB_ERRSPACE.

Comments   If you create an owner-drawn combo box with the CBS_SORT style but without the CBS_HASSTRINGS style, the WM_COMPAREITEM message is sent one or more times to the owner of the combo box so the new item can be properly placed in the list.

To insert a string at a specific location within the list, use the CB_INSERTSTRING message.

See Also   CB_DIR, CB_INSERTSTRING, WM_COMPAREITEM

CB_DELETESTRING

```
CB_DELETESTRING
wParam = (WPARAM) index;   /* item to delete        */
lParam = 0;                /* not used, must be zero */
```

An application sends a CB_DELETESTRING message to delete a string in the list box of a combo box.

Parameters   *index*
    Value of *wParam*. Specifies the zero-based index of the string to delete.

Return Value   The return value is a count of the strings remaining in the list. If the *index* parameter specifies an index greater than the number of items in the list, the return value is CB_ERR.

Comments   If you create the combo box with an owner-draw style but without the CBS_HASSTRINGS style, Windows sends a WM_DELETEITEM message to the owner of the combo box so the application can free any additional data associated with the item.

See Also   CB_RESETCONTENT, WM_DELETEITEM

CB_DIR

Unicode

```
CB_DIR
wParam = (WPARAM) (UINT) uAttrs;          /* file attributes    */
lParam = (LPARAM) (LPCTSTR) lpszFileSpec; /* address of filename */
```

An application sends a CB_DIR message to add a list of file names to the list box of a combo box.

Parameters   *uAttrs*
    Value of *wParam*. Specifies the attributes of the files to be added to the list box. It can be any combination of the following values:

Value	Description
DDL_ARCHIVE	Includes archived files.

DDL_DIRECTORY	Includes subdirectories. Subdirectory names are enclosed in square brackets ([ ]).
DDL_DRIVES	Includes drives. Drives are listed in the form [-*x*-], where *x* is the drive letter.
DDL_EXCLUSIVE	Includes only files with the specified attributes. By default, read-write files are listed even if DDL_READWRITE is not specified.
DDL_HIDDEN	Includes hidden files.
DDL_READONLY	Includes read-only files.
DDL_READWRITE	Includes read-write files with no additional attributes.
DDL_SYSTEM	Includes system files.

lpszFileSpec
Value of *lParam*. Points to the null-terminated string that specifies the filename to add to the list. If the filename contains any wildcards (for example, *.*), all files that match and have the attributes specified by the *uAttrs* parameter are added to the list.

Return Value   The return value is the zero-based index of the last filename added to the list. If an error occurs, the return value is CB_ERR. If insufficient space is available to store the new strings, it is CB_ERRSPACE.

See Also   **DlgDirList**, **DlgDirListComboBox**, CB_ADDSTRING, CB_INSERTSTRING

CB_FINDSTRING   `Unicode`

```
CB_FINDSTRING
wParam = (WPARAM) indexStart;          /* item before start of search */
lParam = (LPARAM) (LPCSTR) lpszFind; /* prefix string address      */
```

An application sends a CB_FINDSTRING message to search the list box of a combo box for an item beginning with the characters in a specified string.

Parameters   *indexStart*
Value of *wParam*. Specifies the zero-based index of the item preceding the first item to be searched. When the search reaches the bottom of the list box, it continues from the top of the list box back to the item specified by the *indexStart* parameter. If *indexStart* is –1, the entire list box is searched from the beginning.

lpszFind
Value of *lParam*. Points to the null-terminated string that contains the prefix to search for. The search is not case sensitive, so this string can contain any combination of uppercase and lowercase letters.

Return Value   The return value is the zero-based index of the matching item. If the search is unsuccessful, it is CB_ERR.

Comments   If you create the combo box with an owner-drawn style but without the CBS_HASSTRINGS style, what the CB_FINDSTRING message does depend on whether your application uses the CBS_SORT style. If you use the CBS_SORT style, WM_COMPAREITEM messages are sent to the owner of the combo box to determine which item matches the specified string. The CB_FINDSTRING message searches for a list item that matches the value of the *lpszFind* parameter.

See Also   CB_FINDSTRINGEXACT, CB_SELECTSTRING, CB_SETCURSEL, WM_COMPAREITEM

CB_FINDSTRINGEXACT

```
CB_FINDSTRINGEXACT
wParam = (WPARAM) indexStart;        /* item before start of search */
lParam = (LPARAM)(LPCSTR)lpszFind; /* address of prefix string    */
```

An application sends a CB_FINDSTRINGEXACT message to find the first list box string in a combo box that matches the string specified in the *lpszFind* parameter.

Parameters   *indexStart*
Value of *wParam*. Specifies the zero-based index of the item preceding the first item to be searched. When the search reaches the bottom of the list box, it continues from the top of the list box back to the item specified by the *indexStart* parameter. If *indexStart* is –1, the entire list box is searched from the beginning.

lpszFind
Value of *lParam*. Points to the null-terminated string to search for. This string can contain a complete filename, including the extension. The search is not case-sensitive, so this string can contain any combination of uppercase and lowercase letters.

Return Value   The return value is the zero-based index of the matching item. If the search is unsuccessful, it is CB_ERR.

Comments   If you create the combo box with an owner-drawn style but without the CBS_HASSTRINGS style, what the CB_FINDSTRINGEXACT message does depends on whether your application uses the CBS_SORT style. If you use the CBS_SORT style, WM_COMPAREITEM messages are sent to the owner of the combo box to determine which item matches the specified string. If you do not use the CBS_SORT style, the CB_FINDSTRINGEXACT message searches for a list item that matches the value of the *lpszFind* parameter.

See Also   CB_FINDSTRING, CB_SELECTSTRING, WM_COMPAREITEM

CB_GETCOUNT

```
CB_GETCOUNT
wParam = 0;      /* not used, must be zero */
lParam = 0;      /* not used, must be zero */
```

An application sends a CB_GETCOUNT message to retrieve the number of items in the list box of a combo box.

Parameters   This message has no parameters.

Return Value   The return value is the number of items in the list box. If an error occurs, it is CB_ERR.

Comments   The index is zero-based, so the returned count is one greater than the index value of the last item.

CB_GETCURSEL

```
CB_GETCURSEL
wParam = 0;      /* not used, must be zero */
lParam = 0;      /* not used, must be zero */
```

An application sends a CB_GETCURSEL message to retrieve the index of the currently selected item, if any, in the list box of a combo box.

Parameters   This message has no parameters.

Return Value   The return value is the zero-based index of the currently selected item. If no item is selected, it is CB_ERR.

See Also   CB_SELECTSTRING, CB_SETCURSEL

CB_GETDROPPEDCONTROLRECT

```
CB_GETDROPPEDCONTROLRECT
wParam = 0;                            /* not used, must be zero   */
lParam = (LPARAM) (RECT FAR*) lprc; /* address of RECT structure */
```

An application sends a CB_GETDROPPEDCONTROLRECT message to retrieve the screen coordinates of the drop-down list box of a combo box.

Parameters

lprc

Value of *lParam*. Points to the **RECT** structure that is to receive the coordinates. The **RECT** structure has the following form:

```
typedef struct tagRECT {      /* rc */
    LONG left;
    LONG top;
    LONG right;
    LONG bottom;
} RECT;
```

For a full description of this structure, see Chapter 3, "Structures."

Return Value   This message always returns CB_OKAY.

CB_GETDROPPEDSTATE

```
CB_GETDROPPEDSTATE
wParam = 0;    /* not used, must be zero */
lParam = 0;    /* not used, must be zero */
```

An application sends a CB_GETDROPPEDSTATE message to determine whether the list box of a combo box is dropped down.

Parameters   This message has no parameters.

Return Value   If the list box is visible, the return value is TRUE; otherwise, it is FALSE.

See Also   CB_SHOWDROPDOWN

CB_GETEDITSEL

```
CB_GETEDITSEL
wParam = (WPARAM) (LPDWORD) lpdwStart; /* receives starting pos. */
lParam = (LPARAM) (LPDWORD) lpdwEnd;   /* receives ending pos.   */
```

An application sends a CB_GETEDITSEL message to get the starting and ending character positions of the current selection in the edit control of a combo box.

Parameters
lpdwStart
Value of *wParam*. Points to a 32-bit value that receives the starting position of the selection. This parameter can be set to NULL.

lpdwEnd
Value of *lParam*. Points to a 32-bit value that receives the ending position of the selection. This parameter can be set to NULL.

Return Value
The return value is a zero-based 32-bit value with the starting position of the selection in the low-order word and with the ending position of the first character after the last selected character in the high-order word.

See Also
CB_SETEDITSEL

CB_GETEXTENDEDUI

```
CB_GETEXTENDEDUI
wParam = 0;    /* not used, must be zero */
lParam = 0;    /* not used, must be zero */
```

An application sends a CB_GETEXTENDEDUI message to determine whether a combo box has the default user interface or the extended user interface.

Parameters
This message has no parameters.

Return Value
If the combo box has the extended user interface, the return value is TRUE; otherwise, it is FALSE.

Comments
By default, the F4 key opens or closes the list and the DOWN ARROW changes the current selection. In a combo box with the extended user interface, the F4 key is disabled and pressing the DOWN ARROW key opens the drop-down list.

See Also
CB_SETEXTENDEDUI

CB_GETITEMDATA

```
CB_GETITEMDATA
wParam = (WPARAM) index;  /* item index          */
lParam = 0;               /* not used, must be zero */
```

An application sends a CB_GETITEMDATA message to a combo box to retrieve the application-supplied 32-bit value associated with the specified item in the combo box.

Parameters   *index*
Value of *wParam*. Specifies the zero-based index of the item.

Return Value   The return value is the 32-bit value associated with the item. If an error occurs, it is CB_ERR.

If the item is in an owner-drawn combo box created without the CBS_HASSTRINGS style, the return value is the 32-bit value contained in the *lParam* parameter of the CB_ADDSTRING or CB_INSERTSTRING message that added the item to the combo box. If the CBS_HASSTRINGS style was not used, the return value is the *lParam* parameter contained in a CB_SETITEMDATA message.

See Also   CB_ADDSTRING, CB_INSERTSTRING, CB_SETITEMDATA

CB_GETITEMHEIGHT

```
CB_GETITEMHEIGHT
wParam = (WPARAM) index;  /* item index          */
lParam = 0;               /* not used, must be zero */
```

An application sends a CB_GETITEMHEIGHT message to determine the height of list items or the selection field in a combo box.

Parameters   *index*
Value of *wParam*. Specifies the component of the combo box whose height is to be retrieved.

This parameter must be –1 to retrieve the height of the selection field. It must be zero to retrieve the height of list items, unless the combo box has the CBS_OWNERDRAWVARIABLE style. In that case, the *index* parameter is the zero-based index of a specific list item.

Return Value   The return value is the height, in pixels, of the list items in a combo box. If the combo box has the CBS_OWNERDRAWVARIABLE style, it is is the height of the item specified by the *index* parameter. If *index* is –1, the return value is the height of the edit control (or static-text) portion of the combo box. If an error occurs, the return value is CB_ERR.

See Also   CB_SETITEMHEIGHT, WM_MEASUREITEM

CB_GETLBTEXT   `Unicode`

```
CB_GETLBTEXT
wParam = (WPARAM) index;                /* item index        */
lParam = (LPARAM) (LPCSTR) lpszBuffer;  /* address of buffer */
```

An application sends a CB_GETLBTEXT message to retrieve a string from the list of a combo box.

Parameters   *index*
    Value of *wParam*. Specifies the zero-based index of the string to retrieve.

    lpszBuffer
    Value of *lParam*. Points to the buffer that receives the string. The buffer must have sufficient space for the string and a terminating null character. You can send a CB_GETLBTEXTLEN message prior to the CB_GETLBTEXT message to retrieve the length, in bytes, of the string.

Return Value   The return value is the length of the string, in bytes, excluding the terminating null character. If the *index* parameter does not specify a valid index, the return value is CB_ERR.

Comments   If you create the combo box with an owner-drawn style but without the CBS_HASSTRINGS style, the buffer pointed to by the *lpszBuffer* parameter of the message receives the 32-bit value associated with the item.

See Also   CB_GETLBTEXTLEN

CB_GETLBTEXTLEN

```
CB_GETLBTEXTLEN
wParam = (WPARAM) index; /* item index            */
lParam = 0;              /* not used, must be zero */
```

An application sends a CB_GETLBTEXTLEN message to retrieve the length, in characters, of a string in the list of a combo box.

Parameters   *index*
Value of *wParam*. Specifies the zero-based index of the string.

Return Value   The return value is the length of the string, in characters, excluding the terminating null character. If the *index* parameter does not specify a valid index, the return value is CB_ERR.

See Also   CB_GETLBTEXT

CB_GETLOCALE

```
CB_GETLOCALE
wParam = 0; /* not used, must be zero */
lParam = 0; /* not used, must be zero */
```

An application sends a CB_GETLOCALE message to retrieve the current locale of the combo box. The locale is used to determine the correct sorting order of displayed text for combo boxes with the CBS_SORT style and text added by using the CB_ADDSTRING message.

Parameters   This message has no parameters.

Return Value   The return value is a 32-bit value that specifies the current locale of the combo box. The high word contains the country code and the low word contains the language identifier.

Comments   The language identifier is made up of a sublanguage identifier and a primary language identifier. The **PRIMARYLANGID** macro obtains the primary language identifier and the **SUBLANGID** macro obtains the sublanguage identifier.

See Also   CB_ADDSTRING, CB_SETLOCALE

CB_INSERTSTRING

Unicode

```
CB_INSERTSTRING
wParam = (WPARAM) index;        /* item index           */
lParam = (LPARAM) (LPCSTR) lpsz; /* address of string to insert */
```

An application sends a CB_INSERTSTRING message to insert a string into the list box of a combo box. Unlike the CB_ADDSTRING message, the CB_INSERTSTRING message does not cause a list with the CBS_SORT style to be sorted.

Parameters

index
Value of *wParam*. Specifies the zero-based index of the position at which to insert the string. If this parameter is –1, the string is added to the end of the list.

lpsz
Value of *lParam*. Points to the null-terminated string to be inserted. If you create the combo box with an owner-drawn style but without the CBS_HASSTRINGS style, the value of the *lpsz* parameter is stored rather than the string it would otherwise point to.

Return Value

The return value is the index of the position at which the string was inserted. If an error occurs, the return value is CB_ERR. If there is insufficient space available to store the new string, it is CB_ERRSPACE.

See Also

CB_ADDSTRING, CB_INSERTSTRING, CB_DIR

CB_LIMITTEXT

```
CB_LIMITTEXT
wParam = (WPARAM) cchLimit;    /* maximum number of characters */
lParam = 0;                    /* not used, must be zero       */
```

An application sends a CB_LIMITTEXT message to limit the length of the text the user may type into the edit control of a combo box.

Parameters

cchLimit
Value of *wParam*. Specifies the maximum number of characters the user can enter. If this parameter is zero, the text length is set to 0x7FFFFFFE characters.

Return Value

The return value is always TRUE.

Comments

If the combo box does not have the CBS_AUTOHSCROLL style, setting the text limit to be larger than the size of the edit control has no effect.

The CB_LIMITTEXT message limits only the text the user can enter. It has no effect on any text already in the edit control when the message is sent, nor does it affect the length of the text copied to the edit control when a string in the list box is selected.

The default limit to the text a user can enter in the edit control is 30,000 characters.

CB_RESETCONTENT

```
CB_RESETCONTENT
wParam = 0;        /* not used, must be zero */
lParam = 0;        /* not used, must be zero */
```

An application sends a CB_RESETCONTENT message to remove all items from the list box and edit control of a combo box.

Parameters   This message has no parameters.

Return Value   This message always returns CB_OKAY.

Comments   If you create the combo box with an owner-drawn style but without the CBS_HASSTRINGS style, the owner of the combo box receives a WM_DELETEITEM message for each item in the combo box.

See Also   CB_DELETESTRING, WM_DELETEITEM

CB_SELECTSTRING   **Unicode**

```
CB_SELECTSTRING
wParam = (WPARAM) indexStart;          /* item before first selection */
lParam = (LPARAM) (LPCSTR) lpszSelect; /* addr. of prefix string      */
```

An application sends a CB_SELECTSTRING message to search the list of a combo box for an item that begins with the characters in a specified string. If a matching item is found, it is selected and copied to the edit control.

Parameters   *indexStart*
            Value of *wParam*. Specifies the zero-based index of the item preceding the first item to be searched. When the search reaches the bottom of the list, it continues from the top of the list back to the item specified by the *indexStart* parameter. If *indexStart* is –1, the entire list is searched from the beginning.

            lpszSelect
            Value of *lParam*. Points to the null-terminated string that contains the prefix to search for. The search is not case sensitive so this string can contain any combination of uppercase and lowercase letters.

Return Value	If the string is found, the return value is the index of the selected item. If the search is unsuccessful, the return value is CB_ERR and the current selection is not changed.
Comments	A string is selected only if the characters from the starting point match the characters in the prefix string.
	If you create the combo box with an owner-drawn style but without the CBS_HASSTRINGS style, what the CB_SELECTSTRING message does depends on whether you use the CBS_SORT style. If the CBS_SORT style is used, the system sends WM_COMPAREITEM messages to the owner of the combo box to determine which item matches the specified string. If you do not use the CBS_SORT style, CB_SELECTSTRING attempts to match the doubleword value against the value of the *lpszFind* parameter.
See Also	CB_FINDSTRING, CB_FINDSTRINGEXACT, CB_SETCURSEL, WM_COMPAREITEM

CB_SETCURSEL

```
CB_SETCURSEL
wParam = (WPARAM) index;   /* item index              */
lParam = 0;                /* not used, must be zero  */
```

An application sends a CB_SETCURSEL message to select a string in the list of a combo box. If necessary, the list scrolls the string into view. The text in the edit control of the combo box changes to reflect the new selection and any previous selection in the list is removed.

Parameters	*index*
	Value of *wParam*. Specifies the zero-based index of the string to select. If the *index* parameter is –1, any current selection in the list is removed and the edit control is cleared.
Return Value	If the message is successful, the return value is the index of the item selected. If the *index* parameter is greater than the number of items in the list or if *index* is set to –1, the return value is CB_ERR and the selection is cleared.
See Also	CB_FINDSTRING, CB_GETCURSEL, CB_SELECTSTRING

CB_SETEDITSEL

```
CB_SETEDITSEL
wParam = 0;                               /* not used, must be zero */
lParam = MAKELPARAM((ichStart), (ichEnd);  /* start and end pos     */
```

An application sends a CB_SETEDITSEL message to select characters in the edit control of a combo box.

Parameters

ichStart

Value of the low-order word of *lParam*. Specifies the starting position. If this parameter is set to –1, the selection, if any, is removed.

ichEnd

Value of the high-order word of *lParam*. Specifies the ending position. If this parameter is set to –1, all text from the starting position to the last character in the edit control is selected.

Return Value

If the message succeeds, the return value is TRUE. If the message is sent to a combo box with the CBS_DROPDOWNLIST style, it is CB_ERR.

Comments

The positions are zero-based. The first character of the edit control is in the zero position. The first character after the last selected character is in the ending position. For example, to select the first four characters of the edit control, use a starting position of 0 and an ending position of 4.

See Also

CB_GETEDITSEL

CB_SETEXTENDEDUI

```
CB_SETEXTENDEDUI
wParam = (WPARAM) (BOOL) fExtended;    /* extended UI flag      */
lParam = 0;                           /* not used, must be zero */
```

An application sends a CB_SETEXTENDEDUI message to select either the default user interface or the extended user interface for a combo box that has the CBS_DROPDOWN or CBS_DROPDOWNLIST style.

Parameters

fExtended

Value of *wParam*. Specifies whether the combo box uses the extended user interface or the default user interface. A value of TRUE selects the extended user interface; a value of FALSE selects the standard user interface.

Return Value   If the operation succeeds, the return value is CB_OKAY. If an error occurs, it is CB_ERR.

Comments   By default, the F4 key opens or closes the list and the DOWN ARROW changes the current selection. In the extended user interface, the F4 key is disabled and the DOWN ARROW key opens the drop-down list.

See Also   CB_GETEXTENDEDUI

CB_SETITEMDATA

```
CB_SETITEMDATA
wParam = (WPARAM) index;          /* item index */
lParam = (LPARAM) (DWORD) dwData;    /* item data  */
```

An application sends a CB_SETITEMDATA message to set the 32-bit value associated with the specified item in a combo box.

Parameters   *index*
    Value of *wParam*. Specifies the item's zero-based index.

dwData
    Value of *lParam*. Specifies the new value to be associated with the item.

Return Value   If an error occurs, the return value is CB_ERR.

Comments   If the specified item is in an owner-drawn combo box created without the CBS_HASSTRINGS style, this message replaces the 32-bit value in the *lParam* parameter of the CB_ADDSTRING or CB_INSERTSTRING message that added the item to the combo box.

See Also   CB_ADDSTRING, CB_GETITEMDATA, CB_INSERTSTRING

CB_SETITEMHEIGHT

```
CB_SETITEMHEIGHT
wParam = (WPARAM) index;          /* item index  */
lParam = (LPARAM) (int) height;   /* item height */
```

An application sends a CB_SETITEMHEIGHT message to set the height of list items or the selection field in a combo box.

Parameters	*index*
	Value of *wParam*. Specifies the component of the combo box for which to set the height.
	This parameter must be −1 to set the height of the selection field. It must be zero to set the height of list items, unless the combo box has the CBS_OWNERDRAWVARIABLE style. In that case, the *index* parameter is the zero-based index of a specific list item.
	height
	Value of *lParam*. Specifies the height, in pixels, of the combo box component identified by *index*.
Return Value	If the index or height is invalid, the return value is CB_ERR.
Comments	The selection field height in a combo box is set independently of the height of the list items. An application must ensure that the height of the selection field is not smaller than the height of a particular list item.
See Also	CB_GETITEMHEIGHT, WM_MEASUREITEM

CB_SETLOCALE

```
CB_SETLOCALE
wParam = (WPARAM) (WORD) wLocaleID; /* locale identifier     */
lParam = 0;                        /* not used, must be zero */
```

An application sends a CB_SETLOCALE message to set the current locale of the combo box. If the combo box has the CBS_SORT style and strings are added using CB_ADDSTRING, the locale of a combo box affects how list items are sorted.

Parameters	*wLocaleID*
	Value of *wParam*. Specifies the locale identifier for the combo box to use for sorting when adding text.
Return Value	The return value is the previous locale identifier. If *wParam* specifies a locale not installed on the system, the return value is CB_ERR and the current combo box locale is not changed.
Comments	Use the **MAKELCID** macro to construct a locale identifier and the **MAKELANGID** macro to construct a language identifier. The language identifier is made up of a primary language identifier and a sublanguage identifier.
See Also	CB_ADDSTRING, CB_GETLOCALE

CB_SHOWDROPDOWN

```
CB_SHOWDROPDOWN
wParam = (WPARAM) (BOOL) fShow;      /* the show/hide flag    */
lParam = 0;                         /* not used, must be zero */
```

An application sends a CB_SHOWDROPDOWN message to show or hide the list box of a combo box that has the CBS_DROPDOWN or CBS_DROPDOWNLIST style.

Parameters   *fShow*
Value of *wParam*. Specifies whether the drop-down list box is to be shown or hidden. A value of TRUE shows the list box; a value of FALSE hides it.

Return Value   The return value is always TRUE.

Comments   This message has no effect on a combo box created with the CBS_SIMPLE style.

See Also   CB_GETDROPPEDSTATE

CBN_CLOSEUP

```
CBN_CLOSEUP
idComboBox = (int) LOWORD(wParam);   /* identifier of combo box */
hwndComboBox = (HWND) lParam;        /* handle of combo box     */
```

The CBN_CLOSEUP notification message is sent when the list box of a combo box has been closed. The parent window of the combo box receives this notification message through the WM_COMMAND message.

Comments   This notification message is not sent to a combo box that has the CBS_SIMPLE style.

In general, you cannot predict the order in which notifications will be sent. In particular, a CBN_SELCHANGE notification may occur either before or after a CBN_CLOSEUP notification.

See Also   CBN_DROPDOWN, CBN_SELCHANGE, WM_COMMAND

CBN_DBLCLK

```
CBN_DBLCLK
idComboBox = (int) LOWORD(wParam);   /* identifier of combo box */
hwndComboBox = (HWND) lParam;        /* handle of combo box      */
```

The CBN_DBLCLK notification message is sent when the user double-clicks a string in the list box of a combo box. The parent window of the combo box receives this notification message through the WM_COMMAND message.

Comments   This notification message occurs only for a combo box with the CBS_SIMPLE style. In a combo box with the CBS_DROPDOWN or CBS_DROPDOWNLIST style, a double-click cannot occur because a single click closes the list box.

See Also   CBN_SELCHANGE, WM_COMMAND

CBN_DROPDOWN

```
CBN_DROPDOWN
idComboBox = (int) LOWORD(wParam);   /* identifier of combo box */
hwndComboBox = (HWND) lParam;        /* handle of combo box      */
```

The CBN_DROPDOWN notification message is sent when the list box of a combo box is about to be made visible. The parent window of the combo box receives this notification message through the WM_COMMAND message.

Comments   This notification message can occur only for a combo box with the CBS_DROPDOWN or CBS_DROPDOWNLIST style.

See Also   CBN_CLOSEUP, WM_COMMAND

CBN_EDITCHANGE

```
CBN_EDITCHANGE
idComboBox = (int) LOWORD(wParam);   /* identifier of combo box */
hwndComboBox = (HWND)lParam;         /* handle of combo box      */
```

The CBN_EDITCHANGE notification message is sent after the user has taken an action that may have altered the text in the edit control portion of a combo box. Unlike the CBN_EDITUPDATE notification message, this notification message is sent after Windows updates the screen. The parent window of the combo box receives this notification message through the WM_COMMAND message.

Comments   If the combo box has the CBS_DROPDOWNLIST style, this notification message does not occur.

See Also   CBN_EDITUPDATE, WM_COMMAND

CBN_EDITUPDATE

```
CBN_EDITUPDATE
idComboBox = (int) LOWORD(wParam);   /* identifier of combo box */
hwndComboBox = (HWND) lParam;        /* handle of combo box     */
```

The CBN_EDITUPDATE notification message is sent when the edit control portion of a combo box is about to display altered text. This notification is sent after the control has formatted the text, but before it displays the text. The parent window of the combo box receives this notification message through the WM_COMMAND message.

Comments   If the combo box has the CBS_DROPDOWNLIST style, this notification message does not occur.

See Also   CBN_EDITCHANGE, WM_COMMAND

CBN_ERRSPACE

```
CBN_ERRSPACE
idComboBox = (int) LOWORD(wParam);   /* identifier of combo box */
hwndComboBox = (HWND) lParam;        /* handle of combo box     */
```

The CBN_ERRSPACE notification message is sent when a combo box cannot allocate enough memory to meet a specific request. The parent window of the combo box receives this notification message through the WM_COMMAND message.

See Also   WM_COMMAND

CBN_KILLFOCUS

```
CBN_KILLFOCUS
idComboBox = (int) LOWORD(wParam);    /* identifier of combo box */
hwndComboBox = (HWND) lParam;         /* handle of combo box      */
```

The CBN_KILLFOCUS notification message is sent when a combo box loses the keyboard focus. The parent window of the combo box receives this notification message through the WM_COMMAND message.

See Also   CBN_SETFOCUS, WM_COMMAND

CBN_SELCHANGE

```
CBN_SELCHANGE
idComboBox = (int) LOWORD(wParam);    /* identifier of combo box */
hwndComboBox = (HWND) lParam;         /* handle of combo box      */
```

The CBN_SELCHANGE notification message is sent when the selection in the list box of a combo box is about to be changed as a result of the user either clicking in the list box or changing the selection by using the arrow keys. The parent window of the combo box receives this message through the WM_COMMAND message.

See Also   CBN_DBLCLK, CBN_SETCURSEL, WM_COMMAND

CBN_SELENDCANCEL

```
CBN_SELENDCANCEL
idComboBox = (int) LOWORD(wParam);    /* identifier of combo box */
hwndComboBox = (HWND) lParam;         /* handle of combo box      */
```

The CBN_SELENDCANCEL notification is sent when the user selects an item, but then selects another control or closes the dialog box. It indicates the user's initial selection is to be ignored. The parent window of the combo box receives this notification message through the WM_COMMAND message.

Comments	In a combo box with the CBS_SIMPLE style, the CBN_SELENDCANCEL notification message is not sent. The CBN_SELENDOK notification message is sent immediately before every CBN_SELCHANGE message.
	If the WS_EX_NOPARENTNOTIFY extended window style is specified for the combo box, the CBN_SELENDCANCEL notification message is not sent.
See Also	CBN_SELENDOK, WM_COMMAND

CBN_SELENDOK

```
CBN_SELENDOK
idComboBox = (int) LOWORD(wParam);    /* identifier of combo box */
hwndComboBox = (HWND) lParam;         /* handle of combo box     */
```

The CBN_SELENDOK notification is sent when the user clicks a list item, or selects an item and then closes the list. It indicates the user's selection is to be processed. The parent window of the combo box receives this notification message through the WM_COMMAND message.

Comments	In a combo box with the CBS_SIMPLE style, the CBN_SELENDOK notification message is sent immediately before every CBN_SELCHANGE message.
	If the WS_EX_NOPARENTNOTIFY extended window style is specified for the combo box, the CBN_SELENDOK notification message is not sent.
See Also	CBN_SELENDCANCEL, WM_COMMAND

CBN_SETFOCUS

```
CBN_SETFOCUS
idComboBox = (int) LOWORD(wParam);    /* identifier of combo box */
hwndComboBox = (HWND) lParam;         /* handle of combo box     */
```

The CBN_SETFOCUS notification message is sent when a combo box receives the keyboard focus. The parent window of the combo box receives this notification message through the WM_COMMAND message.

See Also	CBN_KILLFOCUS, WM_COMMAND

CPL_DBLCLK

```
CPL_DBLCLK
uAppNum = (UINT) lParam1;    /* application number      */
lData = (LONG) lParam2;      /* application-defined value */
```

The CPL_DBLCLK message is sent to a Windows Control Panel dynamic-link library (DLL) when the user double-clicks the icon of an application supported by the DLL.

Parameters
uAppNum
Value of *lParam1*. Specifies the application number. This number must be in the range zero through one less than the value returned in response to the CPL_GETCOUNT message (CPL_GETCOUNT – 1).

lData
Value of *lParam2*. Specifies the value that the Control Panel DLL loaded into the **lData** member of the **CPLINFO** or **NEWCPLINFO** structure for the application. The DLL loads **lData** member in response to the CPL_INQUIRE or CPL_NEWINQUIRE message.

Return Value
If a Control Panel DLL processes this message successfully, the return value is zero; otherwise, it is nonzero.

Comments
In response to this message, a Control Panel DLL must display the dialog box for the application.

See Also
CPL_GETCOUNT, CPL_INQUIRE, CPL_NEWINQUIRE, CPL_SELECT

CPL_EXIT

```
CPL_EXIT
```

The CPL_EXIT message is sent once to a Windows Control Panel dynamic-link library (DLL) before Control Panel calls the **FreeLibrary** function to free the DLL.

Parameters
This function has no parameters.

Return Value
If a Control Panel DLL processes this message successfully, it should return zero.

Comments   This message is sent after the last WM_STOP message is sent.

In response to this message, a Control Panel DLL must free any memory that it has allocated and perform global-level cleanup.

See Also   CPL_STOP, **FreeLibrary**

CPL_GETCOUNT

CPL_GETCOUNT

The CPL_GETCOUNT message is sent to a Windows Control Panel dynamic-link library (DLL) to retrieve the number of applications the DLL services.

Parameters   This function has no parameters.

Return Value   A Control Panel DLL should return the number of applications it services.

Comments   This message is sent immediately after the CPL_INIT message.

See Also   CPL_INIT

CPL_INIT

CPL_INIT

The CPL_INIT message is sent to a Windows Control Panel dynamic-link library (DLL) to prompt the DLL to perform global initialization, especially memory allocation.

Parameters   This function has no parameters.

Return Value   If initialization succeeds, a Control Panel DLL should return nonzero. Otherwise, it should return zero. If the DLL returns zero, Control Panel calls the **FreeLibrary** function and ends communication with the DLL.

Comments   Because this is the only way a Control Panel DLL can signal an error condition, the DLL should allocate memory in response to this message.

This message is sent immediately after the DLL is loaded.

See Also   **FreeLibrary**

CPL_INQUIRE

```
CPL_INQUIRE
uAppNum = (UINT) lParam1;      /* application number            */
lpcpli = (LPCPLINFO) lParam2;  /* structure for application info. */
```

The CPL_INQUIRE message is sent to a Windows Control Panel dynamic-link library (DLL) to request information about an application that the DLL supports.

This message is provided for backward compatibility with Windows, version 3.1. Use the CPL_NEWINQUIRE message instead of the CPL_INQUIRE message for new applications.

Parameters
uAppNum
Value of *lParam1*. Specifies the application number. This number must be in the range zero through one less than the value returned in response to the CPL_GETCOUNT message (CPL_GETCOUNT − 1).

lpcpli
Value of *lParam2*. Points to a **CPLINFO** structure. The DLL must fill this structure with resource identifiers for the icon, short name, description, and any user-defined value associated with the application. The **CPLINFO** structure has the following form:

```
typedef struct tagCPLINFO { /* cpli */
    int  idIcon;
    int  idName;
    int  idInfo;
    LONG lData;
} CPLINFO;
```

For a full description of this structure, see Chapter 3, "Structures."

Return Value
If a Control Panel DLL processes this message successfully, it should return zero.

Comments
This message is sent once for each application serviced by the DLL. It is sent immediately after the CPL_GETCOUNT message. A DLL can perform application-level initialization when it receives this message. If the DLL must allocate memory, it should do so in response to the CPL_INIT message.

See Also
CPL_GETCOUNT, CPL_INIT, CPL_NEWINQUIRE

CPL_NEWINQUIRE

```
CPL_NEWINQUIRE
uAppNum = (UINT) lParam1;        /* application number    */
lpncpli = (LPNEWCPLINFO) lParam2; /* structure for appl. info. */
```

The CPL_NEWINQUIRE message is sent to a Windows Control Panel dynamic-link library (DLL) to request information about an application that the DLL supports.

Parameters

uAppNum
Value of *lParam1*. Specifies the application number. This number must be in the range zero through one less than the value returned in response to the CPL_GETCOUNT message (CPL_GETCOUNT − 1).

lpncpli
Value of *lParam2*. Specifies a far pointer to a **NEWCPLINFO** structure. The DLL should fill this structure with information about the application. The **CPLINFO** structure has the following form:

```
typedef struct tagNEWCPLINFO {  /* ncpli */
    DWORD dwSize;
    DWORD dwFlags;
    DWORD dwHelpContext;
    LONG  lData;
    HICON hIcon;
    char  szName[32];
    char  szInfo[64];
    char  szHelpFile[128];
} NEWCPLINFO;
```

For a full description of this structure, see Chapter 3, "Structures."

Return Value   If a Control Panel DLL processes this message successfully, it should return zero.

Comments   This message is sent once for each application serviced by the DLL. It is sent immediately after the CPL_GETCOUNT message. Upon receiving this message, a DLL can do application-level initialization. If the DLL must allocate memory, it should do so in response to the CPL_INIT message.

See Also   CPL_GETCOUNT, CPL_INIT, CPL_INQUIRE

CPL_SELECT

```
CPL_SELECT
uAppNum = (UINT) lParam1;    /* application number      */
lData = (LONG) lParam2;      /* application-defined value */
```

The CPL_SELECT message from Windows Control Panel is sent to a Control Panel dynamic-link library (DLL) when the user selects the icon of an application supported by the DLL.

Parameters   *uAppNum*
Value of *lParam1*. Specifies the application number.

lData
Value of *lParam2*. Specifies the value that the Control Panel DLL loaded into the **lData** member of the **CPLINFO** or **NEWCPLINFO** structure for the application. The DLL loads **lData** member in response to the CPL_INQUIRE or CPL_NEWINQUIRE message.

Return Value   If a Control Panel DLL processes this message successfully, it should return zero.

See Also   CPL_DBLCLK, CPL_INQUIRE, CPL_NEWINQUIRE

CPL_STOP

```
CPL_STOP
uAppNum = (UINT) lParam1;    /* application number      */
lData = (LONG) lParam2;      /* application-defined value */
```

The CPL_STOP message is sent once for each application when Windows Control Panel closes.

Parameters   *uAppNum*
Value of *lParam1*. Specifies the application number.

lData
Value of *lParam2*. Specifies the value that the Control Panel DLL loaded into the **lData** member of the **CPLINFO** or **NEWCPLINFO** structure for the application. The DLL loads **lData** member in response to the CPL_INQUIRE or CPL_NEWINQUIRE message.

Return Value	If a Control Panel DLL processes this message successfully, it should return zero.
Comments	In response to this message, a Control Panel DLL must perform application-specific cleanup.
See Also	CPL_EXIT, CPL_GETCOUNT, CPL_INQUIRE CPL_NEWINQUIRE

DM_GETDEFID

DM_GETDEFID

An application sends a DM_GETDEFID message to retrieve the identifier of the default push button control for a dialog box.

Parameters	This message has no parameters.
Return Value	If a default push button exists, the high-order word of the return value contains the value DC_HASDEFID and the low-order word contains the control identifier. Otherwise, the return value is zero.
Comments	The **DefDlgProc** function processes this message.
See Also	**DefDlgProc**, DM_SETDEFID

DM_SETDEFID

```
DM_SETDEFID
wParam = idControl; /* identifier of new default push button */
```

An application sends a DM_SETDEFID message to change the identifier of the default push button for a dialog box.

Parameters	*idControl* Value of *wParam*. Specifies the identifier of a push button control that will become the default.
Comments	This message is processed by the **DefDlgProc** function. To set the default push button, the function can send WM_GETDLGCODE and BM_SETSTYLE messages to the given control and the current default push button.
	Using the DM_SETDEFID message can result in more than one button appearing to have the default push button state. When Windows NT brings up a dialog, it draws the first push button in the dialog template with the default state border.

Sending a DM_SETDEFID message to change ,the default button will not always remove the default state border from the first push button. In these cases, the application should send a BM_SETSTYLE message to change the first push button border style.

Return Value   The return value is always TRUE.

See Also   **DefDlgProc**, BM_SETSTYLE, DM_GETDEFID, WM_GETDLGCODE

EM_CANUNDO

```
EM_CANUNDO
wParam = 0; /* not used, must be zero */
lParam = 0; /* not used, must be zero */
```

An application sends an EM_CANUNDO message to determine whether an edit-control operation can be undone; that is, whether the control can respond to the EM_UNDO message.

Parameters   This message has no parameters.

Return Value   If the edit control can correctly process the EM_UNDO message, the return value is TRUE; otherwise, it is FALSE.

See Also   EM_UNDO

EM_EMPTYUNDOBUFFER

```
EM_EMPTYUNDOBUFFER
wParam = 0; /* not used, must be zero */
lParam = 0; /* not used, must be zero */
```

An application sends an EM_EMPTYUNDOBUFFER message to reset the undo flag of an edit control. The undo flag is set whenever an operation within the edit control can be undone.

Parameters   This message has no parameters.

Return Value   This message does not return a value.

Comments   The undo flag is automatically reset whenever the edit control receives a WM_SETTEXT or EM_SETHANDLE message.

See Also   EM_CANUNDO, EM_SETHANDLE, EM_UNDO, WM_SETTEXT

EM_FMTLINES

```
EM_FMTLINES
wParam = (WPARAM) (BOOL) fAddEOL;    /* line break flag        */
lParam = 0;                         /* not used, must be zero */
```

An application sends an EM_FMTLINES message to set the inclusion flag of soft line-break characters on or off within a multiline edit control. A soft line break consists of two carriage returns and a linefeed and is inserted at the end of a line that is broken because of wordwrapping.

Parameters   *fAddEOL*
                        Value of *wParam*. Specifies whether soft-line break characters are to be inserted. A value of TRUE inserts the characters; a value of FALSE removes them.

Return Value   The return value is identical to the *fAddEOL* parameter.

Comments   This message affects only the buffer returned by the EM_GETHANDLE message and the text returned by the WM_GETTEXT message. It has no effect on the display of the text within the edit control.

                        The EM_FMTLINES message does not affect a line that ends with a hard line break. A hard line break consists of one carriage return and a linefeed.

                        Note that the size of the text changes when this message is processed.

See Also   EM_GETHANDLE, WM_GETTEXT

EM_GETFIRSTVISIBLELINE

```
EM_GETFIRSTVISIBLELINE
wParam = 0; /* not used, must be zero */
lParam = 0; /* not used, must be zero */
```

An application sends an EM_GETFIRSTVISIBLELINE message to determine the uppermost visible line in an edit control.

Parameters   This message has no parameters.

Return Value   The return value is the zero-based index of the uppermost visible line in a multiline edit control. For single-line edit controls, the return value is the zero-based index of the first visible character.

EM_GETHANDLE

```
EM_GETHANDLE
wParam = 0; /* not used, must be zero */
lParam = 0; /* not used, must be zero */
```

An application sends an EM_GETHANDLE message to retrieve a handle of the memory currently allocated for a multiline edit control's text.

Parameters   This message has no parameters.

Return Value   The return value is a memory handle identifying the buffer that holds the contents of the edit control. If an error occurs, such as sending the message to a single-line edit control, the return value is zero.

Comments   In a 16-bit Windows-based application, the handle is a local memory handle and can be used only by functions that take a local memory handle as a parameter. The application can send this message to a multiline edit control in a dialog box only if it created the dialog box with the DS_LOCALEDIT style flag set. If the DS_LOCALEDIT style is not set, the return value is still nonzero, but the return value will not be meaningful.

See Also   EM_SETHANDLE

EM_GETLINE   `Unicode`

```
EM_GETLINE
wParam = (WPARAM) line;          /* line number to retrieve    */
lParam = (LPARAM) (LPCSTR) lpch; /* address of buffer for line */
```

An application sends an EM_GETLINE message to copy a line of text from an edit control and place it in a specified buffer.

Parameters   *line*
　　　　　Value of *wParam*. Specifies the zero-based index of the line to retrieve from a multiline edit control. A value of zero specifies the topmost line. This parameter is ignored by a single-line edit control.

lpch
> Value of *lParam*. Points to the buffer that receives a copy of the line. The first word of the buffer specifies the maximum number of characters that can be copied to the buffer.

Return Value   The return value is the number of characters copied. The return value is zero if the line number specified by the *line* parameter is greater than the number of lines in the edit control.

Comments   The copied line does not contain a terminating null character.

See Also   EM_LINELENGTH, WM_GETTEXT

EM_GETLINECOUNT

```
EM_GETLINECOUNT
wParam = 0; /* not used, must be zero */
lParam = 0; /* not used, must be zero */
```

> An application sends an EM_GETLINECOUNT message to retrieve the number of lines in a multiline edit control.

Parameters   This message has no parameters.

Return Value   The return value is an integer specifying the number of lines in the multiline edit control. If no text is in the edit control, the return value is 1.

See Also   EM_GETLINE, EM_GETLINELENGTH

EM_GETMODIFY

```
EM_GETMODIFY
wParam = 0; /* not used, must be zero */
lParam = 0; /* not used, must be zero */
```

> An application sends an EM_GETMODIFY message to determine whether the contents of an edit control have been modified.

Parameters   This message has no parameters.

Return Value   If the contents of edit control have been modified, the return value is TRUE; otherwise, it is FALSE.

Comments   Windows maintains an internal flag indicating whether the contents of the edit control have been changed. This flag is cleared when the edit control is first created; alternatively, an application can send an EM_SETMODIFY message to the edit control to clear the flag.

See Also   EM_SETMODIFY

EM_GETPASSWORDCHAR

```
EM_GETPASSWORDCHAR
wParam = 0; /* not used, must be zero */
lParam = 0; /* not used, must be zero */
```

An application sends an EM_GETPASSWORDCHAR message to retrieve the password character displayed in an edit control when the user enters text.

Parameters   This message has no parameters.

Return Value   The return value specifies the character to be displayed in place of the character typed by the user. The return value is NULL if no password character exists.

Comments   If the edit control is created with the ES_PASSWORD style, the default password character is set to an asterisk (*).

See Also   EM_SETPASSWORDCHAR

EM_GETRECT

```
EM_GETRECT
wParam = 0;                        /* not used, must be zero        */
lParam (LPARAM) (LPRECT) lprc; /* address of structure for rect. */
```

An application sends an EM_GETRECT message to retrieve the formatting rectangle of an edit control. The formatting rectangle is the limiting rectangle of the text. The limiting rectangle is independent of the size of the edit-control window.

Parameters   *lprc*
                    Value of *lParam*. Points to the **RECT** structure that receives the formatting rectangle. The **RECT** structure has the following form:

```
typedef struct tagRECT {     /* rc */
    LONG left;
```

```
                    LONG top;
                    LONG right;
                    LONG bottom;
                } RECT;
```

For a full description of this structure, see Chapter 3, "Structures."

Return Value   The return value is not a meaningful value.

Comments   You can modify the formatting rectangle of a multiline edit control by using the EM_SETRECT and EM_SETRECTNP messages.

See Also   EM_SETRECT, EM_SETRECTNP

EM_GETSEL

```
EM_GETSEL
wParam = (WPARAM) (LPDWORD) lpdwStart; /* receives starting pos. */
lParam = (WPARAM) (LPDWORD) lpdwEnd;   /* receives ending pos.   */
```

An application sends an EM_GETSEL message to get the starting and ending character positions of the current selection in an edit control.

Parameters   *lpdwStart*
Value of *wParam*. Points to a 32-bit value that receives the starting position of the selection. This parameter can be NULL.

lpdwEnd
Value of *lParam*. Points to a 32-bit value that receives the position of the first nonselected character after the end of the selection. This parameter can be NULL.

Return Value   The return value is a zero-based 32-bit value with the starting position of the selection in the low-order word and the position of the first character after the last selected character in the high-order word.

See Also   EM_SETSEL

EM_GETWORDBREAKPROC

```
EM_GETWORDBREAKPROC
wParam = 0; /* not used, must be zero */
lParam = 0; /* not used, must be zero */
```

An application sends an EM_GETWORDBREAKPROC message to an edit control to retrieve the address of the current wordwrap function.

Parameters   This message has no parameters.

Return Value   The return value specifies the address of the application-defined wordwrap function. The return value is NULL if no wordwrap function exists.

Comments   A wordwrap function scans a text buffer that contains text to be sent to the display, looking for the first word that does not fit on the current display line. The wordwrap function places this word at the beginning of the next line on the display. A wordwrap function defines the point at which Windows should break a line of text for multiline edit controls, usually at a space character that separates two words.

See Also   **WordBreakProc**, EM_FMTLINES, EM_SETWORDBREAKPROC

EM_LIMITTEXT

```
EM_LIMITTEXT
wParam = (WPARAM) cchMax;   /* text length          */
lParam = 0;                 /* not used, must be zero */
```

An application sends an EM_LIMITTEXT message to limit the amount of text the user may enter into an edit control.

Parameters   *cchMax*
                    Value of *wParam*. Specifies the maximum number of characters the user can enter. If this parameter is zero, the text length is set to 0x7FFFFFFE characters for single-line edit controls or 0xFFFFFFFF for multiline edit controls.

Return Value   This message does not return a value.

Comments   The EM_LIMITTEXT message limits only the text the user can enter. It has no effect on any text already in the edit control when the message is sent, nor does it affect the length of the text copied to the edit control by the **WM_SETTEXT** message. If an application uses the **WM_SETTEXT** message to place more text into an edit control than is specified in the EM_LIMITTEXT message, the user can edit the entire contents of the edit control.

The default limit to the amount of text a user can enter in an edit control is 30,000 characters.

See Also   WM_SETTEXT

EM_LINEFROMCHAR

```
EM_LINEFROMCHAR
wParam = (WPARAM) ich;  /* character index        */
lParam = 0;             /* not used, must be zero */
```

An application sends an EM_LINEFROMCHAR message to retrieve the index of the line that contains the specified character index in a multiline edit control. A character index is the number of characters from the beginning of the edit control.

Parameters   *ich*
> Value of *wParam*. Specifies the character index of the character contained in the line whose number is to be retrieved. If the *ich* parameter is –1, either the line number of the current line (the line containing the caret) is retrieved or, if there is a selection, the line number of the line containing the beginning of the selection is retrieved.

Return Value   The return value is the zero-based line number of the line containing the character index specified by *ich*.

See Also   EM_LINEINDEX

EM_LINEINDEX

```
EM_LINEINDEX
wParam = (WPARAM) line;  /* line number            */
lParam = 0;              /* not used, must be zero */
```

An application sends an EM_LINEINDEX message to retrieve the character index of a line in a multiline edit control. The character index is the number of characters from the beginning of the edit control to the specified line.

Parameters   *line*
> Value of *wParam*. Specifies the zero-based line number. A value of –1 specifies the current line number (the line that contains the caret).

Return Value   The return value is the character index of the line specified in the *line* parameter, or it is –1 if the specified line number is greater than the number of lines in the edit control.

See Also   EM_LINEFROMCHAR

EM_LINELENGTH

```
EM_LINELENGTH
wParam = (WPARAM) ich;  /* character index        */
lParam = 0;             /* not used, must be zero */
```

An application sends an EM_LINELENGTH message to retrieve the length of a line, in characters, in an edit control.

Parameters   *ich*
                    Value of *wParam*. Specifies the character index of a character in the line whose length is to be retrieved when EM_LINELENGTH is sent to a multiline edit control. If this parameter is –1, the message returns the number of unselected characters on lines containing selected characters. For example, if the selection extended from the fourth character of one line through the eighth character from the end of the next line, the return value would be 10 (three characters on the first line and seven on the next).

Return Value   The return value is the length, in characters, of the line specified by the *ich* parameter when an EM_LINELENGTH message is sent to a multiline edit control. The return value is the length, in characters, of the text in the edit control when an EM_LINELENGTH message is sent to a single-line edit control.

Comments   Use the EM_LINEINDEX message to retrieve a character index for a given line number within a multiline edit control.

See Also   EM_LINEINDEX

EM_LINESCROLL

```
EM_LINESCROLL
wParam = (WPARAM) cxScroll; /* characters to scroll horizontally */
lParam = (LPARAM) cyScroll; /* lines to scroll vertically        */
```

An application sends an EM_LINESCROLL message to scroll the text vertically or horizontally in a multiline edit control.

Parameters	*cxScroll* Value of *wParam*. Specifies the number of characters to scroll horizontally. *cyScroll* Value of *lParam*. Specifies the number of lines to scroll vertically.
Return Value	If the message is sent to a multiline edit control, the return value is TRUE; if the message is sent to a single-line edit control, the return value is FALSE.
Comments	The edit control does not scroll vertically past the last line of text in the edit control. If the current line plus the number of lines specified by the *cyScroll* parameter exceeds the total number of lines in the edit control, the value is adjusted so that the last line of the edit control is scrolled to the top of the edit-control window. The EM_LINESCROLL message can be used to scroll horizontally past the last character of any line.

EM_REPLACESEL   `Unicode`

```
EM_REPLACESEL
wParam = 0;                                    /* not used, must be zero */
1Param = (LPARAM) (LPCTSTR) lpszReplace;       /* address of string      */
```

An application sends an EM_REPLACESEL message to replace the current selection in an edit control with the specified text.

Parameters	*lpszReplace* Value of *lParam*. Points to a null-terminated string containing the replacement text.
Return Value	This message does not return a value.
Comments	Use the EM_REPLACESEL message to replace only a portion of the text in an edit control. To replace all of the text, use the WM_SETTEXT message. If there is no current selection, the replacement text is inserted at the current location of the caret.
See Also	WM_SETTEXT

EM_SCROLLCARET

```
EM_SCROLLCARET
wParam = 0 ;    /* not used now; reserved for future use; must be zero  */
lParam = 0 ;    /* not used now; reserved for future use; must be zero */
```

An application sends an EM_SCROLLCARET message to scroll the caret into view in an edit control.

Parameters   *wParam*
                     This parameter is currently unused. It is reserved for future use. It should be set to zero.

                     lParam
                     This parameter is currently unused. It is reserved for future use. It should be set to zero.

Return Value   The return value is nonzero if the message is sent to an edit control.

Comments   In previous versions of Windows, scrolling the caret into view was done by specifying fScroll = FALSE in the EM_SETSEL message. A Win32 application should use the EM_SCROLLCARET message to scroll the caret into view.

See Also   EM_SETSEL

EM_SCROLL

```
EM_SCROLL
wParam = (WPARAM) (INT) nScroll;    /* scroll action          */
lParam = 0;                         /* not used, must be zero */
```

An application sends an EM_SCROLL message to scroll the text vertically in a multiline edit control. This message is equivalent to sending a WM_VSCROLL message to the edit control.

Parameters   *nScroll*
                     Value of *wParam*. Specifies the action the scroll bar is to take. This parameter may be one of the following values:

Value	Description
SB_LINEDOWN	Scroll down one line.
SB_LINEUP	Scroll up one line.
SB_PAGEDOWN	Scroll down one page.

SB_PAGEUP   Scroll up one page.

Return Value   If the message is successful, the high-order word of the return value is TRUE and the low-order word is the number of lines that the command scrolls. The number returned may not be the same as the actual number of lines scrolled if the scrolling moves to the beginning or the end of the text. If the *nScroll* parameter specifies an invalid value, the return value is FALSE.

Comments   An application should use the EM_LINESCROLL message to scroll to a specific line or character position.

An application should use the EM_SCROLLCARET message to scroll the caret into view.

See Also   EM_LINESCROLL, EM_SCROLLCARET WM_VSCROLL

EM_SETHANDLE

```
EM_SETHANDLE
wParam = (WPARAM) (HLOCAL) hloc; /* handle of memory buffer */
lParam = 0;                      /* not used, must be zero  */
```

An application sends an EM_SETHANDLE message to set the handle of the memory that will be used by a multiline edit control.

Parameters   *hloc*
    Value of *wParam*. Identifies the memory the edit control uses to store the currently displayed text instead of allocating its own memory. If necessary, the control reallocates this memory.

Return Value   This message does not return a value.

Comments   Before an application sets a new memory handle, it should send an EM_GETHANDLE message to retrieve the handle of the current memory buffer and should free that memory.

An edit control automatically reallocates the given buffer whenever it needs additional space for text, or it removes enough text so that additional space is no longer needed.

Sending an EM_SETHANDLE message clears the undo buffer (EM_CANUNDO returns zero) and the internal modification flag (EM_GETMODIFY returns zero). The edit control window is redrawn.

An application can send this message to a multiline edit control in a dialog box only if it has created the dialog box with the DS_LOCALEDIT style flag set.

See Also   EM_CANUNDO, EM_GETHANDLE, EM_GETMODIFY

EM_SETMODIFY

```
EM_SETMODIFY
wParam = (WPARAM) (UINT) fModified;     /* modification flag     */
lParam = 0;                             /* not used, must be zero */
```

An application sends an EM_SETMODIFY message to set or clear the modification flag for an edit control. The modification flag indicates whether the text within the edit control has been modified. It is automatically set whenever the user changes the text. An EM_GETMODIFY message can be sent to retrieve the value of the modification flag.

Parameters   *fModified*

Value of *wParam*. Specifies the new value for the modification flag. A value of TRUE indicates the text has been modified, and a value of FALSE indicates it has not been modified.

Return Value   This message does not return a value.

See Also   EM_GETMODIFY

EM_SETPASSWORDCHAR   `Unicode`

```
EM_SETPASSWORDCHAR
wParam = (WPARAM) (UINT) ch;      /* character to display   */
lParam = 0;                       /* not used, must be zero */
```

An application sends an EM_SETPASSWORDCHAR message to set or remove a password character displayed in a single-line edit control when the user types text. When a password character is set, that character is displayed in place of each character the user types.

Parameters   *ch*

Value of *wParam*. Specifies the character to be displayed in place of the character typed by the user. If this parameter is zero, the characters typed by the user are displayed.

Return Value   This message does not return a value.

Comments   When the EM_SETPASSWORDCHAR message is received by an edit control, the edit control redraws all visible characters by using the character specified by the *ch* parameter.

If the edit control is created with the ES_PASSWORD style, the default password character is set to an asterisk (*). This style is removed if an EM_SETPASSWORDCHAR message is sent with the *ch* parameter set to zero.

See Also   EM_GETPASSWORDCHAR

EM_SETREADONLY

```
EM_SETREADONLY
wParam = (WPARAM) (BOOL) fReadOnly;  /* read-only flag       */
lParam = 0L;                         /* not used, must be zero */
```

An application sends an EM_SETREADONLY message to set or remove the read-only style (ES_READONLY) of an edit control.

Parameters   *fReadOnly*
　　　　Value of *wParam*. Specifies whether to set or remove the ES_READONLY style. A value of TRUE sets the ES_READONLY style; a value of FALSE removes the ES_READONLY style.

Return Value   If the operation succeeds, the return value is nonzero; otherwise, it is zero.

Comments   When an edit control has the ES_READONLY style, the user cannot change the text within the edit control.

To determine whether an edit control has the ES_READONLY style, use the **GetWindowLong** function with the GWL_STYLE flag.

See Also   **GetWindowLong**

EM_SETRECT

```
EM_SETRECT
wParam = 0;                          /* not used, must be zero   */
lParam = (LPARAM) (LPRECT) lprc;     /* address of new rectangle */
```

An application sends an EM_SETRECT message to set the formatting rectangle of a multiline edit control. The formatting rectangle is the limiting rectangle of the text. The limiting rectangle is independent of the size of the edit control window.

When the edit control is first created, the formatting rectangle is the same as the client area of the edit control window. By using the EM_SETRECT message, an application can make the formatting rectangle larger or smaller than the edit control window.

This message is processed only by multiline edit controls.

Parameters   *lprc*

Value of *lParam*. Points to a **RECT** structure that specifies the new dimensions of the rectangle. The **RECT** structure has the following form:

```
typedef struct tagRECT {     /* rc */
    LONG left;
    LONG top;
    LONG right;
    LONG bottom;
} RECT;
```

For a full description of this structure, see Chapter 3, "Structures."

Return Value   This message does not return a value.

Comments   The EM_SETRECT message causes the text of the edit control to be redrawn. To change the size of the formatting rectangle without redrawing the text, use the EM_SETRECTNP message.

If the edit control does not have a horizontal scroll bar, and the formatting rectangle is set to be larger than the edit control window, lines of text exceeding the width of the edit control window (but smaller than the width of the formatting rectangle) are clipped instead of wrapped.

If the edit control contains a border, the formatting rectangle is reduced by the size of the border. If you are adjusting the rectangle returned by an EM_GETRECT message, you must remove the size of the border before using the rectangle with the EM_SETRECT message.

See Also   EM_GETRECT, EM_SETRECTNP

EM_SETRECTNP

```
EM_SETRECTNP
wParam = 0;                          /* not used, must be zero   */
lParam = (LPARAM) (LPRECT) lprc;     /* address of new rectangle */
```

An application sends an EM_SETRECTNP message to set the formatting rectangle of a multiline edit control. The formatting rectangle is the limiting rectangle of the text. The limiting rectangle is independent of the size of the edit control window. When the edit control is first created, the formatting rectangle is the same as the client area of the edit control window. By using the EM_SETRECTNP message, an application can make the formatting rectangle larger or smaller than the edit control window.

The EM_SETRECTNP message is identical to the EM_SETRECT message, except that the edit control window is not redrawn.

This message is processed only by multiline edit controls.

Parameters   *lprc*
     Value of *lParam*. Points to a **RECT** structure that specifies the new dimensions of the rectangle. The **RECT** structure has the following form:

```
typedef struct tagRECT {    /* rc */
    LONG left;
    LONG top;
    LONG right;
    LONG bottom;
} RECT;
```

     For a full description of this structure, see Chapter 3, "Structures."

Return Value   This message does not return a value.

See Also   EM_SETRECT

EM_SETSEL

```
EM_SETSEL
wParam = (WPARAM) (INT) nStart;    /* starting position */
lParam = (LPARAM) (INT) nEnd;      /* ending position   */
```

An application sends an EM_SETSEL message to select a range of characters in an edit control.

Parameters   *nStart*
     Value of *wParam*. Specifies the starting character position of the selection.
     nEnd
     Specifies the ending character position of the selection.

Return Value   This message does not return a value.

Comments   If the *nStart* parameter is 0 and the *nEnd* parameter is –1, all the text in the edit control is selected. If *nStart* is –1, any current selection is removed. The caret is placed at the end of the selection indicated by the greater of the two values *nEnd* and *nStart*.

In previous versions of Windows, the *wParam* parameter is a flag that is FALSE to scroll the caret into view or TRUE to omit the scrolling. A Win32 application should use the EM_SCROLLCARET message to scroll the caret into view.

In previous versions of Windows, the starting and ending positions of the selection are indicated by the low- and high-order words, respectively, of the *lParam* parameter.

See Also   EM_GETSEL, EM_REPLACESEL, EM_SCROLLCARET

EM_SETTABSTOPS

```
EM_SETTABSTOPS
wParam = (WPARAM) cTabs;              /* number of tab stops */
lParam = (LPARAM) (LPWORD) lpwTabs;  /* tab stop array      */
```

An application sends an EM_SETTABSTOPS message to set the tab stops in a multiline edit control. When text is copied to the control, any tab character in the text causes space to be generated up to the next tab stop.

This message is processed only by multiline edit controls.

Parameters   *cTabs*

Value of *wParam*. Specifies the number of tab stops contained in the *lpwTabs* parameter. If this parameter is zero, the *lpwTabs* parameter is ignored and default tab stops are set at every 32 dialog box units. If this parameter is 1, tab stops are set at every *n* dialog box units, where *n* is the distance pointed to by the *lpwTabs* parameter. If the *cTabs* parameter is greater than 1, *lpwTabs* points to an array of tab stops.

lpwTabs

Value of *lParam*. Points to an array of unsigned integers specifying the tab stops, in dialog units. If the *cTabs* parameter is 1, *lpwTabs* points to an unsigned integer containing the distance between all tab stops, in dialog box units.

Return Value   If all the tabs are set, the return value is TRUE; otherwise, it is FALSE.

Comments   The EM_SETTABSTOPS message does not automatically redraw the edit control window. If the application is changing the tab stops for text already in the edit control, it should call the **InvalidateRect** function to redraw the edit control window.

See Also   **GetDialogBaseUnits**, **InvalidateRect**

EM_SETWORDBREAK

The EM_SETWORDBREAK message is not supported. Applications that must replace the default wordwrap function of a multiline edit control with an application-defined wordwrap function should use the EM_SETWORDBREAKPROC message.

EM_SETWORDBREAKPROC

```
EM_SETWORDBREAKPROC
wParam = 0;                                    /* not used, must be zero */
lParam = (LPARAM)(EDITWORDBREAKPROC)ewbprc; /* function address      */
```

An application sends the EM_SETWORDBREAKPROC message to an edit control to replace the default wordwrap function with an application-defined wordwrap function.

Parameters   *ewbprc*
Value of *lParam*. Specifies the address of the application-defined wordwrap function. For more information, see the description of the **WordBreakProc** callback function.

Return Value   This message does not return a value.

Comments   A wordwrap function scans a text buffer that contains text to be sent to the screen, looking for the first word that does not fit on the current screen line. The wordwrap function places this word at the beginning of the next line on the screen.

A wordwrap function defines the point at which Windows should break a line of text for multiline edit controls, usually at a space character that separates two words. Either a multiline or a single-line edit control might call this function when the user presses arrow keys in combination with the CTRL key to move the caret to the next word or previous word. The default wordwrap function breaks a line of text at a space character. The application-defined function may define the wordwrap to occur at a hyphen or a character other than the space character.

See Also   **WordBreakProc**, EM_FMTLINES, EM_GETWORDBREAKPROC

EM_UNDO

```
EM_UNDO
wParam = 0; /* not used, must be zero */
lParam = 0; /* not used, must be zero */
```

An application sends an EM_UNDO message to undo the last edit control operation.

Parameters   This message has no parameters.

Return Value   For a single-line edit control, the return value is always TRUE. For a multiple-line edit control, the return value is TRUE if the undo operation is successful, or FALSE if the undo operation fails.

Comments   An undo operation can also be undone. For example, you can restore deleted text with the first EM_CANUNDO message, and remove the text again with a second EM_CANUNDO message as long as there is no intervening edit operation.

See Also   EM_CANUNDO

EN_CHANGE

```
EN_CHANGE
idEditCtrl = (int) LOWORD(wParam); /* identifier of edit control */
hwndEditCtrl = (HWND) lParam;      /* handle of edit control     */
```

The EN_CHANGE notification message is sent when the user has taken an action that may have altered text in an edit control. Unlike the EN_UPDATE notification message, this notification message is sent after Windows updates the screen. The parent window of the edit control receives this notification message through the WM_COMMAND message.

See Also   EN_UPDATE, WM_COMMAND

EN_ERRSPACE

```
EN_ERRSPACE
idEditCtrl = (int) LOWORD(wParam); /* identifier of edit control */
hwndEditCtrl = (HWND) lParam;      /* handle of edit control     */
```

The EN_ERRSPACE notification message is sent when an edit control cannot allocate enough memory to meet a specific request. The parent window of the edit control receives this notification message through the WM_COMMAND message.

See Also WM_COMMAND

EN_HSCROLL

```
EN_HSCROLL
idEditCtrl = (int) LOWORD(wParam); /* identifier of edit control */
hwndEditCtrl = (HWND) lParam;      /* handle of edit control     */
```

The EN_HSCROLL notification message is sent when the user clicks an edit control's horizontal scroll bar. The parent window of the edit control receives this notification message through the WM_COMMAND message. The parent window is notified before the screen is updated.

See Also EN_VSCROLL, WM_COMMAND

EN_KILLFOCUS

```
EN_KILLFOCUS
idEditCtrl = (int) LOWORD(wParam); /* identifier of edit control */
wNotifyCode = HIWORD(wParam);      /* notification code          */
hwndEditCtrl = (HWND) lParam;      /* handle of edit control      */
```

The EN_KILLFOCUS notification message is sent when an edit control loses the keyboard focus. The parent window of the edit control receives this notification message through the WM_COMMAND message.

Comments In previous versions of Windows, the notication code was in HIWORD(lParam).

See Also EN_SETFOCUS, WM_COMMAND

EN_MAXTEXT

```
EN_MAXTEXT
idEditCtrl = (int) LOWORD(wParam); /* identifier of edit control */
hwndEditCtrl = (HWND) lParam;      /* handle of edit control     */
```

The EN_MAXTEXT notification message is sent when the current text insertion has exceeded the specified number of characters for the edit control. The text insertion has been truncated.

This message is also sent when an edit control does not have the ES_AUTOHSCROLL style and the number of characters to be inserted would exceed the width of the edit control.

This message is also sent when an edit control does not have the ES_AUTOVSCROLL style and the total number of lines resulting from a text insertion would exceed the height of the edit control.

The parent window of the edit control receives this notification message through the WM_COMMAND message.

See Also   EM_LIMITTEXT, WM_COMMAND

EN_SETFOCUS

```
EN_SETFOCUS
idEditCtrl = (int) LOWORD(wParam); /* identifier of edit control */
wNotifyCode = HIWORD(wParam);      /* notification code          */
hwndEditCtrl = (HWND) lParam;      /* handle of edit control     */
```

The EN_SETFOCUS notification message is sent when an edit control receives the keyboard focus. The parent window of the edit control receives this notification message through the WM_COMMAND message.

Comments   In previous versions of Windows, the notication code was in HIWORD(lParam).

See Also   EN_KILLFOCUS, WM_COMMAND

EN_UPDATE

```
EN_UPDATE
idEditCtrl = (int) LOWORD(wParam); /* identifier of edit control */
hwndEditCtrl = (HWND) lParam;      /* handle of edit control     */
```

The EN_UPDATE notification message is sent when an edit control is about to display altered text. This notification is sent after the control has formatted the text but before it displays the text. This makes it possible to resize the edit control window, if necessary. The parent window of the edit control receives this notification message through the WM_COMMAND message.

See Also   EN_CHANGE, WM_COMMAND

EN_VSCROLL

```
EN_VSCROLL
idEditCtrl = (int) LOWORD(wParam); /* identifier of edit control */
hwndEditCtrl = (HWND) lParam;      /* handle of edit control     */
```

The EN_VSCROLL notification message is sent when the user clicks an edit control's vertical scroll bar. The parent window of the edit control receives this notification message through the WM_COMMAND message. The parent window is notified before the screen is updated.

See Also   EN_HSCROLL, WM_COMMAND

FM_GETDRIVEINFO

```
FM_GETDRIVEINFO
wParam = 0;                                          /* not used, must be zero */
lParam = (LPARAM) (LPFMS_GETDRIVEINFO) lpfmsgdi; /* drive data          */
```

A File Manager extension sends an FM_GETDRIVEINFO message to retrieve drive information from the active File Manager window.

Parameters   *lpfmsgdi*

Value of *lParam*. Points to an **FMS_GETDRIVEINFO** structure that receives drive information. The **FMS_GETDRIVEINFO** structure has the following form:

```
typedef struct _FMS_GETDRIVEINFO { /* fmsgdi */
    DWORD dwTotalSpace;
    DWORD dwFreeSpace;
    CHAR  szPath[260];
    CHAR  szVolume[14];
    CHAR  szShare[128];
} FMS_GETDRIVEINFO;
```

For a full description of this structure, see Chapter 3, "Structures."

Return Value   The return value is always nonzero.

Comments   If 0xFFFFFFFF is returned in the **dwTotalSpace** or **dwFreeSpace** member of the **FMS_GETDRIVEINFO** structure, the extension library must compute the value or values.

See Also   **FMExtensionProc**

FM_GETFILESEL

```
FM_GETFILESEL
wParam = (WPARAM) index;                        /* index of selected file */
lParam = (LPARAM) (LPFMS_GETFILESEL) lpfmsgfs; /* file data             */
```

A File Manager extension sends an FM_GETFILESEL message to retrieve information about a selected file from the active File Manager window (either the directory window or the Search Results window).

Parameters   *index*

Value of *wParam*. Specifies the zero-based index of the selected file to retrieve.

lpfmsgfs

Value of *lParam*. Points to an **FMS_GETFILESEL** structure that receives information about the selection. The **FMS_GETFILESEL** structure has the following form:

```
typedef struct _FMS_GETFILESEL { /* fmsgfs */
    FILETIME ftTime;
    DWORD    dwSize;
    BYTE     bAttr;
    CHAR     szName[260];
} FMS_GETFILESEL;
```

For a full description of this structure, see Chapter 3, "Structures."

Return Value   The return value is the zero-based index of the selected file that was retrieved.·

Comments   An extension can use the FM_GETSELCOUNT message to get the count of selected files.

See Also   **FMExtensionProc**, FM_GETFILESELLFN, FM_GETSELCOUNT, FM_GETSELCOUNTLFN

FM_GETFILESELLFN

```
FM_GETFILESELLFN
wParam = (WPARAM) index;                           /* index of selected file */
lParam = (LPARAM) (LPFMS_GETFILESEL) lpfmsgfs; /* selection data          */
```

A File Manager extension sends an FM_GETFILESELLFN message to retrieve information about a selected file from the active File Manager window (either the directory window or the Search Results window). The selected file can have a long filename.

Parameters   *index*
Value of *wParam*. Specifies the zero-based index of the selected file to retrieve.

lpfmsgfs
Value of *lParam*. Points to an **FMS_GETFILESEL** structure that receives information about the selection. The **FMS_GETFILESEL** structure has the following form:

```
typedef struct _FMS_GETFILESEL { /* fmsgfs */
    FILETIME ftTime;
    DWORD    dwSize;
    BYTE     bAttr;
    CHAR     szName[260];
} FMS_GETFILESEL;
```

For a full description of this structure, see Chapter 3, "Structures."

Return Value   The return value is the zero-based index of the selected file that was retrieved.

Comments   Only extensions that support long filenames (for example, network-aware extensions) should use this message.

An extension can use the FM_GETSELCOUNT message to get the count of selected files.

See Also	**FMExtensionProc**, FM_GETFILESEL, FM_GETSELCOUNT, FM_GETSELCOUNTLFN

FM_GETFOCUS

```
FM_GETFOCUS
wParam = 0;     /* not used, must be zero */
lParam = 0;     /* not used, must be zero */
```

A File Manager extension sends a FM_GETFOCUS message to retrieve the type of the File Manager window that has the input focus.

Parameters   This message has no parameters.

Return Value   The return value is the type of File Manager window that has input focus. It can be one of the following values:

Value	Meaning
FMFOCUS_DIR	Directory portion of a directory window
FMFOCUS_TREE	Tree portion of a directory window
FMFOCUS_DRIVES	Drive bar of a directory window
FMFOCUS_SEARCH	Search Results window

FM_GETSELCOUNT

```
FM_GETSELCOUNT
wParam = 0; /* not used, must be zero */
lParam = 0; /* not used, must be zero */
```

A File Manager extension sends a FM_GETSELCOUNT message to retrieve a count of the selected files in the active File Manager window (either the directory window or the Search Results window).

Parameters   This message has no parameters.

Return Value   The return value is the number of selected files.

See Also   FM_GETFILESEL, FM_GETFILESELLFN, FM_GETSELCOUNTLFN

FM_GETSELCOUNTLFN

```
FM_GETSELCOUNTLFN
wParam = 0; /* not used, must be zero */
lParam = 0; /* not used, must be zero */
```

A File Manager extension sends an FM_GETSELCOUNTLFN message to retrieve the number of selected files in the active File Manager window (either the directory window or the Search Results window). The count includes files that have long filenames.

Parameters   This message has no parameters.

Return Value   The return value is the number of selected files.

Comments   Only extensions that support long filenames (for example, network-aware extensions) should use this message.

See Also   FM_GETFILESEL, FM_GETFILESELLFN, FM_GETSELCOUNT

FM_REFRESH_WINDOWS

```
FM_REFRESH_WINDOWS
wParam = (WPARAM) (BOOL) fRepaint;  /* repaint flag          */
lParam = 0;                         /* not used, must be zero */
```

A File Manager extension sends an FM_REFRESH_WINDOWS message to cause File Manager to repaint either its active window or all of its windows.

Parameters   *fRepaint*
Value of *wParam*. Specifies whether File Manager repaints its active window or all of its windows. If this parameter is TRUE, File Manager repaints all of its windows. Otherwise, File Manager repaints only its active window.

Return Value   This message does not return a meaningful value.

Comments   File-system changes caused by an extension are automatically detected by File Manager. An extension should use this message only in situations where drive connections are made or canceled.

See Also   **FMExtensionProc**

FM_RELOAD_EXTENSIONS

```
FM_RELOAD_EXTENSIONS
wParam = 0; /* not used, must be zero */
lParam = 0; /* not used, must be zero */
```

A File Manager extension (or another application) sends an FM_RELOAD_EXTENSIONS message to cause File Manager to reload all extension DLLs listed in the [AddOns] section of the WINFILE.INI file.

Parameters   This message has no parameters.

Return Value   This message does not return a meaningful value.

Comments   Other applications can use the **PostMessage** function to send this message to File Manager. To obtain the appropriate File Manager window handle, an application can specify "WFS_Frame" as the *lpszClassName* parameter in a call to the **FindWindow** function.

See Also   **FindWindow**, **FMExtensionProc**, **PostMessage**

FMEVENT_INITMENU

```
FMEVENT_INITMENU
hmenu = (HMENU) lParam; /* handle of File Manager menu */
```

The FMEVENT_INITMENU message is sent to an extension DLL when the user selects the menu for the extension from the File Manager menu bar. The extension can use this notification to initialize menu items in the menu.

Parameters   *hmenu*
Specifies the handle of the File Manager menu bar.

Return Value   An extension DLL should return zero if it processes this message.

Comments   An extension DLL receives this message only when the user selects the top-level menu. If the extension contains submenus, it must initialize them at the same time it initializes the top-level menu.

See Also   **FMExtensionProc**

FMEVENT_LOAD

```
FMEVENT_LOAD
lpfmsld = (LPFMS_LOAD) lParam;   /* address of struct. with delta */
```

The FMEVENT_LOAD message is sent to an extension DLL when File Manager is loading the DLL.

Parameters   *lpfmsld*
Points to an **FMS_LOAD** structure that specifies the menu-item delta value. An extension DLL should save the menu-item delta value and fill the other structure members with information about the extension. The **FMS_LOAD** structure has the following form:

```
typedef struct _FMS_LOAD { /* fmsld */
    DWORD dwSize;
    CHAR  szMenuName[MENU_TEXT_LEN];
    HMENU hMenu;
    UINT  wMenuDelta;
} FMS_LOAD;
```

For a full description of this structure, see Chapter 3, "Structures."

Return Value   An extension DLL must return TRUE to continue loading the DLL. If the DLL returns FALSE, File Manager calls the **FreeLibrary** function and ends any communication with the extension DLL.

Comments   An application should fill the **dwSize**, **szMenuName**, and **hMenu** members in the **FMS_LOAD** structure. It should also save the value of the **wMenuDelta** member and use it to identify menu items when modifying the menu.

See Also   **FMExtensionProc**

FMEVENT_SELCHANGE

```
FMEVENT_SELCHANGE
```

The FMEVENT_SELCHANGE message is sent to an extension DLL when the user selects a filename in the File Manager directory window or Search Results window.

Parameters   This message has no parameters.

Return Value   An extension DLL should return zero if it processes this message.

Comments   Changes in the tree portion of the directory window do not produce this message.

Because the user can change the selection many times, the extension DLL must return promptly after processing this message to avoid slowing the selection process for the user.

See Also   **FMExtensionProc**

FMEVENT_TOOLBARLOAD

```
FMEVENT_TOOLBARLOAD
lpfmstbl = (LPFMS_TOOLBARLOAD) lParam;    /* toolbar data */
```

The FMEVENT_TOOLBARLOAD message is sent to an extension DLL when File Manager is loading its toolbar. This message allows an extension DLL to add a button to the File Manager toolbar.

Parameters   *lpfmstbl*

Points to an **FMS_TOOLBARLOAD** structure. If the extension DLL adds a button to the toolbar in File Manager, the DLL should fill the structure with information about the button. The **FMS_TOOLBARLOAD** structure has the following form:

```
typedef struct tagFMS_TOOLBARLOAD { /* fmstbl */
    DWORD          dwSize;
    LPEXT_BUTTON   lpButtons;
    WORD           cButtons;
    WORD           cBitmaps;
    WORD           idBitmap;
    HBITMAP        hBitmap;
} FMS_TOOLBARLOAD;
```

For a full description of this structure, see Chapter 3, "Structures."

Return Value   An extension DLL must return TRUE to add the button to the toolbar. If the DLL returns FALSE, File Manager does not add the button.

See Also   **FMExtensionProc**

FMEVENT_UNLOAD

FMEVENT_UNLOAD

The FMEVENT_UNLOAD message is sent to an extension DLL when File Manager is unloading the DLL.

Parameters   This message has no parameters.

Return Value   An extension DLL should return zero if it processes this message.

Comments   The *hwnd* and *hMenu* values passed with the FMEVENT_LOAD and FMEVENT_INITMENU messages may not be valid at the time this message is sent.

See Also   **FMExtensionProc**

FMEVENT_USER_REFRESH

FMEVENT_USER_REFRESH

The FMEVENT_USER_REFRESH message is sent to an extension DLL when the user chooses the Refresh command from the Window menu in File Manager. The extension can use this notification to update its menu.

Parameters   This message has no parameters.

Return Value   An extension DLL should return zero if it processes this message.

See Also   **FMExtensionProc**

LB_ADDFILE   Unicode

```
LB_ADDFILE
wParam = 0;                                  /* not used, must be zero */
lParam = (LPARAM) (LPCTSTR) lpszFilename; /* name of file to add    */
```

An application sends an LB_ADDFILE message to add the specified filename to a list box that contains a directory listing.

Parameters	*lpszFilename*
	Value of *lParam*. Points to the name of the file to add.
Return Value	The return value is the zero-based index of the file that was added, or LB_ERR if an error occurs.
Comments	The list box to which *lpszFilename* is added must have been filled by the **DlgDirList** function.
See Also	**DlgDirList**, LB_ADDSTRING

LB_ADDSTRING   `Unicode`

```
LB_ADDSTRING
wParam = 0;                            /* not used, must be zero   */
lParam = (LPARAM) (LPCTSTR) lpsz;      /* address of string to add */
```

An application sends an LB_ADDSTRING message to add a string to a list box. If the list box does not have the LBS_SORT style, the string is added to the end of the list. Otherwise, the string is inserted into the list and the list is sorted.

Parameters	*lpsz*
	Value of *lParam*. Points to the null-terminated string that is to be added. If you create the list box with an owner-drawn style but without the LBS_HASSTRINGS style, the value of the *lpsz* parameter is stored instead of the string it would otherwise point to.
Return Value	The return value is the zero-based index of the string in the list box. If an error occurs, the return value is LB_ERR. If there is insufficient space to store the new string, the return value is LB_ERRSPACE.
Comments	If you create an owner-drawn list box with the LBS_SORT style but not the LBS_HASSTRINGS style, the system sends the WM_COMPAREITEM message one or more times to the owner of the list box to place the new item properly in the list box.
See Also	LB_DELETESTRING, LB_INSERTSTRING, LB_SELECTSTRING, WM_COMPAREITEM

LB_DELETESTRING

```
LB_DELETESTRING
wParam = (WPARAM) index;      /* index of string to delete */
lParam = 0;                   /* not used, must be zero    */
```

An application sends an LB_DELETESTRING message to delete a string in a list box.

Parameters   *index*
Value of *wParam*. Specifies the zero-based index of the string to be deleted.

Return Value   The return value is a count of the strings remaining in the list. The return value is LB_ERR if the *index* parameter specifies an index greater than the number of items in the list.

Comments   If you create the list box with an owner-drawn style but without the LBS_HASSTRINGS style, the system sends a WM_DELETEITEM message to the owner of the list box so the application can free any additional data associated with the item.

See Also   LB_ADDSTRING, LB_INSERTSTRING, WM_DELETEITEM

LB_DIR   `Unicode`

```
LB_DIR
wParam = (WPARAM) (UINT) uAttrs;        /* file attributes */
lParam = (LPARAM) (LPCTSTR) lpszFileSpec; /* filename address */
```

An application sends an LB_DIR message to add a list of filenames to a list box.

Parameters   *uAttrs*
Value of *wParam*. Specifies the attributes of the files to be added to the list box. This parameter can be a combination of the following values:

Value	Description
DDL_ARCHIVE	Includes archived files.
DDL_DIRECTORY	Includes subdirectories. Subdirectory names are enclosed in square brackets ([ ]).
DDL_DRIVES	Includes drives. Drives are listed in the form [-*x*-], where *x* is the drive letter.

DDL_EXCLUSIVE	Includes only files with the specified attributes. By default, read-write files are listed even if DDL_READWRITE is not specified.
DDL_HIDDEN	Includes hidden files.
DDL_READONLY	Includes read-only files.
DDL_READWRITE	Includes read-write files with no additional attributes.
DDL_SYSTEM	Includes system files.

lpszFileSpec

Value of *lParam*. Points to the null-terminated string that specifies the filename to add to the list. If the filename contains wildcards (for example, *.*), all files that match the wildcards and have the attributes specified by the *uAttrs* parameter are added to the list.

Return Value   The return value is the zero-based index of the last filename added to the list. If an error occurs, the return value is LB_ERR. If there is insufficient space to store the new strings, the return value is LB_ERRSPACE.

See Also   **DlgDirList**

LB_FINDSTRING   `Unicode`

```
LB_FINDSTRING
wParam = (WPARAM) indexStart;          /* item before start of search */
lParam = (LPARAM) (LPCTSTR) lpszFind;  /* search string address       */
```

An application sends an LB_FINDSTRING message to find the first string in a list box that contains the specified prefix.

Parameters   *indexStart*

Value of *wParam*. Specifies the zero-based index of the item before the first item to be searched. When the search reaches the bottom of the list box, it continues from the top of the list box back to the item specified by the *indexStart* parameter. If *indexStart* is –1, the entire list box is searched from the beginning.

lpszFind

Value of *lParam*. Points to the null-terminated string that contains the prefix to search for. The search is case-indepentdent, so this string can contain any combination of uppercase and lowercase letters.

Return Value   The return value is the index of the matching item, or LB_ERR if the search was unsuccessful.

Comments   If you create the list box with an owner-drawn style but without the LBS_HASSTRINGS style, this message returns the index of the item whose long value (supplied as the *lParam* parameter of the LB_ADDSTRING or LB_INSERTSTRING message) matches the value supplied as the *lpszFind* parameter.

See Also   LB_ADDSTRING, LB_INSERTSTRING, LB_SELECTSTRING

LB_FINDSTRINGEXACT

```
LB_FINDSTRINGEXACT
wParam = (WPARAM) indexStart;        /* item before start of search */
lParam = (LPARAM)(LPCSTR)lpszFind; /* address of search string    */
```

An application sends a LB_FINDSTRINGEXACT message to find the first list box string that matches the string specified in the *lpszFind* parameter.

Parameters   *indexStart*
        Value of *wParam*. Specifies the zero-based index of the item before the first item to be searched. When the search reaches the bottom of the list box, it continues from the top of the list box back to the item specified by the *indexStart* parameter. If *indexStart* is &(EN_DASH)1, the entire list box is searched from the beginning.

lpszFind
        Value of *lParam*. Points to the null-terminated string to search for. This string can contain a complete filename, including the extension. The search is not case-sensitive, so this string can contain any combination of uppercase and lowercase letters.

Return Value   The return value is the zero-based index of the matching item, or LB_ERR if the search was unsuccessful.

Comments   If you create the list box with an owner-drawn style but without the LBS_HASSTRINGS style, the action taken by the LB_FINDSTRINGEXACT message depends on whether the LBS_SORT style is used. If the LBS_SORT style is used, the system sends WM_COMPAREITEM messages to the owner of the list box to determine which item matches the specified string. Otherwise, LB_FINDSTRINGEXACT attempts to match the 32-bit value against the value of the *lpszFind* parameter.

See Also   LB_FINDSTRING, LB_SELECTSTRING, WM_COMPAREITEM

LB_GETANCHORINDEX

```
LB_GETANCHORINDEX
wParam = 0; /* not used, must be zero */
lParam = 0; /* not used, must be zero */
```

An application sends an LB_GETANCHORINDEX message to retrieve the index of the anchor item.

Parameters   This message has no parameters.

Return Value   The return value is the index of the current anchor item—that is, the item most recently selected by the user pressing a mouse button.

Comments   In a multiple-selection list box, the anchor item is the first or last item in a block of contiguous selected items.

See Also   LB_SETANCHORINDEX

LB_GETCARETINDEX

```
LB_GETCARETINDEX
wParam = 0; /* not used, must be zero */
lParam = 0; /* not used, must be zero */
```

An application sends an LB_GETCARETINDEX message to determine the index of the item that has the focus rectangle in a multiple-selection list box. The item may or may not be selected.

Parameters   This message has no parameters.

Return Value   The return value is the zero-based index of the list box item that has the focus rectangle. If the list box is a single-selection list box, the return value is the zero-based index of the item that is selected, if any.

See Also   LB_SETCARETINDEX

LB_GETCOUNT

```
LB_GETCOUNT
wParam = 0; /* not used, must be zero */
lParam = 0; /* not used, must be zero */
```

An application sends an LB_GETCOUNT message to retrieve the number of items in a list box.

Parameters   This message has no parameters.

Return Value   The return value is the number of items in the list box, or LB_ERR if an error occurs.

Comments   The returned count is one greater then the index value of the last item (the index is zero-based).

See Also   LB_SETCOUNT

LB_GETCURSEL

```
LB_GETCURSEL
wParam = 0;     /* not used, must be zero */
lParam = 0;     /* not used, must be zero */
```

An application sends an LB_GETCURSEL message to retrieve the index of the currently selected item, if any, in a single-selection list box.

Parameters   This message has no parameters.

Return Value   The return value is the zero-based index of the currently selected item, or LB_ERR if no item is currently selected.

Comments   Use the LB_GETCARETINDEX message to retrieve the index of the item that has the focus rectangle in a multiple-selection list box. An application cannot send the LB_GETCURSEL message to a multiple-selection list box.

See Also   LB_GETCARETINDEX LB_SETCURSEL

LB_GETHORIZONTALEXTENT

```
LB_GETHORIZONTALEXTENT
wParam = 0; /* not used, must be zero */
lParam = 0; /* not used, must be zero */
```

An application sends an LB_GETHORIZONTALEXTENT message to retrieve from a list box the width, in pixels, by which the list box can be scrolled horizontally (the scrollable width) if the list box has a horizontal scroll bar.

Parameters   This message has no parameters.

Return Value   The return value is the scrollable width, in pixels, of the list box.

Comments   To respond to the LB_GETHORIZONTALEXTENT message, the list box must have been defined with the WS_HSCROLL style.

See Also   LB_SETHORIZONTALEXTENT

LB_GETITEMDATA

```
LB_GETITEMDATA
wParam = (WPARAM) index; /* item index            */
lParam = 0;              /* not used, must be zero */
```

An application sends an LB_GETITEMDATA message to retrieve the application-defined 32-bit value associated with the specified list box item.

Parameters   *index*
    Value of *wParam*. Specifies the index of the item.

Return Value   The return value is the 32-bit value associated with the item, or LB_ERR if an error occurs.

Comments   If the item is in an owner-drawn list box created without the LBS_HASSTRINGS style, this 32-bit value was contained in the *lParam* parameter of the LB_ADDSTRING or LB_INSERTSTRING message that added the item to the list box. Otherwise, it is the value in the *lParam* parameter of an LB_SETITEMDATA message.

See Also   LB_ADDSTRING, LB_INSERTSTRING, LB_SETITEMDATA

LB_GETITEMHEIGHT

```
LB_GETITEMHEIGHT
wParam = (WPARAM) index;     /* item index            */
lParam = 0;                  /* not used, must be zero */
```

An application sends an LB_GETITEMHEIGHT message to retrieve the height of items in a list box.

Parameters   *index*

Value of *wParam*. Specifies the zero-based index of the item in the list box. This parameter is used only if the list box has the LBS_OWNERDRAWVARIABLE style; otherwise, set it to zero.

Return Value   The return value is the height, in pixels, of each item in the list box. The return value is the height of the item specified by the *index* parameter if the list box has the LBS_OWNERDRAWVARIABLE style. The return value is LB_ERR if an error occurs.

See Also   LB_SETITEMHEIGHT

LB_GETITEMRECT

```
LB_GETITEMRECT
wParam = (WPARAM) index;             /* item index            */
lParam = (LPARAM) (RECT FAR*) lprc;  /* address of rectangle */
```

An application sends an LB_GETITEMRECT message to retrieve the dimensions of the rectangle that bounds a list box item as it is currently displayed in the list box.

Parameters   *index*

Value of *wParam*. Specifies the zero-based index of the item.

lprc

Value of *lParam*. Points to a **RECT** structure that will receive the client coordinates for the item in the list box. The **RECT** structure has the following form:

```
typedef struct tagRECT {    /* rc */
    LONG left;
    LONG top;
    LONG right;
    LONG bottom;
} RECT;
```

For a full description of this structure, see Chapter 3, "Structures."

Return Value   If an error occurs, the return value is LB_ERR.

LB_GETLOCALE

New

```
LB_GETLOCALE
wParam = 0; /* not used, must be zero */
lParam = 0; /* not used, must be zero */
```

An application sends an LB_GETLOCALE message to retrieve the current locale of the list box. You can use the locale to determine the correct sorting order of displayed text (for list boxes with the LBS_SORT style) and of text added by the LB_ADDSTRING message.

Parameters   This message has no parameters.

Return Value   The return value is a 32-bit value that specifies the current locale of the list box. The high-order word contains the country code and the low-order word contains the language identifier.

Comments   The language identifier consists of a sublanguage identifier and a primary language identifier. Use the **PRIMARYLANGID** macro to extract the primary language identifier from the low-order word of the return value, and the **SUBLANGID** macro to extract the sublanguage identifier.

See Also   **LB_SETLOCALE, PRIMARYLANGID, SUBLANGID**

LB_GETSEL

```
LB_GETSEL
wParam = (WPARAM) index;    /* item index              */
lParam = 0;                 /* not used, must be zero */
```

An application sends an LB_GETSEL message to retrieve the selection state of an item.

Parameters   *index*
        Value of *wParam*. Specifies the zero-based index of the item.

Return Value   If an item is selected, the return value is greater than zero; otherwise, it is zero. If an error occurs, the return value is LB_ERR.

See Also	LB_SETSEL

LB_GETSELCOUNT

```
LB_GETSELCOUNT
wParam = 0; /* not used, must be zero */
lParam = 0; /* not used, must be zero */
```

An application sends an LB_GETSELCOUNT message to retrieve the total number of selected items in a multiple-selection list box.

Parameters   This message has no parameters.

Return Value   The return value is the count of selected items in the list box. If the list box is a single-selection list box, the return value is LB_ERR.

See Also   LB_SETSEL

LB_GETSELITEMS

```
LB_GETSELITEMS
wParam = (WPARAM) cItems;            /* maximum number of items */
lParam = (LPARAM) (LPINT) lpnItems; /* address of buffer        */
```

An application sends an LB_GETSELITEMS message to fill a buffer with an array of integers that specify the item numbers of selected items in a multiple-selection list box.

Parameters   *cItems*
    Value of *wParam*. Specifies the maximum number of selected items whose item numbers are to be placed in the buffer.

lpnItems
    Value of *lParam*. Points to a buffer large enough for the number of integers specified by the *cItems* parameter.

Return Value   The return value is the number of items placed in the buffer. If the list box is a single-selection list box, the return value is LB_ERR.

See Also   LB_GETSELCOUNT

LB_GETTEXT

```
LB_GETTEXT
wParam = (WPARAM) index;                /* item index       */
lParam = (LPARAM) (LPCTSTR) lpszBuffer; /* address of buffer */
```

An application sends an LB_GETTEXT message to retrieve a string from a list box.

Parameters

index
Value of *wParam*. Specifies the zero-based index of the string to retrieve.

lpszBuffer
Value of *lParam*. Points to the buffer that will receive the string. The buffer must have sufficient space for the string and a terminating null character. An LB_GETTEXTLEN message can be sent before the LB_GETTEXT message to retrieve the length, in characters, of the string.

Return Value

The return value is the length of the string, in characters, excluding the terminating null character. If *index* does not specify a valid index, the return value is LB_ERR.

Comments

If you create the list box with an owner-drawn style but without the LBS_HASSTRINGS style, the buffer pointed to by the *lpszBuffer* parameter will receive the 32-bit value associated with the item.

See Also

LB_GETTEXTLEN

LB_GETTEXTLEN

```
LB_GETTEXTLEN
wParam = (WPARAM) index;    /* item index            */
lParam = 0;                 /* not used, must be zero */
```

An application sends an LB_GETTEXTLEN message to retrieve the length of a string in a list box.

Parameters

index
Value of *wParam*. Specifies the zero-based index of the string.

Return Value

The return value is the length of the string, in characters, excluding the terminating null character. If the *index* parameter does not specify a valid index, the return value is LB_ERR.

See Also

LB_GETTEXT

LB_GETTOPINDEX

```
LB_GETTOPINDEX
wParam = 0; /* not used, must be zero */
lParam = 0; /* not used, must be zero */
```

An application sends an LB_GETTOPINDEX message to retrieve the index of the first visible item in a list box. Initially the item with index 0 is at the top of the list box, but if the list box contents have been scrolled another item may be at the top.

Parameters   This message has no parameters.

Return Value   The return value is the index of the first visible item in the list box.

See Also   LB_SETTOPINDEX

LB_INSERTSTRING   `Unicode`

```
LB_INSERTSTRING
wParam = (WPARAM) index;          /* item index                */
lParam = (LPARAM) (LPCTSTR) lpsz; /* address of string to insert */
```

An application sends an LB_INSERTSTRING message to insert a string into a list box. Unlike the LB_ADDSTRING message, the LB_INSERTSTRING message does not cause a list with the LBS_SORT style to be sorted.

Parameters   *index*
Value of *wParam*. Specifies the zero-based index of the position at which to insert the string. If this parameter is –1, the string is added to the end of the list.

lpsz
Value of *lParam*. Points to the null-terminated string to be inserted. If the list was created with an owner-drawn style but without the LBS_HASSTRINGS style, the value of the *lpsz* parameter is stored instead of the string it would otherwise point to.

Return Value   The return value is the index of the position at which the string was inserted. If an error occurs, the return value is LB_ERR. If there is insufficient space to store the new string, the return value is LB_ERRSPACE.

See Also   LB_ADDSTRING, LB_SELECTSTRING

LB_RESETCONTENT

```
LB_RESETCONTENT
wParam = 0; /* not used, must be zero */
lParam = 0; /* not used, must be zero */
```

An application sends an LB_RESETCONTENT to remove all items from a list box.

Parameters   This message has no parameters.

Return Value   This message does not return a value.

Comments   If you create the list box with an owner-drawn style but without the LBS_HASSTRINGS style, the owner of the list box receives a WM_DELETEITEM message for each item in the list box.

See Also   WM_DELETEITEM

LB_SELECTSTRING

Unicode

```
LB_SELECTSTRING
wParam = (WPARAM) indexStart;        /* item before start of search */
lParam = (LPARAM)(LPCTSTR)lpszFind;  /* address of search string    */
```

An application sends an LB_SELECTSTRING message to search a list box for an item that begins with the characters in a specified string. If a matching item is found, the item is selected.

Parameters   *indexStart*
Value of *wParam*. Specifies the zero-based index of the item before the first item to be searched. When the search reaches the bottom of the list box, it continues from the top of the list box back to the item specified by the *indexStart* parameter. If *indexStart* is –1, the entire list box is searched from the beginning.

lpszFind
Value of *lParam*. Points to the null-terminated string that contains the prefix to search for. The search is case independent, so this string can contain any combination of uppercase and lowercase letters.

Return Value   If the search is successful, the return value is the index of the selected item. If the search is unsuccessful, the return value is LB_ERR and the current selection is not changed.

Comments   The list box is scrolled, if necessary, to bring the selected item into view.

Do not use this message with a list box that has the LBS_MULTIPLESEL style.

An item is selected only if its initial characters from the starting point match the characters in the string specified by the *lpszFind* parameter.

If you create the list box with an owner-drawn style but without the LBS_HASSTRINGS style, this message returns the index of the item whose long value (supplied as the *lParam* parameter of the LB_ADDSTRING or LB_INSERTSTRING message) matches the value supplied as the *lParam* parameter of LB_SELECTSTRING.

See Also   LB_ADDSTRING, LB_FINDSTRING, LB_INSERTSTRING

LB_SELITEMRANGE

```
LB_SELITEMRANGE
wParam = (WPARAM) (BOOL) fSelect;   /* selection flag     */
lParam = MAKELPARAM(wFirst, wLast); /* first and last items */
```

An application sends an LB_SELITEMRANGE message to select one or more consecutive items in a multiple-selection list box.

Parameters   *fSelect*
Value of *wParam*. Specifies how to set the selection. If the *fSelect* parameter is TRUE, the string is selected and highlighted; if *fSelect* is zero, the highlight is removed and the string is no longer selected.

wFirst
Value of the low-order word of *lParam*. Specifies the zero-based index of the first item to select.

wLast
Value of the high-order word of *lParam*. Specifies the zero-based index of the last item to select.

Return Value   If an error occurs, the return value is LB_ERR.

Comments   Use this message only with multiple-selection list boxes.

This message can select a range only within the first 65,536 items.

See Also   LB_SELITEMRANGEEX, LB_SETSEL

LB_SELITEMRANGEEX

New

```
LB_SELITEMRANGEEX
wParam = (WPARAM) wFirst; /* first item */
lParam = (LPARAM) wLast); /* last item  */
```

An application sends an LB_SELITEMRANGEEX message to select one or more consecutive items in a multiple-selection list box.

Parameters

wFirst
    Value of *wParam*. Specifies the zero-based index of the first item to select.

wLast
    Value of *lParam*. Specifies the zero-based index of the last item to select.

Return Value   If an error occurs, the return value is LB_ERR.

Comments   If *wFirst* is less than *wLast*, the specified range of items is selected. If *wFirst* is greater than *wLast*, the selection is removed from the specified range of items.

Use this message only with multiple-selection list boxes.

This message can select a range only within the first 65,536 items.

See Also   LB_SELITEMRANGE, LB_SETSEL

LB_SETANCHORINDEX

```
LB_SETANCHORINDEX
wParam = (WPARAM) index; /* index to set as anchor */
lParam = 0;              /* not used, must be zero */
```

An application sends an LB_SETANCHORINDEX message to set the position of the anchor item.

Parameters

index
    Value of *wParam*. Specifies the index of the list box item that will be the anchor.

Return Value   The return value is zero.

Comments   This message sets the anchor by setting the internal value that represents the list box item most recently selected by the user pressing a mouse button. In a multiple-selection list box, the anchor item is the first or last item in a block of contiguous selected items.

See Also   LB_GETANCHORINDEX

LB_SETCARETINDEX

```
LB_SETCARETINDEX
wParam = (WPARAM) index;          /* item index               */
lParam = MAKELPARAM(fScroll, 0);  /* flag for scrolling item */
```

An application sends an LB_SETCARETINDEX message to set the focus rectangle to the item at the specified index in a multiple-selection list box. If the item is not visible, it is scrolled into view.

Parameters   *index*
　　　　　　　　Value of *wParam*. Specifies the zero-based index of the list box item that is to receive the focus rectangle.

　　　　　　　fScroll
　　　　　　　　Value of *lParam*. If this value is FALSE, the item is scrolled until it is fully visible. If this value is TRUE, the item is scrolled until it is at least partially visible.

Return Value   If an error occurs, the return value is LB_ERR.

See Also   LB_GETCARETINDEX

LB_SETCOLUMNWIDTH

```
LB_SETCOLUMNWIDTH
wParam = (WPARAM) cxColumn; /* column width in pixels */
lParam = 0;                 /* not used, must be zero */
```

An application sends an LB_SETCOLUMNWIDTH message to a multiple-column list box (created with the LBS_MULTICOLUMN style) to set the width, in pixels, of all columns in the list box.

Parameters   *cxColumn*
　　　　　　　　Value of *wParam*. Specifies the width, in pixels, of all columns.

Return Value   This message does not return a value.

See Also   LB_SETTABSTOPS

LB_SETCOUNT

```
LB_SETCOUNT
wParam = (WPARAM) (int) cItems; /* count of list box items */
lParam = 0;                     /* not used; must be zero  */
```

An application sends an LB_SETCOUNT message to set the count of items in a list box created with the LBS_NODATA style.

Parameters *cItems*
   Value of *wParam*. Specifies the new count of items in the list box.

Return Value If an error occurs, the return value is LB_ERR. If there is insufficient memory to store the items, the return value is LB_ERRSPACE.

Comments Only list boxes created with the LBS_NODATA style support the LB_SETCOUNT message. All other list boxes return LB_ERR in response to this message.

See Also LB_GETCOUNT

LB_SETCURSEL

```
LB_SETCURSEL
wParam = (WPARAM) index;   /* item index          */
lParam = 0;                /* not used, must be zero */
```

An application sends an LB_SETCURSEL message to select a string and scroll it into view, if necessary. When the new string is selected, the list box removes the highlight from the previously selected string.

Parameters *index*
   Value of *wParam*. Specifies the zero-based index of the string that is selected. If the *index* parameter is -1, the list box is set to have no selection.

Return Value If an error occurs, the return value is LB_ERR. If the *index* parameter is –1, the return value is LB_ERR even though no error occurred.

Comments Use this message only with single-selection list boxes. You cannot use it to set or remove a selection in a multiple-selection list box.

See Also LB_GETCURSEL

LB_SETHORIZONTALEXTENT

```
LB_SETHORIZONTALEXTENT
wParam = (WPARAM) cxExtent; /* horizontal scroll width */
lParam = 0;                 /* not used, must be zero  */
```

An application sends an LB_SETHORIZONTALEXTENT message to set the width, in pixels, by which a list box can be scrolled horizontally (the scrollable width). If the width of the list box is smaller than this value, the horizontal scroll bar horizontally scrolls items in the list box. If the width of the list box is equal to or greater than this value, the horizontal scroll bar is hidden.

Parameters
cxExtent
    Value of *wParam*. Specifies the number of pixels by which the list box can be scrolled.

Return Value
This message does not return a value.

Comments
To respond to the LB_SETHORIZONTALEXTENT message, the list box must have been defined with the WS_HSCROLL style.

See Also
LB_GETHORIZONTALEXTENT

LB_SETITEMDATA

```
LB_SETITEMDATA
wParam = (WPARAM) index;    /* item index                 */
lParam = (LPARAM) dwData;   /* value to associate with item */
```

An application sends an LB_SETITEMDATA message to set a 32-bit value associated with the specified item in a list box.

Parameters
index
    Value of *wParam*. Specifies the zero-based index of the item.

dwData
    Value of *lParam*. Specifies the 32-bit value to be associated with the item.

Return Value
If an error occurs, the return value is LB_ERR.

Comments
If the item is in an owner-drawn list box created without the LBS_HASSTRINGS style, this message replaces the 32-bit value that was contained in the *lParam* parameter of the LB_ADDSTRING or LB_INSERTSTRING message that added the item to the list box.

See Also   LB_ADDSTRING, LB_GETITEMDATA, LB_INSERTSTRING

LB_SETITEMHEIGHT

```
LB_SETITEMHEIGHT
wParam = (WPARAM) index;          /* item index  */
lParam = MAKELPARAM(cyItem, 0); /* item height */
```

An application sends an LB_SETITEMHEIGHT message to set the height, in pixels, of items in a list box. If the list box has the LBS_OWNERDRAWVARIABLE style, this message sets the height of the item specified by the *index* parameter. Otherwise, this message sets the height of all items in the list box.

Parameters   *index*
　　　　　　　　Value of *wParam*. Specifies the zero-based index of the item in the list box. Use this parameter only if the list box has the LBS_OWNERDRAWVARIABLE style; otherwise, set it to zero.

　　　　　　　cyItem
　　　　　　　　Value of *lParam*. Specifies the height, in pixels, of the item.

Return Value   If the index or height is invalid, the return value is LB_ERR.

See Also   LB_GETITEMHEIGHT

LB_SETLOCALE

New

```
LB_SETLOCALE
wParam = (WPARAM) wLocaleID;      /* locale identifier    */
lParam = 0;                       /* not used, must be zero */
```

An application sends an LB_SETLOCALE message to set the current locale of the list box. You can use the locale to determine the correct sorting order of displayed text (for list boxes with the LBS_SORT style) and of text added by the LB_ADDSTRING message.

Parameters   *wLocaleID*
　　　　　　　　Value of *wParam*. Specifies the locale identifier that the list box will use for sorting when adding text.

Return Value	The return value is the previous locale identifier. If the *wLocaleID* parameter specifies a locale that is not installed on the system, the return value is LB_ERR and the current list box locale is not changed.
Comments	Use the **MAKELCID** macro to construct a locale identifier.
See Also	LB_GETLOCALE, **MAKELCID**

LB_SETSEL

```
LB_SETSEL
wParam = (WPARAM) (BOOL) fSelect;    /* selection flag */
lParam = (LPARAM) (UINT) index;      /* item index     */
```

An application sends an LB_SETSEL message to select a string in a multiple-selection list box.

Parameters

fSelect
Value of *wParam*. Specifies how to set the selection. If the *fSelect* parameter is TRUE, the string is selected and highlighted; if *fSelect* is FALSE, the highlight is removed and the string is no longer selected.

index
Value of *lParam*. Specifies the zero-based index of the string to set. If *index* is −1, the selection is added to or removed from all strings, depending on the value of *fSelect*.

Return Value   If an error occurs, the return value is LB_ERR.

Comments   Use this message only with multiple-selection list boxes.

See Also   LB_GETSEL, LB_SELITEMRANGE

LB_SETTABSTOPS

```
LB_SETTABSTOPS
wParam = (WPARAM) cTabs;              /* number of tab stops    */
lParam = (LPARAM) (LPINT) lpnTabs;   /* address of tab-stop array */
```

An application sends an LB_SETTABSTOPS message to set the tab-stop positions in a list box.

Parameters

cTabs
Value of *wParam*. Specifies the number of tab stops in the list box.

lpnTabs

Value of *lParam*. Points to the first member of an array of integers containing the tab stops, in dialog box units. The tab stops must be sorted in ascending order; backward tabs are not allowed.

Return Value   If all the specified tabs are set, the return value is TRUE; otherwise, it is FALSE.

Comments   To respond to the LB_SETTABSTOPS message, the list box must have been created with the LBS_USETABSTOPS style.

If *cTabs* parameter is 0 and *lpnTabs* is NULL, the default tab stop is two dialog box units. If *cTabs* is 1, the list box will have tab stops separated by the distance specified by *lpnTabs*.

If *lpnTabs* points to more than a single value, a tab stop will be set for each value in *lpnTabs*, up to the number specified by *cTabs*.

A dialog box unit is a horizontal or vertical distance. One horizontal dialog box unit is equal to one-fourth of the current dialog box base-width unit. These units are computed based on the height and width of the current system font. The **GetDialogBaseUnits** function returns the current dialog box base units, in pixels.

See Also   **GetDialogBaseUnits**

LB_SETTOPINDEX

```
LB_SETTOPINDEX
wParam = (WPARAM) index;     /* item index             */
lParam = 0;                  /* not used, must be zero */
```

An application sends an LB_SETTOPINDEX message to ensure that a particular item in a list box is visible.

Parameters   *index*

Value of *wParam*. Specifies the zero-based index of the item in the list box.

Return Value   If an error occurs, the return value is LB_ERR.

Comments   The system scrolls the list box contents so that either the specified item appears at the top of the list box or the maximum scroll range has been reached.

See Also   LB_GETTOPINDEX

LBN_DBLCLK

```
LBN_DBLCLK
idListBox = (int) LOWORD(wParam);  /* identifier of list box */
hwndListBox = (HWND) lParam;       /* handle of list box     */
```

An application sends the LBN_DBLCLK notification message when the user double-clicks a string in a list box. The parent window of the list box receives this notification message through the WM_COMMAND message.

Comments   Only a list box that has the LBS_NOTIFY style will send this notification message.

See Also   LBN_SELCHANGE, WM_COMMAND

LBN_ERRSPACE

```
LBN_ERRSPACE
idListBox = (int) LOWORD(wParam);  /* identifier of list box */
hwndListBox = (HWND) lParam;       /* handle of list box     */
```

An application sends the LBN_ERRSPACE notification message when a list box cannot allocate enough memory to meet a specific request. The parent window of the list box receives this notification message through the WM_COMMAND message.

See Also   WM_COMMAND

LBN_KILLFOCUS

```
LBN_KILLFOCUS
idListBox = (int) LOWORD(wParam);  /* identifier of list box */
hwndListBox = (HWND) lParam;       /* handle of list box     */
```

An application sends the LBN_KILLFOCUS notification message when a list box loses the keyboard focus. The parent window of the list box receives this notification message through the WM_COMMAND message.

See Also   LBN_SETFOCUS, WM_COMMAND

LBN_SELCANCEL

```
LBN_SELCANCEL
idListBox = (int) LOWORD(wParam);   /* identifier of list box */
hwndListBox = (HWND) lParam;        /* handle of list box     */
```

An application sends the LBN_SELCANCEL notification message when the user cancels the selection in a list box. The parent window of the list box receives this notification message through the WM_COMMAND message.

Comments   This notification message applies only to a list box that has the LBS_NOTIFY style.

See Also   LBN_DBLCLK, LBN_SELCHANGE, LB_SETCURSEL, WM_COMMAND

LBN_SELCHANGE

```
LBN_SELCHANGE
idListBox = (int) LOWORD(wParam);   /* identifier of list box */
hwndListBox = (HWND) lParam;        /* handle of list box     */
```

An application sends the LBN_SELCHANGE notification message when the selection in a list box is about to change. The parent window of the list box receives this notification message through the WM_COMMAND message.

Comments   This notification message is not sent if the LB_SETCURSEL message changes the selection.

This notification message applies only to a list box that has the LBS_NOTIFY style.

For a multiple-selection list box, the LBN_SELCHANGE notification is sent whenever the user presses an arrow key, even if the selection does not change.

See Also   LBN_DBLCLK, LBN_SELCANCEL, LB_SETCURSEL, WM_COMMAND

LBN_SETFOCUS

```
LBN_SETFOCUS
idListBox = (int) LOWORD(wParam);   /* identifier of list box */
hwndListBox = (HWND) lParam;        /* handle of list box     */
```

An application sends the LBN_SETFOCUS notification message when a list box receives the keyboard focus. The parent window of the list box receives this notification message through the WM_COMMAND message.

See Also   LBN_KILLFOCUS, WM_COMMAND

MCI_BREAK

This MCI command message sets a break key for an MCI device. MCI supports this message directly rather than passing it to the device.

Parameters   **DWORD** *dwFlags*

The following flags apply to all devices:

Value	Meaning
MCI_NOTIFY	

Specifies that MCI should post the MM_MCINOTIFY message when this command completes. The window to receive this message is specified in the **dwCallback** member of the structure identified by *lpBreak*.

MCI_WAIT

Specifies that the break operation should finish before MCI returns control to the application.

MCI_BREAK_KEY

Indicates the **nVirtKey** member of the structure identified by *lpBreak* specifies the virtual key code used for the break key. By default, MCI assigns CTRL+BREAK as the break key. This flag is required if MCI_BREAK_OFF is not specified.

MCI_BREAK_HWND

Indicates the **hwndBreak** member of the structure identified by *lpBreak* contains a window handle which must be the current window in order to enable break detection for that MCI device. This is usually the application's main window. If omitted, MCI does not check the window handle of the current window.

MCI_BREAK_OFF

Used to disable any existing break key for the indicated device

LPMCI_BREAK_PARMS *lpBreak*

Points to the **MCI_BREAK_PARMS** structure. The **MCI_BREAK_PARMS** structure has the following form:

```
typedef struct {
    DWORD  dwCallback;
    int  nVirtKey;
    HWND  hwndBreak;
} MCI_BREAK_PARMS;
```

For a full description of this structure, see Chapter 3, "Structures."

Return Value   Returns zero if successful. Otherwise, it returns an MCI error code.

Comments   You might have to press the break key multiple times to interrupt a wait operation. Pressing the break key after a device wait is broken can send the break to an application. If an application has an action defined for the virtural key code, then it can inadvertantly respond to the break. For example, an application using VK_CANCEL for an accelerator key can respond to the default CTRL+BREAK key if it is pressed after a wait is canceled.

MCI_CLOSE

This MCI command message releases access to a device or device element. All devices respond to this message.

Parameters   **DWORD** *dwFlags*

The following flags apply to all devices:

Value	Meaning
MCI_NOTIFY	Specifies that MCI should post the MM_MCINOTIFY message when this command completes. The window to receive this message is specified in the **dwCallback** member of the structure identified by *lpDefault*.
MCI_WAIT	Specifies that the close operation should finish before MCI returns control to the application.

LPMCI_GENERIC_PARMS *lpDefault*

Points to the **MCI_GENERIC_PARMS** structure. (Devices with extended command sets might replace this data structure with a device-specific data structure.) The **MCI_GENERIC_PARMS** structure has the following form:

```
typedef struct {
    DWORD   dwCallback;
} MCI_GENERIC_PARMS;
```

For a full description of this structure, see Chapter 3, "Structures."

Return Value   Returns zero if successful. Otherwise, it returns an MCI error code.

Comments   Exiting an application without closing any MCI devices it has opened can leave the device opened and unaccessible. Your application should explicitly close each device or device element when it is finished with it. MCI unloads the device when all instances of the device or all device elements are closed.

See Also   MCI_OPEN

MCI_COPY

This MCI command message copies data to the Clipboard. Support of this message by a device is optional. The parameters and flags for this message vary according to the selected device.

Parameters   **DWORD** *dwFlags*
The following flags apply to all devices supporting MCI_COPY:

Value	Meaning
MCI_NOTIFY	
	Specifies that MCI should post the MM_MCINOTIFY message when this command completes. The window to receive this message is specified in the **dwCallback** member of the data structure identified by *lpCopy*.
MCI_WAIT	
	Specifies that the copy should finish before MCI returns control to the application.

LPMCI_GENERIC_PARMS *lpCopy*
Points to an **MCI_GENERIC_PARMS** structure. (Devices with extended command sets might replace this data structure with a device-specific data structure.) The **MCI_GENERIC_PARMS** structure has the following form:

```
typedef struct {
    DWORD  dwCallback;
} MCI_GENERIC_PARMS;
```

For a full description of this structure, see Chapter 3, "Structures."

Return Value   Returns zero if successful. Otherwise, it returns an MCI error code.

See Also   MCI_CUT, MCI_DELETE, MCI_PASTE

MCI_CUE

This MCI command message cues a device so that playback or recording begins with minimum delay. Support of this message by a device is optional. The parameters and flags for this message vary according to the selected device.

Parameters   **DWORD** *dwFlags*
The following flags apply to all devices supporting MCI_CUE:

Value	Meaning
MCI_NOTIFY	
	Specifies that MCI should post the MM_MCINOTIFY message when this command completes. The window to receive this message is specified in the **dwCallback** member of the structure identified by *lpDefault*.
MCI_WAIT	
	Specifies that the cue operation should finish before MCI returns control to the application.

LPMCI_GENERIC_PARMS *lpDefault*
Points to the **MCI_GENERIC_PARMS** structure. (Devices with extended command sets might replace this structure with a device-specific structure.) The **MCI_GENERIC_PARMS** structure has the following form:

```
typedef struct {
    DWORD  dwCallback;
} MCI_GENERIC_PARMS;
```

For a full description of this structure, see Chapter 3, "Structures."

Waveform Audio Extensions

Parameters   **DWORD** *dwFlags*
The following additional flags apply to wave audio devices:

Value	Meaning
MCI_WAVE_INPUT	
	Specifies that a wave input device should be cued.
MCI_WAVE_OUTPUT	
	Specifies that a wave output device should be cued. This is the default flag if a flag is not specified.

LPMCI_GENERIC_PARMS *lpDefault*
Points to the **MCI_GENERIC_PARMS** structure.

Return Value   Returns zero if successful. Otherwise, it returns an MCI error code.

See Also   MCI_SEEK, MCI_PLAY, MCI_RECORD

MCI_CUT

This MCI command message removes data from the MCI element and copies it to the Clipboard. Support of this message by a device is optional. The parameters and flags for this message vary according to the selected device.

Parameters   **DWORD** *dwFlags*
The following flags apply to all devices supporting MCI_CUT:

Value	Meaning
MCI_NOTIFY	
	Specifies that MCI should post the MM_MCINOTIFY message when this command completes. The window to receive this message is specified in the **dwCallback** member of the structure identified by *lpCut*.
MCI_WAIT	
	Specifies that the cut operation should finish before MCI returns control to the application.

LPMCI_GENERIC_PARMS *lpCut*
Points to an **MCI_GENERIC_PARMS** structure. (Devices with extended command sets might replace this structure with a device-specific structure.) The **MCI_GENERIC_PARMS** structure has the following form:

```
typedef struct {
    DWORD  dwCallback;
} MCI_GENERIC_PARMS;
```

For a full description of this structure, see Chapter 3, "Structures."

Return Value   Returns zero if successful. Otherwise, it returns an MCI error code.

See Also   MCI_COPY, MCI_DELETE, MCI_PASTE

MCI_DELETE

This MCI command message removes data from the MCI element. Support of this message by a device is optional. The parameters and flags for this message vary according to the selected device.

Parameters   **DWORD** *dwFlags*

The following flags apply to all devices supporting MCI_DELETE:

Value	Meaning
MCI_NOTIFY	
	Specifies that MCI should post the MM_MCINOTIFY message when this command completes. The window to receive this message is specified in the **dwCallback** member of the structure identified by *lpCut*.
MCI_WAIT	
	Specifies that the delete operation should finish before MCI returns control to the application.

LPMCI_GENERIC_PARMS *lpDelete*

Points to an **MCI_GENERIC_PARMS** structure. (Devices with extended command sets might replace this structure with a device-specific structure.) The **MCI_GENERIC_PARMS** structure has the following form:

```
typedef struct {
    DWORD  dwCallback;
} MCI_GENERIC_PARMS;
```

For a full description of this structure, see Chapter 3, "Structures."

Wave Audio Extensions

Parameters   **DWORD** *dwFlags*

The following extensions apply to wave audio devices:

Value	Meaning
MCI_FROM	
	Specifies that a beginning position is included in the **dwFrom** member of the structure identified by *lpDelete*. The units assigned to the position values is specified with the MCI_SET_TIME_FORMAT flag of the MCI_SET command.
MCI_TO	

Specifies that an ending position is included in the **dwTo** member of the structure identified by *lpDelete*. The units assigned to the position values is specified with the MCI_SET_TIME_FORMAT flag of the MCI_SET command.

LPMCI_WAVE_DELETE_PARMS *lpDelete*
Points to an **MCI_WAVE_DELETE_PARMS** structure. (Devices with extended command sets might replace this structure with a device-specific structure.)

Return Value   Returns zero if successful. Otherwise, it returns an MCI error code.

Comments   The waveform audio device uses this command.

See Also   MCI_COPY, MCI_DELETE, MCI_PASTE

MCI_FREEZE

This MCI command message freezes motion on the display. This command is part of the video overlay command set. The parameters and flags for this message vary according to the selected device.

Parameters   **DWORD** *dwFlags*
The following flags apply to all devices supporting MCI_FREEZE:

Value	Meaning
MCI_NOTIFY	
	Specifies that MCI should post the MM_MCINOTIFY message when this command completes. The window to receive this message is specified in the **dwCallback** member of the structure identified by *lpFreeze*.
MCI_WAIT	
	Specifies that the freeze operation should finish before MCI returns control to the application.
MCI_OVLY_RECT	
	Specifies that the **rc** member of the data structure identified by *lpFreeze* contains a valid rectangle. If this flag is not specified, the device driver will freeze the entire frame.

LPMCI_OVLY_RECT_PARMS *lpFreeze*
Points to a **MCI_OVLY_RECT_PARMS** structure. (Devices with additional parameters might replace this structure with a device-specific structure.) The **MCI_OVLY_RECT_PARMS** structure has the following form:

```
typedef struct {
```

```
        DWORD  dwCallback;
        RECT   rc;
    } MCI_OVLY_RECT_PARMS;
```

For a full description of this structure, see Chapter 3, "Structures."

Return Value   Returns zero if successful. Otherwise, it returns an MCI error code.

See Also   MCI_UNFREEZE

MCI_GETDEVCAPS

This MCI command message is used to obtain static information about a device. All devices must respond to this message. The parameters and flags available for this message depend on the selected device. Information is returned in the **dwReturn** member of the structure identified by *lpCapsParms*.

Parameters   **DWORD** *dwFlags*

The following standard and command-specific flags apply to all devices:

Value	Meaning
MCI_NOTIFY	Specifies that MCI should post the MM_MCINOTIFY message when this command completes. The window to receive this message is specified in the **dwCallback** member of the structure identified by *lpCapsParms*.
MCI_WAIT	Specifies that the query operation should finish before MCI returns control to the application.
MCI_GETDEVCAPS_ITEM	Specifies that the **dwItem** member of the structure identified by *lpCapsParms* contains a constant specifying which device capability to obtain. The following constants define which capability to return in the **dwReturn** member of the structure:
MCI_GETDEVCAPS_CAN_EJECT	The **dwReturn** member is set to TRUE if the device can eject the media; otherwise, it is set to FALSE.
MCI_GETDEVCAPS_CAN_PLAY	The **dwReturn** member is set to TRUE if the device can play the media; otherwise, it is set to FALSE.
	If a device specifies TRUE, it implies the device supports MCI_PAUSE and MCI_STOP as well as MCI_PLAY.

MCI_GETDEVCAPS_CAN_RECORD

The **dwReturn** member is set to TRUE if the device supports recording; otherwise, it is set to FALSE.

If a device specifies TRUE, it implies the device supports MCI_PAUSE and MCI_STOP as well as MCI_RECORD.

MCI_GETDEVCAPS_CAN_SAVE

The **dwReturn** member is set to TRUE if the device can save a file; otherwise, it is set to FALSE.

MCI_GETDEVCAPS_COMPOUND_DEVICE

The **dwReturn** member is set to TRUE if the device uses device elements; otherwise, it is set to FALSE.

MCI_GETDEVCAPS_DEVICE_TYPE

The **dwReturn** member is set to one of the following values indicating the device type:

- MCI_DEVTYPE_ANIMATION
- MCI_DEVTYPE_CD_AUDIO
- MCI_DEVTYPE_DAT
- MCI_DEVTYPE_DIGITAL_VIDEO
- MCI_DEVTYPE_OTHER
- MCI_DEVTYPE_OVERLAY
- MCI_DEVTYPE_SCANNER
- MCI_DEVTYPE_SEQUENCER
- MCI_DEVTYPE_VIDEODISC
- MCI_DEVTYPE_VCR
- MCI_DEVTYPE_WAVEFORM_AUDIO

MCI_GETDEVCAPS_HAS_AUDIO

The **dwReturn** member is set to TRUE if the device has audio output; otherwise, it is set to FALSE.

MCI_GETDEVCAPS_HAS_VIDEO

The **dwReturn** member is set to TRUE if the device has video output; otherwise, it is set to FALSE.

For example, the member is set to TRUE for devices that support the animation or videodisc command set.

MCI_GETDEVCAPS_USES_FILES

The **dwReturn** member is set to TRUE if the device requires a filename as its element name; otherwise, it is set to FALSE.

Only compound devices use files.

LPMCI_GETDEVCAPS_PARMS *lpCapsParms*

Points to the **MCI_GETDEVCAPS_PARMS** structure. (Devices with extended command sets might replace this structure with a device-specific structure.) The **MCI_GETDEVCAPS_PARMS** structure has the following form:

```
typedef struct {
    DWORD   dwCallback;
    DWORD   dwReturn;
    DWORD   dwItem;
} MCI_GETDEVCAPS_PARMS;
```

For a full description of this structure, see Chapter 3, "Structures."

Animation Extensions

Parameters

DWORD *dwFlags*

The following extensions apply to animation devices:

Value	Meaning

MCI_GETDEVCAPS_ITEM

Specifies that the **dwItem** member of the structure identified by *lpCapsParms* contains a constant specifying which device capability to obtain. The following additional device-capability constants are defined for animation devices and specify which value to return in the **dwReturn** member of the structure:

MCI_ANIM_GETDEVCAPS_CAN_REVERSE

The **dwReturn** member is set to TRUE if the device can play in reverse; otherwise, it is set to FALSE.

MCI_ANIM_GETDEVCAPS_CAN_STRETCH

The **dwReturn** member is set to TRUE if the device can stretch the image to fill the frame; otherwise, it is set to FALSE.

MCIMMP returns FALSE.

MCI_ANIM_GETDEVCAPS_FAST_RATE

The **dwReturn** member is set to the standard fast play rate in frames per second.

MCIMMP returns MCIERR_UNSUPPORTED_FUNCTION.

MCI_ANIM_GETDEVCAPS_MAX_WINDOWS

The **dwReturn** member is set to the maximum number of windows that the device can handle simultaneously.

MCI_ANIM_GETDEVCAPS_NORMAL_RATE

The **dwReturn** member is set to the normal rate of play in frames per second.

MCIMMP returns MCIERR_UNSUPPORTED_FUNCTION.

MCI_ANIM_GETDEVCAPS_PALETTES

The **dwReturn** member is set to TRUE if the device can return a palette handle; otherwise, it is set to FALSE.

MCIMMP returns TRUE.

MCI_ANIM_GETDEVCAPS_SLOW_RATE

The **dwReturn** member is set to the standard slow play rate in frames per second.

MCIMMP returns MCIERR_UNSUPPORTED_FUNCTION.

LPMCI_GETDEVCAPS_PARMS *lpCapsParms*
Points to the **MCI_GETDEVCAPS_PARMS** structure.

Videodisc Extensions

Parameters

DWORD *dwFlags*
The following extensions apply to videodisc devices:

Value	Meaning

MCI_GETDEVCAPS_ITEM

Specifies that the **dwItem** member of the structure identified by *lpCapsParms* contains a constant specifying which device capability to obtain. The following additional device-capability constants are defined for videodisc devices and specify which value to return in the **dwReturn** member of the structure:

MCI_VD_GETDEVCAPS_CAN_REVERSE

The **dwReturn** member is set to TRUE if the videodisc player can play in reverse; otherwise, it is set to FALSE.

Some players can play CLV discs in reverse as well as CAV discs.

MCI_VD_GETDEVCAPS_FAST_RATE

The **dwReturn** member is set to the standard fast play rate in frames per second.

MCI_VD_GETDEVCAPS_NORMAL_RATE

The **dwReturn** member is set to the normal play rate in frames per second.

MCI_VD_GETDEVCAPS_SLOW_RATE

The **dwReturn** member is set to the standard slow play rate in frames per second.

MCI_VD_GETDEVCAPS_CLV

Indicates the information requested applies to CLV format discs. By default, the capabilities apply to the current disc.

MCI_VD_GETDEVCAPS_CAV

Indicates the information requested applies to CAV format discs. By default, the capabilities apply to the current disc.

LPMCI_GETDEVCAPS_PARMS *lpCapsParms*
Points to the **MCI_GETDEVCAPS_PARMS** structure.

Video Overlay Extensions

DWORD *dwFlags*
The following extensions apply to video overlay devices:

Value	Meaning
MCI_GETDEVCAPS_ITEM	

Specifies that the **dwItem** member of the structure identified by *lpCapsParms* contains a constant specifying which device capability to obtain. The following additional device-capability constants are defined for video overlay devices and specify which value to return in the **dwReturn** member of the structure:

MCI_OVLY_GETDEVCAPS_CAN_FREEZE

The **dwReturn** member is set to TRUE if the device can freeze the image; otherwise, it is set to FALSE.

MCI_OVLY_GETDEVCAPS_CAN_STRETCH

The **dwReturn** member is set to TRUE if the device can stretch the image to fill the frame; otherwise, it is set to FALSE.

MCI_OVLY_GETDEVCAPS_MAX_WINDOWS

The **dwReturn** member is set to the maximum number of windows that the device can handle simultaneously.

LPMCI_GETDEVCAPS_PARMS *lpCapsParms*
Points to the **MCI_GETDEVCAPS_PARMS** structure.

Waveform Audio Extensions

DWORD *dwFlags*
The following extended flag applies to waveform audio devices:

Value	Meaning
MCI_GETDEVCAPS_ITEM	

Specifies that the **dwItem** member of the structure identified by *lpCapsParms* contains a constant specifying which device capability to obtain. The following additional device-capability constants are defined for waveform audio devices and specify which value to return in the **dwReturn** member of the structure:

MCI_WAVE_GETDEVCAPS_INPUT

The **dwReturn** member is set to the total number of waveform input (recording) devices.

MCI_WAVE_GETDEVCAPS_OUTPUT

The **dwReturn** member is set to the total number of waveform output (playback) devices.

LPMCI_GETDEVCAPS_PARMS *lpCapsParms*
Points to the **MCI_GETDEVCAPS_PARMS** structure.

Return Value   Returns zero if successful. Otherwise, it returns an MCI error code.

MCI_INFO

This MCI command message obtains string information from a device. All
devices respond to this message. The parameters and flags available for this
message depend on the selected device. Information is returned in the
lpstrReturn member of the structure identified by *lpInfo*. The **dwReturnSize**
member specifies the buffer length for the return data.

Parameters   **DWORD** *dwFlags*
The following standard and command-specific flags apply to all devices:

Value	Meaning
MCI_NOTIFY	
	Specifies that MCI should post the MM_MCINOTIFY message when this command completes. The window to receive this message is specified in the **dwCallback** member of the structure identified by *lpInfo*.
MCI_WAIT	
	Specifies that the query operation should finish before MCI returns control to the application.
MCI_INFO_PRODUCT	
	Obtains a description of the hardware associated with a device. Devices should supply a description that identifies both the driver and the hardware used.

LPMCI_INFO_PARMS *lpInfo*
Points to the **MCI_INFO_PARMS** structure. (Devices with extended
command sets might replace this structure with a device-specific structure.)
The **MCI_INFO_PARMS** structure has the following form:

```
typedef struct {
    DWORD  dwCallback;
    LPTSTR lpstrReturn;
    DWORD  dwRetSize;
} MCI_INFO_PARMS;
```

For a full description of this structure, see Chapter 3, "Structures."

Animation Extensions

Parameters

DWORD *dwFlags*

The following additional flags apply to animation devices:

Value	Meaning
MCI_INFO_FILE	
	Obtains the filename of the current file. This flag is only supported by devices that return TRUE to the MCI_GETDEVCAPS_USES_FILES query.
MCI_ANIM_INFO_TEXT	
	Obtains the window caption.

LPMCI_INFO_PARMS *lpInfo*

Points to the **MCI_INFO_PARMS** structure.

Video Overlay Extensions

Parameters

DWORD *dwFlags*

The following additional flags apply to video overlay devices:

Value	Meaning
MCI_INFO_FILE	
	Obtains the filename of the current file. This flag is only supported by devices that return TRUE to the MCI_GETDEVCAPS_USES_FILES query.
MCI_OVLY_INFO_TEXT	
	Obtains the caption of the window associated with the overlay device.

LPMCI_INFO_PARMS *lpInfo*

Points to the **MCI_INFO_PARMS** structure.

Waveform Audio Extensions

Parameters

DWORD *dwFlags*

The following additional flags apply to waveform audio devices:

Value	Meaning
MCI_INFO_FILE	
	Obtains the filename of the current file. This flag is supported by devices that return TRUE to the MCI_GETDEVCAPS_USES_FILES query.
MCI_WAVE_INPUT	
	Obtains the product name of the current input.
MCI_WAVE_OUTPUT	
	Obtains the product name of the current output.

LPMCI_INFO_PARMS *lpInfo*
Points to the **MCI_INFO_PARMS** structure.

Return Value
Returns zero if successful. Otherwise, it returns an MCI error code.

MCI_LOAD

This MCI command message loads a file. Support of this message by a device is optional. The parameters and flags for this message vary according to the selected device.

Parameters

DWORD *dwFlags*
The following flags apply to all devices supporting MCI_LOAD:

Value	Meaning
MCI_NOTIFY	
	Specifies that MCI should post the MM_MCINOTIFY message when this command completes. The window to receive this message is specified in the **dwCallback** member of the structure identified by *lpLoad*.
MCI_WAIT	
	Specifies that the load operation should finish before MCI returns control to the application.
MCI_LOAD_FILE	
	Indicates the **lpfilename** member of the structure identified by *lpLoad* contains a pointer to a buffer containing the file name.

LPMCI_LOAD_PARMS *lpLoad*
Points to the **MCI_LOAD_PARMS** structure. (Devices with additional parameters might replace this structure with a device-specific structure.) The **MCI_LOAD_PARMS** structure has the following form:

```
typedef struct {
    DWORD   dwCallback;
    LPCTSTR  lpfilename;
} MCI_LOAD_PARMS;
```

For a full description of this structure, see Chapter 3, "Structures."

Video Overlay Extensions

Parameters

DWORD *dwFlags*

The following additional flags apply to video overlay devices supporting MCI_LOAD:

Value	Meaning
MCI_OVLY_RECT	

           Specifies that the **rc** member of the structure identified by *lpLoad* contains a valid display rectangle that identifies the area of the video buffer to update.

LPMCI_OVLY_LOAD_PARMS *lpLoad*

Points to a **MCI_OVLY_LOAD_PARMS** structure.

Return Value

Returns zero if successful. Otherwise, it returns an MCI error code.

Comments

This command applies to video overlay devices.

See Also

MCI_SAVE

MCI_OPEN

This MCI command message initializes a device or device element. All devices respond to this message. The parameters and flags available for this message depend on the selected device.

Parameters

DWORD *dwFlags*

The following flags apply to all devices:

Value	Meaning
MCI_NOTIFY	

           Specifies that MCI should post the MM_MCINOTIFY message when this command completes. The window to receive this message is specified in the **dwCallback** member of the structure identified by *lpOpen*.

MCI_WAIT

           Specifies that the open operation should finish before MCI returns control to the application.

MCI_OPEN_ALIAS

           Specifies that an alias is included in the **lpstrAlias** member of the structure identified by *lpOpen*.

MCI_OPEN_SHAREABLE

Specifies that the device or device element should be opened as shareable.

MCI_OPEN_TYPE

Specifies that a device type name or constant is included in the **lpstrDeviceType** member of the structure identified by *lpOpen*.

MCI_OPEN_TYPE_ID

Specifies that the low-order word of the **lpstrDeviceType** member of the associated structure contains a standard MCI device type ID and the high-order word optionally contains the ordinal index for the device. Use this flag with the MCI_OPEN_TYPE flag.

LPMCI_OPEN_PARMS *lpOpen*

Points to the **MCI_OPEN_PARMS** structure. (Devices with extended command sets might replace this structure with a device-specific structure.) The **MCI_OPEN_PARMS** structure has the following form:

```
typedef struct {
    DWORD      dwCallback;
    MCIDEVICEID  wDeviceID;
    LPCTSTR    lpstrDeviceType;
    LPCTSTR    lpstrElementName;
    LPCTSTR    lpstrAlias;
} MCI_OPEN_PARMS;
```

For a full description of this structure, see Chapter 3, "Structures."

Flags for Compound Devices

Parameters   **DWORD** *dwFlags*

The following additional flags apply to compound devices:

Value	Meaning
MCI_OPEN_ELEMENT	

Specifies that an element name is included in the **lpstrElementName** member of the structure identified by *lpOpen*.

MCI_OPEN_ELEMENT_ID

Specifies that the **lpstrElementName** member of the structure identified by *lpOpen* is interpreted as a **DWORD** and has meaning internal to the device. Use this flag with the MCI_OPEN_ELEMENT flag.

LPMCI_OPEN_PARMS *lpOpen*

Points to the **MCI_OPEN_PARMS** structure. (Devices with additional parameters might replace this structure with a device-specific structure.)

Animation Extensions

Parameters   **DWORD** *dwFlags*

The following flags apply to animation devices:

Value	Meaning
MCI_ANIM_OPEN_NOSTATIC	

Specifies that the device should reduce the number of static (system) colors in the palette to two.

MCI_ANIM_OPEN_PARENT

Indicates the parent window handle is specified in the **hWndParent** member of the structure identified by *lpOpen*. The parent window handle is required for some window styles.

MCI_ANIM_OPEN_WS

Indicates a window style is specified in the **dwStyle** member of the structure identified by *lpOpen*. The **dwStyle** value specifies the style of the window that the driver will create and display if the application does not provide one. The style parameter takes an integer which defines the window style. These constants are the same as the ones in WINDOWS.H (such as WS_CHILD, WS_OVERLAPPEDWINDOW, or WS_POPUP).

LPMCI_ANIM_OPEN_PARMS *lpOpen*
Points to the **MCI_ANIM_OPEN_PARMS** structure.

Video Overlay Extensions

Parameters   **DWORD** *dwFlags*
The following flags apply to video overlay devices:

Value	Meaning
MCI_OVLY_OPEN_PARENT	

Indicates the parent window handle is specified in the **hWndParent** member of the structure identified by *lpOpen*.

MCI_OVLY_OPEN_WS

Indicates a window style is specified in the **dwStyle** member of the structure identified by *lpOpen*. The **dwStyle** value specifies the style of the window that the driver will create and display if the application does not provide one. The style parameter takes an integer that defines the window style. These constants are the same as those in WINDOWS.H (for example, WS_CHILD, WS_OVERLAPPEDWINDOW, or WS_POPUP).

LPMCI_OVLY_OPEN_PARMS *lpOpen*
Points to the **MCI_OVLY_OPEN_PARMS** structure.

Waveform Audio Extensions

Parameters   **DWORD** *dwFlags*
The following flags apply to waveform audio devices:

Value	Meaning
MCI_WAVE_OPEN_BUFFER	
	Indicates a buffer length is specified in the **dwBuffer** member of the structure identified by *lpOpen*.

LPMCI_WAVE_OPEN_PARMS *lpOpen*
Points to the **MCI_WAVE_OPEN_PARMS** structure. (Devices with extended command sets might replace this structure with a device-specific structure.)

Return Value   Returns zero if the open succeeds. If an error occurs, it returns the following values:

Value	Meaning
MCIERR_CANNOT_LOAD_DRIVER	
	Error loading media device driver.
MCIERR_DEVICE_OPEN	
	The device name is in use by this task. Use a unique alias.
MCIERR_DUPLICATE_ALIAS	
	The specified alias is an open device in this task.
MCIERR_EXTENSION_NOT_FOUND	
	Cannot deduce a device type from the given extension.
MCIERR_FILENAME_REQUIRED	
	A valid filename is required.
MCIERR_MISSING_PARAMETER	
	Required parameter is missing.
MCIERR_MUST_USE_SHAREABLE	
	The device is already open; use the shareable flag with each open.
MCIERR_NO_ELEMENT_ALLOWED	
	An element name cannot be used with this device.

Comments   If MCI_OPEN_SHAREABLE is not specified when a device or device element is initially opened, then all subsequent MCI_OPEN messages to the device or device element will fail. If the device or device element is already open, and this flag is not specified, the call will fail even if the first open command specified MCI_OPEN_SHAREABLE. Files for the MCIMMP, MCISEQ, and MCIWAVE devices are nonshareable.

Case is ignored in the device name, but there must not be any leading or trailing blanks.

To use automatic type selection (via the [mci extensions] section of the registry file), assign the file name (including file extension) to the **lpstrElementName** member, assign a NULL pointer to the **lpstrDeviceType** member, and set the MCI_OPEN_ELEMENT flag.

See Also   MCI_CLOSE

MCI_PASTE

This MCI command message pastes data from the clipboard into a device element.

Parameters   **DWORD** *dwFlags*

The following flags apply to all devices supporting MCI_PASTE:

Value	Meaning
MCI_NOTIFY	
	Specifies that MCI should post the MM_MCINOTIFY message when this command completes. The window to receive this message is specified in the **dwCallback** member of the structure identified by *lpPaste*.
MCI_WAIT	
	Specifies that the device should complete the operation before MCI returns control to the application.

LPMCI_GENERIC_PARMS *lpPaste*

Points to the **MCI_GENERIC_PARMS** structure. (Devices with extended command sets might replace this structure with a device-specific structure.) The **MCI_GENERIC_PARMS** structure has the following form:

```
typedef struct {
    DWORD  dwCallback;
} MCI_GENERIC_PARMS;
```

For a full description of this structure, see Chapter 3, "Structures."

Return Value   Returns zero if successful. Otherwise, it returns an MCI error code.

See Also   MCI_CUT, MCI_COPY, MCI_DELETE

MCI_PAUSE

This MCI command message pauses the current action.

Parameters

DWORD *dwFlags*

The following flags apply to all devices supporting MCI_PAUSE:

Value	Meaning
MCI_NOTIFY	
	Specifies that MCi should post the MM_MCINOTIFY message when this command completes. The window to receive this message is specified in the **dwCallback** member of the structure identified by *lpPause*.
MCI_WAIT	
	Specifies that the device should be paused before MCi returns control to the application.

LPMCI_GENERIC_PARMS *lpPause*

Points to the **MCI_GENERIC_PARMS** structure. (Devices with extended command sets might replace this structure with a device-specific structure.) The **MCI_GENERIC_PARMS** structure has the following form:

```
typedef struct {
    DWORD  dwCallback;
} MCI_GENERIC_PARMS;
```

For a full description of this structure, see Chapter 3, "Structures."

Return Value

Returns zero if successful. Otherwise, it returns an MCI error code.

Comments

The difference between MCI_STOP and MCI_PAUSE depends upon the device. If possible, MCI_PAUSE suspends device operation but leaves the device ready to resume play immediately.

See Also

MCI_PLAY, MCI_RECORD, MCI_RESUME, MCI_STOP

MCI_PLAY

This MCI command message signals the device to begin transmitting output data. Support of this message by a device is optional. The parameters and flags for this message vary according to the selected device.

Parameters

DWORD *dwFlags*

The following flags apply to all devices supporting MCI_PLAY:

Value	Meaning
MCI_NOTIFY	

Specifies that MCI should post the MM_MCINOTIFY message when this command completes. The window to receive this message is specified in the **dwCallback** member of the structure identified by *lpPlay*.

MCI_WAIT	

Specifies that the play operation should finish before MCI returns control to the application.

MCI_FROM	

Specifies that a starting position is included in the **dwFrom** member of the structure identified by *lpPlay*. The units assigned to the position values is specified with the MCI_SET_TIME_FORMAT flag of the MCI_SET command. If MCI_FROM is not specified, the starting position defaults to the current location.

MCI_TO	

Specifies that an ending position is included in the **dwTo** member of the structure identified by *lpPlay*. The units assigned to the position values is specified with the MCI_SET_TIME_FORMAT flag of the **MCI_SET** command. If MCI_TO is not specified, the end position defaults to the end of the media.

LPMCI_PLAY_PARMS *lpPlay*

Points to an **MCI_PLAY_PARMS** structure. (Devices with extended command sets might replace this structure with a device-specific structure.) The structure has the following form:

```
typedef struct {
    DWORD   dwCallback;
    DWORD   dwFrom;
    DWORD   dwTo;
} MCI_PLAY_PARMS;
```

For a full description of this structure, see Chapter 3, "Structures."

Animation Extensions

Parameters

DWORD *dwFlags*

The following additional flags apply to animation devices:

Value	Meaning
MCI_ANIM_PLAY_FAST	

Specifies to play fast.

MCI_ANIM_PLAY_REVERSE	

Specifies to play in reverse.

MCI_ANIM_PLAY_SCAN

Specifies to scan quickly.

MCI_ANIM_PLAY_SLOW

Specifies to play slowly.

MCI_ANIM_PLAY_SPEED

Specifies that the play speed is included in the **dwSpeed** member in the structure identified by *lpPlay*.

LPMCI_ANIM_PLAY_PARMS *lpPlay*
Points to an **MCI_ANIM_PLAY_PARMS** structure.

Videodisc Extensions

Parameters

DWORD *dwFlags*
The following additional flags apply to videodisc devices:

Value	Meaning
MCI_VD_PLAY_FAST	
	Specifies to play fast.
MCI_VD_PLAY_REVERSE	
	Specifies to play in reverse.
MCI_VD_PLAY_SCAN	
	Specifies to scan quickly.
MCI_VD_PLAY_SLOW	
	Specifies to play slowly.
MCI_VD_PLAY_SPEED	
	Specifies that the play speed is included in the **dwSpeed** member in the structure identified by *lpPlay*.

LPMCI_VD_PLAY_PARMS *lpPlay*
Points to an **MCI_VD_PLAY_PARMS** structure.

Return Value

Returns zero if successful. Otherwise, it returns an MCI error code.

See Also

MCI_CUE, MCI_PAUSE, MCI_RECORD, MCI_RESUME, MCI_SEEK, MCI_STOP

MCI_PUT

This MCI command message sets the source, destination, and frame rectangles. The parameters and flags for this message vary according to the selected device.

Parameters

DWORD *dwFlags*

The following flags apply to all devices supporting MCI_PUT:

Value	Meaning
MCI_NOTIFY	
	Specifies that MCI should post the MM_MCINOTIFY message when this command completes. The window to receive this message is specified in the **dwCallback** member of the structure identified by *lpDest*.
MCI_WAIT	
	Specifies that the operation should finish before MCI returns control to the application.

LPMCI_GENERIC_PARMS *lpDest*

Points to an **MCI_GENERIC_PARMS** structure. (Devices with extended command sets might replace this structure with a device-specific structure.) The **MCI_GENERIC_PARMS** structure has the following form:

```
typedef struct {
    DWORD  dwCallback;
} MCI_GENERIC_PARMS;
```

For a full description of this structure, see Chapter 3, "Structures."

Animation Extensions

Parameters

DWORD *dwFlags*

The following additional flags apply to animation devices supporting MCI_PUT:

Value	Meaning
MCI_ANIM_RECT	
	Specifies that the **rc** member of the structure identified by *lpDest* contains a valid rectangle. If this flag is not specified, the default rectangle matches the coordinates of the image or window being clipped.
MCI_ANIM_PUT_DESTINATION	

Indicates the rectangle defined for MCI_ANIM_RECT specifies the area of the client window used to display an image. The rectangle contains the offset and visible extent of the image relative to the window origin. If the frame is being stretched, the source is stretched to the destination rectangle.

MCI_ANIM_PUT_SOURCE

Indicates the rectangle defined for MCI_ANIM_RECT specifies a clipping rectangle for the animation image. The rectangle contains the offset and extent of the image relative to the image origin.

LPMCI_ANIM_RECT_PARMS *lpDest*
Points to a **MCI_ANIM_RECT_PARMS** structure. (Devices with extended command sets might replace this structure with a device-specific structure.)

Video Overlay Extensions

Parameters

DWORD *dwFlags*
The following additional flags apply to video overlay devices supporting MCI_PUT:

Value	Meaning

MCI_OVLY_RECT

Specifies that the **rc** member of the structure identified by *lpDest* contains a valid display rectangle. If this flag is not specified, the default rectangle matches the coordinates of the video buffer or window being clipped.

MCI_OVLY_PUT_DESTINATION

Indicates the rectangle defined for MCI_OVLY_RECT specifies the area of the client window used to display an image. The rectangle contains the offset and visible extent of the image relative to the window origin. If the frame is being stretched, the source is stretched to the destination rectangle.

MCI_OVLY_PUT_FRAME

Indicates the rectangle defined for MCI_OVLY_RECT specifies the area of the video buffer used to receive the video image. The rectangle contains the offset and extent of the buffer area relative to the video buffer origin.

MCI_OVLY_PUT_SOURCE

Indicates that the rectangle defined for MCI_OVLY_RECT specifies the area of the video buffer used as the source of the digital image. The rectangle contains the offset and extent of the clipping rectangle for the video buffer relative to its origin.

MCI_OVLY_PUT_VIDEO

Indicates that the rectangle defined for MCI_OVLY_RECT specifies the area of the video source capture by the video buffer. The rectangle contains the offset and extent of the clipping rectangle for the video source relative to its origin.

LPMCI_OVLY_RECT_PARMS *lpDest*
Points to a **MCI_OVLY_RECT_PARMS** structure.

Return Value   Returns zero if successful. Otherwise, it returns an MCI error code.

See Also   MCI_WHERE

MCI_RECORD

This MCI command message starts recording from the current position or from the specified position until the specified position. Support of this message by a device is optional. The parameters and flags for this message vary according to the selected device.

Parameters   **DWORD** *dwFlags*
The following flags apply to all devices supporting MCI_RECORD:

Value	Meaning
MCI_NOTIFY	
	Specifies that MCI should post the MM_MCINOTIFY message when this command completes. The window to receive this message is specified in the **dwCallback** member of the structure identified by *lpRecord*.
MCI_WAIT	
	Specifies that recording should finish before MCI returns control to the application.
MCI_RECORD_INSERT	
	Indicates that newly recorded information should be inserted or pasted into the existing data. (Some devices may not support this.) If supported, this is the default.
MCI_FROM	
	Specifies that a starting position is included in the **dwFrom** member of the structure identified by *lpRecord*. The units assigned to the position values is specified with the MCI_SET_TIME_FORMAT flag of the MCI_SET command. If MCI_FROM is not specified, the starting position defaults to the current location.
MCI_RECORD_OVERWRITE	
	Specifies that data should overwrite existing data.

MCIWAVE returns MCIERR_UNSUPPORTED_FUNCTION in response to this flag.

MCI_TO

Specifies that an ending position is included in the **dwTo** member of the structure identified by *lpRecord*. The units assigned to the position values is specified with the MCI_SET_TIME_FORMAT flag of the MCI_SET command. If MCI_TO is not specified, the ending position defaults to the end of the media.

LPMCI_RECORD_PARMS *lpRecord*
Points to the **MCI_RECORD_PARMS** structure. (Devices with extended command sets might replace this structure with a device-specific structure.) The **MCI_RECORD_PARMS** structure has the following form:

```
typedef struct {
    DWORD   dwCallback;
    DWORD   dwFrom;
    DWORD   dwTo;
} MCI_RECORD_PARMS;
```

For a full description of this structure, see Chapter 3, "Structures."

Return Value   Returns zero if successful. Otherwise, it returns an MCI error code.

MCISEQ returns MCIERR_UNSUPPORTED_FUNCTION for this command.

Comments   This command is supported by devices that return TRUE to the MCI_GETDEVCAPS_CAN_RECORD query.

See Also   MCI_CUE, MCI_PAUSE, MCI_PLAY, MCI_RESUME, MCI_SEEK

MCI_RESUME

This MCI command message resumes a paused device. Support of this message by a device is optional.

Parameters   **DWORD** *dwFlags*
The following flags apply to all devices supporting MCI_RESUME:

Value	Meaning
MCI_NOTIFY	
	Specifies that MCI should post the MM_MCINOTIFY message when this command completes. The window to receive this message is specified in the **dwCallback** member of the structure identified by *lpDefault*.
MCI_WAIT	

Specifies that the device should resume before MCI returns control to the application.

LPMCI_GENERIC_PARMS *lpDefault*

Points to the **MCI_GENERIC_PARMS** structure. (Devices with extended command sets might replace this data structure with a device-specific data structure.) The **MCI_GENERIC_PARMS** structure has the following form:

```
typedef struct {
    DWORD  dwCallback;
} MCI_GENERIC_PARMS;
```

For a full description of this structure, see Chapter 3, "Structures."

Return Value   Returns zero if successful. Otherwise, it returns an MCI error code.

Comments   This command resumes playing and recording without changing the stop position set with MCI_PLAY or MCI_RECORD.

See Also   MCI_STOP, MCI_PLAY, MCI_RECORD

MCI_SAVE

This MCI command message saves the current file. Devices which modify files should not destroy the original copy until they receive the save message. Support of this message by a device is optional. The parameters and flags for this message vary according to the selected device.

Parameters   **DWORD** *dwFlags*

The following flags apply to all devices supporting MCI_SAVE:

Value	Meaning
MCI_NOTIFY	
	Specifies that MCI should post the MM_MCINOTIFY message when this command completes. The window to receive this message is specified in the **dwCallback** member of the structure identified by *lpSave*.
MCI_WAIT	
	Specifies that the save operation should finish before MCI returns control to the application.
MCI_SAVE_FILE	
	Indicates the **lpfilename** member of the structure identified by *lpSave* contains a pointer to a buffer containing the destination file name.

LPMCI_SAVE_PARMS *lpSave*
Points to the **MCI_SAVE_PARMS** structure. (Devices with additional parameters might replace this data structure with a device-specific data structure.) The **MCI_SAVE_PARMS** structure has the following form:

```
typedef struct {
    DWORD   dwCallback;
    LPCTSTR lpfilename;
} MCI_SAVE_PARMS;
```

For a full description of this structure, see Chapter 3, "Structures."

Video Overlay Extensions

Parameters

DWORD *dwFlags*
The following additional flags apply to video overlay devices supporting MCI_SAVE:

Value	Meaning
MCI_OVLY_RECT	

Specifies that the **rc** member of the structure identified by *lpSave* contains a valid display rectangle indicating the area of the video buffer to save.

LPMCI_OVLY_SAVE_PARMS *lpSave*
Points to a **MCI_OVLY_SAVE_PARMS** structure.

Return Value

Returns zero if successful. Otherwise, it returns an MCI error code. MCISEQ returns MCIERR_UNSUPPORTED_FUNCTION.

Comments

This command is supported by devices that return true to the MCI_GETDEVCAPS_CAN_SAVE query. MCIWAVE supports this command.

See Also

MCI_LOAD

MCI_SEEK

This MCI command message changes the current position of media as quickly as possible. Video and audio output are disable during the seek. After the seek is complete, the device will be stopped. Support of this message by a device is optional. The parameters and flags for this message vary according to the selected device.

Parameters

DWORD *dwFlags*

The following flags apply to all devices supporting MCI_SEEK:

Value	Meaning
MCI_NOTIFY	
	Specifies that MCI should post the MM_MCINOTIFY message when this command completes. The window to receive this message is specified in the **dwCallback** member of the structure identified by *lpSeek*.
MCI_WAIT	
	Specifies that the seek operation should finish before MCI returns control to the application.
MCI_SEEK_TO_END	
	Specifies to seek to the end of the media.
MCI_SEEK_TO_START	
	Specifies to seek to the start of the media.
MCI_TO	
	Specifies a position is included in the **dwTo** member of the **MCI_SEEK_PARMS** structure. The units assigned to the position values is specified with the MCI_SET_TIME_FORMAT flag of the MCI_SET command. Do not use this flag with MCI_SEEK_END or MCI_SEEK_START.

LPMCI_SEEK_PARMS *lpSeek*

Points to the **MCI_SEEK_PARMS** structure. (Devices with extended command sets might replace this structure with a device-specific structure.) The **MCI_SEEK_PARMS** structure has the following form:

```
typedef struct {
    DWORD  dwCallback;
    DWORD  dwTo;
} MCI_SEEK_PARMS;
```

For a full description of this structure, see Chapter 3, "Structures."

Videodisc Extensions

Parameters

DWORD *dwFlags*

The following additional flag applies to videodisc devices.

Value	Meaning
MCI_VD_SEEK_REVERSE	
	Specifies to seek backward.

LPMCI_SEEK_PARMS *lpSeek*

Points to the **MCI_SEEK_PARMS** structure.

Return Value   Returns zero if successful. Otherwise, it returns an MCI error code.

See Also   MCI_PLAY, MCI_RECORD

MCI_SET

This MCI command message sets device information. Support of this message by a device is optional. The parameters and flags for this message vary according to the selected device.

Parameters   **DWORD** *dwFlags*
The following flags apply to all devices supporting MCI_SET:

Value	Meaning
MCI_NOTIFY	
	Specifies that MCI should post the MM_MCINOTIFY message when this command completes. The window to receive this message is specified in the **dwCallback** member of the structure identified by *lpSet*.
MCI_WAIT	
	Specifies that the set operation should finish before MCI returns control to the application.
MCI_SET_AUDIO	
	Specifies an audio channel number is included in the **dwAudio** member of the structure identified by *lpSet*. This flag must be used with MCI_SET_ON or MCI_SET_OFF. Use one of the following constants to indicate the channel number:

Value	Meaning
MCI_SET_AUDIO_ALL	
	Specifies all audio channels.
MCI_SET_AUDIO_LEFT	
	Specifies the left channel.
MCI_SET_AUDIO_RIGHT	
	Specifies the right channel.

MCI_SET_DOOR_CLOSED	
	Instructs the device to close the media cover (if any).
MCI_SET_DOOR_OPEN	
	Instructs the device to open the media cover (if any).
MCI_SET_TIME_FORMAT	

Specifies a time format parameter is included in the **dwTimeFormat** member of the structure identified by *lpSet*. Specifying MCI_FORMAT_MILLISECONDS indicates that subsequent commands that specify time will use milliseconds for both input and output. Other units are device dependent.

MCI_SET_VIDEO

Sets the video signal on or off. This flag must be used with either MCI_SET_ON or MCI_SET_OFF. Devices that do not have video return MCIERR_UNSUPPORTED_FUNCTION.

MCI_SET_ON

Enables the specified video or audio channel.

MCI_SET_OFF

Disables the specified video or audio channel.

LPMCI_SET_PARMS *lpSet*

Points to the **MCI_SET_PARMS** structure. (Devices with extended command sets might replace this structure with a device-specific structure.) The **MCI_SET_PARMS** structure has the following form:

```
typedef struct {
    DWORD   dwCallback;
    DWORD   dwTimeFormat;
    DWORD   dwAudio;
} MCI_SET_PARMS;
```

For a full description of this structure, see Chapter 3, "Structures."

Animation Extensions

Parameters

DWORD *dwFlags*

The following additional flags apply to animation devices:

Value	Meaning

MCI_SET_TIME_FORMAT

Specifies a time format parameter is included in the **dwTimeFormat** member of the structure identified by *lpSet*. The following constants are defined for the time format:

MCI_FORMAT_MILLISECONDS

Changes the time format to milliseconds.

MCIMMP returns MCIERR_UNSUPPORTED_FUNCTION if the time format is set to MCI_FORMAT_MILLISECONDS.

MCI_FORMAT_FRAMES

Changes the time format to frames.

LPMCI_SET_PARMS *lpSet*

Points to the **MCI_SET_PARMS** structure.

CD Audio Extensions

DWORD *dwFlags*

The following additional flags apply to videodisc devices:

Value	Meaning

MCI_SET_TIME_FORMAT

Specifies a time format parameter is included in the **dwTimeFormat** member of the structure identified by *lpSet*. The following constants are defined for the time format:

MCI_FORMAT_MILLISECONDS

Changes the time format to milliseconds.

MCI_FORMAT_MSF

Changes the time format to minutes, seconds, and frames.

MCI_FORMAT_TMSF

Changes the time format to tracks, minutes, seconds, and frames. (MCI uses continuous track numbers.)

LPMCI_SET_PARMS *lpSet*

Points to the **MCI_SET_PARMS** structure.

MIDI Sequencer Extensions

DWORD *dwFlags*

The following additional flags apply to MIDI sequencer devices:

Value	Meaning

MCI_SEQ_SET_MASTER

Sets the sequencer as a source of synchronization data and indicates that the type of synchronization is specified in the **dwMaster** member of the structure identified by *lpSet*.

MCISEQ returns MCIERR_UNSUPPORTED_FUNCTION.

The following constants are defined for the synchronization type:

Value	Meaning

MCI_SEQ_MIDI

The sequencer will send MIDI format synchronization data.

MCI_SEQ_SMPTE

The sequencer will send SMPTE format synchronization data.

MCI_SEQ_NONE

The sequencer will not send synchronization data.

MCI_SEQ_SET_OFFSET

> Changes the SMPTE offset of a sequence to that specified by the **dwOffset** member of the structure identified by *lpSet*. This only affects sequences with a SMPTE division type.

MCI_SEQ_SET_PORT

> Sets the output MIDI port of a sequence to that specified by the MIDI device ID in the **dwPort** member of the structure identified by *lpSet*. The device will close the previous port (if any), and attempt to open and use the new port. If it fails, it will return an error and re-open the previously used port (if any). The following constants are defined for the ports:

MCI_SEQ_NONE

> Closes the previously used port (if any). The sequencer will behave exactly the same as if a port were open, except no MIDI message will be sent.

MIDI_MAPPER

> Sets the port opened to the MIDI Mapper.

MCI_SEQ_SET_SLAVE

> Sets the sequencer to receive synchronization data and indicates that the type of synchronization is specified in the **dwSlave** member of the structure identified by *lpSet*.
>
> MCISEQ returns MCIERR_UNSUPPORTED_FUNCTION.
>
> The following constants are defined for the synchronization type:

Value	Meaning
MCI_SEQ_FILE	Sets the sequencer to receive synchronization data contained in the MIDI file.
MCI_SEQ_SMPTE	Sets the sequencer to receive SMPTE synchronization data.
MCI_SEQ_MIDI	Sets the sequencer to receive MIDI synchronization data.
MCI_SEQ_NONE	Sets the sequencer to ignore synchronization data in a MIDI stream.

MCI_SEQ_SET_TEMPO

Changes the tempo of the MIDI sequence to that specified by the **dwTempo** member of the structure pointed to by *lpSet*. For sequences with division type PPQN, tempo is specified in beats per minute; for sequences with division type SMPTE, tempo is specified in frames per second.

MCI_SET_TIME_FORMAT

Specifies a time format parameter is included in the **dwTimeFormat** member of the structure identified by *lpSet*. The following constants are defined for the time format:

Value	Meaning
MCI_FORMAT_MILLISECONDS	
	Changes the time format to milliseconds for both input and output.
MCI_FORMAT_SMPTE_24	
	Sets the time format to 24 frame SMPTE.
MCI_FORMAT_SMPTE_25	
	Sets the time format to 25 frame SMPTE.
MCI_FORMAT_SMPTE_30	
	Sets the time format to 30 frame SMPTE.
MCI_FORMAT_SMPTE_30DROP	
	Sets the time format to 30 drop-frame SMPTE.
MCI_SEQ_FORMAT_SONGPTR	
	Sets the time format to song-pointer units.

LPMCI_SEQ_SET_PARMS *lpSet*
Points to the **MCI_SEQ_SET_PARMS** structure.

Videodisc Extensions

Parameters

DWORD *dwFlags*
The following additional flags apply to videodisc devices:

Value	Meaning
MCI_SET_TIME_FORMAT	

Specifies a time format parameter is included in the **dwTimeFormat** member of the structure identified by *lpSet*. The following constants are defined for the time format:

Value	Meaning
MCI_FORMAT_CHAPTERS	
	Changes the time format to chapters.

MCI_FORMAT_FRAMES

> Changes the time format to frames.

MCI_FORMAT_HMS

> Changes the time format to hours, minutes, and seconds.

MCI_FORMAT_MILLISECONDS

> Changes the time format to milliseconds for both input and output.

MCI_VD_FORMAT_TRACK

> Changes the time format to tracks. MCI uses continuous track numbers.

LPMCI_VD_SET_PARMS *lpSet*
Points to the **MCI_VD_SET_PARMS** structure. (Devices with additional parameters might replace this structure with a device-specific structure.)

Waveform Audio Extensions

Parameters

DWORD *dwFlags*
The following additional flags apply to waveform audio devices:

Value	Meaning
MCI_WAVE_INPUT	

> Sets the input used for recording to the **wInput** member of the structure identified by *lpSet*.

MCI_WAVE_OUTPUT

> Sets the output used for playing to the **wOutput** member of the structure identified by *lpSet*.

MCI_WAVE_SET_ANYINPUT

> Specifies that any wave input compatible with the current format can be used for recording.

MCI_WAVE_SET_ANYOUTPUT

> Specifies that any wave output compatible with the current format can be used for playing.

MCI_WAVE_SET_AVGBYTESPERSEC

> Sets the bytes per second used for playing, recording, and saving to the **nAvgBytesPerSec** member of the structure identified by *lpSet*.

MCI_WAVE_SET_BITSPERSAMPLE

> Sets the bits per sample used for playing, recording, and saving to the **nBitsPerSample** member of the structure identified by *lpSet*.

MCI_WAVE_SET_BLOCKALIGN

> Sets the block alignment used for playing, recording, and saving to the **nBlockAlign** member of the structure identified by *lpSet*.

MCI_WAVE_SET_CHANNELS

Specifies the number of channels is indicated in the **nChannels** member of the structure identified by *lpSet*.

MCI_WAVE_SET_FORMATTAG

Sets the format type used for playing, recording, and saving to the **wFormatTag** member of the structure identified by *lpSet*. Specifying WAVE_FORMAT_PCM changes the format to PCM.

MCI_WAVE_SET_SAMPLESPERSEC

Sets the samples per second used for playing, recording, and saving to the **nSamplesPerSec** member of the structure identified by *lpSet*.

MCI_SET_TIME_FORMAT

Specifies a time format parameter is included in the **dwTimeFormat** member of the structure identified by *lpSet*. The following constants are defined for the time format:

Value	Meaning
MCI_FORMAT_BYTES	
	Changes the time format to bytes for input or output.
MCI_FORMAT_MILLISECONDS	
	Changes the time format to milliseconds for input or output.
MCI_FORMAT_SAMPLES	
	Changes the time format to samples for input or output.

LPMCI_WAVE_SET_PARMS *lpSet*
Points to the **MCI_WAVE_SET_PARMS** data structure. This parameter replaces the standard default parameter data structure identified by *lpDefault*.

Return Value   Returns zero if successful. Otherwise, it returns an MCI error code.

MCI_SOUND

This MCI command message plays system sounds identified in the [sounds] section of the registry file. The name of the sound is specified in the buffer pointed to by the **lpstrSoundName** member of the structure identified by *lpInfo*. This is an MCI system message that is not sent to any device.

Parameters   **DWORD** *dwFlags*

The following standard and command-specific flags apply to all devices:

Value	Meaning
MCI_NOTIFY	

MCI_NOTIFY

Specifies that MCI should post the MM_MCINOTIFY message when this command completes. The window to receive this message is specified in the **dwCallback** member of the structure identified by *lpInfo*.

MCI_WAIT

Specifies that the playing of the sound should finish before MCI returns control to the application.

MCI_SOUND_NAME

Indicates that the name of a sound to play is included in the **lpstrSoundName** of the structure identified by *lpSound*. If omitted, the default sound is played.

LPMCI_SOUND_PARMS *lpInfo*

Points to the **MCI_SOUND_PARMS** structure. The **MCI_SOUND_PARMS** structure has the following form:

```
typedef struct {
    DWORD  dwCallback;
    LPCTSTR  lpstrSoundName;
} MCI_SOUND_PARMS;
```

For a full description of this structure, see Chapter 3, "Structures."

Return Value   Returns zero if successful. Otherwise, it returns an MCI error code.

Comments   This command will only play files that fit into available memory. Use the MCI waveform audio device to play longer waveform files.

MCI_STATUS

This MCI command message is used to obtain information about an MCI device. All devices respond to this message. The parameters and flags available for this message depend on the selected device. Information is returned in the **dwReturn** member of the structure identified by *lpStatus*.

Parameters   **DWORD** *dwFlags*

The following standard and command-specific flags apply to all devices:

Value	Meaning
MCI_NOTIFY	

Specifies that MCI should post the MM_MCINOTIFY message when this command completes. The window to receive this message is specified in the **dwCallback** member of the structure identified by *lpStatus*.

MCI_WAIT

Specifies that the status operation should finish before MCI returns control to the application.

MCI_STATUS_ITEM

Specifies that the **dwItem** member of the data structure identified by *lpStatus* contains a constant specifying which status item to obtain. The following constants define which status item to return in the **dwReturn** member of the structure:

Value	Meaning
MCI_STATUS_CURRENT_TRACK	
	The **dwReturn** member is set to the current track number. MCI uses continuous track numbers.
MCI_STATUS_LENGTH	
	The **dwReturn** member is set to the total media length.
MCI_STATUS_MODE	
	The **dwReturn** member is set to the current mode of the device. The modes include the following:

- MCI_MODE_NOT_READY
- MCI_MODE_PAUSE
- MCI_MODE_PLAY
- MCI_MODE_STOP
- MCI_MODE_OPEN
- MCI_MODE_RECORD
- MCI_MODE_SEEK

MCI_STATUS_NUMBER_OF_TRACKS

The **dwReturn** member is set to the total number of playable tracks.

MCI_STATUS_POSITION

The **dwReturn** member is set to the current position.

MCI_STATUS_READY

The **dwReturn** member is set to TRUE if the device is ready; otherwise, it is set to FALSE.

MCI_STATUS_TIME_FORMAT

The **dwReturn** member is set to the current time format of the device. The time formats include:

- MCI_FORMAT_BYTES
- MCI_FORMAT_FRAMES
- MCI_FORMAT_HMS
- MCI_FORMAT_MILLISECONDS
- MCI_FORMAT_MSF
- MCI_FORMAT_SAMPLES
- MCI_FORMAT_TMSF

MCI_STATUS_START

Obtains the starting position of the media. To get the starting position, combine this flag with MCI_STATUS_ITEM and set the **dwItem** member of the structure identified by *lpStatus* to MCI_STATUS_POSITION.

MCI_TRACK

Indicates a status track parameter is included in the **dwTrack** member of the data structure identified by *lpStatus*. You must use this flag with the MCI_STATUS_POSITION or MCI_STATUS_LENGTH constants.

When used with MCI_STATUS_POSITION, MCI_TRACK obtains the starting position of the specified track.

When used with MCI_STATUS_LENGTH, MCI_TRACK obtains the length of the specified track. MCI uses continuous track numbers.

LPMCI_STATUS_PARMS *lpStatus*

Points to the **MCI_STATUS_PARMS** structure. (Devices with extended command sets might replace this structure with a device-specific structure.) The **MCI_STATUS_PARMS** structure has the following form:

```
typedef struct {
    DWORD   dwCallback;
    DWORD   dwReturn;
    DWORD   dwItem;
    DWORD   dwTrack;
} MCI_STATUS_PARMS;
```

For a full description of this structure, see Chapter 3, "Structures."

Animation Extensions

Parameters   **DWORD** *dwFlags*

The following extensions apply to animation devices:

Value	Meaning
MCI_STATUS_ITEM	

    Specifies that the **dwItem** member of the structure identified by *lpStatus* contains a constant specifying which status item to obtain. The following additional status constants are defined for animation devices and indicate which item to return in the **dwReturn** member of the structure:

MCI_ANIM_STATUS_FORWARD

    The **dwReturn** member is set to TRUE if playing forward; otherwise, it is set to FALSE.

MCI_ANIM_STATUS_HPAL

    The **dwReturn** member is set to the handle of the movie palette.

MCI_ANIM_STATUS_HWND

    The **dwReturn** member is set to the handle of the playback window.

MCI_ANIM_STATUS_SPEED

    The **dwReturn** member is set to the animation speed.

MCI_STATUS_MEDIA_PRESENT

    The **dwReturn** member is set to TRUE if the media is inserted in the device; otherwise, it is set to FALSE.

LPMCI_STATUS_PARMS *lpStatus*
Points to the **MCI_STATUS_PARMS** structure.

CD Audio Extensions

Parameters   **DWORD** *dwFlags*

The following extensions applies to CD audio devices:

Value	Meaning
MCI_STATUS_ITEM	

    Specifies that the **dwItem** member of the structure identified by *lpStatus* contains a constant specifying which status item to obtain. The following additional status constants are defined for CD audio devices and indicate which item to return in the **dwReturn** member of the structure:

MCI_STATUS_MEDIA_PRESENT

    The **dwReturn** member is set to TRUE if the media is inserted in the device; otherwise, it is set to FALSE.

LPMCI_STATUS_PARMS *lpStatus*

Points to the **MCI_STATUS_PARMS** data structure. This parameter replaces the standard default parameter data structure.

MIDI Sequencer Extensions

Parameters   DWORD *dwFlags*

The following extensions apply to sequencers:

Value	Meaning

MCI_STATUS_ITEM

Specifies that the **dwItem** member of the structure identified by *lpStatus* contains a constant specifying which status item to obtain. The following additional status constants are defined for sequencers and indicate which item to return in the **dwReturn** member of the structure:

MCI_SEQ_STATUS_DIVTYPE

The **dwReturn** member is set to one of the following values indicating the current division type of a sequence:

- MCI_SEQ_DIV_PPQN
- MCI_SEQ_DIV_SMPTE_24
- MCI_SEQ_DIV_SMPTE_25
- MCI_SEQ_DIV_SMPTE_30
- MCI_SEQ_DIV_SMPTE_30DROP

MCI_SEQ_STATUS_MASTER

The **dwReturn** member is set to the synchronization type used for master operation.

MCI_SEQ_STATUS_OFFSET

The **dwReturn** member is set to the current SMPTE offset of a sequence.

MCI_SEQ_STATUS_PORT

The **dwReturn** member is set to the MIDI device ID for the current port used by the sequence.

MCI_SEQ_STATUS_SLAVE

The **dwReturn** member is set to the synchronization type used for slave operation.

MCI_SEQ_STATUS_TEMPO

The **dwReturn** member is set to the current tempo of a MIDI sequence in beats-per-minute for PPQN files, or frames-per-second for SMPTE files.

MCI_STATUS_MEDIA_PRESENT

The **dwReturn** member is set to TRUE if the media for the device is present; otherwise, it is set to FALSE.

LPMCI_STATUS_PARMS *lpStatus*
Points to the **MCI_STATUS_PARMS** structure. This parameter replaces the standard default parameter structure.

Videodisc Extensions

Parameters   **DWORD** *dwFlags*
The following additional flags apply to videodisc devices:

Value	Meaning

MCI_STATUS_ITEM

Specifies that the **dwItem** member of the structure identified by *lpStatus* contains a constant specifying which status item to obtain. The following additional status constants are defined for videodisc devices and indicate which item to return in the **dwReturn** member of the structure:

MCI_STATUS_MEDIA_PRESENT

The **dwReturn** member is set to TRUE if the media is inserted in the device; otherwise, it is set to FALSE.

MCI_VD_STATUS_DISC_SIZE

The **dwReturn** member is set to the size of the loaded disc in inches (8 or 12).

MCI_VD_STATUS_FORWARD

The **dwReturn** member is set to TRUE if playing forward; otherwise, it is set to FALSE.

MCI_VD_STATUS_MEDIA_TYPE

The **dwReturn** member is set to the media type of the inserted media. The following media types can be returned:

- MCI_VD_MEDIA_CAV

- MCI_VD_MEDIA_CLV

- MCI_VD_MEDIA_OTHER

MCI_STATUS_MODE

The **dwReturn** member is set to the current mode of the device. All devices can return the following constants to indicate the current mode:

- MCI_MODE_NOT_READY
- MCI_MODE_PAUSE
- MCI_MODE_PLAY
- MCI_MODE_STOP
- MCI_VD_MODE_PARK (videodisc devices)

MCI_VD_STATUS_SIDE

The **dwReturn** member is set to 1 or 2 to indicate which side of the disc is loaded. Not all videodisc devices support this flag.

MCI_VD_STATUS_SPEED

The **dwReturn** member is set to the play speed in frames per second.

MCIPIONR returns MCIERR_UNSUPPORTED_FUNCTION.

LPMCI_STATUS_PARMS *lpStatus*

Points to the **MCI_STATUS_PARMS** structure. This parameter replaces the standard default parameter structure.

Waveform Audio Extensions

Parameters   **DWORD** *dwFlags*

The following additional flags apply to waveform audio devices:

Value	Meaning
MCI_STATUS_ITEM	

Specifies that the **dwItem** member of the structure identified by *lpStatus* contains a constant specifying which status item to obtain. The following additional status constants are defined for waveform audio devices and indicate which item to return in the **dwReturn** member of the structure:

MCI_STATUS_MEDIA_PRESENT

The **dwReturn** member is set to TRUE if the media is inserted in the device; otherwise, it is set to FALSE.

MCI_WAVE_INPUT

The **dwReturn** member is set to the wave input device used for recording. If no device is in use and no device has been explicitly set, then the error return is MCI_WAVE_INPUTUNSPECIFIED.

MCI_WAVE_OUTPUT

The **dwReturn** member is set to the wave output device used for playing. If no device is in use and no device has been explicitly set, then the error return is MCI_WAVE_OUTPUTUNSPECIFIED.

MCI_WAVE_STATUS_AVGBYTESPERSEC

The **dwReturn** member is set to the current bytes per second used for playing, recording, and saving.

MCI_WAVE_STATUS_BITSPERSAMPLE

The **dwReturn** member is set to the current bits per sample used for playing, recording, and saving.

MCI_WAVE_STATUS_BLOCKALIGN

The **dwReturn** member is set to the current block alignment used for playing, recording, and saving.

MCI_WAVE_STATUS_CHANNELS

The **dwReturn** member is set to the current channel count used for playing, recording, and saving.

MCI_WAVE_FORMATTAG

The **dwReturn** member is set to the current format tag used for playing, recording, and saving.

MCI_WAVE_STATUS_LEVEL

The **dwReturn** member is set to the current record or playback level. The value is returned as an 8- or 16-bit value, depending on the sample size used. The right or mono channel level is returned in the low-order word. The left channel level is returned in the high-order word.

MCI_WAVE_STATUS_SAMPLESPERSEC

The **dwReturn** member is set to the current samples per second used for playing, recording, and saving.

LPMCI_STATUS_PARMS *lpStatus*
Points to the **MCI_STATUS_PARMS** structure.

Video Overlay Extensions

Parameters   **DWORD** *dwFlags*
The following additional flags apply to video overlay devices:

Value	Meaning
MCI_OVLY_STATUS_HWND	

The **dwReturn** member is set to the handle of the window associated with the video overlay device.

MCI_STATUS_ITEM

Specifies that the **dwItem** member of the structure identified by *lpStatus* contains a constant specifying which status item to obtain. The following additional status constants are defined for video overlay devices and indicate which item to return in the **dwReturn** member of the structure:

MCI_STATUS_MEDIA_PRESENT

The **dwReturn** member is set to TRUE if the media is inserted in the device; otherwise, it is set to FALSE.

LPMCI_STATUS_PARMS *lpStatus*
Points to the **MCI_STATUS_PARMS** structure.

Return Value   Returns zero if successful. Otherwise, it returns an MCI error code.

MCI_STEP

This MCI command message steps the player one or more frames.

Parameters   **DWORD** *dwFlags*
The following flags apply to all devices supporting MCI_STEP:

Value	Meaning
MCI_NOTIFY	
	Specifies that MCI should post the MM_MCINOTIFY message when this command completes. The window to receive this message is specified in the **dwCallback** member of the structure identified by *lpStep*.
MCI_WAIT	
	Specifies that the step operation should finish before MCI returns control to the application.

Animation Extensions

Parameters   **DWORD** *dwFlags*
The following additional flag applies to animation devices.

Value	Meaning
MCI_ANIM_STEP_FRAMES	
	Indicates that the **dwFrames** member of the structure identified by *lpStep* specifies the number of frames to step.
MCI_ANIM_STEP_REVERSE	
	Steps in reverse.

LPMCI_ANIM_STEP_PARMS *lpStep*
Points to the **MCI_ANIM_STEP_PARMS** structure.

Videodisc Extensions

Parameters   **DWORD** *dwFlags*
The following additional flags apply to videodisc devices.

Value	Meaning
MCI_VD_STEP_FRAMES	Indicates that the **dwFrames** member of the structure identified by *lpStep* specifies the number of frames to step.
MCI_VD_STEP_REVERSE	Steps in reverse.

LPMCI_VD_STEP_PARMS *lpStep*
Points to a **MCI_VD_STEP_PARMS** structure. The
MCI_VD_STEP_PARMS structure has the following form:

```
typedef struct {
    DWORD   dwCallback;
    DWORD   dwFrames;
} MCI_VD_STEP_PARMS;
```

For a full description of this structure, see Chapter 3, "Structures."

Return Value   Returns zero if successful. Otherwise, it returns an MCI error code.

Comments   Only devices that return TRUE to the MCI_GETDEVCAPS_HAS_VIDEO capability query support this command at present.

See Also   MCI_CUE, MCI_PLAY, MCI_SEEK

MCI_STOP

This MCI command message stops all play and record sequences, unloads all play buffers, and ceases display of video images. Support of this message by a device is optional. The parameters and flags for this message vary according to the selected device.

Parameters   **DWORD** *dwFlags*
The following flags apply to all devices supporting MCI_STOP:

Value	Meaning
MCI_NOTIFY	Specifies that MCI should post the MM_MCINOTIFY message when this command completes. The window to receive this message is specified in the **dwCallback** member of the structure identified by *lpStop*.
MCI_WAIT	Specifies that the device should stop before MCI returns control to the application.

LPMCI_GENERIC_PARMS *lpStop*

Points to the **MCI_GENERIC_PARMS** structure. (Devices with extended command sets might replace this structure with a device-specific structure.) The **MCI_GENERIC_PARMS** structure has the following form:

```
typedef struct {
    DWORD  dwCallback;
} MCI_GENERIC_PARMS;
```

For a full description of this structure, see Chapter 3, "Structures."

Return Value

Returns zero if successful. Otherwise, it returns an MCI error code.

Comments

The difference between MCI_STOP and MCI_PAUSE depends upon the device. If possible, MCI_PAUSE suspends device operation but leaves the device ready to resume play immediately.

See Also

MCI_PAUSE, MCI_PLAY, MCI_RECORD, MCI_RESUME

MCI_SYSINFO

This MCI command message returns information about MCI devices. MCI supports this message directly rather than passing it to the devices. String information is returned in the application-supplied buffer pointed to by the **lpstrReturn** member of the structure identified by *lpSysInfo*. Numeric information is returned as a **DWORD** placed in the application-supplied buffer. The **dwReturnSize** member specifies the buffer length.

Parameters

DWORD *dwFlags*

The following standard and command-specific flags apply to all devices:

Value	Meaning
MCI_SYSINFO_INSTALLNAME	
	Obtains the name (listed in the registry) used to install the device.
MCI_SYSINFO_NAME	
	Obtains a device name corresponding to the device number specified in the **dwNumbermember** of the structure identified by *lpSysInfo* . If the MCI_SYSINFO_OPEN flag is set, MCI returns the names of open devices.
MCI_SYSINFO_OPEN	
	Obtains the quantity or name of open devices.
MCI_SYSINFO_QUANTITY	

Obtains the number of devices of the specified type that are listed in the [mci] section of the registry file. If the MCI_SYSINFO_OPEN flag is set, the number of open devices is returned.

LPMCI_SYSINFO_PARMS *lpSysInfo*
Points to the **MCI_SYSINFO_PARMS** structure. The **MCI_SYSINFO_PARMS** structure has the following form:

```
typedef struct {
    DWORD   dwCallback;
    LPTSTR  lpstrReturn;
    DWORD   dwRetSize;
    DWORD   dwNumber;
    UINT    wDeviceType;
} MCI_SYSINFO_PARMS;
```

For a full description of this structure, see Chapter 3, "Structures."

Return Value
Returns zero if successful. Otherwise, it returns an MCI error code.

Comments
The **wDeviceType** element of the *lpSysInfo* structure is used to indicate the device type of the query. If the *wDeviceID* parameter is set to MCI_ALL_DEVICE_ID it will override the value of **wDeviceType**.

Integer return values are doublewords returned in the buffer pointed to by the **lpstrReturn** member of **MCI_SYSINFO_PARMS**.

String return values are NULL-terminated strings returned in the buffer pointed to by the **lpstrReturn** member.

MCI_UNFREEZE

This MCI command message restores motion to an area of the video buffer frozen with MCI_FREEZE. This command is part of the video overlay command set. The parameters and flags for this message vary according to the selected device.

Parameters
DWORD *dwFlags*
The following flags apply to all devices supporting MCI_UNFREEZE:

Value	Meaning
MCI_NOTIFY	
	Specifies that MCI should post the MM_MCINOTIFY message when this command completes. The window to receive this message is specified in the **dwCallback** member of the structure identified by *lpFreeze*.
MCI_WAIT	

Specifies that the unfreeze operation should finish before MCI returns control to the application.

MCI_OVLY_RECT

Specifies that the **rc** member of the data structure identified by *lpFreeze* contains a valid display rectangle. This is a required parameter.

LPMCI_OVLY_RECT_PARMS *lpFreeze*
Points to a **MCI_OVLY_RECT_PARMS** structure. (Devices with additional parameters might replace this structure with a device-specific structure.) The **MCI_OVLY_RECT_PARMS** structure has the following form:

```
typedef struct {
    DWORD  dwCallback;
    RECT  rc;
} MCI_OVLY_RECT_PARMS;
```

For a full description of this structure, see Chapter 3, "Structures."

Return Value   Returns zero if successful. Otherwise, it returns an MCI error code.

Comments   This command applies to video overlay devices.

See Also   MCI_FREEZE

MCI_WHERE

This MCI command message obtains the clipping rectangle for the video device. The top and left members of the returned rectangle contain the origin of the clipping rectangle, and the right and bottom members contain the width and height of the clipping rectangle. The parameters and flags for this message vary according to the selected device.

Parameters   **DWORD** *dwFlags*
The following flags apply to all devices supporting MCI_WHERE:

Value	Meaning
MCI_NOTIFY	
	Specifies that MCI should post the MM_MCINOTIFY message when this command completes. The window to receive this message is specified in the **dwCallback** member of the structure identified by *lpQuery*.
MCI_WAIT	
	Specifies that the operation should complete before MCI returns control to the application.

DWORD *lpQuery*

Points to a device-specific structure. For a description of this parameter, see the *lpQuery* description included with the device extensions.

Animation Extensions

DWORD *dwFlags*

The following additional flags apply to animation devices supporting MCI_WHERE:

Value	Meaning

MCI_ANIM_WHERE_DESTINATION

> Obtains the destination display rectangle. The rectangle coordinates are placed in the **rc** member of the data structure identified by *lpQuery*.

MCI_ANIM_WHERE_SOURCE

> Obtains the animation source rectangle. The rectangle coordinates are placed in the **rc** member of the data structure identified by *lpQuery*.

LPMCI_ANIM_RECT_PARMS *lpQuery*

Points to a **MCI_ANIM_RECT_PARMS** structure. The **MCI_ANIM_RECT_PARMS** structure has the following form:

```
typedef struct {
    DWORD  dwCallback;
    RECT   rc;
} MCI_ANIM_RECT_PARMS;
```

For a full description of this structure, see Chapter 3, "Structures."

Video Overlay Extensions

DWORD *dwFlags*

The following additional flags apply to video overlay devices supporting MCI_WHERE:

Value	Meaning

MCI_OVLY_WHERE_DESTINATION

> Obtains the destination display rectangle. The rectangle coordinates are placed in the **rc** member of the structure identified by *lpQuery*.

MCI_OVLY_WHERE_FRAME

> Obtains the overlay frame rectangle. The rectangle coordinates are placed in the **rc** member of the structure identified by *lpQuery*.

MCI_OVLY_WHERE_SOURCE

> Obtains the source rectangle. The rectangle coordinates are placed in the **rc** member of the structure identified by *lpQuery*.

MCI_OVLY_WHERE_VIDEO

Obtains the video rectangle. The rectangle coordinates are placed in the **rc** member of the structure identified by *lpQuery*.

LPMCI_OVLY_RECT_PARMS *lpQuery*
Points to a **MCI_OVLY_RECT_PARMS** structure. The **MCI_OVLY_RECT_PARMS** structure has the following form:

```
typedef struct {
    DWORD  dwCallback;
    RECT  rc;
} MCI_OVLY_RECT_PARMS;
```

For a full description of this structure, see Chapter 3, "Structures."

Return Value   Returns zero if successful. Otherwise, it returns an MCI error code.

Comments   This command applies to animation and video overlay devices.

See Also   MCI_PUT

MCI_WINDOW

This MCI command message specifies the window and the window characteristics for graphic devices. Graphic devices should create a default window when a device is opened but should not display it until they receive the play command. The window command is used to supply an application-created window to the device and to change the display characteristics of an application-supplied or default display window. If the application supplies the display window, it should be prepared to update an invalid rectangle on the window.

Support of this message by a device is optional. The parameters and flags for this message vary according to the selected device.

Parameters   **DWORD** *dwFlags*
The following flags apply to all devices supporting MCI_WINDOW:

Value	Meaning
MCI_NOTIFY	
	Specifies that MCI should post the MM_MCINOTIFY message when this command completes. The window to receive this message is specified in the **dwCallback** member of the structure identified by *lpWindow*.
MCI_WAIT	
	Specifies that the operation should finish before MCI returns control to the application.

DWORD *lpWindow*

Points to a device specific structure. For a description of this parameter, see the *lpWindow* description included with the device extensions.

Animation Extensions

Parameters

DWORD *dwFlags*

The following additional flags apply to animation devices supporting MCI_WINDOW:

Value	Meaning

MCI_ANIM_WINDOW_HWND

Indicates the handle of the window to use for the destination is included in the **hWnd** member of the structure identified by *lpWindow*. Set this to MCI_ANIM_WINDOW_DEFAULT to return to the default window.

MCI_ANIM_WINDOW_STATE

Indicates the **nCmdShow** member of the **MCI_ANIM_WINDOW_PARMS** structure contains parameters for setting the window state. This flag is equivalent to calling **ShowWindow** with the state parameter. The constants are the same as the ones in WINDOWS.H (such as SW_HIDE, SW_MINIMIZE, or SW_SHOWNORMAL.)

MCI_ANIM_WINDOW_TEXT

Indicates the **lpstrText** member of the **MCI_ANIM_WINDOW_PARMS** structure contains a pointer to a buffer containing the caption used for the window.

LPMCI_ANIM_WINDOW_PARMS *lpWindow*

Points to a **MCI_ANIM_WINDOW_PARMS** structure. (Devices with additional parameters might replace this structure with a device-specific structure.) The **MCI_ANIM_WINDOW_PARMS** structure has the following form:

```
typedef struct tagMCI_ANIM_WINDOW_PARMS {
    DWORD   dwCallback;
    DWORD   hWnd;
    UINT    nCmdShow;
    LPCTSTR lpstrText;
} MCI_ANIM_WINDOW_PARMS;
```

For a full description of this structure, see Chapter 3, "Structures."

Video Overlay Extensions

Parameters

DWORD *dwFlags*

The following additional flags apply to video overlay devices supporting MCI_WINDOW:

Value	Meaning

MCI_OVLY_WINDOW_HWND

> Indicates the handle of the window used for the destination is included in the **hWnd** member of the **MCI_OVLY_WINDOW_PARMS** structure. Set this to MCI_OVLY_WINDOW_DEFAULT to return to the default window.

MCI_OVLY_WINDOW_STATE

> Indicates the **nCmdShow** member of the *lpWindow* structure contains parameters for setting the window state. This flag It is equivalent to calling **showwindow** with the state parameter. The constants are the same as those defined in WINDOWS.H (such as SW_HIDE, SW_MINIMIZE, or SW_SHOWNORMAL.)

MCI_OVLY_WINDOW_TEXT

> Indicates the **lpstrText** member of the **MCI_OVLY_WINDOWS_PARMS** structure contains a pointer to buffer containing the caption used for the window.

LPMCI_OVLY_WINDOW_PARMS *lpWindow*

Points to a **MCI_OVLY_WINDOW_PARMS** structure. (Devices with additional parameters might replace this structure with a device-specific structure.) The **MCI_OVLY_WINDOW_PARMS** structure has the following form:

```
typedef struct {
    DWORD   dwCallback;
    HWND    hWnd;
    UINT    nCmdShow;
    LPCTSTR lpstrText;
} MCI_OVLY_WINDOW_PARMS;
```

For a full description of this structure, see Chapter 3, "Structures."

Return Value   Returns zero if successful. Otherwise, it returns an MCI error code.

Comments   This command applies to animation, and video overlay devices.

MIM_CLOSE

This message is sent to a MIDI input callback function when a MIDI input device is closed. The device handle is no longer valid once this message has been sent.

Parameters   **DWORD** *dwParam1*
Currently unused.

DWORD *dwParam2*
Currently unused.

Return Value   None.

See Also   MM_MIM_CLOSE

MIM_DATA

This message is sent to a MIDI input callback function when a MIDI message is received by a MIDI input device.

Parameters   **DWORD** *dwParam1*
Specifies the MIDI message that was received. The message is packed into a DWORD with the first byte of the message in the low-order byte.

DWORD *dwParam2*
Specifies the time that the message was received by the input device driver. The timestamp is specified in milliseconds, beginning at 0 when **midiInStart** was called.

Return Value   None.

Comments   MIDI messages received from a MIDI input port have running status disabled; each message is expanded to include the MIDI status byte.

This message is not sent when a MIDI system-exclusive message is received.

See Also   MM_MIM_DATA, MIM_LONGDATA

MIM_ERROR

This message is sent to a MIDI input callback function when an invalid MIDI message is received.

Parameters   **DWORD** *dwParam1*
Specifies the invalid MIDI message that was received. The message is packed into a DWORD with the first byte of the message in the low-order byte.

DWORD *dwParam2*
Specifies the time that the message was received by the input device driver. The timestamp is specified in milliseconds, beginning at 0 when **midiInStart** was called.

Return Value   None.

See Also   MM_MIM_ERROR

MIM_LONGDATA

This message is sent to a MIDI input callback function when an input buffer has been filled with MIDI system-exclusive data and is being returned to the application.

Parameters

DWORD *dwParam1*
Points to a **MIDIHDR** structure identifying the input buffer. The **MIDIHDR** structure has the following form:

```
typedef struct midihdr_tag {
    LPSTR   lpData;
    DWORD   dwBufferLength;
    DWORD   dwBytesRecorded;
    DWORD   dwUser;
    DWORD   dwFlags;
    struct midihdr_tag *lpNext;
    DWORD   reserved;
} MIDIHDR;
```

For a full description of this structure, see Chapter 3, "Structures."

DWORD *dwParam2*
Specifies the time that the data was received by the input device driver. The timestamp is specified in milliseconds, beginning at 0 when **midiInStart** was called.

Return Value   None.

Comments   The returned buffer may not be full. The **dwBytesRecorded** member of the **MIDIHDR** structure specified by *dwParam1* will specify the number of bytes recorded into the buffer.

See Also   MIM_DATA, MM_MIM_LONGDATA

MIM_LONGERROR

This message is sent to a MIDI input callback function when an invalid MIDI system-exclusive message is received.

Parameters **DWORD** *dwParam1*

Specifies a pointer to a **MIDIHDR** structure identifying the buffer containing the invalid message. The **MIDIHDR** structure has the following form:

```
typedef struct midihdr_tag {
    LPSTR  lpData;
    DWORD  dwBufferLength;
    DWORD  dwBytesRecorded;
    DWORD  dwUser;
    DWORD  dwFlags;
    struct midihdr_tag *lpNext;
    DWORD  reserved;
} MIDIHDR;
```

For a full description of this structure, see Chapter 3, "Structures."

DWORD *dwParam2*

Specifies the time that the data was received by the input device driver. The timestamp is specified in milliseconds, beginning at 0 when **midiInStart** was called.

Return Value None.

Comments The returned buffer may not be full. The **dwBytesRecorded** member of the **MIDIHDR** structure specified by *dwParam1* will specify the number of bytes recorded into the buffer.

See Also MM_MIM_LONGERROR

MIM_OPEN

This message is sent to a MIDI input callback function when a MIDI input device is opened.

Parameters **DWORD** *dwParam1*
Currently unused.

DWORD *dwParam2*
Currently unused.

Return Value None.

See Also MM_MIM_OPEN

MM_JOY1BUTTONDOWN

This message is sent to the window that has captured joystick 1 when a button is pressed.

Parameters   **WPARAM** *wParam*
Indicates which button has changed state. It can be any one of the following combined with any of the flags defined in MM_JOY1MOVE.

Value	Meaning
JOY_BUTTON1CHG	
	Set if first joystick button has changed.
JOY_BUTTON2CHG	
	Set if second joystick button has changed.
JOY_BUTTON3CHG	
	Set if third joystick button has changed.
JOY_BUTTON4CHG	
	Set if fourth joystick button has changed.

LPARAM *lParam*
The low-order word contains the current *x*-position of the joystick. The high-order word contains the current *y*-position.

Return Value   None.

See Also   MM_JOY1BUTTONUP

MM_JOY1BUTTONUP

This message is sent to the window that has captured joystick one when a button is released.

Parameters   **WORD** *wParam*
Indicates which button has changed state. It can be any one of the following combined with any of the flags defined in MM_JOY1MOVE.

Value	Meaning
JOY_BUTTON1CHG	
	Set if first joystick button has changed.
JOY_BUTTON2CHG	

Set if second joystick button has changed.

JOY_BUTTON3CHG

Set if third joystick button has changed.

JOY_BUTTON4CHG

Set if fourth joystick button has changed.

DWORD *lParam*
The low-order word contains the current *x*-position of the joystick. The high-order word contains the current *y*-position.

Return Value   None.

See Also   MM_JOY1BUTTONDOWN

MM_JOY1MOVE

This message is sent to the window that has captured joystick 1 when the joystick position changes.

Parameters

WPARAM *wParam*
Indicates which joystick buttons are pressed. It can be any combination of the following values:

Value	Meaning
JOY_BUTTON1	
	Set if first joystick button is pressed.
JOY_BUTTON2	
	Set if second joystick button is pressed.
JOY_BUTTON3	
	Set if third joystick button is pressed.
JOY_BUTTON4	
	Set if fourth joystick button is pressed.

LPARAM *lParam*
The low-order word contains the current *x*-position of the joystick. The high-order word contains the current *y*-position.

Return Value   None.

See Also   MM_JOY1ZMOVE

MM_JOY1ZMOVE

This message is sent to the window that has captured joystick 1 when the z-axis position changes.

Parameters   **WPARAM** *wParam*
Indicates which joystick buttons are pressed. It can be any combination of the following values:

Value	Meaning
JOY_BUTTON1	
	Set if first joystick button is pressed.
JOY_BUTTON2	
	Set if second joystick button is pressed.
JOY_BUTTON3	
	Set if third joystick button is pressed.
JOY_BUTTON4	
	Set if fourth joystick button is pressed.

LPARAM *lParam*
The low-order word contains the current z-position of the joystick.

Return Value   None.

See Also   MM_JOY1MOVE

MM_JOY2BUTTONDOWN

This message is sent to the window that has captured joystick 2 when a button is pressed.

Parameters   **WPARAM** *wParam*
Indicates which button has changed state. It can be any one of the following combined with any of the flags defined in MM_JOY1MOVE.

Value	Meaning
JOY_BUTTON1CHG	
	Set if first joystick button has changed.
JOY_BUTTON2CHG	
	Set if second joystick button has changed.

JOY_BUTTON3CHG

> Set if third joystick button has changed.

JOY_BUTTON4CHG

> Set if fourth joystick button has changed.

LPARAM *lParam*
The low-order word contains the current *x*-position of the joystick. The high-order word contains the current *y*-position.

Return Value   None.

See Also   MM_JOY2BUTTONUP

MM_JOY2BUTTONUP

This message is sent to the window that has captured joystick 2 when a button is released.

Parameters   **WORD** *wParam*
Indicates which button has changed state. It can be any one of the following combined with any of the flags defined in MM_JOY1MOVE.

Value	Meaning
JOY_BUTTON1CHG	
	Set if first joystick button has changed.
JOY_BUTTON2CHG	
	Set if second joystick button has changed.
JOY_BUTTON3CHG	
	Set if third joystick button has changed.
JOY_BUTTON4CHG	
	Set if fourth joystick button has changed.

DWORD *lParam*
The low-order word contains the current *x*-position of the joystick. The high-order word contains the current *y*-position.

Return Value   None.

See Also   MM_JOY2BUTTONDOWN

MM_JOY2MOVE

This message is sent to the window that has captured joystick 2 when the joystick position changes.

Parameters

WPARAM *wParam*
Indicates which joystick buttons are pressed. It can be any combination of the following values:

Value	Meaning
JOY_BUTTON1	
	Set if first joystick button is pressed.
JOY_BUTTON2	
	Set if second joystick button is pressed.
JOY_BUTTON3	
	Set if third joystick button is pressed.
JOY_BUTTON4	
	Set if fourth joystick button is pressed.

WPARAM *lParam*
The low-order word contains the current *x*-position of the joystick. The high-order word contains the current *y*-position.

Return Value   None.

See Also   MM_JOY2ZMOVE

MM_JOY2ZMOVE

This message is sent to the window that has captured joystick 2 when the *z*-axis position changes.

Parameters

WPARAM *wParam*
Indicates which joystick buttons are pressed. It can be any combination of the following values:

Value	Meaning
JOY_BUTTON1	
	Set if first joystick button is pressed.
JOY_BUTTON2	

Set if second joystick button is pressed.

JOY_BUTTON3

Set if third joystick button is pressed.

JOY_BUTTON4

Set if fourth joystick button is pressed.

LPARAM *lParam*
The low-order word contains the current *z*-position of the joystick.

Return Value   None.

See Also   MM_JOY2MOVE

MM_MCINOTIFY

This message is sent to a window to notify an application that an MCI device has completed an operation. MCI devices send this message only when the MCI_NOTIFY flag is used with an MCI command message or when the **notify** flag is used with an MCI command string.

Parameters   **WORD** *wParam*
Contains one of the following flags:

Value	Meaning

MCI_NOTIFY_ABORTED

Specifies that the device received a command that prevented the current conditions for initiating the callback from being met. If a new command interrupts the current command and it also requests notification, the device sends only this message and not MCI_NOTIFY_SUPERCEDED.

MCI_NOTIFY_SUCCESSFUL

Specifies that the conditions initiating the callback have been met.

MCI_NOTIFY_SUPERSEDED

Specifies that the device received another command with the MCI_NOTIFY flag set and the current conditions for initiating the callback have been superseded.

MCI_NOTIFY_FAILURE

Specifies that a device error occurred while the device was executing the command.

LONG *lParam*
The low-order word specifies the ID of the device initiating the callback.

Return Value   Returns zero if successful. Otherwise, it returns an MCI error code.

Comments   A device returns the flag MCI_NOTIFY_SUCCESSFUL with MM_MCINOTIFY when the action for a command finishes. For example, a CD audio device uses this flag for notification for MCI_PLAY when the device finishes playing. The MCI_PLAY command is successful only when it reaches the specified end position or reaches the end of the media. Similarly, MCI_SEEK and MCI_RECORD do not return MCI_NOTIFY_SUCCESSFUL until they reach the specified end position or reach the end of the media.

A device returns the flag MCI_NOTIFY_ABORTED with MM_MCINOTIFY only when it receives a command that prevents it from meeting the notification conditions. For example, the command MCI_PLAY would not abort notification for a previous play command provided that the new command does not change the play direction or change the ending position for the play command with an active notify. The MCI_RECORD and MCI_SEEK commands behave similarly.

MCI also does not send MCI_NOTIFY_ABORTED when MCI_PLAY or MCI_RECORD is paused with MCI_PAUSE. Sending the MCI_RESUME command will let them continue to meet the callback conditions.

When your application requests notification for a command, check the error return of **mciSendMessage** or **mciSendCommand**. If these functions encounter an error and return a nonzero value, MCI will not set notification for the command.

MM_MIM_CLOSE

This message is sent to a window when a MIDI input device is closed. The device handle is no longer valid once this message has been sent.

Parameters   **WORD** *wParam*
Specifies a handle to the MIDI input device that was closed.

LONG *lParam*
Currently unused.

Return Value   None.

See Also   MIM_CLOSE

MM_MIM_DATA

This message is sent to a window when a MIDI message is received by a MIDI input device.

Parameters   **WORD** *wParam*

Specifies a handle to the MIDI input device that received the MIDI message.

LONG *lParam*

Specifies the MIDI message that was received. The message is packed into a DWORD with the first byte of the message in the low-order byte.

Return Value   None.

Comments   MIDI messages received from a MIDI input port have running status disabled; each message is expanded to include the MIDI status byte.

This message is not sent when a MIDI system-exclusive message is received. No timestamp is available with this message. For timestamped input data, you must use the messages that are sent to low-level callback functions.

See Also   MIM_DATA, MM_MIM_LONGDATA

MM_MIM_ERROR

This message is sent to a window when an invalid MIDI message is received.

Parameters   **WORD** *wParam*

Specifies a handle to the MIDI input device that received the invalid message.

LONG *lParam*

Specifies the invalid MIDI message. The message is packed into a **DWORD** with the first byte of the message in the low-order byte.

Return Value   None.

See Also   MIM_ERROR

MM_MIM_LONGDATA

This message is sent to a window when an input buffer has been filled with MIDI system-exclusive data and is being returned to the application.

Parameters   **WORD** *wParam*

Specifies a handle to the MIDI input device that received the data.

LONG *lParam*

Points to a **MIDIHDR** structure identifying the buffer. The **MIDIHDR** structure has the following form:

```
typedef struct midihdr_tag {
```

```
    LPSTR   lpData;
    DWORD   dwBufferLength;
    DWORD   dwBytesRecorded;
    DWORD   dwUser;
    DWORD   dwFlags;
    struct midihdr_tag *lpNext;
    DWORD   reserved;
} MIDIHDR;
```

For a full description of this structure, see Chapter 3, "Structures."

Return Value   None.

Comments   The returned buffer may not be full. The **dwBytesRecorded** member of the **MIDIHDR** structure specified by *lParam* will specify the number of bytes recorded into the buffer.

No timestamp is available with this message. For timestamped input data, you must use the messages that are sent to low-level callback functions.

See Also   MM_MIM_DATA, MIM_LONGDATA

MM_MIM_LONGERROR

This message is sent to a window when an invalid MIDI system-exclusive message is received.

Parameters   **WORD** *wParam*
Specifies a handle to the MIDI input device that received the invalid message.

LONG *lParam*
Points to a **MIDIHDR** structure identifying buffer containing the invalid message. The **MIDIHDR** structure has the following form:

```
typedef struct midihdr_tag {
    LPSTR   lpData;
    DWORD   dwBufferLength;
    DWORD   dwBytesRecorded;
    DWORD   dwUser;
    DWORD   dwFlags;
    struct midihdr_tag *lpNext;
    DWORD   reserved;
} MIDIHDR;
```

For a full description of this structure, see Chapter 3, "Structures."

Return Value   None.

Comments	The returned buffer may not be full. The **dwBytesRecorded** member of the **MIDIHDR** structure specified by *lParam* will specify the number of bytes recorded into the buffer.
See Also	MIM_LONGERROR

MM_MIM_OPEN

This message is sent to a window when a MIDI input device is opened.

Parameters	**WORD** *wParam* Specifies the handle to the MIDI input device that was opened. **LONG** *lParam* Currently unused.
Return Value	None.
See Also	MIM_OPEN

MM_MOM_CLOSE

This message is sent to a window when a MIDI output device is closed. The device handle is no longer valid once this message has been sent.

Parameters	**WORD** *wParam* Specifies the handle to the MIDI output device. **LONG** *lParam* Currently unused.
Return Value	None.
See Also	MOM_CLOSE

MM_MOM_DONE

This message is sent to a window when the specified system-exclusive buffer has been played and is being returned to the application.

Parameters

WORD *wParam*
Specifies a handle to the MIDI output device that played the buffer.

LONG *lParam*
Points to a **MIDIHDR** structure identifying the buffer. The **MIDIHDR** structure has the following form:

```
typedef struct midihdr_tag {
    LPSTR  lpData;
    DWORD  dwBufferLength;
    DWORD  dwBytesRecorded;
    DWORD  dwUser;
    DWORD  dwFlags;
    struct midihdr_tag *lpNext;
    DWORD  reserved;
} MIDIHDR;
```

For a full description of this structure, see Chapter 3, "Structures."

Return Value   None.

See Also   MOM_DONE

MM_MOM_OPEN

This message is sent to a window when a MIDI output device is opened.

Parameters

WORD *wParam*
Specifies the handle to the MIDI output device.

LONG *lParam*
Currently unused.

Return Value   None.

See Also   MOM_OPEN

MM_WIM_CLOSE

This message is sent to a window when a waveform input device is closed. The device handle is no longer valid once this message has been sent.

Parameters

DWORD *dwParam1*
Currently unused.

DWORD *dwParam2*
Currently unused.

Return Value   None.

See Also   WIM_CLOSE

MM_WIM_DATA

This message is sent to a window when waveform data is present in the input buffer and the buffer is being returned to the application. The message can be sent either when the buffer is full, or after the **waveInReset** function is called.

Parameters   **DWORD** *dwParam1*
Points to a **WAVEHDR** structure identifying the buffer containing the waveform data. The **WAVEHDR** structure has the following form:

```
typedef struct wavehdr_tag {
    LPSTR  lpData;
    DWORD  dwBufferLength;
    DWORD  dwBytesRecorded;
    DWORD  dwUser;
    DWORD  dwFlags;
    DWORD  dwLoops;
    struct wavehdr_tag *lpNext;
    DWORD  reserved;
} WAVEHDR;
```

For a full description of this structure, see Chapter 3, "Structures."

DWORD *dwParam2*
Currently unused.

Return Value   None.

Comments   The returned buffer may not be full. The **dwBytesRecorded** member of the **WAVEHDR** structure specified by *dwParam1* will specify the number of bytes recorded into the buffer.

See Also   WIM_DATA

MM_WIM_OPEN

This message is sent to a window when a waveform input device is opened.

Parameters   **DWORD** *dwParam1*
                    Currently unused.

                    DWORD *dwParam2*
                    Currently unused.

Return Value   None.

See Also   WIM_OPEN

MM_WOM_CLOSE

This message is sent to a window when a waveform output device is closed. The device handle is no longer valid once this message has been sent.

Parameters   **DWORD** *dwParam1*
                    Currently unused.

                    DWORD *dwParam2*
                    Currently unused.

Return Value   None.

See Also   WOM_CLOSE

MM_WOM_DONE

This message is sent to a window when the specified output buffer is being returned to the application. Buffers are returned to the application when they have been played, or as the result of a call to **waveOutReset**.

Parameters   **DWORD** *dwParam1*
                    Points to a **WAVEHDR** structure identifying the buffer. The **WAVEHDR** structure has the following form:

```
typedef struct wavehdr_tag {
    LPSTR  lpData;
    DWORD  dwBufferLength;
    DWORD  dwBytesRecorded;
    DWORD  dwUser;
    DWORD  dwFlags;
    DWORD  dwLoops;
    struct wavehdr_tag *lpNext;
    DWORD  reserved;
} WAVEHDR;
```

For a full description of this structure, see Chapter 3, "Structures."

DWORD *dwParam2*
Currently unused.

Return Value   None.

See Also   WOM_DONE

MM_WOM_OPEN

This message is sent to a window when a waveform output device is opened.

Parameters   **DWORD** *dwParam1*
Currently unused.

DWORD *dwParam2*
Currently unused.

Return Value   None.

See Also   WOM_OPEN

MMIOM_CLOSE

This message is sent to an I/O procedure by **mmioClose** to request that a file be closed.

Parameters   **LONG** *lParam1*
Specifies options contained in the *wFlags* parameter of **mmioClose**.

LONG *lParam2*
Is not used.

Return Value   The return value is zero if the file is successfully closed. Otherwise, the return value specifies an error code.

See Also   **mmioClose**, MMIOM_OPEN

MMIOM_OPEN

This message is sent to an I/O procedure by **mmioOpen** to request that a file be opened or deleted.

Parameters

LONG *lParam1*
Specifies a null-terminated string containing the name of the file to open.

LONG *lParam2*
Is not used.

Return Value

The return value is zero if the operation is successful. Otherwise, the return value specifies an error value. Possible error returns are:

Value	Meaning
MMIOM_CANNOTOPEN	
	Specified file could not be opened.
MMIOM_OUTOFMEMORY	
	Not enough memory to perform operation.

Comments

The **dwFlags** member of the **MMIOINFO** structure contains option flags passed to the **mmioOpen** function. The **lDiskOffset** member of the **MMIOINFO** structure is initialized to zero. If this value is incorrect, then the I/O procedure must correct it.

If the caller passed a **MMIOINFO** structure to **mmioOpen**, the return value will be returned in the **wErrorRet** member.

See Also

mmioOpen, MMIOM_CLOSE

MMIOM_READ

This message is sent to an I/O procedure by **mmioRead** to request that a specified number of bytes be read from an open file.

Parameters

LONG *lParam1*
Points to the buffer to be filled with data read from the file.

LONG *lParam2*
Specifies the number of bytes to read from the file.

Return Value

The return value is the number of bytes actually read from the file. If no more bytes can be read, the return value is zero. If there is an error, the return value is -1.

Comments   The I/O procedure is responsible for updating the **lDiskOffset** member of the **MMIOINFO** structure to reflect the new file position after the read operation.

See Also   mmioRead, MMIOM_WRITE, MMIOM_WRITEFLUSH

MMIOM_SEEK

This message is sent to an I/O procedure by **mmioSeek** to request that the current file position be moved.

Parameters   **LONG** *lParam1*
Specifies the new file position according to the option flag specified in *lParam2*.

LONG *lParam2*
Specifies how the file position is changed. Only one of the following flags can be specified:

Value	Meaning
SEEK_SET	
	Move the file position to be *lParam1* bytes from the beginning of the file.
SEEK_CUR	
	Move the file position to be *lParam1* bytes from the current position. *lParam1* may be positive or negative.
SEEK_END	
	Move the file position to be *lParam1* bytes from the end of the file.

Return Value   The return value is the new file position. If there is an error, the return value is -1.

Comments   The I/O procedure is responsible for maintaining the current file position in the **lDiskOffset** member of the **MMIOINFO** structure.

See Also   **mmioSeek**

MMIOM_WRITE

This message is sent to an I/O procedure by **mmioWrite** to request that data be written to an open file.

Parameters	**LONG** *lParam1*
	Points to a buffer containing the data to write to the file.
	LONG *lParam2*
	Specifies the number of bytes to write to the file.
Return Value	The return value is the number of bytes actually written to the file. If there is an error, the return value is -1.
Comments	The I/O procedure is responsible for updating the **lDiskOffset** member of the **MMIOINFO** structure to reflect the new file position after the write operation.
See Also	**mmioWrite**, MMIOM_READ, MMIOM_WRITEFLUSH

MMIOM_WRITEFLUSH

This message is sent to an I/O procedure by **mmioWrite** to request that data be written to an open file and then that any internal buffers used by the I/O procedure be flushed to disk.

Parameters	**LONG** *lParam1*
	Points to a buffer containing the data to write to the file.
	LONG *lParam2*
	Specifies the number of bytes to write to the file.
Return Value	The return value is the number of bytes actually written to the file. If there is an error, the return value is -1.
Comments	The I/O procedure is responsible for updating the **lDiskOffset** member of the **MMIOINFO** structure to reflect the new file position after the write operation.
	Note that this message is equivalent to the MMIOM_WRITE message except that it additionally requests that the I/O procedure flush its internal buffers, if any. Unless an I/O procedure performs internal buffering, this message can be handled exactly like the MMIOM_WRITE message.
See Also	**mmioWrite**, **mmioFlush**, MMIOM_READ, MMIOM_WRITE

MOM_CLOSE

This message is sent to a MIDI output callback function when a MIDI output device is closed. The device handle is no longer valid once this message has been sent.

Parameters	**DWORD** *dwParam1*
	Currently unused.
	DWORD *dwParam2*
	Currently unused.
Return Value	None.
See Also	MM_MOM_CLOSE

MOM_DONE

This message is sent to a MIDI output callback function when the specified system-exclusive buffer has been played and is being returned to the application.

Parameters

DWORD *dwParam1*

Points to a **MIDIHDR** structure identifying the buffer. The **MIDIHDR** structure has the following form:

```
typedef struct midihdr_tag {
    LPSTR   lpData;
    DWORD   dwBufferLength;
    DWORD   dwBytesRecorded;
    DWORD   dwUser;
    DWORD   dwFlags;
    struct midihdr_tag *lpNext;
    DWORD   reserved;
} MIDIHDR;
```

For a full description of this structure, see Chapter 3, "Structures."

DWORD *dwParam2*
Currently unused.

Return Value   None.

See Also   MM_MOM_DONE

MOM_OPEN

This message is sent to a MIDI output callback function when a MIDI output device is opened.

Parameters   **DWORD** *dwParam1*
Currently unused.

DWORD *dwParam2*
Currently unused.

Return Value   None.

See Also   MM_MOM_OPEN

SBM_ENABLE_ARROWS

```
SBM_ENABLE_ARROWS
wParam = (WPARAM) fuArrowFlags; /* scroll-bar arrow flags */
lParam = 0;                     /* not used, must be zero */
```

An application sends the SBM_ENABLE_ARROWS message to enable or
disable one or both arrows of a scroll bar control.

Parameters   *fuArrowFlags*
Specifies whether the scroll bar arrows are enabled or disabled and indicates
which arrows are enabled or disabled. This parameter can be one of the
following values:

Value	Meaning
ESB_ENABLE_BOTH	Enables both arrows on a scroll bar.
ESB_DISABLE_LTUP	Disables the left arrow on a horizontal scroll bar or the up arrow of a vertical scroll bar.
ESB_DISABLE_RTDN	Disables the right arrow on a horizontal scroll bar or the down arrow of a vertical scroll bar.
ESB_DISABLE_BOTH	Disables both arrows on a scroll bar.

Return Value   If the message succeeds, the return value is TRUE; otherwise, it is FALSE.

SBM_GETPOS

```
SBM_GETPOS
wParam = 0; /* not used, must be zero */
lParam = 0; /* not used, must be zero */
```

An application sends the SBM_GETPOS message to retrieve the current position
of the scroll box of a scroll bar control. The current position is a relative value
that depends on the current scrolling range. For example, if the scrolling range is

0 through 100 and the scroll box is in the middle of the bar, the current position is 50.

Parameters   This message has no parameters.

Return Value   If the message succeeds, the return value is the current position of the scroll box in the scroll bar.

See Also   SBM_GETRANGE, SBM_SETPOS, SBM_SETRANGE, SBM_SETRANGEREDRAW

SBM_GETRANGE

New

```
SBM_GETRANGE
wParam = (WPARAM) (LPINT) lpnMinPos; /* minimum position */
lParam = (LPARAM) (LPINT) lpnMaxPos; /* maximum position */
```

An application sends the SBM_GETRANGE message to a scroll bar control to retrieve the minimum and maximum position values for the control.

Parameters   *lpnMinPos*
Points to a value that receives the minimum scrolling position.

lpnfMaxPos
Points to a value that receives the maximum scrolling position.

Return Value   This message does not return a value.

See Also   SBM_GETPOS, SBM_SETPOS, SBM_SETRANGE, SBM_SETRANGEREDRAW

SBM_SETPOS

New

```
SBM_SETPOS
wParam = (WPARAM) nPos;              /* new position of scroll box */
lParam = (LPARAM) (BOOL) fRedraw; /* redraw flag              */
```

An application sends the SBM_SETPOS message to a scroll bar control to set the position of the scroll box (thumb) and, if requested, redraw the scroll bar to reflect the new position of the scroll box.

Parameters   *nPos*
Specifies the new position of the scroll box. It must be within the scrolling range.

fRedraw
> Specifies whether the scroll bar should be redrawn to reflect the new scroll box position. If this parameter is TRUE, the scroll bar is redrawn. If it is FALSE, the scroll bar is not redrawn.

Return Value
> If the position of the scroll box changed, the return value is the previous position of the scroll box; otherwise, it is zero.

Comments
> Setting the *fRedraw* parameter to FALSE is useful if the scroll bar control is redrawn by a subsequent call to another function.

See Also
> SBM_GETPOS, SBM_GETRANGE, SBM_SETRANGE, SBM_SETRANGEREDRAW

SBM_SETRANGE

New

```
SBM_SETRANGE
wParam = (WPARAM) nMinPos; /* minimum scrolling position */
lParam = (LPARAM) nMaxPos; /* maximum scrolling position */
```

> An application sends the SBM_SETRANGE message to a scroll bar control to set the minimum and maximum position values for the control.

Parameters
> *nMinPos*
> > Specifies the minimum scrolling position.
>
> *fMaxPos*
> > Specifies the maximum scrolling position.

Return Value
> The return value is always zero.

Comments
> The default minimum and maximum position values are 0. The difference between the values specified by the *nMinPos* and *nMaxPos* parameters must not be greater than 32,767.
>
> If the minimum and maximum position values are equal, the scroll bar control is hidden and, in effect, disabled.

See Also
> SBM_GETPOS, SBM_GETRANGE, SBM_SETPOS, SBM_SETRANGEREDRAW

SBM_SETRANGEREDRAW

```
SBM_SETRANGEREDRAW
wParam = (WPARAM) nMinPos; /* minimum scrolling position */
lParam = (LPARAM) nMaxPos  /* maximum scrolling position */
```

An application sends the SBM_SETRANGEREDRAW message to a scroll bar control to set the minimum and maximum position values and to redraw the control.

Parameters

nMinPos
Specifies the minimum scrolling position.

fMaxPos
Specifies the maximum scrolling position.

Return Value

If the position of the scroll box changed, the return value is the previous position of the scroll box; otherwise, it is zero.

Comments

The default minimum and maximum position values are 0. The difference between the values specified by the *nMinPos* and *nMaxPos* parameters must not be greater than 32,767.

If the minimum and maximum position values are equal, the scroll bar control is hidden and, in effect, disabled.

See Also

SBM_GETPOS, SBM_GETRANGE, SBM_SETPOS, SBM_SETRANGE

STM_GETICON

```
STM_GETICON
wParam = 0; /* not used; must be zero */
lParam = 0; /* not used; must be zero */
```

An application sends the STM_GETICON message to retrieve the handle of the icon associated with an icon control.

Parameters

This message has no parameters.

Return Value

The return value is the handle of the icon, or zero if either the icon control has no associated icon or if an error occurred.

See Also

STM_SETICON

STM_SETICON

```
STM_SETICON
wParam = (WPARAM) (HICON) hicon;    /* handle of icon        */
lParam = 0;                         /* not used, must be zero */
```

An application sends the STM_SETICON message to associate an icon with an icon control.

Parameters   *hicon*
Value of *wParam*. Identifies the icon to associate with the icon control.

Return Value   The return value is the handle of the icon previously associated with the icon control, or zero if an error occurs.

See Also   **LoadIcon**, STM_GETICON

WIM_CLOSE

This message is sent to a waveform input callback function when a waveform input device is closed. The device handle is no longer valid once this message has been sent.

Parameters   **DWORD** *dwParam1*
Currently unused.

DWORD *dwParam2*
Currently unused.

Return Value   None.

See Also   MM_WIM_CLOSE

WIM_DATA

This message is sent to a waveform input callback function when waveform data is present in the input buffer and the buffer is being returned to the application. The message can be sent either when the buffer is full, or after the **waveInReset** function is called.

Parameters   **DWORD** *dwParam1*

Points to a **WAVEHDR** structure identifying the buffer containing the waveform data. The **WAVEHDR** structure has the following form:

```
typedef struct wavehdr_tag {
    LPSTR   lpData;
    DWORD   dwBufferLength;
    DWORD   dwBytesRecorded;
    DWORD   dwUser;
    DWORD   dwFlags;
    DWORD   dwLoops;
    struct  wavehdr_tag *lpNext;
    DWORD   reserved;
} WAVEHDR;
```

For a full description of this structure, see Chapter 3, "Structures."

DWORD *dwParam2*
Currently unused.

Return Value   None.

Comments   The returned buffer may not be full. Use the **dwBytesRecorded** member of the **WAVEHDR** structure specified by *dwParam1* to determine the number of bytes recorded into the returned buffer.

See Also   MM_WIM_DATA

WIM_OPEN

This message is sent to a waveform input callback function when a waveform input device is opened.

Parameters   **DWORD** *dwParam1*
Currently unused.

DWORD *dwParam2*
Currently unused.

Return Value   None.

See Also   MM_WIM_OPEN

WM_ACTIVATE

```
WM_ACTIVATE
fActive = LOWORD(wParam);            /* activation flag */
fMinimized = (BOOL) HIWORD(wParam); /* minimized flag  */
hwnd = (HWND) lParam;               /* window handle   */
```

The WM_ACTIVATE message is sent when a window is being activated or deactivated. This message is sent first to the window procedure of the top-level window being deactivated and then to the window procedure of the top-level window being activated.

Parameters

fActive

Value of the low-order word of *wParam*. Specifies whether the window is being activated or deactivated. This parameter can be one of the following values:

Value	Meaning
WA_ACTIVE	Activated by some method other than a mouse click (for example, by a call to the **SetActiveWindow** function or by use of the keyboard interface to select the window).
WA_CLICKACTIVE	Activated by a mouse click.
WA_INACTIVE	Deactivated.

fMinimized

Value of the high-order word of *wParam*. Specifies the minimized state of the window being activated or deactivated. A nonzero value indicates the window is minimized.

hwnd

Value of *lParam*. Identifies the window being activated or deactivated, depending on the value of the *fActive* parameter. If the value of *fActive* is WA_INACTIVE, *hwnd* is the handle of the window being activated. If the value of *fActive* is WA_ACTIVE or WA_CLICKACTIVE, *hwnd* is the handle of the window being deactivated. This handle can be NULL.

Return Value

If an application processes this message, it should return zero.

Default Action

If the window is being activated and is not minimized, the **DefWindowProc** function sets the keyboard focus to the window.

Comments

If the window is activated by a mouse click, it also receives a WM_MOUSEACTIVATE message.

See Also

WM_MOUSEACTIVATE, WM_NCACTIVATE

WM_ACTIVATEAPP

```
WM_ACTIVATEAPP
fActive = (BOOL) wParam;        /* activation flag   */
dwThreadID = (DWORD) lParam:    /* thread identifier */
```

The WM_ACTIVATEAPP message is sent when a window belonging to a different application than the active window is about to be activated. The message is sent to the application whose window is being activated and to the application whose window is being deactivated.

Parameters   *fActive*
Value of *wParam*. Specifies whether the window is being activated or deactivated. This parameter is TRUE if the window is being activated; it is FALSE if the window is being deactivated.

dwThreadID
Value of *lParam*. Specifies a thread identifier. If the *fActive* parameter is TRUE, *dwThreadID* is the identifier of the thread that owns the window being deactivated. If *fActive* is FALSE, *dwThreadID* is the identifier of the thread that owns the window being activated.

Return Value   If an application processes this message, it should return zero.

See Also   WM_ACTIVATE

WM_ASKCBFORMATNAME   `Unicode`

```
WM_ASKCBFORMATNAME
cchName = (DWORD) wParam         /* size of buffer             */
lpszFormatName = (LPTSTR) lParam /* buffer to receive format name */
```

The WM_ASKCBFORMATNAME message is sent to the clipboard owner by a clipboard viewer window to request the name of a CF_OWNERDISPLAY clipboard format.

Parameters   *cchName*
Value of *wParam*. Specifies the size, in characters, of the buffer pointed to by the *lpszFormatName* parameter.

lpszFormatName
Value of *lParam*. Points to the buffer that is to receive the clipboard format name.

Return Value   If an application processes this message, it should return zero.

Comments   In response to this message, the clipboard owner should copy the name of the owner-display format to the specified buffer, not exceeding the buffer size specified by the *cchName* parameter.

A clipboard viewer window sends this message to the clipboard owner to determine the name of the CF_OWNERDISPLAY format—for example, to initialize a menu listing available formats.

WM_CANCELMODE

```
WM_CANCELMODE
```

The WM_CANCELMODE message is sent to the focus window when a dialog box or message box is displayed, enabling the focus window to cancel modes such as mouse capture.

Parameters   This message has no parameters.

Return Value   If an application processes this message, it should return zero.

Default Action   The **DefWindowProc** function cancels internal processing of standard scroll bar input, cancels internal menu processing, and releases the mouse capture.

See Also   **DefWindowProc**, **ReleaseCapture**

WM_CHANGECBCHAIN

```
WM_CHANGECBCHAIN
hwndRemove = (HWND) wParam;      /* handle of window being removed */
hwndNext = (HWND) lParam;        /* handle of next window in chain */
```

The WM_CHANGECBCHAIN message is sent to the first window in the clipboard viewer chain when a window is being removed from the chain.

Parameters   *hwndRemove*
Value of *wParam*. Identifies the window being removed from the clipboard viewer chain.

hwndNext
Value of *lParam*. Identifies the next window in the chain following the window being removed. This parameter is NULL if the window being removed is the last window in the chain.

Return Value   If an application processes this message, it should return zero.

Comments   Each clipboard viewer window saves the handle of the next window in the clipboard viewer chain. Initially, this handle is the return value of the **SetClipboardViewer** function.

When a clipboard viewer window receives the WM_CHANGECBCHAIN message, it should call the **SendMessage** function to pass the message to the next window in the chain, unless the next window is the window being removed. In this case, the clipboard viewer should save the handle specified by *hwndNext* as the next window in the chain.

See Also   **SendMessage**, **SetClipboardViewer**

WM_CHAR   Unicode

```
WM_CHAR
chCharCode = (TCHAR) wParam;      /* character code */
lKeyData = lParam;                /* key data       */
```

The WM_CHAR message is posted to the window with the keyboard focus when a WM_KEYDOWN message is translated by the **TranslateMessage** function. WM_CHAR contains the character code of the key that was pressed.

Parameters   *chCharCode*
Value of *wParam*. Specifies the character code of the key.

lKeyData
Value of *lParam*. Specifies the repeat count, scan code, extended-key flag, context code, previous key-state flag, and transition-state flag, as shown in the following table:

Value	Description
0–15	Specifies the repeat count. The value is the number of times the keystroke is repeated as a result of the user holding down the key.
16–23	Specifies the scan code. The value depends on the original equipment manufacturer (OEM).
24	Specifies whether the key is an extended key, such as a function key or a key on the numeric keypad. The value is 1 if it is an extended key; otherwise, it is 0.
25–28	Reserved.
29	Specifies the context code. The value is 1 if the ALT key is held down while the key is pressed; otherwise, the value is 0.

| 30 | Specifies the previous key state. The value is 1 if the key is down before the message is sent, or it is 0 if the key is up. |
| 31 | Specifies the transition state. The value is 1 if the key is being released, or it is 0 if the key is being pressed. |

Return Value

An application should return zero if it processes this message.

Comments

Because there is not necessarily a one-to-one correspondence between keys pressed and character messages generated, the information in the high-order word of the *lKeyData* parameter is generally not useful to applications. The information in the high-order word applies only to the most recent WM_KEYDOWN message that precedes the posting of the WM_CHAR message.

For enhanced 101- and 102-key keyboards, extended keys are the right ALT and the right CTRL keys on the main section of the keyboard; the INS, DEL, HOME, END, PAGE UP, PAGE DOWN and arrow keys in the clusters to the left of the numeric keypad; and the divide (/) and ENTER keys in the numeric keypad. Some other keyboards may support the extended-key bit in the *lKeyData* parameter.

See Also

TranslateMessage, WM_KEYDOWN

WM_CHARTOITEM

```
WM_CHARTOITEM
nKey = LOWORD(wParam);          /* key value         */
nCaretPos = HIWORD(wParam);     /* caret position    */
hwndListBox = (HWND) lParam;    /* handle of list box */
```

The WM_CHARTOITEM message is sent by a list box with the LBS_WANTKEYBOARDINPUT style to its owner in response to a WM_CHAR message.

Parameters

nKey
Value of the low-order word of *wParam*. Specifies the value of the key the user pressed.

nCaretPos
Value of the high-order word of *wParam*. Specifies the current position of the caret.

hwndListBox
Value of *lParam*. Identifies the list box.

Return Value

The return value specifies the action that the application performed in response to the message. A return value of –1 or –2 indicates that the application handled all aspects of selecting the item and requires no further action by the list box. A return value of 0 or greater specifies the zero-based index of an item in the list box and indicates that the list box should perform the default action for the keystroke on the given item.

Default Action   The **DefWindowProc** function returns –1.

Comments   Only owner-drawn list boxes that do not have the LBS_HASSTRINGS style can receive this message.

See Also   **DefWindowProc**, WM_CHAR, WM_VKEYTOITEM

WM_CHILDACTIVATE

```
WM_CHILDACTIVATE
```

The WM_CHILDACTIVATE message is sent to a multiple document interface (MDI) child window when the user clicks the window's title bar or when the window is activated, moved, or sized.

Parameters   This message has no parameters.

Return Value   If an application processes this message, it should return zero.

See Also   **MoveWindow**, **SetWindowPos**

WM_CHOOSEFONT_GETLOGFONT

```
WM_CHOOSEFONT_GETLOGFONT
wParam = 0;                    /* not used, must be zero        */
lParam = (LPLOGFONT) lplf; /* address of struct. with font data */
```

An application sends a WM_CHOOSEFONT_GETLOGFONT message to the Font dialog box created by the **ChooseFont** function to retrieve the current **LOGFONT** structure.

Parameters   *lplf*
Points to a **LOGFONT** structure that receives information about the current logical font. The **LOGFONT** structure has the following form:

```
typedef struct tagLOGFONT { /* lf */
    LONG lfHeight;
    LONG lfWidth;
    LONG lfEscapement;
    LONG lfOrientation;
```

```
                        LONG lfWeight;
                        BYTE lfItalic;
                        BYTE lfUnderline;
                        BYTE lfStrikeOut;
                        BYTE lfCharSet;
                        BYTE lfOutPrecision;
                        BYTE lfClipPrecision;
                        BYTE lfQuality;
                        BYTE lfPitchAndFamily;
                        CHAR lfFaceName[LF_FACESIZE];
                    } LOGFONT;
```

Return Value   This message does not return a value.

Comments   An application uses this message to retrieve the **LOGFONT** structure while the Font dialog box is open. When the user closes the dialog box, the **ChooseFont** function receives information about the **LOGFONT** structure.

See Also   **ChooseFont**, WM_GETFONT, **LOGFONT**

WM_CLEAR

```
WM_CLEAR
wParam = 0; /* not used, must be zero */
lParam = 0; /* not used, must be zero */
```

An application sends a WM_CLEAR message to an edit control or combo box to delete (clear) the current selection, if any, from the edit control.

Parameters   This message has no parameters.

Return Value   This message does not return a value.

Comments   The deletion performed by the WM_CLEAR message can be undone by sending the edit control an EM_UNDO message.

To delete the current selection and place the deleted contents into the Clipboard, use the WM_CUT message.

When sent to a combo box, the WM_CLEAR message is handled by its edit control. This message has no effect when sent to a combo box with the CBS_DROPDOWNLIST style.

See Also   EM_UNDO, WM_COPY, WM_CUT, WM_PASTE

WM_CLOSE

WM_CLOSE

The WM_CLOSE message is sent as a signal that a window or an application should terminate.

Parameters   This message has no parameters.

Return Value   If an application processes this message, it should return zero.

Default Action   The **DefWindowProc** function calls the **DestroyWindow** function to destroy the window.

Comments   An application can prompt the user for confirmation, prior to destroying a window, by processing the WM_CLOSE message and calling the **DestroyWindow** function only if the user confirms the choice.

See Also   **DefWindowProc**, **DestroyWindow**

WM_COMMAND

```
WM_COMMAND
wNotifyCode = HIWORD(wParam);  /* notification code                    */
wID = LOWORD(wParam);          /* item, control, or accelerator identifier */
hwndCtl = (HWND) lParam;       /* handle of control                    */
```

The WM_COMMAND message is sent when the user selects a command item from a menu, when a control sends a notification message to its parent window, or when an accelerator keystroke is translated.

Parameters   *wNotifyCode*
Value of the high-order word of *wParam*. Specifies the notification code if the message is from a control. If the message is from an accelerator, this parameter is 1. If the message is from a menu, this parameter is 0.

wID
Value of the low-order word of *wParam*. Specifies the identifier of the menu item, control, or accelerator.

hwndCtl
Value of *lParam*. Identifies the control sending the message if the message is from a control. Otherwise, this parameter is NULL.

Return Value   If an application processes this message, it should return zero.

Comments   Accelerator keystrokes that select items from the System menu are translated into WM_SYSCOMMAND messages.

If an accelerator keystroke occurs that corresponds to a menu item when the window that owns the menu is minimized, no WM_COMMAND message is sent. However, if an accelerator keystroke occurs that does not match any of the items in the window's menu or in the System menu, a WM_COMMAND message is sent, even if the window is minimized.

See Also   WM_SYSCOMMAND

WM_COMPACTING

```
WM_COMPACTING
wCompactRatio = wParam; /* compacting ratio */
```

The WM_COMPACTING message is sent to all top-level windows when Windows detects more than 12.5 percent of system time over a 30- to 60-second interval is being spent compacting memory. This indicates that system memory is low.

Parameters   *wCompactRatio*
Value of *wParam*. Specifies the ratio of central processing unit (CPU) time currently spent by Windows compacting memory to CPU time currently spent by Windows performing other operations. For example, 0x8000 represents 50 percent of CPU time spent compacting memory.

Return Value   If an application processes this message, it should return zero.

Comments   When an application receives this message, it should free as much memory as possible, taking into account the current level of activity of the application and the total number of applications running with Windows.

WM_COMPAREITEM

```
WM_COMPAREITEM
idCtl = wParam;                          /* control identifier    */
lpcis = (LPCOMPAREITEMSTRUCT) lParam; /* structure with items */
```

Windows sends the WM_COMPAREITEM message to determine the relative position of a new item in the sorted list of an owner-drawn combo box or list box. Whenever the application adds a new item, Windows sends this message to the owner of a combo box or list box created with the CBS_SORT or LBS_SORT style.

Parameters

idCtl

Value of *wParam*. Specifies the identifier of the control that sent the WM_COMPAREITEM message.

lpcis

Value of *lParam*. Points to a **COMPAREITEMSTRUCT** structure that contains the identifiers and application-supplied data for two items in the combo or list box. The **COMPAREITEMSTRUCT** structure has the following form:

```
typedef struct tagCOMPAREITEMSTRUCT { /* cis */
    UINT  CtlType;
    UINT  CtlID;
    HWND  hwndItem;
    UINT  itemID1;
    DWORD itemData1;
    UINT  itemID2;
    DWORD itemData2;
} COMPAREITEMSTRUCT;
```

Return Value

The return value indicates the relative position of the two items. It may be any of the following:

Value	Meaning
−1	Item 1 precedes item 2 in the sorted order.
0	Items 1 and 2 are equivalent in the sorted order.
1	Item 1 follows item 2 in the sorted order.

Comments

When the owner of an owner-drawn combo box or list box receives this message, the owner returns a value indicating which of the items specified by the **COMPAREITEMSTRUCT** structure will appear before the other. Typically, Windows sends this message several times until it determines the exact position for the new item.

See Also

COMPAREITEMSTRUCT

WM_COPY

```
WM_COPY
wParam = 0; /* not used, must be zero */
lParam = 0; /* not used, must be zero */
```

An application sends the WM_COPY message to an edit control or combo box to copy the current selection to the Clipboard in CF_TEXT format.

Parameters   This message has no parameters.

Return Value   This message does not return a value.

Comments   When sent to a combo box, the WM_COPY message is handled by its edit control. This message has no effect when sent to a combo box with the CBS_DROPDOWNLIST style.

See Also   WM_CLEAR, WM_CUT, WM_PASTE

WM_COPYDATA

New

```
WM_COPYDATA
wParam = (WPARAM) (HWND) hwndFrom;       /* handle of sending window */
lParam = (LPARAM) (PCOPYDATASTRUCT) cds; /* structure with data      */
```

The WM_COPYDATA message is sent when an application passes data to another application.

Parameters   *hwndData*
                    Identifies the window passing the data.

                    cds
                    Points to a **COPYDATASTRUCT** structure that contains the data to be passed. The **COPYDATASTRUCT** has the following form:

```
typedef struct tagCOPYDATASTRUCT {  /* cds */
    DWORD dwData;
    DWORD cbData;
    PVOID lpData;
} COPYDATASTRUCT;
```

                    For a full description of this structure, see Chapter 3, "Structures."

Return Value   If the receiving application processes this message, it should return TRUE; otherwise, it should return FALSE.

Comments   An application must use the **SendMessage** function to send this message, not the **PostMessage** function.

                    The data being passed must not contain pointers or other references to objects not accessible to the application receiving the data.

                    While this message is being sent, the referenced data must not be changed by another thread of the sending process.

The receiving application should consider the data read-only. The *cds* parameter is valid only during the processing of the message. The receiving application should not free the memory referenced by the *cds* parameter. If the receiving application must access the data after **SendMessage** returns, it must copy the data into a local buffer.

See Also   **PostMessage, SendMessage, COPYDATASTRUCT**

WM_CPL_LAUNCH

```
WM_CPL_LAUNCH
hwnd = (HWND) wParam;           /* handle of sending window */
lpszAppName = (LPSTR) lParam;   /* application-name string  */
```

An application sends the WM_CPL_LAUNCH message to Windows Control Panel to request that a Control Panel application be started.

Parameters   *hwnd*
Value of *wParam*. Specifies the handle of the window sending the message. The WM_CPL_LAUNCHED message is sent to this window.

lpszAppName
Value of *lParam*. Specifies a far pointer to a string containing the name of the Control Panel application to open.

Return Value   If the application starts, the return value is TRUE; otherwise, it is FALSE.

See Also   WM_CPL_LAUNCHED

WM_CPL_LAUNCHED

```
WM_CPL_LAUNCHED
fAppStarted = (BOOL) wParam;
```

The WM_CPL_LAUNCHED message is sent when a Windows Control Panel application, started by the WM_CPL_LAUNCH message, has closed. The WM_CPL_LAUNCHED message is sent to the window identified by the *wParam* parameter of the WM_CPL_LAUNCH message that started the application.

Parameters   *fAppStarted*
Value of *wParam*. Specifies whether the application was started. If the application was started, this parameter is TRUE; otherwise, it is FALSE.

Return Value   The value returned by the application is ignored for this message.

See Also   WM_CPL_LAUNCH

WM_CREATE

```
WM_CREATE
lpcs = (LPCREATESTRUCT) lParam; /* structure with creation data */
```

The WM_CREATE message is sent when an application requests that a window be created by calling the **CreateWindowEx** or **CreateWindow** function. The window procedure of the new window receives this message after the window is created, but before the window becomes visible. The message is sent before the **CreateWindowEx** or **CreateWindow** function returns.

Parameters   *lParam*

Value of *lParam*. Points to a **CREATESTRUCT** structure that contains information about the window being created. The members of the **CREATESTRUCT** structure are identical to the parameters of the **CreateWindowEx** function. The **CREATESTRUCT** structure has the following form:

```
typedef struct tagCREATESTRUCT { /* cs */
    LPVOID  lpCreateParams;
    HANDLE  hInstance;
    HMENU   hMenu;
    HWND    hwndParent;
    int     cy;
    int     cx;
    int     y;
    int     x;
    LONG    style;
    LPCSTR  lpszName;
    LPCSTR  lpszClass;
    DWORD   dwExStyle;
} CREATESTRUCT;
```

For a full description of this structure, see Chapter 3, "Structures."

Return Value   If an application processes this message, it should return 0 to continue creation of the window. If the application returns –1, the window is destroyed and the **CreateWindowEx** or **CreateWindow** function returns a NULL handle.

See Also   **CreateWindow**, **CreateWindowEx**, **CREATESTRUCT**, WM_NCCREATE

WM_CTLCOLORBTN

```
WM_CTLCOLORBTN
hdcButton = (HDC) wParam;   /* handle of button display context */
hwndButton = (HWND) lParam; /* handle of button                */
```

The WM_CTLCOLORBTN message is sent to the parent window of a button when the button is about to be drawn. By responding to this message, the parent window can set a button's text and background colors.

Parameters
hdcButton
    Value of *wParam*. Identifies the display context for the button.

hwndButton
    Value of *lParam*. Identifies the button.

Return Value
If an application processes this message, it must return the handle of a brush. Windows uses the brush to paint the background of the button.

Default Action
The **DefWindowProc** function selects the default system colors for the button.

Comments
The WM_CTLCOLORBTN message is never sent between threads. It is sent only within one thread.

The text color of a check box or radio button applies to the box or button, its check mark, and the text. The focus rectangle for these buttons remains the system default color (typically black). The text color of a group box applies to the text but not to the line that defines the box. The text color of a push button applies only to its focus rectangle; it does not affect the color of the text.

See Also
DefWindowProc, WM_CTLCOLORDLG, WM_CTLCOLOREDIT, WM_CTLCOLORLISTBOX, WM_CTLCOLORMSGBOX, WM_CTLCOLORSCROLLBAR, WM_CTLCOLORSTATIC

WM_CTLCOLORDLG

```
WM_CTLCOLORDLG
hdcDlg = (HDC) wParam;   /* handle of dialog box display context */
hwndDlg = (HWND) lParam; /* handle of dialog box                 */
```

The WM_CTLCOLORDLG message is sent to a dialog box before Windows draws the dialog box. By responding to this message, the dialog box can set its text and background colors by using the given display device context handle.

Parameters   *hdcDlg*
        Value of *wParam*. Identifies the device context for the dialog box.

        hwndDlg
        Value of *lParam*. Identifies the dialog box.

Return Value   If an application processes this message, it must return the handle of a brush. Windows uses the brush to paint the background of the dialog box.

Default Action   The **DefWindowProc** function selects the default system colors for the dialog box.

Comments   The WM_CTLCOLORDLG message is never sent between threads. It is sent only within one thread.

        Note that the WM_CTLCOLORDLG message is sent to the dialog itself; all of the other WM_CTLCOLOR* messages are sent to the owner of the control.

See Also   **DefWindowProc**, WM_CTLCOLORBTN, WM_CTLCOLOREDIT, WM_CTLCOLORLISTBOX, WM_CTLCOLORMSGBOX, WM_CTLCOLORSCROLLBAR, WM_CTLCOLORSTATIC

WM_CTLCOLOREDIT   `New`

```
WM_CTLCOLOREDIT
hdcEdit = (HDC) wParam;    /* handle of display context */
hwndEdit = (HWND) lParam; /* handle of static control  */
```

The WM_CTLCOLOREDIT message is sent to the parent window of an edit control when the control is about to be drawn. By responding to this message, the parent window can use the given device context handle to set the text and background colors of the edit control.

Parameters   *hdcEdit*
        Value of *wParam*. Identifies the device context for the edit control window.

        hwndEdit
        Value of *lParam*. Identifies the edit control.

Return Value   If an application processes this message, it must return the handle of a brush. Windows uses the brush to paint the background of the edit control.

Default Action   The **DefWindowProc** function selects the default system colors for the edit control.

Comments   The WM_CTLCOLOREDIT message is never sent between threads, it is only sent within the same thread.

See Also   **DefWindowProc**, WM_CTLCOLORBTN, WM_CTLCOLORDLG, WM_CTLCOLORLISTBOX, WM_CTLCOLORMSGBOX, WM_CTLCOLORSCROLLBAR, WM_CTLCOLORSTATIC

WM_CTLCOLORLISTBOX

```
WM_CTLCOLORLISTBOX
hdcLB = (HDC) wParam;   /* handle of list box display context */
hwndLB = (HWND) lParam; /* handle of list box                 */
```

The WM_CTLCOLORLISTBOX message is sent to the parent window of a list box before Windows draws the list box. By responding to this message, the parent window can set the text and background colors of the list box by using the given display device context handle.

Parameters   *hdcLB*
　　　　　　　　Value of *wParam*. Identifies the device context for the list box.

　　　　　　　hwndLB
　　　　　　　　Value of *lParam*. Identifies the list box.

Return Value   If an application processes this message, it must return the handle of a brush. Windows uses the brush to paint the background of the list box.

Default Action   The **DefWindowProc** function selects the default system colors for the list box.

Comments   The WM_CTLCOLORLISTBOX message is never sent between threads. It is sent only within one thread.

See Also   **DefWindowProc**, WM_CTLCOLORBTN, WM_CTLCOLORDLG, WM_CTLCOLOREDIT, WM_CTLCOLORMSGBOX, WM_CTLCOLORSCROLLBAR, WM_CTLCOLORSTATIC

WM_CTLCOLORMSGBOX

```
WM_CTLCOLORMSGBOX
hdcMB = (HDC) wParam;   /* handle of message box display context */
hwndMB = (HWND) lParam; /* handle of message box                 */
```

The WM_CTLCOLORMSGBOX message is sent to the owner window of a message box before Windows draws the message box. By responding to this message, the owner window can set the text and background colors of the message box by using the given display device context handle.

Parameters   *hdcMB*
                      Value of *wParam*. Identifies the device context for the message box.

                      hwndMB
                      Value of *lParam*. Identifies the message box.

Return Value   If an application processes this message, it must return the handle of a brush. Windows uses the brush to paint the background of the message box.

Default Action   The **DefWindowProc** function selects the default system colors for the message box.

Comments   The WM_CTLCOLORMSGBOX message is never sent between threads. It is sent only within one thread.

See Also   **DefWindowProc**, WM_CTLCOLORBTN, WM_CTLCOLORDLG, WM_CTLCOLOREDIT, WM_CTLCOLORLISTBOX, WM_CTLCOLORSCROLLBAR, WM_CTLCOLORSTATIC

WM_CTLCOLORSCROLLBAR

New

```
WM_CTLCOLORSCROLLBAR
hdcSB  = (HDC) wParam;    /* handle of scroll bar display context */
hwndSB = (HWND) lParam;   /* handle of scroll bar                 */
```

The WM_CTLCOLORSCROLLBAR message is sent to the parent window of a scroll bar control when the control is about to be drawn. By responding to this message, the parent window can use the given display context handle to set the background color of the scroll bar control.

Parameters   *hdcSB*
                      Value of *wParam*. Identifies the display context for the scroll bar control.

                      hwndSB
                      Value of *lParam*. Identifies the scroll bar.

Return Value   If an application processes this message, it must return the handle of a brush. Windows uses the brush to paint the background of the scroll bar control.

Default Action   The **DefWindowProc** function selects the default system colors for the scroll bar control.

Comments	The WM_CTLCOLORSCROLLBAR message is never sent between threads; it is only sent within the same thread.
See Also	**DefWindowProc**, WM_CTLCOLORBTN, WM_CTLCOLORDLG, WM_CTLCOLOREDIT, WM_CTLCOLORLISTBOX, WM_CTLCOLORMSGBOX, WM_CTLCOLORSTATIC

WM_CTLCOLORSTATIC   New

```
WM_CTLCOLORSTATIC
hdcStatic = (HDC) wParam;   /* handle of display context */
hwndStatic = (HWND) lParam; /* handle of static control  */
```

The WM_CTLCOLORSTATIC message is sent to the parent window of a static control when the control is about to be drawn. By responding to this message, the parent window can use the given device context (DC) handle to set the text and background colors of the static control.

Parameters	*hdcStatic*
	    Value of *wParam*. Identifies the DC for the static control window.
	hwndStatic
	    Value of *lParam*. Identifies the static control.

Return Value	If an application processes this message, the return value is the handle of a brush that Windows uses to paint the background of the static control.
Default Action	The **DefWindowProc** function selects the default system colors for the static control.
Comments	The WM_CTLCOLORSCROLLBAR message is never sent between threads; it is sent only within the same thread.
See Also	**DefWindowProc**, WM_CTLCOLORBTN, WM_CTLCOLORDLG, WM_CTLCOLOREDIT, WM_CTLCOLORLISTBOX, WM_CTLCOLORMSGBOX, WM_CTLCOLORSCROLLBAR

WM_CUT

```
WM_CUT
wParam = 0; /* not used, must be zero */
lParam = 0; /* not used, must be zero */
```

An application sends a WM_CUT message to an edit control or combo box to delete (cut) the current selection, if any, in the edit control and copy the deleted text to the Clipboard in CF_TEXT format.

Parameters

This message has no parameters.

Return Value

This message does not return a value.

Comments

The deletion performed by the WM_CUT message can be undone by sending the edit control an EM_UNDO message.

To delete the current selection without placing the deleted text onto the Clipboard, use the WM_CLEAR message.

When sent to a combo box, the WM_CUT message is handled by its edit control. This message has no effect when sent to a combo box with the CBS_DROPDOWNLIST style.

See Also

WM_CLEAR, WM_COPY, WM_PASTE

WM_DDE_ACK

```
WM_DDE_ACK
                                    /* Response to WM_DDE_INITIATE      */
wParam = (WPARAM) hwnd;             /* handle of posting application    */
lParam = MAKELPARAM(aApp, aTopic)   /* application and topic atoms      */

                                    /* Response to WM_DDE_EXECUTE       */
wParam = (WPARAM) hwnd;             /* handle of posting application    */
lParam = (LPARAM) lPackedVal;       /* packed status flags and data handle */

                                    /* Response to all other messages   */
wParam = (WPARAM) hwnd;             /* handle of posting application    */
lParam = (LPARAM) lPackedVal;       /* packed status flags and item     */
```

The WM_DDE_ACK message notifies a dynamic data exchange (DDE) application of the receipt and processing of a WM_DDE_INITIATE, WM_DDE_EXECUTE, WM_DDE_DATA, WM_DDE_ADVISE, WM_DDE_UNADVISE, or WM_DDE_POKE message, and in some cases, of a WM_DDE_REQUEST message.

Parameters

When responding to WM_DDE_INITIATE:
hwnd
    Value of *wParam*. Identifies the server window posting the message.

aApp

Value of the low-order word of *lParam*. Contains an atom that identifies the replying application.

aTopic

Value of the high-order word of *lParam*. Contains an atom that identifies the topic for which a conversation is being established.

When responding to WM_DDE_EXECUTE:

hwnd

Value of *wParam*. Identifies the server window posting the message.

lPackedVal

Value of *lParam*. The component parameters that are packed into *lPackedVal* are extracted by calling the **UnpackDDElParam** function. The Low component is *wStatus*. The High component is the same *hCommands* that was received in the WM_DDE_EXECUTE message.

Parameter	Description
wStatus	Specifies a **DDEACK** structure containing a series of flags that indicate the status of the response. The **DDEACK** structure has the following form:

```
typedef struct { /* ddeack */
    unsigned short bAppReturnCode:8,
    reserved:6,
    fBusy:1,
    fAck:1;
} DDEACK;
```

For a full description of this structure, see Chapter 3, "Structures"

Parameter	Description
hCommands	Identifies a global memory object containing the command string.

When replying to all other messages:

hwnd

Value of *wParam*. Identifies the client or server window posting the message.

lPackedVal

Value of *lParam*. The component parameters that are packed into *lPackedVal* are extracted by calling the **UnpackDDElParam** function. The Low component is *wStatus*. The High component is *aItem*.

Parameter	Description
wStatus	Specifies a **DDEACK** structure containing a series of flags that indicate the status of the response. The **DDEACK** structure has the following form:

```
typedef struct { /* ddeack */
```

```
            unsigned short bAppReturnCode:8,
            reserved:6,
            fBusy:1,
            fAck:1;
        } DDEACK;
```

For a full description of this structure, see Chapter 3, "Structures"

aItem   Contains a global atom that identifies the name of the data item for which the response is sent.

Comments   **Posting**

Except in response to the WM_DDE_INITIATE message, the application posts the WM_DDE_ACK message by calling the **PostMessage** function, not the **SendMessage** function. When responding to WM_DDE_INITIATE, the application sends the WM_DDE_ACK message by calling **SendMessage**. In this case, neither the application-name atom nor the topic-name atom should be NULL (even if the WM_DDE_INITIATE message specified NULL atoms.

When acknowledging any message with an accompanying *aItem* atom, the application posting WM_DDE_ACK can either reuse the *aItem* atom that accompanied the original message, or it can delete it and create a new one.

When acknowledging WM_DDE_EXECUTE, the application that posts WM_DDE_ACK should reuse the *hCommands* object that accompanied the original WM_DDE_EXECUTE message.

All posted WM_DDE_ACK messages must create or reuse the *lPackedVal* parameter by calling the **PackDDElParam** function or the **ReuseDDElParam** function.

If an application has initiated the termination of a conversation by posting WM_DDE_TERMINATE and is awaiting confirmation, the waiting application should not acknowledge (positively or negatively) any subsequent messages sent by the other application. The waiting application should delete any atoms or shared memory objects received in these intervening messages. Memory objects should not be freed if the **fRelease** flag is set to FALSE in WM_DDE_POKE, and WM_DDE_DATA messages.

Receiving

The application that receives a WM_DDE_ACK message should delete all atoms accompanying the message. If the application receives a WM_DDE_ACK in response to a message with an accompanying *hData* object, and the object was sent with the **fRelease** flags set to FALSE, the application is responsible for deleteing the *hData* object.

If the application receives a negative WM_DDE_ACK message posted in reply to a WM_DDE_ADVISE message, the application should delete the *hOptions* object posted with the original WM_DDE_ADVISE message. If the application receives a negative WM_DDE_ACK message posted in reply to a WM_DDE_DATA, WM_DDE_POKE, or WM_DDE_EXECUTE message, the application should delete the *hCommands* object posted with the original WM_DDE_DATA, WM_DDE_POKE, or WM_DDE_EXECUTE message.

The application that receives a posted WM_DDE_ACK message must free the *lPackedVal* parameter by using the **FreeDDElParam** function.

See Also   **FreeDDElParam**, **PackDDElParam**, **PostMessage**, **ReuseDDElParam**, **UnpackDDElParam**, WM_DDE_ADVISE, WM_DDE_DATA, WM_DDE_EXECUTE, WM_DDE_INITIATE, WM_DDE_POKE, WM_DDE_REQUEST, WM_DDE_TERMINATE, WM_DDE_UNADVISE

WM_DDE_ADVISE

```
WM_DDE_ADVISE
wParam = (WPARAM) hwnd;        /* handle of posting application  */
lParam = (LPARAM) lPackedVal; /* packed DDEADVISE and item atom */
```

A dynamic data exchange (DDE) client application posts the WM_DDE_ADVISE message to a DDE server application to request the server to supply an update for a data item whenever the item changes.

Parameters   *hwnd*
Value of *wParam*. Identifies the client window posting the message.

lPackedVal
Value of *lParam*. The component parameters that are packed into *lPackedVal* are extracted by calling the **UnpackDDElParam** function. The Low component is *hOptions*. The High component is *aItem*.

Parameter	Description
hOptions	Identifies a global memory object containing a **DDEADVISE** structure that specifies how the data is to be sent. The **DDEADVISE** structure has the following form:

```
typedef struct { /* ddeadv */
    unsigned short reserved:14,
        fDeferUpd:1,
        fAckReq:1;
    short cfFormat;
} DDEADVISE;
```

For a full description of this structure, see Chapter 3, "Structures" *aItem*   Contains an atom that identifies the data item requested.

Comments   If a client application supports more than one clipboard format for a single topic
and item, it can post multiple WM_DDE_ADVISE messages for the topic and
item, specifying a different clipboard format with each message. Note that a
server can support multiple formats only for hot links, not warm links.

Posting

The client application posts the WM_DDE_ADVISE message by calling the
PostMessage function, not the **SendMessage** function.

The client application allocates *hOptions* by calling the **GlobalAlloc** function
with the GMEM_DDESHARE option. It allocates *aItem* by calling the
GlobalAddAtom function.

The client application must create or reuse the WM_DDE_ADVISE *lPackedVal*
parameter by calling the **PackDDElParam** function or the **ReuseDDElParam**
function with *hOptions* supplied as the Low component and *aItem* supplied as the
High component.

If the receiving (server) application responds with a negative WM_DDE_ACK
message, the posting (client) application must delete the *hOptions* object.

The **fRelease** flag is not used in WM_DDE_ADVISE messages, but their data
freeing behavior is similar to that of WM_DDE_DATA and WM_DDE_POKE
messages where **fRelease** is TRUE.

Receiving

The server application posts the WM_DDE_ACK message to respond positively
or negatively. When posting WM_DDE_ACK, the application can reuse the *aItem*
atom or delete it and create a new one. If the WM_DDE_ACK message is
positive, the application should delete the *hOptions* object; otherwise, the
application should not delete the object.

The server must create or reuse the WM_DDE_ACK *lPackedVal* parameter by
calling the **PackDDElParam** function or the **ReuseDDElParam** function with
wStatus supplied as the Low component and *aItem* supplied as the High
component.

See Also   **FreeDDElParam, GlobalAddAtom, GlobalAlloc, PackDDElParam,
PostMessage, ReuseDDElParam, SendMessage, UnpackDDElParam,**
WM_DDE_DATA, WM_DDE_REQUEST

WM_DDE_DATA

```
WM_DDE_DATA
wParam = (WPARAM) hwnd;        /* handle of posting application */
lParam = (LPARAM) lPackedVal;  /* packed DDEDATA and item atom  */
```

A dynamic data exchange (DDE) server application posts a WM_DDE_DATA message to a DDE client application to pass a data item to the client or to notify the client of the availability of a data item.

Parameters

hwnd

Value of *wParam*. Identifies the server window posting the message.

lPackedVal

Value of *lParam*. The component parameters that are packed into *lPackedVal* are extracted by calling the **UnpackDDElParam** function. The Low component is *hData* or NULL. The High component is *aItem*.

Parameter	Meaning
hData	Identifies a global memory object containing a **DDEDATA** structure with the data and additional information. The handle should be set to NULL if the server is notifying the client that the data-item value has changed during a warm link. A warm link is established by the client sending a WM_DDE_ADVISE message with the *fDeferUpd* bit set. The **DDEDATA** structure has the following form:

```
typedef struct { /* ddedat */
    unsigned short unused:12,
        fResponse:1,
        fRelease:1,
        reserved:1,
        fAckReq:1;
    short cfFormat;
    BYTE  Value[1];
} DDEDATA;
```

For a full description of this structure, see Chapter 3, "Structures"

aItem	Contains an atom that identifies the data item for which the data or notification is sent.

Comments

Posting

The server application posts the WM_DDE_DATA message by calling the **PostMessage** function, not the **SendMessage** function.

The server application allocates *hData* by calling the **GlobalAlloc** function with the GMEM_DDESHARE option. It allocates *aItem* by calling the **GlobalAddAtom** function.

The server must create or reuse the WM_DDE_DATA *lPackedVal* parameter by calling the **PackDDElParam** function or the **ReuseDDElParam** function with *hData* supplied as the Low component and *aItem* supplied as the High component.

If the receiving (client) application responds with a negative WM_DDE_ACK message, the posting (server) application must delete the *hData* object; otherwise, the client must delete the *hData* object after extracting its contents by calling the **UnpackDDElParam** function.

If the server application sets the **fRelease** member of the **DDEDATA** structure to FALSE, the server is responsible for deleting *hData* upon receiving either a positive or negative acknowledgement.

The server application should not set both the **fAckReq** and **fRelease** members of the **DDEDATA** structure to FALSE. If both members are set to FALSE, it is impossible for the server to determine when to delete *hData*.

Receiving

If **fAckReq** is TRUE, the client application should post the WM_DDE_ACK message to respond positively or negatively. When posting WM_DDE_ACK, the client can either reuse the *aItem* atom, or it can delete it and create a new one.

The client must create or reuse the WM_DDE_ACK *lPackedVal* parameter by calling the **PackDDElParam** function or the **ReuseDDElParam** function with *wStatus* supplied as the Low component and *aItem* supplied as the High component.

If **fAckReq** is FALSE, the client application should delete the *aItem* atom.

If the posting (server) application specified *hData* as NULL, the receiving (client) application can request the server to send the actual data by posting a WM_DDE_REQUEST message.

After processing a WM_DDE_DATA message in which *hData* is not NULL, the client should free *hData* by calling the **FreeDDElParam** function, unless one of the following conditions is true:

- The **fRelease** member is FALSE.

- The **fRelease** member is TRUE, but the client application responds with a negative WM_DDE_ACK message.

See Also   **FreeDDElParam**, **GlobalAddAtom**, **GlobalAlloc**, **PostMessage**, **ReuseDDElParam**, **SendMessage**, WM_DDE_ACK, WM_DDE_ADVISE, WM_DDE_POKE, WM_DDE_REQUEST

WM_DDE_EXECUTE

```
WM_DDE_EXECUTE
wParam = (WPARAM) hwnd;        /* handle of posting application   */
lParam = (LPARAM) hCommands;   /* handle to global object         */
```

A dynamic data exchange (DDE) client application posts a WM_DDE_EXECUTE message to a DDE server application to send a string to the server to be processed as a series of commands. The server application is expected to post a WM_DDE_ACK message in response.

Parameters   *hwnd*
　　　　　　Value of *wParam*. Identifies the client window posting the message.

hCommands
　　　　　　Value of *lParam*. Contains a global memory object which references an ANSI or UNICODE command string depending on the types of windows involved in the conversation.

Comments   The command string is a null-terminated string consisting of one or more *opcode* strings enclosed in single brackets ([ ]).

Each *opcode* string has the following syntax, where the *parameters* list is optional:

　　　　opcode parameters

The *opcode* is any application-defined single token. It cannot include spaces, commas, parentheses, brackets, or quotation marks.

The *parameters* list can contain any application-defined value or values. Multiple parameters are separated by commas, and the entire parameter list is enclosed in parentheses. Parameters cannot include commas or parentheses except inside a quoted string. If a bracket or parenthesis character is to appear in a quoted string, it need not be doubled, as was the case under the old rules.

Following are some valid command strings:

```
[connect][download(query1,results.txt)][disconnect]
[query("sales per employee for each district")]
[open("sample.xlm")][run("r1c1")]
[quote_case("This is a "" character")]
[bracket_or_paren_case("()s or []s should be no problem.")]
```

Note that, under old rules, parentheses and brackets had to be doubled, as follows:

```
[bracket_or_paren_case("(())s or [[]]s should be no problem.")]
```

Servers should be able to parse commands in either form.

UNICODE execute strings should always and only be used when both the client and server window handles cause the **IsWindowUnicode** function to return TRUE.

Posting

The client application posts the WM_DDE_EXECUTE message by calling the **PostMessage** function, not the **SendMessage** function.

The client application allocates *hCommands* by calling the **GlobalAlloc** function with the GMEM_DDESHARE option.

When processing the WM_DDE_ACK message that the server posts in reply to a WM_DDE_EXECUTE message, the client application must delete the *hCommands* object sent back in the WM_DDE_ACK message.

Receiving

The server application posts the WM_DDE_ACK message to respond positively or negatively. The server should reuse the *hCommands* object.

Unless specified otherwise by a sub-protocol, the server should not post the WM_DDE_ACK message until all the actions specified by the execute command string are completed. The one exception to this rule is when an execute command string causes the server to terminate the conversation.

See Also   **GlobalAlloc**, **PackDDElParam**, **PostMessage**, **ReuseDDElParam**, **SendMessage**, **UnpackDDElParam**, WM_DDE_ACK

WM_DDE_INITIATE

```
WM_DDE_INITIATE
wParam = (WPARAM) hwnd;             /* handle of posting appl. */
lParam = MAKELPARAM(aApp, aTopic); /* appl. and topic atoms   */
```

A dynamic data exchange (DDE) client application sends a WM_DDE_INITIATE message to initiate a conversation with a server application responding to the specified application and topic names. Upon receiving this message, all server applications with names that match the specified application and that support the specified topic are expected to acknowledge it. (For more information, see the WM_DDE_ACK message.)

Parameters

hwnd
Value of *wParam*. Identifies the client window sending the message.

aApp
Value of the low-order word of *lParam*. Contains an atom that identifies the application with which a conversation is requested. The application name cannot contain slashes (/) or backslashes (\). These characters are reserved for network implementations. If *aApp* is NULL, a conversation with all applications is requested.

aTopic
Value of the high-order word of *lParam*. Contains an atom that identifies the topic for which a conversation is requested. If the topic is NULL, conversations for all available topics are requested.

Comments

If *aApp* is NULL, any server application can respond. If *aTopic* is NULL, any topic is valid. Upon receiving a WM_DDE_INITIATE request with the *aTopic* parameter set to NULL, a server must send a WM_DDE_ACK message for each of the topics it supports.

Sending

The client application sends the WM_DDE_INITIATE message by calling the **SendMessage** function, not the **PostMessage** function. The client broadcasts the message to all top-level windows by setting the first parameter of **SendMessage** to −1.

If the client application has already obtained the window handle of the desired server, it can send WM_DDE_INITIATE directly to the server window by passing the server's window handle as the first parameter of **SendMessage**.

The client application allocates *aApp* and *aTopic* by calling **GlobalAddAtom**.

When **SendMessage** returns, the client application must delete the *aApp* and *aTopic* atoms.

Receiving

To complete the initiation of a conversation, the server application must respond with one or more WM_DDE_ACK messages, where each message is for a separate topic. When sending WM_DDE_ACK message, the server should create new *aApp* and *aTopic* atoms; it should not reuse the atoms sent with the WM_DDE_INITIATE message.

See Also

GlobalAddAtom, GlobalAlloc, PostMessage, SendMessage, WM_DDE_ACK

WM_DDE_POKE

```
WM_DDE_POKE
wParam = (WPARAM) hwnd;        /* handle of posting application  */
lParam = (LPARAM) lPackedVal; /* packed DDEPOKE and item atom   */
```

A dynamic data exchange (DDE) client application posts a WM_DDE_POKE message to a DDE server application. A client uses this message to request the server to accept an unsolicited data item. The server is expected to reply with a WM_DDE_ACK message indicating whether it accepted the data item.

Parameters

hwnd

Value of *wParam*. Identifies the client window posting the message.

lPackedVal

Value of *lParam*. The component parameters that are packed into *lPackedVal* are extracted by calling the **UnpackDDElParam** function. The Low component is *hData*. The High component is *aItem*.

Parameter	Description
hData	Identifies a global memory object containing a **DDEPOKE** structure with the data and additional information. The **DDEPOKE** structure has the following form: ```typedef struct { /* ddepok */ unsigned short unused:13, fRelease:1, fReserved:2; short cfFormat; BYTE Value[1];} DDEPOKE;``` For a full description of this structure, see Chapter 3, "Structures"
aItem	Contains a global atom that identifies the data item for which the data or notification is being sent.

Comments

Posting

The client application posts the WM_DDE_POKE message by using the **PostMessage** function.

The client application must allocate memory for the *hData* object by using the **GlobalAlloc** function with the GMEM_DDESHARE option. The client application must delete the *hData* object if either of the following conditions is true:

- The server application responds with a negative WM_DDE_ACK message.

- The **fRelease** member is FALSE, but the server application responds with either a positive or negative WM_DDE_ACK.

The client application must create the *aItem* atom by using the **GlobalAddAtom** function.

The client application must create or reuse the WM_DDE_POKE *lPackedVal* parameter by calling the **PackDDElParam** function or the **ReuseDDElParam** function with *hData* supplied as the Low component and *aItem* supplied as the High component.

Receiving

The server application should post the WM_DDE_ACK message to respond positively or negatively. When posting WM_DDE_ACK, the server can either reuse the *aItem* atom, or it can delete it and create a new one.

The server must create or reuse the WM_DDE_ACK *lPackedVal* parameter by calling the **PackDDElParam** function or the **ReuseDDElParam** function with *wStatus* supplied as the Low component and *aItem* supplied as the High component.

To free the *hData* object, the server should call the **GlobalFree** function.

To free the *lPackedVal* object, the server should call the **FreeDDElParam** function.

See Also   **FreeDDElParam, GlobalAddAtom, GlobalAlloc, PackDDElParam, PostMessage, ReuseDDElParam, SendMessage, UnpackDDElParam,** WM_DDE_ACK

WM_DDE_REQUEST

```
WM_DDE_REQUEST
wParam = (WPARAM) hwnd;       /* handle of posting application  */
lParam = (LPARAM) lParam;     /* holds cfFormat and aItem       */
```

A dynamic data exchange (DDE) client application posts a WM_DDE_REQUEST message to a DDE server application to request the value of a data item.

Parameters   *hwnd*
Value of *wParam*. Identifies the client window sending the message.

lParam
Holds the *cfFormat* and *aItem* parameters.

Parameter	Description
cfFormat	This is the LOWORD of *lParam*. Specifies a standard or registered clipboard format.
aItem	This is the HIWORD of *lParam*. Contains an atom that identifies the data item requested from the server.

Comments

Posting

The client application posts the WM_DDE_REQUEST message by calling the **PostMessage** function, not the **SendMessage** function.

The client application allocates *aItem* by calling the **GlobalAddAtom** function.

Receiving

If the receiving (server) application can satisfy the request, it responds with a WM_DDE_DATA message containing the requested data. Otherwise, it responds with a negative WM_DDE_ACK message.

When responding with either a WM_DDE_DATA or WM_DDE_ACK message, the server application can either reuse the *aItem* atom or it can delete the atom and create a new one.

See Also

GlobalAddAtom, **PackDDElParam**, **PostMessage**, **ReuseDDElParam**, **SendMessage**, **UnpackDDElParam**, WM_DDE_ACK, WM_DDE_DATA

WM_DDE_TERMINATE

```
WM_DDE_TERMINATE
wParam = (WPARAM) hwnd; /* handle of posting window */
lParam = 0;             /* not used, must be zero   */
```

A dynamic data exchange (DDE) application (client or server) posts a WM_DDE_TERMINATE message to terminate a conversation.

Parameters

hwnd
　　　Value of *wParam*. Identifies the client or server window posting the message.

Comments

Posting

The client or server application posts the WM_DDE_TERMINATE message by calling the **PostMessage** function, not the **SendMessage** function.

While waiting for confirmation of the termination, the posting application should not post any other messages to the receiving application. If the sending application receives messages (other than WM_DDE_TERMINATE) from the receiving application, it should delete any atoms or shared memory objects accompanying the messages, except *hData* objects associated with WM_DDE_POKE or WM_DDE_DATA messages that do not have the **fRelease** flag set.

Receiving

The client or server application should respond by posting a WM_DDE_TERMINATE message.

See Also   **PostMessage**, **SendMessage**, WM_DDE_DATA, WM_DDE_POKE

WM_DDE_UNADVISE

```
WM_DDE_UNADVISE
wParam = (WPARAM) hwnd;          /* handle of posting application  */
lParam = (LPARAM) lParam;        /* format and item atom           */
```

A dynamic data exchange (DDE) client application posts a WM_DDE_UNADVISE message to inform a DDE server application that the specified item or a particular clipboard format for the item should no longer be updated. This terminates the warm or hot link for the specified item.

Parameters   *hwnd*
    Value of *wParam*. Identifies the client window sending the message.

lParam
    Holds the *cfFormat* and *aItem* parameters.

Parameter	Description
cfFormat	This is the LOWORD of *lParam*. Specifies the clipboard format of the item for which the update request is being retracted. If *cfFormat* is NULL, all active WM_DDE_ADVISE conversations for the item are to be terminated.
aItem	This is the HIWORD of *lParam*. Contains a global atom that identifies the item for which the update request is being retracted. When *aItem* is NULL, all active WM_DDE_ADVISE links associated with the conversation are to be terminated.

Comments   **Posting**

The client application posts the WM_DDE_UNADVISE message by calling the **PostMessage** function, not the **SendMessage** function.

The client application allocates *aItem* by calling the **GlobalAddAtom** function.

Receiving

The server application posts the WM_DDE_ACK message to respond positively or negatively. When posting WM_DDE_ACK, the server can either reuse the *aItem* atom or it can delete the atom and create a new one.

See Also   **GlobalAddAtom**, **PackDDElParam**, **PostMessage**, **ReuseDDElParam**, **SendMessage**, **UnpackDDElParam**, WM_DDE_ACK, WM_DDE_ADVISE

WM_DEADCHAR   Unicode

```
WM_DEADCHAR
chCharCode = (TCHAR) wParam;      /* character code */
lKeyData = lParam;               /* key data        */
```

The WM_DEADCHAR message is posted to the window with the keyboard focus when a WM_KEYUP message is translated by the **TranslateMessage** function. WM_DEADCHAR specifies a character code generated by a dead key. A dead key is a key that generates a character, such as the umlaut (double-dot), that is combined with another character to form a composite character. For example, the umlaut-O character (Ö) is generated by typing the dead key for the umlaut character, and then typing the O key.

Parameters   *chCharCode*
Value of *wParam*. Specifies the character code generated by the dead key.

lKeyData
Value of *lParam*. Specifies the repeat count, scan code, extended-key flag, context code, previous key-state flag, and transition-state flag, as shown in the following table:

Value	Description
0–15	Specifies the repeat count. The value is the number of times the keystroke is repeated as a result of the user holding down the key.
16–23	Specifies the scan code. The value depends on the original equipment manufacturer (OEM).
24	Specifies whether the key is an extended key, such as a function key or a key on the numeric keypad. The value is 1 if it is an extended key; otherwise, it is 0.
25–28	Reserved.
29	Specifies the context code. The value is 1 if the ALT key is held down while the key is pressed; otherwise, the value is 0.
30	Specifies the previous key state. The value is 1 if the key is down before the message is sent, or it is 0 if the key is up.

31	Specifies the transition state. The value is 1 if the key is being released, or it is 0 if the key is being pressed.

Return Value   An application should return zero if it processes this message.

Comments   The WM_DEADCHAR message typically is used by applications to give the user feedback about each key pressed. For example, an application can display the accent in the current character position without moving the caret.

Because there is not necessarily a one-to-one correspondence between keys pressed and character messages generated, the information in the high-order word of the *lKeyData* parameter is generally not useful to applications. The information in the high-order word applies only to the most recent WM_KEYDOWN message that precedes the posting of the WM_DEADCHAR message.

For enhanced 101- and 102-key keyboards, extended keys are the right ALT and the right CTRL keys on the main section of the keyboard; the INS, DEL, HOME, END, PAGE UP, PAGE DOWN and arrow keys in the clusters to the left of the numeric keypad; and the divide (/) and ENTER keys in the numeric keypad. Some other keyboards may support the extended-key bit in the *lKeyData* parameter.

See Also   **TranslateMessage**, WM_KEYDOWN, WM_SYSDEADCHAR

WM_DELETEITEM

```
WM_DELETEITEM
idCtl = wParam;                        /* control identifier      */
lpdis = (LPDELETEITEMSTRUCT) lParam; /* structure with item info. */
```

The WM_DELETEITEM message is sent to the owner of an owner-drawn list box or combo box when the list box or combo box is destroyed or when items are removed by the LB_DELETESTRING, LB_RESETCONTENT, CB_DELETESTRING, or CB_RESETCONTENT message.

Parameters   *idCtl*

Value of *wParam*. Specifies the identifier of the control that sent the WM_DELETEITEM message.

lpdis

Value of *lParam*. Points to a **DELETEITEMSTRUCT** structure that contains information about the item deleted from a list box. The **DELETEITEMSTRUCT** structure has the following form:

```
typedef struct tagDELETEITEMSTRUCT { /* ditms */
    UINT CtlType;
    UINT CtlID;
    UINT itemID;
```

```
                    HWND hwndItem;
                    UINT itemData;
              } DELETEITEMSTRUCT;
```

For a full description of this structure, see Chapter 3, "Structures."

Return Value   An application should return TRUE if it processes this message.

See Also   CB_DELETESTRING, CB_RESETCONTENT, LB_DELETESTRING, LB_RESETCONTENT

WM_DESTROY

WM_DESTROY

The WM_DESTROY message is sent when a window is being destroyed. It is sent to the window procedure of the window being destroyed after the window is removed from the screen.

This message is sent first to the window being destroyed and then to the child windows (if any) as they are destroyed. During the processing of the message, it can be assumed that all child windows still exist.

Parameters   This message has no parameters.

Return Value   If an application processes this message, it should return zero.

Comments   If the window being destroyed is part of the clipboard viewer chain (set by calling the **SetClipboardViewer** function), the window must remove itself from the chain by processing the **ChangeClipboardChain** function before returning from the WM_DESTROY message.

See Also   **ChangeClipboardChain**, **DestroyWindow**, **PostQuitMessage**, **SetClipboardViewer**, WM_CLOSE

WM_DESTROYCLIPBOARD

WM_DESTROYCLIPBOARD

The WM_DESTROYCLIPBOARD message is sent to the clipboard owner when the clipboard is emptied by a call to the **EmptyClipboard** function.

Parameters   This message has no parameters.

Return Value   If an application processes this message, it should return zero.

See Also   **EmptyClipboard**

WM_DEVMODECHANGE

```
WM_DEVMODECHANGE
lpszDev = (LPCTSTR) lParam; /* address of device name */
```

The WM_DEVMODECHANGE message is sent to all top-level windows whenever the user changes device-mode settings.

Parameters   *lpszDev*
    Value of *lParam*. Points to the device name specified in the WIN.INI file.

Return Value   An application should return zero if it processes this message.

Comments   Calls to functions that change the WIN.INI file may be mapped to the registry instead. This mapping occurs when WIN.INI and the section being changed are specified in the registry under the following keys:

**HKEY_LOCAL_MACHINE\Software\Description\Microsoft\
    Windows NT\CurrentVersion\IniFileMapping**

The change in the storage location has no effect on the behavior of this message.

See Also   WM_WININICHANGE

WM_DRAWCLIPBOARD

```
WM_DRAWCLIPBOARD
```

The WM_DRAWCLIPBOARD message is sent to the first window in the clipboard viewer chain when the contents of the clipboard change. This enables a clipboard viewer window to display the new contents of the clipboard.

Parameters   This message has no parameters.

Comments   Only clipboard viewer windows receive this message. These are windows that have been added to the clipboard viewer chain by using the **SetClipboardViewer** function.

Each window that receives the WM_DRAWCLIPBOARD message must call the **SendMessage** function to pass the message on to the next window in the clipboard viewer chain. The handle of the next window in the chain is returned by the **SetClipboardViewer** function, and may change in response to a WM_CHANGECBCHAIN message.

See Also   **SendMessage**, **SetClipboardViewer**, WM_CHANGECBCHAIN

WM_DRAWITEM

```
WM_DRAWITEM
idCtl = (UINT) wParam;              /* control identifier     */
lpdis = (LPDRAWITEMSTRUCT) lParam; /* item-drawing information */
```

The WM_DRAWITEM message is sent to the owner window of an owner-drawn button, combo box, list box, or menu when a visual aspect of the button, combo box, list box, or menu has changed.

Parameters   *idCtl*

Value of *wParam*. Specifies the identifier of the control that sent the WM_DRAWITEM message. If the message was sent by a menu, this parameter is zero.

lpdis

Value of *lParam*. Points to a **DRAWITEMSTRUCT** structure containing information about the item to be drawn and the type of drawing required. The **DRAWITEMSTRUCT** structure has the following form:

```
typedef struct tagDRAWITEMSTRUCT {  /* dis */
    UINT  CtlType;
    UINT  CtlID;
    UINT  itemID;
    UINT  itemAction;
    UINT  itemState;
    HWND  hwndItem;
    HDC   hDC;
    RECT  rcItem;
    DWORD itemData;
} DRAWITEMSTRUCT;
```

For a full description of this structure, see Chapter 3, "Structures."

Return Value   If an application processes this message, it should return TRUE.

Default Action   The **DefWindowProc** function draws the focus rectangle for an owner-drawn list box item.

Comments   The **itemAction** member of the **DRAWITEMSTRUCT** structure specifies the drawing operation that an application should perform.

Before returning from processing this message, an application should ensure that the device context identified by the **hDC** member of the **DRAWITEMSTRUCT** structure is in the default state.

See Also   **DefWindowProc**

WM_DROPFILES

```
WM_DROPFILES
hDrop = (HANDLE) wParam;   /* handle of internal drop structure */
```

The WM_DROPFILES message is sent when the user releases the left mouse button while the cursor is in the window of an application that has registered itself as a recipient of dropped files.

Parameters   *hDrop*
                        Value of *wParam*. Identifies an internal structure describing the dropped files. This handle is used by the **DragFinish**, **DragQueryFile**, and **DragQueryPoint** functions to retrieve information about the dropped files.

Return Value   An application should return zero if it processes this message.

See Also   **DragAcceptFiles**, **DragFinish**, **DragQueryFile**, **DragQueryPoint**

WM_ENABLE

```
WM_ENABLE
fEnabled = (BOOL) wParam;   /* enabled/disabled flag */
```

The WM_ENABLE message is sent when an application changes the enabled state of a window. It is sent to the window whose enabled state is changing. This message is sent before the **EnableWindow** function returns, but after the enabled state (WS_DISABLE style bit) of the window has changed.

Parameters   *fEnabled*
                        Value of *wParam*. Specifies whether the window has been enabled or disabled. This parameter is TRUE if the window has been enabled or FALSE if the window has been disabled.

Return Value   If an application processes this message, it should return zero.

See Also   **EnableWindow**

WM_ENDSESSION

```
WM_ENDSESSION
fEndSession = (BOOL) wParam;    /* end-session flag */
```

The WM_ENDSESSION message is sent to an application after Windows processes the results of the WM_QUERYENDSESSION message. The WM_ENDSESSION message informs the application whether the Windows session is ending.

Parameters   *fEndSession*
Value of *wParam*. Specifies whether the session is being ended. If the session is being ended, this parameter is TRUE; otherwise, it is FALSE.

Return Value   If an application processes this message, it should return zero.

Comments   If the *fEndSession* parameter is TRUE, the Windows session can end any time after all applications have returned from processing this message. Therefore, an application should perform all tasks required for termination before returning from this message.

The application need not call the **DestroyWindow** or **PostQuitMessage** function when the session is ending.

See Also   **DestroyWindow**, **PostQuitMessage**, WM_QUERYENDSESSION

WM_ENTERIDLE

```
WM_ENTERIDLE
fuSource = wParam;        /* idle-source flag                       */
hwnd = (HWND) lParam;  /* handle of dialog box or owner window */
```

The WM_ENTERIDLE message informs an application's main window procedure that a modal dialog box or menu is entering an idle state. A modal dialog box or menu enters an idle state when no messages are waiting in its queue after it has processed one or more previous messages.

Parameters   *fuSource*
Value of *wParam*. Specifies whether the message is the result of a dialog box or a menu being displayed. This parameter can be one of the following values:

Value	Meaning
MSGF_DIALOGBOX	The system is idle because a dialog box is displayed.

MSGF_MENU   The system is idle because a menu is displayed.

hwnd
Value of *lParam*. Contains the handle of the dialog box (if *fuSource* is
MSGF_DIALOGBOX) or of the window containing the displayed menu (if
fuSource is MSGF_MENU).

Return Value   An application should return zero if it processes this message.

Comments   The **DefWindowProc** function returns zero.

WM_ENTERMENULOOP   `New`

```
WM_ENTERMENULOOP
wParam = (BOOL) fIsTrackPopupMenu /* flags a popup menu     */
lParam = 0 ;                      /* not used; must be zero */
```

The **WM_ENTERMENULOOP** message informs an application's main window
procedure that a menu modal loop has been entered.

Parameters   *fIsTrackPopupMenu*
Specifies whether the menu involved is a popup menu. Has a value of TRUE if
it is a popup, FALSE if it isn't.

Return Value   An application should return zero if it processes this message.

Comments   The **DefWindowProc** function returns zero.

See Also   WM_EXITMENULOOP

WM_EXITMENULOOP   `New`

```
WM_EXITLOOP
wParam = (BOOL) fIsTrackPopupMenu /* flags a popup menu     */
lParam = 0 ;                      /* not used; must be zero */
```

The **WM_ENTERMENULOOP** message informs an application's main window
procedure that a menu modal loop has been exited.

Parameters   *fIsTrackPopupMenu*
Specifies whether the menu involved is a popup menu. Has a value of TRUE if
it is a popup, FALSE if it isn't.

Return Value   An application should return zero if it processes this message.

Comments   The DefWindowProc function returns zero.

See Also   **WM_ENTERMENULOOP**

WM_ERASEBKGND

```
WM_ERASEBKGND
hdc = (HDC) wParam; /* device-context handle */
```

An application sends the WM_ERASEBKGND message when the window
background must be erased (for example, when a window is resized). The
message is sent to prepare an invalidated portion of a window for painting.

Parameters   *hdc*
                        Value of *wParam*. Identifies the device context.

Return Value   An application should return nonzero if it erases the background; otherwise, it
                    should return zero.

Comments   The **DefWindowProc** function erases the background by using the class
                    background brush specified by the **hbrbackground** member of the **WNDCLASS**
                    structure. If **hbrbackground** is NULL, the application should process the
                    WM_ERASEBKGND message and erase the background.

                    An application should return nonzero in response to WM_ERASEBKGND if it
                    processes the message and erases the background; this indicates that no further
                    erasing is required. If the application returns *zero*, the window will remain marked
                    for erasing. (Typically, this indicates that the **fErase** member of the
                    PAINTSTRUCT structure will be TRUE.)

See Also   **BeginPaint**, WM_ICONERASEBKGND

WM_FONTCHANGE

```
WM_FONTCHANGE
wParam = 0; /* not used, must be zero */
lParam = 0; /* not used, must be zero */
```

An application sends the WM_FONTCHANGE message to all top-level windows
in the system after changing the pool of font resources.

Parameters   This message has no parameters.

Comments   An application that adds or removes fonts from the system (for example, by using the **AddFontResource** or **RemoveFontResource** function) should send this message to all top-level windows.

To send the WM_FONTCHANGE message to all top-level windows, an application can call the **SendMessage** function with the *hwnd* parameter set to HWND_BROADCAST.

See Also   **AddFontResource, RemoveFontResource, SendMessage**

WM_GETDLGCODE

WM_GETDLGCODE

The WM_GETDLGCODE message is sent to the dialog box procedure associated with a control. Normally, Windows handles all arrow-key and TAB-key input to the control. By responding to the WM_GETDLGCODE message, an application can take control of a particular type of input and process the input itself.

Parameters   This message has no parameters.

Return Value   The return value is one or more of the following values, indicating which type of input the application processes.

Value	Meaning
DLGC_BUTTON	Button
DLGC_DEFPUSHBUTTON	Default push button
DLGC_HASSETSEL	EM_SETSEL messages
DLGC_RADIOBUTTON	Radio button
DLGC_STATIC	Static control
DLGC_UNDEFPUSHBUTTON	Non-default push button
DLGC_WANTALLKEYS	All keyboard input
DLGC_WANTARROWS	Direction keys
DLGC_WANTCHARS	WM_CHAR messages
DLGC_WANTMESSAGE	All keyboard input (the application passes this message on to a control)
DLGC_WANTTAB	TAB key

Default Action   The **DefWindowProc** function returns zero.

Comments	Although the **DefWindowProc** function always returns zero in response to the WM_GETDLGCODE message, the window functions for the predefined control classes return a code appropriate for each class.
	The WM_GETDLGCODE message and the returned values are useful only with user-defined dialog controls or standard controls modified by subclassing.
See Also	**DefWindowProc**, EM_SETSEL, WM_CHAR

WM_GETFONT

```
WM_GETFONT
wParam = 0; /* not used, must be zero */
lParam = 0; /* not used, must be zero */
```

An application sends a WM_GETFONT message to a control to retrieve the font with which the control is currently drawing its text.

Parameters	This message has no parameters.
Return Value	The return value is the handle of the font used by the control or NULL if the control is using the system font.
See Also	WM_SETFONT

WM_GETHOTKEY

```
WM_GETHOTKEY
wParam = 0; /* not used, must be zero */
lParam = 0; /* not used, must be zero */
```

An application sends a WM_GETHOTKEY message to determine the hot key associated with a window.

Parameters	This message has no parameters.
Return Value	The return value is the virtual-key code of the hot key, or NULL if no hot key is associated with the window.
See Also	WM_SETHOTKEY

WM_GETMINMAXINFO

```
WM_GETMINMAXINFO
lpmmi = (LPMINMAXINFO) lParam; /* address of structure */
```

The WM_GETMINMAXINFO message is sent to a window when the size or position of the window is about to change. An application can use this message to override the window's default maximized size and position, or its default minimum or maximum tracking size.

Parameters   *lpmmi*

Value of *lParam*. Points to a **MINMAXINFO** structure that contains the default maximized position and dimensions, and the default minimum and maximum tracking sizes. An application can override the defaults by setting the members of this structure. The **MINMAXINFO** structure has the following form:

```
typedef struct tagMINMAXINFO {   /* mmi */
    POINT ptReserved;
    POINT ptMaxSize;
    POINT ptMaxPosition;
    POINT ptMinTrackSize;
    POINT ptMaxTrackSize;
} MINMAXINFO;
```

For a full description of this structure, see Chapter 3, "Structures."

Return Value   If an application processes this message, it should return zero.

Comments   The maximum tracking size is the largest window size that can be produced by using the borders to size the window. The minimum tracking size is the smallest window size that can be produced by using the borders to size the window.

See Also   **MoveWindow, SetWindowPos, MINMAXINFO**

WM_GETTEXT   Unicode

```
WM_GETTEXT
wParam = (WPARAM) cchTextMax;   /* number of characters to copy */
lParam = (LPARAM) lpszText;     /* address of buffer for text   */
```

An application sends a WM_GETTEXT message to copy the text that corresponds to a window into a buffer provided by the caller.

Parameters	*cchTextMax* Value of *wParam*. Specifies the maximum number of characters to be copied, including the terminating null character.
	lpszText Value of *lParam*. Points to the buffer that is to receive the text.
Return Value	The return value is the number of characters copied.
Default Action	The **DefWindowProc** function copies the text associated with the window into the specified buffer and returns the number of characters copied.
Comments	For an edit control, the text to be copied is the contents of the edit control. For a combo box, the text is the contents of the edit control (or static-text) portion of the combo box. For a button, the text is the button name. For other windows, the text is the window title. To copy the text of an item in a list box, an application can use the LB_GETTEXT message.
	When the WM_GETTEXT message is sent to a static control with the SS_ICON style, the handle of the icon will be returned in the first four bytes of the buffer pointed to by *lpszText*. This is true only if the WM_SETTEXT message has been used to set the icon.
See Also	**DefWindowProc**, **GetWindowText**, **GetWindowTextLength**, LB_GETTEXT, WM_GETTEXTLENGTH, WM_SETTEXT

WM_GETTEXTLENGTH

```
WM_GETTEXTLENGTH
wParam = 0; /* not used, must be zero */
lParam = 0; /* not used, must be zero */
```

	An application sends a WM_GETTEXTLENGTH message to determine the length, in characters, of the text associated with a window. The length does not include the terminating null character.
Parameters	This message has no parameters.
Return Value	The return value is the length, in characters, of the text.
Default Action	The **DefWindowProc** function returns the length, in characters, of the text.
Comments	For an edit control, the text to be copied is the contents of the edit control. For a combo box, the text is the contents of the edit control (or static-text) portion of the combo box. For a button, the text is the button name. For other windows, the text is the window title. To determine the length of an item in a list box, an application can use the LB_GETTEXTLEN message.

See Also   **DefWindowProc**, **GetWindowText**, **GetWindowTextLength**,
LB_GETTEXTLEN, WM_GETTEXT

WM_HOTKEY

```
WM_HOTKEY
idHotKey = (int) wParam;    /* identifier of hot-key */
```

The WM_HOTKEY message is posted when the user presses a hot key. The
message is placed at the top of the message queue associated with the thread that
registered the hot key.

Parameters   *idHotKey*
Value of *wParam*. Specifies the identifier of the hot key that generated the
message. If the message was generated by a system-defined hot key, the
idHotKey parameter will be one of the following values:

Value	Meaning
IDHOT_SNAPDESKTOP	The "snap desktop" hot key was pressed.
IDHOT_SNAPWINDOW	The "snap window" hot key was pressed.

See Also   **RegisterHotKey**, WM_GETHOTKEY, WM_SETHOTKEY

WM_HSCROLL

```
WM_HSCROLL
nScrollCode = (int) LOWORD(wParam); /* scroll bar value    */
nPos = (int) HIWORD(wParam);        /* scroll box position */
hwndScrollBar = (HWND) lParam;      /* handle of scroll bar */
```

The WM_HSCROLL message is sent to a window when a scroll event occurs in
the window's standard horizontal scroll bar. This message is also sent to the
owner of a horizontal scroll bar control when a scroll event occurs in the control.

Parameters   *nScrollCode*
Value of the low-order word of *wParam*. Specifies a scroll bar value that
indicates the user's scrolling request. This parameter can be one of the
following values:

Value	Meaning
SB_BOTTOM	Scroll to lower right.

SB_ENDSCROLL	End scroll.
SB_LINEDOWN	Scroll one line down.
SB_LINEUP	Scroll one line up.
SB_PAGEDOWN	Scroll one page down.
SB_PAGEUP	Scroll one page up.
SB_THUMBPOSITION	Scroll to absolute position. The current position is specified by the *nPos* parameter.
SB_THUMBTRACK	Drag scroll box (thumb) to specified position. The current position is specified by the *nPos* parameter.
SB_TOP	Scroll to upper left.

nPos
> Value of the high-order word of *wParam*. Specifies the current position of the scroll box if the *nScrollCode* parameter is SB_THUMBPOSITION or SB_THUMBTRACK; otherwise, *nPos* is not used.

hwndScrollBar
> Value of *lParam*. Identifies the control if WM_HSCROLL is sent by a scroll bar control. If WM_HSCROLL is sent by a window's standard scroll bar, *hwndScrollBar* is not used.

Return Value   If an application processes this message, it should return zero.

Comments   The SB_THUMBTRACK notification code is typically used by applications that provide feedback as the user drags the scroll box.

If an application scrolls the contents of the window, it must also reset the position of the scroll box by using the **SetScrollPos** function.

See Also   **SetScrollPos**, WM_VSCROLL

WM_HSCROLLCLIPBOARD

```
WM_HSCROLLCLIPBOARD
hwndViewer = (HWND) wParam;          /* handle of clipboard viewer */
nScrollCode = (int) LOWORD(lParam); /* scroll bar code            */
nPos = (int) HIWORD(lParam);         /* scroll box position        */
```

> The WM_HSCROLLCLIPBOARD message is sent to the clipboard owner by a clipboard viewer window when the clipboard contains data in the CF_OWNERDISPLAY format and an event occurs in the clipboard viewer's horizontal scroll bar. The owner should scroll the clipboard image and update the scroll bar values.

Parameters   *hwndViewer*
Value of *wParam*. Identifies the clipboard viewer window.

nScrollCode
Value of the low-order word of *lParam*. Specifies a scroll bar event. This parameter can be one of the following values:

Value	Meaning
SB_BOTTOM	Scroll to lower right.
SB_ENDSCROLL	End scroll.
SB_LINEDOWN	Scroll one line down.
SB_LINEUP	Scroll one line up.
SB_PAGEDOWN	Scroll one page down.
SB_PAGEUP	Scroll one page up.
SB_THUMBPOSITION	Scroll to absolute position. The current position is specified by the *nPos* parameter.
SB_TOP	Scroll to upper left.

nPos
Value of the high-order word of *lParam*. Specifies the current position of the scroll box if the *nScrollCode* parameter is SB_THUMBPOSITION; otherwise, the *nPos* parameter is not used.

Return Value   If an application processes this message, it should return zero.

Comments   The clipboard owner can use the **ScrollWindow** function to scroll the image in the clipboard viewer window and invalidate the appropriate region.

See Also   **ScrollWindow**

WM_ICONERASEBKGND

```
WM_ICONERASEBKGND
hdc = (HDC) wParam; /* handle of device context */
```

The WM_ICONERASEBKGND message is sent to a minimized window when the background of the icon must be filled before painting the icon. A window receives this message only if a class icon is defined for the window; otherwise, WM_ERASEBKGND is sent.

Parameters   *hdc*
Value of *wParam*. Identifies the device context of the icon.

Return Value   An application should return nonzero if it processes this message.

Comments   The **DefWindowProc** function fills the icon background with the class background brush of the parent window.

See Also   **DefWindowProc**, WM_ERASEBKGND

WM_INITDIALOG

```
WM_INITDIALOG
hwndFocus = (HWND) wParam; /* handle of control to receive focus */
lInitParam = lParam;       /* initialization parameter          */
```

The WM_INITDIALOG message is sent to the dialog box procedure immediately before a dialog box is displayed. Dialog box procedures typically use this message to initialize controls and carry out any other initialization tasks that affect the appearance of the dialog box.

Parameters   *hwndFocus*
    Value of *wParam*. Identifies the control to receive the default keyboard focus. Windows assigns the default keyboard focus only if the dialog box procedure returns TRUE.

lInitParam
    Value of *lParam*. Specifies additional initialization data. This data is passed to Windows as the *lParamInit* parameter in a call to the **CreateDialogIndirectParam**, **CreateDialogParam**, **DialogBoxIndirectParam**, or **DialogBoxParam** function used to create the dialog box. This parameter is zero if any other dialog box creation function is used.

Return Value   The dialog box procedure should return TRUE to direct Windows to set the keyboard focus to the control given by *hwndFocus*. Otherwise, it should return FALSE to prevent Windows from setting the default keyboard focus.

Comments   The control to receive the default keyboard focus is always the first control in the dialog box that is visible, not disabled, and has the WS_TABSTOP style. When the dialog box procedure returns TRUE, Windows checks the control to ensure that the procedure has not disabled it. If it has been disabled, Windows sets the keyboard focus to the next control that is visible, not disabled, and has the WS_TABSTOP.

An application can return FALSE only if it has set the keyboard focus to one of the controls of the dialog box.

See Also   **CreateDialogIndirectParam**, **CreateDialogParam**, **DialogBoxIndirectParam**, **DialogBoxParam**, **SetFocus**

WM_INITMENU

```
WM_INITMENU
hmenuInit = (HMENU) wParam; /* handle of menu to initialize */
```

The WM_INITMENU message is sent when a menu is about to become active. It occurs when the user clicks an item on the menu bar or presses a menu key. This allows the application to modify the menu before it is displayed.

Parameters   *hmenuInit*
Value of *wParam*. Identifies the menu to be initialized.

Return Value   If an application processes this message, it should return zero.

Comments   A WM_INITMENU message is sent only when a menu is first accessed; only one WM_INITMENU message is generated for each access. For example, moving the mouse across several menu items while holding down the button does not generate new messages. WM_INITMENU does not provide information about menu items.

See Also   WM_INITMENUPOPUP

WM_INITMENUPOPUP

```
WM_INITMENUPOPUP
hmenuPopup = (HMENU) wParam;            /* handle of pop-up menu */
uPos = (UINT) LOWORD(lParam);           /* pop-up item position  */
fSystemMenu = (BOOL) HIWORD(lParam); /* System menu flag       */
```

The WM_INITMENUPOPUP message is sent when a pop-up menu is about to become active. This allows an application to modify the pop-up menu before it is displayed, without changing the entire menu.

Parameters   *hmenuPopup*
Value of *wParam*. Identifies the pop-up menu.

uPos
Value of the low-order word of *lParam*. Specifies the zero-based relative position of the menu item that invokes the pop-up menu.

fSystemMenu
Value of the high-order word of *lParam*. Specifies whether the pop-up menu is the System menu. If the pop-up menu is the System menu (also known as Control menu), this parameter is TRUE; otherwise, it is FALSE.

Return Value   If an application processes this message, it should return zero.

See Also   WM_INITMENU

WM_KEYDOWN

```
WM_KEYDOWN
nVirtKey = (int) wParam;    /* virtual-key code */
lKeyData = lParam;          /* key data         */
```

The WM_KEYDOWN message is posted to the window with the keyboard focus when a nonsystem key is pressed. A nonsystem key is a key that is pressed when the ALT key is *not* pressed.

Parameters   *nVirtKey*
Value of *wParam*. Specifies the virtual-key code of the nonsystem key.

lKeyData
Value of *lParam*. Specifies the repeat count, scan code, extended-key flag, context code, previous key-state flag, and transition-state flag, as shown in the following table:

Value	Description
0–15	Specifies the repeat count. The value is the number of times the keystroke is repeated as a result of the user holding down the key.
16–23	Specifies the scan code. The value depends on the original equipment manufacturer (OEM).
24	Specifies whether the key is an extended key, such as the right-hand ALT and CTRL keys that appear on an enhanced 101- or 102-key keyboard. The value is 1 if it is an extended key; otherwise, it is 0.
25–28	Reserved.
29	Specifies the context code. The value is always 0 for a WM_KEYDOWN message.
30	Specifies the previous key state. The value is 1 if the key is down before the message is sent, or it is 0 if the key is up.
31	Specifies the transition state. The value is always 0 for a WM_KEYDOWN message.

Return Value   An application should return zero if it processes this message.

Default Action   If the F10 key is pressed, the **DefWindowProc** function sets an internal flag. When **DefWindowProc** receives the WM_KEYUP message, the function checks whether the internal flag is set and, if so, sends a WM_SYSCOMMAND message to the top-level window. The *wParam* parameter of the message is set to SC_KEYMENU.

Comments Because of the autorepeat feature, more than one WM_KEYDOWN message may be posted before a WM_KEYUP message is posted. The previous key state (bit 30) can be used to determine whether the WM_KEYDOWN message indicates the first down transition or a repeated down transition.

For enhanced 101- and 102-key keyboards, extended keys are the right ALT and CTRL keys on the main section of the keyboard; the INS, DEL, HOME, END, PAGE UP, PAGE DOWN and arrow keys in the clusters to the left of the numeric keypad; and the divide (/) and ENTER keys in the numeric keypad. Other keyboards may support the extended-key bit in the *lKeyData* parameter.

See Also **DefWindowProc**, WM_CHAR, WM_KEYUP, WM_SYSCOMMAND

WM_KEYUP

```
WM_KEYUP
nVirtKey = (int) wParam;      /* virtual-key code */
lKeyData = lParam;            /* key data         */
```

The WM_KEYUP message is posted to the window with the keyboard focus when a nonsystem key is released. A nonsystem key is a key that is pressed when the ALT key is *not* pressed, or a keyboard key that is pressed when a window has the keyboard focus.

Parameters *nVirtKey*
Value of *wParam*. Specifies the virtual-key code of the nonsystem key.

lKeyData
Value of *lParam*. Specifies the repeat count, scan code, extended-key flag, context code, previous key-state flag, and transition-state flag, as shown in the following table:

Value	Description
0–15	Specifies the repeat count. The value is the number of times the keystroke is repeated as a result of the user holding down the key. The repeat count is always one for a WM_KEYUP message.
16–23	Specifies the scan code. The value depends on the original equipment manufacturer (OEM).
24	Specifies whether the key is an extended key, such as a function key or a key on the numeric keypad. The value is 1 if it is an extended key; otherwise, it is 0.
25–28	Reserved.

29	Specifies the context code. The value is always 0 for a WM_KEYUP message.
30	Specifies the previous key state. The value is always 1 for a WM_KEYUP message.
31	Specifies the transition state. The value is always 1 for a WM_KEYUP message.

Return Value   An application should return zero if it processes this message.

Default Action   The **DefWindowProc** function sends a WM_SYSCOMMAND message to the top-level window if the F10 key or the ALT key was released. The *wParam* parameter of the message is set to SC_KEYMENU.

Comments   For enhanced 101- and 102-key keyboards, extended keys are the right ALT and CTRL keys on the main section of the keyboard; the INS, DEL, HOME, END, PAGE UP, PAGE DOWN and arrow keys in the clusters to the left of the numeric keypad; and the divide (/) and ENTER keys in the numeric keypad. Other keyboards may support the extended-key bit in the *lKeyData* parameter.

See Also   **DefWindowProc**, WM_KEYDOWN, WM_SYSCOMMAND

WM_KILLFOCUS

```
WM_KILLFOCUS
hwndGetFocus = (HWND) wParam; /* handle of window receiving focus */
```

The WM_KILLFOCUS message is sent to a window immediately before it loses the keyboard focus.

Parameters   *hwndGetFocus*
        Value of *wParam*. Identifies the window that receives the keyboard focus (may be NULL).

Return Value   An application should return zero if it processes this message.

Comments   If an application is displaying a caret, the caret should be destroyed at this point.

See Also   **SetFocus**, WM_SETFOCUS

WM_LBUTTONDBLCLK

```
WM_LBUTTONDBLCLK
fwKeys = wParam;          /* key flags                  */
xPos = LOWORD(lParam);    /* horizontal position of cursor */
yPos = HIWORD(lParam);    /* vertical position of cursor   */
```

The WM_LBUTTONDBLCLK message is posted when the user double-clicks the left mouse button while the cursor is in the client area of a window. If the mouse is not captured, the message is posted to the window beneath the cursor. Otherwise, the message is posted to the window that has captured the mouse.

Parameters

fwKeys

Value of *wParam*. Indicates whether various virtual keys are down. This parameter can be any combination of the following values:

Value	Description
MK_CONTROL	Set if the CTRL key is down
MK_LBUTTON	Set if the left mouse button is down
MK_MBUTTON	Set if the middle mouse button is down
MK_RBUTTON	Set if the right mouse button is down
MK_SHIFT	Set if the SHIFT key is down

xPos

Value of the low-order word of *lParam*. Specifies the x-coordinate of the cursor. The coordinate is relative to the upper-left corner of the client area.

yPos

Value of the high-order word of *lParam*. Specifies the y-coordinate of the cursor. The coordinate is relative to the upper-left corner of the client area.

Return Value

If an application processes this message, it should return zero.

Comments

Only windows that have the CS_DBLCLKS style can receive WM_LBUTTONDBLCLK messages, which Windows generates whenever the user presses, releases, and again presses the left mouse button within the system's double-click time limit. Double-clicking the left mouse button actually generates four messages: WM_LBUTTONDOWN, WM_LBUTTONUP, WM_LBUTTONDBLCLK, and WM_LBUTTONUP again.

An application can use the **MAKEPOINTS** macro to convert the *lParam* parameter to a **POINTS** structure.

See Also

GetCapture, GetDoubleClickTime, SetCapture, SetDoubleClickTime, WM_LBUTTONDOWN, WM_LBUTTONUP

WM_LBUTTONDOWN

```
WM_LBUTTONDOWN
fwKeys = wParam;            /* key flags                  */
xPos = LOWORD(lParam);      /* horizontal position of cursor */
yPos = HIWORD(lParam);      /* vertical position of cursor    */
```

The WM_LBUTTONDOWN message is posted when the user presses the left mouse button while the cursor is in the client area of a window. If the mouse is not captured, the message is posted to the window beneath the cursor. Otherwise, the message is posted to the window that has captured the mouse.

Parameters   *fwKeys*
Value of *wParam*. Indicates whether various virtual keys are down. This parameter can be any combination of the following values:

Value	Description
MK_CONTROL	Set if the CTRL key is down
MK_MBUTTON	Set if the middle mouse button is down
MK_RBUTTON	Set if the right mouse button is down
MK_SHIFT	Set if the SHIFT key is down

xPos
Value of the low-order word of *lParam*. Specifies the x-coordinate of the cursor. The coordinate is relative to the upper-left corner of the client area.

yPos
Value of the high-order word of *lParam*. Specifies the y-coordinate of the cursor. The coordinate is relative to the upper-left corner of the client area.

Return Value   If an application processes this message, it should return zero.

Comments   An application can use the **MAKEPOINTS** macro to convert the *lParam* parameter to a **POINTS** structure.

See Also   **GetCapture**, **SetCapture**, WM_LBUTTONDBLCLK, WM_LBUTTONUP

WM_LBUTTONUP

```
WM_LBUTTONUP
fwKeys = wParam;            /* key flags                  */
xPos = LOWORD(lParam);      /* horizontal position of cursor */
yPos = HIWORD(lParam);      /* vertical position of cursor    */
```

The WM_LBUTTONUP message is posted when the user releases the left mouse button while the cursor is in the client area of a window. If the mouse is not captured, the message is posted to the window beneath the cursor. Otherwise, the message is posted to the window that has captured the mouse.

Parameters   *fwKeys*
Value of *wParam*. Indicates whether various virtual keys are down. This parameter can be any combination of the following values:

Value	Description
MK_CONTROL	Set if the CTRL key is down
MK_MBUTTON	Set if the middle mouse button is down
MK_RBUTTON	Set if the right mouse button is down
MK_SHIFT	Set if the SHIFT key is down

xPos
Value of the low-order word of *lParam*. Specifies the x-coordinate of the cursor. The coordinate is relative to the upper-left corner of the client area.

yPos
Value of the high-order word of *lParam*. Specifies the y-coordinate of the cursor. The coordinate is relative to the upper-left corner of the client area.

Return Value   If an application processes this message, it should return zero.

Comments   An application can use the **MAKEPOINTS** macro to convert the *lParam* parameter to a **POINTS** structure.

See Also   **GetCapture**, **SetCapture**, WM_LBUTTONDBLCLK, WM_LBUTTONDOWN

WM_MBUTTONDBLCLK

```
WM_MBUTTONDBLCLK
fwKeys = wParam;          /* key flags                    */
xPos = LOWORD(lParam);    /* horizontal position of cursor */
yPos = HIWORD(lParam);    /* vertical position of cursor   */
```

The WM_MBUTTONDBLCLK message is posted when the user double-clicks the middle mouse button while the cursor is in the client area of a window. If the mouse is not captured, the message is posted to the window beneath the cursor. Otherwise, the message is posted to the window that has captured the mouse.

Parameters

fwKeys

Value of *wParam*. Indicates whether various virtual keys are down. This parameter can be any combination of the following values:

Value	Description
MK_CONTROL	Set if the CTRL key is down
MK_LBUTTON	Set if the left mouse button is down
MK_MBUTTON	Set if the middle mouse button is down
MK_RBUTTON	Set if the right mouse button is down
MK_SHIFT	Set if the SHIFT key is down

xPos

Value of the low-order word of *lParam*. Specifies the x-coordinate of the cursor. The coordinate is relative to the upper-left corner of the client area.

yPos

Value of the high-order word of *lParam*. Specifies the y-coordinate of the cursor. The coordinate is relative to the upper-left corner of the client area.

Return Value

If an application processes this message, it should return zero.

Comments

Only windows that have the CS_DBLCLKS style can receive WM_MBUTTONDBLCLK messages, which Windows generates whenever the user presses, releases, and again presses the middle mouse button within the system's double-click time limit. Double-clicking the middle mouse button actually generates four messages: WM_MBUTTONDOWN, WM_MBUTTONUP, WM_MBUTTONDBLCLK, and WM_MBUTTONUP again.

An application can use the **MAKEPOINTS** macro to convert the *lParam* parameter to a **POINTS** structure.

See Also

GetCapture, GetDoubleClickTime, SetCapture, SetDoubleClickTime, WM_MBUTTONDOWN, WM_MBUTTONUP

WM_MBUTTONDOWN

```
WM_MBUTTONDOWN
fwKeys = wParam;         /* key flags                   */
xPos = LOWORD(lParam);   /* horizontal position of cursor */
yPos = HIWORD(lParam);   /* vertical position of cursor   */
```

The WM_MBUTTONDOWN message is posted when the user presses the middle mouse button while the cursor is in the client area of a window. If the mouse is not captured, the message is posted to the window beneath the cursor. Otherwise, the message is posted to the window that has captured the mouse.

Parameters

fwKeys

Value of *wParam*. Indicates whether various virtual keys are down. This parameter can be any combination of the following values:

Value	Description
MK_CONTROL	Set if the CTRL key is down
MK_LBUTTON	Set if the left mouse button is down
MK_RBUTTON	Set if the right mouse button is down
MK_SHIFT	Set if the SHIFT key is down

xPos

Value of the low-order word of *lParam*. Specifies the x-coordinate of the cursor. The coordinate is relative to the upper-left corner of the client area.

yPos

Value of the high-order word of *lParam*. Specifies the y-coordinate of the cursor. The coordinate is relative to the upper-left corner of the client area.

Return Value

If an application processes this message, it should return zero.

Comments

An application can use the **MAKEPOINTS** macro to convert the *lParam* parameter to a **POINTS** structure.

See Also

GetCapture, **SetCapture**, WM_MBUTTONDBLCLK, WM_MBUTTONUP

WM_MBUTTONUP

```
WM_MBUTTONUP
fwKeys = wParam;         /* key flags                    */
xPos = LOWORD(lParam);   /* horizontal position of cursor */
yPos = HIWORD(lParam);   /* vertical position of cursor   */
```

The WM_MBUTTONUP message is posted when the user releases the middle mouse button while the cursor is in the client area of a window. If the mouse is not captured, the message is posted to the window beneath the cursor. Otherwise, the message is posted to the window that has captured the mouse.

Parameters

fwKeys

Value of *wParam*. Indicates whether various virtual keys are down. This parameter can be any combination of the following values:

Value	Description
MK_CONTROL	Set if the CTRL key is down
MK_LBUTTON	Set if the left mouse button is down
MK_RBUTTON	Set if the right mouse button is down
MK_SHIFT	Set if the SHIFT key is down

xPos

   Value of the low-order word of *lParam*. Specifies the x-coordinate of the cursor. The coordinate is relative to the upper-left corner of the client area.

yPos

   Value of the high-order word of *lParam*. Specifies the y-coordinate of the cursor. The coordinate is relative to the upper-left corner of the client area.

An application can use the **MAKEPOINTS** macro to convert the *lParam* parameter to a **POINTS** structure.

See Also   **GetCapture**, **SetCapture**, WM_MBUTTONDBLCLK, WM_MBUTTONDOWN

WM_MDIACTIVATE

```
WM_MDIACTIVATE
                                        /* Message sent to MDI client    */
wParam = (WPARAM) (HWND) hwndChildAct;  /* child to activate             */
lParam = 0;                             /* not used, must be zero        */

                                        /* Message received by MDI child */
hwndChildDeact = (HWND) wParam;         /* child being deactivated       */
hwndChildAct = (HWND) lParam;           /* child being activated         */
```

An application sends the WM_MDIACTIVATE message to a multiple document interface (MDI) client window to instruct the client window to activate a different MDI child window. As the client window processes this message, it sends WM_MDIACTIVATE to the child window being deactivated and to the child window being activated.

Parameters   In messages sent to an MDI client window:
hwndChildAct
   Value of *wParam*. Identifies the MDI child window to be activated.

In messages received by an MDI child window:
hwndChildDeact
   Value of *wParam*. Identifies the MDI child window being deactivated.

hwndChildAct
Value of *lParam*. Identifies the MDI child window being activated.

Return Value   If an application sends this message to an MDI client window, the return value is zero. An MDI child window should return zero if it processes this message.

Comments   An MDI child window is activated independently of the MDI frame window. When the frame window becomes active, the child window last activated by using the WM_MDIACTIVATE message receives the WM_NCACTIVATE message to draw an active window frame and title bar; the child window does not receive another WM_MDIACTIVATE message.

See Also   WM_MDIGETACTIVE, WM_MDINEXT, WM_NCACTIVATE

WM_MDICASCADE

```
WM_MDICASCADE
wParam = (WPARAM) (UINT) fuCascade;  /* cascade flag         */
lParam = 0;                          /* not used, must be zero */
```

An application sends the WM_MDICASCADE message to a multiple document interface (MDI) client window to arrange all its child windows in a cascade format.

Parameters   *fuCascade*
Value of *wParam*. Specifies a cascade flag. The only flag currently available, MDITILE_SKIPDISABLED, prevents disabled MDI child windows from being cascaded.

Return Value   If the message succeeds, the return value is TRUE; otherwise, it is FALSE.

See Also   WM_MDIICONARRANGE, WM_MDITILE

WM_MDICREATE   `Unicode`

```
WM_MDICREATE
wParam = 0;                                    /* not used, must be zero */
lParam = (LPARAM) (LPMDICREATESTRUCT) lpmdic;  /* creation data          */
```

An application sends the WM_MDICREATE message to a multiple document interface (MDI) client window to create an MDI child window.

Parameters	*lpmdic*

Points to an **MDICREATESTRUCT** structure containing information that Windows uses to create the MDI child window. The **MDICREATESTRUCT** structure has the following form:

```
typedef struct tagMDICREATESTRUCT { /* mdic */
    LPCTSTR szClass;
    LPCTSTR szTitle;
    HANDLE  hOwner;
    int     x;
    int     y;
    int     cx;
    int     cy;
    DWORD   style;
    LPARAM  lParam;
} MDICREATESTRUCT;
```

Return Value

For a full description of this structure, see Chapter 3, "Structures."

If the message succeeds, the return value is the handle of the new child window; otherwise, it is NULL.

Comments

The MDI child window is created with the style bits WS_CHILD, WS_CLIPSIBLINGS, WS_CLIPCHILDREN, WS_SYSMENU, WS_CAPTION, WS_THICKFRAME, WS_MINIMIZEBOX, and WS_MAXIMIZEBOX, plus additional style bits specified in the **MDICREATESTRUCT** structure to which the *lpmdic* parameter points. Windows adds the title of the new child window to the Window menu of the frame window. An application should use this message to create all child windows of the client window.

If an MDI client window receives any message that changes the activation of its child windows while the active child window is maximized, Windows restores the active child window and maximizes the newly activated child window.

When an MDI child window is created, Windows sends the WM_CREATE message to the window. The *lParam* parameter of the WM_CREATE message contains a pointer to a **CREATESTRUCT** structure. The **lpCreateParams** member of this structure contains a pointer to the **MDICREATESTRUCT** structure passed with the WM_MDICREATE message that created the MDI child window.

An application should not send a second WM_MDICREATE message while a WM_MDICREATE message is still being processed. For example, it should not send a WM_MDICREATE message while an MDI child window is processing its WM_MDICREATE message.

See Also

CreateMDIWindow, WM_CREATE, WM_MDIDESTROY

WM_MDIDESTROY

```
WM_MDIDESTROY
wParam = (WPARAM) (HWND) hwndChild; /* handle of child to close   */
lParam = 0;                        /* not used, must be zero      */
```

An application sends the WM_MDIDESTROY message to a multiple document interface (MDI) client window to close an MDI child window.

Parameters   *hwndChild*
                    Value of *wParam*. Identifies the MDI child window to be closed.

Return Value   This message always returns zero.

Comments   This message removes the title of the MDI child window from the MDI frame window and deactivates the child window. An application should use this message to close all MDI child windows.

                    If an MDI client window receives a message that changes the activation of its child windows and the active MDI child window is maximized, Windows restores the active child window and maximizes the newly activated child window.

See Also   WM_MDICREATE

WM_MDIGETACTIVE

```
WM_MDIGETACTIVE
wParam = 0; /* not used, must be zero */
lParam = 0; /* not used, must be zero */
```

An application sends the WM_MDIGETACTIVE message to a multiple document interface (MDI) client window to retrieve the handle of the active MDI child window.

Parameters   This message has no parameters.

Return Value   The return value is the handle of the active MDI child window.

Comments   In Windows version 3.*x*, the return value includes a flag indicating whether the MDI child window is maximized. In the Win32 application programming interface (API), return values do not include this flag. To determine whether the MDI child window is maximized, use the **GetWindowLong** function and a Boolean test, as follows:

```
fMaximized = GetWindowLong(hwndMdiChild, GWL_STYLE) & WS_MAXIMIZE;
```

See Also   **GetWindowLong**

WM_MDIICONARRANGE

```
WM_MDIICONARRANGE
wParam = 0; /* not used, must be zero */
lParam = 0; /* not used, must be zero */
```

An application sends the WM_MDIICONARRANGE message to a multiple document interface (MDI) client window to arrange all minimized MDI child windows. It does not affect child windows that are not minimized.

Parameters   This message has no parameters.

See Also   WM_MDICASCADE, WM_MDITILE

WM_MDIMAXIMIZE

```
WM_MDIMAXIMIZE
wParam = (WPARAM) (HWND) hwndMax; /* handle of child to maximize */
lParam = 0;                       /* not used, must be zero       */
```

An application sends the WM_MDIMAXIMIZE message to a multiple document interface (MDI) client window to maximize an MDI child window. Windows resizes the child window to make its client area fill the client window. Windows places the child window's System menu icon in the rightmost position of the frame window's menu bar, and places the child window's restore icon in the leftmost position. Windows also appends the title bar text of the child window to that of the frame window.

Parameters   *hwndMax*
          Value of *wParam*. Identifies the MDI child window to be maximized.

Return Value   The return value is always zero.

Comments   If an MDI client window receives any message that changes the activation of its child windows while the currently active MDI child window is maximized, Windows restores the active child window and maximizes the newly activated child window.

See Also   WM_MDIRESTORE

WM_MDINEXT

```
WM_MDINEXT
wParam = (WPARAM) (HWND) hwndChild; /* handle of child        */
lParam = (LPARAM) fNext;            /* next or previous child */
```

An application sends the WM_MDINEXT message to a multiple document interface (MDI) client window to activate the next or previous child window.

Parameters

hwndChild
Value of *wParam*. Identifies the MDI child window. Windows activates the child window that is immediately before or after the given child window, depending on the value of the *fNext* parameter. If the *hwndChild* parameter is NULL, Windows activates the child window that is immediately before or after the currently active child window.

fNext
Value of *lParam*. If this parameter is zero, Windows activates the next MDI child window and places the child window identified by the *hwndChild* parameter behind all other child windows. If this parameter is nonzero, Windows activates the previous child window, placing it in front of the child window identified by *hwndChild*.

Return Value
The return value is always zero.

Comments
If an MDI client window receives any message that changes the activation of its child windows while the active MDI child window is maximized, Windows restores the active child window and maximizes the newly activated child window.

See Also
WM_MDIACTIVATE, WM_MDIGETACTIVE

WM_MDIREFRESHMENU

```
WM_MDIREFRESHMENU
wParam = 0; /* not used, must be zero */
lParam = 0; /* not used, must be zero */
```

An application sends the WM_MDIREFRESHMENU message to a multiple document interface (MDI) client window to refresh the Window menu of the MDI frame window.

Parameters
This message has no parameters.

Return Value	If the message succeeds, the return value is the handle of the frame window menu; otherwise, it is NULL.
Comments	After sending this message, an application must call the **DrawMenuBar** function to update the menu bar.
See Also	**DrawMenuBar**, WM_MDISETMENU

WM_MDIRESTORE

```
WM_MDIRESTORE
wParam = (WPARAM) (HWND) hwndRes; /* handle of child to restore */
lParam = 0;                       /* not used, must be zero     */
```

An application sends the WM_MDIRESTORE message to a multiple document interface (MDI) client window to restore an MDI child window from maximized or minimized size.

Parameters	*hwndRes* Value of *wParam.* Identifies the MDI child window to be restored.
Return Value	The return value is always zero.
See Also	WM_MDIMAXIMIZE

WM_MDISETMENU

```
WM_MDISETMENU
wParam = (WPARAM) (HMENU) hmenuFrame;  /* handle of frame menu  */
lParam = (LPARAM) (HMENU) hmenuWindow; /* handle of Window menu */
```

An application sends the WM_MDISETMENU message to a multiple document interface (MDI) client window to replace the entire menu of an MDI frame window, to replace the Window menu of the frame window, or both.

Parameters	*hmenuFrame*
	    Value of *wParam.* Identifies the new frame window menu. If this parameter is NULL, the frame window menu is not changed.
	
	hmenuWindow
	    Value of *lParam.* Identifies the new Window menu. If this parameter is NULL, the Window menu is not changed.

Return Value	If the message succeeds, the return value is the handle of the old frame window menu; otherwise, it is zero.
Comments	After sending this message, an application must call the **DrawMenuBar** function to update the menu bar.
	If this message replaces the Window menu, the MDI child window menu items are removed from the previous Window menu and added to the new Window menu.
	If an MDI child window is maximized and this message replaces the MDI frame window menu, the System menu icon and restore icon are removed from the previous frame window menu and added to the new frame window menu.
See Also	**DrawMenuBar**, WM_MDIREFRESHMENU

WM_MDITILE

```
WM_MDITILE
wParam = (WPARAM) (UINT) fuTile; /* tiling flag           */
lParam = 0;                      /* not used, must be zero */
```

An application sends the WM_MDITILE message to a multiple document interface (MDI) client window to arrange all of its MDI child windows in a tile format.

Parameters

fuTile

Specifies a tiling flag. This parameter can be one of the following values:

Value	Description
MDITILE_HORIZONTAL	Tiles MDI child windows so that they are wide rather than tall.
MDITILE_SKIPDISABLED	Prevents disabled MDI child windows from being tiled.
MDITILE_VERTICAL	Tiles MDI child windows so that they are tall rather than wide.

Return Value   If the message succeeds, the return value is TRUE; otherwise, it is FALSE.

See Also   WM_MDICASCADE, WM_MDIICONARRANGE

WM_MEASUREITEM

```
WM_MEASUREITEM
idCtl = (UINT) wParam;                /* control identifier   */
lpmis = (LPMEASUREITEMSTRUCT) lParam; /* item-size information */
```

The WM_MEASUREITEM message is sent to the owner window of an owner-drawn button, combo box, list box, or menu item when the control or menu is created.

Parameters   *idCtl*

Value of *wParam*. Contains the value of the **CtlID** member of the **MEASUREITEMSTRUCT** structure pointed to by *lpmis*. This value identifies the control that sent the WM_MEASUREITEM message.

If the value is zero, the message was sent by a menu.

If the value is non-zero, the message was sent by a combo box or by a list box.

If the value is non-zero, and the value of the **itemID** member of the **MEASUREITEMSTRUCT** pointed to by *lpmis* is (UINT) –1, the message was sent by a combo edit field.

lpmis

Value of *lParam*. Points to a **MEASUREITEMSTRUCT** structure that contains the dimensions of the owner-drawn control or menu item. The **MEASUREITEMSTRUCT** structure has the following form:

```
typedef struct tagMEASUREITEMSTRUCT {   /* mis */
    UINT  CtlType;
    UINT  CtlID;
    UINT  itemID;
    UINT  itemWidth;
    UINT  itemHeight;
    DWORD itemData;
} MEASUREITEMSTRUCT;
```

For a full description of this structure, see Chapter 3, "Structures."

Return Value   If an application processes this message, it should return TRUE.

Comments   When the owner window receives the WM_MEASUREITEM message, the owner fills in the **MEASUREITEMSTRUCT** structure pointed to by the *lParam* parameter of the messages and returns; this informs Windows of the dimensions of the control. If a list box or combo box is created with the LBS_OWNERDRAWVARIABLE or CBS_OWNERDRAWVARIABLE style, this message is sent to the owner for each item in the control; otherwise, this message is sent once.

Windows sends the WM_MEASUREITEM message to the owner window of combo boxes and list boxes created with the OWNERDRAWFIXED style before sending the WM_INITDIALOG message. As a result, when the owner receives this message, Windows has not yet determined the height and width of the font used in the control; function calls and calculations requiring these values should occur in the main function of the application or library.

See Also   WM_INITDIALOG

WM_MENUCHAR

```
WM_MENUCHAR
chUser = (char) LOWORD(wParam); /* ASCII character */
fuFlag = (UINT) HIWORD(wParam); /* menu flag       */
hmenu = (HMENU) lParam;         /* handle of menu  */
```

The WM_MENUCHAR message is sent when a menu is active and the user presses a key that does not correspond to any mnemonic or accelerator key. This message is sent to the window that owns the menu.

Parameters   *chUser*
Value of the low-order word of *wParam*. Specifies the ASCII character that corresponds to the key the user pressed.

fuFlag
Value of the high-order word of *wParam*. Specifies the type of the active menu. This parameter can be one of the following values:

Value	Meaning
MF_POPUP	Pop-up menu
MF_SYSMENU	System menu

hmenu
Value of *lParam*. Identifies the active menu.

Return Value   An application that processes this message should return one of the following values in the high-order word of the return value:

Value	Meaning
0	Informs Windows that it should discard the character the user pressed and create a short beep on the system speaker.
1	Informs Windows that it should close the active menu.
2	Informs Windows that the low-order word of the return value specifies the zero-based relative position of a menu item. This item is selected by Windows.

Comments

The low-order word is ignored if the high-order word contains 0 or 1. An application should process this message when an accelerator is used to select a menu item that displays a bitmap.

WM_MENUSELECT

```
WM_MENUSELECT
uItem  = (UINT) LOWORD(wParam);   /* menu item or pop-up menu index */
fuFlags = (UINT) HIWORD(wParam);  /* menu flags                    */
hmenu  = (HMENU) lParam;          /* handle of menu clicked on     */
```

The WM_MENUSELECT message is sent to a menu's owner window when the user selects a menu item.

Parameters

uItem

Value of the low-order word of *wParam*. If the selected item is a command item, this parameter contains the identifier of the menu item. If the selected item invokes a pop-up menu, this parameter contains the menu index of the pop-up menu in the main menu, and the *hMenu* parameter then contains the handle of the main (clicked-on) menu; use the **GetSubMenu** function to get the menu handle of the pop-up menu.

fuFlags

Value of the high-order word of *wParam*. Specifies one or more menu flags. This parameter can be a combination of the following values:

Value	Description
MF_BITMAP	Item displays a bitmap.
MF_CHECKED	Item is checked.
MF_DISABLED	Item is disabled.
MF_GRAYED	Item is grayed.
MF_MOUSESELECT	Item is selected with the mouse.
MF_OWNERDRAW	Item is an owner-drawn item.
MF_POPUP	Item invokes a pop-up menu.
MF_SYSMENU	Item is contained in the System menu (also known as Control menu). The *hmenu* parameter identifies the System menu associated with the message.

hmenu

Value of *lParam*. Identifies the menu that was clicked on.

Return Value

If an application processes this message, it should return zero.

Comments   If the *fuFlags* parameter contains 0xFFFF and the *hmenu* parameter contains NULL, Windows has closed the menu because the user pressed the ESC key or clicked outside the menu.

DO NOT use the value –1 for *fuFlags*. That is because *fuFlags* is specified as (UINT) HIWORD(wParam). If HIWORD(wParam) were 0xFFFF, *fuFlags* (because of the UINT cast) would be 0x0000FFFF, not –1.

WM_MOUSEACTIVATE

```
WM_MOUSEACTIVATE
hwndTopLevel = (HWND) wParam;            /* handle of top-level parent */
nHittest = (INT) LOWORD(lParam);         /* hit-test code              */
uMsg =  (UINT) HIGHWORD(lParam);         /* mouse message              */
```

The WM_MOUSEACTIVATE message is sent when the cursor is in an inactive window and the user presses a mouse button. The parent window receives this message only if the child window passes it to the **DefWindowProc** function.

Parameters   *hwndTopLevel*
Value of *wParam*. Identifies the top-level parent window of the window being activated.

nHittest
Value of the low-order word of *lParam*. Specifies the hit-test code returned by the **DefWindowProc** function as a result of processing the WM_NCHITTEST message. For more information, see the description of the WM_NCHITTEST message.

uMsg
Value of the high-order word of *lParam*. Specifies the identifier of the mouse message generated when the user pressed a mouse button. The mouse message is either discarded or posted to the window, depending on the return value.

Return Value   The return value specifies whether the window should be activated and whether the identifier of the mouse message should be discarded. It must be one of the following values:

Value	Meaning
MA_ACTIVATE	Activate the window, and do not discard the mouse message.
MA_NOACTIVATE	Do not activate the window, and do not discard the mouse message.
MA_ACTIVATEANDEAT	Activate the window, and discard the mouse message.

	MA_NOACTIVATEANDEAT	Do not activate the window, but discard the mouse message.

Default Action   The **DefWindowProc** function passes the message to a child window's parent window before any processing occurs. The parent window determines whether to activate the child window. If it activates the child window, the parent window should return TRUE to prevent the system from processing the message further.

See Also   **DefWindowProc**, WM_NCHITTEST

WM_MOUSEMOVE

```
WM_MOUSEMOVE
fwKeys = wParam;         /* key flags                  */
xPos = LOWORD(lParam);   /* horizontal position of cursor */
yPos = HIWORD(lParam);   /* vertical position of cursor   */
```

The WM_MOUSEMOVE message is posted to a window when the cursor moves. If the mouse is not captured, the message is posted to the window that contains the cursor. Otherwise, the message is posted to the window that has captured the mouse.

Parameters   *fwKeys*
Value of *wParam*. Indicates whether various virtual keys are down. This parameter can be any combination of the following values:

Value	Description
MK_CONTROL	Set if the CTRL key is down
MK_LBUTTON	Set if the left mouse button is down
MK_MBUTTON	Set if the middle mouse button is down
MK_RBUTTON	Set if the right mouse button is down
MK_SHIFT	Set if the SHIFT key is down

xPos
Value of the low-order word of *lParam*. Specifies the x-coordinate of the cursor. The coordinate is relative to the upper-left corner of the client area.

yPos
Value of the high-order word of *lParam*. Specifies the y-coordinate of the cursor. The coordinate is relative to the upper-left corner of the client area.

Comments   The **MAKEPOINTS** macro can be used to convert the *lParam* parameter to a **POINTS** structure.

See Also   **GetCapture, SetCapture**

WM_MOVE

```
WM_MOVE
xPos = (int) LOWORD(lParam);    /* horizontal position */
yPos = (int) HIWORD(lParam);    /* vertical position   */
```

The WM_MOVE message is sent after a window has been moved.

Parameters   *xPos*
    Value of the low-order word of *lParam*. Specifies the x-coordinate of the upper-left corner of the client area of the window.

    yPos
    Value of the high-order word of *lParam*. Specifies the y-coordinate of the upper-left corner of the client area of the window.

Return Value   If an application processes this message, it should return zero.

Comments   The *xPos* and *yPos* parameters are given in screen coordinates for overlapped and pop-up windows and in parent-client coordinates for child windows.

An application can use the **MAKEPOINTS** macro to convert the *lParam* parameter to a **POINTS** structure.

See Also   **POINTS**

WM_NCACTIVATE

```
WM_NCACTIVATE
fActive = (BOOL) wParam;
```

The WM_NCACTIVATE message is sent to a window when its nonclient area needs to be changed to indicate an active or inactive state.

Parameters   *fActive*
    Value of *wParam*. Specifies when a title bar or icon needs to be changed to indicate an active or inactive state. If an active title bar or icon is to be drawn, the *fActive* parameter is TRUE . It is FALSE for an inactive title bar or icon.

Return Value   When the *fActive* parameter is FALSE, an application should return TRUE to indicate that Windows should proceed with the default processing, or it should return FALSE to prevent the title bar or icon from being deactivated. When *fActive* is TRUE, the return value is ignored.

Default Action The **DefWindowProc** function draws the title bar or icon title in its active colors when the *fActive* parameter is TRUE and in its inactive colors when *fActive* is FALSE.

See Also **DefWindowProc**

WM_NCCALCSIZE

```
WM_NCCALCSIZE
fCalcValidRects = (BOOL) wParam;          /* valid area flag */
lpncsp = (LPNCCALCSIZE_PARAMS) lParam;  /* address of data */
```

The WM_NCCALCSIZE message is sent when the size and position of a window's client area must be calculated. By processing this message, an application can control the contents of the window's client area when the size or position of the window changes.

Parameters *fCalcValidRects*
Value of *wParam*. Specifies whether the application should indicate which part of the client area contains valid information. Windows will copy the valid information to the specified area within the new client area. If this parameter is TRUE, the application should specify which part of the client area is valid.

lpncsp
Value of *lParam*. Points to an **NCCALCSIZE_PARAMS** structure that contains information an application can use to calculate the new size and position of the client rectangle. The **NCCALCSIZE_PARAMS** structure has the following form:

```
typedef struct tagNCCALCSIZE_PARAMS { /* nccp */
    RECT        rgrc[3];
    PWINDOWPOS  lppos;
} NCCALCSIZE_PARAMS;
```

For a full description of this structure, see Chapter 3, "Structures."

Return Value If the *fCalcValidRects* parameter is FALSE, the application should return zero. If *fCalcValidRects* is TRUE, the application can return zero or a valid combination of the following values:

Value	Meaning
WVR_ALIGNTOP, WVR_ALIGNLEFT, WVR_ALIGNBOTTOM, WVR_ALIGNRIGHT	

These values, used in combination, specify that the client area of the window is to be preserved and aligned appropriately relative to the new position of the window. For example, to align the client area to the lower-left corner, return the WVR_ALIGNLEFT and WVR_ALIGNTOP values.

WVR_HREDRAW, WVR_VREDRAW

These values, used in combination with any other values, cause the window to be completely redrawn if the client rectangle changes size horizontally or vertically. These values are similar to the CS_HREDRAW and CS_VREDRAW class styles.

WVR_REDRAW

This value causes the entire window to be redrawn. It is a combination of WVR_HREDRAW and WVR_VREDRAW values.

WVR_VALIDRECTS

This value indicates that, upon return from WM_NCCALCSIZE, the rectangles specified by the **rgrc[1]** and **rgrc[2]** members of the NCCALCSIZE_PARAMS structure contain valid source and destination area rectangles, respectively. Windows combines these rectangles to calculate the area of the window to be preserved. Windows copies any part of the window image that is within the source rectangle and clips the image to the destination rectangle. Both rectangles are in parent-relative or screen-relative coordinates.

This return value allows an application to implement more elaborate client-area preservation strategies, such as centering or preserving a subset of the client area.

If *fCalcValidRects* is TRUE and an application returns zero, the old client area is preserved and is aligned with the upper-left corner of the new client area.

Default Action   The window may be redrawn, depending on whether the CS_HREDRAW or CS_VREDRAW class style is specified. This is the default, backward-compatible processing of this message by the **DefWindowProc** function (in addition to the usual client rectangle calculation described in the preceding table).

See Also   **DefWindowProc, MoveWindow, SetWindowPos, NCCALCSIZE_PARAMS, RECT**

WM_NCCREATE   `Unicode`

```
WM_NCCREATE
lpcs = (LPCREATESTRUCT) lParam; /* initialization data */
```

The WM_NCCREATE message is sent prior to the WM_CREATE message when a window is first created.

Parameters   *lpcs*

Value of *wParam*. Points to the **CREATESTRUCT** structure for the window. The **CREATESTRUCT** structure has the following form:

```
typedef struct tagCREATESTRUCT { /* cs */
    LPVOID  lpCreateParams;
    HANDLE  hInstance;
    HMENU   hMenu;
    HWND    hwndParent;
    int     cy;
    int     cx;
    int     y;
    int     x;
    LONG    style;
    LPCSTR  lpszName;
    LPCSTR  lpszClass;
    DWORD   dwExStyle;
} CREATESTRUCT;
```

For a full description of this structure, see Chapter 3, "Structures."

Return Value   If an application processes this message, it should return TRUE to continue creation of the window. If the application returns FALSE, the **CreateWindow** or **CreateWindowEx** function will return a NULL handle.

Default Action   The **DefWindowProc** function returns TRUE.

See Also   **CreateWindow**, **CreateWindowEx**, **DefWindowProc**, **CREATESTRUCT**, WM_CREATE

WM_NCDESTROY

WM_NCDESTROY

The WM_NCDESTROY message informs a window that its nonclient area is being destroyed. The **DestroyWindow** function sends the WM_NCDESTROY message to the window following the WM_DESTROY message. WM_DESTROY is used to free the allocated memory object associated with the window.

Parameters   This message has no parameters.

Return Value   If an application processes this message, it should return zero.

Comments   This message frees any memory internally allocated for the window.

See Also   **DestroyWindow**, WM_DESTROY, WM_NCCREATE

WM_NCHITTEST

```
WM_NCHITTEST
xPos = LOWORD(lParam);  /* horizontal position of cursor */
yPos = HIWORD(lParam);  /* vertical position of cursor   */
```

The WM_NCHITTEST message is sent to a window when the cursor moves, or when a mouse button is pressed or released. If the mouse is not captured, the message is sent to the window beneath the cursor. Otherwise, the message is posted to the window that has captured the mouse.

Parameters

xPos
Value of the low-order word of *lParam*. Specifies the x-coordinate of the cursor. The coordinate is relative to the upper left corner of the screen.

yPos
Value of the high-order word of *lParam*. Specifies the y-coordinate of the cursor. The coordinate is relative to the upper left corner of the screen.

Return Value

The return value of the **DefWindowProc** function is one of the following values, indicating the position of the cursor hot spot:

Value	Location of hot spot
HTBORDER	In the border of a window that does not have a sizing border
HTBOTTOM	In the lower horizontal border of a window
HTBOTTOMLEFT	In the lower left corner of a window border
HTBOTTOMRIGHT	In the lower right corner of a window border
HTCAPTION	In a title bar
HTCLIENT	In a client area
HTERROR	On the screen background or on a dividing line between windows (same as HTNOWHERE, except that the **DefWindowProc** function produces a system beep to indicate an error)
HTGROWBOX	In a size box (same as HTSIZE)
HTHSCROLL	In a horizontal scroll bar
HTLEFT	In the left border of a window
HTMENU	In a menu
HTNOWHERE	On the screen background or on a dividing line between windows
HTREDUCE	In a Minimize button
HTRIGHT	In the right border of a window
HTSIZE	In a size box (same as HTGROWBOX)

HTSYSMENU	In a System menu or in a Close button in a child window
HTTOP	In the upper horizontal border of a window
HTTOPLEFT	In the upper left corner of a window border
HTTOPRIGHT	In the upper right corner of a window border
HTTRANSPARENT	In a window currently covered by another window
HTVSCROLL	In the vertical scroll bar
HTZOOM	In a Maximize button

Comments   The **MAKEPOINTS** macro can be used to convert the *lParam* parameter to a **POINTS** structure.

See Also   **DefWindowProc**, **GetCapture**

WM_NCLBUTTONDBLCLK

```
WM_NCLBUTTONDBLCLK
nHittest = (INT) wParam;     /* hit-test code          */
pts = MAKEPOINTS(lParam);    /* position of cursor     */
```

The WM_NCLBUTTONDBLCLK message is posted when the user double-clicks the left mouse button while the cursor is within the nonclient area of a window. This message is posted to the window that contains the cursor. If a window has captured the mouse, this message is not posted.

Parameters   *nHittest*

Value of *wParam*. Specifies the hit-test code returned by the **DefWindowProc** function as a result of processing the WM_NCHITTEST message. For more information, see the description of the WM_NCHITTEST message.

pts

Value of *lParam*. Specifies a **POINTS** structure that contains the x- and y-coordinates of the cursor. The coordinates are relative to the upper-left corner of the screen. The **POINTS** structure has the following form:

```
typedef struct tagPOINTS { /* pts */
    SHORT x;
    SHORT y;
} POINTS;
```

For a full description of this structure, see Chapter 3, "Structures."

Return Value   If an application processes this message, it should return zero.

Default Action	The **DefWindowProc** function tests the given point to find out the location of the cursor and carries out the appropriate action. If appropriate, **DefWindowProc** sends the WM_SYSCOMMAND message to the window.
Comments	A window need not have the CS_DBLCLKS style to receive WM_NCLBUTTONDBLCLK messages.

Windows generates a WM_NCLBUTTONDBLCLK message when the user presses, releases, and again presses the left mouse button within the system's double-click time limit. Double-clicking the left mouse button actually generates four messages: WM_NCLBUTTONDOWN, WM_NCLBUTTONUP, WM_NCLBUTTONDBLCLK, and WM_NCLBUTTONUP again.

An application can use the **MAKEPOINTS** macro to convert the *lParam* parameter to a **POINTS** structure.

See Also   **DefWindowProc**, WM_NCHITTEST, WM_NCLBUTTONDOWN, WM_NCLBUTTONUP, WM_SYSCOMMAND

WM_NCLBUTTONDOWN

```
WM_NCLBUTTONDOWN
nHittest = (INT) wParam;      /* hit-test code          */
pts = MAKEPOINTS(lParam);     /* position of cursor     */
```

The WM_NCLBUTTONDOWN message is posted when the user presses the left mouse button while the cursor is within the nonclient area of a window. This message is posted to the window that contains the cursor. If a window has captured the mouse, this message is not posted.

Parameters   *nHittest*

Value of *wParam*. Specifies the hit-test code returned by the **DefWindowProc** function as a result of processing the WM_NCHITTEST message. For more information, see the description of the WM_NCHITTEST message.

pts

Value of *lParam*. Specifies a **POINTS** structure that contains the x- and y-coordinates of the cursor. The coordinates are relative to the upper-left corner of the screen. The **POINTS** structure has the following form:

```
typedef struct tagPOINTS { /* pts */
    SHORT x;
    SHORT y;
} POINTS;
```

For a full description of this structure, see Chapter 3, "Structures."

Return Value	If an application processes this message, it should return zero.
Default Action	The **DefWindowProc** function tests the given point to find out the location of the cursor and carries out the appropriate action. If appropriate, **DefWindowProc** sends the WM_SYSCOMMAND message to the window.
Comments	An application can use the **MAKEPOINTS** macro to convert the *lParam* parameter to a **POINTS** structure.
See Also	**DefWindowProc**, WM_NCHITTEST, WM_NCLBUTTONDBLCLK, WM_NCLBUTTONUP, WM_SYSCOMMAND

WM_NCLBUTTONUP

```
WM_NCLBUTTONUP
nHittest = (INT) wParam;      /* hit-test code            */
pts = MAKEPOINTS(lParam);     /* mouse-cursor coordinates */
```

The WM_NCLBUTTONUP message is posted when the user releases the left mouse button while the cursor is within the nonclient area of a window. This message is posted to the window that contains the cursor. If a window has captured the mouse, this message is not posted.

Parameters

nHittest

Value of *wParam*. Specifies the hit-test code returned by the **DefWindowProc** function as a result of processing the WM_NCHITTEST message. For more information, see the description of the WM_NCHITTEST message.

pts

Value of *lParam*. Specifies a **POINTS** structure that contains the x- and y-coordinates of the cursor. The coordinates are relative to the upper-left corner of the screen. The **POINTS** structure has the following form:

```
typedef struct tagPOINTS { /* pts */
    SHORT x;
    SHORT y;
} POINTS;
```

For a full description of this structure, see Chapter 3, "Structures."

Return Value   If an application processes this message, it should return zero.

Default Action   The **DefWindowProc** function tests the given point to find out the location of the cursor and carries out the appropriate action. If appropriate, **DefWindowProc** sends the WM_SYSCOMMAND message to the window.

Comments	An application can use the **MAKEPOINTS** macro to convert the *lParam* parameter to a **POINTS** structure.
	If it is appropriate to do so, the system sends the WM_SYSCOMMAND message to the window.
See Also	**DefWindowProc**, WM_NCHITTEST, WM_NCLBUTTONDBLCLK, WM_NCLBUTTONDOWN, WM_SYSCOMMAND

WM_NCMBUTTONDBLCLK

```
WM_NCMBUTTONDBLCLK
nHittest = (INT) wParam;      /* hit-test code            */
pts = MAKEPOINTS(lParam);     /* position of cursor       */
```

The WM_NCMBUTTONDBLCLK message is posted when the user double-clicks the middle mouse button while the cursor is within the nonclient area of a window. This message is posted to the window that contains the cursor. If a window has captured the mouse, this message is not posted.

Parameters

nHittest

Value of *wParam*. Specifies the hit-test code returned by the **DefWindowProc** function as a result of processing the WM_NCHITTEST message. For more information, see the description of the WM_NCHITTEST message.

pts

Value of *lParam*. Specifies a **POINTS** structure that contains the x- and y-coordinates of the cursor. The coordinates are relative to the upper-left corner of the screen. The **POINTS** structure has the following form:

```
typedef struct tagPOINTS { /* pts */
    SHORT x;
    SHORT y;
} POINTS;
```

For a full description of this structure, see Chapter 3, "Structures."

Return Value

If an application processes this message, it should return zero.

Comments

A window need not have the CS_DBLCLKS style to receive WM_NCMBUTTONDBLCLK messages.

Windows generates a WM_NCMBUTTONDBLCLK message when the user presses, releases, and again presses the middle mouse button within the system's double-click time limit. Double-clicking the middle mouse button actually generates four messages: WM_NCMBUTTONDOWN, WM_NCMBUTTONUP, WM_NCMBUTTONDBLCLK, and WM_NCMBUTTONUP again.

An application can use the **MAKEPOINTS** macro to convert the *lParam* parameter to a **POINTS** structure.

If it is appropriate to do so, the system sends the WM_SYSCOMMAND message to the window.

See Also   **DefWindowProc**, WM_NCHITTEST, WM_NCMBUTTONDOWN, WM_NCMBUTTONUP, WM_SYSCOMMAND

WM_NCMBUTTONDOWN

```
WM_NCMBUTTONDOWN
nHittest = (INT) wParam;      /* hit-test code          */
pts = MAKEPOINTS(lParam);     /* position of cursor     */
```

The WM_NCMBUTTONDOWN message is posted when the user presses the middle mouse button while the cursor is within the nonclient area of a window. This message is posted to the window that contains the cursor. If a window has captured the mouse, this message is not posted.

Parameters   *nHittest*
Value of *wParam*. Specifies the hit-test code returned by the **DefWindowProc** function as a result of processing the WM_NCHITTEST message. For more information, see the description of the WM_NCHITTEST message.

pts
Value of *lParam*. Specifies a **POINTS** structure that contains the x- and y-coordinates of the cursor. The coordinates are relative to the upper-left corner of the screen. The **POINTS** structure has the following form:

```
typedef struct tagPOINTS { /* pts */
    SHORT x;
    SHORT y;
} POINTS;
```

For a full description of this structure, see Chapter 3, "Structures."

Return Value   If an application processes this message, it should return zero.

Comments   An application can use the **MAKEPOINTS** macro to convert the *lParam* parameter to a **POINTS** structure.

If it is appropriate to do so, the system sends the WM_SYSCOMMAND message to the window.

See Also   **DefWindowProc**, WM_NCHITTEST, WM_NCMBUTTONDBLCLK, WM_NCMBUTTONUP, WM_SYSCOMMAND

WM_NCMBUTTONUP

```
WM_NCMBUTTONUP
nHittest = (INT) wParam;      /* hit-test code          */
pts = MAKEPOINTS(lParam);     /* position of cursor     */
```

The WM_NCMBUTTONUP message is posted when the user releases the middle mouse button while the cursor is within the nonclient area of a window. This message is posted to the window that contains the cursor. If a window has captured the mouse, this message is not posted.

Parameters   *nHittest*

Value of *wParam*. Specifies the hit-test code returned by the **DefWindowProc** function as a result of processing the WM_NCHITTEST message. For more information, see the description of the WM_NCHITTEST message.

pts

Value of *lParam*. Specifies a **POINTS** structure that contains the x- and y-coordinates of the cursor. The coordinates are relative to the upper-left corner of the screen. The **POINTS** structure has the following form:

```
typedef struct tagPOINTS { /* pts */
    SHORT x;
    SHORT y;
} POINTS;
```

For a full description of this structure, see Chapter 3, "Structures."

Return Value   If an application processes this message, it should return zero.

Comments   An application can use the **MAKEPOINTS** macro to convert the *lParam* parameter to a **POINTS** structure.

If it is appropriate to do so, the system sends the WM_SYSCOMMAND message to the window.

See Also   **DefWindowProc**, WM_NCHITTEST, WM_NCMBUTTONDBLCLK, WM_NCMBUTTONDOWN, WM_SYSCOMMAND

WM_NCMOUSEMOVE

```
WM_NCMOUSEMOVE
nHittest = (INT) wParam;      /* hit-test code          */
pts = MAKEPOINTS(lParam);     /* position of cursor     */
```

The WM_NCMOUSEMOVE message is posted to a window when the cursor is moved within the nonclient area of the window. This message is posted to the window that contains the cursor. If a window has captured the mouse, this message is not posted.

Parameters

nHittest

    Value of *wParam*. Specifies the hit-test code returned by the **DefWindowProc** function as a result of processing the WM_NCHITTEST message. For more information, see the description of the WM_NCHITTEST message.

pts

    Value of *lParam*. Specifies a **POINTS** structure that contains the x- and y-coordinates of the cursor. The coordinates are relative to the upper-left corner of the screen. The **POINTS** structure has the following form:

```
typedef struct tagPOINTS { /* pts */
    SHORT x;
    SHORT y;
} POINTS;
```

    For a full description of this structure, see Chapter 3, "Structures."

Return Value

If an application processes this message, it should return zero.

Comments

If it is appropriate to do so, the system sends the WM_SYSCOMMAND message to the window.

The **MAKEPOINTS** macro can be used to convert the *lParam* parameter to a **POINTS** structure.

See Also

DefWindowProc, WM_NCHITTEST

WM_NCPAINT

```
WM_NCPAINT
hrgn = (HRGN) wParam;    /* update-region handle */
```

An application sends the WM_NCPAINT message to a window when its frame must be painted.

Parameters

hrgn

    Value of *wParam*. Identifies the update region of the window. The update region is clipped to the window frame.

Return Value

An application should return zero if it processes this message.

Comments

The **DefWindowProc** function paints the window frame.

Comments   An application can intercept this message and paint its own custom window frame. The clipping region for a window is always rectangular, even if the shape of the frame is altered.

See Also   **DefWindowProc**, **GetWindowDC**, WM_PAINT

WM_NCRBUTTONDBLCLK

```
WM_NCRBUTTONDBLCLK
nHittest = (INT) wParam;        /* hit-test code          */
pts = MAKEPOINTS(lParam);       /* position of cursor     */
```

The WM_NCRBUTTONDBLCLK message is posted when the user double-clicks the right mouse button while the cursor is within the nonclient area of a window. This message is posted to the window that contains the cursor. If a window has captured the mouse, this message is not posted.

Parameters   *nHittest*
   Value of *wParam*. Specifies the hit-test code returned by the **DefWindowProc** function as a result of processing the WM_NCHITTEST message. For more information, see the description of the WM_NCHITTEST message.

pts
   Value of *lParam*. Specifies a **POINTS** structure that contains the x- and y-coordinates of the cursor. The coordinates are relative to the upper-left corner of the screen. The **POINTS** structure has the following form:

```
typedef struct tagPOINTS { /* pts */
    SHORT x;
    SHORT y;
} POINTS;
```

For a full description of this structure, see Chapter 3, "Structures."

Return Value   If an application processes this message, it should return zero.

Comments   A window need not have the CS_DBLCLKS style to receive WM_NCRBUTTONDBLCLK messages.

Windows generates a WM_NCRBUTTONDBLCLK message when the user presses, releases, and again presses the right mouse button within the system's double-click time limit. Double-clicking the right mouse button actually generates four messages: WM_NCRBUTTONDOWN, WM_NCRBUTTONUP, WM_NCRBUTTONDBLCLK, and WM_NCRBUTTONUP again.

An application can use the **MAKEPOINTS** macro to convert the *lParam* parameter to a **POINTS** structure.

If it is appropriate to do so, the system sends the WM_SYSCOMMAND message to the window.

See Also   **DefWindowProc**, WM_NCHITTEST, WM_NCRBUTTONDOWN, WM_NCRBUTTONUP, WM_SYSCOMMAND

WM_NCRBUTTONDOWN

```
WM_NCRBUTTONDOWN
nHittest = (INT) wParam;      /* hit-test code        */
pts = MAKEPOINTS(lParam);     /* position of cursor   */
```

The WM_NCRBUTTONDOWN message is posted when the user presses the right mouse button while the cursor is within the nonclient area of a window. This message is posted to the window that contains the cursor. If a window has captured the mouse, this message is not posted.

Parameters   *nHittest*

Value of *wParam*. Specifies the hit-test code returned by the **DefWindowProc** function as a result of processing the WM_NCHITTEST message. For more information, see the description of the WM_NCHITTEST message.

pts

Value of *lParam*. Specifies a **POINTS** structure that contains the x- and y-coordinates of the cursor. The coordinates are relative to the upper-left corner of the screen. The **POINTS** structure has the following form:

```
typedef struct tagPOINTS { /* pts */
    SHORT x;
    SHORT y;
} POINTS;
```

For a full description of this structure, see Chapter 3, "Structures."

Return Value   If an application processes this message, it should return zero.

Comments   An application can use the **MAKEPOINTS** macro to convert the *lParam* parameter to a **POINTS** structure.

If it is appropriate to do so, the system sends the WM_SYSCOMMAND message to the window.

See Also   **DefWindowProc**, WM_NCHITTEST, WM_NCRBUTTONDBLCLK, WM_NCRBUTTONUP, WM_SYSCOMMAND

WM_NCRBUTTONUP

```
WM_NCRBUTTONUP
nHittest = (INT) wParam;      /* hit-test code           */
pts = MAKEPOINTS(lParam);     /* position of cursor      */
```

The WM_NCRBUTTONUP message is posted when the user releases the right mouse button while the cursor is within the nonclient area of a window. This message is posted to the window that contains the cursor. If a window has captured the mouse, this message is not posted.

Parameters

nHittest

Value of *wParam*. Specifies the hit-test code returned by the **DefWindowProc** function as a result of processing the WM_NCHITTEST message. For more information, see the description of the WM_NCHITTEST message.

pts

Value of *lParam*. Specifies a **POINTS** structure that contains the x- and y-coordinates of the cursor. The coordinates are relative to the upper-left corner of the screen. The **POINTS** structure has the following form:

```
typedef struct tagPOINTS { /* pts */
    SHORT x;
    SHORT y;
} POINTS;
```

For a full description of this structure, see Chapter 3, "Structures."

Return Value

If an application processes this message, it should return zero.

Comments

An application can use the **MAKEPOINTS** macro to convert the *lParam* parameter to a **POINTS** structure.

If it is appropriate to do so, the system sends the WM_SYSCOMMAND message to the window.

See Also

DefWindowProc, WM_NCHITTEST, WM_NCRBUTTONDBLCLK, WM_NCRBUTTONDOWN, WM_SYSCOMMAND

WM_NEXTDLGCTL

```
WM_NEXTDLGCTL
wCtlFocus = wParam;                /* identifies control for focus */
fHandle = (BOOL) LOWORD(lParam); /* wParam handle flag           */
```

The WM_NEXTDLGCTL message is sent to a dialog box procedure to set the keyboard focus to a different control in the dialog box.

Parameters   *wCtlFocus*

Value of *wParam*. If the *fHandle* parameter is TRUE, the *wCtlFocus* parameter identifies the control that receives the focus. If *fHandle* is FALSE, *wCtlFocus* is a flag that indicates whether the next or previous control with the WS_TABSTOP style receives the focus. If *wCtlFocus* is zero, the next control receives the focus; otherwise, the previous control with the WS_TABSTOP style receives the focus.

fHandle

Value of *lParam*. Contains a flag that indicates how Windows uses the *wCtlFocus* parameter. If the *fHandle* parameter is TRUE, *wCtlFocus* is a handle associated with the control that receives the focus; otherwise, *wCtlFocus* is a flag that indicates whether the next or previous control with the WS_TABSTOP style receives the focus.

Return Value   An application should return zero if it processes this message.

Comments   The effect of this message differs from that of the **SetFocus** function because WM_NEXTDLGCTL modifies the border around the control.

Do not use the **SendMessage** function to send a WM_NEXTDLGCTL message if your application will concurrently process other messages that set the focus. Use the **PostMessage** function instead.

See Also   **PostMessage, SendMessage, SetFocus**

WM_PAINT

WM_PAINT

An application sends the WM_PAINT message when Windows or another application makes a request to paint a portion of an application's window. The message is sent when the **UpdateWindow** or **RedrawWindow** function is called, or by the **DispatchMessage** function when the application obtains a WM_PAINT message by using the **GetMessage** or **PeekMessage** function.

Parameters   This message has no parameters.

Return Value   An application should return zero if it processes this message.

Comments   The **DefWindowProc** function validates the update region. The function may also send the WM_NCPAINT message to the window procedure if the window frame must be painted and send the WM_ERASEBKGND message if the window background must be erased.

The system sends this message when there are no other messages in the application's message queue. **DispatchMessage** determines where to send the message; **GetMessage** determines which message to dispatch. **GetMessage** returns the WM_PAINT message when there are no other messages in the application's message queue, and **DispatchMessage** sends the message to the appropriate window procedure.

A window may receive internal paint messages as a result of calling **RedrawWindow** with the RDW_INTERNALPAINT flag set. In this case, the window may not have an update region. An application should call the **GetUpdateRect** function to determine whether the window has an update region. If **GetUpdateRect** returns zero, the application should not call the **BeginPaint** and **EndPaint** functions.

An application must check for any necessary internal painting by looking at its internal data structures for each WM_PAINT message, because a WM_PAINT message may have been caused by both a non-NULL update region and a call to **RedrawWindow** with the RDW_INTERNALPAINT flag set.

Windows sends an internal WM_PAINT message only once. After an internal WM_PAINT message is returned from the **GetMessage** or **PeekMessage** function or is sent to a window by **UpdateWindow**, Windows does not post or send further WM_PAINT messages until the window is invalidated or until **RedrawWindow** is called again with the RDW_INTERNALPAINT flag set.

See Also   **BeginPaint**, **DispatchMessage**, **EndPaint**, **GetMessage**, **PeekMessage**, **RedrawWindow**, **UpdateWindow**, WM_ERASEBKGND, WM_NCPAINT

WM_PAINTCLIPBOARD

```
WM_PAINTCLIPBOARD
hwndViewer = (HWND) wParam;      /* handle of clipboard viewer   */
hglbPs = (HGLOBAL) lParam;       /* handle of PAINTSTRUCT object */
```

The WM_HSCROLLCLIPBOARD message is sent to the clipboard owner by a clipboard viewer window when the clipboard contains data in the CF_OWNERDISPLAY format and the clipboard viewer's client area needs repainting.

Parameters   *hwndViewer*
    Value of *wParam*. Identifies the clipboard viewer window.

hglbPs

Value of *lParam*. Identifies a global DDESHARE object that contains a **PAINTSTRUCT** structure. The structure defines the part of the client area to paint. The **PAINTSTRUCT** structure has the following form:

```
typedef struct tagPAINTSTRUCT { /* ps */
    HDC  hdc;
    BOOL fErase;
    RECT rcPaint;
    BOOL fRestore;
    BOOL fIncUpdate;
    BYTE rgbReserved[32];
} PAINTSTRUCT;
```

For more information about the **PaintStruct** structure, see Chapter 3, "Structures."

Return Value   If an application processes this message, it should return zero.

Comments   To determine whether the entire client area or just a portion of it needs repainting, the clipboard owner must compare the dimensions of the drawing area given in the **rcpaint** member of the **PAINTSTRUCT** structure to the dimensions given in the most recent WM_SIZECLIPBOARD message.

The clipboard owner must use the **GlobalLock** function to lock the memory that contains the **PAINTSTRUCT** structure. Before returning, the clipboard owner must unlock that memory by using the **GlobalUnlock** function.

See Also   **GlobalLock**, **GlobalUnlock**, WM_SIZECLIPBOARD

WM_PAINTICON

WM_PAINTICON

The WM_PAINTICON message is sent to a minimized window when the icon is to be painted. A window receives this message only if a class icon is defined for the window. Otherwise, WM_PAINT is sent instead.

Parameters   This message has no parameters.

Return Value   An application should return zero if it processes this message.

Comments   The **DefWindowProc** function draws the class icon.

For compatibility with Windows 3.*x*, the *wParam* parameter is TRUE. However, this value has no significance.

See Also   **DefWindowProc**, WM_ICONERASEBKGND, WM_PAINT

WM_PALETTECHANGED

```
WM_PALETTECHANGED
hwndPalChg = (HWND) wParam; /* handle of window that changed palette */
```

The WM_PALETTECHANGED message is sent to all top-level and overlapped windows after the window with the keyboard focus has realized its logical palette, thereby changing the system palette. This message enables a window without the keyboard focus that uses a color palette to realize its logical palette and update its client area.

Parameters   *hwndPalChg*
Value of *wParam*. Identifies the window that caused the system palette to change.

Comments   This message must be sent to all top-level and overlapped windows, including the one that changed the system palette. If any child windows use a color palette, this message must be passed on to them as well.

To avoid creating an infinite loop, a window that receives this message must not realize its palette, unless it determines that *wParam* does not contain its own window handle.

See Also   WM_PALETTEISCHANGING, WM_QUERYNEWPALETTE

WM_PALETTEISCHANGING

```
WM_PALETTEISCHANGING
hwndRealize = (HWND) wParam; /* window to realize palette */
```

The WM_PALETTEISCHANGING message informs applications that an application is going to realize its logical palette.

Parameters   *hwndRealize*
Value of *wParam*. Identifies the window that is going to realize its logical palette.

Return Value   If an application processes this message, it should return zero.

Comments   The application changing its palette does not wait for acknowledgment of this message before changing the palette and sending the WM_PALETTECHANGED message. As a result, the palette may already be changed by the time an application receives this message.

If the application either ignores or fails to process this message and a second application realizes its palette while the first is using palette indices, there is a strong possibility that the user will see unexpected colors during subsequent drawing operations.

See Also   WM_PALETTECHANGED, WM_QUERYNEWPALETTE

WM_PARENTNOTIFY

```
WM_PARENTNOTIFY
fwEvent = LOWORD(wParam);  /* event flags                    */
idChild = HIWORD(wParam);  /* identifier of child window      */
lValue = lParam;           /* child handle, or cursor coordinates */
```

The WM_PARENTNOTIFY message is sent to the parent of a child window when the child window is created or destroyed or when the user clicks a mouse button while the cursor is over the child window. When the child window is being created, the system sends WM_PARENTNOTIFY just before the **CreateWindow** or **CreateWindowEx** function that creates the window returns. When the child window is being destroyed, Windows sends the message before any processing to destroy the window takes place.

Parameters   *fwEvent*

Value of the low-order word of *wParam*. Specifies the event for which the parent is being notified. This parameter can be one of the following values:

Value	Meaning
WM_CREATE	The child window is being created.
WM_DESTROY	The child window is being destroyed.
WM_LBUTTONDOWN	The user has placed the cursor over the child window and has clicked the left mouse button.
WM_MBUTTONDOWN	The user has placed the cursor over the child window and has clicked the middle mouse button.
WM_RBUTTONDOWN	The user has placed the cursor over the child window and has clicked the right mouse button.

idChild

Value of the high-order word of *wParam*. If the *fwEvent* parameter is the WM_CREATE or WM_DESTROY value, *idChild* specifies the identifier of the child window. Otherwise, *idChild* is undefined.

lValue

Contains the handle of the child window, if the *fwEvent* parameter is the WM_CREATE or WM_DESTROY value; otherwise, *lValue* contains the x-

and y-coordinates of the cursor. The x-coordinate is in the low-order word and the y-coordinate is in the high-order word.

Return Value   If an application processes this message, it should return zero.

Comments   This message is also sent to all ancestor windows of the child window, including the top-level window.

All child windows, except those that have the WS_EX_NOPARENTNOTIFY extended window style, send this message to their parent windows. By default, child windows in a dialog box have the WS_EX_NOPARENTNOTIFY style, unless the **CreateWindowEx** function is called to create the child window without this style.

See Also   **CreateWindow**, **CreateWindowEx**, WM_CREATE, WM_DESTROY, WM_LBUTTONDOWN, WM_MBUTTONDOWN, WM_RBUTTONDOWN

WM_PASTE

```
WM_PASTE
wParam = 0; /* not used, must be zero */
lParam = 0; /* not used, must be zero */
```

An application sends a WM_PASTE message to an edit control or combo box to copy the current contents of the Clipboard to the edit control at the current caret position. Data is inserted only if the Clipboard contains data in CF_TEXT format.

Parameters   This message has no parameters.

Return Value   This message does not return a value.

Comments   When sent to a combo box, the WM_PASTE message is handled by its edit control. This message has no effect when sent to a combo box with the CBS_DROPDOWNLIST style.

See Also   WM_CLEAR, WM_COPY, WM_CUT

WM_POWER

```
WM_POWER
fwPowerEvt = wParam;      /* power-event notification message */
```

The WM_POWER message is sent when the system, typically a battery-powered personal computer, is about to enter the suspended mode.

Parameters   *fwPowerEvt*
Value of *wParam*. Specifies a power-event notification message. This parameter can be one of the following values:

Value	Meaning
PWR_SUSPENDREQUEST	Indicates that the system is about to enter the suspended mode.
PWR_SUSPENDRESUME	Indicates that the system is resuming operation after having entered the suspended mode normally —that is, the system sent a PWR_SUSPENDREQUEST notification message to the application before the system was suspended. An application should perform any necessary recovery actions.
PWR_CRITICALRESUME	Indicates that the system is resuming operation after entering the suspended mode without first sending a PWR_SUSPENDREQUEST notification message to the application. An application should perform any necessary recovery actions.

Return Value   The value an application should return depends on the value of the *wParam* parameter. If *wParam* is PWR_SUSPENDREQUEST, the return value is PWR_FAIL to prevent the system from entering the suspended state; otherwise, it is PWR_OK. If *wParam* is PWR_SUSPENDRESUME or PWR_CRITICALRESUME, the return value is zero.

Comments   This message is sent only to an application that is running on a system that conforms to the advanced power management (APM) basic input/output system (BIOS) specification. The message is sent by the power-management driver to each window returned by the **EnumWindows** function.

The suspended mode is the state in which the greatest amount of power savings occurs, but all operational data and parameters are preserved. Random-access memory (RAM) contents are preserved, but many devices are likely to be turned off.

See Also   **EnumWindows**

WM_QUERYDRAGICON

WM_QUERYDRAGICON

The WM_QUERYDRAGICON message is sent to a minimized (iconic) window which is about to be dragged by the user but which does not have an icon defined for its class. An application can return the handle of an icon or cursor. The system displays this cursor or icon while the user drags the icon.

Parameters   This message has no parameters.

Return Value   An application should return the handle of a cursor or icon that Windows is to display while the user drags the icon. The cursor or icon must be compatible with the display driver's resolution. If the application returns NULL, the system displays the default cursor.

Default Action   The **DefWindowProc** function returns the handle of the default cursor.

Comments   When the user drags the icon of a window without a class icon, Windows replaces the icon with a default cursor. If the application requires a different cursor to be displayed during dragging, it must return the handle of the cursor or icon compatible with the display driver's resolution. If an application returns the handle of a color cursor or icon, the system converts the cursor or icon to black and white. The application can call the **LoadCursor** or **LoadIcon** function to load a cursor or icon from the resources in its executable file and to retrieve this handle.

See Also   **DefWindowProc**, **LoadCursor**, **LoadIcon**

WM_QUERYENDSESSION

```
WM_QUERYENDSESSION
nSource = (UINT) wParam;    /* source of end-session request */
```

The WM_QUERYENDSESSION message is sent when the user chooses to end the Windows session or when an application calls the **ExitWindows** function. If any application returns zero, the Windows session is not ended. Windows stops sending WM_QUERYENDSESSION messages as soon as one application returns zero.

After processing this message, Windows sends the WM_ENDSESSION message with the *wParam* parameter set to the results of the WM_QUERYENDSESSION message.

Parameters   *nSource*
    Value of *wParam*. Specifies the source of the request to end the Windows session. This parameter is zero if the request occurred because the user clicked the Logoff or Shutdown button in the Windows NT Security dialog box. This

parameter is nonzero if the user clicked the End Task button in the Task List dialog box.

Return Value   If an application can terminate conveniently, it should return TRUE; otherwise, it should return FALSE.

Default Action   The **DefWindowProc** function returns TRUE.

See Also   **DefWindowProc**, **ExitWindows**, WM_ENDSESSION

WM_QUERYNEWPALETTE

WM_QUERYNEWPALETTE

The WM_QUERYNEWPALETTE message informs a window that it is about to receive the keyboard focus, giving the window the opportunity to realize its logical palette when it receives the focus.

Parameters   This message has no parameters.

Return Value   If the window realizes its logical palette, it must return TRUE; otherwise, it must return FALSE.

See Also   WM_PALETTECHANGED, WM_PALETTEISCHANGING

WM_QUERYOPEN

WM_QUERYOPEN

The WM_QUERYOPEN message is sent to an icon when the user requests that the window be restored to its previous size and position.

Parameters   This message has no parameters.

Return Value   If the icon can be opened, an application that processes this message should return TRUE; otherwise, it should return FALSE to prevent the icon from being opened.

Default Action   The **DefWindowProc** function returns TRUE.

Comments   While processing this message, the application should not perform any action that would cause an activation or focus change (for example, creating a dialog box).

See Also   **DefWindowProc**

WM_QUEUESYNC

```
WM_QUEUESYNC
wParam = 0; /* not used, must be zero */
lParam = 0; /* not used, must be zero */
```

The WM_QUEUESYNC message is sent by a computer-based training (CBT) application to separate user-input messages from other messages sent through the WH_JOURNALPLAYBACK hook procedure.

Parameters   This message has no parameters.

Return Value   A CBT application should return zero if it processes this message.

Comments   Whenever a CBT application uses the WH_JOURNALPLAYBACK hook procedure, the first and last messages are WM_QUEUESYNC. This allows the CBT application to intercept and examine user-initiated messages without doing so for events that it sends.

If an application specifies a NULL window handle, the message is posted to the message queue of the active window.

WM_QUIT

```
WM_QUIT
nExitCode = (int) wParam;    /* exit code */
```

The WM_QUIT message indicates a request to terminate an application and is generated when the application calls the **PostQuitMessage** function. It causes the **GetMessage** function to return zero.

Parameters   *nExitCode*
          Value of *wParam*. Specifies the exit code given in the **PostQuitMessage** function.

Return Value   This message does not have a return value, because it causes the message loop to terminate before the message is sent to the application's window procedure.

See Also   **GetMessage**, **PostQuitMessage**

WM_RBUTTONDBLCLK

```
WM_RBUTTONDBLCLK
fwKeys = wParam;           /* key flags                    */
xPos = LOWORD(lParam);     /* horizontal position of cursor */
yPos = HIWORD(lParam);     /* vertical position of cursor   */
```

The WM_RBUTTONDBLCLK message is posted when the user double-clicks the right mouse button while the cursor is in the client area of a window. If the mouse is not captured, the message is posted to the window beneath the cursor. Otherwise, the message is posted to the window that has captured the mouse.

Parameters

fwKeys
Value of *wParam*. Indicates whether various virtual keys are down. This parameter can be any combination of the following values:

Value	Description
MK_CONTROL	Set if the CTRL key is down
MK_LBUTTON	Set if the left mouse button is down
MK_MBUTTON	Set if the middle mouse button is down
MK_RBUTTON	Set if the right mouse button is down
MK_SHIFT	Set if the SHIFT key is down

xPos
Value of the low-order word of *lParam*. Specifies the x-coordinate of the cursor. The coordinate is relative to the upper-left corner of the client area.

yPos
Value of the high-order word of *lParam*. Specifies the y-coordinate of the cursor. The coordinate is relative to the upper-left corner of the client area.

Return Value

If an application processes this message, it should return zero.

Comments

Only windows that have the CS_DBLCLKS style can receive WM_RBUTTONDBLCLK messages, which Windows generates whenever the user presses, releases, and again presses the right mouse button within the system's double-click time limit. Double-clicking the right mouse button actually generates four messages: WM_RBUTTONDOWN, WM_RBUTTONUP, WM_RBUTTONDBLCLK, and WM_RBUTTONUP again.

An application can use the **MAKEPOINTS** macro to convert the *lParam* parameter to a **POINTS** structure.

See Also

GetCapture, GetDoubleClickTime, SetCapture, SetDoubleClickTime,
WM_RBUTTONDOWN, WM_RBUTTONUP

WM_RBUTTONDOWN

```
WM_RBUTTONDOWN
fwKeys = wParam;          /* key flags                    */
xPos = LOWORD(lParam);    /* horizontal position of cursor */
yPos = HIWORD(lParam);    /* vertical position of cursor   */
```

The WM_RBUTTONDOWN message is posted when the user presses the right mouse button while the cursor is in the client area of a window. If the mouse is not captured, the message is posted to the window beneath the cursor. Otherwise, the message is posted to the window that has captured the mouse.

Parameters

fwKeys

Value of *wParam*. Indicates whether various virtual keys are down. This parameter can be any combination of the following values:

Value	Description
MK_CONTROL	Set if the CTRL key is down
MK_LBUTTON	Set if the left mouse button is down
MK_MBUTTON	Set if the middle mouse button is down
MK_SHIFT	Set if the SHIFT key is down

xPos

Value of the low-order word of *lParam*. Specifies the x-coordinate of the cursor. The coordinate is relative to the upper-left corner of the client area.

yPos

Value of the high-order word of *lParam*. Specifies the y-coordinate of the cursor. The coordinate is relative to the upper-left corner of the client area.

Return Value

If an application processes this message, it should return zero.

Comments

An application can use the **MAKEPOINTS** macro to convert the *lParam* parameter to a **POINTS** structure.

See Also

GetCapture, **SetCapture**, WM_RBUTTONDBLCLK, WM_RBUTTONUP

WM_RBUTTONUP

```
WM_RBUTTONUP
fwKeys = wParam;          /* key flags                    */
xPos = LOWORD(lParam);    /* horizontal position of cursor */
yPos = HIWORD(lParam);    /* vertical position of cursor   */
```

The WM_RBUTTONUP message is posted when the user releases the right mouse button while the cursor is in the client area of a window. If the mouse is not captured, the message is posted to the window beneath the cursor. Otherwise, the message is posted to the window that has captured the mouse.

Parameters

fwKeys
Value of *wParam*. Indicates whether various virtual keys are down. This parameter can be any combination of the following values:

Value	Description
MK_CONTROL	Set if the CTRL key is down
MK_LBUTTON	Set if the left mouse button is down
MK_MBUTTON	Set if the middle mouse button is down
MK_SHIFT	Set if the SHIFT key is down

xPos
Value of the low-order word of *lParam*. Specifies the x-coordinate of the cursor. The coordinate is relative to the upper-left corner of the client area.

yPos
Value of the high-order word of *lParam*. Specifies the y-coordinate of the cursor. The coordinate is relative to the upper-left corner of the client area.

Return Value   If an application processes this message, it should return zero.

Comments   An application can use the **MAKEPOINTS** macro to convert the *lParam* parameter to a **POINTS** structure.

See Also   **GetCapture**, **SetCapture**, WM_RBUTTONDBLCLK, WM_RBUTTONDOWN

WM_RENDERALLFORMATS

WM_RENDERALLFORMATS

The WM_RENDERALLFORMATS message is sent to the clipboard owner before it is destroyed, if the clipboard owner has delayed rendering one or more clipboard formats. For the contents of the clipboard to remain available to other applications, the clipboard owner must render data in all the formats it is capable of generating, and place the data on the clipboard by calling the **SetClipboardData** function.

Parameters   This message has no parameters.

Return Value   If an application processes this message, it should return zero.

Comments	When responding to a WM_RENDERFORMAT or WM_RENDERALLFORMATS message, the clipboard owner must not open the clipboard before calling **SetClipboardData**.
	When the application returns, the system removes any unrendered formats from the list of available clipboard formats. For information about delayed rendering, see the **SetClipboardData** function.
See Also	**SetClipboardData**, WM_RENDERFORMAT

WM_RENDERFORMAT

```
WM_RENDERFORMAT
uFormat = (UINT) wParam;     /* clipboard format */
```

The WM_RENDERFORMAT message is sent to the clipboard owner if it has delayed rendering a specific clipboard format, and if an application has requested data in that format. The clipboard owner must render data in the specified format and place it on the clipboard by calling the **SetClipboardData** function.

Parameters	*uFormat* Specifies the clipboard format to be rendered.
Return Value	If an application processes this message, it should return zero.
Comments	When responding to a WM_RENDERFORMAT or WM_RENDERALLFORMATS message, the clipboard owner must not open the clipboard before calling **SetClipboardData**.
See Also	**SetClipboardData**, WM_RENDERALLFORMATS

WM_SETCURSOR

```
WM_SETCURSOR
hwnd = (HWND) wParam;         /* handle of window with cursor */
nHittest = LOWORD(lParam);   /* hit-test code                */
wMouseMsg = HIWORD(lParam);  /* mouse-message identifier     */
```

The WM_SETCURSOR message is sent to a window if the mouse causes the cursor to move within a window and mouse input is not captured.

Parameters	*hwnd* Value of *wParam*. Identifies the window that contains the cursor.

nHittest
Value of the low-order word of *lParam*. Specifies the hit-test code.

wMouseMsg
Value of the high-order word of *lParam*. Specifies the identifier of the mouse message.

Default Action   The **DefWindowProc** function passes the WM_SETCURSOR message to a parent window before processing. If the parent window returns TRUE, further processing is halted. Passing the message to a window's parent window gives the parent window control over the cursor's setting in a child window. The **DefWindowProc** function also uses this message to set the cursor to an arrow if it is not in the client area, or to the registered class cursor if it is in the client area. If the low-order word of the *lParam* parameter is HTERROR and the high-order word of *lParam* specifies that one of the mouse buttons is pressed, **DefWindowProc** calls the **MessageBeep** function.

Comments   The high-order word of *lParam* is zero when the window enters menu mode.

See Also   **DefWindowProc**, **MessageBeep**

WM_SETFOCUS

```
WM_SETFOCUS
hwndLoseFocus = (HWND) wParam; /* handle of window losing focus */
```

The WM_SETFOCUS message is sent to a window after it has gained the keyboard focus.

Parameters   *hwndLoseFocus*
Value of *wParam*. Identifies the window that has lost the keyboard focus (may be NULL).

Return Value   An application should return zero if it processes this message.

Comments   To display a caret, an application should call the appropriate caret functions when it receives the WM_SETFOCUS message.

See Also   **SetFocus**, WM_KILLFOCUS

WM_SETFONT

```
WM_SETFONT
wParam = (WPARAM) hfont;              /* handle of font */
lParam = MAKELPARAM(fRedraw, 0);     /* redraw flag    */
```

An application sends a WM_SETFONT message to specify the font that a control is to use when drawing text.

Parameters   *hfont*
Value of *wParam*. Identifies the font. If this parameter is NULL, the control uses the default system font to draw text.

fRedraw
Value of *lParam*. Specifies whether the control should be redrawn immediately upon setting the font. Setting the *fRedraw* parameter to TRUE causes the control to redraw itself.

Return Value   This message does not return a value.

Comments   The WM_SETFONT message applies to all controls, not just those in dialog boxes.

The best time for the owner of a dialog box control to set the font of the control is when it receives the WM_INITDIALOG message. The application should call the **DeleteObject** function to delete the font when it is no longer needed; for example, after it destroys the control.

The size of the control does not change as a result of receiving this message. To avoid clipping text that does not fit within the boundaries of the control, the application should correct the size of the control window before it sets the font.

When a dialog box uses the DS_SETFONT style to set the text in its controls, Windows sends the WM_SETFONT message to the dialog box procedure before it creates the controls. An application can create a dialog box that contains the DS_SETFONT style by calling any of the following functions:

- **CreateDialogIndirect**
- **CreateDialogIndirectParam**
- **DialogBoxIndirect**
- **DialogBoxIndirectParam**

See Also   **CreateDialogIndirect**, **CreateDialogIndirectParam**, **DeleteObject**, **DialogBoxIndirect**, **DialogBoxIndirectParam**, WM_INITDIALOG, WM_SETFONT, **DLGTEMPLATE**

WM_SETHOTKEY

```
WM_SETHOTKEY
wParam = (WPARAM) vkey;      /* virtual-key code of hot key */
lParam = 0;                  /* not used, must be zero      */
```

An application sends a WM_SETHOTKEY message to a window to associate a hot key with the window. When the user presses the hot key, the system activates the window.

Parameters

vkey

Value of *wParam*. Specifies the virtual-key code of the hot key to associate with the window. Setting this parameter to NULL removes the hot key associated with a window.

Return Value

The return value is one of the following:

Value	Meaning
2	The function is successful, but another window already has the same hot key.
1	The function is successful and no other window has the same hot key.
0	The function is unsuccessful—the window is invalid.
−1	The function is unsuccessful—the hot key is invalid.

Comments

A hot key cannot be associated with a child window.

VK_ESCAPE, VK_SPACE, and VK_TAB are invalid hot keys.

When the user presses the hot key, the system generates a WM_SYSCOMMAND message with *wParam* equal to SC_HOTKEY.

A window can only have one hot key. If the window already has a hot key associated with it, the new hot key replaces the old one. If more than one window has the same hot key, the window that is activated by the hot key is random.

See Also

RegisterHotKey, WM_GETHOTKEY, WM_SYSCOMMAND

WM_SETREDRAW

```
WM_SETREDRAW
wParam = (WPARAM) fRedraw; /* state of redraw flag   */
lParam = 0;               /* not used, must be zero */
```

An application sends the WM_SETREDRAW message to a window to allow changes in that window to be redrawn or to prevent changes in that window from being redrawn.

Parameters   *fRedraw*

Value of *wParam*. Specifies the state of the redraw flag. If this parameter is TRUE, the redraw flag is set. If the parameter is FALSE, the flag is cleared.

Return Value   An application should return zero if it processes this message.

Comments   This message sets or clears the redraw flag. If the redraw flag is cleared, the contents of the given window is not updated after each change, and the window is not repainted until the redraw flag is set. For example, an application that must add several items to a list box can clear the redraw flag, add the items, and then set the redraw flag. Finally, the application can call the **InvalidateRect** function to cause the list box to be repainted.

See Also   **InvalidateRect**

WM_SETTEXT   Unicode

```
WM_SETTEXT
wParam = 0;                          /* not used, must be zero      */
lParam = (LPARAM)(LPCTSTR)lpsz; /* address of window-text string */
```

An application sends a WM_SETTEXT message to set the text of a window.

Parameters   *lpsz*

Value of *wParam*. Points to a null-terminated string that is the window text.

Return Value   The return value is TRUE if the text is set. It is LB_ERRSPACE (for a list box) or CB_ERRSPACE (for a combo box) if insufficient space is available to set the text in the edit control. It is CB_ERR if this message is sent to a combo box without an edit control.

Default Action   The **DefWindowProc** function sets and displays the window text.

Comments   For an edit control, the text is the contents of the edit control. For a combo box, the text is the contents of the edit-control portion of the combo box. For a button, the text is the button name. For other windows, the text is the window title.

This message does not change the current selection in the list box of a combo box. An application should use the CB_SELECTSTRING message to select the item in a list box that matches the text in the edit control.

See Also   **DefWindowProc**, CB_SELECTSTRING, WM_GETTEXT

WM_SHOWWINDOW

```
WM_SHOWWINDOW
fShow = (BOOL) wParam;        /* show/hide flag */
fnStatus = (int) lParam;      /* status flag    */
```

The WM_SHOWWINDOW message is sent to a window when the window is about to be hidden or shown.

Parameters

fShow

Value of *wParam*. Specifies whether a window is being shown. It is TRUE if the window is being shown or FALSE if the window is being hidden.

fnStatus

Value of *lParam*. Specifies the status of the window being shown. The *fnStatus* parameter is zero if the message is sent because of a call to the **ShowWindow** function; otherwise, *fnStatus* is one of the following values:

Value	Meaning
SW_PARENTCLOSING	Window's owner window is being minimized.
SW_PARENTOPENING	Window's owner window is being restored.

Return Value

If an application processes this message, it should return zero.

Default Action

The **DefWindowProc** function hides or shows the window, as specified by the message.

Comments

If a window has the WS_VISIBLE style when it is created, the window receives this message after it is created, but before it is displayed. A window also receives this message when its visibility state is changed by the **ShowWindow** or **ShowOwnedPopups** function.

The WM_SHOWWINDOW message is not sent under the following circumstances:

- When a top-level, overlapped window is created with the WS_MAXIMIZE or WS_MINIMIZE style.
- When the SW_SHOWNORMAL flag is specified in the call to the **ShowWindow** function.

See Also

DefWindowProc, **ShowOwnedPopups**, **ShowWindow**

WM_SIZE

```
WM_SIZE
fwSizeType = wParam;       /* resizing flag               */
nWidth = LOWORD(lParam);   /* width of client area        */
nHeight = HIWORD(lParam);  /* height of client area       */
```

The WM_SIZE message is sent to a window after its size has changed.

Parameters   *fwSizeType*
Value of *wParam*. Specifies the type of resizing requested. This parameter can be one of the following values:

Value	Meaning
SIZE_MAXIMIZED	Window has been maximized.
SIZE_MINIMIZED	Window has been minimized.
SIZE_RESTORED	Window has been resized, but neither the SIZE_MINIMIZED nor SIZE_MAXIMIZED value applies.
SIZE_MAXHIDE	Message is sent to all pop-up windows when some other window is maximized.
SIZE_MAXSHOW	Message is sent to all pop-up windows when some other window has been restored to its former size.

nWidth
Value of the low-order word of *lParam*. Specifies the new width of the client area.

nHeight
Value of the high-order word of *lParam*. Specifies the new height of the client area.

Return Value   If an application processes this message, it should return zero.

Comments   If the **SetScrollPos** or **MoveWindow** function is called for a child window as a result of the WM_SIZE message, the *bRedraw* parameter should be nonzero to cause the window to be repainted.

Note that the *nWidth* and *nHeight* parameters are limited to one word. Although a window can be created with a dword height or width that is a doubleword, the WM_SIZE message cannot use values of that size.

See Also   **MoveWindow, SetScrollPos**

WM_SIZECLIPBOARD

```
WM_SIZECLIPBOARD
hwndViewer = (HWND) wParam;   /* handle of clipboard viewer */
hglbRc = (HGLOBAL) lParam;    /* handle of RECT object      */
```

The **WM_SIZECLIPBOARD** message is sent to the clipboard owner by a clipboard viewer window when the clipboard contains data in the CF_OWNERDISPLAY format and the clipboard viewer's client area has changed size.

Parameters

hwndViewer
   Value of *wParam*. Identifies the clipboard viewer window.

hglbRc
   Value of *lParam*. Identifies a global memory object that contains a **RECT** structure. The structure specifies the new dimensions of the clipboard viewer's client area. The **RECT** structure has the following form:

```
typedef struct tagRECT {    /* rc */
    LONG left;
    LONG top;
    LONG right;
    LONG bottom;
} RECT;
```

For a full description of this structure, see Chapter 3, "Structures.."

Comments
When the clipboard viewer window is about to be destroyed or resized, a WM_SIZECLIPBOARD message is sent with a null rectangle (0, 0, 0, 0) as the new size. This permits the clipboard owner to free its display resources.

The clipboard owner must use the **GlobalLock** function to lock the memory object that contains the **RECT** structure. Before returning, the clipboard owner must unlock the object by using the **GlobalUnlock** function.

See Also
   GlobalLock, **GlobalUnlock**

WM_SPOOLERSTATUS

```
WM_SPOOLERSTATUS
fwJobStatus = wParam;         /* job-status flag            */
cJobsLeft = LOWORD(lParam);   /* number of jobs remaining   */
```

The WM_SPOOLERSTATUS message is sent from Windows Print Manager whenever a job is added to or removed from the Print Manager queue.

Parameters   *fwJobStatus*
Value of *wParam*. Specifies the SP_JOBSTATUS flag.

cJobsLeft
Value of the low-order word of *lParam*. Specifies the number of jobs remaining in the Print Manager queue.

Return Value   An application should return zero if it processes this message.

Comments   This message is for informational purposes only.

WM_SYSCHAR   `Unicode`

```
WM_SYSCHAR
chCharCode = (TCHAR) wParam;    /* character code */
lKeyData = lParam;              /* key data       */
```

The WM_SYSCHAR message is posted to the window with the keyboard focus when a WM_SYSKEYDOWN message is translated by the **TranslateMessage** function. It specifies the character code of a system character key—that is, a character key that is pressed while the ALT key is down.

Parameters   *chCharCode*
Value of *wParam*. Specifies the character code of the System-menu key.

lKeyData
Value of *lParam*. Specifies the repeat count, scan code, extended-key flag, context code, previous key-state flag, and transition-state flag, as shown in the following table:

Value	Meaning
0–15	Specifies the repeat count. The value is the number of times the keystroke is repeated as a result of the user holding down the key.
16–23	Specifies the scan code. The value depends on the original equipment manufacturer (OEM).
24	Specifies whether the key is an extended key, such as a function key or a key on the numeric keypad. The value is 1 if it is an extended key; otherwise, it is 0.
25–28	Reserved.
29	Specifies the context code. The value is 1 if the ALT key is held down while the key is pressed; otherwise, the value is 0.

30	Specifies the previous key state. The value is 1 if the key is down before the message is sent, or it is 0 if the key is up.
31	Specifies the transition state. The value is 1 if the key is being released, or it is 0 if the key is being pressed.

Return Value   An application should return zero if it processes this message.

Comments   When the context code is zero, the message can be passed to the **TranslateAccelerator** function, which will handle it as though it were a standard key message instead of a system character-key message. This allows accelerator keys to be used with the active window even if the active window does not have the keyboard focus.

For enhanced 101- and 102-key keyboards, extended keys are the right ALT and CTRL keys on the main section of the keyboard; the INS, DEL, HOME, END, PAGE UP, PAGE DOWN and arrow keys in the clusters to the left of the numeric keypad; the PRINT SCRN key; the BREAK key; the NUMLOCK key; and the divide (/) and ENTER keys in the numeric keypad. Other keyboards may support the extended-key bit in the *lKeyData* parameter.

See Also   **TranslateAccelerator**, **TranslateMessage**, WM_SYSKEYDOWN

WM_SYSCOLORCHANGE

WM_SYSCOLORCHANGE

The WM_SYSCOLORCHANGE message is sent to all top-level windows when a change is made to a system color setting.

Parameters   This message has no parameters.

Comments   Windows sends a WM_PAINT message to any window that is affected by a system color change.

Applications that have brushes using the existing system colors should delete those brushes and recreate them using the new system colors.

See Also   WM_PAINT

WM_SYSCOMMAND

```
WM_SYSCOMMAND
uCmdType = wParam;        /* command value              */
xPos = LOWORD(lParam);    /* horizontal position of cursor */
yPos = HIWORD(lParam);    /* vertical position of cursor   */
```

The WM_SYSCOMMAND message is sent when the user chooses a command from the System menu (also known as Control menu) or when the user chooses the Maximize button or Minimize button.

Parameters

uCmdType

Value of *wParam*. Specifies the type of system command requested. This parameter can be one of the following values:

Value	Meaning
SC_CLOSE	Closes the window.
SC_HOTKEY	Activates the window associated with the application-specified hot key. The low-order word of *lParam* identifies the window to activate.
SC_HSCROLL	Scrolls horizontally.
SC_KEYMENU	Retrieves a menu through a keystroke.
SC_MAXIMIZE (or SC_ZOOM)	Maximizes the window.
SC_MINIMIZE (or SC_ICON)	Minimizes the window.
SC_MOUSEMENU	Retrieves a menu through a mouse click.
SC_MOVE	Moves the window.
SC_NEXTWINDOW	Moves to the next window.
SC_PREVWINDOW	Moves to the previous window.
SC_RESTORE	Restores the window to its normal position and size.
SC_SCREENSAVE	Executes the screen saver application specified in the [boot] section of the SYSTEM.INI file.
SC_SIZE	Sizes the window.
SC_TASKLIST	Executes or activates Windows Task Manager.
SC_VSCROLL	Scrolls vertically.

xPos

    Value of the low-order word of *lParam*. Specifies the x-coordinate of the cursor, in screen coordinates, if a System menu command is chosen with the mouse. Otherwise, this parameter is not used.

yPos

    Value of the high-order word of *lParam*. Specifies the y-coordinate of the cursor, in screen coordinates, if a System menu command is chosen with the mouse. Otherwise, this parameter is not used.

Return Value   If an application processes this message, it should return zero.

Default Action   The **DefWindowProc** function carries out the System menu request for the predefined actions specified in the preceding table.

Comments   In WM_SYSCOMMAND messages, the four low-order bits of the *uCmdType* parameter are used internally by Windows. To obtain the correct result when testing the value of *uCmdType*, an application must combine the value 0xFFF0 with the *uCmdType* value by using the bitwise AND operator.

The menu items in a System menu can be modified by using the **GetSystemMenu**, **AppendMenu**, **InsertMenu**, and **ModifyMenu** functions. Applications that modify the System menu must process WM_SYSCOMMAND messages.

An application can carry out any system command at any time by passing a WM_SYSCOMMAND message to the **DefWindowProc** function. Any WM_SYSCOMMAND messages not handled by the application must be passed to **DefWindowProc**. Any command values added by an application must be processed by the application and cannot be passed to **DefWindowProc**.

Accelerator keys that are defined to choose items from the System menu are translated into WM_SYSCOMMAND messages; all other accelerator keystrokes are translated into WM_COMMAND messages.

See Also   **AppendMenu**, **DefWindowProc**, **GetSystemMenu**, **InsertMenu**, **ModifyMenu**, **WM_COMMAND**

WM_SYSDEADCHAR   **Unicode**

```
WM_SYSDEADCHAR
chCharCode = (TCHAR) wParam;      /* character code */
lKeyData = lParam;                /* key data       */
```

    The WM_SYSDEADCHAR message is sent to the window with the keyboard focus when a WM_SYSKEYDOWN message is translated by the

TranslateMessage function. WM_SYSDEADCHAR specifies the character code of a system dead key—that is, a dead key that is pressed while holding down the ALT key.

Parameters

chCharCode
Value of *wParam*. Specifies the character code generated by the system dead key—that is, a dead key that is pressed while holding down the ALT key.

lKeyData
Value of *lParam*. Specifies the repeat count, scan code, extended-key flag, context code, previous key-state flag, and transition-state flag, as shown in the following table:

Value	Description
0–15	Specifies the repeat count. The value is the number of times the keystroke is repeated as a result of the user holding down the key.
16–23	Specifies the scan code. The value depends on the original equipment manufacturer (OEM).
24	Specifies whether the key is an extended key, such as a function key or a key on the numeric keypad. The value is 1 if it is an extended key; otherwise, it is 0.
25–28	Reserved.
29	Specifies the context code. The value is 1 if the ALT key is held down while the key is pressed; otherwise, the value is 0.
30	Specifies the previous key state. The value is 1 if the key is down before the message is sent, or it is 0 if the key is up.
31	Specifies the transition state. The value is 1 if the key is being released, or it is 0 if the key is being pressed.

Return Value

An application should return zero if it processes this message.

See Also

TranslateMessage, WM_DEADCHAR, WM_SYSKEYDOWN

WM_SYSKEYDOWN

```
WM_SYSKEYDOWN
nVirtKey = (int) wParam;    /* virtual-key code */
lKeyData = lParam;          /* key data         */
```

The WM_SYSKEYDOWN message is posted to the window with the keyboard focus when the user holds down the ALT key and then presses another key. It also occurs when no window currently has the keyboard focus; in this case, the WM_SYSKEYDOWN message is sent to the active window. The window that receives the message can distinguish between these two contexts by checking the context code in the *lKeyData* parameter.

Parameters

nVirtKey
Value of *wParam*. Specifies the virtual-key code of the key being pressed.

lKeyData
Value of *lParam*. Specifies the repeat count, scan code, extended-key flag, context code, previous key-state flag, and transition-state flag, as shown in the following table:

Value	Description
0–15	Specifies the repeat count. The value is the number of times the keystroke is repeated as a result of the user holding down the key.
16–23	Specifies the scan code. The value depends on the original equipment manufacturer (OEM).
24	Specifies whether the key is an extended key, such as a function key or a key on the numeric keypad. The value is 1 if it is an extended key; otherwise, it is 0.
25–28	Reserved.
29	Specifies the context code. The value is 1 if the ALT key is down while the key is pressed; it is 0 if the WM_SYSKEYDOWN message is posted to the active window because no window has the keyboard focus.
30	Specifies the previous key state. The value is 1 if the key is down before the message is sent, or it is 0 if the key is up.
31	Specifies the transition state. The value is always 0 for a WM_SYSKEYDOWN message.

Return Value

An application should return zero if it processes this message.

Default Action

The **DefWindowProc** function examines the given key and generates a WM_SYSCOMMAND message if the key is either TAB or ENTER.

Comments

When the context code is zero, the message can be passed to the **TranslateAccelerator** function, which will handle it as though it were a normal key message instead of a system character-key message. This allows accelerator keys to be used with the active window even if the active window does not have the keyboard focus.

Because of automatic repeat, more than one WM_SYSKEYDOWN message may occur before a WM_SYSKEYUP message is sent. The previous key state (bit 30) can be used to determine whether the WM_SYSKEYDOWN message indicates the first down transition or a repeated down transition.

For enhanced 101- and 102-key keyboards, enhanced keys are the right ALT and CTRL keys on the main section of the keyboard; the INS, DEL, HOME, END, PAGE UP, PAGE DOWN and arrow keys in the clusters to the left of the numeric keypad;

and the divide (/) and ENTER keys in the numeric keypad. Other keyboards may support the extended-key bit in the *lParam* parameter.

See Also   **DefWindowProc**, **TranslateAccelerator**, WM_SYSCOMMAND, WM_SYSKEYUP

WM_SYSKEYUP

```
WM_SYSKEYUP
nVirtKey = (int) wParam;    /* virtual-key code */
lKeyData = lParam;          /* key data         */
```

The WM_SYSKEYUP message is posted to the window with the keyboard focus when the user releases a key that was pressed while the ALT key was held down. It also occurs when no window currently has the keyboard focus; in this case, the WM_SYSKEYUP message is sent to the active window. The window that receives the message can distinguish between these two contexts by checking the context code in the *lKeyData* parameter.

Parameters   *nVirtKey*
Value of *wParam*. Specifies the virtual-key code of the key being released.

lKeyData
Value of *lParam*. Specifies the repeat count, scan code, extended-key flag, context code, previous key-state flag, and transition-state flag, as shown in the following table:

Value	Description
0–15	Specifies the repeat count. The value is the number of times the keystroke is repeated as a result of the user holding down the key. The repeat count is always one for a WM_SYSKEYUP message.
16–23	Specifies the scan code. The value depends on the original equipment manufacturer (OEM).
24	Specifies whether the key is an extended key, such as a function key or a key on the numeric keypad. The value is 1 if it is an extended key; otherwise, it is 0.
25–28	Reserved.
29	Specifies the context code. The value is 1 if the ALT key is down while the key is released; it is 0 if the WM_SYSKEYDOWN message is posted to the active window because no window has the keyboard focus.
30	Specifies the previous key state. The value is always 1 for a WM_SYSKEYUP message.
31	Specifies the transition state. The value is always 1 for a WM_SYSKEYUP message.

Return Value   An application should return zero if it processes this message.

Default Action   The **DefWindowProc** function sends a WM_SYSCOMMAND message to the
top-level window if the F10 key or the ALT key was released. The *wParam*
parameter of the message is set to SC_KEYMENU.

Comments   When the context code is zero, the message can be passed to the
TranslateAccelerator function, which will handle it as though it were a normal
key message instead of a system character-key message. This allows accelerator
keys to be used with the active window even if the active window does not have
the keyboard focus.

For enhanced 101- and 102-key keyboards, extended keys are the right ALT and
CTRL keys on the main section of the keyboard; the INS, DEL, HOME, END, PAGE
UP, PAGE DOWN and arrow keys in the clusters to the left of the numeric keypad;
and the divide (/) and ENTER keys in the numeric keypad. Other keyboards may
support the extended-key bit in the *lKeyData* parameter.

For non-USA enhanced 102-key keyboards, the right ALT key is handled as a
CTRL+ALT key. The following shows the sequence of messages that result when
the user presses and releases this key:

WM_KEYDOWN	VK_CONTROL
WM_KEYDOWN	VK_MENU
WM_KEYUP	VK_CONTROL
WM_SYSKEYUP	VK_MENU

See Also   **DefWindowProc**, **TranslateAccelerator**, WM_SYSCOMMAND,
WM_SYSKEYDOWN

WM_TIMECHANGE

```
WM_TIMECHANGE
wParam = 0; /* not used, must be zero */
lParam = 0; /* not used, must be zero */
```

An application sends the WM_TIMECHANGE message to all top-level windows
after changing the system time.

Parameters   This message has no parameters.

Return Value   An application should return zero if it processes this message.

Comments   An application that changes the system time should send this message to all top-level windows. To send the WM_TIMECHANGE message to all top-level windows, an application can use the **SendMessage** function with the *hwnd* parameter set to HWND_TOPMOST.

See Also   **SendMessage**

WM_TIMER

```
WM_TIMER
wTimerID = wParam;              /* timer identifier        */
tmprc = (TIMERPROC *) lParam; /* address of timer callback */
```

The WM_TIMER message is posted to the installing thread's message queue or sent to the appropriate **TimerProc** callback function after each interval specified in the **SetTimer** function used to install a timer.

Parameters   *wTimerID*
    Value of *wParam*. Specifies the timer identifier.

tmprc
    Value of *lParam*. Points to an application-defined callback function that was passed to the **SetTimer** function when the timer was installed. If the *tmprc* parameter is not NULL, Windows passes the WM_TIMER message to the specified callback function rather than posting the message to the thread's message queue.

Return Value   An application should return zero if it processes this message.

Comments   The **DispatchMessage** function forwards this message when no other messages are in the thread's message queue.

See Also   **DispatchMessage, SetTimer, TimerProc**

WM_UNDO

```
WM_UNDO
```

An application sends a WM_UNDO message to an edit control to undo the last operation. When this message is sent to an edit control, the previously deleted text is restored or the previously added text is deleted.

Parameters   This message has no parameters.

Return Value   If the message succeeds, the return value is TRUE; otherwise, it is FALSE.

See Also   WM_CLEAR, WM_COPY, WM_CUT, WM_PASTE

WM_USER

WM_USER

The WM_USER constant is used by applications to help define private messages.

Comments   The WM_USER constant is used to distinguish between message values that are reserved for use by Windows and values that can be used by an application to send messages within a private window class. There are five ranges of message numbers:

Range	Meaning
0 through WM_USER – 1	Messages reserved for use by Windows
WM_USER through 0x7FFF	Integer messages for use by private window classes
0x8000 through 0xBFFF	Messages reserved for future use by Windows
0xC000 through 0xFFFF	String messages for use by applications
Greater than 0xFFFF	Reserved by Windows for future use

Message numbers in the first range (0 through WM_USER – 1) are defined by Windows. Values in this range that are not explicitly defined are reserved for future use by Windows.

Message numbers in the second range (WM_USER through 0x7FFF) can be defined and used by an application to send messages within a private window class. These values cannot be used to define messages that are meaningful throughout an application, because some predefined window classes already define values in this range. For example, predefined control classes such as BUTTON, EDIT, LISTBOX, and COMBOBOX may use these values. Messages in this range should not be sent to other applications unless the applications have been designed to exchange messages and to attach the same meaning to the message numbers.

Message numbers in the third range (0x8000 through 0xBFFF) are reserved for future use by Windows.

Message numbers in the fourth range (0xC000 through 0xFFFF) are defined at run time when an application calls the **RegisterWindowMessage** function to retrieve a message number for a string. All applications that register the same string can use the associated message number for exchanging messages. The actual message number, however, is not a constant and cannot be assumed to be the same in different Windows sessions.

Message numbers in the fifth range (greater than 0xFFFF) are reserved for future use by Windows.

See Also   **RegisterWindowMessage**

WM_VKEYTOITEM

```
WM_VKEYTOITEM
vkey = LOWORD(wParam);      /* virtual-key code  */
nCaretPos = HIWORD(wParam); /* caret position    */
hwndLB = lParam;            /* handle of list box */
```

The WM_VKEYTOITEM message is sent by a list box with the LBS_WANTKEYBOARDINPUT style to its owner in response to a WM_KEYDOWN message.

Parameters   *vkey*
Value of the low-order word of *wParam*. Specifies the virtual-key code of the key the user pressed.

nCaretPos
Value of the high-order word of *wParam*. Specifies the current position of the caret.

hwndLB
Value of *lParam*. Identifies the list box.

Return Value   The return value specifies the action that the application performed in response to the message. A return value of –2 indicates that the application handled all aspects of selecting the item and requires no further action by the list box. A return value of –1 indicates that the list box should perform the default action in response to the keystroke. A return value of 0 or greater specifies the index of an item in the list box and indicates that the list box should perform the default action for the keystroke on the given item.

Default Action   The **DefWindowProc** function returns –1.

See Also   **DefWindowProc**, WM_CHARTOITEM, WM_KEYDOWN

WM_VSCROLL

```
WM_VSCROLL
nScrollCode = (int) LOWORD(wParam);  /* scroll bar value    */
nPos = (int) HIWORD(wParam);         /* scroll box position */
hwndScrollBar = (HWND) lParam;       /* handle of scroll bar */
```

The WM_VSCROLL message is sent to a window when a scroll event occurs in the window's standard vertical scroll bar. This message is also sent to the owner of a vertical scroll bar control when a scroll event occurs in the control.

Parameters   *nScrollCode*

Value of the low-order word of *wParam*. Specifies a scroll bar value that indicates the user's scrolling request. This parameter can be one of the following values:

Value	Meaning
SB_BOTTOM	Scroll to lower right.
SB_ENDSCROLL	End scroll.
SB_LINEDOWN	Scroll one line down.
SB_LINEUP	Scroll one line up.
SB_PAGEDOWN	Scroll one page down.
SB_PAGEUP	Scroll one page up.
SB_THUMBPOSITION	Scroll to absolute position. The current position is specified by the *nPos* parameter.
SB_TOP	Scroll to upper left.

nPos

Value of the high-order word of *wParam*. Specifies the current position of the scroll box if the *nScrollCode* parameter is SB_THUMBPOSITION or SB_THUMBTRACK; otherwise, *nPos* is not used.

hwndScrollBar

Value of *lParam*. Identifies the control if WM_VSCROLL is sent by a scroll bar control. If WM_VSCROLL is sent by a window's standard scroll bar, *hwndScrollBar* is not used.

Return Value   If an application processes this message, it should return zero.

Comments   The SB_THUMBTRACK notification code is typically used by applications that provide feedback as the user drags the scroll box.

If an application scrolls the contents of the window, it must also reset the position of the scroll box by using the **SetScrollPos** function.

See Also   **SetScrollPos**, **WM_HSCROLL**

WM_VSCROLLCLIPBOARD

```
WM_VSCROLLCLIPBOARD
hwndViewer = (HWND) wParam;          /* handle of clipboard viewer */
nScrollCode = (int) LOWORD(lParam);  /* scroll bar code            */
nPos = (int) HIWORD(lParam);         /* scroll box position        */
```

The WM_VSCROLLCLIPBOARD message is sent to the clipboard owner by a clipboard viewer window when the clipboard contains data in the CF_OWNERDISPLAY format and an event occurs in the clipboard viewer's vertical scroll bar. The owner should scroll the clipboard image and update the scroll bar values.

Parameters   *hwndViewer*
Value of *wParam*. Identifies the clipboard viewer window.

nScrollCode
Value of the low-order word of *lParam*. Specifies a scroll bar event. This parameter can be one of the following values:

Value	Meaning
SB_BOTTOM	Scroll to lower right.
SB_ENDSCROLL	End scroll.
SB_LINEDOWN	Scroll one line down.
SB_LINEUP	Scroll one line up.
SB_PAGEDOWN	Scroll one page down.
SB_PAGEUP	Scroll one page up.
SB_THUMBPOSITION	Scroll to absolute position. The current position is specified by the *nPos* parameter.
SB_TOP	Scroll to upper left.

nPos
Value of the high-order word of *lParam*. Specifies the current position of the scroll box if the *nScrlCode* parameter is SB_THUMBPOSITION; otherwise, the *nPos* parameter is not used.

Return Value   If an application processes this message, it should return zero.

Comments   The clipboard owner can use the **ScrollWindow** function to scroll the image in the clipboard viewer window and invalidate the appropriate region.

See Also   **ScrollWindow**

WM_WINDOWPOSCHANGED

```
WM_WINDOWPOSCHANGED
lpwp = (LPWINDOWPOS) lParam; /* points to size and position data */
```

The WM_WINDOWPOSCHANGED message is sent to a window whose size, position, or place in the Z order has changed as a result of a call to **SetWindowPos** or another window-management function.

Parameters

lpwp

Value of *lParam*. Points to a **WINDOWPOS** structure that contains information about the window's new size and position. The **WINDOWPOS** structure has the following form:

```
typedef struct tagWINDOWPOS { /* wp */
    HWND hwnd;
    HWND hwndInsertAfter;
    int  x;
    int  y;
    int  cx;
    int  cy;
    UINT flags;
} WINDOWPOS;
```

For a full description of this structure, see Chapter 3, "Structures."

Return Value

If an application processes this message, it should return zero.

Default Action

The **DefWindowProc** function sends the WM_SIZE and WM_MOVE messages to the window.

Comments

The WM_SIZE and WM_MOVE messages are not sent if an application handles the WM_WINDOWPOSCHANGED message without calling **DefWindowProc**. It is more efficient to perform any move or size change processing during the WM_WINDOWPOSCHANGED message without calling **DefWindowProc**.

See Also

DefWindowProc, EndDeferWindowPos, SetWindowPos, WINDOWPOS, WM_MOVE, WM_SIZE, WM_WINDOWPOSCHANGING

WM_WINDOWPOSCHANGING

```
WM_WINDOWPOSCHANGING
lpwp = (LPWINDOWPOS) lParam; /* points to size and position data */
```

The WM_WINDOWPOSCHANGING message is sent to a window whose size, position, or place in the Z order is about to change as a result of a call to **SetWindowPos** or another window-management function.

Parameters

lpwp

Value of *lParam*. Points to a **WINDOWPOS** structure that contains information about the window's new size and position. The **WINDOWPOS** structure has the following form:

```
typedef struct tagWINDOWPOS { /* wp */
    HWND hwnd;
    HWND hwndInsertAfter;
    int  x;
    int  y;
    int  cx;
    int  cy;
    UINT flags;
} WINDOWPOS;
```

For a full description of this structure, see Chapter 3, "Structures."

Return Value

If an application processes this message, it should return zero.

Default Action

For a window with the WS_OVERLAPPED or WS_THICKFRAME style, the **DefWindowProc** function sends the WM_GETMINMAXINFO message to the window. This is done to validate the new size and position of the window and to enforce the CS_BYTEALIGNCLIENT and CS_BYTEALIGN client styles. An application can override this by not passing the WM_WINDOWPOSCHANGING message to the **DefWindowProc** function.

Comments

While this message is being processed, modifying any of the values in the **WINDOWPOS** structure affects the window's new size, position, or place in the Z order. An application can prevent changes to the window by setting or clearing the appropriate bits in the **flags** member of the **WINDOWPOS** structure.

See Also

DefWindowProc, EndDeferWindowPos, SetWindowPos, WINDOWPOS, WM_GETMINMAXINFO, WM_MOVE, WM_SIZE, WM_WINDOWPOSCHANGED

WM_WININICHANGE

```
WM_WININICHANGE
wParam = 0;                                 /* not used, must be zero */
lParam = (LPARAM) (LPCTSTR) pszSection; /* section-name string    */
```

An application sends the WM_WININICHANGE message to all top-level windows after making a change to the WIN.INI file. The **SystemParametersInfo** function sends the WM_WININICHANGE message after an application uses the function to change a setting in WIN.INI.

Parameters   *pszSection*
Value of *lParam*. Points to a string containing the name of the section that has changed. The string does not include the square brackets that enclose the section name.

Return Value   An application should return zero if it processes this message.

Comments   To send the WM_WININICHANGE message to all top-level windows, an application can use the **SendMessage** function with the *hwnd* parameter set to HWND_BROADCAST.

Some applications send this message with *lParam* set to NULL. If an application receives this message with an *lParam* value of NULL, it should check all sections in WIN.INI that affect the application.

Calls to functions that change WIN.INI may be mapped to the registry instead. This mapping occurs when WIN.INI and the section being changed are specified in the registry under the following keys:

HKEY_LOCAL_MACHINE\Software\Microsoft
 Windows NT\CurrentVersion\IniFileMapping

The change in the storage location has no effect on the behavior of this message.

See Also   **SendMessage**, **SystemParametersInfo**, WM_DEVMODECHANGE

WOM_CLOSE

This message is sent to a waveform output callback function when a waveform output device is closed. The device handle is no longer valid once this message has been sent.

Parameters   **DWORD** *dwParam1*
                       Currently unused.

                       DWORD *dwParam2*
                       Currently unused.

Return Value   None.

See Also   MM_WOM_CLOSE

WOM_DONE

This message is sent to a waveform output callback function when the specified output buffer is being returned to the application. Buffers are returned to the application when they have been played, or as the result of a call to **waveOutReset**.

Parameters   **DWORD** *dwParam1*
                       Points to a **WAVEHDR** structure identifying the buffer. The **WAVEHDR** structure has the following form:

```
typedef struct wavehdr_tag {
    LPSTR   lpData;
    DWORD   dwBufferLength;
    DWORD   dwBytesRecorded;
    DWORD   dwUser;
    DWORD   dwFlags;
    DWORD   dwLoops;
    struct wavehdr_tag *lpNext;
    DWORD   reserved;
} WAVEHDR;
```

For a full description of this structure, see Chapter 3, "Structures."

                       DWORD *dwParam2*
                       Currently unused.

Return Value   None.

See Also   MM_WOM_DONE

WOM_OPEN

This message is sent to a waveform output callback function when a waveform output device is opened.

Parameters   **DWORD** *dwParam1*
                    Currently unused.
                  DWORD *dwParam2*
                    Currently unused.

Return Value   None.

See Also   MM_WOM_OPEN

C H A P T E R   3

Structures

ABC

```
typedef struct _ABC { /* abc */
    int     abcA;
    UINT    abcB;
    int     abcC;
} ABC;
```

The **ABC** structure contains the width of a character in a TrueType ® font.

Members   **abcA**

Specifies the "A" spacing of the character. The "A" spacing is the distance to add to the current position before drawing the character glyph.

abcB

Specifies the "B" spacing of the character. The "B" spacing is the width of the drawn portion of the character glyph.

abcC

Specifies the "C" spacing of the character. The "C" spacing is the distance to add to the current position to provide white space to the right of the character glyph.

Comments   The total width of a character is the summation of the "A," "B," and "C" spaces. Either the "A" or the "C" space can be negative to indicate underhangs or overhangs.

See Also   **GetCharABCWidths**

ABCFLOAT

New

```
typedef struct _ABCFLOAT { /* abcf */
    FLOAT   abcfA;
    FLOAT   abcfB;
    FLOAT   abcfC;
} ABCFLOAT;
```

The **ABCFLOAT** structure contains the A, B, and C widths of a font character.

Members   **abcfA**

Specifies the "A" spacing of the character. The "A" spacing is the distance to add to the current position before drawing the character glyph.

abcfB
Specifies the "B" spacing of the character. The "B" spacing is the width of the drawn portion of the character glyph.

abcfC
Specifies the "C" spacing of the character. The "C" spacing is the distance to add to the current position to provide white space to the right of the character glyph.

Comments   The A, B, and C widths are measured along the base line of the font.

The character increment (total width) of a character is the sum of the "A," "B," and "C" spaces. Either the "A" or the "C" space can be negative to indicate underhangs or overhangs.

See Also   **GetCharABCWidthsFloat**

ACCEL

New

```
typedef struct tagACCEL { /* accl */
    BYTE    fVirt;
    WORD    key;
    WORD    cmd;
} ACCEL;
```

The **ACCEL** structure defines an accelerator key used in an accelerator table.

Members   **fVirt**
Specifies the accelerator flags. This member can be a combination of the following values:

Value	Meaning
FALT	The ALT key must be held down when the accelerator key is pressed.
FCONTROL	The CTRL key must be held down when the accelerator key is pressed.
FNOINVERT	Specifies that no top-level menu item is highlighted when the accelerator is used. If this flag is not specified, a top-level menu item will be highlighted, if possible, when the accelerator is used.
FSHIFT	The SHIFT key must be held down when the accelerator key is pressed.
FVIRTKEY	The **key** member specifies a virtual-key code. If this flag is not specified, **key** is assumed to specify an ASCII character code.

key

Specifies the accelerator key. This member can be either a virtual-key code or an ASCII character code.

cmd

Specifies the accelerator identifier. This value is placed in the low-order word of the *wParam* parameter of the WM_COMMAND or WM_SYSCOMMAND message when the accelerator is pressed.

See Also   **WM_COMMAND, WM_SYSCOMMAND**

ACCESS_ALLOWED_ACE

`New`

```
typedef struct _ACCESS_ALLOWED_ACE { /* aaace */
    ACE_HEADER Header;
    ACCESS_MASK Mask;
    DWORD SidStart;
} ACCESS_ALLOWED_ACE;
```

The **ACCESS_ALLOWED_ACE** structure defines an access-control entry (ACE) for the discretionary access-control list (ACL) that controls access to an object. An access-allowed ACE allows access to an object for a specific subject identified by a security identifier (SID).

Members   **Header**

Specifies an **ACE_HEADER** structure.

Mask

Specifies an **ACCESS_MASK** structure that specifies the access rights granted by this ACE.

SidStart

Specifies an SID. The access rights specified by the **Mask** member are granted to any subject possessing an enabled SID matching this field.

Comments   ACE structures must be aligned on doubleword boundaries. All Windows memory-management functions return doubleword-aligned handles to memory.

See Also   **AddAccessAllowedAce, AddAce, GetAce, ACCESS_DENIED_ACE, ACCESS_MASK, ACE_HEADER, ACL, SID, SYSTEM_ALARM_ACE, SYSTEM_AUDIT_ACE**

ACCESS_DENIED_ACE

`New`

```
typedef struct _ACCESS_DENIED_ACE { /* adace */
    ACE_HEADER  Header;
    ACCESS_MASK Mask;
    DWORD       SidStart;
} ACCESS_DENIED_ACE;
```

The **ACCESS_DENIED_ACE** structure defines an access-control entry (ACE) for the discretionary access-control list (ACL) controlling access to an object. An access-denied ACE denies access to an object for a specific subject identified by a security identifier (SID).

Members

Header
Specifies an **ACE_HEADER** structure.

Mask
Specifies an **ACCESS_MASK** structure specifying the access rights explicitly denied by this ACE.

SidStart
Specifies an SID. The access rights specified by the **Mask** member are denied to any subject possessing an enabled SID matching this field.

Comments
ACE structures must be aligned on doubleword boundaries. All Windows memory-management functions return doubleword-aligned handles to memory.

See Also
AddAccessDeniedAce, ACCESS_ALLOWED_ACE, ACCESS_MASK, ACE_HEADER, ACL, SID, SYSTEM_ALARM_ACE, SYSTEM_AUDIT_ACE

ACCESS_MASK

`New`

```
typedef DWORD ACCESS_MASK;
```

The **ACCESS_MASK** structure is one doubleword value containing standard, specific, and generic rights. These rights are used in access-control entries (ACEs) and are the primary means of specifying the requested or granted access to an object.

The bits in this value are allocated as follows:

Bits	Meaning
0 through 15	Specific rights. Contain the access mask specific to the object type associated with the mask.
16 through 23	Standard rights. Contains the object's standard access rights and can be a combination of the following predefined flags:

Bit	Flag	Meaning
16	DELETE	Delete access
17	READ_CONTROL	Read access to the owner, group, and discretionary access-control list (ACL) of the security descriptor
18	WRITE_DAC	Write access to the discretionary access-control list (ACL)
19	WRITE_OWNER	Write access to owner
20	SYNCHRONIZE	Synchronize access

Bits	Meaning
24	Access system security (ACCESS_SYSTEM_SECURITY). This flag is not a typical access type. It is used to indicate access to a system ACL. This type of access requires the calling process to have a specific privilege.
25	Maximum allowed (MAXIMUM_ALLOWED)
26 through 27	Reserved
28	Generic all (GENERIC_ALL)
29	Generic execute (GENERIC_EXECUTE)
30	Generic write (GENERIC_WRITE)
31	Generic read (GENERIC_READ)

The following constants represent the specific and standard access rights:

```
#define SPECIFIC_RIGHTS_ALL         0x0000FFFF
#define STANDARD_RIGHTS_REQUIRED    0x000F0000
#define STANDARD_RIGHTS_ALL         0x001F0000
```

See Also   **GENERIC_MAPPING**

ACE

An **ACE** is an access-control entry (ACE) in an access-control list (ACL).

Following are the currently defined **ACE** types:

ACE type	Structure	ACL Type
Access allowed	**ACCESS_ALLOWED_ACE**	Discretionary
Access denied	**ACCESS_DENIED_ACE**	Discretionary
System alarm	**SYSTEM_ALARM_ACE**	System
System audit	**SYSTEM_AUDIT_ACE**	System

System-alarm ACEs are not supported in the current version of Windows NT.

Comments

An ACL contains a list of ACEs. An ACE defines access to an object for a specific user or group or defines the types of access that generate system-administration messages or alarms for a specific user or group. The user or group is identified by a security identifier (SID).

Each ACE starts with an **ACE_HEADER** structure. The format of the data following the header varies according to the ACE type specified in the header.

See Also

AddAce, ACCESS_ALLOWED_ACE, ACCESS_DENIED_ACE, ACL, SYSTEM_ALARM_ACE, SYSTEM_AUDIT_ACE

ACE_HEADER

```
typedef struct _ACE_HEADER { /* acehdr */
    BYTE AceType;
    BYTE AceFlags;
    WORD AceSize;
} ACE_HEADER;
```

The **ACE_HEADER** structure describes the type and size of an access-control entry (ACE).

Members

AceType

Specifies the ACE type. This member can be one of the following values:

Value	ACE type
ACCESS_ALLOWED_ACE_TYPE	Access-allowed (defined by the **ACCESS_ALLOWED_ACE** structure)

ACCESS_DENIED_ACE_TYPE	Access-denied (defined by the **ACCESS_DENIED_ACE** structure)
SYSTEM_AUDIT_ACE_TYPE	System-audit (defined by the **SYSTEM_AUDIT_ACE** structure)

System-alarm ACEs are not supported in the current version of Windows NT. Applications cannot use the SYSTEM_ALARM_ACE_TYPE value or **SYSTEM_ALARM_ACE** structure.

AceFlags

Specifies a set of ACE type-specific control flags. This member can be a combination of the following values:

Value	Meaning
CONTAINER_INHERIT_ACE	The ACE is inherited by container objects, such as directories.
INHERIT_ONLY_ACE	The ACE does not apply to the container object, but to objects contained by it.
NO_PROPAGATE_INHERIT_ACE	The OBJECT_INHERIT_ACE and CONTAINER_INHERIT_ACE bits are not propagated to an inherited ACE.
OBJECT_INHERIT_ACE	The ACE is inherited by noncontainer objects, such as files created within the container object to which the ACE is assigned.
FAILED_ACCESS_ACE_FLAG	Used with system-audit and system-alarm ACEs to indicate a message is generated for failed access attempts.
SUCCESSFUL_ACCESS_ACE_FLAG	Used with system-audit and system-alarm ACEs to indicate a message is generated for successful access attempts.

AceSize

Specifies the size, in bytes, of the ACE.

Comments   An ACE defines access to an object for a specific user or group or defines the types of access that generate system-administration messages or alarms for a specific user or group. The user or group is identified by a security identifier (SID).

See Also   **ACCESS_ALLOWED_ACE, ACCESS_DENIED_ACE, ACL, SYSTEM_ALARM_ACE, SYSTEM_AUDIT_ACE**

ACL

```
typedef struct _ACL { /* acl */
    BYTE AclRevision;
    BYTE Sbz1;
    WORD AclSize;
    WORD AceCount;
    WORD Sbz2;
} ACL;
```

The **ACL** structure is the header of an access-control list (ACL). A complete ACL consists of an **ACL** structure followed by an ordered list of zero or more access-control entries (ACEs).

Members

AclRevision

Specifies the ACL's revision level. This value should be ACL_REVISION. All ACEs in an ACL must be at the same revision level.

Sbz1

Specifies a zero byte of padding that aligns the **AclRevision** member on a 16-bit boundary.

AclSize

Specifies the size, in bytes, of the ACL. This value includes both the **ACL** structure and all the ACEs.

AceCount

Specifies the number of ACEs stored in the ACL.

Sbz2

Specifies two zero bytes of padding that align the **ACL** structure on a 32-bit boundary.

Comments

An ACL includes a sequential list of zero or more ACEs. The individual ACEs in an ACL are numbered from 0 to n, where $n+1$ is the number of ACEs in the ACL. When editing an ACL, an application refers to an ACE within the ACL by its index.

There are two types of ACL: discretionary and system.

A discretionary ACL is controlled by the owner of an object or anyone granted WRITE_DAC access to the object. It specifies the access particular users and groups can have to an object. For example, the owner of a file can use a discretionary ACL to control which users and groups can and cannot have access to the file.

An object may also have system-level security information associated with it, in the form of a system ACL controlled by a system administrator. A system ACL can allow the system administrator to audit any attempts to gain access to an object.

Three ACE structures are currently defined:

ACE structure	Description
ACCESS_ALLOWED_ACE	Grants specified rights to a user or group. This ACE is stored in a discretionary ACL.
ACCESS_DENIED_ACE	Denies specified rights to a user or group. This ACE is stored in a discretionary ACL.
SYSTEM_AUDIT_ACE	Specifies what types of access will cause system-level audits. This ACE is stored in a system ACL.

A fourth ACE structure, **SYSTEM_ALARM_ACE**, is not currently supported by Windows NT.

The **ACL** structure is to be treated as though it were opaque and applications are not to attempt to work with its members directly. To ensure that ACLs are semantically correct, applications can use the functions listed in the **SeeAlso** section to create and manipulate ACLs.

Each **ACL** and **ACE** structure begins on a doubleword boundary.

See Also   **AddAce, DeleteAce, GetAclInformation, GetSecurityDescriptorDacl, GetSecurityDescriptorSacl, InitializeAcl, IsValidAcl, SetAclInformation, SetSecurityDescriptorDacl, SetSecurityDescriptorSacl**

ACL_INFORMATION_CLASS

New

```
typedef enum tagACL_INFORMATION_CLASS { /* aclic */
    AclRevisionInformation = 1,
    AclSizeInformation
} ACL_INFORMATION_CLASS;
```

The **ACL_INFORMATION_CLASS** enumerated type indicates the type of information being assigned to or retrieved from an access-control list (ACL).

See Also   **GetAclInformation, SetAclInformation, ACL, ACL_REVISION_INFORMATION, ACL_SIZE_INFORMATION**

ACL_REVISION_INFORMATION

`New`

```
typedef struct _ACL_REVISION_INFORMATION {
    DWORD    AclRevision;
} ACL_REVISION_INFORMATION;
```

The **ACL_REVISION_INFORMATION** structure contains revision information about an **ACL** structure.

Members

AclRevision
Specifies a revision number. The current revision number is ACL_REVISION.

See Also

GetAclInformation, SetAclInformation, ACL, ACL_INFORMATION_CLASS, ACL_SIZE_INFORMATION

ACL_SIZE_INFORMATION

`New`

```
typedef struct _ACL_SIZE_INFORMATION {
    DWORD    AceCount;
    DWORD    AclBytesInUse;
    DWORD    AclBytesFree;
} ACL_SIZE_INFORMATION;
```

The **ACL_SIZE_INFORMATION** structure contains information about the size of an **ACL** structure.

Members

AceCount
Specifies the number of access-control entries (ACEs) in the access-control list (ACL).

AclBytesInUse
Specifies the number of bytes in the ACL actually used to store the ACEs and **ACL** structure. This may be less than the total number of bytes allocated to the ACL.

AclBytesFree
Specifies the number of unused bytes in the ACL.

See Also

GetAclInformation, SetAclInformation, ACL, ACL_INFORMATION_CLASS, ACL_REVISION_INFORMATION

ACTION_HEADER

```
typedef struct _ACTION_HEADER {
    ULONG    transport_id;
    USHORT   action_code;
    USHORT   reserved;
} ACTION_HEADER;
```

The **ACTION_HEADER** structure contains information about an action. This action is an extension to the standard transport interface.

Members

transport_id
Specifies the transport provider. This member can be used to check the validity of the request by the transport.

This member is always a four-character string. All strings starting with the letter M are reserved, as shown in the following example:

String	Meaning
M000	All transports
MNBF	NBF
MABF	AsyBEUI
MXNS	XNS, etc.

action_code
Specifies the action.

reserved
Reserved.

Comments

The scope of the action is determined by the **ncb_lsn** and **ncb_num** members of the **NCB** structure, as follows:

	ncb_lsn = 0	ncb_lsn != 0
ncb_num = 0	Action applies to control channel associated with the valid LANadapter.	Action applies to connection identifier associated with the valid local session number.
ncb_num != 0	Action applies to address associated with the valid LAN adapter.	Illegal combination.

See Also

NCB

ADAPTER_STATUS

```
typedef struct _ADAPTER_STATUS { /* adptst */
    UCHAR    adapter_address[6];
    UCHAR    rev_major;
    UCHAR    reserved0;
    UCHAR    adapter_type;
    UCHAR    rev_minor;
    WORD     duration;
    WORD     frmr_recv;
    WORD     frmr_xmit;
    WORD     iframe_recv_err;
    WORD     xmit_aborts;
    DWORD    xmit_success;
    DWORD    recv_success;
    WORD     iframe_xmit_err;
    WORD     recv_buff_unavail;
    WORD     t1_timeouts;
    WORD     ti_timeouts;
    DWORD    reserved1;
    WORD     free_ncbs;
    WORD     max_cfg_ncbs;
    WORD     max_ncbs;
    WORD     xmit_buf_unavail;
    WORD     max_dgram_size;
    WORD     pending_sess;
    WORD     max_cfg_sess;
    WORD     max_sess;
    WORD     max_sess_pkt_size;
    WORD     name_count;
} ADAPTER_STATUS;
```

The **ADAPTER_STATUS** structure contains information about a network adapter. This structure is pointed to by the **ncb_buffer** member of the **NCB** structure. **ADAPTER_STATUS** is followed by as many **NAME_BUFFER** structures as are required to describe the network adapters on the system.

Members

adapter_address
Specifies the adapter's encoded address.

rev_major
Specifies the major software-release level. This value is 3 for IBM NetBIOS 3.*x*.

reserved0
Reserved. This value is always 0.

adapter_type

Specifies the adapter type. This value is 0xFF for a Token Ring adapter or 0xFE for an Ethernet adapter.

rev_minor

Specifies the minor software-release level. This value is 0 for IBM NetBIOS *x*.0.

duration

Specifies the duration of the reporting period, in minutes.

frmr_recv

Specifies the number of FRMR frames received.

frmr_xmit

Specifies the number of FRMR frames transmitted.

iframe_recv_err

Specifies the number of I frames received in error.

xmit_aborts

Specifies the number of aborted transmissions.

xmit_success

Specifies the number of successfully transmitted packets.

recv_success

Specifies the number of successfully received packets.

iframe_xmit_err

Specifies the number of I frames transmitted in error.

recv_buff_unavail

Specifies the number of times a buffer was not available to service a request from a remote computer.

ti_timeouts

Specifies the number of times the DLC T1 timer expired.

reserved1

Reserved. This value is always 0.

free_ncbs

Specifies the current number of free network-control blocks.

max_cfg_ncbs

Undefined for IBM NetBIOS 3.0.

max_ncbs

Undefined for IBM NetBIOS 3.0.

xmit_buf_unavail

Undefined for IBM NetBIOS 3.0.

max_dgram_size

Specifies the maximum size of a datagram packet. This value is always at least 512 bytes.

pending_sess
Specifies the number of pending sessions.

max_cfg_sess
Specifies the configured maximum pending sessions.

max_sess
Undefined for IBM NetBIOS 3.0.

max_sess_pkt_size
Specifies the maximum size of a session data packet.

name_count
Specifies the number of names in the local names table.

See Also   **NAME_BUFFER**, **NCB**

ADDJOB_INFO_1   `New, Unicode`

```
typedef struct _ADDJOB_INFO_1 { /* aji1 */
    LPTSTR  Path;
    DWORD   JobId;
} ADDJOB_INFO_1;
```

The **ADDJOB_INFO_1** structure identifies a print job as well as the directory and file in which an application can store that job.

Members   **Path**
Points to a null-terminated string that contains the path and filename that the application can use to store the print job.

JobId
Identifies the print job.

See Also   **AddJob**

AUXCAPS

```
typedef struct auxcaps_tag {
    WORD  wMid;
    WORD  wPid;
    MMVERSION  vDriverVersion;
    TCHAR  szPname[MAXPNAMELEN];
    WORD  wTechnology;
    DWORD  dwSupport;
} AUXCAPS;
```

The **AUXCAPS** structure describes the capabilities of an auxiliary output device.

Members

wMid

Specifies a manufacturer identifier for the device driver for the auxiliary audio device. Manufacturer identifiers are defined in Appendix D, "Manufacturer and Product Identifiers" in the *Microsoft Win32 Programmer's Reference, Volume 2*.

wPid

Specifies a product identifier for the auxiliary audio device. Product identifiers are defined in Appendix D, "Manufacturer and Product Identifiers" in the *Microsoft Win32 Programmer's Reference, Volume 2*.

vDriverVersion

Specifies the version number of the device driver for the auxiliary audio device. The high-order byte is the major version number, and the low-order byte is the minor version number.

szPname

Specifies the product name in a null-terminated string.

wTechnology

Specifies the type of the auxiliary audio output. This member can be one of the following values:

Value	Meaning
AUXCAPS_AUXIN	Audio output from auxiliary input jacks
AUXCAPS_CDAUDIO	Audio output from an internal CD-ROM drive

dwSupport

Specifies optional functionality supported by the auxiliary audio device. This member can be one or both of the following values:

Value	Meaning
AUXCAPS_LRVOLUME	Supports separate left and right volume control.
AUXCAPS_VOLUME	Supports volume control.

Comments   If a device supports volume changes, the AUXCAPS_VOLUME flag is set for the **dwSupport** member. If a device supports separate volume changes on the left and right channels, both the AUXCAPS_VOLUME and the AUXCAPS_LRVOLUME flags are set for this member.

See Also   **auxGetDevCaps**

BITMAP

```
typedef struct tagBITMAP {  /* bm */
    LONG    bmType;
    LONG    bmWidth;
    LONG    bmHeight;
    LONG    bmWidthBytes;
    WORD    bmPlanes;
    WORD    bmBitsPixel;
    LPVOID  bmBits;
} BITMAP;
```

The **BITMAP** structure defines the type, width, height, color format, and bit values of a bitmap.

Members   **bmType**
Specifies the bitmap type. This member must be zero.

bmWidth
Specifies the width, in pixels, of the bitmap. The width must be greater than zero.

bmHeight
Specifies the height, in pixels, of the bitmap. The height must be greater than zero.

bmWidthBytes
Specifies the number of bytes in each scan line. This value must be divisible by 2, because Windows assumes that the bit values of a bitmap form an array that is word aligned.

bmPlanes
Specifies the count of color planes.

bmBitsPixel
Specifies the number of bits required to indicate the color of a pixel.

bmBits
Points to the location of the bit values for the bitmap. The **bmBits** member must be a long pointer to an array of character (1-byte) values.

Comments   The currently used bitmap formats are monochrome and color. The monochrome bitmap uses a one-bit, one-plane format. Each scan is a multiple of 32 bits.

Scans are organized as follows for a monochrome bitmap of height *n*:

```
Scan 0
Scan 1
    .
    .
    .
Scan n-2
Scan n-1
```

The pixels on a monochrome device are either black or white. If the corresponding bit in the bitmap is 1, the pixel is set to the foreground color; if the corresponding bit in the bitmap is zero, the pixel is set to the background color.

All devices that have the RC_BITBLT device capability support bitmaps. For more information, see the **GetDeviceCaps** function.

Each device has a unique color format. In order to transfer a bitmap from one device to another, use the **GetDIBits** and **SetDIBits** functions.

See Also   **CreateBitmapIndirect, GetDeviceCaps, GetDIBits, GetObject, SetDIBits**

BITMAPCOREHEADER

```
typedef struct tagBITMAPCOREHEADER { /* bmch */
        DWORD   bcSize;
        WORD    bcWidth;
        WORD    bcHeight;
        WORD    bcPlanes;
        WORD    bcBitCount;
} BITMAPCOREHEADER;
```

The **BITMAPCOREHEADER** structure contains information about the dimensions and color format of a device-independent bitmap (DIB).

Members   **bcSize**
        Specifies the number of bytes required by the structure.

bcWidth
        Specifies the width of the bitmap, in pixels.

bcHeight
        Specifies the height of the bitmap, in pixels.

bcPlanes
> Specifies the number of planes for the target device. This value must be 1.

bcBitCount
> Specifies the number of bits per pixel. This value must be 1, 4, 8, or 24.

Comments　　The **BITMAPCOREINFO** structure combines the **BITMAPCOREHEADER** structure and a color table to provide a complete definition of the dimensions and colors of a DIB. For more information about specifying a device-independent bitmap, see the description of the **BITMAPCOREINFO** structure.

An application should use the information stored in the **bcSize** member to locate the color table in a **BITMAPCOREINFO** structure, using a method such as the following:

```
pColor = ((LPBYTE) pBitmapCoreInfo +
          (WORD) (pBitmapCoreInfo -> bcSize))
```

See Also　　**BITMAPCOREINFO**

BITMAPCOREINFO

```
typedef struct _BITMAPCOREINFO {     /* bmci */
      BITMAPCOREHEADER  bmciHeader;
      RGBTRIPLE         bmciColors[1];
} BITMAPCOREINFO;
```

The **BITMAPCOREINFO** structure defines the dimensions and color information for a device-independent bitmap (DIB).

Members　　**bmciHeader**
> Specifies a **BITMAPCOREHEADER** structure that contains information about the dimensions and color format of a DIB.

bmciColors
> Specifies an array of **RGBTRIPLE** structures that define the colors in the bitmap.

Comments　　A DIB consists of two parts: a **BITMAPCOREINFO** structure describing the dimensions and colors of the bitmap, and an array of bytes defining the pixels of the bitmap. The bits in the array are packed together, but each scan line must be padded with zeroes to end on a **LONG** boundary. The origin of the bitmap is the lower left corner.

The **bcBitCount** member of the **BITMAPCOREHEADER** structure determines the number of bits that define each pixel and the maximum number of colors in the bitmap. This member can be one of the following values:

Value	Meaning
1	The bitmap is monochrome, and the **bmciColors** member contains two entries. Each bit in the bitmap array represents a pixel. If the bit is clear, the pixel is displayed with the color of the first entry in the **bmciColors** table; if the bit is set, the pixel has the color of the second entry in the table.
4	The bitmap has a maximum of 16 colors, and the **bmciColors** member contains up to 16 entries. Each pixel in the bitmap is represented by a 4-bit index into the color table. For example, if the first byte in the bitmap is 0x1F, the byte represents two pixels. The first pixel contains the color in the second table entry, and the second pixel contains the color in the sixteenth table entry.
8	The bitmap has a maximum of 256 colors, and the **bmciColors** member contains up to 256 entries. In this case, each byte in the array represents a single pixel.
24	The bitmap has a maximum of 2^{24} colors, and the **bmciColors** member is NULL. Each 3-byte triplet in the bitmap array represents the relative intensities of red, green, and blue, respectively, for a pixel.

The colors in the **bmciColors** table should appear in order of importance.

Alternatively, for functions that use DIBs, the **bmciColors** member can be an array of 16-bit unsigned integers that specify indices into the currently realized logical palette, instead of explicit RGB values. In this case, an application using the bitmap must call the DIB functions (**CreateDIBitmap**, **CreateDIBPatternBrush**, and **CreateDIBSection**) with the *iUsage* parameter set to DIB_PAL_COLORS.

Note The **bmciColors** member should not contain palette indices if the bitmap is to be stored in a file or transferred to another application. Unless the application has exclusive use and control of the bitmap, the bitmap color table should contain explicit RGB values.

See Also   **BITMAPCOREHEADER, RGBTRIPLE**

BITMAPFILEHEADER

```
typedef struct tagBITMAPFILEHEADER { /* bmfh */
        WORD    bfType;
        DWORD   bfSize;
        WORD    bfReserved1;
        WORD    bfReserved2;
        DWORD   bfOffBits;
} BITMAPFILEHEADER;
```

The **BITMAPFILEHEADER** data structure contains information about the type, size, and layout of a file that contains a device-independent bitmap (DIB).

Members

bfType

Specifies the file type. It must be BM.

bfSize

Specifies the size of the file, in a doubleword value. This value can be obtained by dividing the length of the file, in bytes, by 4.

bfReserved1

Reserved; must be zero.

bfReserved2

Reserved; must be zero.

bfOffBits

Specifies the offset, in bytes, from the **BITMAPFILEHEADER** to the bitmap bits.

Comments

A **BITMAPINFO** or **BITMAPCOREINFO** structure immediately follows the **BITMAPFILEHEADER** structure in the DIB file.

See Also

BITMAPCOREINFO, **BITMAPINFO**

BITMAPINFO

```
typedef struct tagBITMAPINFO { /* bmi */
    BITMAPINFOHEADER bmiHeader;
    RGBQUAD          bmiColors[1];
} BITMAPINFO;
```

The **BITMAPINFO** structure defines the dimensions and color information for a Windows device-independent bitmap (DIB).

Members

bmiHeader

Specifies a **BITMAPINFOHEADER** structure that contains information about the dimensions and color format of a device-independent bitmap.

bmiColors

Specifies an array of **RGBQUAD** or **DWORD** data types that define the colors in the bitmap.

Comments

A device-independent bitmap consists of two distinct parts: a **BITMAPINFO** structure describing the dimensions and colors of the bitmap, and an array of bytes defining the pixels of the bitmap. The bits in the array are packed together, but each scan line must be padded with zeroes to end on a **LONG** boundary. If height is positive the origin of the bitmap is the lower-left corner. If the height is negative then the origin is the upper-left corner.

The **biBitCount** member of the **BITMAPINFOHEADER** structure determines the number of bits that define each pixel and the maximum number of colors in the bitmap. This member can be one of the following values:

Value	Meaning
1	The bitmap is monochrome, and the **bmiColors** member contains two entries. Each bit in the bitmap array represents a pixel. If the bit is clear, the pixel is displayed with the color of the first entry in the **bmiColors** table; if the bit is set, the pixel has the color of the second entry in the table.
4	The bitmap has a maximum of 16 colors, and the **bmiColors** member contains up to 16 entries. Each pixel in the bitmap is represented by a 4-bit index into the color table. For example, if the first byte in the bitmap is 0x1F, the byte represents two pixels. The first pixel contains the color in the second table entry, and the second pixel contains the color in the sixteenth table entry.
8	The bitmap has a maximum of 256 colors, and the **bmiColors** member contains up to 256 entries. In this case, each byte in the array represents a single pixel.
16	The bitmap has a maximum of 2^{16} colors. The **biCompression** member of the **BITMAPINFOHEADER** must be BI_BITFIELDS. The **bmiColors** member contains 3 DWORD color masks which specify the red, green, and blue components, respectively, of each pixel. Bits set in the DWORD mask must be contiguous and should not overlap the bits of another mask. All the bits in the pixel do not have to be used. Each **WORD** in the array represents a single pixel.
24	The bitmap has a maximum of 2^{24} colors, and the **bmiColors** member is NULL. Each 3-byte triplet in the bitmap array represents the relative intensities of blue, green, and red, respectively, of a pixel.
32	The bitmap has a maximum of 2^{32} colors. The **biCompression** member of the **BITMAPINFOHEADER** must be BI_BITFIELDS. The **bmiColors** member contains 3 DWORD color masks which specify the red, green, and blue components, respectively, of each pixel. Bits set in the DWORD mask must be contiguous and should not overlap the bits of another mask. All the bits in the pixel do not have to be used. Each **DWORD** in the array represents a single pixel.

The **biClrUsed** member of the **BITMAPINFOHEADER** structure specifies the number of color indices in the color table that are actually used by the bitmap. If the **biClrUsed** member is set to zero, the bitmap uses the maximum number of colors corresponding to the value of the **biBitCount** member.

The colors in the **bmiColors** table should appear in order of importance.

Alternatively, for functions that use DIBs, the **bmiColors** member can be an array of 16-bit unsigned integers that specify indices into the currently realized logical palette, instead of explicit RGB values. In this case, an application using the bitmap must call the DIB functions (**CreateDIBitmap**, **CreateDIBPatternBrush**, and **CreateDIBSection**) with the *iUsage* parameter set to DIB_PAL_COLORS.

If the bitmap is a packed bitmap (that is, a bitmap in which the bitmap array immediately follows the **BITMAPINFO** header and which is referenced by a single pointer), the **biClrUsed** member must be set to an even number when using the DIB_PAL_COLORS mode so the DIB bitmap array starts on a DWORD boundary.

Note The **bmiColors** member should not contain palette indices if the bitmap is to be stored in a file or transferred to another application. Unless the application has exclusive use and control of the bitmap, the bitmap color table should contain explicit RGB values.

See Also   **BITMAPINFOHEADER, RGBQUAD**

BITMAPINFOHEADER

```
typedef struct tagBITMAPINFOHEADER{ /* bmih */
    DWORD  biSize;
    LONG   biWidth;
    LONG   biHeight;
    WORD   biPlanes;
    WORD   biBitCount
    DWORD  biCompression;
    DWORD  biSizeImage;
    LONG   biXPelsPerMeter;
    LONG   biYPelsPerMeter;
    DWORD  biClrUsed;
    DWORD  biClrImportant;
} BITMAPINFOHEADER;
```

The **BITMAPINFOHEADER** structure contains information about the dimensions and color format of a device-independent bitmap (DIB).

Members   **biSize**
Specifies the number of bytes required by the structure.

biWidth
Specifies the width of the bitmap, in pixels.

biHeight

Specifies the height of the bitmap, in pixels. If **biHeight** is negative then the origin of the bitmap is the upper-left hand corner and the height is the absolute value of **biHeight**.

biPlanes

Specifies the number of planes for the target device. This value must be set to 1.

biBitCount

Specifies the number of bits per pixel. This value must be 1, 4, 8, 16, 24, or 32.

biCompression

Specifies the type of compression for a compressed bitmap. It can be one of the following values:

Value	Description
BI_RGB	An uncompressed format.
BI_RLE8	A run-length encoded format for bitmaps with 8 bits per pixel. The compression format is a 2-byte format consisting of a count byte followed by a byte containing a color index. For more information, see the following Comments section.
BI_RLE4	A run-length encoded format for bitmaps with 4 bits per pixel. The compression format is a 2-byte format consisting of a count byte followed by two word-length color indices. For more information, see the following Comments section.
BI_BITFIELDS	Specifies the bitmap is not compressed and the color table consists of 3 DWORD color masks which specify the red, green, and blue components, respectively, of each pixel. This is valid when used with 16 and 32 bits per pixel bitmaps.

biSizeImage

Specifies the size, in bytes, of the image. This may be set to 0 if the bitmap is not compressed.

biXPelsPerMeter

Specifies the horizontal resolution, in pixels per meter, of the target device for the bitmap. An application can use this value to select a bitmap from a resource group that best matches the characteristics of the current device.

biYPelsPerMeter

Specifies the vertical resolution, in pixels per meter, of the target device for the bitmap.

biClrUsed

Specifies the number of color indices in the color table that are actually used by the bitmap. If this value is zero, the bitmap uses the maximum number of colors corresponding to the value of the **biBitCount** member for the compression mode specified by **biCompression**.

If **biClrUsed** is nonzero and the **biBitCount** member is less than 16, the **biClrUsed** member specifies the actual number of colors the graphics engine or device driver accesses. If **biBitCount** is 16 or greater, then **biClrUsed** member specifies the size of the color table used to optimize performance of Windows color palettes. For **biBitCount** equal to 16 or 32 the optimal color palette starts immediately following the 3 DWORD masks.

If the bitmap is a packed bitmap (that is, a bitmap in which the bitmap array immediately follows the **BITMAPINFO** header and which is referenced by a single pointer), the **biClrUsed** member must be 0 or the actual size of the color table.

biClrImportant

Specifies the number of color indices that are considered important for displaying the bitmap. If this value is zero, all colors are important.

Comments

The **BITMAPINFO** data structure combines the **BITMAPINFOHEADER** structure and a color table to provide a complete definition of the dimensions and colors of a Windows DIB. For more information about Windows DIBs, see the description of the **BITMAPINFO** data structure.

An application should use the information stored in the **biSize** member to locate the color table in a **BITMAPINFO** structure, as follows:

```
pColor = ((LPSTR)pBitmapInfo +
    (WORD)(pBitmapInfo->bmiHeader.biSize));
```

Windows supports formats for compressing bitmaps that define their colors with 8 bits per pixel and with 4 bits per pixel. Compression reduces the disk and memory storage required for the bitmap. The following paragraphs describe these formats.

When the **biCompression** member is BI_RLE8, the bitmap is compressed by using a run-length encoding (RLE) format for an 8-bit bitmap. This format can be compressed in encoded or absolute modes. Both modes can occur anywhere in the same bitmap.

- Encoded mode consists of two bytes: the first byte specifies the number of consecutive pixels to be drawn using the color index contained in the second byte. In addition, the first byte of the pair can be set to zero to indicate an escape that denotes an end of line, end of bitmap, or delta. The interpretation of the escape depends on the value of the second byte of the pair. Following are the meanings of the second byte of the escape.

Value	Meaning
0	End of line.
1	End of bitmap.
2	Delta. The two bytes following the escape contain unsigned values indicating the horizontal and vertical offsets of the next pixel from the current position.

- In absolute mode, the first byte is zero and the second byte is a value in the range 03H through FFH. The second byte represents the number of bytes that follow, each of which contains the color index of a single pixel. When the second byte is 2 or less, the escape has the same meaning as in encoded mode. In absolute mode, each run must be aligned on a WORD boundary.

The following example shows the hexadecimal values of an 8-bit compressed bitmap.

```
03 04 05 06 00 03 45 56 67 00 02 78 00 02 05 01
02 78 00 00 09 1E 00 01
```

This bitmap would expand as follows (two-digit values represent a color index for a single pixel):

```
04 04 04
06 06 06 06 06
45 56 67
78 78
move current position 5 right and 1 down
78 78
end of line
1E 1E 1E 1E 1E 1E 1E 1E 1E
end of RLE bitmap
```

When the **biCompression** member is BI_RLE4, the bitmap is compressed by using a run-length encoding format for a 4-bit bitmap, which also uses encoded and absolute modes:

- In encoded mode, the first byte of the pair contains the number of pixels to be drawn using the color indices in the second byte. The second byte contains two color indices, one in its high-order nibble (that is, its high-order four bits) and one in its low-order nibble. The first of the pixels is drawn using the color specified by the high-order nibble, the second is drawn using the color in the low-order nibble, the third is drawn using the color in the high-order nibble, and so on, until all the pixels specified by the first byte have been drawn.

- In absolute mode, the first byte is zero, the second byte contains the number of color indices that follow, and subsequent bytes contain color indices in their high- and low-order four bits, one color index for each pixel. In absolute mode, each run must be aligned on a WORD boundary. The end-of-line, end-of-bitmap, and delta escapes also apply to BI_RLE4 compression.

  The following example shows the hexadecimal values of a 4-bit compressed bitmap.

```
03 04 05 06 00 06 45 56 67 00 04 78 00 02 05 01
04 78 00 00 09 1E 00 01
```

This bitmap would expand as follows (single-digit values represent a color index for a single pixel):

```
0 4 0
0 6 0 6 0
4 5 5 6 6 7
7 8 7 8
move current position 5 right and 1 down
7 8 7 8
end of line
1 E 1 E 1 E 1 E 1
end of RLE bitmap
```

See Also   **BITMAPINFO**

BY_HANDLE_FILE_INFORMATION   New

```
typedef struct _BY_HANDLE_FILE_INFORMATION { /* bhfi */
    DWORD    dwFileAttributes;
    FILETIME ftCreationTime;
    FILETIME ftLastAccessTime;
    FILETIME ftLastWriteTime;
    DWORD    dwVolumeSerialNumber;
    DWORD    nFileSizeHigh;
    DWORD    nFileSizeLow;
    DWORD    nNumberOfLinks;
    DWORD    nFileIndexHigh;
    DWORD    nFileIndexLow;
} BY_HANDLE_FILE_INFORMATION;
```

The **BY_HANDLE_FILE_INFORMATION** structure contains information retrieved by the **GetFileInformationByHandle** function.

Members   **dwFileAttributes**

Specifies the file's attributes. This member can be one or more of the following:

Value	Meaning
FILE_ATTRIBUTE_ARCHIVE	
	The file is an archive file. Applications use this flag to mark files for backup or removal.
FILE_ATTRIBUTE_DIRECTORY	
	The file is a directory.
FILE_ATTRIBUTE_HIDDEN	

The file is hidden. It is not included in an ordinary directory listing.

FILE_ATTRIBUTE_NORMAL

The file has no other attributes set. This attribute is valid only if used alone.

FILE_ATTRIBUTE_READONLY

The file is a read-only file. Applications can read the file but cannot write to it or delete it.

FILE_ATTRIBUTE_SYSTEM

The file is part of or is used exclusively by the operating system.

FILE_ATTRIBUTE_TEMPORARY

The file is a temporary file. Applications can write to the file only if absolutely necessary. Most of the file's data remains in memory without being flushed to the media because the file will soon be deleted.

FILE_ATTRIBUTE_ATOMIC_WRITE

The file is an atomic write file. Applications write to the file using atomic write semantics. If any write operation flushes data to the medium, all write operations up to that point are also flushed, as well as any file system structures. This ensures that the data is retrievable at a later time.

FILE_ATTRIBUTE_XACTION_WRITE

Reserved for future use. Do not specify.

ftCreationTime

Specifies the time the file was created. If the underlying file system does not support this time field, **ftCreationTime** is zero. The file allocation table (FAT) file system does not record file creation time, but the high-performance (HPFS) and New Technology (NTFS) file systems do.

ftLastAccessTime

Specifies the time the file was last accessed. If the underlying file system does not support this time field, **ftLastAccessTime** is zero. The FAT file system does not record last access time, but HPFS and NTFS do.

ftLastWriteTime

Specifies the last time the file was written to.

dwVolumeSerialNumber

Specifies the serial number of the volume that contains the file.

nFileSizeHigh

Specifies the high-order word of the file size.

nFileSizeLow

Specifies the low-order word of the file size.

nNumberOfLinks

Specifies the number of links to this file. For FAT and HPFS file systems, this member is always 1. For NTFS, it may be more than one.

nFileIndexHigh

Specifies the high order word of a unique identifier associated with the file.

nFileIndexLow

Specifies the low order word of a unique identifier associated with the file. This identifier and the volume serial number uniquely identify a file. This number may change when the system is restarted or when the file is opened. After a process opens a file, the identifier is constant until the file is closed. An application can use this identifier and the volume serial number to determine whether two handles refer to the same file.

See Also   **GetFileInformationByHandle**

CBT_CREATEWND   `Unicode`

```
typedef struct tagCBT_CREATEWND { /* cbtcw */
    LPCREATESTRUCT lpcs;
    HWND           hwndInsertAfter;
} CBT_CREATEWND;
```

The **CBT_CREATEWND** structure contains information passed to a WH_CBT hook procedure before a window is created.

Members   **lpcs**

Points to a **CREATESTRUCT** structure that contains initialization parameters for the window about to be created. The **CREATESTRUCT** structure has the following form:

```
typedef struct tagCREATESTRUCT { /* cs */
    LPVOID lpCreateParams;
    HANDLE hInstance;
    HMENU  hMenu;
    HWND   hwndParent;
    int    cy;
    int    cx;
    int    y;
    int    x;
    LONG   style;
    LPCSTR lpszName;
    LPCSTR lpszClass;
    DWORD  dwExStyle;
} CREATESTRUCT;
```

hwndInsertAfter
Identifies the window whose position in the Z order precedes that of the window being created.

See Also   **CBTProc**, **SetWindowsHookEx**

CBTACTIVATESTRUCT

```
typedef struct tagCBTACTIVATESTRUCT { /* cas */
    BOOL fMouse;
    HWND hWndActive;
} CBTACTIVATESTRUCT;
```

The **CBTACTIVATESTRUCT** structure contains information passed to a WH_CBT hook procedure before a window is activated.

Members   **fMouse**
Specifies whether the window is being activated as a result of a mouse click. This value is TRUE if a mouse click is causing the activation or FALSE if it is not.

hWndActive
Identifies the active window.

See Also   **SetWindowsHookEx**

CHAR_INFO

New

```
typedef struct _CHAR_INFO { /* chi */
    union {                  /* Unicode or ANSI character  */
        WCHAR UnicodeChar;
        CHAR AsciiChar;
    } Char;
    WORD Attributes;         /* text and background colors */
} CHAR_INFO, *PCHAR_INFO;
```

The **CHAR_INFO** structure specifies the Unicode or ANSI character and the foreground (text) and background color attributes of a screen buffer character cell. This structure is used by console functions to read from and write to a console screen buffer.

Members   **Char**
Specifies either the Unicode (wide-character) or ANSI character of a screen buffer character cell, depending on whether the Unicode or ANSI version of the function is used.

Attributes
Specifies the foreground (text) and background colors in which a screen buffer character cell is drawn.

See Also   **ReadConsoleOutput**, **ScrollConsoleScreenBuffer**, **WriteConsoleOutput**

CHARSET

```
typedef struct tagCHARSET { /* chst */
    DWORD aflBlock[3];
    DWORD flLang;
} CHARSET;
```

The **CHARSET** structure specifies the Unicode ™ blocks and the character sets supported by a given font.

Members   **aflBlock**
Specifies which (if any) of the 96 Unicode blocks are supported by a font. If the font contains at least one character in the given block, the corresponding bit is set.

flLang
Identifies the character set supported by the font. This member can be one of the following values:

Value	Meaning
CS_UGL	Supports the Universal Glyph List (UGL) character set.
CS_LATIN	Supports the Latin character set.
CS_GREEK	Supports the Greek character set.
CS_WIN30	Supports the Windows 3.0 character set.

Bits 0 and 31 of **flLang** are reserved and must be set to zero.

CHOOSECOLOR

```
typedef struct {    /* cc */
    DWORD           lStructSize;
    HWND            hwndOwner;
    HWND            hInstance;
    DWORD           rgbResult;
    LPDWORD         lpCustColors;
    DWORD           Flags;
    DWORD           lCustData;
    LPCCHOOKPROC    lpfnHook;
    LPCSTR          lpTemplateName;
} CHOOSECOLOR;
```

The **CHOOSECOLOR** structure contains information the operating system uses to initialize the system-defined Color dialog box. After the user closes the dialog box, the system returns information about the user's selection in this structure.

Members

lStructSize
Specifies the length, in bytes, of the structure.

hwndOwner
Identifies the window that owns the dialog box. This member can be any valid window handle, or NULL if the dialog box has no owner.

hInstance
Identifies a data block that contains the dialog box template specified by the **lpTemplateName** member. This member is used only if the **Flags** member specifies the CC_ENABLETEMPLATE flag; otherwise, this member is ignored.

rgbResult
Specifies the color initially selected when the dialog box is created, and contains the user's color selection when the dialog box is closed. When the dialog box is created, if the CC_RGBINIT flag is set in the **Flags** member and the value of this member is not among the colors available, the system selects the nearest solid color available. If this member is NULL, the color initially selected is black.

lpCustColors
Points to an array of 16 DWORDs that contain RGB values for the custom color boxes in the dialog box. If the user modifies these colors, the system updates the array with the new RGB values. An application should save these values for future calls to the **ChooseColor** function.

Flags
Specifies the dialog box initialization flags. This member may be a combination of the following values:

Value	Meaning
CC_ENABLEHOOK	Enables the hook function specified in the **lpfnHook** member.
CC_ENABLETEMPLATE	Causes the system to create the dialog box by using the dialog box template identified by the **hInstance** and **lpTemplateName** members.
CC_ENABLETEMPLATEHANDLE	Indicates that the **hInstance** member identifies a data block that contains a pre-loaded dialog box template. The system ignores the **lpTemplateName** member if this flag is specified.
CC_FULLOPEN	Causes the entire dialog box to appear when the dialog box is created, including the portion that allows the user to create custom colors. If this flag is not specified, the user must choose the Define Custom Color button to see this portion of the dialog box.
CC_PREVENTFULLOPEN	Disables the Define Custom Colors button, preventing the user from creating custom colors.
CC_RGBINIT	Causes the dialog box to use the color specified in the **rgbResult** member as the initial color selection.
CC_SHOWHELP	Causes the dialog box to show the Help button. The **hwndOwner** member must not be NULL if this option is specified.

lCustData

Specifies application-defined data the system passes to the hook function identified by the **lpfnHook** member. The system passes the data in the *lParam* parameter of the WM_INITDIALOG message.

lpfnHook

Points to a hook function that processes messages intended for the dialog box. An application must specify the CC_ENABLEHOOK flag in the **Flags** member to enable the function; otherwise, the system ignores this structure member. The hook function must return FALSE to pass a message to the standard color dialog box procedure, or TRUE to discard the message.

lpstrTemplateName

Points to a null-terminated string that names the dialog box template resource to be substituted for the standard dialog box template. An application can use the **MAKEINTRESOURCE** macro for numbered dialog box resources. This member is used only if the **Flags** member specifies the CC_ENABLETEMPLATE flag; otherwise, this member is ignored.

See Also   ChooseColor, WM_INITDIALOG

CHOOSEFONT

Unicode

```
typedef struct {    /* cf */
    DWORD          lStructSize;
    HWND           hwndOwner;
    HDC            hDC;
    LPLOGFONT      lpLogFont;
    INT            iPointSize;
    DWORD          Flags;
    DWORD          rgbColors;
    DWORD          lCustData;
    LPCFHOOKPROC   lpfnHook;
    LPCTSTR        lpTemplateName;
    HANDLE         hInstance;
    LPTSTR         lpszStyle;
    WORD           nFontType;
    WORD           ___MISSING_ALIGNMENT__;
    INT            nSizeMin;
    INT            nSizeMax;
} CHOOSEFONT;
```

The **CHOOSEFONT** structure contains information the operating system uses to initialize the system-defined Font dialog box. After the user closes the dialog box, the system returns information about the user's selection in this structure.

Members

lStructSize
Specifies the length, in bytes, of the structure.

hwndOwner
Identifies the window that owns the dialog box. This member can be any valid window handle, or NULL if the dialog box has no owner.

hDC
Identifies the device context (or information context) of the printer whose fonts will be listed in the dialog box. This member is used only if the **Flags** member specifies the CF_PRINTERFONTS flag; otherwise, this member is ignored.

lpLogFont
Points to a **LOGFONT** structure. If an application initializes the members of this structure before calling **ChooseFont** and also sets the CF_INITTOLOGFONTSTRUCT flag, the **ChooseFont** function initializes the dialog with a font that is the closest possible match. After the user closes the

dialog box, **ChooseFont** sets the members of the **LOGFONT** structure based on the user's final selection.

iPointSize

Specifies the size of the selected font in units of 1/10 of a point. **ChooseFont** sets this value after the user closes the dialog box.

Flags

Specifies the dialog box initialization flags. This member may be a combination of the following values:

Value	Meaning
CF_APPLY	Specifies that **ChooseFont** should enable the Apply button.
CF_ANSIONLY	Specifies that **ChooseFont** should allow only the selection of fonts using the Windows character set. (If this flag is set, the user will not be able to select a font that contains only symbols.)
CF_BOTH	Causes the dialog box to list the available printer and screen fonts. The **hDC** member identifies the device context (or information context) associated with the printer.
CF_TTONLY	Specifies that **ChooseFont** should enumerate only and allow the selection of TrueType fonts.
CF_EFFECTS	Specifies that **ChooseFont** should enable strikeout, underline, and color effects. If this flag is set, the **lfStrikOut**, **lfUnderline**, and **rgbColors** members can be set before calling **ChooseFont**, and **ChooseFont** can set these members after the user closes the dialog box.
CF_ENABLEHOOK	Enables the hook function specified in the **lpfnHook** member of this structure.
CF_ENABLETEMPLATE	Indicates that **hInstance** member identifies a data block that contains a dialog box template identified by **lpTemplateName**.
CF_ENABLETEMPLATEHANDLE	Indicates that **hInstance** member identifies a data block that contains a preloaded dialog box template. The system ignores the **lpTemplateName** member if this flag is specified.
CF_FIXEDPITCHONLY	Specifies **ChooseFont** should select only fixed-pitch fonts.

CF_FORCEFONTEXIST	Specifies that **ChooseFont** should indicate an error condition if the user attempts to select a font or style that does not exist.
CF_INITTOLOGFONTSTRUCT	Specifies that **ChooseFont** should use the LOGFONT structure pointed to by **lpLogFont** to initialize the dialog box controls.
CF_LIMITSIZE	Specifies that **ChooseFont** should select only font sizes within the range specified by the **nSizeMin** and **nSizeMax** members.
CF_NOOEMFONTS	See the CF_NOVECTORFONTS description.
CF_NOFACESEL	Specifies that **ChooseFont** should not allow font selections.
CF_NOSTYLESEL	Specifies that **ChooseFont** should not allow style selections.
CF_NOSIZESEL	Specifies that **ChooseFont**w should not allow size selections.
CF_NOSIMULATIONS	Specifies that **ChooseFont** should not allow graphics device interface (GDI) font simulations.
CF_NOVECTORFONTS	Specifies that **ChooseFont** should not allow vector-font selections.
CF_PRINTERFONTS	Causes the dialog box to list only the fonts supported by the printer associated with the device context (or information context) identified by the **hDC** member.
CF_SCALABLEONLY	Specifies that **ChooseFont** should allow only the selection of scalable fonts. (Scalable fonts include: vector fonts, scalable printer fonts, TrueType fonts, and fonts scaled by other algorithms or technologies.)
CF_SCREENFONTS	Causes the dialog box to list only the screen fonts supported by the system.
CF_SHOWHELP	Causes the dialog box to show the Help button. The **hwndOwner** member must not be NULL if this option is specified.

CF_USESTYLE	Specifies that **lpszStyle** member points to a buffer that contains style data that **ChooseFont** should use to initialize the Font Style selection. When the user closes the dialog box, **ChooseFont** copies style data for the user's selection to this buffer.
CF_WYSIWYG	Specifies that **ChooseFont** should allow only the selection of fonts available on both the printer and the display. If this flag is set, the CF_BOTH and CF_SCALABLEONLY flags should also be set.

rgbColors

If the CF_EFFECTS flag is set, this member contains an RGB value that **ChooseFont** should use to set the text color. After the user closes the dialog box, this member contains the RGB value of the color the user selected.

lCustData

Specifies application-defined data the application passes to the hook function.

lpfnHook

Points to a hook function that processes messages intended for the dialog box. An application must specify the CF_ENABLEHOOK flag in the **Flags** member to enable the function; otherwise, the system ignores this member. The hook function must return FALSE to pass a message to the standard dialog box procedure, or TRUE to discard the message.

lpTemplateName

Points to a null-terminated string that names the dialog box template resource to be substituted for the standard dialog box template. An application can use the **MAKEINTRESOURCE** macro for numbered dialog box resources. This member is used only if the **Flags** member specifies the CF_ENABLETEMPLATE flag; otherwise, this member is ignored.

hInstance

Identifies a data block that contains the dialog box template specified by the **lpstrTemplateName** member. This member is used only if the **Flags** member specifies the CF_ENABLETEMPLATE flag; otherwise, this member is ignored.

lpszStyle

Points to a buffer that contains style data. If the CF_USESTYLE flag is set, that **ChooseFont** uses the data in this buffer to initialize the style control. When the user closes the dialog box, that **ChooseFont** copies the string in the style control into this buffer.

nFontType

Specifies the type of the selected font. This member may contain one of the values in the following list:

Value	Meaning
SIMULATED_FONTTYPE	The font is simulated by graphics device interface (GDI).
PRINTER_FONTTYPE	The font is a printer font.
SCREEN_FONTTYPE	The font is a screen font.

nSizeMin

Specifies the minimum point size a user can select. **ChooseFont** recognizes this member only if the CF_LIMITSIZE flag is set.

nSizeMax

Specifies the maximum point size a user can select. **ChooseFont** recognizes this member only if the CF_LIMITSIZE flag is set.

See Also   **ChooseFont**

COLORADJUSTMENT

```
typedef struct  tagCOLORADJUSTMENT {    /* ca */
    WORD   caSize;
    WORD   caFlags;
    WORD   caIlluminantIndex;
    WORD   caRedGamma;
    WORD   caGreenGamma;
    WORD   caBlueGamma;
    WORD   caReferenceBlack;
    WORD   caReferenceWhite;
    SHORT  caContrast;
    SHORT  caBrightness;
    SHORT  caColorfulness;
    SHORT  caRedGreenTint;
} COLORADJUSTMENT;
```

The **COLORADJUSTMENT** structure defines the color adjustment values used by the **StretchBlt** and **StretchDIBits** functions when the stretchblt mode is HALFTONE.

Members   *caSize*

Specifies the size of the structure in bytes.

caFlags

Specifies how the output image should be prepared. This member may be set to NULL or any combination of the following values:

Value	Meaning
CA_NEGATIVE	Specifies that the negative of the original image should be displayed.
CA_LOG_FILTER	Specifies that a logarithmic function should be applied to the final density of the output colors. This will increase the color contrast when the luminance is low.

caIlluminantIndex
  Specifies the luminance of the light source under which the image object is viewed. This member may be set to one of the following values:

- ILLUMINANT_EQUAL_ENERGY

- ILLUMINANT_A

- ILLUMINANT_B

- ILLUMINANT_C

- ILLUMINANT_D50

- ILLUMINANT_D55

- ILLUMINANT_D65

- ILLUMINANT_D75

- ILLUMINANT_F2

- ILLUMINANT_TURNGSTEN

- ILLUMINANT_DAYLIGHT

- ILLUMINANT_FLUORESCENT

- ILLUMINANT_NTSC

caRedGamma
  Specifies the n-th power gamma-correction value for the red primary of the source colors. The value must be in the range from 2,500 to 65,000. A value of 10,000 means no gamma-correction.

caGreenGamma
  Specifies the n-th power gamma-correction value for the green primary of the source colors. The value must be in the range from 2,500 to 65,000. A value of 10,000 means no gamma-correction.

caBlueGamma
  Specifies the n-th power gamma-correction value for the blue primary of the source colors. The value must be in the range from 2,500 to 65,000. A value of 10,000 means no gamma-correction.

caReferenceBlack
  Specifies the black reference for the source colors. Any colors that are darker than this are treated as black. The value must be in the range from 0 to 4,000.

caReferenceWhite

Specifies the white reference for the source colors. Any colors that are lighter than this are treated as white. The value must be in the range from 6,000 to 10,000.

caContrast

Specifies the amount of contrast to be applied to the source object. The value must be in the range from -100 to 100. A value of 0 means no contrast adjustment.

caBrightness

Specifies the amount of brightness to be applied to the source object. The value must be in the range from -100 to 100. A value of 0 means no brightness adjustment.

caColorfulness

Specifies the amount of colorfulness to be applied to the source object. The value must be in the range from -100 to 100. A value of 0 means no colorfulness adjustment.

caRedGreenTint

Specifies the amount of red or green tint adjustment to be applied to the source object. The value must be in the range from -100 to 100. Positive numbers would adjust towards red and negative numbers adjust towards green. A 0 means no tint adjustment.

See Also   **SetStretchBltMode StretchBlt StretchDIBits**

CLIENTCREATESTRUCT

```
typedef struct tagCLIENTCREATESTRUCT { /* ccs */
    HANDLE hWindowMenu;
    UINT   idFirstChild;
} CLIENTCREATESTRUCT;
```

The **CLIENTCREATESTRUCT** structure contains information about the menu and first multiple document interface (MDI) child window of an MDI client window. An application passes a pointer to this structure as the *lpvParam* parameter of the **CreateWindow** function when creating an MDI client window.

Members   **hWindowMenu**

Identifies the handle of the MDI application's Window menu. An MDI application can retrieve this handle from the menu of the MDI frame window by using the **GetSubMenu** function.

idFirstChild

Specifies the child window identifier of the first MDI child window created. Windows increments the identifier for each additional MDI child window the application creates, and reassigns identifiers when the application destroys a window to keep the range of identifiers contiguous. These identifiers are used in WM_COMMAND messages sent to the application's MDI frame window when a child window is chosen from the Window menu; they should not conflict with any other command identifiers.

See Also   **CreateWindow**, **GetSubMenu**, **MDICREATESTRUCT**

COLORREF

The **COLORREF** value is a 32-bit value used to specify an RGB color.

Comments   When specifying an explicit RGB color, the **COLORREF** value has the following hexadecimal form:

```
0x00bbggrr
```

The low-order byte contains a value for the relative intensity of red; the second byte contains a value for green; and the third byte contains a value for blue. The high-order byte must be zero. The maximum value for a single byte is 0xFF.

See Also   **GetBValue**, **GetGValue**, **GetRValue**, **RGB**

COMMPROP

```
typedef struct _COMMPROP { /* cmmp */
    WORD   wPacketLength;       /* packet size, in bytes   */
    WORD   wPacketVersion;      /* packet version          */
    DWORD  dwServiceMask;       /* services implemented    */
    DWORD  dwReserved1;         /* reserved                */
    DWORD  dwMaxTxQueue;        /* max Tx bufsize, in bytes */
    DWORD  dwMaxRxQueue;        /* max Rx bufsize, in bytes */
    DWORD  dwMaxBaud;           /* max baud rate, in bps    */
    DWORD  dwProvSubType;       /* specific provider type   */
    DWORD  dwProvCapabilities;  /* capabilities supported   */
    DWORD  dwSettableParams;    /* changable parameters     */
    DWORD  dwSettableBaud;      /* allowable baud rates     */
    WORD   wSettableData;       /* allowable byte sizes     */
    WORD   wSettableStopParity; /* stop bits/parity allowed */
    DWORD  dwCurrentTxQueue;    /* Tx buffer size, in bytes */
    DWORD  dwCurrentRxQueue;    /* Rx buffer size, in bytes */
    DWORD  dwProvSpec1;         /* provider-specific data   */
    DWORD  dwProvSpec2;         /* provider-specific data   */
    WCHAR  wcProvChar[1];       /* provider-specific data   */
} COMMPROP;
```

The **COMMPROP** structure is used in the **GetCommProperties** function to return information about a given communications driver.

Members

wPacketLength

Specifies the size, in bytes, of the entire data packet, regardless of the amount of data requested.

wPacketVersion

Specifies the version of the structure.

dwServiceMask

Specifies a bitmask indicating which services are implemented by this provider. The SP_SERIALCOMM bit is always set for communications providers.

dwReserved1

Reserved; do not use.

dwMaxTxQueue

Specifies the maximum size, in bytes, of the driver's internal output buffer. A value of zero indicates that no maximum value is imposed by the serial provider. See the Comments section below for further discussion of a zero value.

dwMaxRxQueue

Specifies the maximum size, in bytes, of the driver's internal input buffer. A value of zero indicates that no maximum value is imposed by the serial provider. See the Comments section below for further discussion of a zero value.

dwMaxBaud

Specifies the maximum allowable baud rate, in bits per second (bps). This member can be one of the following values:

Value	Meaning
BAUD_075	75 bps
BAUD_110	110 bps
BAUD_134_5	134.5 bps
BAUD_150	150 bps
BAUD_300	300 bps
BAUD_600	600 bps
BAUD_1200	1200 bps
BAUD_1800	1800 bps
BAUD_2400	2400 bps
BAUD_4800	4800 bps
BAUD_7200	7200 bps
BAUD_9600	9600 bps
BAUD_14400	14400 bps
BAUD_19200	19200 bps
BAUD_38400	38400 bps
BAUD_56K	56K bps
BAUD_128K	128K bps
BAUD_USER	Programmable baud rates available

dwProvSubType

Specifies the specific communications provider type.

Value	Meaning
PST_UNSPECIFIED	Unspecified
PST_RS232	RS-232 serial port
PST_PARALLELPORT	Parallel port
PST_RS422	RS-422 port
PST_RS423	RS-423 port
PST_RS449	RS-449 port
PST_FAX	Fax device

PST_SCANNER	Scanner device
PST_NETWORK_BRIDGE	Unspecified network bridge
PST_LAT	LAT protocol
PST_TCPIP_TELNET	TCP/IP Telnet protocol
PST_X25	X.25 standards

dwProvCapabilities

Specifies a bitmask indicating the capabilities offered by the provider. This member can be one of the following values:

Flag	Meaning
PCF_DTRDSR	DTR (data-terminal-ready)/DSR (data-set-ready) supported
PCF_RTSCTS	RTS (request-to-send)/CTS (clear-to-send) supported
PCF_RLSD	RLSD (receive-line-signal-detect supported)
PCF_PARITY_CHECK	Parity checking supported
PCF_XONXOFF	XON/XOFF flow control supported
PCF_SETXCHAR	Settable XON/XOFF supported
PCF_TOTALTIMEOUTS	Total (elapsed) timeouts supported
PCF_INTTIMEOUTS	Interval timeouts supported
PCF_SPECIALCHARS	Special character support provided
PCF_16BITMODE	Special 16-bit mode supported

dwSettableParams

Specifies a bitmask indicating the communications parameter that can be changed. This member can be one of the following values:

Flag	Meaning
SP_PARITY	Parity
SP_BAUD	Baud rate
SP_DATABITS	Data bits
SP_STOPBITS	Stop bits
SP_HANDSHAKING	Handshaking (flow control)
SP_PARITY_CHECK	Parity checking
SP_RLSD	RLSD (receive-line-signal-detect)

dwSettableBaud

Specifies a bitmask indicating the baud rates that can be set. For values, see the **dwMaxBaud** member.

wSettableData

Specifies a bitmask indicating the number of data bits that can be set. This member can be one of the following values:

Flag	Meaning
DATABITS_5	5 data bits
DATABITS_6	6 data bits
DATABITS_7	7 data bits
DATABITS_8	8 data bits
DATABITS_16	Special wide path through serial hardware lines

wSettableStopParity

Specifies a bitmask indicating the stop bit and parity settings that can be selected. This member can be one of the following values:

Flag	Meaning
STOPBITS_10	1 stop bit
STOPBITS_15	1.5 stop bits
STOPBITS_20	2 stop bits
PARITY_NONE	No parity
PARITY_ODD	Odd parity
PARITY_EVEN	Even parity
PARITY_MARK	Mark parity
PARITY_SPACE	Space parity

dwCurrentTxQueue

Specifies the size, in bytes, of the driver's internal output buffer. A value of zero indicates that the value is unavailable.

dwCurrentRxQueue

Specifies the size, in bytes, of the driver's internal input buffer. A value of zero indicates that the value is unavailable.

dwProvSpec1

Specifies provider-specific data. Applications should ignore this member unless they have detailed information about the format of the data required by the provider.

dwProvSpec2

Specifies provider-specific data. Applications should ignore this member unless they have detailed information about the format of the data required by the provider.

wcProvChar
> Specifies provider-specific data. Applications should ignore this member unless they have detailed information about the format of the data required by the provider.

Comments
> A zero value for **dwMaxTxQueue** and **dwMaxRxQueue** indicates that no maximum value is imposed by the serial provider. What does this really mean ? In the case of the transmit buffer, for example, it means that the serial driver is using a buffer provided as a parameter by a caller of the **WriteFile** function. The serial buffer doesn't have its own separate write buffer in such a situation, and no maximum values can be imposed on a non-existent entity.

See Also
> **GetCommProperties**

COMMTIMEOUTS

```
typedef struct _COMMTIMEOUTS { /* ctmo */
    DWORD ReadIntervalTimeout;
    DWORD ReadTotalTimeoutMultiplier;
    DWORD ReadTotalTimeoutConstant;
    DWORD WriteTotalTimeoutMultiplier;
    DWORD WriteTotalTimeoutConstant;
} COMMTIMEOUTS,*LPCOMMTIMEOUTS;
```

> The **COMMTIMEOUTS** structure is used in the **SetCommTimeouts** and **GetCommTimeouts** functions to set and query the timeout parameters for a communications device. The parameters determine the behavior of **ReadFile**, **WriteFile**, **ReadFileEx**, and **WriteFileEx** operations on the device.

Members
> **ReadIntervalTimeout**
> > Specifies the maximum time, in milliseconds, allowed to elapse between the arrival of two characters on the communications line. During a **ReadFile** operation, the time period begins when the first character is received. If the interval between the arrival of any two characters exceeds this amount, the **ReadFile** operation is completed and any buffered data is returned. A value of zero indicates that interval timeouts are not used.
> >
> > A value of MAXDWORD, combined with zero values for both the **ReadTotalTimeoutConstant** and **ReadTotalTimeoutMultiplier** members, specifies that the read operation is to return immediately with the characters that have already been received, even if no characters have been received.

> **ReadTotalTimeoutMultiplier**
> > Specifies the multiplier, in milliseconds, used to calculate the total timeout period for read operations. For each read operation, this value is multiplied by the requested number of bytes to read.

ReadTotalTimeoutConstant

Specifies the constant, in milliseconds, used to calculate the total timeout period for read operations. For each read operation, this value is added to the product of the **ReadTotalTimeoutMultiplier** member and the requested number of bytes.

A value of zero for both the **ReadTotalTimeoutMultiplier** and **ReadTotalTimeoutConstant** members indicates that total timeouts are not used for read operations.

WriteTotalTimeoutMultiplier

Specifies the multiplier, in milliseconds, used to calculate the total timeout period for write operations. For each write operation, this value is multiplied by the number of bytes to be written.

WriteTotalTimeoutConstant

Specifies the constant, in milliseconds, used to calculate the total timeout period for write operations. For each write operation, this value is added to the product of the **WriteTotalTimeoutMultiplier** member and the number of bytes to be written.

A value of zero for both the **WriteTotalTimeoutMultiplier** and **WriteTotalTimeoutConstant** members indicates that total timeouts are not used for write operations.

See Also   **GetCommTimeouts**, **SetCommTimeouts**

COMPAREITEMSTRUCT

```
typedef struct tagCOMPAREITEMSTRUCT { /* cis */
    UINT  CtlType;
    UINT  CtlID;
    HWND  hwndItem;
    UINT  itemID1;
    DWORD itemData1;
    UINT  itemID2;
    DWORD itemData2;
} COMPAREITEMSTRUCT;
```

The **COMPAREITEMSTRUCT** structure supplies the identifiers and application-supplied data for two items in a sorted owner-draw list box or combo box.

Whenever an application adds a new item to an owner-drawn list box or combo box created with the CBS_SORT or LBS_SORT style, Windows sends the owner a WM_COMPAREITEM message. The *lParam* parameter of the message contains a long pointer to a **COMPAREITEMSTRUCT** structure. Upon receiving the message, the owner compares the two items and returns a value indicating which item sorts before the other.

Members   **CtlType**

Specifies ODT_LISTBOX (an owner-drawn list box) or ODT_COMBOBOX (an owner-drawn combo box).

CtlID

Specifies the identifier of the list box or combo box.

hwndItem

Identifies the control.

itemID1

Specifies the index of the first item in the list box or combo box being compared.

itemData1

Specifies application-supplied data for the first item being compared. (This value was passed as the *lParam* parameter of the message that added the item to the list box or combo box.)

itemID2

Specifies the index of the second item in the list box or combo box being compared.

itemData2

Specifies application-supplied data for the second item being compared. This value was passed as the *lParam* parameter of the message that added the item to the list box or combo box.

See Also   WM_COMPAREITEM

COMSTAT

```
typedef struct _COMSTAT { /* cst */
    DWORD fCtsHold : 1;    /* Tx waiting for CTS signal    */
    DWORD fDsrHold : 1;    /* Tx waiting for DSR signal    */
    DWORD fRlsdHold : 1;   /* Tx waiting for RLSD signal   */
    DWORD fXoffHold : 1;   /* Tx waiting, XOFF char rec'd  */
    DWORD fXoffSent : 1;   /* Tx waiting, XOFF char sent   */
    DWORD fEof : 1;        /* EOF character sent           */
    DWORD fTxim : 1;       /* character waiting for Tx     */
    DWORD fReserved : 25;  /* reserved                     */
    DWORD cbInQue;         /* bytes in input buffer        */
    DWORD cbOutQue;        /* bytes in output buffer       */
} COMSTAT, *LPCOMSTAT;
```

The **COMSTAT** structure contains information about a communications device. This structure is filled in by the **ClearCommError** function.

Members

fCtsHold

Specifies whether transmission is waiting for the CTS (clear-to-send) signal to be sent. If this member is TRUE, transmission is waiting.

fDsrHold

Specifies whether transmission is waiting for the DSR (data-set-ready) signal to be sent. If this member is TRUE, transmission is waiting.

fRlsdHold

Specifies whether transmission is waiting for the RLSD (receive-line-signal-detect) signal to be sent. If this member is TRUE, transmission is waiting.

fXoffHold

Specifies whether transmission is waiting because the XOFF character was received. If this member is TRUE, transmission is waiting.

fXoffSent

Specifies whether transmission is waiting because the XOFF character was transmitted. If this member is TRUE, transmission is waiting. Transmission halts when the XOFF character is transmitted to a system that takes the next character as XON, regardless of the actual character.

fEof

Specifies whether the EOF character has been received. If this member is TRUE, the EOF character has been received.

fTxim

Specifies whether a character is waiting to be transmitted. If this member is TRUE, a character is waiting to be transmitted.

fReserved

Reserved; do not use.

cbInQue

Specifies the number of bytes received by the serial provider but not yet read by a **ReadFile** operation.

cbOutQue

Specifies the number of bytes of user data remaining to be transmitted for all write operations. This value will be 0 when doing a non-overlapped write.

See Also

ClearCommError

CONSOLE_CURSOR_INFO

New

```
typedef struct _CONSOLE_CURSOR_INFO { /* cci */
    DWORD  dwSize;
    BOOL   bVisible;
} CONSOLE_CURSOR_INFO, *PCONSOLE_CURSOR_INFO;
```

The **CONSOLE_CURSOR_INFO** structure contains information about the console cursor.

Members

dwSize
Specifies a number between 1 and 100, indicating the percentage of the character cell that is filled by the cursor. The cursor appearance varies, ranging from completely filling the cell to showing up as a horizontal line at the bottom of the cell.

bVisible
Specifies the visibility of the cursor. If the cursor is visible, this member is TRUE.

See Also   **GetConsoleCursorInfo, SetConsoleCursorInfo**

CONSOLE_SCREEN_BUFFER_INFO

New

```
typedef struct _CONSOLE_SCREEN_BUFFER_INFO { /* csbi */
    COORD       dwSize;
    COORD       dwCursorPosition;
    WORD        wAttributes;
    SMALL_RECT  srWindow;
    COORD       dwMaximumWindowSize;
} CONSOLE_SCREEN_BUFFER_INFO ;
```

The **CONSOLE_SCREEN_BUFFER_INFO** structure contains information about a console screen buffer.

Members

dwSize
Specifies the size, in character columns and rows, of the screen buffer.

dwCursorPosition
Specifies the column and row coordinates of the cursor in the screen buffer.

wAttributes
Specifies the foreground (text) and background color attributes to be used for characters that are written to a screen buffer by the **WriteFile** and **WriteConsole** functions, or echoed to a screen buffer by the **ReadFile** and

ReadConsole functions. The attribute values are some combination of the following values: FOREGROUND_BLUE, FOREGROUND_GREEN, FOREGROUND_RED, FOREGROUND_INTENSITY, BACKGROUND_BLUE, BACKGROUND_GREEN, BACKGROUND_RED, and BACKGROUND_INTENSITY. For example, the following combination of values produces red text on a white background.

```
FOREGROUND_RED | BACKGROUND_RED | BACKGROUND_GREEN | BACKGROUND_BLUE
```

srWindow

Specifies a **SMALL_RECT** structure that contains the screen buffer coordinates of the upper left and lower right corners of the display window. The **SMALL_RECT** structure has the following form:

```
typedef struct _SMALL_RECT { /* srct */
    SHORT Left;
    SHORT Top;
    SHORT Right;
    SHORT Bottom;
} SMALL_RECT;
```

dwMaximumWindowSize

Specifies the maximum size of the console window, given the current screen buffer size and font and the screen size.

See Also   **GetConsoleScreenBufferInfo**

CONTEXT

New

The **CONTEXT** structure contains processor-specific register data. Currently, there is a **CONTEXT** structure for Intel ® processors and one for MIPS ® processors. This structure is defined in the header file.

CONVCONTEXT

```
typedef struct tagCONVCONTEXT {    /* cc */
    UINT  cb;
    UINT  wFlags;
    UINT  wCountryID;
    int   iCodePage;
    DWORD dwLangID;
    DWORD dwSecurity;
    SECURITY_QUALITY_OF_SERVICE qos;  /* client side's quality of service */
} CONVCONTEXT;
```

The **CONVCONTEXT** structure contains information supplied by a dynamic data exchange (DDE) client application. The information is useful for specialized or cross-language DDE conversations.

Members

cb

Specifies the size, in bytes, of the structure.

wFlags

Specifies conversation context flags. Currently, no flags are defined for this member.

wCountryID

Specifies the country-code identifier for topic-name and item-name strings.

iCodePage

Specifies the code page for topic-name and item-name strings. Non-multilingual clients should set this member to CP_WINANSI. Unicode clients should set this value to CP_WINUNICODE.

dwLangID

Specifies the language identifier for topic-name and item-name strings.

dwSecurity

Specifies a private (application-defined) security code.

qos

Specifies the quality of service a DDE client wants from the system during a given conversation. The quality of service level specified lasts for the duration of the conversation. It cannot be changed once the conversation is started.

CONVINFO

```
typedef struct tagCONVINFO {  /* ci */
    DWORD       cb;
    DWORD       hUser;
    HCONV       hConvPartner;
    HSZ         hszSvcPartner;
    HSZ         hszServiceReq;
    HSZ         hszTopic;
    HSZ         hszItem;
    UINT        wFmt;
    UINT        wType;
    UINT        wStatus;
    UINT        wConvst;
    UINT        wLastError;
    HCONVLIST   hConvList;
    CONVCONTEXT ConvCtxt;
    HWND        hwnd;
    HWND        hwndPartner;
} CONVINFO;
```

The **CONVINFO** structure contains information about a dynamic data exchange (DDE) conversation.

Members

cb

Specifies the length, in bytes, of the structure.

hUser

Identifies application-defined data.

hConvPartner

Identifies the partner application in the DDE conversation. This member is set to zero if the partner has not registered itself (using the **DdeInitialize** function) to make DDE Management Library (DDEML) function calls. An application should not pass this member to any DDEML function except **DdeQueryConvInfo**.

hszSvcPartner

Identifies the service name of the partner application.

hszServiceReq

Identifies the service name of the server application that was requested for connection.

hszTopic

Identifies the name of the requested topic.

hszItem

Identifies the name of the requested item. This member is transaction specific.

wFmt

Specifies the format of the data being exchanged. This member is transaction specific.

wType

Specifies the type of the current transaction. This member is transaction specific; it can be one of the following values:

Value	Meaning
XTYP_ADVDATA	Informs a client that advise data from a server has arrived.
XTYP_ADVREQ	Requests a server send updated data to the client during an advise loop. This transaction results when the server calls the **DdePostAdvise** function.
XTYP_ADVSTART	Requests a server begin an advise loop with a client.
XTYP_ADVSTOP	Notifies a server an advise loop is stopping.
XTYP_CONNECT	Requests a server establish a conversation with a client.
XTYP_CONNECT_CONFIRM	Notifies a server a conversation with a client has been established.
XTYP_DISCONNECT	Notifies a server a conversation has terminated.
XTYP_EXECUTE	Requests a server execute a command sent by a client.
XTYP_MONITOR	Notifies an application registered as APPCMD_MONITOR that DDE data is being transmitted.
XTYP_POKE	Requests a server accept unsolicited data from a client.
XTYP_REGISTER	Notifies other DDEML applications that a server has registered a service name.
XTYP_REQUEST	Requests a server send data to a client.
XTYP_UNREGISTER	Notifies other DDEML applications that a server has unregistered a service name.
XTYP_WILDCONNECT	Requests a server establish multiple conversations with the same client.
XTYP_XACT_COMPLETE	Notifies a client that an asynchronous data transaction has been completed.

wStatus

Specifies the status of the current conversation. This member can be a combination of the following values:

Value	Meaning
ST_ADVISE	One or more links are in progress.
ST_BLOCKED	The conversation is blocked.
ST_BLOCKNEXT	The conversation will block after calling the next callback.
ST_CLIENT	The conversation handle passed to the **DdeQueryConvInfo** function is a client-side handle. If the handle is zero, the conversation handle passed to the **DdeQueryConvInfo** function is a server-side handle.
ST_CONNECTED	The conversation is connected.
ST_INLIST	The conversation is a member of a conversation list.
ST_ISLOCAL	Both sides of the conversation are using the DDEML.
ST_ISSELF	Both sides of the conversation are using the same instance of the DDEML.
ST_TERMINATED	The conversation has been terminated by the partner.

wConvst

Specifies the conversation state. This member can be one of the following values:

Value	Meaning
XST_ADVACKRCVD	The advise transaction has just been completed.
XST_ADVDATAACKRCVD	The advise data transaction has just been completed.
XST_ADVDATASENT	Advise data has been sent and is awaiting an acknowledgement.
XST_ADVSENT	An advise transaction is awaiting an acknowledgement.
XST_CONNECTED	The conversation has no active transactions.
XST_DATARCVD	The requested data has just been received.
XST_EXECACKRCVD	An execute transaction has just been completed.
XST_EXECSENT	An execute transaction is awaiting an acknowledgement.
XST_INCOMPLETE	The last transaction failed.
XST_INIT1	Mid-initiate state 1.
XST_INIT2	Mid-initiate state 2.
XST_NULL	Pre-initiate state.
XST_POKEACKRCVD	A poke transaction has just been completed.
XST_POKESENT	A poke transaction is awaiting an acknowledgement.

XST_REQSENT	A request transaction is awaiting an acknowledgement.
XST_UNADVACKRCVD	An unadvise transaction has just been completed.
XST_UNADVSENT	An unadvise transaction is awaiting an acknowledgement.

wLastError
Specifies the error value associated with the last transaction.

hConvList
Identifies the conversation list if the handle of the current conversation is in a conversation list. This member is NULL if the conversation is not in a conversation list.

ConvCtxt
Specifies the conversation context.

hwnd
Identifies the window of the calling application involved in the conversation.

hwndPartner
Identifies the window of the partner application involved in the current conversation.

See Also   **CONVCONTEXT**

COORD

New

```
typedef struct _COORD { /* coord. */
    SHORT X;    /* horizontal coordinate   */
    SHORT Y;    /* vertical coordinate     */
} COORD;
```

The **COORD** structure defines the coordinates of a character cell in a console screen buffer. The origin of the coordinate system (0,0) is at the top, left cell of the buffer.

Members   **X**
Horizontal or column value.

Y
Vertical or row value.

COPYDATASTRUCT

New

```
typedef struct tagCOPYDATASTRUCT {   /* cds */
    DWORD dwData;
    DWORD cbData;
    PVOID lpData;
} COPYDATASTRUCT;
```

The **COPYDATASTRUCT** structure contains data to be passed to another application by the WM_COPYDATA message.

Members

dwData
Specifies up to 32 bits of data to be passed to the receiving application.

cbData
Specifies the size, in bytes, of the data pointed to by the **lpData** member.

lpData
Points to data to be passed to the receiving application. This member can be NULL.

See Also   WM_COPYDATA

CPINFO

New

```
struct tagCPINFO {
    UINT MaxCharSize;
    BYTE DefaultChar[MAX_DEFAULTCHAR];
    BYTE LeadByte[MAX_LEADBYTES];
} CPINFO;
```

The **CPINFO** structure contains information about a code page.

Members

MaxCharSize
Specifies the maximum length, in bytes, of a character in this code page.

DefaultChar
Specifies the default character used in translations into this code page as determined by the translation options specified in the **WideCharToMultiByte** function.

LeadByte
Specifies lead-byte ranges in a variable-length array. If there are no lead bytes in this code page, every element of the array is NULL. If there are lead bytes, a

starting value and an ending value are given for each range. Ranges are inclusive.

Comments   Lead bytes are unique to double-byte character sets. A lead byte introduces a double-byte character. Lead bytes occupy a specific range of byte values.

The maximum number of lead-byte ranges for any code page is 5. Each range requires 2 bytes to describe, plus a double-byte terminating null character. Therefore, a value of 12 for the **LeadByte** member designates 5 lead-byte ranges.

See Also   **GetCPInfo**, **WideCharToMultiByte**

CPLINFO

```
typedef struct tagCPLINFO { /* cpli */
    int  idIcon;
    int  idName;
    int  idInfo;
    LONG lData;
} CPLINFO;
```

The **CPLINFO** structure contains resource information and a user-defined value for a Control Panel application.

Members   **idIcon**
Specifies an icon resource identifier for the application icon. This icon is displayed in the Control Panel window.

idName
Specifies a string resource identifier for the application name. The name is the short string displayed below the application icon in the Control Panel window. The name is also displayed in the Settings menu of Control Panel.

idInfo
Specifies a string resource identifier for the application description. The description is the descriptive string displayed at the bottom of the Control Panel window when the application icon is selected.

lData
Specifies user-defined data for the application.

See Also   CPL_INQUIRE, **NEWCPLINFO**

CREATE_PROCESS_DEBUG_INFO

New

```
typedef struct _CREATE_PROCESS_DEBUG_INFO { /* cpdi */
    HANDLE hFile;
    HANDLE hProcess;
    HANDLE hThread;
    LPVOID lpBaseOfImage;
    DWORD dwDebugInfoFileOffset;
    DWORD nDebugInfoSize;
    LPVOID lpThreadLocalBase;
    LPTHREAD_START_ROUTINE lpStartAddress;
    LPVOID lpImageName;
    WORD fUnicode;
} CREATE_PROCESS_DEBUG_INFO;
```

The **CREATE_PROCESS_DEBUG_INFO** structure contains process creation information that can be used by a debugger.

Members

hFile

Identifies an open handle of the process's image file. If **hFile** is NULL, the handle is not valid. Otherwise, the debugger can use **hFile** to read from and write to the image file.

hProcess

Identifies an open handle of the process. If **hProcess** is NULL, the handle is not valid. Otherwise, the debugger can use **hProcess** to read from and write to the process's memory.

hThread

Identifies an open handle of the initial thread of the process identified by the **hProcess** member. If **hThread** is NULL, the handle is not valid. Otherwise, the debugger has THREAD_GET_CONTEXT, THREAD_SET_CONTEXT, and THREAD_SUSPEND_RESUME access to the thread. This allows the debugger to read from and write to the registers of the thread and control execution of the thread.

lpBaseOfImage

Points to the base address of the executable image that the process is running.

dwDebugInfoFileOffset

Specifies the offset to the debugging information in the file identified by the **hFile** member. The kernel expects the debugging information to be in Microsoft ® CodeView ® version 4.0 format. This format is currently a derivative of COFF (Common Object File Format).

nDebugInfoSize

Specifies the size, in bytes, of the debugging information in the file. If this value is zero, there is no debugging information.

lpThreadLocalBase

Specifies the base address of a per-thread data block. At offset 0x2C within this block there exists an array of **LPVOID**s. There is one **LPVOID** for each DLL/EXE loaded at process initialization, and that **LPVOID** points to thread local storage. This gives a debugger access to per-thread data in its debuggee's threads using the same algorithms that a compiler would use.

lpStartAddress

Points to the starting address of the thread. This value may only be an approximation of the thread's starting address, because any application with appropriate access to the thread can change the thread's context by using the **SetThreadContext** function.

lpImageName

Provides an optional pointer to the file name associated with the *hFile* parameter. The **lpImageName** parameter may be NULL, or may contain the address of a string pointer in the debuggee's address space. That address may in turn either be NULL, or point to the actual file name. If **fUnicode** is a non-zero value, the name string is Unicode; otherwise it is ANSI.

This parameter is strictly optional. Debuggers must be prepared to handle the case where **lpImageName** is NULL, OR *lpImageName (in the debuggee's address space) is NULL. Specifically, this release of Windows NT will never provide an image name for a create process event, and will not likely pass an image name for the first DLL event. This version of Windows NT will also never provide this information in the case of debug events that originate from a call to the **DebugActiveProcess** function.

fUnicode

Indicates whether a file name specified by **lpImageName** is Unicode or ANSI. A non-zero value indicates Unicode; zero indicates ANSI.

See Also   **CREATE_THREAD_DEBUG_INFO, DEBUG_EVENT, LOAD_DLL_DEBUG_INFO**

CREATE_THREAD_DEBUG_INFO

`New`

```
typedef struct _CREATE_THREAD_DEBUG_INFO { /* ctdi */
    HANDLE hThread;
    LPVOID lpThreadLocalBase;
    LPTHREAD_START_ROUTINE lpStartAddress;
} CREATE_THREAD_DEBUG_INFO;
```

The **CREATE_THREAD_DEBUG_INFO** structure contains thread-creation information that can be used by a debugger.

Members

hThread

Identifies a handle of the thread whose creation caused the debugging event. If **hThread** is NULL, the handle is not valid. Otherwise, the debugger has THREAD_GET_CONTEXT, THREAD_SET_CONTEXT, and THREAD_SUSPEND_RESUME access to the thread. This allows the debugger to read from and write to the registers of the thread and control execution of the thread.

lpThreadLocalBase

Specifies the base address of a per-thread data block. At offset 0x2C within this block there exists an array of **LPVOID**s. There is one **LPVOID** for each DLL/EXE loaded at process initialization, and that **LPVOID** points to thread local storage. This gives a debugger access to per-thread data in its debuggee's threads using the same algorithms that a compiler would use.

lpStartAddress

Points to the starting address of the thread. This value may only be an approximation of the thread's starting address, because any application with appropriate access to the thread can change the thread's context by using the **SetThreadContext** function.

See Also

CREATE_PROCESS_DEBUG_INFO, DEBUG_EVENT, LOAD_DLL_DEBUG_INFO

CREATESTRUCT

```
typedef struct tagCREATESTRUCT { /* cs */
    LPVOID lpCreateParams;
    HANDLE hInstance;
    HMENU  hMenu;
    HWND   hwndParent;
    int    cy;
    int    cx;
    int    y;
    int    x;
    LONG   style;
    LPCSTR lpszName;
    LPCSTR lpszClass;
    DWORD  dwExStyle;
} CREATESTRUCT;
```

The **CREATESTRUCT** structure defines the initialization parameters passed to the window procedure of an application.

Members

lpCreateParams

Points to data to be used for creating the window.

hInstance

Identifies the module that owns the new window.

hMenu

Identifies the menu to be used by the new window.

hwndParent

Identifies the parent window, if the window is a child window. If the window is owned, this member identifies the owner window. If the window is not a child or owned window, this member is NULL.

cy

Specifies the height of the new window, in pixels.

cx

Specifies the width of the new window, in pixels.

y

Specifies the y-coordinate of the upper-left corner of the new window. If the new window is a child window, coordinates are relative to the parent window. Otherwise, the coordinates are relative to the screen origin.

x

Specifies the x-coordinate of the upper-left corner of the new window. If the new window is a child window, coordinates are relative to the parent window. Otherwise, the coordinates are relative to the screen origin.

style

Specifies the style for the new window.

lpszName

Points to a null-terminated string that specifies the name of the new window.

lpszClass

Points to a null-terminated string that specifies the class name of the new window.

dwExStyle

Specifies the extended style for the new window.

See Also   **CreateWindow, CreateWindowEx**

CWPSTRUCT

New

```
typedef struct tagCWPSTRUCT { /* cwps */
    LPARAM lParam;
    WPARAM wParam;
    DWORD  message;
    HWND   hwnd;
} CWPSTRUCT;
```

The **CWPSTRUCT** structure defines the message parameters passed to a WH_CALLWNDPROC hook procedure.

Members

lParam

Specifies additional information about the message. The exact meaning depends on the **message** value.

wParam

Specifies additional information about the message. The exact meaning depends on the **message** value.

message

Specifies the message.

hwnd

Identifies the window to receive the message.

See Also

SetWindowsHook, **SetWindowsHookEx**

DCB

```
typedef struct _DCB { /* dcb */
    DWORD DCBlength;              /* sizeof(DCB)                  */
    DWORD BaudRate;              /* current baud rate            */
    DWORD fBinary: 1;            /* binary mode, no EOF check    */
    DWORD fParity: 1;            /* enable parity checking       */
    DWORD fOutxCtsFlow:1;        /* CTS output flow control      */
    DWORD fOutxDsrFlow:1;        /* DSR output flow control      */
    DWORD fDtrControl:2;         /* DTR flow control type        */
    DWORD fDsrSensitivity:1;     /* DSR sensitivity              */
    DWORD fTXContinueOnXoff:1;   /* XOFF continues Tx            */
    DWORD fOutX: 1;              /* XON/XOFF out flow control    */
    DWORD fInX: 1;               /* XON/XOFF in flow control     */
    DWORD fErrorChar: 1;         /* enable error replacement     */
    DWORD fNull: 1;              /* enable null stripping        */
    DWORD fRtsControl:2;         /* RTS flow control             */
    DWORD fAbortOnError:1;       /* abort reads/writes on error  */
    DWORD fDummy2:17;            /* reserved                     */
    WORD wReserved;              /* not currently used           */
    WORD XonLim;                 /* transmit XON threshold       */
    WORD XoffLim;                /* transmit XOFF threshold      */
    BYTE ByteSize;               /* number of bits/byte, 4-8     */
    BYTE Parity;                 /* 0-4=no,odd,even,mark,space   */
    BYTE StopBits;               /* 0,1,2 = 1, 1.5, 2            */
    char XonChar;                /* Tx and Rx XON character      */
    char XoffChar;               /* Tx and Rx XOFF character     */
    char ErrorChar;              /* error replacement character  */
```

```
    char EofChar;          /* end of input character      */
    char EvtChar;          /* received event character    */
} DCB;
```

The **DCB** structure defines the control setting for a serial communications device.

Members

DCBlength

Specifies the length, in bytes, of the **DCB** structure.

BaudRate

Specifies the baud rate at which the communications device operates.

fBinary

Specifies whether binary mode is enabled. Windows NT does not support non-binary mode transfers, so this member should be set TRUE. Trying to set it to FALSE, under Windows NT, will not work.

Under Windows 3.1, if this member is FALSE, non-binary mode is enabled, and the character specified by the **EofChar** member is recognized on input and remembered as the end of data.

fParity

Specifies whether parity checking is enabled. If this member is TRUE, parity checking is performed and errors are reported.

fOutxCtsFlow

Specifies whether the CTS (clear-to-send) signal is monitored for output flow control. If this member is TRUE, when CTS is turned off, output is suspended until CTS is sent again.

fOutxDsrFlow

Specifies whether the DSR (data-set-ready) signal is monitored for output flow control. If this member is TRUE, when DSR is turned off, output is suspended until DSR is sent again.

fDtrControl

Specifies the DTR (data-terminal-ready) flow control. This member can be one of the following values:

Value	Description
DTR_CONTROL_DISABLE	

Disables the DTR line on device open and leaves it disabled.

DTR_CONTROL_ENABLE

Enables the DTR line on device open and leaves it on.

DTR_CONTROL_HANDSHAKE

Enables DTR handshaking. If handshaking is enabled, it is an error for the application to adjust the line by using the **EscapeCommFunction** function.

fDsrSensitivity

Specifies whether the communications driver is sensitive to the state of the DSR signal. If this member is TRUE, the driver ignores any bytes received, unless the DSR modem input line is high.

fTXContinueOnXoff

Specifies whether transmission stops when the input buffer is full and the driver has transmitted the **XoffChar** character. If this member is TRUE, transmission continues after the input buffer has come within **XoffLim** bytes of being full and the driver has transmitted the **XoffChar** character to stop receiving bytes. If this member is FALSE, transmission does not continue until the input buffer is within **XonLim** bytes of being empty and the driver has transmitted the **XonChar** character to resume reception.

fOutX

Specifies whether XON/XOFF flow control is used during transmission. If this member is TRUE, transmission stops when the **XoffChar** character is received and starts again when the **XonChar** character is received.

fInX

Specifies whether XON/XOFF flow control is used during reception. If this member is TRUE, the **XoffChar** character is sent when the input buffer comes within **XoffLim** bytes of being full, and the **XonChar** character is sent when the input buffer comes within **XonLim** bytes of being empty.

fErrorChar

Specifies whether bytes received with parity errors are replaced with the character specified by the **ErrorChar** member. If this member is TRUE, and the **fParity** member is TRUE, replacement occurs.

fNull

Specifies whether null bytes are discarded. If this member is TRUE, null bytes are discarded when received.

fRtsControl

Specifies the RTS (request-to-send) flow control. If this flag is zero, the default is RTS_CONTROL_HANDSHAKE. This member can be one of the following values:

Value	Meaning
RTS_CONTROL_DISABLE	Disables the RTS line when the device is opened and leaves it disabled.
RTS_CONTROL_ENABLE	Enables the RTS line when the device is opened and leaves it on.
RTS_CONTROL_HANDSHAKE	

Enables RTS handshaking. The driver raises the RTS line when the "type-ahead" (input) buffer is less than one-half full and lowers the RTS line when the buffer is more than three-quarters full. If handshaking is enabled, it is an error for the application to adjust the line by using the **EscapeCommFunction** function.

RTS_CONTROL_TOGGLE

Specifies that the RTS line will be high if bytes are available for transmission. After all buffered bytes have been sent, the RTS line will be low.

fAbortOnError

Specifies whether read and write operations are terminated if an error occurs. If this member is TRUE, the driver terminates all read and write operations with an error status if an error occurs. The driver will not accept any further communications operations until the application has acknowledged the error by calling the **ClearCommError** function.

fdummy2

Reserved; do not use.

wReserved

Not used; must be set to zero.

XonLim

Specifies the minimum number of bytes allowed in the input buffer before the XON character is sent.

XoffLim

Specifies the maximum number of bytes allowed in the input buffer before the XOFF character is sent. To calculate the maximum number of bytes allowed, this value is subtracted from the size, in bytes, of the input buffer.

ByteSize

Specifies the number of bits in the bytes transmitted and received.

Parity

Specifies the parity scheme to be used. This member can be one of the following values:

Value	Meaning
EVENPARITY	Even
MARKPARITY	Mark
NOPARITY	No parity
ODDPARITY	Odd

StopBits

Specifies the number of stop bits to be used. This member can be one of the following values:

Value	Meaning
ONESTOPBIT	1 stop bit
ONE5STOPBITS	1.5 stop bits
TWOSTOPBITS	2 stop bits

XonChar

Specifies the value of the XON character for both transmission and reception.

XoffChar

Specifies the value of the XOFF character for both transmission and reception.

ErrorChar

Specifies the value of the character used to replace bytes received with a parity error.

EofChar

Specifies the value of the character used to signal the end of data.

EvtChar

Specifies the value of the character used to signal an event.

Comments   When a **DCB** structure is used to configure the 8250, the following restrictions apply to the values specified for the the **ByteSize** and **StopBits** members:

- The number of data bits must be 5 to 8 bits.

- The use of 5 data bits with 2 stop bits is an invalid combination, as is 6, 7, or 8 data bits with 1.5 stop bits.

See Also   **BuildCommDCB, GetCommState, SetCommState**

DDEACK

```
typedef struct { /* ddeack */
    unsigned short bAppReturnCode:8,
    reserved:6,
    fBusy:1,
    fAck:1;
} DDEACK;
```

The **DDEACK** structure contains status flags that a dynamic data exchange (DDE) application passes to its partner as part of the WM_DDE_ACK message. The flags provide details about the application's response to a WM_DDE_ADVISE, WM_DDE_DATA, WM_DDE_EXECUTE, WM_DDE_REQUEST, WM_DDE_POKE, or WM_DDE_UNADVISE message.

Members

bAppReturnCode

Specifies an application-defined return code.

fBusy

Indicates whether the application was busy and unable to respond to the partner's message at the time the message was received. A nonzero value indicates the partner was busy and unable to respond. The **fBusy** member is defined only when the **fAck** member is zero.

fAck

Indicates whether the application accepted the message from its partner. A nonzero value indicates the partner accepted the message.

See Also

WM_DDE_ACK, WM_DDE_ADVISE, WM_DDE_DATA, WM_DDE_EXECUTE, WM_DDE_REQUEST, WM_DDE_POKE, WM_DDE_UNADVISE

DDEADVISE

```
typedef struct { /* ddeadv */
    unsigned short reserved:14,
        fDeferUpd:1,
        fAckReq:1;
    short cfFormat;
} DDEADVISE;
```

The **DDEADVISE** structure contains flags that specify how a dynamic data exchange (DDE) server application should send data to a client application during an advise loop. A client passes the handle of a **DDEADVISE** structure to a server as part of a WM_DDE_ADVISE message.

Members

fDeferUpd

Indicates whether the server should defer sending updated data to the client. If this value is nonzero, the server should send a WM_DDE_DATA message with a NULL data handle whenever the data item changes. In response, the client can post a WM_DDE_REQUEST message to the server to get a handle of the updated data.

fAckReq

Indicates whether the server should set the **fAckReq** flag in the WM_DDE_DATA messages it posts to the client. If this value is nonzero, the server should set the **fAckReq** bit.

cfFormat

Specifies the client application's preferred data format. The format must be a standard or registered clipboard format. The following standard clipboard formats can be used:

                    CF_BITMAP
                    CF_DIB
                    CF_DIF
                    CF_ENHMETAFILE
                    CF_METAFILEPICT
                    CF_OEMTEXT
                    CF_PALETTE
                    CF_PENDATA
                    CF_RIFF
                    CF_SYLK
                    CF_TEXT
                    CF_TIFF
                    CF_WAVE
                    CF_UNICODETEXT

See Also   WM_DDE_ADVISE, WM_DDE_DATA, WM_DDE_UNADVISE

DDEDATA

```
typedef struct { /* ddedat */
    unsigned short unused:12,
        fResponse:1,
        fRelease:1,
        reserved:1,
        fAckReq:1;
    short cfFormat;
    BYTE  Value[1];
} DDEDATA;
```

The **DDEDATA** structure contains the data, and information about the data, sent as part of a WM_DDE_DATA message.

Members   **fResponse**
Indicates whether the application receiving the WM_DDE_DATA message should acknowledge receipt of the data by sending a WM_DDE_ACK message. If this value is nonzero, the application should send the acknowledgment.

fRelease
Indicates whether the application receiving the WM_DDE_POKE message should free the data. If this value is nonzero, the application should free the data.

fAckReq

Indicates whether the data was sent in response to a WM_DDE_REQUEST message or a WM_DDE_ADVISE message. If this value is nonzero, the data was sent in response to a WM_DDE_REQUEST message.

cfFormat

Specifies the format of the data. The format should be a standard or registered clipboard format. The following standard clipboard formats can be used:

CF_BITMAP
CF_DIB
CF_DIF
CF_ENHMETAFILE
CF_METAFILEPICT
CF_OEMTEXT
CF_PALETTE
CF_PENDATA
CF_RIFF
CF_SYLK
CF_TEXT
CF_TIFF
CF_WAVE
CF_UNICODETEXT

Value[1]

Contains the data. The length and the type of data depends on the **cfFormat** member.

See Also   WM_DDE_ACK, WM_DDE_ADVISE, WM_DDE_DATA, WM_DDE_POKE, WM_DDE_REQUEST

DDELN

```
typedef struct { /* ddeln */
    unsigned short unused:13,
        fRelease:1,
        fDeferUpd:1,
        fAckReq:1;
    short cfFormat;
} DDELN;
```

The **DDELN** structure is obsolete. Win32 applications should use the **DDEADVISE** structure.

See Also   **DDEADVISE**, WM_DDE_ADVISE, WM_DDE_UNADVISE

DDEML_MSG_HOOK_DATA

```
typedef struct tagDDEML_MSG_HOOK_DATA { /* dmhd */
    UINT  uiLo;
    UINT  uiHi;
    DWORD cbData;
    DWORD Data[8];
} DDEML_MSG_HOOK_DATA;
```

The **DDEML_MSG_HOOK_DATA** structure contains information about a dynamic data exchange (DDE) message, and provides read access to the data referenced by the message. This structure is intended to be used by a DDE Management Library (DDEML) monitoring application.

Members

uiLo

Specifies the unpacked low-order word of the *lParam* parameter associated with the DDE message.

uiHi

Specifies the unpacked high-order word of the *lParam* parameter associated with the DDE message.

cbData

Specifies the amount, in bytes, of data being passed with the message. This value can be greater than 32.

Data

Contains the first 32 bytes of data being passed with the message (8 * sizeof(DWORD)).

See Also

MONCBSTRUCT, MONCONVSTRUCT, MONERRSTRUCT, MONHSZSTRUCT, MONLINKSTRUCT, MONMSGSTRUCT

DDEPOKE

```
typedef struct { /* ddepok */
    unsigned short unused:13,
        fRelease:1,
        fReserved:2;
    short cfFormat;
    BYTE  Value[1];
} DDEPOKE;
```

The **DDEPOKE** structure contains the data, and information about the data, sent as part of a WM_DDE_POKE message.

Members

fRelease

Indicates whether the application receiving the WM_DDE_POKE message should free the data. If this value is nonzero, the application should free the data.

fReserved

Reserved; do not use.

cfFormat

Specifies the format of the data. The format should be a standard or registered clipboard format. The following standard clipboard formats can be used:

CF_BITMAP
CF_DIB
CF_DIF
CF_ENHMETAFILE
CF_METAFILEPICT
CF_OEMTEXT
CF_PALETTE
CF_PENDATA
CF_RIFF
CF_SYLK
CF_TEXT
CF_TIFF
CF_WAVE
CF_UNICODETEXT

Value

Contains the data. The length and type of data depends on the value of the **cfFormat** member.

See Also

WM_DDE_POKE

DDEUP

```
typedef struct { /* ddeup */
    unsigned short unused:12,
        fAck:1,
        fRelease:1,
        fReserved:1,
        fAckReq:1;
    short cfFormat;
    BYTE rgb[1];
} DDEUP;
```

The **DDEUP** structure is obsolete. Win32 applications should use the **DDEDATA** and **DDEPOKE** structures.

See Also   **DDEDATA**, **DDEPOKE**, WM_DDE_DATA, WM_DDE_POKE

DEBUG_EVENT

New

```
typedef struct _DEBUG_EVENT { /* de */
    DWORD dwDebugEventCode;
    DWORD dwProcessId;
    DWORD dwThreadId;
    union {
        EXCEPTION_DEBUG_INFO Exception;
        CREATE_THREAD_DEBUG_INFO CreateThread;
        CREATE_PROCESS_DEBUG_INFO CreateProcessInfo;
        EXIT_THREAD_DEBUG_INFO ExitThread;
        EXIT_PROCESS_DEBUG_INFO ExitProcess;
        LOAD_DLL_DEBUG_INFO LoadDll;
        UNLOAD_DLL_DEBUG_INFO UnloadDll;
        OUTPUT_DEBUG_STRING_INFO DebugString;
        RIP_INFO RipInfo;
    } u;
} DEBUG_EVENT;
```

The **DEBUG_EVENT** structure describes a debugging event.

Members   **dwDebugEventCode**
Specifies a debugging event code that identifies the type of debugging event. This parameter can be one of the following values:

Value	Meaning

EXCEPTION_DEBUG_EVENT

Reports an exception debugging event. The value of **u.Exception** specifies an **EXCEPTION_DEBUG_INFO** structure.

CREATE_THREAD_DEBUG_EVENT

Reports a create-thread debugging event. The value of **u.CreateThread** specifies a **CREATE_THREAD_DEBUG_INFO** structure.

CREATE_PROCESS_DEBUG_EVENT

Reports a create-process debugging event. The value of **u.CreateProcessInfo** specifies a **CREATE_PROCESS_DEBUG_INFO** structure.

EXIT_THREAD_DEBUG_EVENT

Reports an exit-thread debugging event. The value of **u.ExitThread** specifies an **EXIT_THREAD_DEBUG_INFO** structure.

EXIT_PROCESS_DEBUG_EVENT

Reports an exit-process debugging event. The value of **u.ExitProcess** specifies an **EXIT_PROCESS_DEBUG_INFO** structure.

LOAD_DLL_DEBUG_EVENT

Reports a load-DLL debugging event. The value of **u.LoadDll** specifies a **LOAD_DLL_DEBUG_INFO** structure.

UNLOAD_DLL_DEBUG_EVENT

Reports an unload-DLL debugging event. The value of **u.UnloadDll** specifies an **UNLOAD_DLL_DEBUG_INFO** structure.

OUTPUT_DEBUG_STRING_EVENT

Reports an output-debugging-string debugging event. The value of **u.DebugString** specifies an **OUTPUT_DEBUG_STRING_INFO** structure.

RIP_EVENT

Reports a RIP-debugging event (system debugging error). The value of **u.RipInfo** specifies a **RIP_INFO** structure.

dwProcessId

Specifies the identifier of the process in which the debugging event occurred. A debugger uses this value to locate the debugger's per-process structure. These values are not necessarily small integers that can be used as table indices.

dwThreadId

Specifies the identifier of the thread in which the debugging event occurred. A debugger uses this value to locate the debugger's per-thread structure. These values are not necessarily small integers that can be used as table indices.

u

Specifies additional information relating to the debugging event. This union takes on the type and value appropriate to the type of debugging event, as described in the **dwDebugEventCode** member.

Comments

If the **WaitForDebugEvent** function succeeds, it fills in the members of a **DEBUG_EVENT** structure.

See Also

WaitForDebugEvent

DEBUGHOOKINFO

```
typedef struct tagDEBUGHOOKINFO { /* dh */
    DWORD   idThread;
    LPARAM  reserved;
    LPARAM  lParam;
    WPARAM  wParam;
    int     code;
} DEBUGHOOKINFO;
```

The **DEBUGHOOKINFO** structure contains debugging information.

Members

idThread

Identifies the thread containing the filter function.

reserved

Not used.

lParam

Specifies the value to be passed to the hook in the *lParam* parameter of the **DebugProc** callback function.

wParam

Specifies the value to be passed to the hook in the *wParam* parameter of the **DebugProc** callback function.

code

Specifies the value to be passed to the hook in the *nCode* parameter of the **DebugProc** callback function.

See Also

DebugProc, SetWindowsHook

DELETEITEMSTRUCT

```
typedef struct tagDELETEITEMSTRUCT { /* ditms */
    UINT CtlType;
    UINT CtlID;
    UINT itemID;
    HWND hwndItem;
    UINT itemData;
} DELETEITEMSTRUCT;
```

The **DELETEITEMSTRUCT** structure describes a deleted owner-drawn list-box or combo-box item. When an item is removed from the list box or combo box or when the list box or combo box is destroyed, Windows sends the WM_DELETEITEM message to the owner for each deleted item. The *lParam* parameter of the message contains a pointer to this structure.

Members

CtlType

Specifies ODT_LISTBOX (an owner-drawn list box) or ODT_COMBOBOX (an owner-drawn combo box).

CtlID

Specifies the identifier of the list box or combo box.

itemID

Specifies index of the item in the list box or combo box being removed.

hwndItem

Identifies the control.

itemData

Specifies application-defined data for the item. This value is passed to the control in the *lParam* parameter of the message that adds the item to the list box or combo box.

See Also

WM_DELETEITEM

DEVMODE

```
typedef struct _devicemode {    /* dvmd */
    TCHAR  dmDeviceName[32];
    WORD   dmSpecVersion;
    WORD   dmDriverVersion;
    WORD   dmSize;
    WORD   dmDriverExtra;
    DWORD  dmFields;
    short  dmOrientation;
    short  dmPaperSize;
    short  dmPaperLength;
    short  dmPaperWidth;
    short  dmScale;
    short  dmCopies;
    short  dmDefaultSource;
    short  dmPrintQuality;
    short  dmColor;
    short  dmDuplex;
    short  dmYResolution;
    short  dmTTOption;
    short  dmCollate;
    TCHAR  dmFormName[32];
    WORD   dmUnusedPadding;
    USHORT dmBitsPerPel;
    DWORD  dmPelsWidth;
    DWORD  dmPelsHeight;
    DWORD  dmDisplayFlags;
    DWORD  dmDisplayFrequency;
} DEVMODE;
```

The **DEVMODE** data structure contains information about the device initialization and environment of a printer.

Members

dmDeviceName

Specifies the name of the device the driver supports; for example, "PCL/HP LaserJet" in the case of PCL/HP LaserJet ®. This string is unique among device drivers.

dmSpecVersion

Specifies the version number of the initialization data specification on which the structure is based.

dmDriverVersion

Specifies the printer driver version number assigned by the printer driver developer.

dmSize

Specifies the size, in bytes, of the **DEVMODE** structure *except* the **dmDriverData** (device-specific) member. If an application manipulates only the driver-independent portion of the data, it can use this member to determine the length of the structure without having to account for different versions.

dmDriverExtra

Contains the number of bytes of private driver-data that follow this structure. If a device driver does not use device-specific information, set this member to zero.

dmFields

Specifies which of the remaining members in the **DEVMODE** structure have been initialized. Bit 0 (defined as DM_ORIENTATION) corresponds to **dmOrientation**; bit 1 (defined as DM_PAPERSIZE) specifies **dmPaperSize**, and so on. A printer driver supports only those members that are appropriate for the printer technology.

dmOrientation

Selects the orientation of the paper. This member can be either DMORIENT_PORTRAIT (1) or DMORIENT_LANDSCAPE (2).

dmPaperSize

Selects the size of the paper to print on. This member can be set to zero if the length and width of the paper are both set by the **dmPaperLength** and **dmPaperWidth** members. Otherwise, the **dmPaperSize** member can be set to one of the following predefined values:

Value	Meaning
DMPAPER_LETTER	Letter, 8 1/2- by 11-inches
MPAPER_LEGAL	Legal, 8 1/2- by 14-inches
DMPAPER_A4	A4 Sheet, 210- by 297-millimeters
DMPAPER_CSHEET	C Sheet, 17- by 22-inches
DMPAPER_DSHEET	D Sheet, 22- by 34-inches
DMPAPER_ESHEET	E Sheet, 34- by 44-inches
DMPAPER_LETTERSMALL	Letter Small, 8 1/2- by 11-inches
DMPAPER_TABLOID	Tabloid, 11- by 17-inches
DMPAPER_LEDGER	Ledger, 17- by 11-inches
DMPAPER_STATEMENT	Statement, 5 1/2- by 8 1/2-inches
DMPAPER_EXECUTIVE	Executive, 7 1/4- by 10 1/2-inches
DMPAPER_A3	A3 sheet, 297- by 420-millimeters
DMPAPER_A4SMALL	A4 small sheet, 210- by 297-millimeters
DMPAPER_A5	A5 sheet, 148- by 210-millimeters
DMPAPER_B4	B4 sheet, 250- by 354-millimeters

DMPAPER_B5	B5 sheet, 182- by 257-millimeter paper
DMPAPER_FOLIO	Folio, 8 1/2- by 13-inch paper
DMPAPER_QUARTO	Quarto, 215- by 275-millimeter paper
DMPAPER_10X14	10- by 14-inch sheet
DMPAPER_11X17	11- by 17-inch sheet
DMPAPER_NOTE	Note, 8 1/2- by 11-inches
DMPAPER_ENV_9	#9 Envelope, 3 7/8- by 8 7/8-inches
DMPAPER_ENV_10	#10 Envelope, 4 1/8- by 9 1/2-inches
DMPAPER_ENV_11	#11 Envelope, 4 1/2- by 10 3/8-inches
DMPAPER_ENV_12	#12 Envelope, 4 3/4- by 11-inches
DMPAPER_ENV_14	#14 Envelope, 5- by 11 1/2-inches
DMPAPER_ENV_DL	DL Envelope, 110- by 220-millimeters
DMPAPER_ENV_C5	C5 Envelope, 162- by 229-millimeters
DMPAPER_ENV_C3	C3 Envelope, 324- by 458-millimeters
DMPAPER_ENV_C4	C4 Envelope, 229- by 324-millimeters
DMPAPER_ENV_C6	C6 Envelope, 114- by 162-millimeters
DMPAPER_ENV_C65	C65 Envelope, 114- by 229-millimeters
DMPAPER_ENV_B4	B4 Envelope, 250- by 353-millimeters
DMPAPER_ENV_B5	B5 Envelope, 176- by 250-millimeters
DMPAPER_ENV_B6	B6 Envelope, 176- by 125-millimeters
DMPAPER_ENV_ITALY	Italy Envelope, 110- by 230-millimeters
DMPAPER_ENV_MONARCH	Monarch Envelope, 3 7/8- by 7 1/2-inches
DMPAPER_ENV_PERSONAL	6 3/4 Envelope, 3 5/8- by 6 1/2-inches
DMPAPER_FANFOLD_US	US Std Fanfold, 14 7/8- by 11-inches

| DMPAPER_FANFOLD_STD_GERMAN | German Std Fanfold, 8 1/2- by 12-inches |
| DMPA PER_FANFOLD_LGL_GERMAN | German Legal Fanfold, 8 1/2- by 13-inches |

dmPaperLength

Overrides the length of the paper specified by the **dmPaperSize** member, either for custom paper sizes or for devices such as dot-matrix printers, which can print on a page of arbitrary length. These values, along with all other values in this structure that specify a physical length, are in tenths of a millimeter.

dmPaperWidth

Overrides the width of the paper specified by the **dmPaperSize** member.

dmScale

Specifies the factor by which the printed output is to be scaled. The apparent page size is scaled from the physical page size by a factor of **dmScale**/100. For example, a letter-sized page with a **dmScale** value of 50 would contain as much data as a page of 17- by 22-inches because the output text and graphics would be half their original height and width.

dmCopies

Selects the number of copies printed if the device supports multiple-page copies.

dmDefaultSource

Reserved; must be zero.

dmPrintQuality

Specifies the printer resolution. There are four predefined device-independent values:

DMRES_HIGH
DMRES_MEDIUM
DMRES_LOW
DMRES_DRAFT

If a positive value is given, it specifies the number of dots per inch (DPI) and is therefore device dependent.

dmColor

Switches between color and monochrome on color printers. Following are the possible values:

DMCOLOR_COLOR
DMCOLOR_MONOCHROME

dmDuplex

Selects duplex or double-sided printing for printers capable of duplex printing. Following are the possible values:

    DMDUP_SIMPLEX
    DMDUP_HORIZONTAL
    DMDUP_VERTICAL

dmYResolution

Specifies the y-resolution, in dots per inch, of the printer. If the printer initializes this member, the **dmPrintQuality** member specifies the x-resolution, in dots per inch, of the printer.

dmTTOption

Specifies how TrueType ® fonts should be printed. This member can be one of the following values:

Value	Meaning
DMTT_BITMAP	Prints TrueType fonts as graphics. This is the default action for dot-matrix printers.
DMTT_DOWNLOAD	Downloads TrueType fonts as soft fonts. This is the default action for Hewlett-Packard printers that use Printer Control Language (PCL).
DMTT_SUBDEV	Substitute device fonts for TrueType fonts. This is the default action for PostScript ® printers.

dmUnusedPadding

Used to align the structure to a DWORD boundary. This should not be used or referenced. Its name and usage is reserved, and can change in future releases.

dmCollate

Specifies whether collation should be used when printing multiple copies. This member can be be one of the following values:

Value	Meaning
DMCOLLATE_TRUE	Collate when printing multiple copies.
DMCOLLATE_FALSE	Do NOT collate when printing multiple copies.

Using DMCOLLATE_FALSE provides faster, more efficient output, since the data is sent to a page printer just once, no matter how many copies are required. The printer is told to simply print the page again.

dmFormName

Specifies the name of the form to use; for example, "Letter" or "Legal". A complete set of names can be retrieved through the **EnumForms** function.

dmBitsPerPel

Specifies in bits per pixel the color resolution of the display device. For example: 4 bits for 16 colors, 8 bits for 256 colors, or 16 bits for 65536 colors.

dmPelsWidth

Specifies the width, in pixels, of the visible device surface.

dmPelsHeight
Specifies the height, in pixels, of the visible device surface.

dmDisplayFlags
Specifies the device's display mode. The following are valid flags:

Value	Meaning
DM_GRAYSCALE	Specifies that the display is a NON-color device. If this flag is not set, color is assumed.
DM_INTERLACED	Specifies that the display mode is interlaced. If the flag is not set, NON-interlaced is assumed.

dmDisplayFrequency
Specifies the frequency, in hertz (cycles per second), of the display device in a particular mode.

Comments
A device driver's private data will follow the **dmDisplayMode** member. The number of bytes of private data is specified by the **dmDriverExtra** member.

See Also
AdvancedDocumentProperties, **CreateDC**, **CreateIC**, **DeviceCapabilitiesEx**, **DocumentProperties**, **OpenPrinter**

DEVNAMES

```
typedef struct tagDEVNAMES { /* dvnm */
    WORD wDriverOffset;
    WORD wDeviceOffset;
    WORD wOutputOffset;
    WORD wDefault;
    /* driver, device, and port-name strings follow wDefault */
} DEVNAMES;
```

The **DEVNAMES** structure contains strings that identify the driver, device, and output-port names for a printer. The **PrintDlg** function uses these strings to initialize members in the system-defined Print dialog box. When the user closes the dialog box, information about the selected printer is returned in this structure.

Members
wDriverOffset
(Input/Output) Specifies the offset to a null-terminated string that contains the MS-DOS filename (without the extension) of the device driver. On input, this string is used to determine the printer to display initially in the dialog box.

wDeviceOffset
(Input/Output) Specifies the offset to the null-terminated string (maximum of 32 bytes including the null) that contains the name of the device. This string

must be identical to the **dmDeviceName** member of the **DEVMODE** structure.

wOutputOffset

(Input/Output) Specifies the offset to the null-terminated string that contains the MS-DOS device name for the physical output medium (output port).

wDefault

Specifies whether the strings contained in the **DEVNAMES** structure identify the default printer. This string is used to verify that the default printer has not changed since the last print operation. On input, if the DN_DEFAULTPRN flag is set, the other values in the **DEVNAMES** structure are checked against the current default printer. If any of the strings do not match, a warning message is displayed informing the user that the document may need to be reformatted.

On output, the **wDefault** member is changed only if the Print Setup dialog box was displayed and the user chose the OK button. The DN_DEFAULTPRN flag is set if the default printer was selected. If a specific printer is selected, the flag is not set. All other bits in this member are reserved for internal use by the Print Dialog box procedure.

See Also   **PrintDlg**

DISK_GEOMETRY

`New`

```
typedef struct _DISK_GEOMETRY {
   MEDIA_TYPE  MediaType;
   LARGE_INTEGER  Cylinders;
   DWORD  TracksPerCylinder;
   DWORD  SectorsPerTrack;
   DWORD  BytesPerSector;
} DISK_GEOMETRY ;
```

The **DISK_GEOMETRY** structure describes the geometry of disk devices and media.

Members   **MediaType**

The type of media. See **MEDIA_TYPE**.

Cylinders

The number of cylinders.

TracksPerCylinder

The number of tracks per cylinder.

SectorsPerTrack

The number of sectors per track.

BytesPerSector
The number of bytes per sector

Comments   The **DeviceIoControl** function receives a **DISK_GEOMETRY** structure in response to an **IOCTL_DISK_GET_DRIVE_GEOMETRY** device i/o operation. The **DeviceIoControl** function receives an array of **DISK_GEOMETRY** structures in response to an **IOCTL_DISK_GET_MEDIA_TYPES** device i/o operation.

See Also   **DeviceIoControl, IOCTL_DISK_GET_DRIVE_GEOMETRY, IOCTL_DISK_GET_MEDIA_TYPES, MEDIA_TYPE**

DISK_PERFORMANCE   New

```
typedef struct _DISK_PERFORMANCE {
        LARGE_INTEGER BytesRead;
        LARGE_INTEGER BytesWritten;
        LARGE_INTEGER ReadTime;
        LARGE_INTEGER WriteTime;
        DWORD ReadCount;
        DWORD WriteCount;
        DWORD QueueDepth;
} DISK_PERFORMANCE ;
```

The **DISK_PERFORMANCE** structure provides disk performance information.

Members   **BytesRead**
Specifies the number of bytes read.

BytesWritten
Specifies the number of bytes written.

ReadTime
Specifies the time it took to complete the read.

WriteTime
The time it took to complete the write.

ReadCount
Specifies the number of read operations.

WriteCount
Specifies the number of write operations.

QueueDepth
Specifies the depth of the queue.

Comments   The **DeviceIoControl** function receives a **DISK_PERFORMANCE** structure in response to an **IOCTL_DISK_PERFORMANCE** device i/o operation.

See Also   **DeviceIoControl, IOCTL_DISK_PERFORMANCE**

DLGITEMTEMPLATE

```
typedef struct { /* dlit */
    DWORD style;
    DWORD dwExtendedStyle;
    WORD  x;
    WORD  y;
    WORD  cx;
    WORD  cy;
    WORD  id;
} DLGITEMTEMPLATE;
```

The **DLGITEMTEMPLATE** structure defines the dimensions and style of a control in a dialog box. One or more of these structures are combined with a **DLGTEMPLATE** structure to form a dialog box template.

Members

style

Specifies the style of the control. This member can be a combination of window style values (such as WS_BORDER) and one or more of the control style values (such as BS_PUSHBUTTON and ES_LEFT).

dwExtendedStyle

Specifies extended styles for a window. This member is not used to create controls in dialog boxes, but applications that use dialog box templates can use it to create other types of windows.

x

Specifies the x-coordinate, in dialog units, of the upper left corner of the control. This coordinate is always relative to the upper left corner of the dialog box's client area.

y

Specifies the y-coordinate, in dialog units, of the upper left corner of the control. This coordinate is always relative to the upper left corner of the dialog box's client area.

cx

Specifies the width, in dialog units, of the control.

cy

Specifies the height, in dialog units, of the control.

id

Specifies the control identifier.

Comments   In a dialog box template, the **DLGITEMTEMPLATE** structure is always immediately followed by three variable-length arrays specifying the class, title, and creation data for the control. Each array consists of one or more 16-bit elements.

The class array follows the **DLGITEMTEMPLATE** structure. When the first element of this array is 0xFFFF, the array has one additional element that specifies an atom value identifying a registered window class. When the first element has any other value, Windows assumes the array is a null-terminated Unicode string that specifies the name of a registered window class. Following are the class atom values for predefined controls:

Value	Meaning
0x0080	Button
0x0081	Edit
0x0082	Static
0x0083	List box
0x0084	Scroll bar
0x0085	Combo box

The title array follows the class array. When the first element is 0xFFFF, the array has one additional element that specifies the identifier of a resource, such as an icon, in an executable file. Resource identifiers are usually given for controls, such as static icon controls, that load and display an icon or other resources rather than text. When the first element is any other value, Windows assumes the array is a null-terminated Unicode string that specifies the initial text for the control.

The creation data array follows the text array. This array can contain any number of elements; the control's window procedure must understand the content and format of the data. Windows passes this data to the control when it calls the **CreateWindowEx** function.

The **x**, **y**, **cx**, and **cy** members specify values in dialog units. You can convert these values to screen units (pixels) by using the **MapDialogRect** function.

See Also   **CreateDialogIndirect**, **CreateDialogIndirectParam**, **CreateWindowEx**, **DialogBoxIndirect**, **DialogBoxIndirectParam**, **MapDialogRect**

DLGTEMPLATE

```
typedef struct { /* dltt */
    DWORD style;
    DWORD dwExtendedStyle;
    WORD  cdit;
    WORD  x;
    WORD  y;
    WORD  cx;
    WORD  cy;
} DLGTEMPLATE;
```

The **DLGTEMPLATE** structure defines the dimensions and style of a dialog box. This structure, always the first in a dialog box template, also specifies the number of controls in the dialog box and therefore specifies the number of subsequent **DLGITEMTEMPLATE** structures in the template.

Members

style

Specifies the style of the dialog box. This member can be a combination of window style values (such as WS_CAPTION and WS_SYSMENU) and one or more of the following dialog box style values:

Value	Meaning
DS_ABSALIGN	Specifies that the dialog box position is relative to the upper-left corner of the screen. If this style is not given, the position is relative to the upper-left corner of the owner window's client area.
DS_MODALFRAME	Specifies a dialog box with a modal dialog box border.
DS_NOIDLEMSG	Prevents Windows from sending the WM_ENTERIDLE messages to the owner window when no messages are in the application queue. This value applies to modal dialog boxes only.
DS_SETFONT	Specifies that a font other than the system font is used to draw text in the dialog box and its controls. When this value is given, the dialog box template must specify a point size and typeface name as described in the "Comments" section.
DS_SETFOREGROUND	Specifies that the application creating the dialog box is to be made the foreground task. Windows calls the **SetForegroundWindow** function to set the foreground task.

The DS_LOCALEDIT and DS_SYSMODAL styles are not fully supported in Windows NT. DS_LOCALEDIT applies only to applications written for

Windows 3.*x*. DS_SYSMODAL creates a dialog box having the WS_EX_TOPMOST style but does not cause the system to disable all other windows.

dwExtendedStyle

Specifies extended styles for a window. This member is not used to create dialog boxes, but applications that use dialog box templates can use it to create other types of windows.

cdit

Specifies the number of items in the dialog box.

x

Specifies the *x*-coordinate, in dialog units, of the upper left corner of the dialog box.

y

Specifies the *y*-coordinate, in dialog units, of the upper left corner of the dialog box

cx

Specifies the width, in dialog units, of the dialog box.

cy

Specifies the height, in dialog units, of the dialog box.

Comments

In a dialog box template, the **DLGTTEMPLATE** structure is always immediately followed by three variable-length arrays that specify the menu, class, and title for the dialog box. When the DS_SETFONT style is given, these arrays are also followed by a 16-bit value specifying point size and another variable-length array specifying a typeface name. Each array consists of one or more 16-bit elements.

The menu array follows the **DLGTEMPLATE** structure. When the first element of this array is 0x0000, the dialog box has no menu and the array has no other elements. When the first element is 0xFFFF, the array has one additional element that specifies the resource identifier for a menu resource in an executable file. If the first element has any other value, Windows assumes the array is a null-terminated Unicode string that specifies the name of the menu resource in an executable file.

The class array follows the menu array. When the first element of the array is 0x0000, Windows uses the predefined dialog box class for the dialog box. When the first element is 0xFFFF, the array has one additional element that specifies the atom value identifying a registered window class. When the first element has any other value, Windows assumes the array is a null-terminated Unicode string that specifies the name of a registered window class.

The title array follows the class array. When the first element of the array is 0x0000, the dialog box has no title. When the first element has any other value,

Windows assumes the array is a null-terminated Unicode string that specifies the title.

The 16-bit point size value and the typeface array follow the title array, but only if the **style** member gives the DS_SETFONT style. The point size value specifies the size in points of the font to use for the text in the dialog box and its controls. The typeface array is a null-terminated Unicode string specifying the name of the typeface for the font. When these values are given, Windows creates a font having the given size and typeface (if possible) and sends a WM_SETFONT message to the dialog box procedure and the control window procedures as it creates the dialog box and controls.

Every dialog box template also contains the number of **DLGITEMTEMPLATE** structures as given by the **cdit** member. These structures define the dimensions and style of the controls in the dialog box.

The **x**, **y**, **cx**, and **cy** members specify values in dialog units. You can convert these values to screen units (pixels) by using the **MapDialogRect** function.

See Also   **CreateDialogIndirect, CreateDialogIndirectParam, DialogBoxIndirect, DialogBoxIndirectParam, MapDialogRect**

DOCINFO   `Unicode`

```
typedef struct {    /* di */
    int    cbSize;
    LPTSTR lpszDocName;
    LPTSTR lpszOutput;
} DOCINFO;
```

The **DOCINFO** structure contains the input and output filenames used by the **StartDoc** function.

Members   **cbSize**
Specifies the size, in bytes, of the structure.

lpszDocName
Points to a null-terminated string that specifies the name of the document.

pszOutput
Points to a null-terminated string that specifies the name of an output file. If this pointer is NULL, the output will be sent to the device identified by the DC handle which was passed to the **StartDoc** function.

See Also   **StartDoc**

DOC_INFO_1

```
typedef struct _DOC_INFO_1 { /* dci1 */
    LPTSTR pDocName;
    LPTSTR pOutputFile;
    LPTSTR pDatatype;
} DOC_INFO_1;
```

The **DOC_INFO_1** structure describes a document that will be printed.

Members

pDocName
Points to a null-terminated string that specifies the name of the document.

pOutputFile
Points to a null-terminated string that specifies the name of an output file.

pDatatype
Points to a null-terminated string that identifies the type of data used to record the document.

See Also

StartDocPrinter

DRAWITEMSTRUCT

```
typedef struct tagDRAWITEMSTRUCT {  /* dis */
    UINT  CtlType;
    UINT  CtlID;
    UINT  itemID;
    UINT  itemAction;
    UINT  itemState;
    HWND  hwndItem;
    HDC   hDC;
    RECT  rcItem;
    DWORD itemData;
} DRAWITEMSTRUCT;
```

The **DRAWITEMSTRUCT** structure provides information the owner window must have to determine how to paint an owner-drawn control or menu item. The owner window of the owner-drawn control or menu item receives a pointer to this structure as the *lParam* parameter of the WM_DRAWITEM message.

Members

CtlType
Specifies the control type. This member can be one of the following values:

Value	Meaning
ODT_BUTTON	Owner-drawn button
ODT_COMBOBOX	Owner-drawn combo box
ODT_LISTBOX	Owner-drawn list box
ODT_MENU	Owner-drawn menu item

CtlID

Specifies the identifier of the combo box, list box, or button. This member is not used for a menu item.

itemID

Specifies the menu item identifier for a menu item or the index of the item in a list box or combo box. For an empty list box or combo box, this member can be −1. This allows the application to draw only the focus rectangle at the coordinates specified by the **rcItem** member even though there are no items in the control. This indicates to the user whether the list box or combo box has the focus. How the bits are set in the **itemAction** member determines whether the rectangle is to be drawn as though the list box or combo box has the focus.

itemAction

Specifies the drawing action required. This member can be one or more of the following values:

Value	Meaning
ODA_DRAWENTIRE	The entire control needs to be drawn.
ODA_FOCUS	The control has lost or gained the keyboard focus. The **itemState** member should be checked to determine whether the control has the focus.
ODA_SELECT	The selection status has changed. The **itemState** member should be checked to determine the new selection state.

itemState

Specifies the visual state of the item *after* the current drawing action takes place. This member can be a combination of the following values:

Value	Meaning
ODS_CHECKED	The menu item is to be checked. This bit is used only in a menu.
ODS_DISABLED	The item is to be drawn as disabled.
ODS_FOCUS	The item has the keyboard focus.
ODS_GRAYED	The item is to be grayed. This bit is used only in a menu.
ODS_SELECTED	The menu item's status is selected.

hwndItem

Identifies the control for combo boxes, list boxes, and buttons. For menus, this member identifies the menu containing the item.

hDC

Identifies a device context (DC); this DC must be used when performing drawing operations on the control.

rcItem

Specifies a rectangle that defines the boundaries of the control to be drawn. This rectangle is in the DC specified by the **hDC** member. Windows automatically clips anything the owner window draws in the DC for combo boxes, list boxes, and buttons, but does not clip menu items. When drawing menu items, the owner window must not draw outside the boundaries of the rectangle defined by the **rcItem** member.

itemData

Specifies the application-defined 32-bit value associated with the menu item. For a control, this parameter specifies the value last assigned to the list box or combo box by the LB_SETITEMDATA or CB_SETITEMDATA message. If the list box or combo box has the LB_HASSTRINGS or CB_HASSTRINGS style, this value is initially zero. Otherwise, this value is initially the value that was passed to the list box or combo box in the *lParam* parameter of one of the following messages:

CB_ADDSTRING
CB_INSERTSTRING
LB_ADDSTRING
LB_INSERTSTRING

DRIVE_LAYOUT_INFORMATION

New

```
typedef struct _DRIVE_LAYOUT_INFORMATION {
    DWORD   PartitionCount;
    DWORD   Signature;
    PARTITION_INFORMATION   PartitionEntry[1];
} DRIVE_LAYOUT_INFORMATION;
```

The **DRIVE_LAYOUT_INFORMATION** structure provides information about a drive's partitions.

Members

PartitionCount

The number of partitions on the drive.

Signature

A drive signature value.

PartitionEntry[1]
A variable-sized array of **PARTITION_INFORMATION** structures, one structure for each partition on the drive.

Comments   The **DeviceIoControl** function receives a **DRIVE_LAYOUT_INFORMATION** structure in response to an **IOCTL_GET_DRIVE_LAYOUT** device i/o operation. The **DeviceIoControl** function uses a **DRIVE_LAYOUT_INFORMATION** structure as input to an **IOCTL_SET_DRIVE_LAYOUT** device i/o operation.

See Also   **DeviceIoControl, IOCTL_DISK_GET_DRIVE_LAYOUT, IOCTL_DISK_SET_DRIVE_LAYOUT, PARTITION_INFORMATION**

DRIVER_INFO_1

New, Unicode

```
typedef struct _DRIVER_INFO_1 { /* dri1 */
    LPTSTR pName;
} DRIVER_INFO_1;
```

The **DRIVER_INFO_1** structure identifies a printer driver.

Members   **pName**
Points to a null-terminated string that specifies the name of a printer driver.

See Also   **EnumPrinterDrivers**

DRIVER_INFO_2

New, Unicode

```
typedef struct _DRIVER_INFO_2 { /* dri2 */
    DWORD  cVersion;
    LPTSTR pName;
    LPTSTR pEnvironment;
    LPTSTR pDriverPath;
    LPTSTR pDataFile;
    LPTSTR pConfigFile;
} DRIVER_INFO_2;
```

The **DRIVER_INFO_2** structure identifies a printer driver, the driver version number, the environment for which the driver was written, the name of the file in which the driver is stored, and so on.

Members   **cVersion**
Specifies a printer-driver version number.

pName

Points to a null-terminated string that specifies the name of the driver (for example, "QMS 810").

pEnvironment

Points to a null-terminated string that specifies the environment for which the driver was written (for example, "W32X86" or "W32MIPS").

pDriverPath

Points to null-terminated string that specifies a filename or full path and filename for the file that contains the device driver (for example, "c:\drivers\pscript.dll").

pDataFile

Points to a null-terminated string that specifies a filename or a full path and filename for the file that contains driver data (for example, "c:\driversQMS810.PPD").

pConfigFile

Points to a null-terminated string that specifies a filename or a full path and filename for the device-driver's configuration DLL (for example, "c:\drivers\PSCRPTUI.DLL").

See Also   **AddPrinterDriver, GetPrinterDriver**

ENHMETAHEADER

New

```
typedef struct tagENHMETAHEADER { /* enmh */
    DWORD iType;
    DWORD nSize;
    RECTL rclBounds;
    RECTL rclFrame;
    DWORD dSignature;
    DWORD nVersion;
    DWORD nBytes;
    DWORD nRecords;
    WORD  nHandles;
    WORD  sReserved;
    DWORD nDescription;
    DWORD offDescription;
    DWORD nPalEntries;
    SIZEL szlDevice;
    SIZEL szlMillimeters;
} ENHMETAHEADER;
```

The **ENHMETAHEADER** structure contains enhanced-metafile data such as the dimensions of the picture stored in the enhanced metafile, the count of records in the enhanced metafile, the resolution of the device on which the picture was created, and so on.

This structure is always the first record in an enhanced metafile.

Members

iType
Specifies the record type. This member must specify the value assigned to the EMR_HEADER constant.

nSize
Specifies the structure size, in bytes.

rclBounds
Specifies the dimensions, in device units, of the smallest rectangle that can be drawn around the picture stored in the metafile. This rectangle is supplied by graphics device interface (GDI). Its dimensions include the right and bottom edges.

rclFrame
Specifies the dimensions, in .01 millimeter units, of a rectangle that surrounds the picture stored in the metafile. This rectangle must be supplied by the application that creates the metafile. Its dimensions include the right and bottom edges.

dSignature
Specifies a doubleword signature. This member must specify the value assigned to the ENHMETA_SIGNATURE constant.

nVersion
Specifies the metafile version. For the first release of Windows NT, the version value is 0x10000.

nBytes
Specifies the size of the enhanced metafile, in bytes.

nRecords
Specifies the number of records in the enhanced metafile.

nHandles
Specifies the number of handles in the enhanced-metafile handle table. (Index zero in this table is reserved.)

sReserved
Reserved; must be zero.

nDescription
Specifies the number of characters in the array that contains the description of the enhanced metafile's contents. This member should be set to zero if the enhanced metafile does not contain a description string.

offDescription
Specifies the offset from the beginning of the **ENHMETAHEADER** structure to the array that contains the description of the enhanced metafile's contents.

This member should be set to zero if the enhanced metafile does not contain a description string.

nPalEntries

Specifies the number of entries in the enhanced metafile's palette.

szlDevice

Specifies the resolution of the reference device, in pixels.

szlMillimeters

Specifies the resolution of the reference device, in millimeters.

See Also   **ENHMETARECORD**

ENHMETARECORD

New

```
typedef struct tagENHMETARECORD { /* enmr */
    DWORD iType;
    DWORD nSize;
    DWORD dParm[1];
} ENHMETARECORD;
```

The **ENHMETARECORD** structure contains data that describes a graphics device interface (GDI) function used to create part of a picture in an enhanced-format metafile.

Members   **iType**

Specifies the record type.

nSize

Specifies the size of the record, in bytes.

dParm

Specifies an array of parameters passed to the GDI function identified by the record.

See Also   **ENHMETAHEADER**

ENUMLOGFONT

```
typedef struct tagENUMLOGFONT { /* elf */
    LOGFONT elfLogFont;
    BYTE    elfFullName[LF_FULLFACESIZE];
    BYTE    elfStyle[LF_FACESIZE];
} ENUMLOGFONT;
```

The **ENUMLOGFONT** structure defines the attributes of a font, the complete name of a font, and the style of a font.

Members

elfLogFont

Specifies a **LOGFONT** structure that defines the attributes of a font.

The **LOGFONT** structure has the following format:

```
typedef struct tagLOGFONT { /* lf */
    LONG lfHeight;
    LONG lfWidth;
    LONG lfEscapement;
    LONG lfOrientation;
    LONG lfWeight;
    BYTE lfItalic;
    BYTE lfUnderline;
    BYTE lfStrikeOut;
    BYTE lfCharSet;
    BYTE lfOutPrecision;
    BYTE lfClipPrecision;
    BYTE lfQuality;
    BYTE lfPitchAndFamily;
    CHAR lfFaceName[LF_FACESIZE];
} LOGFONT;
```

elfFullName

Specifies a unique name for the font. For example "ABC Font Company TrueType Bold Italic Sans Serif".

elfStyle

Specifies the style of the font. For example "Bold Italic"

See Also   **EnumFontFamProc, LOGFONT**

ENUM_SERVICE_STATUS

```
typedef struct _ENUM_SERVICE_STATUS { /* ess */
    LPTSTR lpServiceName;
    LPTSTR lpDisplayName;
    SERVICE_STATUS ServiceStatus;
} ENUM_SERVICE_STATUS, *LPENUM_SERVICE_STATUS;
```

The **ENUM_SERVICE_STATUS** structure is used by the **EnumDependentServices** and **EnumServicesStatus** functions to return the name of a service in a service control manager database and to return information about that service.

Members

lpServiceName

Points to a null-terminated string that names a service in a service control manager database. The maximum string length is 256 characters. The service control manager database preserves the case of the characters, but service name comparisons are always case insensitive. A forward-slash (/), back-slash (\), comma, and space are invalid service name characters.

lpDisplayName

Points to a NULL-terminated string that is to be used by user interface programs to identify the service. This string has a maximum length of 256 characters. The name is case-preserved in the Service Control Manager. Display name comparisons are always case-insensitive.

ServiceStatus

Specifies a **SERVICE_STATUS** structure in which status information about the **lpServiceName** service is returned. The **SERVICE_STATUS** structure has the following form:

```
typedef struct _SERVICE_STATUS { /* ss */
    DWORD dwServiceType;
    DWORD dwCurrentState;
    DWORD dwControlsAccepted;
    DWORD dwWin32ExitCode;
    DWORD dwServiceSpecificExitCode;
    DWORD dwCheckPoint;
    DWORD dwWaitHint;
} SERVICE_STATUS, *LPSERVICE_STATUS;
```

For a full description of this structure, see SERVICE_STATUS.

See Also   **EnumDependentServices**, **EnumServicesStatus**

EVENTLOGRECORD

New

```
typedef struct _EVENTLOGRECORD { /* evlr         */
    DWORD  Length;
    DWORD  Reserved;
    DWORD  RecordNumber;
    DWORD  TimeGenerated;
    DWORD  TimeWritten;
    DWORD  EventID;
    WORD   EventType;
    WORD   NumStrings;
    WORD   EventCategory;
    WORD   ReservedFlags;
    DWORD  ClosingRecordNumber;
    DWORD  StringOffset;
```

```
    DWORD   UserSidLength;
    DWORD   UserSidOffset;
    DWORD   DataLength;
    DWORD   DataOffset;
    //
    // Then follow:
    //
    // WCHAR SourceName[]
    // WCHAR Computername[]
    // SID   UserSid
    // WCHAR Strings[]
    // BYTE  Data[]
    // CHAR  Pad[]
    // DWORD Length;
    //
} EVENTLOGRECORD;
```

The **EVENTLOGRECORD** structure contains information about an event record.

Members

Length

Specifies the length, in bytes, of this event record. Note that this value is stored at both ends of the entry to ease moving forward or backward through the log. The length includes any pad bytes inserted at the end of the record for DWORD alignment.

Reserved

Reserved.

RecordNumber

Contains a record number that can be used with the EVENTLOG_SEEK_READ flag passed in a call to the **ReadEventLog** function to begin reading at a specified record.

TimeGenerated

The time at which this entry was submitted. This time is measured in the number of seconds elapsed since 00:00:00 January 1, 1970.

TimeWritten

Specifies the time at which this entry was received by the service to be written to the logfile. This time is measured in the number of seconds elapsed since 00:00:00 January 1, 1970.

EventID

Identifies the event. This is specific to the source that generated the event log entry, and is used, together with **SourceName**, to identify a message in a message file that is presented to the user while viewing the log.

EventType

Specifies the type of event. This member can be one of the following values:

Value	Meaning
EVENTLOG_ERROR_TYPE	Error event
EVENTLOG_WARNING_TYPE	Warning event
EVENTLOG_INFORMATION_TYPE	Information event
EVENTLOG_AUDIT_SUCCESS	Success Audit event
EVENTLOG_AUDIT_FAILURE	Failure Audit event

For more information about event types, see Chapter 65, "Event Logging," in the *Microsoft Win32 Programmer's Reference, Volume 2.*

NumStrings
Specifies the number of strings present in the log (at the position indicated by **StringOffset**). These strings are merged into the message before it is displayed to the user.

EventCategory
Specifies a subcategory for this event. This subcategory is source specific.

ReservedFlags
Reserved.

ClosingRecordNumber
Reserved.

StringOffset
Specifies the offset of the strings within this event log entry.

UserSiDLength
Specifies the length, in bytes, of the **UserSiD** member. This value can be zero if no security identifier was provided.

UserSiDOffset
Specifies the offset of the security identifier within this event record.

DataLength
Specifies the length, in bytes, of the event-specific data (at the position indicated by **DataOffset**).

DataOffset
Specifies the offset of the event-specific information within this log. This information could be something specific (a disk driver might log the number of retries, for example), followed by binary information specific to the event being logged and to the source that generated the entry.

SourceName
Contains the variable-length null-terminated string specifying the name of the source (application, service, driver, subsystem) that generated the entry. This is the name used to retrieve from the registry the name of the file containing the message strings for this source. It is used, together with the event identifier, to get the message string that describes this event.

Computername

Contains the variable-length null-terminated string specifying the name of the computer that generated this event. There may also be some pad bytes after this field to ensure that the UserSid is aligned on a DWORD boundary.

UserSiD

Specifies the security identifier of the active user at the time this event was logged. This member may be empty if the **UserSiDLength** member is zero.

The defined members are followed by the replacement strings for the message identified by the event identifier, the binary information, some pad bytes to make sure the full entry is on a **DWORD** boundary, and finally the length of the log entry again. Because the strings and the binary information can be of any length, no structure members are defined to reference them.

The event identifier together with **SourceName** and a language identifier identify a message string that describes the event in more detail. The strings are used as replacement strings and are merged into the message string to make a complete message. The message strings are contained in a message file specified in the source entry in the registry.

The binary information is information that is specific to the event. It could be the contents of the processor registers when a device driver got an error, a dump of an invalid packet that was received from the network, a dump of all the structures in a program (when the data area was detected to be corrupt), and so on. This information should be useful to the writer of the device driver or the application in tracking down bugs or unauthorized breaks into the application.

See Also   **ReadEventLog**

EVENTMSG

```
typedef struct tagEVENTMSG {      /* em */
    UINT  message;
    UINT  paramL;
    UINT  paramH;
    DWORD time;
    HWND  hwnd;
} EVENTMSG;
```

The **EVENTMSG** structure contains information about a hardware message sent to the system message queue. This structure is used to store message information for the **JournalPlaybackProc** callback function.

Members   **message**

Specifies the message.

paramL

Specifies additional information about the message. The exact meaning depends on the **message** value.

paramH

Specifies additional information about the message. The exact meaning depends on the **message** value.

time

Specifies the time at which the message was posted.

hwnd

Identifies the window to which the message was posted.

See Also   **JournalPlaybackProc**, **SetWindowsHookEx**

EXCEPTION_DEBUG_INFO

New

```
typedef struct _EXCEPTION_DEBUG_INFO { /* exdi */
    EXCEPTION_RECORD ExceptionRecord;
    DWORD dwFirstChance;
} EXCEPTION_DEBUG_INFO;
```

The **EXCEPTION_DEBUG_INFO** structure contains exception information that could be used by a debugger.

Members   **ExceptionRecord**

Contains an **EXCEPTION_RECORD** structure with information specific to the exception. This includes the exception code, flags, address, a pointer to a related exception, extra parameters, and so on.

dwFirstChance

Indicates whether the debugger has previously encountered the exception specified by **ExceptionRecord**. If **dwFirstChance** is nonzero, this is the first time the debugger has encountered the exception. Debuggers typically handle breakpoint and single-step exceptions when they are first encountered. If **dwFirstChance** is zero, the debugger has previously encountered the exception. This occurs only if, during the search for structured exception handlers, either no handler was found or the exception was continued.

See Also   **DEBUG_EVENT**

EXCEPTION_POINTERS

`New`

```
typedef struct _EXCEPTION_POINTERS { /* exp */
    PEXCEPTION_RECORD ExceptionRecord;
    PCONTEXT ContextRecord;
} EXCEPTION_POINTERS;
```

The **EXCEPTION_POINTERS** structure contains an exception record with a machine-independent description of an exception and a context record with a machine-dependent description of the processor context at the time of the exception.

Members

ExceptionRecord
Points to an **EXCEPTION_RECORD** structure that contains a machine-independent description of the exception.

ContextRecord
Points to a **CONTEXT** structure that contains a processor-specific description of the state of the processor at the time of the exception.

See Also   **GetExceptionInformation, CONTEXT, EXCEPTION_RECORD**

EXCEPTION_RECORD

`New`

```
typedef struct _EXCEPTION_RECORD { /* exr */
    DWORD ExceptionCode;
    DWORD ExceptionFlags;
    struct _EXCEPTION_RECORD *ExceptionRecord;
    PVOID ExceptionAddress;
    DWORD NumberParameters;
    DWORD ExceptionInformation[EXCEPTION_MAXIMUM_PARAMETERS];
} EXCEPTION_RECORD;
```

The **EXCEPTION_RECORD** structure describes an exception.

Members

ExceptionCode
Specifies the reason the exception occurred. This is the code generated by a hardware exception, or the code specified in the **RaiseException** function for a software-generated exception. Following are the exception codes likely to occur due to common programming errors:

Value	Meaning
EXCEPTION_ACCESS_VIOLATION	

The thread tried to read from or write to a virtual address for which it does not have the appropriate access.

EXCEPTION_BREAKPOINT

A breakpoint was encountered.

EXCEPTION_DATATYPE_MISALIGNMENT

The thread tried to read or write data that is misaligned on hardware that does not provide alignment. For example, 16-bit values must be aligned on 2-byte boundaries; 32-bit values on 4-byte boundaries, and so on.

EXCEPTION_SINGLE_STEP

A trace trap or other single-instruction mechanism signaled that one instruction has been executed.

EXCEPTION_ARRAY_BOUNDS_EXCEEDED

The thread tried to access an array element that is out of bounds and the underlying hardware supports bounds checking.

EXCEPTION_FLT_DENORMAL_OPERAND

One of the operands in a floating-point operation is denormal. A denormal value is one that is too small to represent as a standard floating-point value.

EXCEPTION_FLT_DIVIDE_BY_ZERO

The thread tried to divide a floating-point value by a floating-point divisor of zero.

EXCEPTION_FLT_INEXACT_RESULT

The result of a floating-point operation cannot be represented exactly as a decimal fraction.

EXCEPTION_FLT_INVALID_OPERATION

This exception represents any floating-point exception not included in this list.

EXCEPTION_FLT_OVERFLOW

The exponent of a floating-point operation is greater than the magnitude allowed by the corresponding type.

EXCEPTION_FLT_STACK_CHECK

The stack overflowed or underflowed as the result of a floating-point operation.

EXCEPTION_FLT_UNDERFLOW

The exponent of a floating-point operation is less than the magnitude allowed by the corresponding type.

EXCEPTION_INT_DIVIDE_BY_ZERO

The thread tried to divide an integer value by an integer divisor of zero.

EXCEPTION_INT_OVERFLOW

The result of an integer operation caused a carry out of the most significant bit of the result.

EXCEPTION_PRIV_INSTRUCTION

The thread tried to execute an instruction whose operation is not allowed in the current machine mode.

STATUS_NONCONTINUABLE_EXCEPTION

The thread tried to continue execution after a noncontinuable exception occurred.

ExceptionFlags

Specifies the exception flags. This member can be either zero, indicating a continuable exception, or EXCEPTION_NONCONTINUABLE indicating a noncontinuable exception. Any attempt to continue execution after a noncontinuable exception causes the STATUS_NONCONTINUABLE_EXCEPTION exception.

ExceptionRecord

Points to an associated **EXCEPTION_RECORD** structure. Exception records can be chained together to provide additional information when nested exceptions occur.

ExceptionAddress

Specifies the address where the exception occurred.

NumberParameters

Specifies the number of parameters associated with the exception. This is the number of defined elements in the **ExceptionInformation** array.

ExceptionInformation

Specifies an array of additional 32-bit arguments that describe the exception. The **RaiseException** function can specify this array of arguments. For most exception codes, the array elements are undefined. For the following exception code, the array elements are defined as follows:

Exception code	Array contents
EXCEPTION_ACCESS_VIOLATION	

The first element of the array contains a read-write flag that indicates the type of operation that caused the access violation. If this value is zero, the thread attempted to read the inaccessible data. If this value is 1, the thread attempted to write to an inaccessible address.

The second array element specifies the virtual address of the inaccessible data.

See Also

GetExceptionInformation, UnhandledExceptionFilter, EXCEPTION_DEBUG_INFO, EXCEPTION_POINTERS

EXIT_PROCESS_DEBUG_INFO

`New`

```
typedef struct _EXIT_PROCESS_DEBUG_INFO { /* epdi */
    DWORD dwExitCode;
} EXIT_PROCESS_DEBUG_INFO;
```

The **EXIT_PROCESS_DEBUG_INFO** structure contains an exiting process's exit code.

Members   **dwExitCode**
Specifies the exit code for the process.

See Also   **DEBUG_EVENT**

EXIT_THREAD_DEBUG_INFO

`New`

```
typedef struct _EXIT_THREAD_DEBUG_INFO { /* etdi */
    DWORD dwExitCode;
} EXIT_THREAD_DEBUG_INFO;
```

The **EXIT_THREAD_DEBUG_INFO** structure contains an exiting thread's exit code.

Members   **dwExitCode**
Specifies the exit code for the thread.

See Also   **DEBUG_EVENT**

EXTLOGFONT

`New, Unicode`

```
typedef struct tagEXTLOGFONT {
    LOGFONT elfLogFont;
    BYTE    elfFullName[LF_FULLFACESIZE];
    BYTE    elfStyle[LF_FACESIZE];
    DWORD   elfVersion;
    DWORD   elfStyleSize;
    DWORD   elfMatch;
    DWORD   elfReserved;
    BYTE    elfVendorId[ELF_VENDOR_SIZE];
    DWORD   elfCulture;
    PANOSE  elfPanose;
```

```
} EXTLOGFONT;
```

The **EXTLOGFONT** structure defines the attributes of a font.

Members

elfLogFont

Specifies some of the attributes of the given font. This member is a **LOGFONT** structure.

```
typedef struct tagLOGFONT { /* lf */
    LONG lfHeight;
    LONG lfWidth;
    LONG lfEscapement;
    LONG lfOrientation;
    LONG lfWeight;
    BYTE lfItalic;
    BYTE lfUnderline;
    BYTE lfStrikeOut;
    BYTE lfCharSet;
    BYTE lfOutPrecision;
    BYTE lfClipPrecision;
    BYTE lfQuality;
    BYTE lfPitchAndFamily;
    CHAR lfFaceName[LF_FACESIZE];
} LOGFONT;
```

elfFullName

Specifies a unique name for the font (for example, ABC Font Company TrueType Bold Italic Sans Serif).

elfStyle

Specifies the style of the font (for example, Bold Italic).

elfVersion

Reserved. Must be zero for the first release of Windows NT.

elfStyleSize

This member only has meaning for hinted fonts. It specifies the point size at which the font is hinted. If set to zero, which is its default value, the font is hinted at the point size corresponding to the **lfHeight** member of the **LOGFONT** structure specified by **elfLogFont**.

elfMatch

A unique identifier for an enumerated font. This will be filled in by graphics device interface (GDI) upon font enumeration.

elfReserved

Reserved; must be zero.

elfVendorId

A 4-byte identifier of the font vendor.

elfCulture

Reserved; must be zero.

elfPanose

Specifies the shape of the font. If all members of this structure are set to zero, the **elfPanose** member is ignored by the font mapper. The **PANOSE** structure has the following form:

```
typedef struct tagPANOSE { /* pnse */
    DWORD ulCulture;
    BYTE  bFamilyType;
    BYTE  bSerifStyle;
    BYTE  bWeight;
    BYTE  bProportion;
    BYTE  bContrast;
    BYTE  bStrokeVariation;
    BYTE  bArmStyle;
    BYTE  bLetterform;
    BYTE  bMidline;
    BYTE  bXHeight;
} PANOSE
```

See Also   **ExtCreateFontIndirect**

EXTLOGPEN

`New`

```
typedef struct tagEXTLOGPEN { /* exlp */
    UINT     elpPenStyle;
    UINT     elpWidth;
    UINT     elpBrushStyle;
    COLORREF elpColor;
    LONG     elpHatch;
    DWORD    elpNumEntries;
    DWORD    elpStyleEntry[1];
} EXTLOGPEN;
```

The **EXTLOGPEN** structure defines the pen style, width, and brush attributes for an extended pen. This structure is used by the **GetObject** function when it retrieves a description of a pen that was created when an application called the **ExtCreatePen** function.

Members   **elpPenStyle**

Specifies a combination of pen type, style, end cap style, and join style. The values from each category can be retrieved by using a bitwise AND with the appropriate mask.

The **elpPenStyle** member masked with PS_TYPE_MASK has one of the following pen type values:

Value	Meaning
PS_GEOMETRIC	The pen is geometric.
PS_COSMETIC	The pen is cosmetic.

The **elpPenStyle** member masked with PS_STYLE_MASK has one of the following pen styles values:

Value	Meaning
PS_SOLID	The pen is solid.
PS_DASH	The pen is dashed.
PS_DOT	The pen is dotted.
PS_DASHDOT	The pen has alternating dashes and dots.
PS_DASHDOTDOT	The pen has alternating dashes and double dots.
PS_NULL	The pen is invisible.
PS_USERSTYLE	The pen will use a styling array supplied by the user.
PS_INSIDEFRAME	The pen is solid. When this pen is used in any GDI drawing function that takes a bounding rectangle, the dimensions of the figure are shrunk so that it fits entirely in the bounding rectangle, taking into account the width of the pen. This applies only to PS_GEOMETRIC pens.

The following category applies only to PS_GEOMETRIC pens. The **elpPenStyle** member masked with PS_ENDCAP_MASK has one of the following end cap values:

Value	Meaning
PS_ENDCAP_ROUND	Line end caps are round.
PS_ENDCAP_SQUARE	Line end caps are square.
PS_ENDCAP_FLAT	Line end caps are flat.

The following category applies only to PS_GEOMETRIC pens. The **elpPenStyle** member masked with PS_JOIN_STYLE has one of the following join values:

Value	Meaning
PS_JOIN_BEVEL	Line joins are beveled.
PS_JOIN_MITER	Line joins are mitered when they are within the current **SetMiterLimit** limit. A join is beveled when it would exceed the limit.
PS_JOIN_ROUND	Line joins are round.

elpWidth
Specifies the width of the pen.

If the **elpPenStyle** member specifies geometric lines, this value is the width, in logical units, of the line. Otherwise, the lines are cosmetic and this value is 1.

elpBrushStyle

Specifies the brush style of the pen. The **elpBrushStyle** member values can be one of the following:

Value	Description
BS_DIBPATTERN	Specifies a pattern brush defined by a device-independent bitmap (DIB) specification. If **elpBrushStyle** is BS_DIBPATTERN, the **elpHatch** member contains a handle to a packed DIB.
BS_DIBPATTERNPT	Specifies a pattern brush defined by a device-independent bitmap (DIB) specification. If **elpBrushStyle** is BS_DIBPATTERNPT, the **elpHatch** member contains a pointer to a packed DIB.
BS_HATCHED	Specifies a hatched brush.
BS_HOLLOW	Specifies a hollow or NULL brush.
BS_PATTERN	Specifies a pattern brush defined by a memory bitmap.
BS_SOLID	Specifies a solid brush.

elpColor

If **elpBrushStyle** is BS_SOLID or BS_HATCHED, **elpColor** specifies the color in which the pen is to be drawn. For BS_HATCHED, the **SetBkMode** and **SetBkColor** functions determine the background color.

If **elpBrushStyle** is BS_HOLLOW or BS_PATTERN, **elpColor** is ignored.

If **elpBrushStyle** is BS_DIBPATTERN or BS_DIBPATTERNPT, the low-order word of **elpColor** specifies whether the **bmiColors** members of the **BITMAPINFO** structure contain explicit red, green, blue (RGB) values or indexes into the currently realized logical palette. The **elpColor** value must be one of the following:

Value	Meaning
DIB_PAL_COLORS	The color table consists of an array of 16-bit indexes into the currently realized logical palette.
DIB_RGB_COLORS	The color table contains literal RGB values.

elpHatch

If **elpBrushStyle** is BS_PATTERN, **elpHatch** is a handle to the bitmap that defines the pattern.

If **elpBrushStyle** is BS_SOLID or BS_HOLLOW, **elpHatch** is ignored.

If **elpBrushStyle** is BS_DIBPATTERN, the **elpHatch** member is a handle to a packed DIB. To obtain this handle, an application calls the **GlobalAlloc** function to allocate a block of global memory and then fills the memory with the packed DIB. A packed DIB consists of a **BITMAPINFO** structure immediately followed by the array of bytes that define the pixels of the bitmap.

If **elpBrushStyle** is BS_DIBPATTERNPT, the **elpHatch** member is a pointer to a packed DIB.

If **elpBrushStyle** is BS_HATCHED, the **elpHatch** member specifies the orientation of the lines used to create the hatch. It can be any one of the following values:

Value	Meaning
HS_BDIAGONAL	45-degree upward hatch (left to right)
HS_CROSS	Horizontal and vertical crosshatch
HS_DIAGCROSS	45-degree crosshatch
HS_FDIAGONAL	45-degree downward hatch (left to right)
HS_HORIZONTAL	Horizontal hatch
HS_VERTICAL	Vertical hatch

elpNumEntries
Specifies the number of entries in the style array in the **elpStyleEntry** member. This value is zero if **elpPenStyle** does not specify PS_USERSTYLE.

elpStyleEntry
Specifies a user-supplied style array. The array is specified with a finite length, but it is used as if it repeated indefinitely. The first entry in the array specifies the length of the first dash. The second entry specifies the length of the first gap. Thereafter, lengths of dashes and gaps alternate.

If **elpWidth** specifies geometric lines, the lengths are in logical units. Otherwise, the lines are cosmetic and lengths are in device units.

See Also   **ExtCreatePen**, **GetObject**, **SetBkColor**, **SetBkMode**

EXT_BUTTON

New

```
typedef struct tagEXT_BUTTON { /* extbtn */
    WORD idCommand;
    WORD idsHelp;
    WORD fsStyle;
} EXT_BUTTON;
```

The **EXT_BUTTON** structure contains information about a button that a File Manager extension dynamic-link library is adding to the toolbar of File Manager.

Members	**idCommand**
	Specifies the command identifier for the button.
	idsHelp
	Specifies the identifier of the Help string for the button.
	fsStyle
	Specifies the style of the button.
See Also	FMEVENT_TOOLBARLOAD, **FMS_TOOLBARLOAD**

FILETIME

```
typedef struct _FILETIME { /* ft */
    DWORD dwLowDateTime;
    DWORD dwHighDateTime;
} FILETIME;
```

The **FILETIME** structure is a 64-bit value representing the number of 100-nanosecond intervals since January 1, 1601.

Members	**dwLowDateTime**
	Specifies the low-order 32 bits of the file time.
	dwHighDateTime
	Specifies the high-order 32 bits of the file time.
See Also	**CompareFileTime, DosDateTimeToFileTime, FileTimeToDosDateTime, FileTimeToLocalFileTime, FileTimeToSystemTime, GetFileTime, LocalFileTimeToFileTime, SetFileTime, SystemTimeToFileTime**

FIND_NAME_BUFFER

New

```
typedef struct _FIND_NAME_BUFFER { /* fnb */
    UCHAR length;
    UCHAR access_control;
    UCHAR frame_control;
    UCHAR destination_addr[6];
    UCHAR source_addr[6];
    UCHAR routing_info[18];
} FIND_NAME_BUFFER;
```

The **FIND_NAME_BUFFER** structure contains information about a local network session. One or more **FIND_NAME_BUFFER** structures follows a

FIND_NAME_HEADER structure when an application specifies NCBFINDNAME in the **ncb_command** member of the **NCB** structure.

Members

length
Specifies the length, in bytes, of the **FIND_NAME_BUFFER** structure. Although this structure always occupies 33 bytes, not all of the structure is necessarily valid.

access_control
Specifies the access control for the LAN header.

frame_control
Specifies the frame control for the LAN header.

destination_addr[6]
Specifies the destination address of the remote node where the name was found.

source_addr[6]
Specifies the source address for the remote node where the name was found.

routing_info[18]
Specifies additional routing information.

See Also   **FILE_NAME_HEADER, NCB**

FIND_NAME_HEADER   New

```
typedef struct _FIND_NAME_HEADER { /* fnh */
    WORD  node_count;
    UCHAR reserved;
    UCHAR unique_group;
} FIND_NAME_HEADER;
```

The **FIND_NAME_HEADER** structure contains information about a network name. **FIND_NAME_HEADER** is followed by as many **FIND_NAME_BUFFER** structures as are required to describe the name.

Members

node_count
Specifies the number of nodes on which the specified name was found. The **FIND_NAME_HEADER** structure is followed by the number of **FIND_NAME_BUFFER** structures specified by the **node_count** member.

reserved
Reserved.

unique_group
Specifies whether the name is unique. This value is 0 to specify a unique name or 1 to specify a group.

Comments   The **FIND_NAME_HEADER** structure is pointed to by the **ncb_buffer** member of the **NCB** structure when an application issues an NCBFINDNAME command.

See Also   **FIND_NAME_BUFFER**, **NCB**

FINDREPLACE

`Unicode`

```
typedef struct {    /* fr */
    DWORD         lStructSize;
    HWND          hwndOwner;
    HINSTANCE     hInstance;
    DWORD         Flags;
    LPSTR         lpstrFindWhat;
    LPSTR         lpstrReplaceWith;
    WORD          wFindWhatLen;
    WORD          wReplaceWithLen;
    DWORD         lCustData;
    LPFRHOOKPROC  lpfnHook;
    LPCSTR        lpTemplateName;
} FINDREPLACE;
```

The **FINDREPLACE** structure contains information the operating system uses to initialize the system-defined Find and Replace dialog boxes. After the user closes the dialog box, the system returns information about the user-defined find or replace parameters in this structure.

Members   **lStructSize**
Specifies the length, in bytes, of the structure.

hwndOwner
Identifies the window that owns the dialog box. This member can be any valid window handle, but it must not be NULL.

hInstance
Identifies a data block that contains a dialog box template specified by the **lpstrTemplateName** member. This member is used only if the **Flags** member specifies the FR_ENABLETEMPLATE flag; otherwise, this member is ignored.

Flags
Specifies the dialog box initialization flags. This member may be a combination of the following values:

Value	Meaning
FR_DIALOGTERM	

Indicates that the dialog box is closing. The window handle returned by the **FindText** or **ReplaceText** function is not valid if this flag is set.

FR_DOWN

Determines the direction of searches through a document. If this flag is set, the search direction is down; if the flag is clear, the search direction is up. Initially, this flag specifies the state of the Up and Down controls; after the user closes the dialog box, this flag specifies the user's selection.

FR_ENABLEHOOK

Enables the hook function specified in the **lpfnHook** member of this structure. This flag is used only to initialize the dialog box.

FR_ENABLETEMPLATE

Causes the system to create the dialog box by using the dialog box template identified by the **hInstance** and **lpTemplateName** members. This flag is used only to initialize the dialog box.

FR_ENABLETEMPLATEHANDLE

Indicates that the **hInstance** member identifies a data block that contains a preloaded dialog box template. The system ignores the **lpTemplateName** member if this flag is specified.

FR_FINDNEXT

Indicates that the application should search for the next occurrence of the string specified by the **lpstrFindWhat** member.

FR_HIDEUPDOWN

Causes the system to hide the Direction check box and the Up and Down controls.

FR_HIDEMATCHCASE

Causes the system to hide the Match Case check box.

FR_HIDEWHOLEWORD

Causes the system to hide the Match Whole Word Only check box.

FR_MATCHCASE

Set for case-sensitive searches.

FR_NOMATCHCASE

Disables the Match Case check box. This flag is used only to initialize the dialog box.

FR_NOUPDOWN

Disables the direction radio buttons. This flag is used only to initialize the dialog box.

FR_NOWHOLEWORD

Disables the Whole Word check box. This flag is used only to initialize the dialog box.

FR_REPLACE

Indicates that the application should replace the current occurrence of the string specified in the **lpstrFindWhat** member with the string specified in the **lpstrReplaceWith** member.

FR_REPLACEALL

Indicates that the application should replace all occurrences of the string specified in the **lpstrFindWhat** member with the string specified in the **lpstrReplaceWith** member.

FR_SHOWHELP

Causes the dialog box to show the Help button. The **hwndOwner** member must not be NULL if this option is specified.

FR_WHOLEWORD

Checks the Whole Word check box. Only whole words matching the search string will be considered.

lpstrFindWhat

Specifies the string to search for. If there is a string specified when the dialog box starts, the dialog box initializes the Find What: text control with this string. If the FR_FINDNEXT flag is set when the dialog box is opened, the application should search for an occurrence of this string by using the FR_DOWN, FR_WHOLEWORD, and FR_MATCHCASE flags to further define the direction and type of search. The application must allocate a buffer for the string. This buffer should be at least 80 characters long.

lpstrReplaceWith

Specifies the replacement string for replace operations. The **FindText** function ignores this member.

wFindWhatLen

Specifies the length, in bytes, of the buffer pointed to by the **lpstrFindWhat** member points.

wReplaceWithLen

Specifies the length, in bytes, of the buffer pointed to by the **lpstrReplaceWith** member.

lCustData

Specifies application-defined data the system passes to the hook function identified by the **lpfnHook** member. The system passes the data in the *lParam* parameter of the WM_INITDIALOG message.

lpfnHook

Points to a hook function that processes messages intended for the dialog box. An application must specify the FR_ENABLEHOOK flag in the **Flags** member to enable the function; otherwise, the system ignores this structure member. The hook function should return FALSE to pass a message on to the standard dialog procedure, or TRUE to discard the message.

If the hook function returns FALSE in response to the WM_INITDIALOG message, it is responsible for displaying the dialog. This is done by calling the **ShowWindow** and **UpdateWindow** functions (note: remember to put these calls after any other paint operations). The following code snippet provides an example:

```
/* we've returned FALSE in response to WM_INITDIALOG */
/* we've performed any other paint operations */
/* now we display the dialog */
ShowWindow(hDlg, SW_SHOWNORMAL);
UpdateWindow(hDlg);
```

If the hook function returns FALSE in response to the WM_INITDIALOG message, but fails to display the dialog, the dialog will not be shown.

lpstrTemplateName

Points to a null-terminated string that names the dialog box template resource to be substituted for the standard dialog box template. An application can use the **MAKEINTRESOURCE** macro for numbered dialog resources. This member is used only if the **Flags** member specifies the FR_ENABLETEMPLATE flag; otherwise, this member is ignored.

See Also **FindText**, **ReplaceText**, WM_INITDIALOG

FIXED

```
typedef struct _FIXED { /* fix */
    WORD  fract;
    short value;
} FIXED;
```

The **FIXED** structure contains the integral and fractional parts of a fixed-point real number.

Members **fract**
Specifies the fractional part of the number.

value
Specifies the integer part of the number.

Comments The **FIXED** structure is used to describe the elements of the **MAT2** structure.

FMS_GETDRIVEINFO

```
typedef struct _FMS_GETDRIVEINFO { /* fmsgdi */
    DWORD dwTotalSpace;
    DWORD dwFreeSpace;
    CHAR  szPath[260];
    CHAR  szVolume[14];
    CHAR  szShare[128];
} FMS_GETDRIVEINFO;
```

The **FMS_GETDRIVEINFO** structure contains information about the drive selected in the active File Manager window (the directory window or the Search Results window).

Members

dwTotalSpace

Specifies the total amount of storage space, in bytes, on the disk associated with the drive.

dwFreeSpace

Specifies the amount of free storage space, in bytes, on the disk associated with the drive.

szPath

Specifies the null-terminated path of the current directory.

szVolume

Specifies the null-terminated volume label of the disk associated with the drive.

szShare

Specifies the null-terminated name of the sharepoint (if the drive is being accessed through a network).

See Also

FMExtensionProc, FM_GETDRIVEINFO

FMS_GETFILESEL

```
typedef struct _FMS_GETFILESEL { /* fmsgfs */
    FILETIME ftTime;
    DWORD    dwSize;
    BYTE     bAttr;
    CHAR     szName[260];
} FMS_GETFILESEL;
```

The **FMS_GETFILESEL** structure contains information about a selected file in the active File Manager window (the directory window or the Search Results window).

Members

ftTime

Specifies the time and date the file was created.

dwSize

Specifies the size, in bytes, of the file.

bAttr

Specifies the attributes of the file.

szName

Specifies the null-terminated full path and filename of the selected file.

See Also

FMExtensionProc

FMS_LOAD

```
typedef struct _FMS_LOAD { /* fmsld */
    DWORD dwSize;
    CHAR  szMenuName[MENU_TEXT_LEN];
    HMENU hMenu;
    UINT  wMenuDelta;
} FMS_LOAD;
```

The **FMS_LOAD** structure contains information that File Manager uses to add a custom menu provided by a File Manager extension DLL. The structure also provides a delta value that the extension DLL can use to manipulate the custom menu after File Manager has loaded the menu.

Members

dwSize

Specifies the length, in bytes, of the structure.

szMenuName

Specifies the null-terminated name for a menu item that appears on the menu bar in File Manager.

hMenu

Identifies the pop-up menu added to the menu bar in File Manager.

wMenuDelta

Specifies the menu-item delta value. To avoid conflicts with its own menu items, File Manager renumbers the menu-item identifiers in the pop-up menu identified by the **hMenu** member by adding this delta value to each identifier. An extension DLL that must modify a menu item must identify the item by adding the delta value to the menu item's identifier. The value of this member can vary from session to session.

See Also   **FMExtensionProc**

FMS_TOOLBARLOAD

New

```
typedef struct tagFMS_TOOLBARLOAD { /* fmstbl */
    DWORD        dwSize;
    LPEXT_BUTTON lpButtons;
    WORD         cButtons;
    WORD         cBitmaps;
    WORD         idBitmap;
    HBITMAP      hBitmap;
} FMS_TOOLBARLOAD;
```

The **FMS_TOOLBARLOAD** structure contains information about custom buttons to be added to the File Manager toolbar. The buttons are provided by a File Manager extension DLL.

Members   **dwSize**

Specifies the size, in bytes, of the structure. File Manager sets the size before calling the extension and checks the size after the extension procedure returns.

lpButtons

Points to an array of **EXT_BUTTON** structures that specify the style, command identifier, and Help string identifier for each toolbar button.

cButtons

Specifies the number of **EXT_BUTTON** structures in the array pointed to by the **lpButtons** member. This number equals the number of buttons and separators to add to the toolbar.

cBitmaps

Specifies the number of buttons represented by the given bitmap.

idBitmap

Specifies the identifier of a bitmap resource in the executable file for the extension DLL. The bitmap resource contains images for the number of buttons specified by **cBitmaps**. File Manager loads the bitmap resource, then uses it to display the buttons.

hBitmap

Specifies the handle of a bitmap that the File Manager will use to obtain and display button images if **idBitmap** is 0.

See Also   FMEVENT_TOOLBARLOAD, **EXT_BUTTON**

FOCUS_EVENT_RECORD

`New`

```
typedef struct _FOCUS_EVENT_RECORD { /* fer */
    BOOL bSetFocus;
} FOCUS_EVENT_RECORD;
```

The **FOCUS_EVENT_RECORD** structure is used to report focus events in a console **INPUT_RECORD** structure. These events are used internally and should be ignored.

Members   **bSetFocus**
Used internally.

See Also   **INPUT_RECORD**

FORM_INFO_1

`New, Unicode`

```
typedef struct _FORM_INFO_1 { /* fil */
    LPTSTR pName;
    SIZEL  Size;
    RECTL  ImageableArea;
} FORM_INFO_1;
```

The **FORM_INFO_1** structure identifies a form, specifies its dimensions, and specifies the dimensions of its printable area.

Members   **pName**
Points to a null-terminated string that specifies the name of the form.

Size
Specifies the width and height, in thousandths of millimeters, of the form.

ImageableArea
Specifies the width and height, in thousandths of millimeters, of the form.

See Also   **AddForm**, **GetForm**, **SetForm**

FORMAT_PARAMETERS

New

```
typedef struct _FORMAT_PARAMETERS{
    MEDIA_TYPE MediaType;
    DWORD StartCylinderNumber;
    DWORD EndCylinderNumber;
    DWORD StartHeadNumber;
    DWORD EndHeadNumber;
} FORMAT_PARAMETERS ;
```

The **FORMAT_PARAMETERS** structure provides information used in formatting a contiguous set of disk tracks.

Members

MediaType
Specifies the media type. See **MEDIA_TYPE**.

StartCylinderNumber
Specifies the cylinder number at which to begin the format.

EndCylinderNumber
Specifies the cylinder number at which to end the format.

StartHeadNumber
Specifies the beginning head location.

EndHeadNumber
Specifies the ending head location.

Comments
The **DeviceIoControl** function uses a **FORMAT_PARAMETERS** structure as input to an **IOCTL_DISK_FORMAT_TRACKS** device i/o operation.

See Also
DeviceIoControl, **IOCTL_DISK_FORMAT_TRACKS**, **MEDIA_TYPE**

GENERIC_MAPPING

New

```
typedef struct _GENERIC_MAPPING { /* gm */
    ACCESS_MASK GenericRead;
    ACCESS_MASK GenericWrite;
    ACCESS_MASK GenericExecute;
    ACCESS_MASK GenericAll;
} GENERIC_MAPPING;
```

The **GENERIC_MAPPING** structure defines the mapping of generic access rights to specific and standard access rights for an object. When a client application requests generic access to an object, that request is mapped to the access rights defined in this structure.

Members

GenericRead
Specifies an access mask defining read access to an object.

GenericWrite
Specifies an access mask defining write access to an object.

GenericExecute
Specifies an access mask defining execute access to an object.

GenericAll
Specifies an access mask defining all possible types of access to an object.

See Also   **AccessCheck, AccessCheckAndAuditAlarm, CreatePrivateObjectSecurity, MapGenericMask, SetPrivateObjectSecurity, ACCESS_MASK**

GLYPHMETRICS

```
typedef struct _GLYPHMETRICS { /* glmt */
    UINT  gmBlackBoxX;
    UINT  gmBlackBoxY;
    POINT gmptGlyphOrigin;
    short gmCellIncX;
    short gmCellIncY;
} GLYPHMETRICS;
```

The **GLYPHMETRICS** structure contains information about the placement and orientation of a glyph in a character cell.

Members

gmBlackBoxX
Specifies the width of the smallest rectangle that completely encloses the glyph (its "black box").

gmBlackBoxY
Specifies the height of the smallest rectangle that completely encloses the glyph (its "black box").

gmptGlyphOrigin
Specifies the x- and y-coordinates of the upper left corner of the smallest rectangle that completely encloses the glyph.

gmCellIncX
Specifies the horizontal distance from the origin of the current character cell to the origin of the next character cell.

gmCellIncY
Specifies the vertical distance from the origin of the current character cell to the origin of the next character cell.

Comments   Values in the **GLYPHMETRICS** structure are specified in logical units.

See Also   **GetGlyphOutline**

HANDLETABLE

```
typedef struct tagHANDLETABLE { /* ht */
    HGDIOBJ objectHandle[1];
} HANDLETABLE;
```

The **HANDLETABLE** structure is an array of handles, each of which identifies a graphics device interface (GDI) object.

Members   **objectHandle[1]**
Contains an array of handles.

HELPWININFO   `Unicode`

```
typedef struct {     /* hi */
    int    wStructSize;
    int    x;
    int    y;
    int    dx;
    int    dy;
    int    wMax;
    TCHAR  rgchMember[2];
} HELPWININFO;
```

The **HELPWININFO** structure contains the size and position of either a primary or a secondary Help window. An application can set this information by calling the **WinHelp** function with the HELP_SETWINPOS value.

Members   **wStructSize**
Specifies the size of the **HELPWININFO** structure.

x
Specifies the x-coordinate of the upper left corner of the window.

y
Specifies the y-coordinate of the upper left corner of the window.

dx
  Specifies the width of the window.

dy
  Specifies the height of the window.

wMax
  Specifies how the window is to be shown. This member must be one of the following values:

Value	Action
SW_HIDE	Hides the window and passes activation to another window.
SW_SHOWNORMAL	Activates and displays the window. Whether the window is minimized or maximized, Windows restores it to its original size and position.
SW_SHOWMINIMIZED	Activates the window and displays it as an icon.
SW_SHOWMAXIMIZED	Activates the window and displays it as a maximized window.
SW_SHOWNOACTIVATE	Displays a window in its most recent size and position. The window that is currently active remains active.
SW_SHOW	Activates a window and displays it in its current size and position.
SW_MINIMIZE	Minimizes the specified window and activates the top-level window in the Z order.
SW_SHOWMINNOACTIVE	Displays the window as an icon. The window that is currently active remains active.
SW_SHOWNA	Displays the window in its current state. The window that is currently active remains active.
SW_RESTORE	Same as SW_SHOWNORMAL.

rgchMember
  Specifies the name of the window.

Comments   Microsoft Windows Help divides the display into 1024 units in both the x- and y-directions. To create a secondary window that fills the upper left quadrant of the display, for example, an application would specify zero for the **x** and **y** members and 512 for the **dx** and **dy** members.

See Also   **WinHelp**

HSZPAIR

```
typedef struct tagHSZPAIR {    /* hp */
    HSZ hszSvc;
    HSZ hszTopic;
} HSZPAIR;
```

The **HSZPAIR** structure contains a dynamic data exchange (DDE) service name and topic name. A DDE server application can use this structure during an XTYP_WILDCONNECT transaction to enumerate the service-topic pairs that it supports.

Members

hszSvc
Identifies a service name.

hszTopic
Identifies a topic name.

ICONINFO

```
typedef struct _ICONINFO { /* ii */
    BOOL    fIcon;
    DWORD   xHotspot;
    DWORD   yHotspot;
    HBITMAP hbmMask;
    HBITMAP hbmColor;
} ICONINFO;
```

The **ICONINFO** structure contains information about an icon or a cursor.

Members

fIcon
Specifies whether this structure defines an icon or a cursor. A value of TRUE specifies an icon; FALSE specifies a cursor.

xHotspot
Specifies the x-coordinate of a cursor's hot spot. If this structure defines an icon, the hot spot is always in the center of the icon, and this member is ignored.

yHotspot
Specifies the y-coordinate of the cursor's hot spot. If this structure defines an icon, the hot spot is always in the center of the icon, and this member is ignored.

hbmMask

Specifies the icon bitmask bitmap. If this structure defines a black and white icon, this bitmask is formatted so that the upper half is the icon AND bitmask, and the lower half is the icon XOR bitmask. Under this condition, the height should be an even multiple of two. If this structure defines a color icon, this mask defines the AND bitmask of the icon ONLY.

hbmColor

Identifies the icon color bitmap. This member can be optional if this structure defines a black and white icon. After the AND bitmask of **hbmMask** is applied with SRCAND to the destination, the color bitmap is applied (using XOR) to the destination by using SRCINVERT.

See Also   **CreateIconIndirect**, **GetIconInfo**

INPUT_RECORD

```
typedef struct _INPUT_RECORD { /* ir */
    WORD EventType;
    union {
        KEY_EVENT_RECORD KeyEvent;
        MOUSE_EVENT_RECORD MouseEvent;
        WINDOW_BUFFER_SIZE_RECORD WindowBufferSizeEvent;
        MENU_EVENT_RECORD MenuEvent;
        FOCUS_EVENT_RECORD FocusEvent;
    } Event;
} INPUT_RECORD;
```

The **INPUT_RECORD** structure is used to report input events in the console input buffer. These records can be read from the input buffer by using the **ReadConsoleInput** or **PeekConsoleInput** function, or written to the input buffer by using the **WriteConsoleInput** function.

Members   **EventType**

Identifies the type of input event and the event record stored in the **Event** member. This member can have one of the following values:

Value	Meaning
KEY_EVENT	The **Event** member contains a **KEY_EVENT_RECORD** structure with information about a keyboard input event. The **KEY_EVENT_RECORD** structure has the following form:

```
typedef struct _KEY_EVENT_RECORD { /* ker */
    BOOL bKeyDown;
```

```
        WORD wRepeatCount;
        WORD wVirtualKeyCode;
        WORD wVirtualScanCode;
        union {
            WCHAR UnicodeChar;
            CHAR  AsciiChar;
        } uChar;
        DWORD dwControlKeyState;
    } KEY_EVENT_RECORD;
```

MOUSE_EVENT

The **Event** member contains a **MOUSE_EVENT_RECORD** structure with information about a mouse movement or button press event. The **MOUSE_EVENT_RECORD** structure has the following form:

```
typedef struct _MOUSE_EVENT_RECORD { /* mer */
    COORD dwMousePosition;
    DWORD dwButtonState;
    DWORD dwControlKeyState;
    DWORD dwEventFlags;
} MOUSE_EVENT_RECORD;
```

WINDOW_BUFFER_SIZE_EVENT

The **Event** member contains a **WINDOW_BUFFER_SIZE_RECORD** structure with information a user action to change the console window size. The **WINDOW_BUFFER_SIZE_RECORD** structure has the following form:

```
typedef struct _WINDOW_BUFFER_SIZE_RECORD { /* wbsr */
    COORD dwSize;
} WINDOW_BUFFER_SIZE_RECORD;
```

MENU_EVENT

The **Event** member contains a **MENU_EVENT_RECORD** structure. These events are used internally, and should be ignored. The **MENU_EVENT_RECORD** structure has the following form:

```
typedef struct _MENU_EVENT_RECORD { /* mer */
    UINT dwCommandId;
} MENU_EVENT_RECORD, *PMENU_EVENT_RECORD;
```

FOCUS_EVENT

The **Event** member contains a **FOCUS_EVENT_RECORD** structure. These events are used internally, and should be ignored. The **FOCUS_EVENT_RECORD** structure has the following form:

```
typedef struct _FOCUS_EVENT_RECORD { /* fer */
    BOOL bSetFocus;
```

```
                              } FOCUS_EVENT_RECORD;
```

Event

Contains a **KEY_EVENT_RECORD, MOUSE_EVENT_RECORD,
WINDOW_BUFFER_SIZE_RECORD, MENU_EVENT_RECORD,** or
FOCUS_EVENT_RECORD structure, depending on the event type specified
by the **EventType** member.

See Also   **PeekConsoleInput, ReadConsoleInput, WriteConsoleInput**

JOB_INFO_1   New, Unicode

```
typedef struct _JOB_INFO_1 {     /* ji1 */
    DWORD   JobId;
    LPTSTR  pPrinterName;
    LPTSTR  pMachineName;
    LPTSTR  pUserName;
    LPTSTR  pDocument;
    LPTSTR  pDatatype;
    LPTSTR  pStatus;
    DWORD   Status;
    DWORD   Priority;
    DWORD   Position;
    DWORD   TotalPages;
    DWORD   PagesPrinted;
    SYSTEMTIME Submitted;
} JOB_INFO_1;
```

The **JOB_INFO_1** structure specifies print-job information such as the job-
identifier value, the name of the printer for which the job is spooled, the name of
the machine that created the print job, the name of the user that owns the print job,
and so on.

Members   **JobId**

Specifies a job identifier.

pPrinterName

Points to a null-terminated string that specifies the name of the printer for
which the job is spooled.

pMachineName

Points to a null-terminated string that specifies the name of the machine that
created the print job.

pUserName

Points to a null-terminated string that specifies the name of the user that owns the print job.

pDocument

Points to a null-terminated string that specifies the name of the print job (for example, "MS-WORD: Review.doc").

pDatatype

Points to a null-terminated string that specifies the type of data used to record the print job.

pStatus

Points to a null-terminated string that specifies the status of the print job.

Status

Specifies the job status. This member can be one or more of the following values:

JOB_STATUS_DELETING
JOB_STATUS_ERROR
JOB_STATUS_OFFLINE
JOB_STATUS_PAPEROUT
JOB_STATUS_PAUSED
JOB_STATUS_PRINTED
JOB_STATUS_PRINTING
JOB_STATUS_SPOOLING

Priority

Specifies the job priority.

Position

Specifies the job's position in the print queue.

TotalPages

Specifies how many pages the document contains.

PagesPrinted

Specifies the number of pages that have printed.

Submitted

Specifies the time that this document was spooled.

See Also   **EnumJobs, GetJob, SetJob**

JOB_INFO_2

```
typedef struct _JOB_INFO_2 { /* ji2 */
    DWORD       JobId;
    LPTSTR      pPrinterName;
    LPTSTR      pMachineName;
    LPTSTR      pUserName;
    LPTSTR      pDocument;
    LPTSTR      pNotifyName;
    LPTSTR      pDatatype;
    LPTSTR      pPrintProcessor;
    LPTSTR      pParameters;
    LPTSTR      pDriverName;
    LPDEVMODE   pDevMode;
    LPTSTR      pStatus;
    PSECURITY_DESCRIPTOR pSecurityDescriptor;
    DWORD       Status;
    DWORD       Priority;
    DWORD       Position;
    DWORD       StartTime;
    DWORD       UntilTime;
    DWORD       TotalPages;
    DWORD       Size;
    SYSTEMTIME  Submitted;
    DWORD       Time;
    DWORD       PagesPrinted ;
} JOB_INFO_2;
```

The **JOB_INFO_2** structure describes a full set of values associated with a job.

Members

JobId
Specifies a job ID value.

pPrinterName
Points to a null-terminated string that specifies the name of the printer for which the job is spooled.

pMachineName
Points to a null-terminated string that specifies the name of the machine that created the print job.

pUserName
Points to a null-terminated string that specifies the name of the user who owns the print job.

pDocument
Points to a null-terminated string that specifies the name of the print job (for example, "MS-WORD: Review.doc").

pNotifyName

Points to a null-terminated string that specifies the name of the user who should be notified when the job has been printed or when an error occurs while printing the job.

pDatatype

Points to a null-terminated string that specifies the type of data used to record the print job.

pPrintProcessor

Points to a null-terminated string that specifies the name of the print processor that should be used to print the job.

pParameters

Points to a null-terminated string that specifies print-processor parameters.

pDriverName

Points to a null-terminated string that specifies the name of the printer driver that should be used to process the print job.

pDevMode

Points to a **DEVMODE** structure that contains device-initialization and environment data for the printer driver.

pStatus

Points to a null-terminated string that specifies the status of the print job.

pSecurityDescriptor

Points to a **SECURITY_DESCRIPTOR** structure that defines the print-job's owner and group, as well as other access-related data.

Status

Specifies the job status. This member can be one or more of the following values:

JOB_STATUS_PAUSED
JOB_STATUS_ERROR
JOB_STATUS_DELETING
JOB_STATUS_SPOOLING
JOB_STATUS_PRINTING
JOB_STATUS_OFFLINE
JOB_STATUS_PAPEROUT
JOB_STATUS_PRINTED

Priority

Specifies the job priority.

Position

Specifies the job's position in the print queue.

StartTime

Specifies the earliest time that the job can be printed.

UntilTime

Specifies the the latest time that the job can be printed.

TotalPages

Specifies the number of pages required for the job.

Size

Specifies the size, in bytes, of the job.

Submitted

Specifies the time when the job was submitted.

Time

Specifies the total time (in seconds) elapsed since the job began printing.

PagesPrinted

Specifies the number of pages that have printed.

See Also   **EnumJobs**, **GetJob**, **SetJob**

JOYCAPS   `Unicode`

```
typedef struct joyinfo_tag {
    WORD   wMid;
    WORD   wPid;
    TCHAR  szPname[MAXPNAMELEN];
    UINT   wXmin;
    UINT   wXmax;
    UINT   wYmin;
    UINT   wYmax;
    UINT   wZmin;
    UINT   wZmax;
    UINT   wNumButtons;
    UINT   wPeriodMin;
    UINT   wPeriodMax;
} JOYCAPS;
```

The **JOYCAPS** structure stores joystick-capability information.

Members   **wMid**

Specifies the manufacturer identifier of the joystick. Manufacturer identifiers are defined in Appendix D, "Manufacturer and Product Identifiers" in the *Microsoft Win32 Programmer's Reference, Volume 2*.

wPid

Specifies the product identifier of the joystick. Product identifiers are defined in Appendix D, "Manufacturer and Product Identifiers" in the *Microsoft Win32 Programmer's Reference, Volume 2*.

szPname

Specifies the product name of the joystick, stored as a null-terminated string.

wXmin

Specifies the minimum x-position of the joystick.

wXmax

Specifies the maximum x-position of the joystick.

wYmin

Specifies the minimum y-position of the joystick.

wYmax

Specifies the maximum y-position of the joystick.

wZmin

Specifies the minimum z-position of the joystick.

wZmax

Specifies the maximum z-position of the joystick.

wNumButtons

Specifies the number of buttons on the joystick.

wPeriodMin

Specifies the smallest polling interval supported when captured by the **joySetCapture** function.

wPeriodMax

Specifies the largest polling interval supported when captured by **joySetCapture**.

See Also   **joyGetDevCaps**

JOYINFO

```
typedef struct joyinfo_tag {
    UINT  wXpos;
    UINT  wYpos;
    UINT  wZpos;
    UINT  wButtons;
} JOYINFO;
```

The **JOYINFO** structure stores joystick-position and button-state information.

Members   **wXpos**

Specifies the current x-position of the joystick.

wYpos

Specifies the current y-position of the joystick.

wZpos

Specifies the current z-position of the joystick.

wButtons

Specifies the current state of the joystick buttons. This member can be any combination of the following bit flags:

Value	Meaning
JOY_BUTTON1	Set if button 1 is pressed
JOY_BUTTON2	Set if button 2 is pressed
JOY_BUTTON3	Set if button 3 is pressed
JOY_BUTTON4	Set if button 4 is pressed

See Also   joyGetPos

KERNINGPAIR

```
typedef struct tagKERNINGPAIR { /* kp */
    WORD wFirst;
    WORD wSecond;
    int  iKernAmount;
} KERNINGPAIR;
```

The **KERNINGPAIR** structure defines a kerning pair.

Members   **wFirst**

Specifies the character code for the first character in the kerning pair.

wSecond

Specifies the character code for the second character in the kerning pair.

iKernAmount

Specifies the amount this pair will be kerned if they appear side by side in the same font and size. This value is typically negative, because pair kerning usually results in two characters being set more tightly than normal. The value is given in logical units—that is, it depends on the current mapping mode.

See Also   **GetKerningPairs**

KEY_EVENT_RECORD

```
typedef struct _KEY_EVENT_RECORD { /* ker */
    BOOL bKeyDown;
    WORD wRepeatCount;
    WORD wVirtualKeyCode;
    WORD wVirtualScanCode;
    union {
        WCHAR UnicodeChar;
        CHAR  AsciiChar;
    } uChar;
    DWORD dwControlKeyState;
} KEY_EVENT_RECORD;
```

The **KEY_EVENT_RECORD** structure is used to report keyboard input events in a console **INPUT_RECORD** structure.

Members

bKeyDown

Specifies TRUE if the key is being pressed, FALSE if the key is being released.

wRepeatCount

Specifies a count indicating that a key is being held down. For example, when a key is held down, you might get five events with this member equal to 1, one event with this member equal to 5, or multiple events with this member greater than or equal to 1.

wVirtualKeyCode

Specifies the virtual-key code that identifies the given key in a device-independent manner.

wVirtualScanCode

Specifies the virtual scan code of the given key that represents the device-dependent value generated by the keyboard hardware.

uChar

Specifies the translated Unicode or ASCII character, depending on whether the wide-character (Unicode) or ANSI version of the **ReadConsoleInput** function was used.

dwControlKeyState

Indicates the state of the control keys. This member can be a combination of the following values:

Value	Meaning
RIGHT_ALT_PRESSED	The right ALT key is pressed.
LEFT_ALT_PRESSED	The left ALT key is pressed.

RIGHT_CTRL_PRESSED	The right CTRL key is pressed.
LEFT_CTRL_PRESSED	The left CTRL key is pressed.
SHIFT_PRESSED	The SHIFT key is pressed.
NUMLOCK_ON	The NUM LOCK light is on.
SCROLLLOCK_ON	The SCROLL LOCK light is on.
CAPSLOCK_ON	The CAPS LOCK light is on.
ENHANCED_KEY	The key is enhanced.

Comments

Enhanced keys for the IBM 101- and 102-key keyboards are the INS, DEL, HOME, END, PAGE UP, PAGE DOWN, and direction keys in the clusters to the left of the keypad; and the divide (/) and ENTER keys in the keypad.

Keyboard input events are generated when any key, including control keys, is pressed or released. However, the ALT key when pressed and released without combining with another character, has special meaning to Windows and is not passed through to the application. Also, the CTRL+C key combination is not passed through if the input handle is in processed mode (ENABLE_PROCESSED_INPUT).

See Also

PeekConsoleInput, **ReadConsoleInput**, **WriteConsoleInput**, **INPUT_RECORD**

LANA_ENUM

```
typedef struct _LANA_ENUM { /* le */
    UCHAR length;
    UCHAR lana[MAX_LANA];
} LANA_ENUM;
```

The **LANA_ENUM** structure contains the numbers for the current LAN adapters.

Members

length
Specifies the number of valid entries in the array of LAN adapter numbers.

lana
Specifies an array of LAN adapter numbers.

Comments

The **LANA_ENUM** structure is pointed to by the **ncb_buffer** member of the **NCB** structure when an application issues the NCBENUM command. The NCBENUM command is not part of the IBM NetBIOS 3.0 specification.

See Also

NCB

LARGE_INTEGER

```
typedef struct _LARGE_INTEGER { /* li */
    DWORD LowPart;
    LONG  HighPart;
} LARGE_INTEGER;
```

The **LARGE_INTEGER** structure is used to represent a 64-bit signed integer value.

Members   **LowPart**
                 Specifies the low-order 32 bits.

                 HighPart
                 Specifies the high-order 32 bits.

See Also   **LUID, ULARGE_INTEGER**

LDT_ENTRY

New

```
typedef struct _LDT_ENTRY { /* ldte */
    WORD LimitLow;
    WORD BaseLow;
    union {
        struct {
            BYTE BaseMid;
            BYTE Flags1;
            BYTE Flags2;
            BYTE BaseHi;
        } Bytes;
        struct {
            DWORD BaseMid : 8;
            DWORD Type : 5;
            DWORD Dpl : 2;
            DWORD Pres : 1;
            DWORD LimitHi : 4;
            DWORD Sys : 1;
            DWORD Reserved_0 : 1;
            DWORD Default_Big : 1;
            DWORD Granularity : 1;
            DWORD BaseHi : 8;
        } Bits;
    } HighWord;
} LDT_ENTRY, *PLDT_ENTRY;
```

The **LDT_ENTRY** structure describes an entry in the descriptor table. This structure is valid only on x86-based systems.

Members

LimitLow
Contains the low 16 bits of the address of the last byte in the segment.

BaseLow
Contains the low 16 bits of the base address of the segment.

HighWord
Contains the high two words of the descriptor. This member may be interpreted as bytes or collections of bits, depending on the level of detail required.

The members of the **Bits** structure are as follows:

Member	Contents
BaseMid	Middle bits (16–23) of the base address of the segment.
Type	Bitmask that indicates the type of segment. This can be one of the following values:

Value	Meaning
0	Read-only data segment
1	Read-write data segment
2	Unused segment
3	Read-write expand-down data segment
4	Execute-only code segment
5	Executable-readable code segment
6	Execute-only "conforming" code segment
7	Executable-readable "conforming" code segment

Member	Contents
Dpl	The privilege level of the descriptor. This member is an integer value in the range 0 (most privileged) through 3 (least privileged).
Pres	The present flag. This member is 1 if the segment is present in physical memory; 0 if not.
LimitHi	High bits (16–19) of the address of the last byte in the segment.
Sys	Space that is available to system programmers. This member might be used for marking segments in some system-specific way.
Reserved_0	Reserved.
Default_Big	Size of segment. If the segment is a data segment, this member contains 1 if the segment is larger than 64K, 0 if the segment is smaller than or equal to 64K.

If the segment is a code segment, this member contains 1 if the segment is a code segment and runs with the default (native mode) instruction set. This member contains 0 if the code segment is an 80286 code segment and runs with 16-bit offsets and the 80286-compatible instruction set.

Granularity   Granularity. This member contains 0 if the segment is byte granular, 1 if the segment is page granular.

BaseHi   High bits (24–31) of the base address of the segment.

The members of the **Bytes** structure are as follows:

Member	Contents
BaseMid	Middle bits (16–23) of the base address of the segment.
Flags1	Values of the **Type**, **Dpl**, and **Pres** members in the **Bits** structure.
Flags2	Values of the **LimitHi**, **Sys**, **Reserved_0**, **Default_Big**, and **Granularity** members in the **Bits** structure.
BaseHi	High bits (24–31) of the base address of the segment.

Comments   The **GetThreadSelectorEntry** function fills this structure with information from an entry in the descriptor table. You can use this information to convert a segment-relative address to a linear virtual address.

The base address of a segment is the address of offset 0 in the segment. To calculate this value, combine **BaseLow**, **BaseMid**, and **BaseHi**.

The limit of a segment is the address of the last byte that can be addressed in the segment. To calculate this value, combine **LimitLow** and **LimitHi**.

See Also   **GetThreadSelectorEntry**

LIST_ENTRY

New

```
typedef struct _LIST_ENTRY { /* le */
    struct _LIST_ENTRY *Flink;
    struct _LIST_ENTRY *Blink;
} LIST_ENTRY;
```

The **LIST_ENTRY** structure is available for any entry in a double-linked list.

Members   **Flink**
Points to the preceding entry in a double-linked list.

Blink
Points to the next entry in a double-linked list.

Comments   This structure can be used as the beginning of a double-linked list or as any subsequent entry in the list.

LOAD_DLL_DEBUG_INFO

```
typedef struct _LOAD_DLL_DEBUG_INFO { /* lddi */
    HANDLE hFile;
    LPVOID lpBaseOfDll;
    DWORD  dwDebugInfoFileOffset;
    DWORD  nDebugInfoSize;
    LPVOID lpImageName;
    WORD fUnicode;
} LOAD_DLL_DEBUG_INFO;
```

The **LOAD_DLL_DEBUG_INFO** structure contains information about a dynamic-link library (DLL) that has just been loaded.

Members   **hFile**
Identifies a handle of the DLL. If **hFile** is NULL, the handle is not valid. Otherwise, **hFile** is opened for reading and read-sharing in the context of the debugger.

lpBaseOfDll
Points to the base address of the DLL in the address space of the process loading the DLL.

dwDebugInfoFileOffset
Specifies the offset to the debugging information in the file identified by the **hFile** member. The kernel expects the debugging information to be in CodeView 4.0 format. This format is currently a derivative of Common Object File Format (COFF).

nDebugInfoSize
Specifies the size, in bytes, of the debugging information in the file. If this value is zero, there is no debugging information.

lpImageName
Provides an optional pointer to the file name associated with the *hFile* parameter. The **lpImageName** parameter may be NULL, or may contain the address of a string pointer in the debuggee's address space. That address may in turn either be NULL, or point to the actual file name. If **fUnicode** is a non-zero value, the name string is Unicode; otherwise it is ANSI.

This parameter is strictly optional. Debuggers must be prepared to handle the case where **lpImageName** is NULL, OR ***lpImageName** (in the debuggee's address space) is NULL. Specifically, this release of Windows NT will never provide an image name for a create process event, and will not likely pass an image name for the first DLL event. This version of Windows NT will also never provide this information in the case of debug events that originate from a call to the **DebugActiveProcess** function.

fUnicode

Indicates whether a file name specified by **lpImageName** is Unicode or ANSI. A non-zero value indicates Unicode; zero indicates ANSI.

See Also   **CREATE_PROCESS_DEBUG_INFO, CREATE_THREAD_DEBUG_INFO, DEBUG_EVENT**

LOGBRUSH

```
typedef struct tagLOGBRUSH { /* lb */
    UINT      lbStyle;
    COLORREF  lbColor;
    LONG      lbHatch;
} LOGBRUSH;
```

The **LOGBRUSH** structure defines the style, color, and pattern of a physical brush. It is used by the **CreateBrushIndirect** and **ExtCreatePen** functions.

Members   **lbStyle**

Specifies the brush style. The **lbStyle** member must be one of the following styles:

Value	Meaning
BS_DIBPATTERN	A pattern brush defined by a device-independent bitmap (DIB) specification. If **lbStyle** is BS_DIBPATTERN, the **lbHatch** member contains a handle to a packed DIB.
BS_DIBPATTERNPT	A pattern brush defined by a device-independent bitmap (DIB) specification. If **lbStyle** is BS_DIBPATTERNPT, the **lbHatch** member contains a pointer to a packed DIB.
BS_HATCHED	Hatched brush.
BS_HOLLOW	Hollow brush.
BS_NULL	Same as BS_HOLLOW.
BS_PATTERN	Pattern brush defined by a memory bitmap.
BS_SOLID	Solid brush.

lbColor

Specifies the color in which the brush is to be drawn. If **lbStyle** is the BS_HOLLOW or BS_PATTERN style, **lbColor** is ignored.

If **lbStyle** is BS_DIBPATTERN or BS_DIBPATTERNBT, the low-order word of **lbColor** specifies whether the **bmiColors** members of the **BITMAPINFO** structure contain explicit red, green, blue (RGB) values or indices into the currently realized logical palette. The **lbColor** member must be one of the following values:

Value	Meaning
DIB_PAL_COLORS	The color table consists of an array of 16-bit indices into the currently realized logical palette.
DIB_RGB_COLORS	The color table contains literal RGB values.

lbHatch

Specifies a hatch style. The meaning depends on the brush style defined by **lbStyle**.

If **lbStyle** is BS_DIBPATTERN, the **lbHatch** member contains a handle to a packed DIB. If **lbStyle** is BS_DIBPATTERNPT, the **lbHatch** member contains a pointer to a packed DIB.

If **lbStyle** is BS_HATCHED, the **lbHatch** member specifies the orientation of the lines used to create the hatch. It can be one of the following values:

Value	Meaning
HS_BDIAGONAL	A 45-degree upward, left-to-right hatch
HS_CROSS	Horizontal and vertical cross-hatch
HS_DIAGCROSS	45-degree crosshatch
HS_FDIAGONAL	A 45-degree downward, left-to-right hatch
HS_HORIZONTAL	Horizontal hatch
HS_VERTICAL	Vertical hatch

If **lbStyle** is BS_PATTERN, **lbHatch** is a handle to the bitmap that defines the pattern.

If **lbStyle** is BS_SOLID or BS_HOLLOW, **lbHatch** is ignored.

Comments   Although **lbColor** controls the foreground color of a hatch brush, the **SetBkMode** and **SetBkColor** functions control the background color.

See Also   **CreateBrushIndirect, ExtCreatePen, SetBkColor, SetBkMode**

LOGFONT

```
typedef struct tagLOGFONT { /* lf */
    LONG lfHeight;
    LONG lfWidth;
    LONG lfEscapement;
    LONG lfOrientation;
    LONG lfWeight;
    BYTE lfItalic;
    BYTE lfUnderline;
    BYTE lfStrikeOut;
    BYTE lfCharSet;
    BYTE lfOutPrecision;
    BYTE lfClipPrecision;
    BYTE lfQuality;
    BYTE lfPitchAndFamily;
    CHAR lfFaceName[LF_FACESIZE];
} LOGFONT;
```

The **LOGFONT** structure defines the attributes of a font.

Members

lfHeight

Specifies the height, in logical units, of the font. The font height can be specified in one of three ways. If **lfHeight** is greater than zero, it is transformed into device units and matched against the cell height of the available fonts. If it is zero, a reasonable default size is used. If it is less than zero, it is transformed into device units and the absolute value is matched against the character height of the available fonts. For all height comparisons, the font mapper looks for the largest font that does not exceed the requested size; if there is no such font, it looks for the smallest font available. This mapping occurs when the font is actually used for the first time.

lfWidth

Specifies the average width, in logical units, of characters in the font. If **lfWidth** is zero, the aspect ratio of the device is matched against the digitization aspect ratio of the available fonts to find the closest match, determined by the absolute value of the difference.

lfEscapement

Specifies the angle, in tenths of degrees, of each line of text written in the font (relative to the bottom of the page).

lfOrientation

Specifies the angle, in tenths of degrees, of each character's base line (relative to the bottom of the page).

lfWeight

Specifies the weight of the font, in the range 0 through 1000 (for example, 400 is normal and 700 is bold). If **lfWeight** is zero, a default weight is used.

lfItalic

Specifies an italic font if set to TRUE.

lfUnderline

Specifies an underlined font if set to TRUE.

lfStrikeOut

Specifies a strikeout font if set to TRUE.

lfCharSet

Specifies the character set. The following values are predefined:

ANSI_CHARSET
OEM_CHARSET
SYMBOL_CHARSET
UNICODE_CHARSET

The OEM character set is system dependent.

Fonts with other character sets may exist in the system. If an application uses a font with an unknown character set, it should not attempt to translate or interpret strings that are to be rendered with that font.

lfOutPrecision

Specifies the output precision. The output precision defines how closely the output must match the requested font's height, width, character orientation, escapement, and pitch. It can be one of the following values:

OUT_CHARACTER_PRECIS
OUT_DEFAULT_PRECIS
OUT_STRING_PRECIS
OUT_STROKE_PRECIS

lfClipPrecision

Specifies the clipping precision. The clipping precision defines how to clip characters that are partially outside the clipping region. It can be one of the following values:

CLIP_CHARACTER_PRECIS
CLIP_DEFAULT_PRECIS
CLIP_STROKE_PRECIS

lfQuality

Specifies the output quality. The output quality defines how carefully graphics device interface (GDI) must attempt to match the logical-font attributes to those of an actual physical font. It can be one of the following values:

Value	Meaning
DEFAULT_QUALITY	Appearance of the font does not matter.
DRAFT_QUALITY	Appearance of the font is less important than when PROOF_QUALITY is used. For GDI fonts, scaling is enabled, which means that more font sizes are available, but the quality may be lower. Bold, italic, underline, and strikeout fonts are synthesized if necessary.
PROOF_QUALITY	Character quality of the font is more important than exact matching of the logical-font attributes. For GDI fonts, scaling is disabled and the font closest in size is chosen. Although the chosen font size may not be mapped exactly when PROOF_QUALITY is used, the quality of the font is high and there is no distortion of appearance. Bold, italic, underline, and strikeout fonts are synthesized if necessary.

lfPitchAndFamily

Specifies the pitch and family of the font. The two low-order bits specify the pitch of the font and can be one of the following values:

DEFAULT_PITCH
FIXED_PITCH
VARIABLE_PITCH

Bits 4 through 7 of the member specify the font family and can be one of the following values:

FF_DECORATIVE
FF_DONTCARE
FF_MODERN
FF_ROMAN
FF_SCRIPT
FF_SWISS

The proper value can be obtained by using the Boolean OR operator to join one pitch constant with one family constant.

Font families describe the look of a font in a general way. They are intended for specifying fonts when the exact typeface desired is not available. The values for font families are as follows:

Value	Meaning
FF_DECORATIVE	Novelty fonts. Old English is an example.
FF_DONTCARE	Don't care or don't know.
FF_MODERN	Fonts with constant stroke width (fixed-pitch), with or without serifs. Fixed-pitch fonts are usually modern. Pica, Elite, and CourierNew ® are examples.

FF_ROMAN	Fonts with variable stroke width (proportionally spaced) and with serifs. MS ® Serif is an example.
FF_SCRIPT	Fonts designed to look like handwriting. Script and Cursive are examples.
FF_SWISS	Fonts with variable stroke width (proportionally spaced) and without serifs. MS ® Sans Serif is an example.

lfFaceName
Points to a null-terminated string that specifies the typeface name of the font. The length of this string must not exceed 32 characters. The **EnumFonts** function can be used to enumerate the typeface names of all currently available fonts. If **lfFaceName** is NULL, GDI uses a default typeface.

See Also   **CreateFontIndirect**

LOGPALETTE

```
typedef struct tagLOGPALETTE { /* lgpl */
    WORD         palVersion;
    WORD         palNumEntries;
    PALETTEENTRY palPalEntry[1];
} LOGPALETTE;
```

The **LOGPALETTE** structure defines a logical color palette.

Members

palVersion
Specifies the Windows version number for the structure (currently 0x300).

palNumEntries
Specifies the number of entries in the logical color palette.

palPalEntry
Specifies an array of **PALETTEENTRY** structures that define the color and usage of each entry in the logical palette. The **PALETTEENTRY** structure has the following form:

```
typedef struct tagPALETTEENTRY { /* pe */
    BYTE peRed;
    BYTE peGreen;
    BYTE peBlue;
    BYTE peFlags;
} PALETTEENTRY;
```

Comments
The colors in the palette-entry table should appear in order of importance because entries earlier in the logical palette are most likely to be placed in the system palette.

See Also   **CreatePalette**

LOGPEN

```
typedef struct tagLOGPEN { /* lgpn */
    UINT     lopnStyle;
    POINT    lopnWidth;
    COLORREF lopnColor;
} LOGPEN;
```

The **LOGPEN** structure defines the style, width, and color of a pen, a drawing object used to draw lines and borders. The **CreatePenIndirect** function uses the **LOGPEN** structure.

Members   **lopnStyle**

Specifies the pen style, which can be one of the following values:

Value	Meaning
PS_SOLID	Pen is solid.
PS_DASH	Pen is dashed.
PS_DOT	Pen is dotted.
PS_DASHDOT	Pen has alternating dashes and dots.
PS_DASHDOTDOT	Pen has dashes and double dots.
PS_NULL	Pen is invisible.
PS_INSIDEFRAME	Pen is solid. When this pen is used in any graphics device interface (GDI) drawing function that takes a bounding rectangle, the dimensions of the figure are shrunk so that it fits entirely in the bounding rectangle, taking into account the width of the pen. This applies only to geometric pens.

lopnWidth

Specifies the **POINT** structure that contains the pen width, in logical units. If the **pointer** member is NULL, the pen is one pixel wide on raster devices. The **y** member in the **POINT** structure for **lopnWidth** is not used.

lopnColor

Specifies the pen color.

Comments   If the width of the pen is greater than 1 and the pen style is PS_INSIDEFRAME, the line is drawn inside the frame of all GDI objects except polygons and polylines. If the pen color does not match an available red, green, blue (RGB) value, the pen is drawn with a logical (dithered) color. If the pen width is less than or equal to 1, the PS_INSIDEFRAME style is identical to the PS_SOLID style.

See Also   **CreatePenIndirect, RGB**

LUID

```
typedef LARGE_INTEGER LUID
```

An **LUID** is a 64-bit value guaranteed to be unique only on the system on which it was generated. The uniqueness of a locally unique identifier (LUID) is guaranteed only until the system is restarted.

An **LUID** is not for direct manipulation. Applications are to use functions and structures to manipulate **LUID** values.

See Also   **AllocateLocallyUniqueId, LookupPrivilegeName, LookupPrivilegeValue, PrivilegeCheck, LUID_AND_ATTRIBUTES, PRIVILEGE_SET**

LUID_AND_ATTRIBUTES

```
typedef struct _LUID_AND_ATTRIBUTES { /* luaa */
    LUID  Luid;
    DWORD Attributes;
} LUID_AND_ATTRIBUTES;
```

The **LUID_AND_ATTRIBUTES** structure represents a locally unique identifier (LUID) and its attributes.

Members   **Luid**
             Specifies an **LUID** value.

             Attributes
             Specifies attributes of the LUID. This value contains up to 32 one-bit flags. Its meaning is dependent on the definition and use of the LUID.

Comments   An **LUID_AND_ATTRIBUTES** structure can represent an LUID whose attributes change frequently, such as when it is used to represent privileges in the **PRIVILEGE_SET** structure. Privileges are represented by **LUIDs** and have attributes indicating whether they are currently enabled or disabled.

See Also   **AllocateLocallyUniqueId, LUID, PRIVILEGE_SET, TOKEN_PRIVILEGES**

MAT2

```
typedef struct _MAT2 { /* mt2 */
    FIXED eM11;
    FIXED eM12;
    FIXED eM21;
    FIXED eM22;
} MAT2;
```

The **MAT2** structure contains the values for a transformation matrix used by the **GetGlyphOutline** function.

Members

eM11

Specifies a fixed-point value for the *M11* component of a 3 by 3 transformation matrix.

eM12

Specifies a fixed-point value for the *M12* component of a 3 by 3 transformation matrix.

eM21

Specifies a fixed-point value for the *M21* component of a 3 by 3 transformation matrix.

eM22

Specifies a fixed-point value for the *M22* component of a 3 by 3 transformation matrix.

Comments

The identity matrix produces a transformation in which the transformed graphical object is identical to the source object. In the identity matrix, the value of **eM11** is 1, the value of **eM12** is zero, the value of **eM21** is zero, and the value of **eM22** is 1.

See Also

GetGlyphOutline

MCI_ANIM_OPEN_PARMS

```
typedef struct {
    DWORD      dwCallback;
    MCIDEVICEID wDeviceID;
    LPCTSTR    lpstrDeviceType;
    LPCTSTR    lpstrElementName;
    LPCSTR     lpstrAlias;
    DWORD      dwStyle;
    HWND       hWndParent;
} MCI_ANIM_OPEN_PARMS;
```

The **MCI_ANIM_OPEN_PARMS** structure contains information for the MCI_OPEN command message. When assigning data to the members in this structure, set the corresponding Media Control Interface (MCI) flags in the *fdwCommand* parameter of the **mciSendCommand** function to validate the members.

Members

dwCallback
Specifies a window handle used for the MCI_NOTIFY flag.

wDeviceID
Specifies the device identifier returned to the user.

lpstrDeviceType
Points to the name or constant identifier of the device type.

lpstrElementName
Points to the device-element name (usually a path).

lpstrAlias
Points to an optional device alias.

dwStyle
Specifies the window style.

hWndParent
Identifies the window to use as the parent window.

Comments

You can use the **MCI_OPEN_PARMS** structure in place of **MCI_ANIM_OPEN_PARMS** if you are not using the extended data members.

See Also

MCI_OPEN

MCI_ANIM_PLAY_PARMS

```
typedef struct {
    DWORD   dwCallback;
    DWORD   dwFrom;
    DWORD   dwTo;
    DWORD   dwSpeed;
} MCI_ANIM_PLAY_PARMS;
```

The **MCI_ANIM_PLAY_PARMS** structure contains parameters for the MCI_PLAY command message for animation devices. When assigning data to the members in this structure, set the corresponding Media Control Interface (MCI) flags in the *fdwCommand* parameter of the **mciSendCommand** function to validate the members.

Members

dwCallback
Specifies a window handle used for the MCI_NOTIFY flag.

dwFrom
Specifies the position to play from.

dwTo
Specifies the position to play to.

dwSpeed
Specifies the play rate, in frames per second.

Comments

You can use the **MCI_PLAY_PARMS** structure in place of **MCI_ANIM_PLAY_PARMS** if you are not using the extended data members.

See Also

MCI_PLAY

MCI_ANIM_RECT_PARMS

```
typedef struct {
    DWORD   dwCallback;
    RECT   rc;
} MCI_ANIM_RECT_PARMS;
```

The **MCI_ANIM_RECT_PARMS** structure contains parameters for the MCI_PUT and MCI_WHERE command messages for animation devices. When assigning data to the members in this structure, set the corresponding Media Control Interface (MCI) flags in the *fdwCommand* parameter of the **mciSendCommand** function to validate the members.

Members

dwCallback

Specifies a window handle used for the MCI_NOTIFY flag.

rc

Specifies a rectangle.

See Also   MCI_PUT, MCI_WHERE

MCI_ANIM_STEP_PARMS

```
typedef struct {
    DWORD   dwCallback;
    DWORD   dwFrames;
} MCI_ANIM_STEP_PARMS;
```

The **MCI_ANIM_STEP_PARMS** structure contains parameters for the MCI_STEP command message for animation devices. When assigning data to the members in this structure, set the corresponding Media Control Interface (MCI) flags in the *fdwCommand* parameter of the **mciSendCommand** function to validate the members.

Members

dwCallback

Specifies a window handle used for the MCI_NOTIFY flag.

dwFrames

Specifies the number of frames to step.

See Also   MCI_STEP

MCI_ANIM_UPDATE_PARMS

```
typedef struct {
    DWORD   dwCallback;
    RECT    rc;
    HDC     hDC;
} MCI_ANIM_UPDATE_PARMS;
```

The **MCI_ANIM_UPDATE_PARMS** structure contains parameters for the MCI_UPDATE command message for animation devices. When assigning data to the members in this structure, set the corresponding Media Control Interface (MCI) flags in the *fdwCommand* parameter of the **mciSendCommand** function to validate the members.

Members	**dwCallback**
	Specifies a window handle used for the MCI_NOTIFY flag.
	rc
	Specifies a window rectangle.
	hDC
	Identifies the device context.
See Also	MCI_UPDATE

MCI_ANIM_WINDOW_PARMS

```
typedef struct tagMCI_ANIM_WINDOW_PARMS {
    DWORD  dwCallback;
    DWORD  hWnd;
    UINT  nCmdShow;
    LPCTSTR  lpstrText;
} MCI_ANIM_WINDOW_PARMS;
```

The **MCI_ANIM_WINDOW_PARMS** structure contains parameters for the MCI_WINDOW command message for animation devices. When assigning data to the members in this structure, set the corresponding Media Control Interface (MCI) flags in the *fdwCommand* parameter of the **mciSendCommand** function to validate the members.

Members	**dwCallback**
	Specifies a window handle used for the MCI_NOTIFY flag.
	hWnd
	Identifies the display window.
	nCmdShow
	Specifies how the window is displayed.
	lpstrText
	Points to a null-terminated string containing the window caption.
See Also	MCI_WINDOW

MCI_BREAK_PARMS

```
typedef struct {
    DWORD  dwCallback;
    int  nVirtKey;
    HWND  hwndBreak;
} MCI_BREAK_PARMS;
```

The **MCI_BREAK_PARMS** structure contains parameters for the MCI_BREAK command message. When assigning data to the members in this structure, set the corresponding Media Control Interface (MCI) flags in the *fdwCommand* parameter of the **mciSendCommand** function to validate the members.

Members

dwCallback
Specifies a window handle used for the MCI_NOTIFY flag.

nVirtKey
Specifies the virtual-key code used for the break key.

hwndBreak
Identifies the window that must be the current window for break detection.

See Also   MCI_BREAK

MCI_GENERIC_PARMS

```
typedef struct {
    DWORD  dwCallback;
} MCI_GENERIC_PARMS;
```

The **MCI_GENERIC_PARMS** structure contains information for the Media Control Interface (MCI) command messages that have empty parameter lists. When assigning data to the members in this structure, set the corresponding MCI flags in the *fdwCommand* parameter of the **mciSendCommand** function to validate the members.

Members

dwCallback
Specifies a window handle used for the MCI_NOTIFY flag.

MCI_GETDEVCAPS_PARMS

```
typedef struct {
    DWORD   dwCallback;
    DWORD   dwReturn;
    DWORD   dwItem;
} MCI_GETDEVCAPS_PARMS;
```

The **MCI_GETDEVCAPS_PARMS** structure contains parameters for the MCI_GETDEVCAPS command message. When assigning data to the members in this structure, set the corresponding Media Control Interface (MCI) flags in the *fdwCommand* parameter of the **mciSendCommand** function to validate the members.

Members

dwCallback
Specifies a window handle used for the MCI_NOTIFY flag.

dwReturn
Contains the return information on exit.

dwItem
Specifies the capability being queried.

See Also   MCI_GETDEVCAPS

MCI_INFO_PARMS   Unicode

```
typedef struct {
    DWORD   dwCallback;
    LPTSTR  lpstrReturn;
    DWORD   dwRetSize;
} MCI_INFO_PARMS;
```

The **MCI_INFO_PARMS** structure contains parameters for the MCI_INFO command message. When assigning data to the members in this structure, set the corresponding Media Control Interface (MCI) flags in the *fdwCommand* parameter of the **mciSendCommand** function to validate the members.

Members

dwCallback
Specifies a window handle used for the MCI_NOTIFY flag.

lpstrReturn
Points to a user-defined buffer for the return string.

dwRetSize
Specifies the size, in bytes, of the buffer for the return string.

See Also   MCI_INFO

MCI_LOAD_PARMS

```
typedef struct {
    DWORD   dwCallback;
    LPCTSTR lpfilename;
} MCI_LOAD_PARMS;
```

The **MCI_LOAD_PARMS** structure contains information for the MCI_LOAD command message. When assigning data to the members in this structure, set the corresponding Media Control Interface (MCI) flags in the *fdwCommand* parameter of the **mciSendCommand** function to validate the members.

Members   dwCallback
Specifies a window handle used for the MCI_NOTIFY flag.

lpfilename
Points to a null-terminated string containing the filename of the device element to load.

See Also   MCI_LOAD

MCI_OPEN_PARMS

```
typedef struct {
    DWORD   dwCallback;
    MCIDEVICEID  wDeviceID;
    LPCTSTR lpstrDeviceType;
    LPCTSTR lpstrElementName;
    LPCTSTR lpstrAlias;
} MCI_OPEN_PARMS;
```

The **MCI_OPEN_PARMS** structure contains information for the MCI_OPEN command message. When assigning data to the members in this structure, set the corresponding Media Control Interface (MCI) flags in the *fdwCommand* parameter of the **mciSendCommand** function to validate the members.

Members   dwCallback
Specifies a window handle used for the MCI_NOTIFY flag.

wDeviceID
Contains the device identifier returned to the user.

lpstrDeviceType
Points to the name or constant identifier of the device type.

lpstrElementName
Points to the device-element name (usually a path).

lpstrAlias
Points to an optional device alias.

See Also   MCI_OPEN

MCI_OVLY_LOAD_PARMS   Unicode

```
typedef struct {
    DWORD  dwCallback;
    LPCTSTR  lpfilename;
    RECT  rc;
} MCI_OVLY_LOAD_PARMS;
```

The **MCI_OVLY_LOAD_PARMS** structure contains parameters for the MCI_LOAD command message for video overlay devices. When assigning data to the members in this structure, set the corresponding Media Control Interface (MCI) flags in the *fdwCommand* parameter of the **mciSendCommand** function to validate the members.

Members   **dwCallback**
Specifies a window handle used for the MCI_NOTIFY flag.

lpfilename
Points to the buffer containing a null-terminated string.

rc
Specifies a rectangle.

See Also   MCI_LOAD

MCI_OVLY_OPEN_PARMS

Unicode

```
typedef struct {
    DWORD  dwCallback;
    MCIDEVICEID  wDeviceID;
    LPCTSTR  lpstrDeviceType;
    LPCTSTR  lpstrElementName;
    LPCTSTR  lpstrAlias;
    DWORD  dwStyle;
    HWND  hWndParent;
} MCI_OVLY_OPEN_PARMS;
```

The **MCI_OVLY_OPEN_PARMS** structure contains information for the MCI_OPEN command message for video overlay devices. When assigning data to the members in this structure, set the corresponding Media Control Interface (MCI) flags in the *fdwCommand* parameter of the **mciSendCommand** function to validate the members.

Members

dwCallback
Specifies a window handle used for the MCI_NOTIFY flag.

wDeviceID
Specifies the device identifier returned to the user.

lpstrDeviceType
Points to the name or constant identifier of the device type obtained from the SYSTEM.INI file.

lpstrElementName
Points to the device-element name (usually a path).

lpstrAlias
Points to an optional device alias.

dwStyle
Specifies the window style.

hWndParent
Identifies the window to use as the parent window.

Comments

You can use the **MCI_OPEN_PARMS** structure in place of **MCI_OVLY_OPEN_PARMS** if you are not using the extended data members.

See Also

MCI_OPEN

MCI_OVLY_RECT_PARMS

```
typedef struct {
    DWORD  dwCallback;
    RECT   rc;
} MCI_OVLY_RECT_PARMS;
```

The **MCI_OVLY_RECT_PARMS** structure contains parameters for the MCI_PUT and MCI_WHERE command messages for video overlay devices. When assigning data to the members in this structure, set the corresponding Media Control Interface (MCI) flags in the *fdwCommand* parameter of the **mciSendCommand** function to validate the members.

Members

dwCallback
Specifies a window handle used for the MCI_NOTIFY flag.

rc
Specifies a rectangle.

See Also   MCI_PUT, MCI_WHERE

MCI_OVLY_SAVE_PARMS   `Unicode`

```
typedef struct {
    DWORD   dwCallback;
    LPCTSTR lpfilename;
    RECT    rc;
} MCI_OVLY_SAVE_PARMS;
```

The **MCI_OVLY_SAVE_PARMS** structure contains parameters for the MCI_SAVE command message for video overlay devices. When assigning data to the members in this structure, set the corresponding Media Control Interface (MCI) flags in the *fdwCommand* parameter of the **mciSendCommand** function to validate the members.

Members

dwCallback
Specifies a window handle used for the MCI_NOTIFY flag.

lpfilename
Points to the buffer containing a null-terminated string.

rc
Specifies a rectangle.

See Also   MCI_SAVE

MCI_OVLY_WINDOW_PARMS

`Unicode`

```
typedef struct {
    DWORD   dwCallback;
    HWND    hWnd;
    UINT    nCmdShow;
    LPCTSTR lpstrText;
} MCI_OVLY_WINDOW_PARMS;
```

The **MCI_OVLY_WINDOW_PARMS** structure contains parameters for the MCI_WINDOW command message for video overlay devices. When assigning data to the members in this structure, set the corresponding Media Control Interface (MCI) flags in the *fdwCommand* parameter of the **mciSendCommand** function to validate the members.

Members

dwCallback
Specifies a window handle used for the MCI_NOTIFY flag.

hWnd
Identifies the display window.

nCmdShow
Specifies how the window is displayed.

lpstrText
Points to a null-terminated buffer containing the window caption.

See Also   MCI_WINDOW

MCI_PLAY_PARMS

```
typedef struct {
    DWORD   dwCallback;
    DWORD   dwFrom;
    DWORD   dwTo;
} MCI_PLAY_PARMS;
```

The **MCI_PLAY_PARMS** structure contains parameters for the MCI_PLAY command message. When assigning data to the members in this structure, set the corresponding Media Control Interface (MCI) flags in the *fdwCommand* parameter of the **mciSendCommand** function to validate the members.

Members

dwCallback
Specifies a window handle used for the MCI_NOTIFY flag.

dwFrom
Specifies the position to play from.

dwTo
Specifies the position to play to.

See Also   MCI_PLAY

MCI_RECORD_PARMS

```
typedef struct {
    DWORD  dwCallback;
    DWORD  dwFrom;
    DWORD  dwTo;
} MCI_RECORD_PARMS;
```

The **MCI_RECORD_PARMS** structure contains parameters for the MCI_RECORD command message. When assigning data to the members in this structure, set the corresponding Media Control Interface (MCI) flags in the *fdwCommand* parameter of the **mciSendCommand** function to validate the members.

Members   **dwCallback**
Specifies a window handle used for the MCI_NOTIFY flag.

dwFrom
Specifies the position to play from.

dwTo
Specifies the position to play to.

See Also   MCI_RECORD

MCI_SAVE_PARMS

Unicode

```
typedef struct {
    DWORD   dwCallback;
    LPCTSTR lpfilename;
} MCI_SAVE_PARMS;
```

The **MCI_SAVE_PARMS** structure contains information for the MCI_SAVE command message. When assigning data to the members in this structure, set the corresponding Media Control Interface (MCI) flags in the *fdwCommand* parameter of the **mciSendCommand** function to validate the members.

Members   **dwCallback**
                    Specifies a window handle used for the MCI_NOTIFY flag.

                    lpfilename
                    Points to the buffer containing a null-terminated string.

See Also   MCI_SAVE

MCI_SEEK_PARMS

```
typedef struct {
    DWORD  dwCallback;
    DWORD  dwTo;
} MCI_SEEK_PARMS;
```

The **MCI_SEEK_PARMS** structure contains parameters for the MCI_SEEK command message. When assigning data to the members in this structure, set the corresponding Media Control Interface (MCI) flags in the *fdwCommand* parameter of the **mciSendCommand** function to validate the members.

Members   **dwCallback**
                    Specifies a window handle used for the MCI_NOTIFY flag.

                    dwTo
                    Specifies the position to seek to.

See Also   MCI_SEEK

MCI_SEQ_SET_PARMS

```
typedef struct {
    DWORD  dwCallback;
    DWORD  dwTimeFormat;
    DWORD  dwAudio;
    DWORD  dwTempo;
    DWORD  dwPort;
    DWORD  dwSlave;
    DWORD  dwMaster;
    DWORD  dwOffset;
} MCI_SEQ_SET_PARMS;
```

The **MCI_SEQ_SET_PARMS** structure contains parameters for the MCI_SET command message for Musical Instrument Digital Interface (MIDI) sequencer devices. When assigning data to the members in this structure, set the corresponding Media Control Interface (MCI) flags in the *fdwCommand* parameter of the **mciSendCommand** function to validate the members.

Members   **dwCallback**
Specifies a window handle used for the MCI_NOTIFY flag.

dwTimeFormat
Specifies the time format of the sequencer.

dwAudio
Specifies the audio output channel.

dwTempo
Specifies the tempo.

dwPort
Specifies the output port.

dwSlave
Specifies the type of synchronization used by the sequencer for slave operation.

dwMaster
Specifies the type of synchronization used by the sequencer for master operation.

dwOffset
Specifies the data offset.

See Also   MCI_SET

MCI_SET_PARMS

```
typedef struct {
    DWORD  dwCallback;
    DWORD  dwTimeFormat;
    DWORD  dwAudio;
} MCI_SET_PARMS;
```

The **MCI_SET_PARMS** structure contains parameters for the MCI_SET command message. When assigning data to the members in this structure, set the corresponding Media Control Interface (MCI) flags in the *fdwCommand* parameter of the **mciSendCommand** function to validate the members.

Members   **dwCallback**
Specifies a window handle used for the MCI_NOTIFY flag.

dwTimeFormat
Specifies the time format used by the device.

dwAudio
Specifies the audio output channel.

See Also   MCI_SET

MCI_SOUND_PARMS

```
typedef struct {
    DWORD   dwCallback;
    LPCTSTR lpstrSoundName;
} MCI_SOUND_PARMS;
```

The **MCI_SOUND_PARMS** structure contains parameters for the MCI_SOUND command message. When assigning data to the members in this structure, set the corresponding Media Control Interface (MCI) flags in the *fdwCommand* parameter of the **mciSendCommand** function to validate the members.

Members   dwCallback
Specifies a window handle used for the MCI_NOTIFY flag.

lpstrSoundName
Points to a null-terminated string containing the name of the sound or the name of the file containing the sound to be played.

See Also   MCI_SOUND

MCI_STATUS_PARMS

```
typedef struct {
    DWORD   dwCallback;
    DWORD   dwReturn;
    DWORD   dwItem;
    DWORD   dwTrack;
} MCI_STATUS_PARMS;
```

The **MCI_STATUS_PARMS** structure contains parameters for the MCI_STATUS command message. When assigning data to the members in this structure, set the corresponding Media Control Interface (MCI) flags in the *fdwCommand* parameter of the **mciSendCommand** function to validate the members.

Members   dwCallback
Specifies a window handle used for the MCI_NOTIFY flag.

dwReturn
Contains the return information on exit.

dwItem
Specifies the capability being queried.

dwTrack
Specifies the length or number of tracks.

See Also   MCI_STATUS

MCI_SYSINFO_PARMS

Unicode

```
typedef struct {
    DWORD  dwCallback;
    LPTSTR lpstrReturn;
    DWORD  dwRetSize;
    DWORD  dwNumber;
    UINT   wDeviceType;
} MCI_SYSINFO_PARMS;
```

The **MCI_SYSINFO_PARMS** structure contains parameters for the MCI_SYSINFO command message. When assigning data to the members in this structure, set the corresponding Media Control Interface (MCI) flags in the *fdwCommand* parameter of the **mciSendCommand** function to validate the members.

Members   **dwCallback**
Specifies a window handle used for the MCI_NOTIFY flag.

lpstrReturn
Points to a user-defined buffer for the return string. When the MCI_SYSINFO_QUANTITY flag is used, **lpstrReturn** is evaluated as a LPDWORD, and a doubleword value is stored.

dwRetSize
Specifies the size, in bytes, of the buffer for the return string.

dwNumber
Specifies a number indicating the device position in the MCI device table or in the list of open devices if the MCI_SYSINFO_OPEN flag is set.

wDeviceType
Specifies the type of device.

See Also   MCI_SYSINFO

MCI_VD_ESCAPE_PARMS

Unicode

```
typedef struct {
    DWORD   dwCallback;
    LPCTSTR lpstrCommand;
} MCI_VD_ESCAPE_PARMS;
```

The **MCI_VD_ESCAPE_PARMS** structure contains parameters for the MCI_ESCAPE command message for videodisc devices. When assigning data to the members in this structure, set the corresponding Media Control Interface (MCI) flags in the *fdwCommand* parameter of the **mciSendCommand** function to validate the members.

Members

dwCallback
Specifies a window handle used for the MCI_NOTIFY flag.

lpstrCommand
Points to a null-terminated buffer containing the command to send to the device.

See Also   MCI_ESCAPE

MCI_VD_PLAY_PARMS

```
typedef struct {
    DWORD   dwCallback;
    DWORD   dwFrom;
    DWORD   dwTo;
    DWORD   dwSpeed;
} MCI_VD_PLAY_PARMS;
```

The **MCI_VD_PLAY_PARMS** structure contains parameters for the MCI_PLAY command message for videodiscs. When assigning data to the members in this structure, set the corresponding Media Control Interface (MCI) flags in the *fdwCommand* parameter of the **mciSendCommand** function to validate the members.

Members

dwCallback
Specifies a window handle used for the MCI_NOTIFY flag.

dwFrom
Specifies the position to play from.

dwTo

Specifies the position to play to.

dwSpeed

Specifies the playing speed, in frames per second.

Comments   You can use the **MCI_PLAY_PARMS** structure in place of
MCI_VD_PLAY_PARMS if you are not using the extended data members.

See Also   MCI_PLAY

MCI_VD_STEP_PARMS

```
typedef struct {
    DWORD  dwCallback;
    DWORD  dwFrames;
} MCI_VD_STEP_PARMS;
```

The **MCI_VD_STEP_PARMS** structure contains parameters for the MCI_STEP
command message for videodiscs. When assigning data to the members in this
structure, set the corresponding Media Control Interface (MCI) flags in the
fdwCommand parameter of the **mciSendCommand** function to validate the
members.

Members   **dwCallback**

Specifies a window handle used for the MCI_NOTIFY flag.

dwFrames

Specifies the number of frames to step.

See Also   MCI_STEP

MCI_WAVE_DELETE_PARMS

```
typedef struct {
    DWORD  dwCallback;
    DWORD  dwFrom;
    DWORD  dwTo;
} MCI_WAVE_DELETE_PARMS;
```

The **MCI_WAVE_DELETE_PARMS** structure contains parameters for the
MCI_DELETE command message for waveform audio devices. When assigning
data to the members in this structure, set the corresponding Media Control

Interface (MCI) flags in the *fdwCommand* parameter of the **mciSendCommand** function to validate the members.

Members

dwCallback
Specifies a window handle used for the MCI_NOTIFY flag.

dwFrom
Specifies the starting position for the delete operation.

dwTo
Specifies the end position for the delete operation.

See Also   MCI_DELETE

MCI_WAVE_OPEN_PARMS   `Unicode`

```
typedef struct {
    DWORD  dwCallback;
    MCIDEVICEID  wDeviceID;
    LPCTSTR  lpstrDeviceType;
    LPCTSTR  lpstrElementName;
    LPCTSTR  lpstrAlias;
    DWORD  dwBufferSeconds;
} MCI_WAVE_OPEN_PARMS;
```

The **MCI_WAVE_OPEN_PARMS** structure contains information for the MCI_OPEN command message for waveform audio devices. When assigning data to the members in this structure, set the corresponding Media Control Interface (MCI) flags in the *fdwCommand* parameter of the **mciSendCommand** function to validate the members.

Members

dwCallback
Specifies a window handle used for the MCI_NOTIFY flag.

wDeviceID
Specifies the device identifier returned to the user.

lpstrDeviceType
Points to the name or constant identifier of the device type obtained.

lpstrElementName
Points to the device-element name (usually a path).

lpstrAlias
Points to an optional device alias.

dwBufferSeconds
Specifies the buffer length, in seconds.

Comments   You can use the **MCI_OPEN_PARMS** structure in place of
                   MCI_WAVE_OPEN_PARMS if you are not using the extended data members.

See Also   MCI_OPEN

MCI_WAVE_SET_PARMS

```
typedef struct {
    DWORD  dwCallback;
    DWORD  dwTimeFormat;
    DWORD  dwAudio;
    UINT   wInput;
    UINT   wOutput;
    WORD   wFormatTag;
    WORD   wReserved2;
    WORD   nChannels;
    WORD   wReserved3;
    DWORD  nSamplesPerSec;
    DWORD  nAvgBytesPerSec;
    WORD   nBlockAlign;
    WORD   wReserved4;
    WORD   wBitsPerSample;
    WORD   wReserved5;
} MCI_WAVE_SET_PARMS;
```

The **MCI_WAVE_SET_PARMS** structure contains parameters for the
MCI_SET command message for waveform audio devices. When assigning data
to the members in this structure, set the corresponding Media Control Interface
(MCI) flags in the *fdwCommand* parameter of the **mciSendCommand** function to
validate the members.

Members   **dwCallback**
                   Specifies a window handle used for the MCI_NOTIFY flag.

                   dwTimeFormat
                   Specifies the time format used by the device.

                   dwAudio
                   Specifies the channel used for audio output.

                   wInput
                   Specifies the channel used for audio input.

                   wOutput
                   Specifies the channel used for output.

                   wFormatTag
                   Specifies the interpretation of the waveform data.

wReserved2
Reserved; do not use.

nChannels
Specifies monaural (1) or stereo data (2).

wReserved3
Reserved; do not use.

nSamplesPerSec
Specifies the samples per second used for the waveform.

nAvgBytesPerSec
Specifies the sample rate, in bytes per second.

nBlockAlign
Specifies the block alignment of the data.

wReserved4
Reserved; do not use.

wBitsPerSample
Specifies the number of bits per sample.

wReserved5
Reserved; do not use.

See Also   MCI_SET

MDICREATESTRUCT   Unicode

```
typedef struct tagMDICREATESTRUCT { /* mdic */
    LPCTSTR szClass;
    LPCTSTR szTitle;
    HANDLE  hOwner;
    int     x;
    int     y;
    int     cx;
    int     cy;
    DWORD   style;
    LPARAM  lParam;
} MDICREATESTRUCT;
```

The **MDICREATESTRUCT** structure contains information about the class, title, owner, location, and size of a multiple document interface (MDI) child window.

Members   **szClass**
Points to a null-terminated string specifying the name of the window class of the MDI child window. The class name must have been registered by a previous call to the **RegisterClass** function.

szTitle

Points to a null-terminated string that represents the title of the MDI child window. Windows displays the title in the child window's title bar.

hOwner

Identifies the instance of the application creating the MDI client window.

x

Specifies the initial horizontal position, in client coordinates, of the MDI child window. If this parameter is CW_USEDEFAULT, the MDI child window is assigned the default horizontal position.

y

Specifies the initial vertical position, in client coordinates, of the MDI child window. If this parameter is CW_USEDEFAULT, the MDI child window is assigned the default vertical position.

cx

Specifies the initial width, in device units, of the MDI child window. If this parameter is CW_USEDEFAULT, the MDI child window is assigned the default width.

cy

Specifies the initial height, in device units, of the MDI child window. If this parameter is set to CW_USEDEFAULT, the MDI child window is assigned the default height.

style

Specifies the style of the MDI child window. If the MDI client window was created with the MDIS_ALLCHILDSTYLES window style, this parameter can be any combination of the window styles listed in the description of the **CreateWindow** function. Otherwise, this parameter can be one or more of the following values:

Value	Description
WS_MINIMIZE	Creates an MDI child window that is initially minimized.
WS_MAXIMIZE	Creates an MDI child window that is initially maximized.
WS_HSCROLL	Creates an MDI child window that has a horizontal scroll bar.
WS_VSCROLL	Creates an MDI child window that has a vertical scroll bar.

lParam

Specifies an application-defined 32-bit value.

Comments

When the MDI child window is created, Windows sends the WM_CREATE message to the window. The *lParam* parameter of WM_CREATE contains a pointer to a **CREATESTRUCT** structure. The **lpCreateParams** member of this structure contains a pointer to the **MDICREATESTRUCT** structure passed with the WM_MDICREATE message that created the MDI child window.

See Also   **CLIENTCREATESTRUCT, CREATESTRUCT**

MEASUREITEMSTRUCT

```
typedef struct tagMEASUREITEMSTRUCT {    /* mis */
    UINT  CtlType;
    UINT  CtlID;
    UINT  itemID;
    UINT  itemWidth;
    UINT  itemHeight;
    DWORD itemData;
} MEASUREITEMSTRUCT;
```

The **MEASUREITEMSTRUCT** structure informs Windows of the dimensions of an owner-drawn control. This allows Windows to process user interaction with the control correctly.

Members   **CtlType**

Specifies the control type. This member can be one of the following values:

Value	Description
ODT_BUTTON	Owner-drawn button
ODT_COMBOBOX	Owner-drawn combo box
ODT_LISTBOX	Owner-drawn list box
ODT_MENU	Owner-drawn menu

CtlID

Specifies the identifier of the combo box, list box, or button. This member is not used for a menu.

itemID

Specifies the menu item identifier for a menu item or the list box item identifier for a variable-height list box or combo box. This member is not used for a fixed-height list box or combo box, or for a button.

itemWidth

Specifies the width, in pixels, of a menu item. Before returning from the message, the owner of the owner-drawn menu item must fill this member.

itemHeight

Specifies the height, in pixels, of an individual item in a list box or a menu. Before returning from the message, the owner of the owner-drawn combo box, list box, or menu item must fill out this member.

itemData

Specifies the application-defined 32-bit value associated with the menu item. For a control, this parameter specifies the value last assigned to the list box or combo box by the LB_SETITEMDATA or CB_SETITEMDATA message. If the list box or combo box has the LB_HASSTRINGS or CB_HASSTRINGS style, this value is initially zero. Otherwise, this value is initially the value passed to the list box or combo box in the *lParam* parameter of one of the following messages:

CB_ADDSTRING
CB_INSERTSTRING
LB_ADDSTRING
LB_INSERTSTRING

Comments   The owner window of an owner-drawn control receives a pointer to the **MEASUREITEMSTRUCT** structure as the *lParam* parameter of a WM_MEASUREITEM message. The owner-drawn control sends this message to its owner window when the control is created. The owner then fills in the appropriate members in the structure for the control and returns. This structure is common to all owner-drawn controls.

If an application does not fill the appropriate members of **MEASUREITEMSTRUCT**, the control or menu item may not be drawn properly.

See Also   WM_MEASUREITEM

MEDIA_TYPE

`New`

```
typedef enum _MEDIA_TYPE {
    Unknown,              // Format is unknown
    F5_1Pt2_512,          // 5.25", 1.2MB,   512 bytes/sector
    F3_1Pt44_512,         // 3.5",  1.44MB,  512 bytes/sector
    F3_2Pt88_512,         // 3.5",  2.88MB,  512 bytes/sector
    F3_20Pt8_512,         // 3.5",  20.8MB,  512 bytes/sector
    F3_720_512,           // 3.5",  720KB,   512 bytes/sector
    F5_360_512,           // 5.25", 360KB,   512 bytes/sector
    F5_320_512,           // 5.25", 320KB,   512 bytes/sector
    F5_320_1024,          // 5.25", 320KB,   1024 bytes/sector
    F5_180_512,           // 5.25", 180KB,   512 bytes/sector
    F5_160_512,           // 5.25", 160KB,   512 bytes/sector
    RemovableMedia,       // Removable media other than floppy
    FixedMedia            // Fixed hard disk media
} MEDIA_TYPE;
```

The **MEDIA_TYPE** enumerated type provides a set of enumerators to describe various forms of device media. The comments above explain the enumerators.

Comments

The *MediaType* member of the **DISK_GEOMETRY** data structure is of type **MEDIA_TYPE**. The **DeviceIoControl** function receives a **DISK_GEOMETRY** structure in response to an **IOCTL_DISK_GET_DRIVE_GEOMETRY** device i/o operation. The **DeviceIoControl** function receives an array of **DISK_GEOMETRY** structures in response to an **IOCTL_DISK_GET_MEDIA_TYPES** device i/o operation.

See Also

DeviceIoControl, IOCTL_DISK_GET_DRIVE_GEOMETRY, IOCTL_DISK_GET_MEDIA_TYPES, DISK_GEOMETRY

MEMORY_BASIC_INFORMATION

```
typedef struct _MEMORY_BASIC_INFORMATION { /* mbi */
    PVOID BaseAddress;              /* base address of region    */
    PVOID AllocationBase;           /* allocation base address   */
    DWORD AllocationProtect;        /* initial access protection */
    DWORD RegionSize;               /* size, in bytes, of region */
    DWORD State;                    /* committed, reserved, free */
    DWORD Protect;                  /* current access protection */
    DWORD Type;                     /* type of pages             */
} MEMORY_BASIC_INFORMATION;
typedef MEMORY_BASIC_INFORMATION *PMEMORY_BASIC_INFORMATION;
```

The **MEMORY_BASIC_INFORMATION** structure contains information about a range of pages in the process's virtual address space. The **VirtualQuery** and **VirtualQueryEx** functions use this structure.

Members

BaseAddress
Points to the base address of the region of pages.

AllocationBase
Points to the base address of a range of pages allocated by the **VirtualAlloc** function. The page pointed to by the **BaseAddress** member is contained within this allocation range.

AllocationProtect
Specifies the access protection given when the region was initially allocated. One of the following flags is specified:

Value	Meaning
PAGE_NOACCESS	Disables all access to the committed region of pages. An attempt to read from, write to, or execute in the committed region results in an access violation exception, called a general protection (GP) fault.
PAGE_READONLY	Enables read access to the committed region of pages. An attempt to write to the committed region results in an access violation. If the system differentiates between read-only access and execution access, an attempt to execute code in the committed region results in an access violation.
PAGE_READWRITE	Enables both read and write access to the committed region of pages.

RegionSize

Specifies the size, in bytes, of the region beginning at the base address in which all pages have identical attributes.

State

Specifies the state of the pages in the region. One of the following states is indicated:

State	Meaning
MEM_COMMIT	Indicates committed pages for which physical storage has been allocated, either in memory or in the paging file on disk.
MEM_RESERVE	Indicates reserved pages where a range of the process's virtual address space is reserved without allocating any physical storage. For reserved pages, the information in the **Protect** member is undefined.
MEM_FREE	Indicates free pages not accessible to the calling process and available to be allocated. For free pages, the information in the **AllocationBase**, **AllocationProtect**, **Protect**, and **Type** members is undefined.

Protect

Specifies the access protection of the pages in the region. One of the flags listed for the **AllocationProtect** member is specified.

Type

Specifies the type of pages in the region. This value is always the MEM_PRIVATE flag, indicating that the memory is not shared by other processes.

See Also   **VirtualQuery**, **VirtualQueryEx**

MEMORYSTATUS

```
typedef struct _MEMORYSTATUS { /* mst */
    DWORD dwLength;         /* sizeof(MEMORYSTATUS)       */
    DWORD dwMemoryLoad;     /* percent of memory in use   */
    DWORD dwTotalPhys;      /* bytes of physical memory   */
    DWORD dwAvailPhys;      /* free physical memory bytes */
    DWORD dwTotalPageFile;  /* bytes of paging file       */
    DWORD dwAvailPageFile;  /* free bytes of paging file  */
    DWORD dwTotalVirtual;   /* user bytes of address space */
    DWORD dwAvailVirtual;   /* free user bytes            */
} MEMORYSTATUS, *LPMEMORYSTATUS;
```

The **MEMORYSTATUS** structure contains information about current memory availability. The **GlobalMemoryStatus** function uses this structure.

Members

dwLength

Indicates the size of this structure. The calling process should set this member prior to calling the **GlobalMemoryStatus** function.

dwMemoryLoad

Specifies a number between 0 and 100 that gives a general idea of current memory utilization, in which 0 indicates no memory use and 100 indicates full memory use.

dwTotalPhys

Indicates the total number of bytes of physical memory.

dwAvailPhys

Indicates the number of bytes of physical memory available.

dwTotalPageFile

Indicates the total number of bytes that can be stored in the paging file. Note that this number does not represent the actual physical size of the paging file on disk.

dwAvailPageFile

Indicates the number of bytes available in the paging file.

dwTotalVirtual

Indicates the total number of bytes that can be described in the user mode portion of the virtual address space of the calling process.

dwAvailVirtual

Indicates the number of bytes of unreserved and uncommitted memory in the user mode portion of the virtual address space of the calling process.

MENU_EVENT_RECORD

```
typedef struct _MENU_EVENT_RECORD { /* mer */
    UINT dwCommandId;
} MENU_EVENT_RECORD, *PMENU_EVENT_RECORD;
```

The **MENU_EVENT_RECORD** structure reports menu events in a console **INPUT_RECORD** structure. These events are used internally and should be ignored.

Members   **dwCommandId**
                 Used internally.

See Also   **INPUT_RECORD**

MENUITEMTEMPLATE

```
typedef struct {    /* mit */
    WORD mtOption;
    WORD mtID;
    WCHAR mtString[1];
} MENUITEMTEMPLATE;
```

The **MENUITEMTEMPLATE** structure defines a menu item in a menu template.

Members   **mtOption**
                 Specifies a mask of one or more of the following predefined menu options that control the appearance of the menu item.

Value	Meaning
MF_CHECKED	Indicates that the menu item has a check mark next to it.
MF_GRAYED	Indicates that the menu item is initially inactive and drawn with a gray effect.
MF_HELP	Indicates that the menu item has a vertical separator to its left.
MF_MENUBARBREAK	Indicates that the menu item is placed in a new column. The old and new columns are separated by a bar.
MF_MENUBREAK	Indicates that the menu item is placed in a new column.

| MF_OWNERDRAW | Indicates that the owner window of the menu is responsible for drawing all visual aspects of the menu item, including highlighted, checked, and inactive states. This option is not valid for an item in a menu bar. |
| MF_POPUP | Indicates that the item is a pop-up item (a pop-up item invokes a pop-up menu when the user chooses the item). |

mtID
Specifies the menu item identifier of a command item; a command item sends a command message to its owner window. The **MENUITEMTEMPLATE** structure for a pop-up menu item does not contain the **mtID** member.

mtString
Specifies the null-terminated string for the menu item.

See Also   **LoadMenuIndirect**, **MENUITEMTEMPLATEHEADER**

MENUITEMTEMPLATEHEADER

```
typedef struct {     /* mith */
    WORD versionNumber;
    WORD offset;
} MENUITEMTEMPLATEHEADER;
```

The **MENUITEMTEMPLATEHEADER** structure defines the header for a menu template. A complete menu template consists of a header and one or more menu item lists.

Members   **versionNumber**
Specifies the version number. This member should be zero.

offset
Specifies the offset, in bytes, from the end of the header. The menu item list begins at this offset. Usually, this member is zero, and the menu item list follows immediately after the header.

Comments   One or more **MENUITEMTEMPLATE** structures are combined to form the menu item list.

See Also   **LoadMenuIndirect**, **MENUITEMTEMPLATE**

METAFILEPICT

```
typedef struct tagMETAFILEPICT { /* mfp */
    LONG      mm;
    LONG      xExt;
    LONG      yExt;
    HMETAFILE hMF;
} METAFILEPICT;
```

The **METAFILEPICT** structure defines the metafile picture format used for exchanging metafile data through the clipboard.

Members

mm

Specifies the mapping mode in which the picture is drawn.

xExt

Specifies the size of the metafile picture for all modes except the MM_ISOTROPIC and MM_ANISOTROPIC modes. (For more information about these modes, see the **yExit** member.) The x-extent specifies the width of the rectangle within which the picture is drawn. The coordinates are in units that correspond to the mapping mode.

yExt

Specifies the size of the metafile picture for all modes except the MM_ISOTROPIC and MM_ANISOTROPIC modes. The y-extent specifies the height of the rectangle within which the picture is drawn. The coordinates are in units that correspond to the mapping mode.

For MM_ISOTROPIC and MM_ANISOTROPIC modes, which can be scaled, the **xExt** and **yExt** members contain an optional suggested size in MM_HIMETRIC units. For MM_ANISOTROPIC pictures, **xExt** and **yExt** can be zero when no suggested size is supplied. For MM_ISOTROPIC pictures, an aspect ratio must be supplied even when no suggested size is given. (If a suggested size is given, the aspect ratio is implied by the size.) To give an aspect ratio without implying a suggested size, set **xExt** and **yExt** to negative values whose ratio is the appropriate aspect ratio. The magnitude of the negative **xExt** and **yExt** values is ignored; only the ratio is used.

hMF

Identifies a memory metafile.

See Also   **SetClipboardData**

METAHEADER

```
typedef struct tagMETAHEADER {   /* mh */
    WORD  mtType;
    WORD  mtHeaderSize;
    WORD  mtVersion;
    DWORD mtSize;
    WORD  mtNoObjects;
    DWORD mtMaxRecord;
    WORD  mtNoParameters;
} METAHEADER;
```

The **METAHEADER** structure contains information about a metafile.

Members

mtType

Specifies whether the metafile is in memory or recorded in a disk file. This member can be one of the following values:

Value	Meaning
1	Metafile is in memory.
2	Metafile is in a disk file.

mtHeaderSize

Specifies the size, in words, of the metafile header.

mtVersion

Specifies the Windows version number. The version number for metafiles that support device-independent bitmaps (DIBs) is 0x0300. Otherwise, the version number is 0x0100.

mtSize

Specifies the size, in words, of the file.

mtNoObjects

Specifies the maximum number of objects that exist in the metafile at the same time.

mtMaxRecord

Specifies the size, in words, of the largest record in the metafile.

mtNoParameters

Reserved.

See Also   **METARECORD**

METARECORD

```
typedef struct tagMETARECORD {   /* mr */
    DWORD rdSize;
    WORD  rdFunction;
    WORD  rdParm[1];
} METARECORD;
```

The **METARECORD** structure contains a metafile record.

Members   **rdSize**
                 Specifies the size, in words, of the record.

                 rdFunction
                 Specifies the function number.

                 rdParm
                 Specifies an array of words containing the function parameters, in reverse of
                 the order they are passed to the function.

See Also   **METAHEADER**

MIDIHDR

```
typedef struct midihdr_tag {
    LPSTR  lpData;
    DWORD  dwBufferLength;
    DWORD  dwBytesRecorded;
    DWORD  dwUser;
    DWORD  dwFlags;
    struct midihdr_tag *lpNext;
    DWORD  reserved;
} MIDIHDR;
```

The **MIDIHDR** structure defines the header used to identify a Musical Instrument
Digital Interface (MIDI) system-exclusive data buffer.

Members   **lpData**
                 Points to the system-exclusive data buffer.

                 dwBufferLength
                 Specifies the length of the data buffer.

                 dwBytesRecorded
                 Specifies the amount of data in the buffer, if the header is used in input.

dwUser

Specifies user data.

dwFlags

Specifies flags giving information about the data buffer. This member can be one of the following values:

Value	Meaning
MHDR_DONE	Set by the device driver to indicate that it is finished with the data buffer and is returning it to the application.
MHDR_PREPARED	Set by Windows to indicate that the data buffer has been prepared with **midiInPrepareHeader** or **midiOutPrepareHeader**.

lpNext

Reserved; do not use.

reserved

Reserved; do not use.

MIDIINCAPS

`Unicode`

```
typedef struct midiincaps_tag {
    WORD   wMid;
    WORD   wPid;
    MMVERSION  vDriverVersion;
    TCHAR  szPname[MAXPNAMELEN];
} MIDIINCAPS;
```

The **MIDIINCAPS** structure describes the capabilities of a Musical Instrument Digital Interface (MIDI) input device.

Members

wMid

Specifies a manufacturer identifier for the device driver for the MIDI input device. Manufacturer identifiers are defined in Appendix D, "Manufacturer and Product Identifiers" in the *Microsoft Win32 Programmer's Reference, Volume 2*.

wPid

Specifies a product identifier for the MIDI input device. Product identifiers are defined in Appendix D, "Manufacturer and Product Identifiers" in the *Microsoft Win32 Programmer's Reference, Volume 2*.

vDriverVersion

Specifies the version number of the device driver for the MIDI input device. The high-order byte is the major version number, and the low-order byte is the minor version number.

szPname
Specifies the product name in a null-terminated string.

See Also   **midiInGetDevCaps**

MIDIOUTCAPS

```
typedef struct midioutcaps_tag {
    WORD    wMid;
    WORD    wPid;
    MMVERSION  vDriverVersion;
    TCHAR   szPname[MAXPNAMELEN];
    WORD    wTechnology;
    WORD    wVoices;
    WORD    wNotes;
    WORD    wChannelMask;
    DWORD   dwSupport;
} MIDIOUTCAPS;
```

The **MIDIOUTCAPS** structure describes the capabilities of a Musical Instrument Digital Interface (MIDI) output device.

Members   **wMid**
Specifies a manufacturer identifier for the device driver for the MIDI output device. Manufacturer identifiers are defined in Appendix D, "Manufacturer and Product Identifiers" in the *Microsoft Win32 Programmer's Reference, Volume 2.*

wPid
Specifies a product identifier for the MIDI output device. Product identifiers are defined in Appendix D, "Manufacturer and Product Identifiers" in the *Microsoft Win32 Programmer's Reference, Volume 2.*

vDriverVersion
Specifies the version number of the device driver for the MIDI output device. The high-order byte is the major version number, and the low-order byte is the minor version number.

szPname
Specifies the product name in a null-terminated string.

wTechnology
Specifies the type of the MIDI output device. This member can be one of the following values:

Value	Meaning
MOD_MIDIPORT	MIDI hardware port

MOD_SQSYNTH	Square wave synthesizer
MOD_FMSYNTH	FM synthesizer
MOD_MAPPER	Microsoft MIDI Mapper

wVoices

Specifies the number of voices supported by an internal synthesizer device. If the device is a port, this member is not meaningful and is set to zero.

wNotes

Specifies the maximum number of notes that may be played simultaneously by an internal synthesizer device. If the device is a port, this member is not meaningful and is set to zero.

wChannelMask

Specifies the channels that an internal synthesizer device responds to, where the least significant bit refers to channel 0 and the most significant bit to channel 15. Port devices transmit on all channels; if the device is a port, this member is set to 0xFFFF.

dwSupport

Specifies optional functionality supported by the device. This member can be one or more of the following values:

Value	Meaning
MIDICAPS_VOLUME	Supports volume control.
MIDICAPS_LRVOLUME	Supports separate left and right volume control.
MIDICAPS_CACHE	Supports patch caching.

Comments

If a device supports volume changes, the MIDICAPS_VOLUME flag is set for the **dwSupport** member. If a device supports separate volume changes on the left and right channels, both the MIDICAPS_VOLUME and the MIDICAPS_LRVOLUME flags are set for this member.

See Also

midiOutGetDevCaps

MINMAXINFO

```
typedef struct tagMINMAXINFO {   /* mmi */
    POINT ptReserved;
    POINT ptMaxSize;
    POINT ptMaxPosition;
    POINT ptMinTrackSize;
    POINT ptMaxTrackSize;
} MINMAXINFO;
```

The **MINMAXINFO** structure contains information about a window's maximized size and position and its minimum and maximum tracking size.

Members

ptReserved
Reserved for internal use.

ptMaxSize
Specifies the maximized width (*point*.**x**) and the maximized height (*point*.**y**) of the window.

ptMaxPosition
Specifies the position of the left side of the maximized window (*point*.**x**) and the position of the top of the maximized window (*point*.**y**).

ptMinTrackSize
Specifies the minimum tracking width (*point*.**x**) and the minimum tracking height (*point*.**y**) of the window.

ptMaxTrackSize
Specifies the maximum tracking width (*point*.**x**) and the maximum tracking height (*point*.**y**) of the window.

See Also   **POINT**, WM_GETMINMAXINFO

MMCKINFO

```
typedef struct _MMCKINFO {
    FOURCC  ckid;
    DWORD   cksize;
    FOURCC  fccType;
    DWORD   dwDataOffset;
    DWORD   dwFlags;
} MMCKINFO;
```

The **MMCKINFO** structure contains information about a chunk in a Resource Interchange File Format (RIFF) file.

Members

ckid
Specifies the identifier of the chunk.

cksize
Specifies the size of the data member of the chunk. The size of the data member does not include the 4-byte chunk identifier, the 4-byte chunk size, or the optional pad byte at the end of the field.

fccType
Specifies the form type for RIFF chunks or the list type for LIST chunks.

dwDataOffset

Specifies the file offset of the beginning of the chunk's data member, relative to the beginning of the file.

dwFlags

Specifies flags giving additional information about the chunk. This value can be MMIO_DIRTY, which specifies that the length of the chunk may have changed and should be updated by the **mmioAscend** function. This flag is set when a chunk is created by the **mmioCreateChunk** function.

MMIOINFO

```
typedef struct _MMIOINFO {
    DWORD    dwFlags;
    FOURCC   fccIOProc;
    LPMMIOPROC pIOProc;
    UINT     wErrorRet;
    HANDLE   htask;
    LONG     cchBuffer;
    LPSTR    pchBuffer;
    LPSTR    pchNext;
    LPSTR    pchEndRead;
    LPSTR    pchEndWrite;
    LONG     lBufOffset;
    LONG     lDiskOffset;
    DWORD    adwInfo[3];
    DWORD    dwReserved1;
    DWORD    dwReserved2;
    HMMIO    hmmio;
} MMIOINFO;
```

This **MMIOINFO** structure contains the current state of a file opened by using the **mmioOpen** function.

Members   **dwFlags**

Specifies flags indicating how a file was opened. This member can be one of the following values:

Value	Meaning
MMIO_READ	The file was opened for reading only.
MMIO_WRITE	The file was opened for writing only.
MMIO_READWRITE	The file was opened for both reading and writing.
MMIO_COMPAT	The file was opened in compatibility mode, allowing any process on a given computer to open the file any number of times.

MMIO_EXCLUSIVE	The file was opened in exclusive mode, denying other processes both read and write access to the file.
MMIO_DENYWRITE	Other processes are denied write access to the file.
MMIO_DENYREAD	Other processes are denied read access to the file.
MMIO_DENYNONE	Other processes are not denied read or write access to the file.
MMIO_CREATE	The **mmioOpen** function was directed to create the file or truncate it to zero length if it already existed.
MMIO_ALLOCBUF	The file's input and output (I/O) buffer was allocated by the **mmioOpen** or **mmioSetBuffer** function.

fccIOProc

Specifies the four-character code identifying the file's I/O procedure. If the I/O procedure is not an installed I/O procedure, **fccIOProc** is NULL.

pIOProc

Points to the file's I/O procedure.

wErrorRet

Contains the extended error value from the **mmioOpen** function, if **mmioOpen** returns NULL. This member does not receive extended error information from any other functions.

htask

Identifies the task.

cchBuffer

Specifies the size of the file's I/O buffer, in characters. If the file does not have an I/O buffer, this member is zero.

pchBuffer

Points to the file's I/O buffer. If the file does not have an I/O buffer, **pchBuffer** is NULL.

pchNext

Points to the next location to be read from or written to in the I/O buffer. If no more bytes can be read without calling the **mmioAdvance** or **mmioRead** function, this member points to **pchEndRead**. If no more bytes can be written without calling the **mmioAdvance** or **mmioWrite** function, this member points to **pchEndWrite**.

pchEndRead

Points to the location that is one byte past the last location in the buffer that can be read from.

pchEndWrite

Points to the location that is one byte past the last location in the buffer that can be written to.

lBufOffset

Reserved for internal use by multimedia file I/O functions; do not use.

lDiskOffset

Specifies the current file position. The current file position is an offset, in bytes, from the beginning of the file. I/O procedures are responsible for maintaining this member.

adwInfo

Contains state information maintained by the I/O procedure. I/O procedures can also use this member to transfer information from the caller to the I/O procedure when the caller opens a file.

dwReserved1

Reserved for internal use by multimedia file I/O functions; do not use.

dwReserved2

Reserved for internal use by multimedia file I/O functions; do not use.

hmmio

Identifies the open file. File I/O procedures can use this type **HMMIO** handle when calling other multimedia file I/O functions.

See Also   **mmioGetInfo**

MMTIME

```
typedef struct mmtime_tag {
    WORD   wType;
    union {
        DWORD   ms;
        DWORD   sample;
        DWORD   cb;
        struct {
            BYTE   hour;
            BYTE   min;
            BYTE   sec;
            BYTE   frame;
            BYTE   fps;
            BYTE   dummy;
        } smpte;
        struct {
            DWORD   songptrpos;
        } midi;
    } u;
} MMTIME;
```

The **MMTIME** structure is a general-purpose structure for timing information.

Members   **wType**

Specifies the type of the union. This member can be one of the following values:

Value	Meaning
TIME_MS	Time counted in milliseconds
TIME_SAMPLES	Number of wave samples
TIME_BYTES	Current byte offset
TIME_SMPTE	Society of Motion Picture and Television Engineers (SMPTE) time
TIME_MIDI	Musical Instrument Digital Interface (MIDI) time

u

Specifies the contents of the union. The following members are contained in the **u** union:

Member	Meaning
ms	Milliseconds. Used when the **wType** member of the **MMTIME** structure is TIME_MS.
sample	Samples. Used when **wType** is TIME_SAMPLES.
cb	Byte count. Used when **wType** is TIME_BYTES.
smpte	SMPTE time. Used when **wType** is TIME_SMPTE. The following members are contained in the **smpte** structure:

Member	Meaning
hour	Hours
min	Minutes
sec	Seconds
frame	Frames
fps	Frames per second (24, 25, 29[30 drop] or 30)
dummy	Dummy byte for alignment

midi   MIDI time. Used when **wType** is TIME_MIDI. The following member is contained in the **midi** structure:

Member	Meaning
songptrpos	Song pointer position

MONCBSTRUCT

```
typedef struct tagMONCBSTRUCT { /* mcbst */
    UINT    cb;
    DWORD   dwTime;
    HANDLE  hTask;
    DWORD   dwRet;
    UINT    wType;
    UINT    wFmt;
    HCONV   hConv;
    HSZ     hsz1;
    HSZ     hsz2;
    HDDEDATA hData;
    DWORD    dwData1;
    DWORD    dwData2;
    CONVCONTEXT cc;
    DWORD   cbData;
    DWORD   Data[8];
} MONCBSTRUCT;
```

The **MONCBSTRUCT** structure contains information about the current dynamic data exchange (DDE) transaction. A DDE debugging application can use this structure when monitoring transactions that the system passes to the DDE callback functions of other applications.

Members

cb
Specifies the length, in bytes, of the structure.

dwTime
Specifies the Windows time that the transaction occurred. Windows time is the number of milliseconds that have elapsed since the system was booted.

hTask
Identifies the task (application instance) containing the DDE callback function that received the transaction.

dwRet
Specifies the value returned by the DDE callback function that processed the transaction.

wType
Identifies the transaction type.

wFmt
Specifies the format of the data exchanged (if any) during the transaction.

hConv
Identifies the conversation in which the transaction took place.

hsz1

Identifies a string.

hsz2

Identifies a string.

hData

Identifies the data exchanged (if any) during the transaction.

dwData1

Specifies additional data.

dwData2

Specifies additional data.

cc

Specifies a **CONVCONTEXT** structure containing language information used to share data in different languages.

cbData

Specifies the amount, in bytes, of data being passed with the transaction. This value may be more than 32 bytes.

Data

Contains the first 32 bytes of data being passed with the transaction (8 * sizeof(DWORD)).

See Also   **CONVCONTEXT, MONERRSTRUCT, MONHSZSTRUCT, MONLINKSTRUCT, MONMSGSTRUCT**

MONCONVSTRUCT

```
typedef struct tagMONCONVSTRUCT { /* mcvst */
    UINT    cb;
    BOOL    fConnect;
    DWORD   dwTime;
    HANDLE  hTask;
    HSZ     hszSvc;
    HSZ     hszTopic;
    HCONV   hConvClient;
    HCONV   hConvServer;
} MONCONVSTRUCT;
```

The **MONCONVSTRUCT** structure contains information about a conversation. A DDE monitoring application can use this structure to obtain information about a conversation that has been established or has terminated.

Members   **cb**

Specifies the length, in bytes, of the structure.

fConnect
> Indicates whether the conversation is currently established. A value of TRUE indicates the conversation is established; FALSE indicates it is not.

dwTime
> Specifies the Windows time at which the conversation was established or terminated. Windows time is the number of milliseconds that have elapsed since the system was booted.

hTask
> Identifies a task (application instance) that is a partner in the conversation.

hszSvc
> Identifies the service name on which the conversation is established.

hszTopic
> Identifies the topic name on which the conversation is established.

hConvClient
> Identifies the client conversation handle.

hConvServer
> Identifies the server conversation handle.

Comments   In Windows NT, string handles are local to the process; therefore, the **hszSvc** and **hszTopic** members are global atoms.

In Windows NT, conversation handles are local to the instance; therefore, the **hConvClient** and **hConvServer** members are window handles.

The **hConvClient** and **hConvServer** members of the **MONCONVSTRUCT** structure do not hold the same value as would be seen by the applications engaged in the conversation. Instead, they hold a globally unique pair of values that identify the conversation.

See Also   **MONCBSTRUCT, MONERRSTRUCT, MONHSZSTRUCT, MONLINKSTRUCT, MONMSGSTRUCT**

MONERRSTRUCT

```
typedef struct tagMONERRSTRUCT { /* mest */
    UINT    cb;
    UINT    wLastError;
    DWORD   dwTime;
    HANDLE  hTask;
} MONERRSTRUCT;
```

The **MONERRSTRUCT** structure contains information about the current dynamic data exchange (DDE) error. A DDE monitoring application can use this structure to monitor errors returned by DDE Management Library functions.

Members

cb
Specifies the length, in bytes, of the structure.

wLastError
Identifies the current error.

dwTime
Specifies the Windows time that the error occurred. Windows time is the number of milliseconds that have elapsed since the system was booted.

hTask
Identifies the task (application instance) that called the DDE function that caused the error.

See Also   **MONCBSTRUCT, MONCONVSTRUCT, MONHSZSTRUCT, MONLINKSTRUCT, MONMSGSTRUCT**

MONHSZSTRUCT

```
typedef struct tagMONHSZSTRUCT { /* mhst */
    UINT   cb;
    BOOL   fsAction;
    DWORD  dwTime;
    HSZ    hsz;
    HANDLE hTask;
    char   str[1];
} MONHSZSTRUCT;
```

The **MONHSZSTRUCT** structure contains information about a DDE string handle. A DDE monitoring application can use this structure when monitoring the activity of the string manager component of the DDE Management Library.

Members

cb
Specifies the length, in bytes, of the structure.

fsAction
Specifies the action being performed on the string handle specified by the **hsz** member.

Value	Meaning
MH_CLEANUP	An application is freeing its DDE resources, causing the system to delete string handles the application had created. (The application called the **DdeUninitialize** function.)

MH_CREATE	An application is creating a string handle. (The application called the **DdeCreateStringHandle** function.)
MH_DELETE	An application is deleting a string handle. (The application called the **DdeFreeStringHandle** function.)
MH_KEEP	An application is increasing the use count of a string handle. (The application called the **DdeKeepStringHandle** function.)

dwTime
Specifies the Windows time when the action specified by the **fsAction** member takes place. Windows time is the number of milliseconds that have elapsed since the system was booted.

hsz
Identifies the string. In Windows NT, string handles are local to the process; therefore, this member is a global atom.

hTask
Identifies the task (application instance) performing the action on the string handle.

str
Points to the string identified by the **hsz** member.

See Also   **MONCBSTRUCT, MONCONVSTRUCT, MONERRSTRUCT, MONLINKSTRUCT, MONMSGSTRUCT**

MONITOR_INFO_1   New, Unicode

```
typedef struct _MONITOR_INFO_1 { /* mi1 */
    LPTSTR pName;
} MONITOR_INFO_1;
```

The **MONITOR_INFO_1** structure identifies an installed monitor.

Members   **pName**
Points to a null-terminated string that identifies an installed monitor.

See Also   **EnumMonitors MONITOR_INFO_2**

MONITOR_INFO_2

```
typedef struct _MONITOR_INFO_2 { /* mi2 */
    LPTSTR pName;
    LPTSTR pEnvironment ;
    LPTSTR pDLLName ;
} MONITOR_INFO_2;
```

The **MONITOR_INFO_2** structure identifies a monitor.

Members

pName
Points to a null-terminated string that is the name of the monitor.

pEnvironment
Points to a null-terminated environment string specifying the environment this DLL is designed to run in.

pDLLName
Points to a null-terminated string that is the name of the monitor DLL.

See Also

EnumMonitors MONITOR_INFO_1

MONLINKSTRUCT

```
typedef struct tagMONLINKSTRUCT { /* mlst */
    UINT   cb;
    DWORD  dwTime;
    HANDLE hTask;
    BOOL   fEstablished;
    BOOL   fNoData;
    HSZ    hszSvc;
    HSZ    hszTopic;
    HSZ    hszItem;
    UINT   wFmt;
    BOOL   fServer;
    HCONV  hConvServer;
    HCONV  hConvClient;
} MONLINKSTRUCT;
```

The **MONLINKSTRUCT** structure contains information about a dynamic data exchange (DDE) advise loop. A DDE monitoring application can use this structure to obtain information about an advise loop that has started or ended.

Members

cb
Specifies the length, in bytes, of the structure.

dwTime

Specifies the Windows time when the advise loop was started or ended. Windows time is the number of milliseconds that have elapsed since the system was booted.

hTask

Identifies a task (application instance) that is a partner in the advise loop.

fEstablished

Indicates whether an advise loop was successfully established. A value of TRUE indicates an advise loop was established; FALSE indicates it was not.

fNoData

Indicates whether the XTYPF_NODATA flag is set for the advise loop. A value of TRUE indicates the flag is set; FALSE indicates it is not.

hszSvc

Identifies the service name of the server in the advise loop. In Windows NT, string handles are local to the process; therefore, this member is a global atom.

hszTopic

Identifies the topic name on which the advise loop is established. In Windows NT, string handles are local to the process; therefore, this member is a global atom.

hszItem

Identifies the item name that is the subject of the advise loop. In Windows NT, string handles are local to the process; therefore, this member is a global atom.

wFmt

Specifies the format of the data exchanged (if any) during the advise loop.

fServer

Indicates whether the link notification came from the server. A value of TRUE indicates the notification came from the server; FALSE indicates otherwise.

hConvServer

Identifies the server conversation.

hConvClient

Identifies the client conversation.

Comments

In Windows NT, string handles are local to the process; therefore, the **hszSvc**, **hszTopic**, and **hszItem** members are actually global atoms.

The **hConvClient** and **hConvServer** members of the **MONCONVSTRUCT** structure do not hold the same value as would be seen by the applications engaged in the conversation. Instead, they hold a globally unique pair of values that identify the conversation.

See Also

MONCBSTRUCT, MONERRSTRUCT, MONHSZSTRUCT, MONMSGSTRUCT

MONMSGSTRUCT

```
typedef struct tagMONMSGSTRUCT { /* mmst */
    UINT   cb;
    HWND   hwndTo;
    DWORD  dwTime;
    HANDLE hTask;
    UINT   wMsg;
    WPARAM wParam;
    LPARAM lParam;
    DDEML_MSG_HOOK_DATA dmhd;
} MONMSGSTRUCT;
```

The **MONMSGSTRUCT** structure contains information about a DDE message. A DDE monitoring application can use this structure to obtain information about a DDE message that was sent or posted.

Members

cb

Specifies the length, in bytes, of the structure.

hwndTo

Identifies the window that receives the DDE message.

dwTime

Specifies the Windows time at which the message was sent or posted. Windows time is the number of milliseconds that have elapsed since the system was booted.

hTask

Identifies the task (application instance) containing the window that receives the DDE message.

wMsg

Specifies the identifier of the DDE message.

wParam

Specifies the *wParam* parameter of the DDE message.

lParam

Specifies the *lParam* parameter of the DDE message.

dmhd

Specifies a **DDEML_MSG_HOOK_DATA** structure that contains additional information about the DDE message.

See Also

DDEML_MSG_HOOK_DATA, MONCBSTRUCT, MONCONVSTRUCT, MONERRSTRUCT, MONHSZSTRUCT, MONLINKSTRUCT

MOUSE_EVENT_RECORD

```
typedef struct _MOUSE_EVENT_RECORD { /* mer */
    COORD dwMousePosition;
    DWORD dwButtonState;
    DWORD dwControlKeyState;
    DWORD dwEventFlags;
} MOUSE_EVENT_RECORD;
```

The **MOUSE_EVENT_RECORD** structure is used in a console **INPUT_RECORD** structure to report mouse input events.

Members

dwMousePosition

Specifies the location of the cursor in terms of the screen buffer's character-cell coordinates.

dwButtonState

Indicates the status of the mouse buttons. The least significant bit corresponds to the leftmost mouse button. The next least significant bit corresponds to the rightmost mouse button. The next bit indicates the next-to-leftmost mouse button. The bits then correspond left-to-right to the mouse buttons. A bit is 1 if the button was pressed.

dwControlKeyState

Indicates the state of the control keys. This member can be a combination of the following values:

Value	Meaning
RIGHT_ALT_PRESSED	The right ALT key is pressed.
LEFT_ALT_PRESSED	The left ALT key is pressed.
RIGHT_CTRL_PRESSED	The right CTRL key is pressed.
LEFT_CTRL_PRESSED	The left CTRL key is pressed.
SHIFT_PRESSED	The SHIFT key is pressed.
NUMLOCK_ON	The NUM LOCK light is on.
SCROLLLOCK_ON	The SCROLL LOCK light is on.
CAPSLOCK_ON	The CAPS LOCK light is on.
ENHANCED_KEY	The key is enhanced.

dwEventFlags

Indicates the type of mouse event. If this value is zero, it indicates a mouse button being pressed or released. Otherwise, the value is one of the following:

Value	Meaning
MOUSE_MOVED	A change in mouse position occurred.

DOUBLE_CLICK	The second click (button press) of a double-click occurred. The first click is returned as a regular button-press event.

Comments   Mouse events are placed in the input buffer when the console is in mouse mode (ENABLE_MOUSE_INPUT).

Mouse events are generated whenever the user moves the mouse, or presses or releases one of the mouse buttons. Mouse events are placed in a console's input buffer only when the console group has the keyboard focus and the cursor is within the borders of the console's window.

See Also   **PeekConsoleInput**, **ReadConsoleInput**, **WriteConsoleInput**

MOUSEHOOKSTRUCT

```
typedef struct tagMOUSEHOOKSTRUCT { /* ms */
    POINT pt;
    HWND  hwnd;
    UINT  wHitTestCode; ·
    DWORD dwExtraInfo;
} MOUSEHOOKSTRUCT;
```

The **MOUSEHOOKSTRUCT** structure contains information about a mouse event.

Members   **pt**
Specifies a **POINT** structure that contains the x- and y-coordinates of the cursor, in screen coordinates.

hwnd
Identifies the window that will receive the mouse message corresponding to the mouse event.

wHitTextCode
Specifies the hit-test code. For a list of hit-test codes, see the description of the WM_NCHITTEST message.

dwExtraInfo
Specifies extra information associated with the message.

See Also   **GetMessageExtraInfo**, **SetWindowsHook**

MSG

```
typedef struct tagMSG {       /* msg */
    HWND    hwnd;
    UINT    message;
    WPARAM  wParam;
    LPARAM  lParam;
    DWORD   time;
    POINT   pt;
} MSG;
```

The **MSG** structure contains message information from a thread's message queue.

Members

hwnd
Identifies the window whose window procedure receives the message.

message
Specifies the message number.

wParam
Specifies additional information about the message. The exact meaning depends on the value of the **message** member.

lParam
Specifies additional information about the message. The exact meaning depends on the value of the **message** member.

time
Specifies the time at which the message was posted.

pt
Specifies the cursor position, in screen coordinates, when the message was posted.

See Also

GetMessage, **PeekMessage**

MULTIKEYHELP

`Unicode`

```
typedef struct tagMULTIKEYHELP { /* mkh */
    DWORD mkSize;
    BYTE  mkKeylist;
    TCHAR szKeyphrase[1];
} MULTIKEYHELP;
```

The **MULTIKEYHELP** structure specifies a keyword table and an associated keyword to be used by the Windows Help application.

Members   **mkSize**
             Specifies the length, in bytes, of the **MULTIKEYHELP** structure.

             mkKeylist
             Specifies a single character that identifies the keyword table to be searched.

             szKeyphrase[]
             Contains a null-terminated text string that specifies the keyword to be located
             in the keyword table.

See Also   **WinHelp**

NAME_BUFFER

```
typedef struct _NAME_BUFFER { /* nb */
    UCHAR name[NCBNAMSZ];
    UCHAR name_num;
    UCHAR name_flags;
} NAME_BUFFER;
```

The **NAME_BUFFER** structure contains information about a local network
name. One or more **NAME_BUFFER** structures follows an
ADAPTER_STATUS structure when an application specifies NCBASTAT in the
ncb_command member of the **NCB** structure.

Members   **name**
             Specifies the local network name. This is the value in the **ncb_name** member
             of the **NCB** structure.

             name_num
             Specifies the number for the local network name. This is the value in the
             ncb_num member of the **NCB** structure.

             name_flags
             Specifies the current state of the name table entry. This member can be one of
             the following values:

Value	Meaning
REGISTERING	The name specified by the **name** member is being added to the network.
REGISTERED	The name specified by the **name** member has been successfully added to the network.
DEREGISTERED	The name specified by the **name** member has an active session when an NCBDELNAME command is issued. The name will be removed from the name table when the session is closed.

DUPLICATE	A duplicate name was detected during registration.
DUPLICATE_DEREG	A duplicate name was detected with a pending deregistration.
GROUP_NAME	The name specified by the **name** member was created using the NCBADDGRNAME command.
UNIQUE_NAME	The name specified by the **name** member was created with using the NCBADDNAME command.

See Also   **ADAPTER_STATUS**, **NCB**

NCB

```
typedef struct _NCB { /* ncb */
    UCHAR   ncb_command;
    UCHAR   ncb_retcode;
    UCHAR   ncb_lsn;
    UCHAR   ncb_num;
    PUCHAR  ncb_buffer;
    WORD    ncb_length;
    UCHAR   ncb_callname[NCBNAMSZ];
    UCHAR   ncb_name[NCBNAMSZ];
    UCHAR   ncb_rto;
    UCHAR   ncb_sto;
    void (*ncb_post) (struct _NCB *);
    UCHAR   ncb_lana_num;
    UCHAR   ncb_cmd_cplt;
    UCHAR   ncb_reserve[10];
    HANDLE  ncb_event;
} NCB;
```

The **NCB** structure describes a network-control block. A pointer to this structure is passed to the **Netbios** function.

Members   **ncb_command**

Specifies the command code and a flag that indicates whether the NCB is processed asynchronously. The most significant bit contains the flag. If the ASYNCH constant is combined with a command code (by using the OR operator), the NCB is processed asynchronously. The following command codes are supported:

Code	Meaning
NCBACTION	Enables extensions to the transport interface. NCBACTION commands are mapped to TdiAction. When this value is specified, the **ncb_buffer** member points to a buffer to be filled with an **ACTION_HEADER** structure, which is optionally followed by data. NCBACTION commands cannot be canceled by using NCBCANCEL.
NCBADDGRNAME	Add a group name to the local name table.
NCBADDNAME	Add a unique name to the local name table.
NCBASTAT	Retrieve the status of the adapter. When this value is specified, the **ncb_buffer** member points to a buffer to be filled with an **ADAPTER_STATUS** structure, followed by an array of **NAME_BUFFER** structures.
NCBCALL	Open a session with another name.
NCBCANCEL	Cancel a previous command.
NCBCHAINSEND	Send the contents of two data buffers to the specified session partner. For Windows NT, this is equivalent to the NCBCHAINSENDNA command.
NCBCHAINSENDNA	Send the contents of two data buffers to the specified session partner and do not wait for acknowledgment. For Windows NT, this is equivalent to the NCBCHAINSEND command.
NCBDELNAME	Delete a name from the local name table.
NCBDGRECV	Receive a datagram from any name.
NCBDGRECVBC	Receive broadcast datagram from any host.
NCBDGSEND	Send datagram to a specified name.
NCBDGSENDBC	Send a broadcast datagram to every host on the local area network (LAN).
NCBENUM	Enumerate LAN adapter (LANA) numbers. When this value is specified, the **ncb_buffer** member points to a buffer to be filled with a **LANA_ENUM** structure.
NCBFINDNAME	Determine the location of a name on the network. When this value is specified, the **ncb_buffer** member points to a buffer to be filled with a **FIND_NAME_HEADER** structure followed by one or more **FIND_NAME_BUFFER** structures.
NCBHANGUP	Close a specified session.
NCBLANSTALERT	Notify the user of LAN failures that last for more than one minute.
NCBLISTEN	Enable a session to be opened with another name.
NCBRECV	Receive data from the specified session partner.

NCBRECVANY	Receive data from any session corresponding to a specified name.
NCBRESET	Reset a LAN adapter. An adapter must be reset before any other NCB command that specifies the same number in the **ncb_lana_num** member will be accepted.
	The IBM Netbios 3.0 specification documents several NCB_RESET NCB's. Win32 implements the "NCB.RESET Using the Dynamic Link Routine Interface". Particular values can be passed in specific bytes of the NCB. More specifically:

- If **ncb_lsn** is not 0x00, all resources associated with **ncb_lana_num** are to be freed.

- If **ncb_lsn** is 0x00, all resources associated with **ncb_lana_num** are to be freed, and new resources are to be allocated. The byte **ncb_callname**[0] specifies the maximum number of sessions, and the byte **ncb_callname**[2] specifies the maximum number of names. A non-zero value for the byte **ncb_callname**[3] requests that the application use NAME_NUMBER_1.

NCBSEND	Send data to the specified session partner. For Windows NT, this is equivalent to the NCBSENDNA command.
NCBSENDNA	Send data to specified session partner and do not wait for an acknowledgment. For Windows NT, this is equivalent to the NCBSEND command.
NCBSSTAT	Retrieve the status of the session. When this value is specified, the **ncb_buffer** member points to a buffer to be filled with a **SESSION_HEADER** structure, followed by one or more **SESSION_BUFFER** structures.
NCBTRACE	Activate or deactivate NCB tracing. Support for this command in the system is optional and system-specific.
NCBUNLINK	Unlink the adapter.

ncb_retcode
Specifies the return code. This value is set to NRC_PENDING while an asynchronous operation is in progress. The return codes can be one of the following:

Return code	Meaning
NRC_GOODRET	The operation succeeded.
NRC_BUFLEN	An illegal buffer length was supplied.
NRC_ILLCMD	An illegal command was supplied.
NRC_CMDTMO	The command was timed out.

NRC_INCOMP	The message was incomplete. The application is to issue another command.
NRC_BADDR	The buffer address was illegal.
NRC_SNUMOUT	The session number was out of range.
NRC_NORES	No resource was available.
NRC_SCLOSED	The session was closed.
NRC_CMDCAN	The command was canceled.
NRC_DUPNAME	A duplicate name existed in the local name table.
NRC_NAMTFUL	The name table was full.
NRC_ACTSES	The command finished; the name has active sessions and is no longer registered.
NRC_LOCTFUL	The local session table was full.
NRC_REMTFUL	The remote session table was full. The request to open a session was rejected.
NRC_ILLNN	An illegal name number was specified.
NRC_NOCALL	The system did not find the name that was called.
NRC_NOWILD	Wildcards are not permitted in the **ncb_name** member.
NRC_INUSE	The name was already in use on the remote adapter.
NRC_NAMERR	The name was deleted.
NRC_SABORT	The session ended abnormally.
NRC_NAMCONF	A name conflict was detected.
NRC_IFBUSY	The interface was busy.
NRC_TOOMANY	Too many commands were outstanding; the application can retry the command later.
NRC_BRIDGE	The **ncb_lana_num** member did not specify a valid network number.
NRC_CANOCCR	The command finished while a cancel operation was occurring.
NRC_CANCEL	The NCBCANCEL command was not valid; the command was not canceled.
NRC_DUPENV	The name was defined by another local process.
NRC_ENVNOTDEF	The environment was not defined. A reset command must be issued.
NRC_OSRESNOTAV	Operating system resources were exhausted. The application can retry the command later.
NRC_MAXAPPS	The maximum number of applications was exceeded.
NRC_NOSAPS	No SAPs available for netbios.
NRC_NORESOURCES	The requested resources were not available.
NRC_INVADDRESS	The NCB address was not valid.

This return code is not part of the IBM NetBIOS 3.0 specification. This return code is not returned in the NCB; instead, it is returned by the **Netbios** function.

NRC_INVDDID	The NCB DDID was invalid.
NRC_LOCKFAIL	The attempt to lock the user area failed.
NRC_OPENERR	An error occurred during an open operation being performed by the device driver. This return code is not part of the IBM NetBIOS 3.0 specification.
NRC_SYSTEM	A system error occurred.
NRC_PENDING	An asynchronous operation is not yet finished.

ncb_lsn
Specifies the local session number. This number uniquely identifies a session within an environment.

ncb_buffer
Points to the message buffer.

ncb_length
Specifies the size, in bytes, of the message buffer.

ncb_callname
Specifies the string that contains the remote name. Trailing space characters should be supplied to bring the length of the string specified by the NCBNAMSZ command.

ncb_name Specifies the string that contains the local name. Trailing space characters should be supplied to bring the length of the string specified by the NCBNAMSZ command.

ncb_rto
Specifies the receive time-out period, in 500-millisecond units, for the session. A value of 0 implies no timeout. Specified only for NCBRECV commands.

ncb_sto
Specifies the send time-out period, in 500-millisecond units, for the session. A value of 0 implies no timeout. Specified only for NCBSEND and NCBCHAINSEND commands.

ncb_post
Specifies the address of the routine to call when the asynchronous NCB finishes. The completion routine is passed a pointer to the completed network-control block.

ncb_lana_num
Specifies the LAN adapter number. This zero-based number corresponds to a particular transport provider using a particular LAN adapter board.

ncb_cmd_cplt

Specifies the command-complete flag. This value is the same as the **ncb_retcode** member.

ncb_reserve

Reserved. This member must be set to zero.

ncb_event

Specifies a handle to a Windows event that is set to the signaled state when the asynchronous network-control block finishes. The event is signaled if the **Netbios** function returns a nonzero value.

The **ncb_event** member must be zero if the **ncb_command** member does not have the ASYNCH value set or if **ncb_post** is non-zero. Otherwise, NRC_ILLCMD is returned.

The event specified by **ncb_event** is set to the non-signalled state by the system when an asynchronous NetBIOS command is accepted, and is set to the signalled state when the asynchronous NetBIOS command finishes.

Using **ncb_event** to submit asynchronous requests requires fewer system resources than using **ncb_post**. Also, when **ncb_event** is nonzero, the pending request is canceled if the thread terminates before the request is processed. This is not true for requests sent by using **ncb_post**.

Only manual reset events should be used with **Netbios**. A given event should not be associated with more than one active asynchronous NetBIOS command.

See Also   **ADAPTER_STATUS, FIND_NAME_BUFFER, FIND_NAME_HEADER, LANA_ENUM, NAME_BUFFER, Netbios, SESSION_HEADER**

NCCALCSIZE_PARAMS

```
typedef struct tagNCCALCSIZE_PARAMS { /* nccp */
    RECT        rgrc[3];
    PWINDOWPOS  lppos;
} NCCALCSIZE_PARAMS;
```

The **NCCALCSIZE_PARAMS** structure contains information that an application can use while processing the WM_NCCALCSIZE message to calculate the size, position, and valid contents of the client area of a window.

Members   **rgrc**

Specifies an array of rectangles. The first contains the new coordinates of a window that has been moved or resized. The second contains the coordinates of the window before it was moved or resized. The third contains the coordinates of the window's client area before the window was moved or resized. If the window is a child window, the coordinates are relative to the

client area of the parent window. If the window is a top-level window, the
coordinates are relative to the screen origin.

lppos

Points to a **WINDOWPOS** structure that contains the size and position values
specified in the operation that moved or resized the window. The
WINDOWPOS structure has the following form:

```
typedef struct tagWINDOWPOS { /* wp */
    HWND hwnd;
    HWND hwndInsertAfter;
    int  x;
    int  y;
    int  cx;
    int  cy;
    UINT flags;
} WINDOWPOS;
```

See Also

MoveWindow, **RECT**, **SetWindowPos**, **WINDOWPOS**, WM_NCCALCSIZE

NETRESOURCE

Unicode

```
typedef struct _NETRESOURCE {   /* nr */
    DWORD   dwScope;
    DWORD   dwType;
    DWORD   dwDisplayType;
    DWORD   dwUsage;
    LPTSTR  lpLocalName;
    LPTSTR  lpRemoteName;
    LPTSTR  lpComment;
    LPTSTR  lpProvider;
} NETRESOURCE;
```

The **NETRESOURCE** structure is returned during enumeration of resources on
the network and during enumeration of currently connected resources.

Members

dwScope

Specifies the scope of the enumeration. Currently, this member can be one of
the following values:

Value	Meaning
RESOURCE_CONNECTED	Currently connected resources (**dwUsage** is undefined)
RESOURCE_GLOBALNET	Resources on the network

RESOURCE_REMEMBERED   Remembered (persistent) connections
                             (**dwUsage** is undefined)

dwType

Specifies a bitmask that gives the resource type. Currently, this member can be one of the following values:

Value	Meaning
RESOURCETYPE_ANY	All resources
RESOURCETYPE_DISK	Disk resources
RESOURCETYPE_PRINT	Print resources

dwDisplayType

Specifies how the network object should be displayed in a network browsing user interface. Currently, this member can be the following values:

Value	Meaning
RESOURCEDISPLAYTYPE_DOMAIN	
The object should be displayed as a domain.	
RESOURCEDISPLAYTYPE_GENERIC	
The method used to display the object does not matter.	
RESOURCEDISPLAYTYPE_SERVER	
The object should be displayed as a server.	
RESOURCEDISPLAYTYPE_SHARE	
The object should be displayed as a sharepoint.	

dwUsage

Specifies a bitmask that gives the resource usage. This member is defined only if **dwScope** is **RESOURCE_GLOBALNET**. Currently, this member can be one of the following values:

Value	Meaning
RESOURCEUSAGE_CONNECTABLE	This is a connectable resource; the name pointed to by the **lpRemoteName** member can be passed to the **WNetAddConnection** function to make a network connection.
RESOURCEUSAGE_CONTAINER	This is a container resource; the name pointed to by the **lpRemoteName** member can be passed to the **WNetOpenEnum** function to enumerate the resources in the container.

lpLocalName

Points to the name of a local device if the **dwScope** member is RESOURCE_CONNECTED or RESOURCE_REMEMBERED. This member is NULL if the connection does not use a device. Otherwise, it is undefined.

lpRemoteName

Points to a remote network name if the entry is a network resource.

If the entry is a current or remembered connection, **lpRemoteName** points to the network name associated with the name pointed to by the **lpLocalName** member.

lpComment

Points to a provider-supplied comment.

lpProvider

Points to the name of the provider owning this resource. This member can be NULL if the provider name is unknown.

See Also   **WNetCloseEnum, WNetEnumResource, WNetOpenEnum**

NEWCPLINFO

```
typedef struct tagNEWCPLINFO {  /* ncpli */
    DWORD dwSize;
    DWORD dwFlags;
    DWORD dwHelpContext;
    LONG  lData;
    HICON hIcon;
    char  szName[32];
    char  szInfo[64];
    char  szHelpFile[128];
} NEWCPLINFO;
```

The **NEWCPLINFO** structure contains resource information and a user-defined value for a Control Panel application.

Members   **dwSize**

Specifies the length of the structure, in bytes.

dwFlags

Specifies Control Panel flags.

dwHelpContext

Specifies the context number for the topic in the help project (.HPJ) file that displays when the user selects help for the application.

lData

Specifies data defined by the application.

hIcon

Identifies an icon resource for the application icon. This icon is displayed in the Control Panel window.

szName

Specifies a null-terminated string that contains the application name. The name is the short string displayed below the application icon in the Control Panel window. The name is also displayed in the Settings menu of Control Panel.

szInfo

Specifies a null-terminated string containing the application description. The description displayed at the bottom of the Control Panel window when the application icon is selected.

szHelpFile

Specifies a null-terminated string that contains the path of the help file, if any, for the application.

See Also   **CPLINFO**, CPL_NEWINQUIRE

NEWTEXTMETRIC

`Unicode`

```
typedef struct tagNEWTEXTMETRIC { /* ntm */
    LONG   tmHeight;
    LONG   tmAscent;
    LONG   tmDescent;
    LONG   tmInternalLeading;
    LONG   tmExternalLeading;
    LONG   tmAveCharWidth;
    LONG   tmMaxCharWidth;
    LONG   tmWeight;
    LONG   tmOverhang;
    LONG   tmDigitizedAspectX;
    LONG   tmDigitizedAspectY;
    BYTE   tmFirstChar;
    BYTE   tmLastChar;
    BYTE   tmDefaultChar;
    BYTE   tmBreakChar;
    BYTE   tmItalic;
    BYTE   tmUnderlined;
    BYTE   tmStruckOut;
    BYTE   tmPitchAndFamily;
    BYTE   tmCharSet;
    DWORD  ntmFlags;
    UINT   ntmSizeEM;
    UINT   ntmCellHeight;
```

```
    UINT  ntmAvgWidth;
} NEWTEXTMETRIC;
```

The **NEWTEXTMETRIC** structure contains data that describes a physical font.

Members

tmHeight

Specifies the height (ascent + descent) of characters.

tmAscent

Specifies the ascent (units above the base line) of characters.

tmDescent

Specifies the descent (units below the base line) of characters.

tmInternalLeading

Specifies the amount of leading (space) inside the bounds set by the **tmHeight** member. Accent marks and other diacritical characters may occur in this area. The designer may set this member to zero.

tmExternalLeading

Specifies the amount of extra leading (space) that the application adds between rows. Since this area is outside the font, it contains no marks and is not altered by text output calls in either OPAQUE or TRANSPARENT mode. The designer may set this member to zero.

tmAveCharWidth

Specifies the average width of characters in the font (generally defined as the width of the letter x). This value does not include overhang required for bold or italic characters.

tmMaxCharWidth

Specifies the width of the widest character in the font.

tmWeight

Specifies the weight of the font.

tmOverhang

Specifies the extra width per-string that may be added to some synthesized fonts. When synthesizing some attributes, such as bold or italic, graphics device interface (GDI) or a device may have to add width to a string on both a per-character and per-string basis. For example, GDI makes a string bold by expanding the spacing of each character and overstriking by an offset value; it italicizes a font by shearing the string. In either case, there is an overhang past the basic string. For bold strings, the overhang is the distance by which the overstrike is offset. For italic strings, the overhang is the amount the top of the font is sheared past the bottom of the font.

The **tmOverhang** member enables the application to determine how much of the character width returned by a **GetTextExtentPoint** function call on a single character is the actual character width and how much is the per-string extra width. The actual width is the extent minus the overhang.

tmDigitizedAspectX

Specifies the horizontal aspect of the device for which the font was designed.

tmDigitizedAspectY

Specifies the vertical aspect of the device for which the font was designed. The ratio of the **tmDigitizedAspectX** and **tmDigitizedAspectY** members is the aspect ratio of the device for which the font was designed.

tmFirstChar

Specifies the value of the first character defined in the font.

tmLastChar

Specifies the value of the last character defined in the font.

tmDefaultChar

Specifies the value of the character to be substituted for characters that are not in the font.

tmBreakChar

Specifies the value of the character to be used to define word breaks for text justification.

tmItalic

Specifies an italic font if it is nonzero.

tmUnderlined

Specifies an underlined font if it is nonzero.

tmStruckOut

Specifies a strikeout font if it is nonzero.

tmPitchAndFamily

Specifies the pitch and family of the selected font. The low-order bit (bit 0) specifies the pitch of the font. If it is 1, the font is variable pitch. If it is 0, the font is fixed pitch. Bits 1 and 2 specify the font type. If both bits are 0, the font is a raster font; if bit 1 is 1 and bit 2 is 0, the font is a vector font; if bit 1 is 0 and bit 2 is set, or if both bits are 1, the font is some other type. Bit 3 is 1 if the font is a device font; otherwise, it is 0.

The four high-order bits designate the font family. The **tmPitchAndFamily** member can be combined with the hexadecimal value 0xF0 by using the bitwise AND operator and can then be compared with the font family names for an identical match. For more information about the font families, see the **LOGFONT** structure.

tmCharSet

Specifies the character set of the font.

ntmFlags

Specifies whether the font is italic, underscored, outlined, bold, and so forth. The following list shows the bits corresponding to each font type:

Bit	Meaning
0	Italic
1	Underscore
2	Negative
3	Outline
4	Strikeout
5	Bold

ntmSizeEM

Specifies the size of the em square for the font. This value is in "notional units" (that is, the units for which the font was designed).

ntmCellHeight

Specifies the height, in notional units, of the font. This value should be compared with the value of the **ntmSizeEM** member.

ntmAvgWidth

Specifies the average width of characters in the font, in notional units. This value should be compared with the value of the **ntmSizeEM** member.

Comments   The last four members of the **NEWTEXTMETRIC** structure are not included in the **TEXTMETRIC** structure; in all other respects, the structures are identical.

The sizes in the **NEWTEXTMETRIC** structure are typically given in logical units; that is, they depend on the current mapping mode of the display context.

See Also   **EnumFonts**, **GetTextMetrics**

OFSTRUCT

```
typedef struct _OFSTRUCT { /* of */
    BYTE cBytes;
    BYTE fFixedDisk;
    WORD nErrCode;
    WORD Reserved1;
    WORD Reserved2;
    BYTE szPathName[OFS_MAXPATHNAME];
} OFSTRUCT;
```

The **OFSTRUCT** structure contains information about a file that the **OpenFile** function opened or attempted to open.

Members   **cBytes**

Specifies the length, in bytes, of the **OFSTRUCT** structure.

fFixedDisk

Specifies whether the file is on a fixed disk. This member is nonzero if the file is on a fixed disk.

nErrCode

Specifies the MS-DOS error code if the **OpenFile** function failed.

Reserved1

Reserved; do not use.

Reserved2

Reserved; do not use.

szPathName

Specifies the path and filename of the file. This string consists of characters from the Windows character set.

See Also   **OpenFile**

OPENFILENAME   `Unicode`

```
typedef struct tagOFN { /* ofn */
    DWORD       lStructSize;
    HWND        hwndOwner;
    HINSTANCE   hInstance;
    LPCSTR      lpstrFilter;
    LPSTR       lpstrCustomFilter;
    DWORD       nMaxCustFilter;
    DWORD       nFilterIndex;
    LPSTR       lpstrFile;
    DWORD       nMaxFile;
    LPSTR       lpstrFileTitle;
    DWORD       nMaxFileTitle;
    LPSTR       lpstrInitialDir;
    LPCSTR      lpstrTitle;
    DWORD       Flags;
    WORD        nFileOffset;
    WORD        nFileExtension;
    LPCSTR      lpstrDefExt;
    DWORD       lCustData;
    LPOFNHOOKPROC lpfnHook;
    LPCSTR      lpTemplateName;
} OPENFILENAME;
```

The **OPENFILENAME** structure contains information the operating system uses to initialize the system-defined Open or Save As dialog box. After the user closes the dialog box, the system returns information about the user's selection in this structure.

Members

lStructSize

Specifies the length, in bytes, of the structure.

hwndOwner

Identifies the window that owns the dialog box. This member can be any valid window handle, or NULL if the dialog box has no owner.

hInstance

Identifies a data block that contains a dialog box template specified by the **lpstrTemplateName** member. This member is used only if the **Flags** member specifies the OFN_ENABLETEMPLATE flag; otherwise, this member is ignored.

lpstrFilter

Points to a buffer containing pairs of null-terminated filter strings. The first string in each pair describes a filter (for example, "Text Files"), the second specifies the filter pattern (for example, "*.TXT"). Multiple filters can be specified for a single item by separating the filter-pattern strings with a semicolon (for example, "*.TXT;*.DOC;*.BAK"). The last string in the buffer must be terminated by two NULL characters. If this parameter is NULL, the dialog box will not display any filters. The filter strings are assumed to be in the proper order—the operating system does not change the order.

lpstrCustomFilter

Points to a buffer containing a pair of user-defined filter strings. The first string describes the filter, and the second specifies the filter pattern (for example "WinWord, *.docnn"). The buffer is terminated by two NULL characters. The operating system copies the strings to the buffer when the user closes the dialog box. The system uses the strings to initialize the user-defined file filter the next time the dialog box is created. If this parameter is NULL, the dialog box lists but does not save user-defined filter strings.

nMaxCustFilter

Specifies the size, in characters, of the buffer identified by the **lpstrCustomFilter** member. This buffer should be at least 40 characters long. This parameter is ignored if the **lpstrCustomFilter** member is NULL or points to a NULL string.

nFilterIndex

Specifies an index into the buffer pointed to by the **lpstrFilter** member. The operating system uses the index value to obtain a pair of strings to use as the initial filter description and filter pattern for the dialog box. The first pair of strings has an index value of 1. When the user closes the dialog box, the system copies the index of the selected filter strings into this location. If the **nFilterIndex** member is 0, the custom filter is used. If the **nFilterIndex** member is 0 and the **lpstrCustomFilter** member is NULL, the system uses the first filter in the buffer identified by the **lpstrFilter** member. If all three members are 0 or NULL, the system does not use any filters and does not show any files in the file list control of the dialog box.

lpstrFile

Points to a buffer that contains a filename used to initialize the File Name edit control. The first character of this buffer must be NULL if initialization is not necessary. When the **GetOpenFileName** or **GetSaveFileName** function returns, this buffer contains the drive designator, path, filename, and extension of the selected file.

If the buffer is too small, the dialog box procedure copies the required size into this member.

nMaxFile

Specifies the size, in characters, of the buffer pointed to by the **lpstrFile** member. The **GetOpenFileName** and **GetSaveFileName** functions return FALSE if the buffer is too small to contain the file information. The buffer should be at least 256 characters long. This member is ignored if the **lpstrFile** member is NULL.

lpstrFileTitle

Points to a buffer that receives the title of the selected file. For Windows versions 3.0 and 3.1, this buffer receives the filename and extension without path information. This application should use this string to display the file title. If this member is NULL, the function does not copy the file title.

nMaxFileTitle

Specifies the maximum length of the string that can be copied into the **lpstrFileTitle** buffer. This member is ignored if **lpstrFileTitle** is NULL.

lpstrInitialDir

Points to a string that specifies the initial file directory. If this member is NULL, the system uses the current directory as the initial directory.

lpstrTitle

Points to a string to be placed in the title bar of the dialog box. If this member is NULL, the system uses the default title (that is, "Save As" or "Open").

Flags

Specifies the dialog box creation flags. This member may be a combination of the following values:

Value	Meaning
OFN_ALLOWMULTISELECT	
	Specifies that the File Name list box allows multiple selections. (If the dialog box is created by using a private template, the LBS_EXTENDEDSEL constant must appear in the definition of the File Name list box.)
OFN_CREATEPROMPT	
	Specifies that the dialog box function should ask whether the user wants to create a file that does not currently exist. (This flag automatically sets the OFN_PATHMUSTEXIST and OFN_FILEMUSTEXIST flags.)

OFN_ENABLEHOOK

Enables the hook function specified in the **lpfnHook** member.

OFN_ENABLETEMPLATE

Causes the operating system to create the dialog box by using the dialog box template identified by the **hInstance** and **lpTemplateName** members.

OFN_ENABLETEMPLATEHANDLE

Indicates that the **hInstance** member identifies a data block that contains a preloaded dialog box template. The operating system ignores the **lpTemplateName** member if this flag is specified.

OFN_EXTENSIONDIFFERENT

Specifies that the user typed a filename extension that differs from the extension specified by the **lpstrDefExt** member. The function does not set this flag if **lpstrDefExt** is NULL.

OFN_FILEMUSTEXIST

Specifies that the user can type only names of existing files in the File Name entry field. If this flag is set and the user enters an invalid filename in the File Name entry field, the dialog box function displays a warning in a message box. The setting of this flag causes the OFN_PATHMUSTEXIST flag to be set.

OFN_HIDEREADONLY

Hides the Read Only check box.

OFN_NOCHANGEDIR

Causes the dialog box to set the current directory back to what it was when the dialog box was called.

OFN_NONETWORKBUTTON

Hides and disables the Network button.

OFN_NOREADONLYRETURN

Specifies that the returned file does not have the Read Only check box checked and is not in a write-protected directory.

OFN_NOTESTFILECREATE

Specifies that the file is not created before the dialog box is closed. This flag should be set if the application saves the file on a create-nonmodify network share point. When an application sets this flag, the library does not check for write protection, a full disk, an open drive door, or network protection. Applications using this flag must perform file operations carefully, because a file cannot be reopened once it is closed.

OFN_NOVALIDATE

Specifies that the common dialog boxes allow invalid characters in the returned filename. Typically, the calling application uses a hook function that checks the filename by using the FILEOKSTRING registered message. If the text box in the edit control is empty or contains nothing but spaces, the lists of files and directories are updated. If the text box in the edit control contains anything else, the **nFileOffset** and **nFileExtension** members are set to values generated by parsing the text. No default extension is added to the text, nor is text copied to the **lpstrFileTitle** buffer.

If the value specified by the **nFileOffset** member is negative, the filename is invalid. If the value specified by **nFileOffset** is not negative, the filename is valid, and the **nFileOffset** and **nFileExtension** members can be used as if the OFN_NOVALIDATE flag had not been set.

OFN_OVERWRITEPROMPT

Causes the Save As dialog box to generate a message box if the selected file already exists. The user must confirm whether to overwrite the file.

OFN_PATHMUSTEXIST

Specifies that the user can type only valid path and filenames. If this flag is set and the user types an invalid path and filename in the File Name entry field, the dialog box function displays a warning in a message box.

OFN_READONLY

Causes the Read Only check box to be checked initially when the dialog box is created. Indicates the state of the Read Only check box when the dialog box is closed.

OFN_SHAREAWARE

Specifies that if a call to the **OpenFile** function fails because of a network sharing violation, the error is ignored and the dialog box returns the given filename. If this flag is not set, the registered message for SHAREVISTRING is sent to the hook function, with a pointer to a null-terminated string for the path and filename in the *lParam* parameter. The hook function responds with one of the following values:

Value	Meaning
OFN_SHAREFALLTHROUGH	Specifies that the filename is returned by the dialog box.
OFN_SHARENOWARN	Specifies no further action.
OFN_SHAREWARN	Specifies that the user receives the standard warning message for this error, the same result as if there were no hook function.
OFN_SHOWHELP	Causes the dialog box to show the Help button. The **hwndOwner** member must not be NULL if this option is specified.

nFileOffset

Specifies a zero-based offset from the beginning of the path to the filename in the string to which the **lpstrFile** member points. For example, if **lpstrFile** points to the following string, "c:\dir1\dir2\file.ext", this member contains the value 13.

nFileExtension

Specifies a zero-based offset from the beginning of the path to the filename extension in the string pointed to by the **lpstrFile** member. For example, if **lpstrFile** points to the following string, "c:\dir1\dir2\file.ext", this member contains the value 18. If the user did not type an extension *and* **lpstrDefExt** is NULL, this member specifies an offset to the terminating null character. If the user typed "." as the last character in the filename, this member specifies 0.

lpstrDefExt

Points to a buffer that contains the default extension. The **GetOpenFileName** and **GetSaveFileName** functions append this extension to the filename if the user fails to type an extension. This string can be any length, but only the first three characters are appended. The string should not contain a period (.). If this member is NULL and the user fails to type an extension, no extension is appended.

lCustData

Specifies application-defined data that the operating system passes to the hook function identified by the **lpfnHook** member. The system passes the data in the *lParam* parameter of the WM_INITDIALOG message.

lpfnHook

Points to a hook function that processes messages intended for the dialog box. An application must specify the OFN_ENABLEHOOK flag in the **Flags** member to enable the function; otherwise, the operating system ignores this structure member. The hook function should return FALSE to pass a message to the standard dialog box procedure, or TRUE to discard the message.

lpstrTemplateName

Points to a null-terminated string that names the dialog box template resource to be substituted for the standard dialog box template. An application can use the **MAKEINTRESOURCE** macro for numbered dialog box resources. This member is used only if the **Flags** member specifies the OFN_ENABLETEMPLATE flag; otherwise, this member is ignored.

See Also   **GetOpenFileName, GetSaveFileName**

OUTLINETEXTMETRIC

```
typedef struct _OUTLINETEXTMETRIC { /* otm */
    UINT      otmSize;
    TEXTMETRIC otmTextMetrics;
    BYTE      otmFiller;
    PANOSE    otmPanoseNumber;
    UINT      otmfsSelection;
    UINT      otmfsType;
    UINT      otmsCharSlopeRise;
    UINT      otmsCharSlopeRun;
    UINT      otmItalicAngle;
    UINT      otmEMSquare;
    UINT      otmAscent;
    int       otmDescent;
    int       otmLineGap;
    UINT      otmsCapEmHeight;
    UINT      otmsXHeight;
    RECT      otmrcFontBox;
    int       otmMacAscent;
    int       otmMacDescent;
    UINT      otmMacLineGap;
    UINT      otmusMinimumPPEM;
    POINT     otmptSubscriptSize;
    POINT     otmptSubscriptOffset;
    POINT     otmptSuperscriptSize;
    POINT     otmptSuperscriptOffset;
    UINT      otmsStrikeoutSize;
    int       otmsStrikeoutPosition;
    int       otmsUnderscoreSize;
    UINT      otmsUnderscorePosition;
    PSTR      otmpFamilyName;
    PSTR      otmpFaceName;
    PSTR      otmpStyleName;
    PSTR      otmpFullName;
} OUTLINETEXTMETRIC;
```

The **OUTLINETEXTMETRIC** structure contains metrics describing a
TrueType ® font.

Members   **otmSize**

Specifies the size, in bytes, of the **OUTLINETEXTMETRIC** structure.

otmTextMetrics

Specifies a **TEXTMETRIC** structure containing further information about the
font.

otmFiller

Specifies a value that causes the structure to be byte aligned.

otmPanoseNumber

Specifies the PANOSE number for this font.

otmfsSelection

Specifies the nature of the font pattern. This member can be a combination of the following bits:

Bit	Meaning
0	Italic
1	Underscore
2	Negative
3	Outline
4	Strikeout
5	Bold

otmfsType

Specifies whether the font is licensed. Licensed fonts must not be modified or exchanged. If bit 1 is set, the font may not be embedded in a document. If bit 1 is clear, the font can be embedded. If bit 2 is set, the embedding is read-only.

otmsCharSlopeRise

Specifies the slope of the cursor. This value is 1 if the slope is vertical. Applications can use this value and the value of the **otmsCharSlopeRun** member to create an italic cursor that has the same slope as the main italic angle (specified by the **otmItalicAngle** member).

otmsCharSlopeRun

Specifies the slope of the cursor. This value is zero if the slope is vertical. Applications can use this value and the value of the **otmsCharSlopeRise** member to create an italic cursor that has the same slope as the main italic angle (specified by the **otmItalicAngle** member).

otmItalicAngle

Specifies the main italic angle of the font, in counterclockwise degrees from vertical. Regular (roman) fonts have a value of zero. Italic fonts typically have a negative italic angle (that is, they lean to the right).

otmEMSquare

Specifies the number of logical units defining the x- or y-dimension of the em square for this font. (The number of units in the x- and y-directions are always the same for an em square.)

otmAscent

Specifies the maximum distance characters in this font extend above the base line. This is the typographic ascent for the font.

otmDescent

Specifies the maximum distance characters in this font extend below the base line. This is the typographic descent for the font.

otmLineGap

Specifies typographic line spacing.

otmsCapEmHeight

Not supported.

otmsXHeight

Not supported.

otmrcFontBox

Specifies the bounding box for the font.

otmMacAscent

Specifies the maximum distance characters in this font extend above the base line for the Macintosh ® computer.

otmMacDescent

Specifies the maximum distance characters in this font extend below the base line for the Macintosh ® computer.

otmMacLineGap

Specifies line-spacing information for the Macintosh ® computer.

otmusMinimumPPEM

Specifies the smallest recommended size for this font, in pixels per em-square.

otmptSubscriptSize

Specifies the recommended horizontal and vertical size for subscripts in this font.

otmptSubscriptOffset

Specifies the recommended horizontal and vertical offset for subscripts in this font. The subscript offset is measured from the character origin to the origin of the subscript character.

otmptSuperscriptSize

Specifies the recommended horizontal and vertical size for superscripts in this font.

otmptSuperscriptOffset

Specifies the recommended horizontal and vertical offset for superscripts in this font. The superscript offset is measured from the character base line to the base line of the superscript character.

otmsStrikeoutSize

Specifies the width of the strikeout stroke for this font. Typically, this is the width of the em dash for the font.

otmsStrikeoutPosition

Specifies the position of the strikeout stroke relative to the base line for this font. Positive values are above the base line and negative values are below.

otmsUnderscoreSize

Specifies the thickness of the underscore character for this font.

otmsUnderscorePosition

Specifies the position of the underscore character for this font.

otmpFamilyName

Specifies the offset from the beginning of the structure to a string specifying the family name for the font.

otmpFaceName

Specifies the offset from the beginning of the structure to a string specifying the typeface name for the font. (This typeface name corresponds to the name specified in the **LOGFONT** structure.)

otmpStyleName

Specifies the offset from the beginning of the structure to a string specifying the style name for the font.

otmpFullName

Specifies the offset from the beginning of the structure to a string specifying the full name for the font. This name is unique for the font and often contains a version number or other identifying information.

Comments   The sizes returned in **OUTLINETEXTMETRIC** are given in logical units; that is, they depend on the current mapping mode of the specified display context.

See Also   **GetOutlineTextMetrics**

OUTPUT_DEBUG_STRING_INFO

```
typedef struct _OUTPUT_DEBUG_STRING_INFO { /* odsi */
    LPSTR lpDebugStringData;
    WORD  fUnicode;
    WORD  nDebugStringLength;
} OUTPUT_DEBUG_STRING_INFO;
```

The **OUTPUT_DEBUG_STRING_INFO** structure contains the address, format, and length, in bytes, of a debugging string.

Members   **lpDebugStringData**

Points to the address of the debugging string in the calling process's address space. The debugger can use the **ReadProcessMemory** function to retrieve the value of the string.

fUnicode

Specifies the format of the debugging string. If this value is zero, the debugging string is 8-bit ASCII; if it is nonzero, the string is 16-bit Unicode ™.

nDebugStringLength

Specifies the length, in bytes, of the debugging string. The length includes the string's terminating null character.

See Also   **DEBUG_EVENT**

OVERLAPPED

```
typedef struct _OVERLAPPED { /* o */
    DWORD   Internal;
    DWORD   InternalHigh;
    DWORD   Offset;
    DWORD   OffsetHigh;
    HANDLE  hEvent;
} OVERLAPPED;
```

The **OVERLAPPED** structure contains information used in asynchronous input and output.

Members   **Internal**

Reserved for operating system use. This member specifies a system-dependent status. This member is valid when the **GetOverlappedResult** function returns without setting the extended error information to ERROR_IO_PENDING.

InternalHigh

Reserved for operating system use. This member specifies the length of the data transferred. This member is valid when the **GetOverlappedResult** function returns TRUE.

Offset

Specifies a file position to start the transfer. The file position is a byte offset from the start of the file. The calling process sets this member before calling the **ReadFile** or **WriteFile** function. This member is ignored when the functions read from and write to named pipes and communication devices.

OffsetHigh

Specifies the high word of the byte offset at which to start the transfer. This member is ignored when the functions read from and write to named pipes and communication devices.

hEvent

Identifies an event set to the signaled state when the transfer has been completed. The calling process sets this member before calling the **ReadFile**, **WriteFile**, **ConnectNamedPipe** or **TransactNamedPipe** function.

See Also   **ConnectNamedPipe, CreateFile, GetOverlappedResult, ReadFile, ReadFileEx, WriteFile, WriteFileEx**

PAINTSTRUCT

```
typedef struct tagPAINTSTRUCT { /* ps. */
    HDC  hdc;
    BOOL fErase;
    RECT rcPaint;
    BOOL fRestore;
    BOOL fIncUpdate;
    BYTE rgbReserved[32];
} PAINTSTRUCT;
```

The **PAINTSTRUCT** structure contains information for an application. This information can be used to paint the client area of a window owned by that application.

Members

hdc
Identifies the display DC to be used for painting.

fErase
Specifies whether the background must be erased. This value is nonzero if the application should erase the background. The application is responsible for erasing the background if a window class is created without a background brush. For more information, see the description of the **hbrBackground** member of the **WNDCLASS** structure.

rcPaint
Specifies a **RECT** structure that specifies the upper-left and lower-right corners of the rectangle in which the painting is requested.

fRestore
Reserved; used internally by Windows.

fIncUpdate
Reserved; used internally by Windows.

rgbReserved
Reserved; used internally by Windows.

See Also   **BeginPaint**, **RECT**, **WNDCLASS**

PALETTEENTRY

```
typedef struct tagPALETTEENTRY { /* pe */
    BYTE peRed;
    BYTE peGreen;
    BYTE peBlue;
    BYTE peFlags;
} PALETTEENTRY;
```

The **PALETTEENTRY** structure specifies the color and usage of an entry in a logical color palette. A logical palette is defined by a **LOGPALETTE** structure.

Members

peRed
Specifies a red intensity value for the palette entry.

peGreen
Specifies a green intensity value for the palette entry.

peBlue
Specifies a blue intensity value for the palette entry.

peFlags
Specifies how the palette entry is to be used. The **peFlags** member may be set to NULL or one of these values:

Value	Meaning
PC_EXPLICIT	Specifies that the low-order word of the logical palette entry designates a hardware palette index. This flag allows the application to show the contents of the display device palette.
PC_NOCOLLAPSE	Specifies that the color be placed in an unused entry in the system palette instead of being matched to an existing color in the system palette. If there are no unused entries in the system palette, the color is matched normally. Once this color is in the system palette, colors in other logical palettes can be matched to this color.
PC_RESERVED	Specifies that the logical palette entry be used for palette animation; this prevents other windows from matching colors to the palette entry since the color frequently changes. If an unused system-palette entry is available, this color is placed in that entry. Otherwise, the color is available for animation.

See Also   **LOGPALETTE**

PANOSE

```
typedef struct tagPANOSE { /* pnse */
    DWORD ulCulture;
    BYTE bFamilyType;
    BYTE bSerifStyle;
    BYTE bWeight;
    BYTE bProportion;
    BYTE bContrast;
    BYTE bStrokeVariation;
    BYTE bArmStyle;
    BYTE bLetterform;
    BYTE bMidline;
    BYTE bXHeight;
} PANOSE
```

The **PANOSE** structure describes the PANOSE font-classification values for a TrueType ® font. These characteristics are then used to associate the font with other fonts of similar appearance but different names.

Members

ulCulture

Specifies the culture-specific classification scheme of the **PANOSE** number. The culture number specifies how to interpret the subsequent ten members for Latin fonts. The culture number can have the following values:

Value	Meaning
PAN_ANY	Any
PAN_CULTURE_LATIN	Latin

bFamilyType

For Latin fonts, **bFamilyType** can have one of the following values:

Value	Meaning
PAN_ANY	Any
PAN_NO_FIT	No fit
PAN_FAMILY_TEXT_DISPLAY	Text and display
PAN_FAMILY_SCRIPT	Script
PAN_FAMILY_DECORATIVE	Decorative
PAN_FAMILY_PICTORIAL	Pictorial

bSerifStyle

Specifies the serif style. For Latin fonts, **bSerifStyle** can have one of the following values:

Value	Meaning
PAN_ANY	Any
PAN_NO_FIT	No fit
PAN_SERIF_COVE	Cove
PAN_SERIF_OBTUSE_COVE	Obtuse cove
PAN_SERIF_SQUARE_COVE	Square cove
PAN_SERIF_OBTUSE_SQUARE_COVE	Obtuse square cove
PAN_SERIF_SQUARE	Square
PAN_SERIF_THIN	Thin
PAN_SERIF_BONE	Bone
PAN_SERIF_EXAGGERATED	Exaggerated
PAN_SERIF_TRIANGLE	Triangle
PAN_SERIF_NORMAL_SANS	Normal sans serif
PAN_SERIF_OBTUSE_SANS	Obtuse sans serif
PAN_SERIF_PERP_SANS	Perp sans serif
PAN_SERIF_FLARED	Flared
PAN_SERIF_ROUNDED	Rounded

bWeight

For Latin fonts, **bWeight** can have one of the following values:

Value	Meaning
PAN_ANY	Any
PAN_NO_FIT	No fit
PAN_WEIGHT_VERY_LIGHT	Very light
PAN_WEIGHT_LIGHT	Light
PAN_WEIGHT_THIN	Thin
PAN_WEIGHT_BOOK	Book
PAN_WEIGHT_MEDIUM	Medium
PAN_WEIGHT_DEMI	Demibold
PAN_WEIGHT_BOLD	Bold
PAN_WEIGHT_HEAVY	Heavy
PAN_WEIGHT_BLACK	Black
PAN_WEIGHT_NORD	Nord

bProportion

For Latin fonts, **bProportion** can have one of the following values:

Value	Meaning
PAN_ANY	Any
PAN_NO_FIT	No fit
PAN_PROP_OLD_STYLE	Old style
PAN_PROP_MODERN	Modern
PAN_PROP_EVEN_WIDTH	Even width
PAN_PROP_EXPANDED	Expanded
PAN_PROP_CONDENSED	Condensed
PAN_PROP_VERY_EXPANDED	Very expanded
PAN_PROP_VERY_CONDENSED	Very condensed
PAN_PROP_MONOSPACED	Monospaced

bContrast

For Latin fonts, **bContrast** can have one of the following values:

Value	Meaning
PAN_ANY	Any
PAN_NO_FIT	No fit
PAN_CONTRAST_NONE	None
PAN_CONTRAST_VERY_LOW	Very low
PAN_CONTRAST_LOW	Low
PAN_CONTRAST_MEDIUM_LOW	Medium low
PAN_CONTRAST_MEDIUM	Medium
PAN_CONTRAST_MEDIUM_HIGH	Medium high
PAN_CONTRAST_HIGH	High
PAN_CONTRAST_VERY_HIGH	Very high

bStrokeVariation

For Latin fonts, **bStrokeVariation** can have one of the following values:

Value	Meaning
PAN_ANY	Any
PAN_NO_FIT	No fit
PAN_STROKE_GRADUAL_DIAG	Gradual/diagonal
PAN_STROKE_GRADUAL_TRAN	Gradual/transitional
PAN_STROKE_GRADUAL_VERT	Gradual/vertical
PAN_STROKE_GRADUAL_HORZ	Gradual/horizontal
PAN_STROKE_RAPID_VERT	Rapid/vertical
PAN_STROKE_RAPID_HORZ	Rapid/horizontal

PAN_STROKE_INSTANT_VERT	Instant/vertical

bArmStyle

For Latin fonts, **bArmStyle** can have one of the following values:

Value	Meaning
PAN_ANY	Any
PAN_NO_FIT	No fit
PAN_STRAIGHT_ARMS_HORZ	Straight arms/horizontal
PAN_STRAIGHT_ARMS_WEDGE	Straight arms/wedge
PAN_STRAIGHT_ARMS_VERT	Straight arms/vertical
PAN_STRAIGHT_ARMS_SINGLE_SERIF	Straight arms/single-serif
PAN_STRAIGHT_ARMS_DOUBLE_SERIF	Straight arms/double-serif
PAN_BENT_ARMS_HORZ	Non-straight arms/horizontal
PAN_BENT_ARMS_WEDGE	Non-straight arms/wedge
PAN_BENT_ARMS_VERT	Non-straight arms/vertical
PAN_BENT_ARMS_SINGLE_SERIF	Non-straight arms/single-serif
PAN_BENT_ARMS_DOUBLE_SERIF	Non-straight arms/double-serif

bLetterform

For Latin fonts, **bLetterform** can have one of the following values:

Value	Meaning
PAN_ANY	Any
PAN_NO_FIT	No fit
PAN_LETT_NORMAL_CONTACT	Normal/contact
PAN_LETT_NORMAL_WEIGHTED	Normal/weighted
PAN_LETT_NORMAL_BOXED	Normal/boxed
PAN_LETT_NORMAL_FLATTENED	Normal/flattened
PAN_LETT_NORMAL_ROUNDED	Normal/rounded
PAN_LETT_NORMAL_OFF_CENTER	Normal/off center
PAN_LETT_NORMAL_SQUARE	Normal/square
PAN_LETT_OBLIQUE_CONTACT	Oblique/contact
PAN_LETT_OBLIQUE_WEIGHTED	Oblique/weighted
PAN_LETT_OBLIQUE_BOXED	Oblique/boxed
PAN_LETT_OBLIQUE_FLATTENED	Oblique/flattened
PAN_LETT_OBLIQUE_ROUNDED	Oblique/rounded
PAN_LETT_OBLIQUE_OFF_CENTER	Oblique/off center
PAN_LETT_OBLIQUE_SQUARE	Oblique/square

bMidline

For Latin fonts, **bMidline** can have one of the following values:

Value	Meaning
PAN_ANY	Any
PAN_NO_FIT	No fit
PAN_MIDLINE_STANDARD_TRIMMED	Standard/trimmed
PAN_MIDLINE_STANDARD_POINTED	Standard/pointed
PAN_MIDLINE_STANDARD_SERIFED	Standard/serifed
PAN_MIDLINE_HIGH_TRIMMED	High/trimmed
PAN_MIDLINE_HIGH_POINTED	High/pointed
PAN_MIDLINE_HIGH_SERIFED	High/serifed
PAN_MIDLINE_CONSTANT_TRIMMED	Constant/trimmed
PAN_MIDLINE_CONSTANT_POINTED	Constant/pointed
PAN_MIDLINE_CONSTANT_SERIFED	Constant/serifed
PAN_MIDLINE_LOW_TRIMMED	Low/trimmed
PAN_MIDLINE_LOW_POINTED	Low/pointed
PAN_MIDLINE_LOW_SERIFED	Low/serifed

bXHeight

For Latin fonts, **bXHeight** can have one of the following values:

Value	Meaning
PAN_ANY	Any
PAN_NO_FIT	No fit
PAN_XHEIGHT_CONSTANT_SMALL	Constant/small
PAN_XHEIGHT_CONSTANT_STD	Constant/standard
PAN_XHEIGHT_CONSTANT_LARGE	Constant/large
PAN_XHEIGHT_DUCKING_SMALL	Ducking/small
PAN_XHEIGHT_DUCKING_STD	Ducking/standard
PAN_XHEIGHT_DUCKING_LARGE	Ducking/large

PARTITION_INFORMATION

```
typedef struct _PARTITION_INFORMATION {
    BYTE PartitionType;
    BOOLEAN BootIndicator;
    BOOLEAN RecognizedPartition;
    BOOLEAN RewritePartition;
    LARGE_INTEGER StartingOffset;
    LARGE_INTEGER PartitionLength;
    LARGE_INTEGER HiddenSectors;
} PARTITION_INFORMATION ;
```

The **PARTITION_INFORMATION** function provides information about a disk partition.

Members

PartitionType

Specifies the type of partition. This member can take on one of the following values:

Value	Meaning
PARTITION_ENTRY_UNUSED	Entry unused.
PARTITION_FAT_12	Specifies a partition with 12-bit FAT entries.
PARTITION_XENIX_1	Specifies a Xenix type 1 partition.
PARTITION_XENIX_2	Specifies a Xenix type 2 partition.
PARTITION_FAT_16	Specifies a partition with 16-bit FAT entries.
PARTITION_EXTENDED	Specifies an extended partition entry.
PARTITION_HUGE	Specifies an MS-DOS V4 huge partition.
PARTITION_IFS	Specifies an IFS partition.
PARTITION_UNIX	Specifies a Unix partition.
VALID_NTFT	Specifies an NTFT partition.

BootIndicator

The boot sector of the disk.

RecognizedPartition

The partition is recognized.

RewritePartition

The rewrite partition.

StartingOffset

The starting offset.

PartitionLength

The partition length.

HiddenSectors
> The number of hidden sectors.

Comments

The **DeviceIoControl** function receives a **PARTITION_INFORMATION** structure in response to an **IOCTL_DISK_GET_PARTITION_INFO** or **IOCTL_DISK_GET_DRIVE_LAYOUT** device i/o operation. The **DeviceIoControl** function uses a **PARTITION_INFORMATION** structure as input to an **IOCTL_DISK_SET_DRIVE_LAYOUT** device i/o operation.

See Also

IOCTL_DISK_GET_DRIVE_LAYOUT,
IOCTL_DISK_GET_PARTITION_INFO,
IOCTL_DISK_SET_DRIVE_LAYOUT

PCMWAVEFORMAT

```
typedef struct pcmwaveformat_tag {
    WAVEFORMAT  wf;
    WORD  wBitsPerSample;
} PCMWAVEFORMAT;
```

The **PCMWAVEFORMAT** structure describes the data format for pulse code modulated (PCM) waveform data.

Members

wf
> Specifies a **WAVEFORMAT** structure containing general information about the format of the waveform data.

wBitsPerSample
> Specifies the number of bits per sample.

See Also

WAVEFORMAT

PERF_COUNTER_BLOCK

New

```
typedef struct _PERF_COUNTER_BLOCK { /* pcd */
    DWORD ByteLength;
} PERF_COUNTER_BLOCK;
```

The **PERF_COUNTER_BLOCK** structure contains the length, in bytes, of the performance-counter data. This structure is followed by data for the number of counters specified in the **PERF_OBJECT_TYPE** structure.

Members   **ByteLength**
                   Specifies the length, in bytes, of this structure, including the counters that
                   follow.

Comments   This structure is part of the performance data provided by the **RegQueryValueEx**
                   function when the **HKEY_PERFORMANCE_DATA** key is used.

See Also   **RegQueryValueEx**

PERF_COUNTER_DEFINITION   `New`

```
typedef struct _PERF_COUNTER_DEFINITION { /* pcd */
    DWORD   ByteLength;
    DWORD   CounterNameTitleIndex;
    LPWSTR  CounterNameTitle;
    DWORD   CounterHelpTitleIndex;
    LPWSTR  CounterHelpTitle;
    DWORD   DefaultScale;
    DWORD   DetailLevel;
    DWORD   CounterType;
    DWORD   CounterSize;
    DWORD   CounterOffset;
} PERF_COUNTER_DEFINITION;
```

The **PERF_COUNTER_DEFINITION** structure describes a performance
counter. The Unicode names in this structure must appear in a message file.

Members   **ByteLength**
                   Contains the length, in bytes, of this structure.

                   CounterNameTitleIndex
                   Contains the index of the counter name in the title database of the registry.

                   CounterNameTitle
                   Points to the name of the counter. This member contains NULL, initially, but
                   can contain a pointer to the actual string once the string is located.

                   CounterHelpTitleIndex
                   Contains the index to the counter's Help title in the title database of the
                   registry.

                   CounterHelpTitle
                   Points to the title of Help. This member contains NULL, initially, but can
                   contain a pointer to the actual string once the string is located.

DefaultScale

Specifies the power of 10 by which to scale a chart line, assuming the vertical axis is 100. If this value is zero, the scale value is 1; if this value is 1, the scale value is 10; if this value is –1, the scale value is .10, and so on.

DetailLevel

Specifies the level of detail for the counter. Applications use this value to control display complexity. This member can be one of the following values:

Detail level	Meaning
PERF_DETAIL_NOVICE	Data can be understood by the uninformed user.
PERF_DETAIL_ADVANCED	Data designed for the advanced user.
PERF_DETAIL_EXPERT	Data designed for the expert user.
PERF_DETAIL_WIZARD	Data designed for the system designer.

CounterType

Specifies the type of counter. This member is some combination of the following values.

The following values indicate the counter's data size:

Value	Meaning
PERF_SIZE_DWORD	The counter data is a doubleword.
PERF_SIZE_LARGE	The counter data is a large integer.
PERF_SIZE_ZERO	The counter data is a zero-length field.
PERF_SIZE_VARIABLE_LEN	The size of the counter data is in the **CounterSize** member.

The following values indicate the additional contents of this member:

Value	Meaning
PERF_TYPE_NUMBER	The counter data is a number value but not a counter.
PERF_TYPE_COUNTER	The counter data is an increasing numeric value.
PERF_TYPE_TEXT	The counter data is a text field.
PERF_TYPE_ZERO	The counter data is always zero.

If PERF_TYPE_NUMBER is specified, one of the following values is also specified to indicate the format of the number:

Value	Meaning
PERF_NUMBER_HEX	The counter data should be displayed as a hexadecimal value.
PERF_NUMBER_DECIMAL	The counter data should be displayed as a decimal value.

PERF_NUMBER_DEC_1000	The counter data should be divided by 1000 and displayed as a decimal value.

If PERF_TYPE_COUNTER is specified, one of the following values is also specified to indicate the type of counter:

Value	Meaning
PERF_COUNTER_VALUE	The counter value is valid without additional calculation. That is, it should be displayed as is.
PERF_COUNTER_RATE	The counter value should be divided by the elapsed time.
PERF_COUNTER_FRACTION	The counter value should be divided by the base value indicated by the next counter if it is of type PERF_COUNTER_BASE or by the value of the counter subtype.
PERF_COUNTER_BASE	The counter value is the base value to use in fractions.
PERF_COUNTER_ELAPSED	The counter value is a start time to be subtracted from the current time.
PERF_COUNTER_QUEUELEN	The performance application should use the **Queuelen** counter; that is, the Queue Length Space-Time Product formula. The next counter is the number currently in the queue. Multiply by the current time (units specified by this counter's subtype). Add the product to this counter. To obtain the average queue length, divide the result by the delta time.
PERF_COUNTER_HISTOGRAM	The counter value begins or ends a histogram.

If PERF_TYPE_COUNTER is specified, one of the following values is also specified to indicate the subtype of counter:

Value	Meaning
PERF_TIMER_TICK	Use the frequency of the high-resolution performance counter as the base.
PERF_TIMER_100NS	Use the time base units of the 100-nanosecond timer as the base.
PERF_OBJECT_TIMER	Use the object-timer frequency as the base unit. This value is system defined in this counter's PERF_OBJECT_TYPE definition.

If PERF_TYPE_TEXT is specified, one of the following values is also specified to indicate the type of text:

Value	Meaning
PERF_TEXT_UNICODE	The counter data contains Unicode text.
PERF_TEXT_ASCII	The counter data contains ASCII text.

The following values indicate how to use the counter data in a calculation:

Value	Meaning
PERF_DELTA_COUNTER	Compute the difference between the previous counter value and the current counter value before proceeding.
PERF_DELTA_BASE	Compute the difference between the previous base value and the current base value before proceeding.
PERF_INVERSE_COUNTER	After other calculations, the counter should be inverted before displaying or converting to a percentage.
PERF_MULTI_COUNTER	This is a sum of counters from several sources, the number of which is indicated by the next counter.

The following values indicate the display suffix of the counter data:

Value	Meaning
PERF_DISPLAY_NO_SUFFIX	There is no display suffix.
PERF_DISPLAY_PER_SEC	The display suffix is '/sec'.
PERF_DISPLAY_PERCENT	The display suffix is '%'.
PERF_DISPLAY_SECONDS	The display suffix is 'secs'.
PERF_DISPLAY_NOSHOW	The counter value should not be displayed.

CounterSize
Specifies the counter size, in bytes.

CounterOffset
Specifies the offset from the start of the **PERF_COUNTER_BLOCK** structure to the first byte of this counter.

Comments   This structure is part of the performance data provided by the **RegQueryValueEx** function when the **HKEY_PERFORMANCE_DATA** key is used.

PERF_DATA_BLOCK

```
typedef struct _PERF_DATA_BLOCK { /* pdb */
    WCHAR         Signature[4];
    DWORD         LittleEndian;
    DWORD         Version;
    DWORD         Revision;
    DWORD         TotalByteLength;
    DWORD         HeaderLength;
    DWORD         NumObjectTypes;
    DWORD         DefaultObject;
    SYSTEMTIME    SystemTime;
    LARGE_INTEGER PerfTime;
    LARGE_INTEGER PerfFreq;
    LARGE_INTEGER PerfTime100nSec;
    DWORD         SystemNameLength;
    DWORD         SystemNameOffset;
} PERF_DATA_BLOCK;
```

The **PERF_DATA_BLOCK** structure describes the performance data provided by **RegQueryValueEx** function. The data starts with a **PERF_DATA_BLOCK** structure and is followed by a **PERF_OBJECT_TYPE** structure and other object-specific data for each type of object monitored.

Members

Signature
Contains the Unicode string PERF.

LittleEndian
Contains zero if the processor is big endian, one if little endian.

Version
Contains the version of the **PERF_** structures. This value is greater than or equal to one.

Revision
Contains the revision of the **PERF_** structures. This value is greater than or equal to zero.

TotalByteLength
Contains the total length, in bytes, of performance data.

HeaderLength
Contains the length, in bytes, of this structure.

NumObjectTypes
Contains the number of object types being monitored.

DefaultObject

Contains the object title index of the default object whose performance data is to be displayed. This value can be –1 to indicate that no data is to be displayed.

SystemTime

Contains the time when the system is monitored. This value is in Universal Time Convention (UTC) format.

PerfTime

Contains the performance-counter value for the system being monitored. This value is in counts.

PerfFreq

Contains the performance-counter frequency for the system being monitored. This value is in counts per second.

PerfTime100nSec

Contains the performance-counter value for the system being monitored. This value is in 100 nanosecond units.

SystemNameLength

Contains the length, in bytes, of the system name.

SystemNameOffset

Contains the offset, from the beginning of this structure, to the name of the system being monitored.

PERF_INSTANCE_DEFINITION

`New`

```
typedef struct _PERF_INSTANCE_DEFINITION { /* pid */
    DWORD ByteLength;
    DWORD ParentObjectTitleIndex;
    DWORD ParentObjectInstance;
    DWORD UniqueID;
    DWORD NameOffset;
    DWORD NameLength;
} PERF_INSTANCE_DEFINITION;
```

The **PERF_INSTANCE_DEFINITION** structure contains the instance-specific information for a block of performance data. There is one **PERF_INSTANCE_DEFINITION** structure for each instance specified in the **PERF_DATA_BLOCK** structure.

Members   **ByteLength**

Specifies the length, in bytes, of this structure, including the subsequent name.

ParentObjectTitleIndex

Specifies the index of the name of the "parent" object in the title database. For example, if the object is a thread, the parent object type is a process; if the object is a logical drive, the parent is a physical drive.

ParentObjectInstance

Specifies the index to an instance of the parent object type that is the parent of this instance. This member may be zero or greater.

UniqueID

Specifies the unique identifier used instead of the instance name. This value is PERF_NO_UNIQUE_ID if there is no such identifier.

NameOffset

Specifies the offset from the beginning of this structure to the Unicode name of this instance.

NameLength

Specifies the length, in bytes, of the instance name. This value is zero if the instance does not have a name.

PERF_OBJECT_TYPE

New

```
typedef struct _PERF_OBJECT_TYPE {  /* pot */
    DWORD   TotalByteLength;
    DWORD   DefinitionLength;
    DWORD   HeaderLength;
    DWORD   ObjectNameTitleIndex;
    LPWSTR  ObjectNameTitle;
    DWORD   ObjectHelpTitleIndex;
    LPWSTR  ObjectHelpTitle;
    DWORD   DetailLevel;
    DWORD   NumCounters;
    DWORD   DefaultCounter;
    DWORD   NumInstances;
    DWORD   CodePage;
    LARGE_INTEGER PerfTime;
    LARGE_INTEGER PerfFreq;
} PERF_OBJECT_TYPE;
```

The **PERF_OBJECT_TYPE** structure describes the object-specific performance information. This structure is followed by a list of **PERF_COUNTER_DEFINITION** structures, one for each counter defined for the type of object.

Members

TotalByteLength

Contains the length, in bytes, of the object-specific data. This value includes this structure, the **PERF_COUNTER_DEFINITION** structures, and the **PERF_INSTANCE_DEFINITION** and **PERF_COUNTER_BLOCK** for each instance. This member specifies the offset from the beginning of this structure to the next **PERF_OBJECT_TYPE** structure, if one exists.

DefinitionLength

Contains the length, in bytes, of the object-specific data. This value includes this structure and the **PERF_COUNTER_DEFINITION** structures for this object. This is the offset from the beginning of the **PERF_OBJECT_TYPE** structure to the first **PERF_INSTANCE_DEFINITION** structure or to the **PERF_COUNTER_DEFINITION** structures, if there is no instance data.

HeaderLength

Contains the length, in bytes, of this structure. This value is the offset to the first **PERF_COUNTER_DEFINITION** structure for this object.

ObjectNameTitleIndex

Contains the index to the object name in the title database.

ObjectNameTitle

Points to the name of the object. This member initially contains NULL, but can contain a pointer to the actual string once the string is located.

ObjectHelpTitleIndex

Contains the index to the object's Help title in the title database.

ObjectHelpTitle

Points to the title of Help. This member initially contains NULL, but can contain a pointer to the actual string once the string is located.

DetailLevel

Specifies the level of detail. Applications use this value to control display complexity. This value is the minimum detail level of all the counters for a given object. This member can be one of the following values:

Detail level	Meaning
PERF_DETAIL_NOVICE	No technical ability is required to understand the counter data.
PERF_DETAIL_ADVANCED	The counter data is provided for advanced users.
PERF_DETAIL_EXPERT	The counter data is provided for expert users.
PERF_DETAIL_WIZARD	The counter data is provided for system designers.

NumCounters

Specifies the number of counters in each counter block. There is one counter block per instance.

DefaultCounter

Specifies the default counter whose information is to be displayed when this object is selected. This value is typically greater than or equal to zero. However, this value may be –1 to indicate that there is no default.

NumInstances

Specifies the number of object instances for which counters are being provided.

CodePage

Specifies the code page. This value is zero if the instance strings are in Unicode. Otherwise, this value is the code-page identifier of the instance names.

PerfTime

Specifies the current value, in counts, of the high-resolution performance counter.

PerfFreq

Specifies the current frequency, in counts per second, of the high-resolution performance counter.

Comments   If there is only one instance of the object type, the counter definitions are followed by a single **PERF_COUNTER_BLOCK** structure. This structure is followed by data for each counter. (The **PERF_COUNTER_BLOCK** structure contains the total length of the structure and the counter data that follows it.)

If there is more than one instance of the object type, the list of counter definitions is followed by a **PERF_INSTANCE_DEFINITION** structure and a **PERF_COUNTER_BLOCK** structure for each instance. The **PERF_INSTANCE_DEFINITION** structure includes the name, the identifier, and the name of the parent of the instance.

Following the counter data, there is a **PERF_INSTANCE_DEFINITION** structure and a **PERF_COUNTER_BLOCK** structure for each instance specified in the **PERF_DATA_BLOCK** structure that begins the performance-data area.

POINT

```
typedef struct tagPOINT { /* pt */
    LONG x;
    LONG y;
} POINT;
```

The **POINT** structure defines the x- and y- coordinates of a point.

Members   **x**

Specifies the x-coordinate of the point.

y

Specifies the y-coordinate of the point.

See Also   **ChildWindowFromPoint, GetBrushOrgEx, PtInRect, SetBrushOrgEx, WindowFromPoint**

POINTFX

```
typedef struct tagPOINTFX { /* ptfx */
    FIXED x;
    FIXED y;
} POINTFX;
```

The **POINTFX** structure contains the coordinates of points that describe the outline of a character in a TrueType ® font.

Members   **x**

Specifies the x-component of a point on the outline of a TrueType character.

y

Specifies the y-component of a point on the outline of a TrueType character.

Comments   The **POINTFX** structure is a member of the **TTPOLYCURVE** and **TTPOLYGONHEADER** structures.

See Also   **FIXED, TTPOLYCURVE, TTPOLYGONHEADER**

POINTL

```
typedef struct _POINTL { /* ptl */
    LONG x;
    LONG y;
} POINTL;
```

The **POINTL** structure contains the coordinates of a point.

Members   **x**

Specifies the horizontal (x) coordinate of the point.

y

Specifies the vertical (y) coordinate of the point.

POINTS

```
typedef struct tagPOINTS { /* pts */
    SHORT x;
    SHORT y;
} POINTS;
```

The **POINTS** structure defines the coordinates of a point.

Members

x

Specifies the x-coordinate of the point.

y

Specifies the y-coordinate of the point.

See Also   **ChildWindowFromPoint**, **PtInRect**, **WindowFromPoint**, **POINT**

POLYTEXT

New, Unicode

```
typedef struct _POLYTEXT { /* ptxt */
    int   x;
    int   y;
    UINT  n;
    TCHAR *lpwstr;
    UINT  uiFlags;
    RECT  rcl;
    int   *pdx;
} POLYTEXT;
```

The **POLYTEXT** structure describes how the **PolyTextOut** function should draw a string of text.

Members

x

Specifies the horizontal reference point for the string. The string is aligned to this point using the current text-alignment mode.

y

Specifies the vertical reference point for the string. The string is aligned to this point using the current text-alignment mode.

n

Specifies the number of characters in the string.

uiFlags

Specifies whether the string is to be opaque or clipped and whether the string is accompanied by an array of character-width values. This member can be one or more of the following values:

Value	Meaning
ETO_OPAQUE	The rectangles given for each string is to be opaqued with the current background color.
ETO_CLIPPED	Each string is to be clipped to its given rectangle.
ETO_DELTAVECTOR	Each string is accompanied by an array of character widths, as in **ExtTextOut**.

lpwstr

Points to a string of text to be drawn by the **PolyTextOut** function.

rcl

Specifies a rectangle structure that contains the dimensions of the opaquing or clipping rectangle. This member is ignored if neither of the ETO_OPAQUE nor the ETO_CLIPPED value is specified for the **uiFlags** member.

pdx

Specifies in an array the width value for each character in the string. This member is ignored unless the ETO_DELTAVECTOR value is specified for the **uiFlags** member.

See Also   **PolyTextOut**

PORT_INFO_1   `New, Unicode`

```
typedef struct _PORT_INFO_1 { /* pi1 */
    LPSTR pName;
} PORT_INFO_1;
```

The **PORT_INFO_1** structure identifies a supported printer port.

Members   **pName**

Points to a null-terminated string that identifies a supported printer port (for example, "LPT1:").

See Also   **EnumPorts**

PREVENT_MEDIA_REMOVAL

`New`

```
typedef struct _PREVENT_MEDIA_REMOVAL{
    BOOLEAN PreventMediaRemoval;
} PREVENT_MEDIA_REMOVAL ;
```

The **PREVENT_MEDIA_REMOVAL** structure provides removeable media locking data.

Members

PreventMediaRemoval
Specifies whether the media is to be locked (if TRUE) or not (if FALSE).

Comments

The **DeviceIoControl** function uses a **PREVENT_MEDIA_REMOVAL** structure as input to an **IOCTL_DISK_MEDIA_REMOVAL** device i/o operation.

See Also

DeviceIoControl, IOCTL_DISK_MEDIA_REMOVAL

PRINTDLG

`Unicode`

```
typedef struct tagPD {   /* pd */
    DWORD        lStructSize;
    HWND         hwndOwner;
    HANDLE       hDevMode;
    HANDLE       hDevNames;
    HDC          hDC;
    DWORD        Flags;
    WORD         nFromPage;
    WORD         nToPage;
    WORD         nMinPage;
    WORD         nMaxPage;
    WORD         nCopies;
    HINSTANCE    hInstance;
    DWORD        lCustData;
    LPPRINTHOOKPROC lpfnPrintHook;
    LPSETUPHOOKPROC lpfnSetupHook;
    LPCSTR       lpPrintTemplateName;
    LPCSTR       lpSetupTemplateName;
    HANDLE       hPrintTemplate;
    HANDLE       hSetupTemplate;
} PRINTDLG;
```

The **PRINTDLG** structure contains information the operating system uses to initialize the system-defined Print dialog boxes. After the user closes the dialog box, the system returns information about the user-defined print parameters in this structure.

Members

lStructSize

Specifies the length, in bytes, of the structure.

hwndOwner

Identifies the window that owns the dialog box. This member can be any valid window handle, or NULL if the dialog box has no owner.

hDevMode

Identifies a movable global memory object that contains a **DEVMODE** structure. Before the call to the **PrintDlg** function, the structure members may contain data used to initialize the dialog controls. When **PrintDlg** returns, the structure members specify the state of the dialog box controls.

If the application uses the structure to initialize the dialog box controls, it must allocate space for and create the **DEVMODE** structure. (The application should allocate a movable block of memory.)

If the application does not use the structure to initialize the dialog box controls, the **hDevMode** member may be NULL. In this case, **PrintDlg** allocates memory for the structure, initializes its members, and returns a handle that identifies it.

If the device driver for the specified printer does not support extended device modes, the **hDevMode** member is NULL when **PrintDlg** returns.

If the device name (specified by the **dmDeviceName** member of the **DEVMODE** structure) does not appear in the [devices] section of WIN.INI, **PrintDlg** returns an error.

Because this structure is a movable global memory object, the value of **hDevMode** may change during the execution of **PrintDlg**.

For a discussion of how the system resolves a possible data collision between an **hDevMode** value and an **hDevNames** value, see the Comments section.

hDevNames

Identifies a movable global memory object that contains a **DEVNAMES** structure. This structure contains three strings that specify the driver name, the printer name, and the output-port name. Before the call to **PrintDlg**, the structure members contain strings used to initialize dialog box controls. When **PrintDlg** returns, the structure members contain the strings typed by the user. The calling application uses these strings to create a device context or an information context.

If the application uses the structure to initialize the dialog box controls, it must allocate space for and create the **DEVMODE** structure. (The application should allocate a movable block of global memory.)

If the application does not use the structure to initialize the dialog box controls, the **hDevNames** member may be NULL. In this case, **PrintDlg** allocates memory for the structure, initializes its members (by using the printer name specified in the **DEVMODE** structure), and returns a handle that identifies it. **PrintDlg** uses the first port name that appears in the [devices] section of WIN.INI when it initializes the members in the **DEVNAMES** structure. For example, if the following string appears in the [devices] section:

```
PCL / HP LaserJet=HPPCL,LPT1:,LPT2:
```

The function uses "LPT1:" as the port name.

If both the **hDevMode** and **hDevNames** members are NULL, **PrintDlg** initializes **hDevNames** using the current default printer.

Because this structure is a movable global memory object, the value of **hDevNames** may change during the execution of **PrintDlg**.

Please refer to the Comments section below for a discussion of how the system resolves a possible data collision between an **hDevNames** value and an **hDevMode** value.

hDC

Identifies a device context or an information context, depending on whether the **Flags** member specifies the PD_RETURNDC or the PC_RETURNIC flag. If neither flag is specified, the value of this member is undefined. If both flags are specified, PD_RETURNDC has priority.

Flags

Specifies the dialog box initialization flags. This member may be a combination of the following values:

Value	Meaning
PD_ALLPAGES	
	Indicates that the All radio button was selected when the user closed the dialog box. (This value is used as a placeholder, to indicate that the PD_PAGENUMS and PD_SELECTION flags are not set. This value can be set on input and on output.)
PD_COLLATE	
	Causes the Collate check box to be in the checked state when the dialog box is created. When the **PrintDlg** function returns, this flag indicates the state the Collate check box was left in by the user.
PD_DISABLEPRINTTOFILE	
	Disables the Print to File check box.
PD_ENABLEPRINTHOOK	
	Enables the hook function specified in the **lpfnPrintHook** member of this structure.
PD_ENABLEPRINTTEMPLATE	

Causes the operating system to create the dialog box by using the dialog box template identified by the **hInstance** and **lpPrintTemplateName** members.

PD_ENABLEPRINTTEMPLATEHANDLE

Indicates that the **hInstance** member identifies a data block that contains a preloaded dialog box template. The system ignores the **lpPrintTemplateName** member if this flag is specified.

PD_ENABLESETUPHOOK

Enables the hook function specified in the **lpfnSetupHook** member of this structure.

PD_ENABLESETUPTEMPLATE

Causes the operating system to create the dialog box by using the dialog template box identified by the **hInstance** and **lpSetupTemplateName** members.

PD_ENABLESETUPTEMPLATEHANDLE

Indicates that the **hInstance** member identifies a data block that contains a preloaded dialog box template. The operating system ignores the **lpSetupTemplateName** member if this flag is specified.

PD_HIDEPRINTTOFILE

Hides and disables the Print to File check box.

PD_NOPAGENUMS

Disables the Pages radio button and the associated edit control.

PD_NOSELECTION

Disables the Selection radio button.

PD_NOWARNING

Prevents the warning message from being displayed when there is no default printer.

PD_PAGENUMS

Causes the Pages radio button to be in the selected state when the dialog box is created. When the **PrintDlg** function returns, this flag is set if the Pages radio button is in the selected state.

PD_PRINTSETUP

Causes the system to display the Print Setup dialog box rather than the Print dialog box.

PD_PRINTTOFILE

Causes the Print to File check box to be in the checked state when the dialog box is created. When the **PrintDlg** function returns, the **pOutput** member of the **DEVNAMES** structure points to the "FILE:" string.

PD_RETURNDC

Causes the **PrintDlg** function to return a device context matching the selections the user made in the dialog box. The device context is returned in the **hDC** member.

PD_RETURNDEFAULT

Without displaying a dialog box the **PrintDlg** function to return **DEVMODE** and **DEVNAME** structures that are initialized for the system default printer. It is assumed that both the **hDevNames** and **hDevMode** members are NULL; otherwise, the function returns an error. If the system default printer is supported by an old printer driver (earlier than Windows 3.0), only the **hDevNames** member is returned— the **hDevMode** member is NULL.

PD_RETURNIC

Similar to the PD_RETURNDC flag except that this flag returns an information context rather than a device context. If neither PD_RETURNDC nor PD_RETURNIC is specified, the **hDC** parameter is undefined on output.

PD_SELECTION

Causes the Selection radio button to be in the selected state when the dialog box is created. When the **PrintDlg** function returns, this flag is set if the Selection radio button is in the selected state. If neither PD_PAGENUMS nor PD_SELECTION is specified, the All radio button is in the selected state.

PD_SHOWHELP

Causes the dialog box to show the Help button. The **hwndOwner** member must not be NULL if this option is specified.

PD_USEDEVMODECOPIES

If a printer driver does not support multiple copies, setting this flag disables the Copies edit control; if a driver does support multiple copies, setting this flag indicates the the **PrintDlg** function should store the requested number of copies in the **dmCopies** member of the **DEVMODE** structure and store the value 1 in the **nCopies** member of the **PRINTDLG** structure.

If this flag is not set, the **PrintDlg** structure stores the value 1 in the **dmCopies** member of the **DEVMODE** structure and stores the requested number of copies in the **nCopies** member of the **PRINTDLG** structure.

nFromPage

Specifies the initial value for the starting page edit control. When the **PrintDlg** function returns, this member specifies the page to begin printing. This value is valid only if the PD_PAGENUMS flag is specified.

nToPage

Specifies the initial value for the ending page edit control. When the **PrintDlg** function returns, this member specifies the last page to print. This value is valid only if the PD_PAGENUMS flag is specified.

nMinPage

Specifies the minimum value for the range of pages specified in the From and To page edit controls.

nMaxPage

Specifies the maximum value for the range of pages specified in the From and To page edit controls.

nCopies

Before the call to the **PrintDlg** function, this member contains a value used to initialize the Copies edit control *if* the **hDevMode** member is NULL; otherwise, the **dmCopies** member of the **DEVMODE** structure contains the value used to initialize this control.

When the **PrintDlg** function returns, the value specified by this member depends on the printer-driver version. For printer drivers earlier than Windows version 3.0, this member specifies the number of copies requested by the user in the dialog box's Copies edit control. For Windows version 3.0 and later printer drivers, this member specifies the number of copies requested by the user *if* the PD_USEDEVMODECOPIES flag was not set; otherwise, this member specifies the value 1, and the actual requested copy count appears in the **DEVMODE** structure.

hInstance

Identifies a data block that contains the preloaded dialog box template specified by the **lpstrTemplateName** member. This member is used only if the **Flags** member specifies the PD_ENABLEPRINTTEMPLATE or PD_ENABLESETUPTEMPLATE flag; otherwise, this member is ignored.

lCustData

Specifies application-defined data that the operating system passes to the hook function pointed to by the **lpfnHook** member. The system passes the data in the **lParam** parameter of the WM_INITDIALOG message.

lpfnPrintHook

Points to the exported function that hooks dialog messages if the application alters the Print dialog box. This member is ignored unless the PD_ENABLEPRINTHOOK flag is specified in the **Flags** member.

lpfnSetupHook

Points to the exported function that hooks dialog messages if the application alters the Print Setup dialog box. This member is ignored unless the PD_ENABLESETUPHOOK flag is specified in the **Flags** member.

lpPrintTemplateName

Points to a hook function that processes messages intended for the dialog box. An application must specify the PD_ENABLEPRINTTEMPLATE or PD_ENABLEPRINTERTEMPLATEHANDLE constant in the **Flags** member to enable the function; otherwise, the system ignores this structure member. The hook function should return FALSE to pass a message to the standard dialog box procedure, or TRUE to discard the message.

lpSetupTemplateName

Points to a hook function that processes messages intended for the dialog box. An application must specify the PD_ENABLESETUPTEMPLATE or PD_ENABLESETUPTEMPLATEHANDLE constant in the **Flags** member to enable the function; otherwise, the system ignores this structure member. The hook function should return FALSE to pass a message to the standard dialog box procedure, or TRUE to discard the message.

hPrintTemplate

Identifies the global memory object that contains the preloaded dialog box template to be used instead of the default Print Dialog box.

hSetupTemplate

Identifies the global memory object that contains the preloaded dialog box template to be used instead of the default Setup dialog box.

Comments   There is the possibility of a data collision between an **hDevNames** value and an **hDevMode** value. That is because the **wDeviceOffset** member of the **DEVNAMES** structure is supposed to be identical to the **dmDeviceName** of the **DEVMODE** structure. If it is not, the system resolves the data collision by using the **wDeviceOffset** value.

See Also   **CreateDC, CreateIC, PrintDlg DEVMODE DEVNAMES**

PRINTER_DEFAULTS

New, Unicode

```
typedef struct _PRINTER_DEFAULTS {  /* pd */
    LPTSTR       pDatatype;
    LPDEVMODE    pDevMode;
    ACCESS_MASK  DesiredAccess;
} PRINTER_DEFAULTS;
```

The **PRINTER_DEFAULTS** structure specifies the default data type, environment, initialization data, and acces rights for a printer.

Members   **pDatatype**

Points to a null-terminated string that specifies the default data type for a printer.

pDevMode

Points to a **DEVMODE** structure that identifies the default environment and initialization data for a printer.

DesiredAccess

Specifies desired access rights for a printer. The **OpenPrinter** function uses this member to set access rights to the printer. These rights can affect the operation of the **SetPrinter** and **DeletePrinter** functions.

This member can be set to PRINTER_ADMINISTER, PRINTER_USE, or any generic security value (for example, WRITE_DACL). If an application wishes to open a printer to perform administrative tasks, such as the **SetPrinter** function, it must open the printer with PRINTER_ADMINISTER access.

See Also   **OpenPrinter**, **DEVMODE**

PRINTER_INFO_1

New, Unicode

```
typedef struct _PRINTER_INFO_1 { /* pri1 */
    DWORD  Flags;
    LPTSTR pDescription;
    LPTSTR pName;
    LPTSTR pComment;
} PRINTER_INFO_1;
```

The **PRINTER_INFO_1** structure specifies general printer information.

Members   **Flags**

Specifies whether or not the structure contains valid data. This member can be either of the following values:

PRINTER_ENUM_CONTAINER
NULL

pDescription

Points to a null-terminated string that describes the contents of the structure.

pName

Points to a null-terminated string that names the contents of the structure.

pComment

Points to a null-terminated string that contains additional data describing the structure.

See Also   **EnumPrinters**, **PRINTER_INFO_2**

PRINTER_INFO_2

```
typedef struct _PRINTER_INFO_2 { /* pri2 */
    LPTSTR    pServerName;
    LPTSTR    pPrinterName;
    LPTSTR    pShareName;
    LPTSTR    pPortName;
    LPTSTR    pDriverName;
    LPTSTR    pComment;
    LPTSTR    pLocation;
    LPDEVMODE pDevMode;
    LPTSTR    pSepFile;
    LPTSTR    pPrintProcessor;
    LPTSTR    pDatatype;
    LPTSTR    pParameters;
    PSECURITY_DESCRIPTOR pSecurityDescriptor;
    DWORD     Attributes;
    DWORD     Priority;
    DWORD     DefaultPriority;
    DWORD     StartTime;
    DWORD     UntilTime;
    DWORD     Status;
    DWORD     cJobs;
    DWORD     AveragePPM;
} PRINTER_INFO_2;
```

The **PRINTER_INFO_2** structure specifies detailed printer information.

Members

pServerName

Points to a null-terminated string identifying the server that controls the printer. If this string is NULL, the printer is controlled locally.

pPrinterName

Points to a null-terminated string that specifies the name of the printer.

pShareName

Points to a null-terminated string that identifies the sharepoint for the printer. (This string is used only if the PRINTER_ATTRIBUTE_SHARED constant was set for the **Attributes** member.)

pPortName

Points to a null-terminated string that identifies the port(s) used to transmit data to the printer. If a printer is connected to more than one port, the names of each port must be separated by commas (for example, "LPT1:,LPT2:,LPT3:").

pDriverName

Points to a null-terminated string that specifies the name of the printer driver.

pComment

Points to a null-terminated string that provides a brief description of the printer.

pLocation

Points to a null-terminated string that specifies the physical location of the printer (for example, "Bldg. 38, Room 1164").

pDevMode

Points to a **DEVMODE** structure that defines default printer data such as the paper orientation and the resolution.

pSepFile

Points to a null-terminated string that specifies the name of the file used to create the separator page. This page is used to separate print jobs sent to the printer.

pPrintProcessor

Points to a null-terminated string that specifies the name of the print processor used by the printer.

pDatatype

Points to a null-terminated string that specifies the data type used to record the print job.

pParameters

Points to a null-terminated string that specifies the default print-processor parameters.

pSecurityDescriptor

Points to a **SECURITY_DESCRIPTOR** structure that defines the print job's owner and group as well as other access-related data.

Attributes

Specifies the printer attributes. This member can be one of the following values:

PRINTER_ATTRIBUTE_QUEUED
PRINTER_ATTRIBUTE_DIRECT
PRINTER_ATTRIBUTE_DEFAULT
PRINTER_ATTRIBUTE_SHARED

Priority

Specifies a priority value that the spooler uses to route print jobs.

DefaultPriority

Specifies the default priority value assigned to each print job.

StartTime

Specifies the earliest time at which the printer will print a job. (This value is specified in minutes elapsed since 12:00 A.M.)

UntilTime

Specifies the latest time at which the printer will print a job. (This value is specified in minutes elapsed since 12:00 A.M.)

Status

Specifies the printer status. This member can be one of the following values:

PRINTER_STATUS_PAUSED
PRINTER_STATUS_PENDING_DELETION

cJobs

Specifies the number of print jobs that have been queued for the printer.

AveragePPM

Specifies the average number of pages-per-minute that have been printed on the printer.

See Also   **EnumPrinters, PRINTER_INFO_1**

PRINTPROCESSOR_INFO_1

`New, Unicode`

```
typedef struct _PRINTPROCESSOR_INFO_1 { /* ppi1 */
    LPSTR pName;
} PRINTPROCESSOR_INFO_1;
```

The **PRINTPROCESSOR_INFO_1** structure specifies the name of an installed print processor.

Members   **pName**

Points to a null-terminated string that specifies the name of an installed print processor.

See Also   **EnumPrintProcessors**

PRIVILEGE_SET

```
typedef struct _PRIVILEGE_SET { /* ps */
    DWORD PrivilegeCount;
    DWORD Control;
    LUID_AND_ATTRIBUTES Privilege[ANYSIZE_ARRAY];
} PRIVILEGE_SET;
```

The **PRIVILEGE_SET** structure specifies a set of privileges. It is also used to indicate which, if any, privileges are held by a user or group requesting access to an object.

Members

PrivilegeCount

Specifies the number of privileges in the privilege set.

Control

Specifies a control flag related to the privileges. The PRIVILEGE_SET_ALL_NECESSARY control flag is currently defined. It indicates that all of the specified privileges must be held by the process requesting access. If this flag is not set, the presence of any privileges in the user's access token grants the access.

Privilege[]

Specifies an array of **LUID_AND_ATTRIBUTES** structures describing the set's privileges. The following attributes are defined for privileges:

Attribute	Description
SE_PRIVILEGE_ENABLED_BY_DEFAULT	
	The privilege is enabled by default.
SE_PRIVILEGE_ENABLED	
	The privilege is enabled.
SE_PRIVILEGE_USED_FOR_ACCESS	
	The privilege was used to gain access to an object or service. This flag is used to identify the relevant privileges in a set passed by a client application that may contain unnecessary privileges.

Comments

A privilege is used to control access to an object or service more strictly than is typical with discretionary access control. A system manager uses privileges to control which users are able to manipulate system resources. An application uses privileges when it changes a system-wide resource, such as when it changes the system time or shuts down the system.

See Also

PrivilegeCheck, LUID, LUID_AND_ATTRIBUTES

PROCESS_INFORMATION

```
typedef struct _PROCESS_INFORMATION { /* pi */
    HANDLE hProcess;
    HANDLE hThread;
    DWORD dwProcessId;
    DWORD dwThreadId;
} PROCESS_INFORMATION;
```

The **PROCESS_INFORMATION** structure is filled in by the **CreateProcess** function with information about a newly created process and its primary thread.

Members   **hProcess**
Returns a handle to the newly created process. The handle is used to specify the process in all functions that perform operations on the process object.

hThread
Returns a handle to the primary thread of the newly created process. The handle is used to specify the thread in all functions that perform operations on the thread object.

dwProcessId
Returns a global process identifiers that can be used to identify a process. The value is valid from the time the process is created until the time the process is terminated.

dwThreadId
Returns a global thread identifiers that can be used to identify a thread. The value is valid from the time the thread is created until the time the thread is terminated.

See Also   **CreateProcess**

PROVIDOR_INFO_1   New, Unicode

```
typedef struct _PROVIDOR_INFO_1 { /* pi1 */
    LPTSTR pName;
    LPTSTR pEnvironment ;
    LPTSTR pDLLName ;
} PROVIDOR_INFO_1;
```

The **PROVIDOR_INFO_1** structure identifies a print provider.

Members   **pName**
Points to a null-terminated string that is the name of the print provider.

pEnvironment
Points to a null-terminated environment string specifying the environment this DLL is designed to run in.

pDLLName
Points to a null-terminated string that is the name of the provider DLL.

See Also   **MONITOR_INFO_2**

QUERY_SERVICE_CONFIG

```
typedef struct _QUERY_SERVICE_CONFIG { /* qsc */
    DWORD dwServiceType;
    DWORD dwStartType;
    DWORD dwErrorControl;
    LPTSTR lpBinaryPathName;
    LPTSTR lpLoadOrderGroup;
    DWORD dwTagId;
    LPTSTR lpDependencies;
    LPTSTR lpServiceStartName;
    LPTSTR lpDisplayName;
} QUERY_SERVICE_CONFIG, LPQUERY_SERVICE_CONFIG;
```

The **QUERY_SERVICE_CONFIG** structure is used by the **QueryServiceConfig** function to return configuration information about an installed service.

Members

dwServiceType

Indicates the type of service. One of the following values is specified.

Type	Meaning
SERVICE_WIN32_OWN_PROCESS	Specifies a service that runs in its own Win32 process.
SERVICE_WIN32_SHARE_PROCESS	Specifies a service that shares a Win32 process with other services.
SERVICE_KERNEL_DRIVER	Specifies a Windows NT device driver.
SERVICE_FILE_SYSTEM_DRIVER	Specifies a Windows NT file system driver.

dwStartType

Specifies when to start the service. One of the following values is specified.

Value	Meaning
SERVICE_BOOT_START	Specifies a device driver started by the operating system loader. This value is valid only if the service type is SERVICE_KERNEL_DRIVER or SERVICE_FILE_SYSTEM_DRIVER.
SERVICE_SYSTEM_START	Specifies a device driver started by the **IoInitSystem** function. This value is valid only if the service type is SERVICE_KERNEL_DRIVER or SERVICE_FILE_SYSTEM_DRIVER.

SERVICE_AUTO_START	Specifies a device driver or Win32 service started by the service control manager automatically during system startup.
SERVICE_DEMAND_START	Specifies a device driver or Win32 service started by the service control manager when a process calls the **StartService** function.
SERVICE_DISABLED	Specifies a device driver or Win32 service that can no longer be started.

dwErrorControl

Specifies the severity of the error if this service fails to start during system startup and determines the action taken by the startup program if failure occurs. This value should be the SERVICE_ERROR_NORMAL flag, which causes the startup program to log the error but continue the startup process. The SERVICE_ERROR_SEVERE and SERVICE_ERROR_CRITICAL flags are not currently supported.

lpBinaryPathName

Points to a null-terminated string that contains the fully qualified path to the service binary file.

lpLoadOrderGroup

Points to a null-terminated string that names the load ordering group of which this service is a member. If the pointer is NULL or if it points to an empty string, the service does not belong to a group. The registry has a list of load ordering groups at HKEY_LOCAL_MACHINE\System\ CurrentControlSet\Control\ServiceGroupOrder. The startup program uses this list to load groups of services in a specified order with respect to the other groups in the list. You can place a service in a group so that another service can depend on the group.

The order in which a service starts is determined by these criteria:

1. The order of groups in the registry's load-ordering group list. Services in groups in the load-ordering group list are started first, followed by services in groups not in the load-ordering group list and then services that do not belong to a group.

2. The service's dependencies listed in the *lpszDependencies* parameter and the dependencies of other services dependent on the service.

dwTagId

Specifies a unique tag value for this service in the group specified by the *lpLoadOrderGroup* parameter. A value of zero indicates that the service has not been assigned a tag. You can use a tag for ordering service startup within a load order group by specifying a tag order vector in the registry at HKEY_LOCAL_MACHINE\System\ CurrentControlSet\Control\GroupOrderList. Tags are only evaluated for SERVICE_KERNEL_DRIVER and SERVICE_FILE_SYSTEM_DRIVER

type services that have SERVICE_BOOT_START or
SERVICE_SYSTEM_START start types.

lpDependencies

Points to an array of null-separated names of services or load ordering groups
that must start before this service. The array is doubly null-terminated. If the
pointer is NULL or if it points to an empty string, the service has no
dependencies. If a group name is specified, it must be prefixed by the
SC_GROUP_IDENTIFIER (defined in the WINSVC.H file) character to
differentiate it from a service name, because services and service groups share
the same name space. Dependency on a service means that this service can
only run if the service it depends on is running. Dependency on a group means
that this service can run if at least one member of the group is running after an
attempt to start all members of the group.

lpServiceStartName

Points to a null-terminated string. If the service type is
SERVICE_WIN32_OWN_PROCESS or
SERVICE_WIN32_SHARE_PROCESS, this name is the account name in the
form of "DomainName\Username", which the service process will be logged
on as when it runs. If the account belongs to the built-in domain, ".\Username"
can be specified. If NULL is specified, the service will be logged on as the
LocalSystem account.

If the service type is SERVICE_KERNEL_DRIVER or
SERVICE_FILE_SYSTEM_DRIVER, this name is the Windows NT driver
object name (that is, \FileSystem\Rdr or \Driver\Xns) which the input and
output (I/O) system uses to load the device driver. If NULL is specified, the
driver is run with a default object name created by the I/O system based on the
service name.

lpDisplayName

Points to a NULL-terminated string that is to be used by user interface
programs to identify the service. This string has a maximum length of 256
characters. The name is case-preserved in the Service Control Manager.
Display name comparisons are always case-insensitive.

Comments   The configuration information for a service is initially specified when the service
is created by a call to the **CreateService** function. The information can be
modified by calling the **ChangeServiceConfig** function.

See Also   **ChangeServiceConfig, CreateService, QueryServiceConfig**

QUERY_SERVICE_LOCK_STATUS

```
typedef struct _QUERY_SERVICE_LOCK_STATUS { /* qsls */
    DWORD fIsLocked;
    LPTSTR lpLockOwner;
    DWORD dwLockDuration;
} QUERY_SERVICE_LOCK_STATUS, * LPQUERY_SERVICE_LOCK_STATUS ;
```

The **QUERY_SERVICE_LOCK_STATUS** structure is used by the **QueryServiceLockStatus** function to return information about the lock status of a Service Control Manager database.

Members

fIsLocked

Specifies whether the database is locked. If this member is nonzero, the database is locked. If it is zero, the database is unlocked.

lpLockOwner

Points to a null-terminated string containing the name of the user who acquired the lock.

dwLockDuration

Specifies the time, in seconds, since the lock was first acquired.

See Also

QueryServiceLockStatus

RASTERIZER_STATUS

```
typedef struct _RASTERIZER_STATUS {     /* rs */
    short nSize;
    short wFlags;
    short nLanguageID;
} RASTERIZER_STATUS;
```

The **RASTERIZER_STATUS** structure contains information about whether TrueType ® is installed. This structure is filled when an application calls the **GetRasterizerCaps** function.

Members

nSize

Specifies the size, in bytes, of the **RASTERIZER_STATUS** structure.

wFlags

Specifies whether at least one TrueType font is installed and whether TrueType is enabled. This value is TT_AVAILABLE and/or TT_ENABLED if TrueType is on the system.

nLanguageID
Specifies the language in the system's SETUP.INF file.

See Also   **GetRasterizerCaps**

REASSIGN_BLOCKS   `New`

```
typedef struct _REASSIGN_BLOCKS {
    WORD    Reserved;
    WORD    Count;
    DWORD BlockNumber[1];
} REASSIGN_BLOCKS ;
```

The **REASSIGN_BLOCKS** structure provides disk block reassignment data. It is a variable-length structure whose last member is an array of block numbers to be reassigned.

Members   **Reserved**
This member is reserved. Do not use it. Set it to zero.

Count
Specifies the number of blocks to be reassigned. This is the number of elements that are in the **BlockNumber** member array.

BlockNumber[1]
An array of **Count** block numbers, one for each block to be reassigned.

Comments   The **DeviceIoControl** function uses a **REASSIGN_BLOCKS** structure as input to an **IOCTL_DISK_REASSIGN_BLOCKS** device i/o operation.

See Also   **DeviceIoControl, IOCTL_DISK_REASSIGN_BLOCKS**

RECT

```
typedef struct tagRECT {    /* rc */
    LONG left;
    LONG top;
    LONG right;
    LONG bottom;
} RECT;
```

The **RECT** structure defines the coordinates of the upper-left and lower-right corners of a rectangle.

Members   **left**
                   Specifies the x-coordinate of the upper-left corner of the rectangle.

                   top
                   Specifies the y-coordinate of the upper-left corner of the rectangle.

                   right
                   Specifies the x-coordinate of the lower-right corner of the rectangle.

                   bottom
                   Specifies the y-coordinate of the lower-right corner of the rectangle.

Comments   When the **RECT** structure is passed to the **FillRect** function, the rectangle is
                   filled up to, but not including, the right column and bottom row of pixels.

See Also   **RECTL, SMALL_RECT**

RECTL

```
typedef struct _RECTL { /* rcl */
    LONG left;
    LONG top;
    LONG right;
    LONG bottom;
} RECTL;
```

The **RECTL** structure defines the coordinates of the upper-left and lower-right
corners of a rectangle.

Members   **left**
                   Specifies the x-coordinate of the upper-left corner of the rectangle.

                   top
                   Specifies the y-coordinate of the upper-left corner of the rectangle.

                   right
                   Specifies the x-coordinate of the lower-right corner of the rectangle.

                   bottom
                   Specifies the y-coordinate of the lower-right corner of the rectangle.

Comments   When the **RECTL** structure is passed to the **FillRect** function, the rectangle is
                   filled up to, but not including, the right column and bottom row of pixels.

See Also   **RECT, SMALL_RECT**

RGBQUAD

```
typedef struct tagRGBQUAD { /* rgbq */
    BYTE    rgbBlue;
    BYTE    rgbGreen;
    BYTE    rgbRed;
    BYTE    rgbReserved;
} RGBQUAD;
```

The **RGBQUAD** structure describes a color consisting of relative intensities of red, green, and blue.

Members

rgbBlue
Specifies the intensity of blue in the color.

rgbGreen
Specifies the intensity of green in the color.

rgbRed
Specifies the intensity of red in the color.

rgbReserved
Reserved; must be zero.

Comments
The **bmiColors** member of the **BITMAPINFO** structure consists of an array of **RGBQUAD** structures.

See Also
CreateDIBitmap, CreateDIBSection, GetDIBits, SetDIBits, SetDIBitsToDevice, StretchDIBits

RGBTRIPLE

```
typedef struct tagRGBTRIPLE { /* rgbt */
    BYTE rgbtBlue;
    BYTE rgbtGreen;
    BYTE rgbtRed;
} RGBTRIPLE;
```

The **RGBTRIPLE** structure describes a color consisting of relative intensities of red, green, and blue. The **bmciColors** member of the **BITMAPCOREINFO** structure consists of an array of **RGBTRIPLE** structures.

Members

rgbtBlue
Specifies the intensity of blue in the color.

rgbtGreen
Specifies the intensity of green in the color.

rgbtRed
Specifies the intensity of red in the color.

RGNDATA

New

```
typedef struct _RGNDATA { /* rgnd */
    RGNDATAHEADER rdh;
    char          Buffer[1];
} RGNDATA;
```

The **RGNDATA** structure contains a header and an array of rectangles that compose a region. These rectangles, sorted top to bottom left to right, do not overlap.

Members

rdh
Specifies a **RGNDATAHEADER** structure. The members of this structure specify the type of region (whether it is rectangular or trapezoidal), the number of rectangles that make up the region, the size of the buffer that contains the rectangle structures, and so on.

Buffer
Specifies an arbitrary-size buffer that contains the **RECT** structures that make up the region.

See Also   **RECT, RGNDATAHEADER**

RGNDATAHEADER

New

```
typedef struct _RGNDATAHEADER { /* rgndh */
    DWORD dwSize;
    DWORD iType;
    DWORD nCount;
    DWORD nRgnSize;
    RECT  rcBound;
} RGNDATAHEADER;
```

The **RGNDATAHEADER** structure describes the data returned by the **GetRegionData** function.

Members

dwSize
Specifies the size, in bytes, of the header.

iType
Specifies the type of region. This value must be RDH_RECTANGLES.

nCount
Specifies the number of rectangles that make up the region.

nRgnSize
Specifies the size of the buffer required to receive the **RECT** structure that specifies the coordinates of the rectangles that make up the region. If the size is not known, this member can be zero.

rcBound
Specifies a bounding rectangle for the region.

See Also   **RECT, RGNDATA**

RIP_INFO

```
typedef struct _RIP_INFO { /* ri */
    DWORD  dwError;
    DWORD  dwType;
} RIP_INFO;
```

The **RIP_INFO** structure contains the error and address, format, and length, in bytes, of a debugging string.

Members

dwError
Specifies the error that caused the RIP debug event. For more information about exception handling, see Chapter 63, "Errors."

dwType
Specifies additional information about the type of error that caused the RIP debug event. This may be one of the following values:

Value	Meaning
SLE_ERROR	Indicates that invalid data was passed to the function that failed. This caused the application to fail.
SLE_MINORERROR	Indicates that invalid data was passed to the function, but the error probably will not cause the application to fail.
SLE_WARNING	Indicates that potentially invalid data was passed to the function, but the function completed processing.
0	Indicates that only **dwError** was set.

See Also   **DEBUG_EVENT**

SECURITY_ATTRIBUTES

`New`

```
typedef struct _SECURITY_ATTRIBUTES { /* sa */
    DWORD  nLength;
    LPVOID lpSecurityDescriptor;
    BOOL   bInheritHandle;
} SECURITY_ATTRIBUTES;
```

The **SECURITY_ATTRIBUTES** structure contains the security descriptor for an object and specifies whether the handle retrieved by specifying this structure is inheritable.

Members

nLength

Specifies the length, in bytes, of this structure. This value is to be set to the size of the **SECURITY_ATTRIBUTES** structure.

lpSecurityDescriptor

Points to a security descriptor for the object that controls the sharing of it. If NULL is specified for this member, the object may be assigned the default security descriptor of the calling process.

bInheritHandle

Specifies whether the returned handle is inherited when a new process is created. If this member is TRUE, the new process inherits the handle.

Comments

A pointer to a **SECURITY_ATTRIBUTES** structure is used as a parameter in most kernel and window-management functions in the Win32 API that return a handle of an object.

See Also

SECURITY_DESCRIPTOR

SECURITY_DESCRIPTOR

`New`

```
typedef PVOID PSECURITY_DESCRIPTOR;
```

The **SECURITY_DESCRIPTOR** structure contains the security information associated with an object. Applications use this structure to set and query an object's security status.

Applications are not to modify the **SECURITY_DESCRIPTOR** structure directly. For creating and manipulating a security descriptor, use the functions listed in the See Also section.

Comments   A security descriptor includes information that specifies the following components of an object's security:

- An owner (SID)
- A primary group (SID)
- A discretionary ACL
- A system ACL
- Qualifiers for the preceding items

Security descriptors use access-control lists (ACLs) and security identifiers (SIDs) to specify the information in this list.

A security descriptor can be in absolute or self-relative form. In self-relative form, all members of the structure are located contiguously in memory. In absolute form, the structure only contains pointers to the members.

See Also   **GetSecurityDescriptorControl, GetSecurityDescriptorDacl, GetSecurityDescriptorGroup, GetSecurityDescriptorLength, GetSecurityDescriptorOwner, GetSecurityDescriptorSacl, InitializeSecurityDescriptor, IsValidSecurityDescriptor, SetSecurityDescriptorDacl, SetSecurityDescriptorGroup, SetSecurityDescriptorOwner, SetSecurityDescriptorSacl**

SECURITY_DESCRIPTOR_CONTROL

New

```
typedef WORD SECURITY_DESCRIPTOR_CONTROL;
```

The **SECURITY_DESCRIPTOR_CONTROL** structure contains a set of bit flags that qualify the meaning of a security descriptor or its individual members.

Each security descriptor has an associated **SECURITY_DESCRIPTOR_CONTROL** structure. Applications can use the Win32 API functions to set and retrieve a security descriptor's **SECURITY_DESCRIPTOR_CONTROL** values. These functions are listed in the See Also section.

The following constants are defined for setting and retrieving **SECURITY_DESCRIPTOR_CONTROL** bit flags:

Value	Meaning
SE_OWNER_DEFAULTED	Instead of the original provider of the security descriptor, a default mechanism provided the security descriptor's owner security identifier (SID). This can affect the treatment of the SID with respect to inheritance of an owner. This flag is ignored if the owner member is NULL. The **SetSecurityDescriptorOwner** function sets this flag.
SE_GROUP_DEFAULTED	Instead of the the original provider of the security descriptor, a default mechanism provided the security descriptor's group SID. This can affect the treatment of the SID with respect to inheritance of a primary group. This flag is ignored if the group member is NULL. The **SetSecurityDescriptorGroup** function sets this flag.
SE_DACL_PRESENT	The security descriptor contains a discretionary access-control list (ACL). If this flag is set and the discretionary ACL is NULL, an empty ACL is being explicitly specified. An empty ACL has a size but no access-control entries (ACEs). A NULL ACL has no pointer to an ACL. This flag allows functions to determine whether a security descriptor points to a NULL ACL or no ACL at all. The **SetSecurityDescriptorDacl** function sets this flag.
SE_DACL_DEFAULTED	Instead of the the original provider of the security descriptor, a default mechanism provided the discretionary ACL. This can affect the treatment of the ACL with respect to inheritance of an ACL. If the SE_DACL_PRESENT flag is not set, this flag is ignored. The **SetSecurityDescriptorDacl** function sets this flag.
SE_SACL_PRESENT	The security descriptor contains a system ACL. If this flag is set and the Sacl member is NULL, an empty ACL is being explicitly specified. This flag allows functions to determine whether a security descriptor points to a NULL ACL or no ACL at all. The **SetSecurityDescriptorSacl** function sets this flag.
SE_SACL_DEFAULTED	Instead of the the original provider of the security descriptor, a default mechanism provided the ACL. This can affect the treatment of the ACL with respect to inheritance of an ACL. If the SE_SACL_PRESENT flag is not set, this flag is ignored. The **SetSecurityDescriptorSacl** function sets this flag.

SE_SELF_RELATIVE	The security descriptor is in self-relative form and all members of the security descriptor are contiguous in memory. All pointer members are expressed as offsets from the beginning of the security descriptor. This form is useful for treating security descriptors as opaque structures for transmission in a communications protocol or for storage on secondary media.

See Also   **GetSecurityDescriptorControl, GetSecurityDescriptorDacl, GetSecurityDescriptorGroup, GetSecurityDescriptorOwner, GetSecurityDescriptorSacl, SetSecurityDescriptorDacl, SetSecurityDescriptorGroup, SetSecurityDescriptorOwner, SetSecurityDescriptorSacl**

SECURITY_IMPERSONATION_LEVEL   New

```
typedef enum tagSECURITY_IMPERSONATION_LEVEL { /* sil */
    SecurityAnonymous,
    SecurityIdentification,
    SecurityImpersonation,
    SecurityDelegation
} SECURITY_IMPERSONATION_LEVEL;
```

The **SECURITY_IMPERSONATION_LEVEL** enumerated type specifies impersonation levels. Security impersonation levels govern the degree to which a server process can act on behalf of a client process.

Value	Meaning
SecurityAnonymous	The server process cannot obtain identification information about the client and it cannot impersonate the client. It is defined with no value given, and thus, by ANSI C rules, defaults to a value of 0.
SecurityIdentification	The server process can obtain information about the client, such as security identifiers and privileges, but it cannot use kernel functions. This is useful for servers that export their own objects—for example, tables and views exported by a database product. Using the retrieved client-security information, the server can make access-validation decisions without being able to utilize other services using the client's security context.
SecurityImpersonation	The server process can impersonate the client's security context on its local system. The server cannot impersonate the client on remote systems.

SecurityDelegation	This impersonation level is not supported in the current version of Windows NT.

Comments   Impersonation is the ability of a process to take on the security attributes of another process.

See Also   **CreatePrivateObjectSecurity, DuplicateToken, GetTokenInformation, ImpersonateSelf, OpenThreadToken**

SECURITY_INFORMATION

New

```
typedef DWORD SECURITY_INFORMATION;
```

The **SECURITY_INFORMATION** structure identifies the object-related security information being set or queried. This security information includes:

- The owner of an object
- The primary group of an object
- The discretionary access-control list (ACL) of an object
- The system ACL of an object

Each item of security information is designated by a bit flag. The following values specify the bits:

Value	Meaning
OWNER_SECURITY_INFORMATION	Indicates the owner identifier of the object is being referenced.
GROUP_SECURITY_INFORMATION	Indicates the primary group identifier of the object is being referenced.
DACL_SECURITY_INFORMATION	Indicates the discretionary ACL of the object is being referenced.
SACL_SECURITY_INFORMATION	Indicates the system ACL of the object is being referenced.

See Also   **GetFileSecurity, GetKernelObjectSecurity, GetPrivateObjectSecurity, GetUserObjectSecurity, SetFileSecurity, SetKernelObjectSecurity, SetPrivateObjectSecurity, SetUserObjectSecurity**

SECURITY_QUALITY_OF_SERVICE

`New`

```
typedef struct _SECURITY_QUALITY_OF_SERVICE { /* sqos */
    DWORD Length;
    SECURITY_IMPERSONATION_LEVEL ImpersonationLevel;
    SECURITY_CONTEXT_TRACKING_MODE ContextTrackingMode;
    BOOLEAN EffectiveOnly;
} SECURITY_QUALITY_OF_SERVICE;
```

The **SECURITY_QUALITY_OF_SERVICE** data structure contains information used to support client impersonation. A client can specify this information when it connects to a server; the information determines whether or not the server may impersonate the client, and if so, to what extent.

Members

Length

Specifies the size, in bytes, of this structure.

ImpersonationLevel

Specifies what the server may be told about the client, and how the server may represent, or impersonate, the client. Security impersonation levels govern the degree to which a server process can act on behalf of a client process. This member is a **SECURITY_IMPERSONATION_LEVEL** enumerated type value. The **SECURITY_IMPERSONATION_LEVEL** enumerated type is defined as follows :

```
typedef enum tagSECURITY_IMPERSONATION_LEVEL { /* sil */
    SecurityAnonymous,
    SecurityIdentification,
    SecurityImpersonation,
    SecurityDelegation
} SECURITY_IMPERSONATION_LEVEL;
```

ContextTracking Mode

Specifies whether the server is to be given a snapshot of the client's security context (called static tracking), or is to be continually updated to track changes to the client's security context (called dynamic tracking). The value SECURITY_STATIC_TRACKING specifies static tracking, and the value SECURITY_DYNAMIC_TRACKING specifies dynamic tracking. Not all communications mechanisms support dynamic tracking; those that do not will default to static tracking.

Effective Only

Specifies whether or not the server may enable or disable privileges and groups that the client's security context may include.

See Also   **SECURITY_IMPERSONATION_LEVEL**

SERVICE_STATUS

```
typedef struct _SERVICE_STATUS { /* ss */
    DWORD dwServiceType;
    DWORD dwCurrentState;
    DWORD dwControlsAccepted;
    DWORD dwWin32ExitCode;
    DWORD dwServiceSpecificExitCode;
    DWORD dwCheckPoint;
    DWORD dwWaitHint;
} SERVICE_STATUS, *LPSERVICE_STATUS;
```

The **SERVICE_STATUS** structure contains information about a service. The **ControlService**, **EnumDependentServices**, **EnumServicesStatus**, and **QueryServiceStatus** functions use this structure to return information about a service. A service uses this structure in the **SetServiceStatus** function to report its current status to the service control manager.

Members

dwServiceType

Indicates the type of service. One of the following values is specified.

Type	Meaning
SERVICE_WIN32_OWN_PROCESS	Specifies a service that runs in its own Win32 process.
SERVICE_WIN32_SHARE_PROCESS	Specifies a service that shares a Win32 process with other services.
SERVICE_KERNEL_DRIVER	Specifies a Windows NT device driver.
SERVICE_FILE_SYSTEM_DRIVER	Specifies a Windows NT file system driver.

dwCurrentState

Indicates the current state of the service. One of the following values is specified.

Value	Meaning
SERVICE_STOPPED	The service is not running.
SERVICE_START_PENDING	The service is starting.
SERVICE_STOP_PENDING	The service is stopping.
SERVICE_RUNNING	The service is running.
SERVICE_CONTINUE_PENDING	The service continue is pending.
SERVICE_PAUSE_PENDING	The service pause is pending.
SERVICE_PAUSED	The service is paused.

dwControlsAccepted

Specifies the control codes that the service will accept and process. A user interface process can control a service by specifying a control command in the **ControlService** function. By default, all services accept the SERVICE_CONTROL_INTERROGATE command. Any or all of the following flags can be specified to enable the other control codes.

Value	Meaning
SERVICE_ACCEPT_STOP	
	The service can be stopped. This enables the SERVICE_CONTROL_STOP command.
SERVICE_ACCEPT_PAUSE_CONTINUE	
	The service can be paused and continued. This enables the SERVICE_CONTROL_PAUSE and SERVICE_CONTROL_CONTINUE commands.
SERVICE_ACCEPT_SHUTDOWN	
	The service is notified when system shutdown occurs. This enables the system to send a SERVICE_CONTROL_SHUTDOWN command to the service. The **ControlService** function cannot send this control code.

dwWin32ExitCode

Specifies a Win32 error code that the service uses to report an error that occurs when it is starting or stopping. To return an error code specific to the service, the service must set this value to ERROR_SERVICE_SPECIFIC_ERROR to indicate that the **dwServiceSpecificExitCode** member contains the error code. The service should set this value to NO_ERROR when it is running and on normal termination.

dwServiceSpecificExitCode

Specifies a service specific error code that the service returns when an error occurs while the service is starting or stopping. This value is ignored unless the **dwWin32ExitCode** member is set to ERROR_SERVICE_SPECIFIC_ERROR.

dwCheckPoint

Specifies a value that the service increments periodically to report its progress during a lengthy start, stop, or continue operation. For example, the service should increment this value as it completes each step of its initialization when it is starting up. The user interface program that invoked the operation on the service uses this value to track the progress of the service during a lengthy operation. This value is not valid and should be zero when the service does not have a start, stop, or continue operation pending .

dwWaitHint

Specifies the amount of time, in milliseconds, that the service expects a pending start, stop, or continue operation to take before completion. The user interface program that invoked the operation waits this amount of time before calling **QueryServiceStatus** to see if the operation has been completed. If the operation has not been completed but **dwCheckPoint** has been incremented indicating that the service is making progress, the user interface program should wait this amount of time again. When the service does not have a start, stop, or continue operation pending, this value is not valid and should be zero.

See Also   **ControlService, EnumDependentServices, EnumServicesStatus, QueryServiceStatus, SetServiceStatus**

SERVICE_TABLE_ENTRY

```
typedef struct _SERVICE_TABLE_ENTRY { /* ste */
    LPTSTR lpServiceName;
    LPSERVICE_MAIN_FUNCTION lpServiceProc;
} SERVICE_TABLE_ENTRY, *LPSERVICE_TABLE_ENTRY;
```

The **SERVICE_TABLE_ENTRY** structure is used by the **StartServiceCtrlDispatcher** function to specify the **SERVICE_MAIN_FUNCTION** function for a Win32 service that can run in the calling process.

Members   **lpServiceName**
Points to a null-terminated string that names a service that can run in this service process. This string is ignored if the service is installed in the service control manager database as a SERVICE_WIN32_OWN_PROCESS service type. For a SERVICE_WIN32_SHARE_PROCESS service process, this string names the service that uses the **ServiceMain** function pointed to by the **lpServiceProc** member.

lpServiceProc
Points to a **ServiceMain** function.

See Also   **ServiceMain, StartServiceCtrlDispatcher**

SESSION_BUFFER

```
typedef struct _SESSION_BUFFER { /* sb */
    UCHAR lsn;
    UCHAR state;
    UCHAR local_name[NCBNAMSZ];
    UCHAR remote_name[NCBNAMSZ];
    UCHAR rcvs_outstanding;
    UCHAR sends_outstanding;
} SESSION_BUFFER;
```

The **SESSION_BUFFER** structure contains information about a local network session. One or more **SESSION_BUFFER** structures follows a **SESSION_HEADER** structure when an application specifies NCBSSTAT in the **ncb_command** member of the **NCB** structure.

Members

lsn

Specifies the local session number.

state

Specifies the state of the session. This member can be one of the following values:

Value	Meaning
LISTEN_OUTSTANDING	The session is waiting for a call from a remote computer.
CALL_PENDING	The session is attempting to connect to a remote computer.
SESSION_ESTABLISHED	The session connected and is able to transfer data.
HANGUP_PENDING	The session is being deleted due to a command by the local user.
HANGUP_COMPLETE	The session was deleted due to a command by the local user.
SESSION_ABORTED	The session was abandoned due to a network or user problem.

local_name

Specifies the 16-byte NetBIOS name on the local computer used for this session.

remote_name

Specifies the 16-byte NetBIOS name on the remote computer used for this session.

rcvs_outstanding

Specifies the number of pending NCBRECV commands.

sends_outstanding
Specifies the number of pending NCBSEND and NCBCHAINSEND commands.

See Also   **NCB, SESSION_HEADER**

SESSION_HEADER

```
typedef struct _SESSION_HEADER { /* sh */
    UCHAR sess_name;
    UCHAR num_sess;
    UCHAR rcv_dg_outstanding;
    UCHAR rcv_any_outstanding;
} SESSION_HEADER;
```

The **SESSION_HEADER** structure contains information about a network session. This structure is pointed to by the **ncb_buffer** member of the **NCB** structure. **SESSION_HEADER** is followed by as many **SESSION_BUFFER** structures as are required to describe the current network sessions.

Members   **sess_name**
Specifies the name number of the session. This value corresponds to the **ncb_num** member of the **NCB** structure.

num_sess
Specifies the number of sessions that have the name specified by the **sess_name** member.

rcv_dg_outstanding
Specifies the number of outstanding NCBDGRECV and NCBDGRECVBC commands.

rcv_any_outstanding
Specifies the number of outstanding NCBRECVANY commands.

See Also   **NCB SESSION_BUFFER**

SET_PARTITION_INFORMATION

```
typedef struct _SET_PARTITION_INFORMATION {
    BYTE PartitionType;
} SET_PARTITION_INFORMATION ;
```

The **SetPartitionInformation** structure provides information used to set a disk partition's type.

Members

PartitionType

Specifies the type of partition. This member can take on one of the following values:

Value	Meaning
PARTITION_ENTRY_UNUSED	Entry unused.
PARTITION_FAT_12	Specifies a partition with 12-bit FAT entries.
PARTITION_XENIX_1	Specifies a Xenix type 1 partition.
PARTITION_XENIX_2	Specifies a Xenix type 2 partition.
PARTITION_FAT_16	Specifies a partition with 16-bit FAT entries.
PARTITION_EXTENDED	Specifies an extended partition entry.
PARTITION_HUGE	Specifies an MS-DOS V4 huge partition.
PARTITION_IFS	Specifies an IFS partition.
PARTITION_UNIX	Specifies a Unix partition.
VALID_NTFT	Specifies an NTFT partition.

Comments

The **DeviceIoControl** function uses a **SET_PARTITION_INFORMATION** structure as input to an **IOCTL_DISK_SET_PARTITION_INFO** device i/o operation.

See Also

DeviceIoControl, IOCTL_DISK_SET_PARTITION_INFO, IOCTL_DISK_GET_PARTITION_INFO, PARTITION_INFORMATION

SID

`New`

```
typedef PVOID PSID;
```

The **SID** structure is a variable-length structure used to uniquely identify users or groups. SID stands for security identifier.

Applications are not to modify the **SID** structure directly. To create and manipulate a security identifier, use the functions listed in the See Also section.

See Also

AllocateAndInitializeSid, CopySid, EqualSid, FreeSid, GetLengthSid, GetSidIdentifierAuthority, GetSidLengthRequired, GetSidSubAuthority, GetSidSubAuthorityCount, InitializeSid, IsValidSid, LookupAccountName, LookupAccountSid

SID_AND_ATTRIBUTES

`New`

```
typedef struct _SID_AND_ATTRIBUTES { /* saa */
    PSID  Sid;
    DWORD Attributes;
} SID_AND_ATTRIBUTES ;
```

The **SID_AND_ATTRIBUTES** structure represents a security identifier (SID) and its attributes. SIDs are used to uniquely identify users or groups.

Members

Sid
Points to an **SID** structure.

Attributes
Specifies attributes of the SID. This value contains up to 32 one-bit flags. Its meaning depends on the definition and use of the SID.

Comments

A group is represented by an SID. SIDs have attributes that indicate whether they are currently enabled, disabled, or mandatory, and how they are used. An **SID_AND_ATTRIBUTES** structure can represent an SID whose attributes change frequently. For example, it is used to represent groups in the **TOKEN_GROUPS** structure.

See Also

SID, TOKEN_GROUPS, TOKEN_USER

SID_IDENTIFIER_AUTHORITY

`New`

```
typedef struct _SID_IDENTIFIER_AUTHORITY { /* sia */
    BYTE Value[6];
} SID_IDENTIFIER_AUTHORITY ;
```

The **SID_IDENTIFIER_AUTHORITY** structure represents the top-level authority of a security identifier (SID).

Members

Value
An array of six bytes specifying a SID's top-level authority.

Comments

The identifier authority value identifies the agency that issued the SID. Some identifier authorities are predefined:

Identifier authority	Value
SECURITY_NULL_SID_AUTHORITY	0
SECURITY_WORLD_SID_AUTHORITY	1

SECURITY_LOCAL_SID_AUTHORITY	2
SECURITY_CREATOR_SID_AUTHORITY	3
SECURITY_NT_AUTHORITY	5

An SID must contain a top-level authority and at least one relative identifier (RID) value.

See Also   **AllocateAndInitializeSid**, **GetSidIdentifierAuthority**, **InitializeSid**, **SID**

SID_NAME_USE

```
typedef enum tagSID_NAME_USE {
    SidTypeUser = 1,
    SidTypeGroup,
    SidTypeDomain,
    SidTypeAlias,
    SidTypeWellKnownGroup,
    SidTypeDeletedAccount,
    SidTypeInvalid,
    SidTypeUnknown
} SID_NAME_USE;
```

The **SID_NAME_USE** enumerated type lists the uses of security identifiers (SIDs). The enumerators indicate what a SID represents.

Value	Meaning
SidTypeUser	Indicates a user SID.
SidTypeGroup	Indicates a group SID.
SidTypeDomain	Indicates a domain SID.
SidTypeAlias	Indicates an alias SID.
SidTypeWellKnownGroup	Indicates an SID for a well-known group.
SidTypeDeletedAccount	Indicates an SID for a deleted account.
SidTypeInvalid	Indicates an invalid SID.
SidTypeUnknown	Indicates an unknown SID type.

See Also   **LookupAccountName**, **LookupAccountSid**

SINGLE_LIST_ENTRY

New

```
typedef struct _SINGLE_LIST_ENTRY { /* sle */
    struct _SINGLE_LIST_ENTRY *Next;
} SINGLE_LIST_ENTRY;
```

The **SINGLE_LIST_ENTRY** structure is available for any entry in a single-linked list.

Members

Next

Points to the next entry in a single-linked list.

Comments

This structure can be used as the beginning of a single-linked list or as any subsequent entry in the list.

SIZE

```
typedef struct tagSIZE { /* siz */
    LONG cx;
    LONG cy;
} SIZE;
```

The **SIZE** structure specifies the width and height of a rectangle.

Members

cx

Specifies the rectangle's width.

cy

Specifies the rectangle's height.

Comments

The rectangle dimensions stored in this structure may correspond to viewport extents, window extents, text extents, bitmap dimensions, or the aspect-ratio filter for some extended functions.

See Also

GetAspectRatioFilterEx, GetBitmapDimensionEx, GetTextExtentPoint, GetViewportExtEx, GetWindowExtEx, ScaleViewportExtEx, ScaleWindowExtEx, SetBitmapDimensionEx, SetViewportExtEx, SetWindowExtEx

SMALL_RECT

```
typedef struct _SMALL_RECT { /* srct */
    SHORT Left;
    SHORT Top;
    SHORT Right;
    SHORT Bottom;
} SMALL_RECT;
```

The **SMALL_RECT** structure defines the coordinates of the upper-left and lower-right corners of a rectangle. This structure is used by console functions to specify rectangular areas of console screen buffers, where the coordinates specify the rows and columns of screen buffer character cells.

Members   **Left**
    Specifies the x-coordinate of the upper-left corner of the rectangle.

Top
    Specifies the y-coordinate of the upper-left corner of the rectangle.

Right
    Specifies the x-coordinate of the lower-right corner of the rectangle.

Bottom
    Specifies the y-coordinate of the lower-right corner of the rectangle.

See Also   **RECT, RECTL**

STARTUPINFO   New, Unicode

```
typedef struct _STARTUPINFO { /* si */
    DWORD   cb;
    LPTSTR  lpReserved;
    LPTSTR  lpDesktop;
    LPTSTR  lpTitle;
    DWORD   dwX;
    DWORD   dwY;
    DWORD   dwXSize;
    DWORD   dwYSize;
    DWORD   dwXCountChars;
    DWORD   dwYCountChars;
    DWORD   dwFillAttribute;
    DWORD   dwFlags;
    WORD    wShowWindow;
    WORD    cbReserved2;
```

```
    LPBYTE  lpReserved2;
    HANDLE  hStdInput;
    HANDLE  hStdOutput;
    HANDLE  hStdError;
} STARTUPINFO, *LPSTARTUPINFO;
```

The **STARTUPINFO** structure is used in the **CreateProcess** function to specify main window properties if a new window is created for the new process. For graphical user interface (GUI) processes, this affects the first window created by the **CreateWindow** function. For console processes, this affects the console window if a new console is created for the process. A process can use the **GetStartupInfo** function to retrieve the **STARTUPINFO** structure specified when it was created.

Members

cb

Specifies the size, in bytes, of the structure.

lpReserved

Reserved. Set this member to NULL before passing the structure to **CreateProcess**.

lpDesktop

If non-NULL, this parameter refers to the name of a desktop to start the process in. If the desktop exists, the new process is associated with this desktop. If the desktop does not exist, a desktop with default attributes is created by this name for the new process.

lpTitle

For console processes, this is the title displayed in the title bar if a new console window is created. If NULL, the name of the executable file is used as the window title instead. This parameter must be NULL for GUI or console processes that do not create a new console window.

dwX, dwY

Ignored unless **dwFlags** specifies STARTF_USEPOSITION. Specifies the x and y offsets, in pixels, of the upper left corner of a window if a new window is created. The offsets are from the upper left corner of the screen. For GUI processes, the specified position is used the first time **CreateWindow** is called to create an overlapped window if the *x* parameter of **CreateWindow** is CW_USEDEFAULT.

dwXSize, dwYSize

Ignored unless **dwFlags** specifies STARTF_USESIZE. Specifies the width (**dwXSize**) and height (**dwYSize**), in pixels, of the window if a new window is created. For GUI processes, this is used only the first time **CreateWindow** is called to create an overlapped window if the *nWidth* parameter of **CreateWindow** is CW_USEDEFAULT.

dwXCountChars, dwYCountChars

Ignored unless **dwFlags** specifies STARTF_USECOUNTCHARS. For console processes, specifies the screen buffer width (**dwXCountChars**) and height (**dwYCountChars**), in character columns and rows, if a new console window is created. These values are ignored in GUI processes.

dwFillAttribute

Ignored unless **dwFlags** specifies STARTF_USEFILLATTRIBUTE. For console processes, specifies the initial text and background colors if a new console window is created. These values are ignored in GUI processes.

dwFlags

This is a bit field that determines whether certain **STARTUPINFO** members are used when the process creates a window. Any combination of the following values can be specified:

Value	Meaning
STARTF_USESHOWWINDOW	If not specified, the **wShowWindow** member is ignored.
STARTF_USEPOSITION	If not specified, the **dwX** and **dwY** members are ignored.
STARTF_USESIZE	If not specified, the **dwXSize** and **dwYSize** members are ignored.
STARTF_USECOUNTCHARS	If not specified, the **dwXCountChars** and **dwYCountChars** members are ignored.
STARTF_USEFILLATTRIBUTE	If not specified, the **dwFillAttribute** member is ignored.
STARTF_FORCEONFEEDBACK	If specified, the cursor is in feedback mode for two seconds after **CreateProcess** is called. If during those two seconds, the process makes the first GUI call, the system gives five more seconds to the process. If during those five seconds, the process shows a window, the system gives five more seconds to the process to finish drawing the window. The system turns the feedback cursor off after the first call to **GetMessage**, regardless of whether the process is drawing. For more information on feedback, see the Comments section.
STARTF_FORCEOFFFEEDBACK	If specified, the feedback cursor is forced off while the process is starting. The normal cursor is displayed. For more information on feedback, see the Comments section.
STARTF_SCREENSAVER	

If specified, the system will treat this application as a screen saver. To wit:

- The system allows the application to initialize at the foreground priority of the priority class passed to the **CreateProcess** function.

- When the application looks for input via the **GetMessage** or **PeekMessage** function for the first time, the system changes it to the idle priority class. That lets background applications get priority over it.

- When the user moves the mouse or hits a key, the system gives the application the foreground priority of the priority class originally passed to the **CreateProcess** function.

Creating a screen saver with NORMAL_PRIORITY_CLASS lets the screen saver initialize and terminate over other normal priority applications.

STARTF_USESTDHANDLES

If specified, sets the process' standard input, standard output, and standard error handles to the handles specified in the **hStdInput**, **hStdOutput**, and **hStdError** fields of the **STARTUPINFO** structure. The **CreateProcess** function's *fInheritHandles* flag must be set to TRUE for this to work properly.

If not specified, any handles specified in the aforementioned standard handle fields of the **STARTUPINFO** structure are ignored.

wShowWindow

Ignored unless **dwFlags** specifies STARTF_USESHOWWINDOW. For GUI processes, specifies the default value the first time **ShowWindow** is called, if the *nCmdShow* parameter of **ShowWindow** is SW_SHOWDEFAULT. Can be any of the SW_ constants defined in WINUSER.H.

In previous versions of Windows, the **WinMain** function had an *nCmdShow* parameter that applications were encouraged to pass to the **CreateWindow** or **ShowWindow** function. The *nCmdShow* parameter is no longer available through **WinMain**. Now applications are encouraged to use SW_SHOWDEFAULT as the default **ShowWindow** command, in which case, **ShowWindow** uses the **wShowWindow** member of the process's **STARTUPINFO** structure.

cbReserved2

Reserved; must be zero.

lpReserved2

Reserved; must be NULL.

hStdInput

Ignored unless **dwFlags** specifies STARTF_USESTDHANDLES. Specifies a handle that will be used as the process' standard input handle if STARTF_USESTDHANDLES is specified.

hStdOutput

Ignored unless **dwFlags** specifies STARTF_USESTDHANDLES. Specifies a handle that will be used as the process' standard output handle if STARTF_USESTDHANDLES is specified.

hStdError

Ignored unless **dwFlags** specifies STARTF_USESTDHANDLES. Specifies a handle that will be used as the process' standard error handle if STARTF_USESTDHANDLES is specified.

Comments

If a GUI process is being started and neither STARTF_FORCEONFEEDBACK or STARTF_FORCEOFFFEEDBACK is specified, the process feedback cursor is used. A GUI process is one whose subsystem is specified as "windows".

WIN32_STREAM_ID

`New`

```
struct WIN32_STREAM_ID {
    DWORD dwStreamId;
    DWORD dwStreamAttributes;
    DWORD dwStreamSizeLow;
    DWORD dwStreamSizeHigh;
    DWORD dwStreamNameSize ;
    CHAR  cStreamName[ ] ;
}
```

Members

dwStreamId

Specifies the type of data. This member can be one of the following values:

Value	Meaning
BACKUP_DATA	Standard data
BACKUP_EA_DATA	Extended attribute data
BACKUP_SECURITY_DATA	Windows NT security descriptor data
BACKUP_ALTERNATE_DATA	Alternative data streams
BACKUP_LINK	Hard link information

dwStreamAttributes

Specifies the attributes of data to facilitate cross-operating system transfer. This member must be one or more of the following values:

Value	Description
STREAM_MODIFIED_WHEN_READ	Attribute set if the stream contains data that is modified when read. Allows the backup application to know that verification of data will fail.
STREAM_CONTAINS_SECURITY	Stream contains security data (general attributes). Allows the stream to be ignored on cross-operations restore.
STREAM_USER_ATTRIBUTE_ONE	Unused by the **BackupRead** and **BackupWrite** functions, but can be used by an application.
STREAM_USER_ATTRIBUTE_TWO	Unused by **BackupRead** and **BackupWrite**, but can be used by an application.

dwStreamSizeLow
Specifies the low-order 32 bits of the size, in bytes, of data.

dwStreamSizeHigh
Specifies the high-order 32 bits of the size needed to support large files.

dwStreamNameSize
Specifies the length of the name of the alternative data stream.

cStreamName
Specifies the name of the alternative data stream, in Unicode ™.

See Also   **BackupRead**, **BackupSeek**, **BackupWrite**

String

```
String {
    WCHAR  szKey[];
    BYTE   Padding[];
    String Value[];
} String;
```

The **String** structure depicts the organization of data in a file-version resource. This structure is not a true C data structure because it contains variable-length members. This structure was created solely to depict the organization of data in a version resource and does not appear in any of the header files shipped with the Microsoft ® Win32 ™ Software Development Kit (SDK).

The **String** structure contains a string that describes a specific aspect of a file.

Members	**szKey**

Specifies an arbitrary 7-bit ASCII English string. The **szKey** member can be one of the following values:

String	Description
Comments	**Value** contains any additional information that should be displayed for diagnostic purposes. This string is optional and can be of an arbitrary length.
CompanyName	**Value** identifies the company that produced the file. For example, "Microsoft Corporation" or "Standard Microsystems Corporation, Inc." This string is required.
FileDescription	**Value** describes the file in such a way that it can be presented to users. This string may be presented in a list box when the user is choosing files to install. For example, "Keyboard driver for AT-style keyboards" or "Microsoft Word for Windows". This string is required.
FileVersion	**Value** identifies the version of this file. For example, **Value** could be "3.00A" or "5.00.RC2". This string is required.
InternalName	**Value** identifies the file's internal name, if one exists. For example, this string would contain the module name for Windows dynamic-link libraries (DLLs), a virtual device name for Windows virtual devices, or a device name for MS-DOS device drivers. This string is required.
LegalCopyright	**Value** describes all copyright notices, trademarks, and registered trademarks that apply to the file. This should include the full text of all notices, legal symbols, copyright dates, trademark numbers, and so on. This string is optional. In English, this string should be in the format "Copyright Microsoft Corp. 1990–1992".
LegalTrademarks	**Value** describes all trademarks and registered trademarks that apply to the file. This should include the full text of all notices, legal symbols, trademark numbers, and so on. This string is optional. In English, this string should be in the format "Windows is a trademark of Microsoft Corporation".
OriginalFilename	**Value** identifies the original name of the file, not including a path. This enables an application to determine whether a file has been renamed by a user. This name may not be MS-DOS 8.3-format if the file is specific to a non-FAT file system. This string is required.
PrivateBuild	**Value** describes by whom, where, and why this private version of the file was built. This string should only be present if the VS_FF_PRIVATEBUILD flag is set in the **dwFileFlags** member of the **VS_FIXEDFILEINFO** structure. For example, **Value** could be "Built by OSCAR on \OSCAR2".

ProductName	**Value** identifies the name of the product with which this file is distributed. For example, this string could be "Microsoft Windows". This string is required.
ProductVersion	**Value** identifies the version of the product with which this file is distributed. For example, **Value** could be "3.00A" or "5.00.RC2". This string is required.
SpecialBuild	**Value** describes how this version of the file differs from the normal version. This entry should only be present if the VS_FF_SPECIALBUILD flag is set in the **dwFileFlags** member of the **VS_FIXEDFILEINFO** structure. For example, **Value** could be "Private build for Olivetti solving mouse problems on M250 and M250E computers".

Padding
Contains as many zero bytes as necessary to align the **Value** member on a 32-bit boundary.

Value
Specifies a zero-terminated string formatted in the language and code page indicated by the current **StringTable** structure. See the **szKey** description for more information.

Comments   For example, a **String** structure may have an **szKey** value of "CompanyName" and a **Value** of "Microsoft Corporation". Another **String** structure with the same **szKey** value could contain a **Value** of "Microsoft GmbH". This might occur if the second **String** structure were associated with a **StringTable** structure whose **szKey** value is 04070000, that is, German/ASCII.

See Also   **StringTable, VS_VERSION_INFO**

StringFileInfo

```
StringFileInfo {
    WCHAR       szKey[];
    BYTE        Padding[];
    StringTable Children[];
};
```

The **StringFileInfo** structure depicts the organization of data in a file-version resource. This structure is not a true C data structure because it contains variable-length members. This structure was created solely to depict the organization of data in a version resource and does not appear in any of the header files shipped with the Microsoft ® Win32 ™ Software Development Kit (SDK).

The **StringFileInfo** structure contains version information that must be displayed in a particular language and code page. A code page is an ordered character set.

Members   **szKey**
Contains "StringFileInfo".

Padding
Contains as many zero bytes as necessary to align the **Children** member on a 32-bit boundary.

Children
Specifies a list of one or more **StringTable** structures. Each **StringTable** structure's **szKey** member indicates the appropriate language and code-page formatting.

Comments   The **Children** member of the **VS_VERSION_INFO** structure may contain zero or more **StringFileInfo** structures.

See Also   **StringTable**, **VS_VERSION_INFO**

StringTable

```
StringTable {
    WCHAR  szKey[];
    BYTE   Padding[];
    String Children[];
};
```

The **StringTable** structure depicts the organization of data in a file-version resource. This structure is not a true C data structure because it contains variable-length members. This structure was created solely to depict the organization of data in a version resource and does not appear in any of the header files shipped with the Microsoft ® Win32 ™ Software Development Kit (SDK).

The **StringTable** structure contains language and code-page formatting information for the strings specified by the **Children** member. A code page is an ordered character set.

An executable file or dynamic-link library (DLL) that supports multiple languages should have a version resource for each language, rather than a single version resource that contains strings in several languages.

Members   **szKey**
Specifies an 8-digit hexadecimal number stored as a string. The four most significant digits represent the language identifier, and the four least significant digits represent the code page for which the data is formatted.

Each Microsoft Standard Language identifier contains two parts: the low-order 10 bits specify the major language and the high-order 6 bits specify the sublanguage. The following language identifiers are valid:

Identifier	Language
0x0401	Arabic
0x0402	Bulgarian
0x0403	Catalan
0x0404	Traditional Chinese
0x0804	Simplified Chinese
0x0405	Czech
0x0406	Danish
0x0407	German
0x0807	Swiss German
0x0408	Greek
0x0409	U.S. English
0x0809	U.K. English
0x040A	Castilian Spanish
0x080A	Mexican Spanish
0x040B	Finnish
0x040C	French
0x080C	Belgian French
0x0C0C	Canadian French
0x100C	Swiss French
0x040D	Hebrew
0x040E	Hungarian
0x040F	Icelandic
0x0410	Italian
0x0810	Swiss Italian
0x0411	Japanese
0x0412	Korean
0x0413	Dutch
0x0813	Belgian Dutch
0x0414	Norwegian—Bokmål
0x0814	Norwegian—Nynorsk
0x0415	Polish
0x0416	Brazilian Portuguese

0x0816	Portuguese
0x0417	Rhaeto-Romanic
0x0418	Romanian
0x0419	Russian
0x041A	Croato-Serbian (Latin)
0x081A	Serbo-Croatian (Cyrillic)
0x041B	Slovak
0x041C	Albanian
0x041D	Swedish
0x041E	Thai
0x041F	Turkish
0x0420	Urdu
0x0421	Bahasa

The code-page value can be one of the following or any IBM-registered code page:

Code page	Description
0	7-bit ASCII
932	Windows, Japan (Shift—JIS X-0208)
949	Windows, Korea (Shift—KSC 5601)
950	Windows, Taiwan (GB5)
1200	Unicode
1250	Windows, Latin-2 (Eastern European)
1251	Windows, Cyrillic
1252	Windows, Multilingual (ANSI)
1253	Windows, Greek
1254	Windows, Turkish
1255	Windows, Hebrew
1256	Windows, Arabic

Files designed for the English version of Windows would normally be marked with a code-page value of 1252.

Padding

Contains as many zero bytes as necessary to align the **Children** member on a 32-bit boundary.

Children

Specifies a list of zero or more **String** structures.

Comments

The **Children** member of the **StringFileInfo** structure contains at least one **StringTable** structure with an **szKey** value of "04090000". This value indicates that the language is U.S. English and the code page is generic 7-bit ASCII.

See Also

String, **StringFileInfo**, **VS_VERSION_INFO**

SYSTEM_ALARM_ACE

New

Reserved for future use.

SYSTEM_AUDIT_ACE

New

```
typedef struct _SYSTEM_AUDIT_ACE { /* sada */
    ACE_HEADER  Header;
    ACCESS_MASK Mask;
    DWORD       SidStart;
} SYSTEM_AUDIT_ACE;
```

The **SYSTEM_AUDIT_ACE** structure defines an access-control entry (ACE) for the system access-control list (ACL) specifying what types of access cause system-level notifications. A system-audit ACE causes an audit message to be logged when a specified user or group attempts to gain access to an object. The user or group is identified by a security identifier (SID).

Members

Header

Specifies an **ACE_HEADER** structure.

Mask

Specifies an **ACCESS_MASK** structure that gives the access rights causing audit messages to be generated. The SUCCESSFUL_ACCESS_ACE_FLAG and FAILED_ACCESS_ACE_FLAG flags in the **AceFlags** member of the **ACE_HEADER** structure indicate whether messages are generated for successful access attempts, unsuccessful access attempts, or both.

SidStart

Specifies an SID. An access attempt of a kind specified by the **Mask** member by any user or group whose SID matches the **SidStart** member causes the system to generate an audit message. If an application does not specify an SID for this member, audit messages are generated for the specified access rights for all users and groups.

Comments

Audit messages are stored in an event log that can be manipulated by using the Win32 API event-logging functions or by using Windows NT Event Viewer (EVENTVWR.EXE).

ACE structures should be aligned on doubleword boundaries. All Windows memory-management functions return doubleword-aligned handles to memory.

See Also

ACCESS_ALLOWED_ACE, ACCESS_DENIED_ACE, ACCESS_MASK, ACE_HEADER, ACL, SYSTEM_ALARM_ACE

SYSTEM_INFO

New

```
typedef struct _SYSTEM_INFO { /* sinf */
    DWORD   dwOemId;
    DWORD   dwPageSize;
    LPVOID  lpMinimumApplicationAddress;
    LPVOID  lpMaximumApplicationAddress;
    DWORD   dwActiveProcessorMask;
    DWORD   dwNumberOfProcessors;
    DWORD   dwProcessorType;
    DWORD   dwReserved1;
    DWORD   dwReserved2;
} SYSTEM_INFO;
```

The **SYSTEM_INFO** structure contains information about the current computer system. This information includes the processor type, page size, original equipment manufacturer (OEM) identifier, and other such information.

Members

dwOemId

Returns a computer identifier that is specific to a particular OEM.

dwPageSize

Returns the page size and specifies the granularity of page protection and commitment.

lpMinimumApplicationAddress

Returns the lowest memory address accessible to applications and dynamic-link libraries (DLLs).

lpMaximumApplicationAddress

Returns the highest memory address accessible to applications and DLLs.

dwActiveProcessorMask

Returns a mask representing the set of processors configured into the system. Bit 0 is processor 0; bit 31 is processor 31.

dwNumberOfProcessors

Returns the number of processors in the system.

dwProcessorType

Returns the type of the current processors in the system. All processors are assumed to be of the same type, have the same stepping, and are configured with the same options.

The following processor type constants are currently defined :

PROCESSOR_INTEL_386
PROCESSOR_INTEL_486
PROCESSOR_INTEL_860
PROCESSOR_MIPS_R2000
PROCESSOR_MIPS_R3000
PROCESSOR_MIPS_R4000
PROCESSOR_ALPHA_21064

dwReserved1

Reserved.

dwReserved2

Reserved.

SYSTEMTIME

```
typedef struct _SYSTEMTIME {  /* st */
    WORD wYear;
    WORD wMonth;
    WORD wDayOfWeek;
    WORD wDay;
    WORD wHour;
    WORD wMinute;
    WORD wSecond;
    WORD wMilliseconds;
} SYSTEMTIME;
```

The **SYSTEMTIME** structure represents a date and time using individual members for the month, day, year, weekday, hour, minute, second, and millisecond.

Members

wYear
Specifies the current year.

wMonth
Specifies the current month; January = 1.

wDayOfWeek
Specifies the current day of the week; Sunday = 0, Monday = 1, etc.

wDay
Specifies the current day of the month.

wHour
Specifies the current hour.

wMinute
Specifies the current minute.

wSecond
Specifies the current second.

wMilliseconds
Specifies the current millisecond.

See Also

GetLocalTime, GetSystemTime, SetLocalTime, SetSystemTime, FILETIME

TAPE_CREATE_PARTITION

```
typedef struct _TAPE_CREATE_PARTITION {   /* tcp */
    ULONG Method;
    ULONG Count;
    ULONG Size;
} TAPE_CREATE_PARTITION;
```

The **TAPE_CREATE_PARTITION** structure describes the size and number of tape partitions of a specified type.

Members

Method

Specifies the type of partition. This member must have one of the following values:

Value	Meaning
TAPE_PARTITION_FIXED	Indicates that the partition parameters are fixed by the device.
TAPE_PARTITION_INITIATOR	Indicates that the number of partitions is specified by **Count** and the partition sizes are specified in the **Size** array.
TAPE_PARTITION_SELECT	Indicates that the number of partitions is specified by **Count** and the partition sizes are defined by the device.

Count

Specifies the number of partitions to create and the number of elements in the **Size** array.

Size

Specifies the size, in megabytes, of each partition. If this value is zero, the partition is the size of the rest of the storage space on the tape.

TAPE_ERASE

```
typedef struct _TAPE_ERASE { /* ter */
    ULONG Type;
} TAPE_ERASE;
```

The **TAPE_ERASE** structure describes the partition to be erased.

Members   **Type**
Specifies how to erase the tape. This member must have one of the following values:

Value	Description
TAPE_ERASE_LONG	Erases the entire partition.
TAPE_ERASE_SHORT	Erases only the partition's header block.

TAPE_GET_DRIVE_PARAMETERS   `New`

```
typedef struct _TAPE_GET_DRIVE_PARAMETERS { /* tgdp */
    BOOLEAN ECC;
    BOOLEAN Compression;
    BOOLEAN DataPadding;
    BOOLEAN ReportSetmarks;
    ULONG   DefaultBlockSize;
    ULONG   MaximumBlockSize;
    ULONG   MinimumBlockSize;
    ULONG   MaximumPartitionCount;
    ULONG   FeaturesLow;
    ULONG   FeaturesHigh;
    ULONG   EOTWarningZoneSize;
} TAPE_GET_DRIVE_PARAMETERS;
```

The **TAPE_GET_DRIVE_PARAMETERS** structure describes the tape drive.

Members   **ECC**
Specifies whether the device supports hardware error correction. This member is TRUE if hardware error correction is supported.

Compression
Specifies whether hardware data compression is enabled or disabled. This member is TRUE if hardware data compression is enabled.

DataPadding
Specifies whether data padding is enabled or disabled. Data padding keeps the tape streaming at a constant speed. This member is TRUE if data padding is enabled.

ReportSetmarks
Specifies whether setmark reporting is enabled or disabled. This member is TRUE if setmark reporting is enabled.

DefaultBlockSize
Specifies the device's default fixed block size.

MaximumBlockSize
Specifies the device's maximum block size.

MinimumBlockSize
Specifies the device's minimum block size.

MaximumPartitionCount
Specifies the maximum number of partitions that can be created on the device.

FeaturesLow
Specifies the low-order 32 bits of the device features flag. This member can have one or more of following bits set:

Value	Meaning
TAPE_DRIVE_COMPRESSION	Device supports hardware data compression.
TAPE_DRIVE_ECC	Device supports hardware error correction.
TAPE_DRIVE_ERASE_BOP_ONLY	Device performs the erase operation from the beginning-of-partition marker only.
TAPE_DRIVE_ERASE_LONG	Device performs a long erase operation.
TAPE_DRIVE_ERASE_IMMEDIATE	Device performs an immediate erase operation— that is, it returns when the erase operation begins.
TAPE_DRIVE_ERASE_SHORT	Device performs a short erase operation.
TAPE_DRIVE_FIXED	Device creates fixed data partitions.
TAPE_DRIVE_FIXED_BLOCK	Device supports fixed-length block mode.
TAPE_DRIVE_INITIATOR	Device creates initiator-defined partitions.
TAPE_DRIVE_PADDING	Device supports data padding.
TAPE_DRIVE_GET_ABSOLUTE_BLK	Device provides the current device-specific block address.
TAPE_DRIVE_GET_LOGICAL_BLK	Device provides the current logical block address (and logical tape partition).
TAPE_DRIVE_REPORT_SMKS	Device supports setmark reporting.
TAPE_DRIVE_SELECT	Device creates select data partitions.
TAPE_DRIVE_SET_EOT_WT_SIZE	Device supports setting the end-of-medium warning size.
TAPE_DRIVE_TAPE_CAPACITY	Device returns the maximum capacity of the tape.

TAPE_DRIVE_TAPE_REMAINING	Device returns the remaining capacity of the tape.
TAPE_DRIVE_VARIABLE_BLOCK	Device supports variable-length block mode.
TAPE_DRIVE_WRITE_PROTECT	Device returns an error if the tape is write-enabled or write-protected.

FeaturesHigh

Contains the high-order 32 bits of the device features flag. This member can have one or more of the following bits set:

Value	Meaning
TAPE_DRIVE_ABS_BLK_IMMED	Device moves the tape to a device-specific block address and returns as soon as the move begins.
TAPE_DRIVE_ABSOLUTE_BLK	Device moves the tape to a device specific block address.
TAPE_DRIVE_END_OF_DATA	Device moves the tape to the end-of-data marker in a partition.
TAPE_DRIVE_FILEMARKS	Device moves the tape forward (or backward) a specified number of filemarks.
TAPE_DRIVE_LOAD_UNLOAD	Device enables and disables the device for further operations.
TAPE_DRIVE_LOAD_UNLOAD_IMMED	Device supports immediate load and unload operations.
TAPE_DRIVE_LOCK_UNLOCK	Device enables and disables the tape ejection mechanism.
TAPE_DRIVE_LOCK_UNLK_IMMED	Device supports immediate lock and unlock operations.
TAPE_DRIVE_LOG_BLK_IMMED	Device moves the tape to a logical block address in a partition and returns as soon as the move begins.
TAPE_DRIVE_LOGICAL_BLK	Device moves the tape to a logical block address in a partition.
TAPE_DRIVE_RELATIVE_BLKS	Device moves the tape forward (or backward) a specified number of blocks.
TAPE_DRIVE_REVERSE_POSITION	Device moves the tape backward over blocks, filemarks, or setmarks.

TAPE_DRIVE_REWIND_IMMEDIATE	Device supports immediate rewind operation.
TAPE_DRIVE_SEQUENTIAL_FMKS	Device moves the tape forward (or backward) to the first occurrence of a specified number of consecutive filemarks.
TAPE_DRIVE_SEQUENTIAL_SMKS	Device moves the tape forward (or backward) to the first occurrence of a specified number of consecutive setmarks.
TAPE_DRIVE_SET_BLOCK_SIZE	Device supports setting the size of a fixed-length logical block or setting the variable-length block mode.
TAPE_DRIVE_SET_COMPRESSION	Device enables and disables hardware data compression.
TAPE_DRIVE_SET_ECC	Device enables and disables hardware error correction.
TAPE_DRIVE_SET_PADDING	Device enables and disables data padding.
TAPE_DRIVE_SET_REPORT_SMKS	Device enables and disables the reporting of setmarks.
TAPE_DRIVE_SETMARKS	Device moves the tape forward (or reverse) a specified number of setmarks.
TAPE_DRIVE_SPACE_IMMEDIATE	Device supports immediate spacing.
TAPE_DRIVE_TENSION	Device supports tape tensioning.
TAPE_DRIVE_TENSION_IMMED	Device supports immediate tape tensioning.
TAPE_DRIVE_WRITE_FILEMARKS	Device writes filemarks.
TAPE_DRIVE_WRITE_LONG_FMKS	Device writes long filemarks.
TAPE_DRIVE_WRITE_MARK_IMMED	Device supports immediate writing of short and long filemarks.
TAPE_DRIVE_WRITE_SETMARKS	Device writes setmarks.
TAPE_DRIVE_WRITE_SHORT_FMKS	Device writes short filemarks.

EOTWarningZoneSize
Indicates the number of bytes between the end-of-tape warning and the physical end of the tape.

TAPE_GET_MEDIA_PARAMETERS

New

```
typedef struct _TAPE_GET_MEDIA_PARAMETERS {  /* tgmp */
    LARGE_INTEGER   Capacity;
    LARGE_INTEGER   Remaining;
    DWORD   BlockSize;
    DWORD   PartitionCount;
    BOOLEAN WriteProtected;
} TAPE_GET_MEDIA_PARAMETERS;
```

The **TAPE_GET_MEDIA_PARAMETERS** structure describes the tape in the tape drive.

Members

Capacity
Specifies the total number of bytes on the tape.

Remaining
Specifies the number of bytes between the current position and the end of the tape.

BlockSize
Specifies the number of bytes per block. Block sizes are typically multiples of 512 bytes, in the range 512 bytes through 32 kilobytes.

PartitionCount
Specifies the number of partitions on the tape.

WriteProtected
Specifies whether the tape is write-protected. If this member is TRUE, the tape is write-protected.

Comments
The **GetTapeParameters** function fills the **RemainingLow**, **RemainingHigh**, **CapacityLow**, and **CapacityHigh** members with estimates of the tape remaining and the total capacity.

TAPE_GET_POSITION

New

```
typedef struct _TAPE_GET_POSITION { /* tgpos */
    ULONG Type;
    ULONG Partition;
    ULONG OffsetLow;
    ULONG OffsetHigh;
} TAPE_GET_POSITION;
```

The **TAPE_GET_POSITION** structure describes the position of the tape.

Members

Type

Specifies the type of position. This member must be one of the following values:

Value	Description
TAPE_ABSOLUTE_POSITION	Position specified by the **OffsetLow** and **OffsetHigh** members is an absolute number of blocks from the beginning of the partition specified by the **Partition** member.
TAPE_LOGICAL_POSITION	Position specified by **OffsetLow** and **OffsetHigh** is relative to the current position in the partition specified by **Partition**.

Partition

Specifies the partition to position within. If this member is zero, the current partition is assumed.

OffsetLow

Specifies the low-order 32 bits of the block address.

OffsetHigh

Specifies the high-order 32 bits of the block address. If the high-order 32 bits are not required, this parameter should be zero.

TAPE_SET_POSITION

`New`

```
typedef struct _TAPE_SET_POSITION { /* tspos */
    ULONG Method;
    ULONG Partition;
    ULONG OffsetLow;
    ULONG OffsetHigh;
} TAPE_SET_POSITION;
```

The **TAPE_SET_POSITION** structure describes how and where to position the tape.

Members

Method

Specifies the type of positioning. This member must be one of the following values:

Value	Description
TAPE_ABSOLUTE_BLOCK	Moves the tape to the device-specific block address specified by the **OffsetLow** and **OffsetHigh** members. The the **Partition** member is ignored.
TAPE_LOGICAL_BLOCK	Moves the tape to the block address specified by **OffsetLow** and **OffsetHigh** in the partition specified by **Partition**.
TAPE_REWIND	Moves the tape to the beginning of the current partition. The **Partition**, **OffsetLow**, and **OffsetHigh** members are ignored.
TAPE_SPACE_END_OF_DATA	Moves the tape to the end of the data on the partition specified by **Partition**.
TAPE_SPACE_FILEMARKS	Moves the tape forward (or backward) the number of filemarks specified by **OffsetLow** and **OffsetHigh** in the current partition. The **Partition** member is ignored.
TAPE_SPACE_RELATIVE_BLOCKS	Moves the tape forward (or backward) the number of blocks specified by **OffsetLow** and **OffsetHigh** in the current partition. The **Partition** members is ignored.
TAPE_SPACE_SEQUENTIAL_FMKS	Moves the tape forward (or backward) to the first occurrence of n filemarks in the current partition, where n is the number specified by **OffsetLow** and **OffsetHigh**. The **Partition** parameter is ignored.
TAPE_SPACE_SEQUENTIAL_SMKS	Moves the tape forward (or backward) to the first occurrence of n setmarks in the current partition, where n is the number specified by **OffsetLow** and **OffsetHigh**. The **Partition** member is ignored.
TAPE_SPACE_SETMARKS	Moves the tape forward (or backward) the number of setmarks specified by **OffsetLow** and **OffsetHigh** in the current partition. The **Partition** member is ignored.

Partition

Specifies the partition to position within. If this member is zero, the current partition is assumed.

OffsetLow

Specifies the low-order 32 bits of the block address or count for the position operation specified by the **Method** member.

OffsetHigh

Specifies the high-order 32 bits of the block address or count for the position operation specified by the **Method** member. If the high-order 32 bits are not required, this parameter should be zero.

Comments   If the positioning is relative, a positive offset moves the tape forward (toward the end of the tape) and a negative offset moves the tape backward (toward the beginning of the tape).

TAPE_PREPARE

New

```
typedef struct _TAPE_PREPARE { /* tp */
    ULONG Operation;
} TAPE_PREPARE;
```

The **TAPE_PREPARE** structure describes how to prepare the tape.

Members   **Operation**

Specifies how to prepare the tape. This member must be one of the following values:

Value	Description
TAPE_LOCK	Locks the tape ejection mechanism. This prevents the tape from being ejected accidentally during a tape operation.
TAPE_TENSION	Moves to the end of the tape and rewinds to the beginning of the tape. This value is ignored if the tape device does not support this action.
TAPE_UNLOAD	Rewinds and unloads the tape.
TAPE_UNLOCK	Unlocks the tape ejection mechanism.

TAPE_SET_DRIVE_PARAMETERS

```
typedef struct _TAPE_SET_DRIVE_PARAMETERS {  /* tsdp */
    BOOLEAN ECC;
    BOOLEAN Compression;
    BOOLEAN DataPadding;
    BOOLEAN ReportSetmarks;
    ULONG   EOTWarningZoneSize;
} TAPE_SET_DRIVE_PARAMETERS;
```

The **TAPE_SET_DRIVE_PARAMETERS** structure describes the tape drive.

Members

ECC

Specifies whether the device supports hardware error correction. This member is TRUE if hardware error correction is supported.

Compression

Specifies whether hardware data compression is enabled or disabled. This member is TRUE if hardware data compression is enabled.

DataPadding

Specifies whether data padding is enabled or disabled. Data padding keeps the tape streaming at a constant speed. This member is TRUE if data padding is enabled.

ReportSetmarks

Specifies whether setmark reporting is enabled or disabled. This member is TRUE if setmarks are enabled.

EOTWarningZoneSize

Specifies the number of bytes between the end-of-tape warning and the physical end of the tape.

TAPE_SET_MEDIA_PARAMETERS

```
typedef struct _TAPE_SET_MEDIA_PARAMETERS { /* tsmp */
    ULONG BlockSize;
} TAPE_SET_MEDIA_PARAMETERS;
```

The **TAPE_SET_MEDIA_PARAMETERS** structure describes the tape in the tape drive.

Members   **BlockSize**

Specifies the number of bytes per block. Block sizes should be powers of 2 : values like 256, 512, 1024, and 204k. Maximum and minimum block sizes can be obtained by calling the **GetTapeParameters** function.

See Also   **GetTapeParameters**, **SetTapeParameters**

TAPE_WRITE_MARKS

`New`

```
typedef struct _TAPE_WRITE_MARKS { /* twm */
    ULONG Type;
    ULONG Count;
} TAPE_WRITE_MARKS;
```

The **TAPE_WRITE_MARKS** structure describes the type and number of tapemarks to write.

Members   **Type**

Specifies the type of tapemark to write. This member can be one of the following values:

Value	Description
TAPE_LONG_FILEMARKS	Writes long filemarks.
TAPE_SEQUENTIAL_FILEMARKS	Writes sequential filemarks.
TAPE_SETMARKS	Writes setmarks.
TAPE_SHORT_FILEMARKS	Writes short filemarks.

Count

Specifies the number of tapemarks to write.

TEXTMETRIC

`Unicode`

```
typedef struct tagTEXTMETRIC { /* tm */
    LONG tmHeight;
    LONG tmAscent;
    LONG tmDescent;
    LONG tmInternalLeading;
    LONG tmExternalLeading;
    LONG tmAveCharWidth;
    LONG tmMaxCharWidth;
    LONG tmWeight;
    LONG tmOverhang;
```

```
      LONG tmDigitizedAspectX;
      LONG tmDigitizedAspectY;
      BYTE tmFirstChar;
      BYTE tmLastChar;
      BYTE tmDefaultChar;
      BYTE tmBreakChar;
      BYTE tmItalic;
      BYTE tmUnderlined;
      BYTE tmStruckOut;
      BYTE tmPitchAndFamily;
      BYTE tmCharSet;
} TEXTMETRIC;
```

The **TEXTMETRIC** structure contains basic information about a physical font. All sizes are given in logical units; that is, they depend on the current mapping mode of the display context.

Members

tmHeight
Specifies the height (ascent + descent) of characters.

tmAscent
Specifies the ascent (units above the base line) of characters.

tmDescent
Specifies the descent (units below the base line) of characters.

tmInternalLeading
Specifies the amount of leading (space) inside the bounds set by the **tmHeight** member. Accent marks and other diacritical characters may occur in this area. The designer may set this member to zero.

tmExternalLeading
Specifies the amount of extra leading (space) that the application adds between rows. Since this area is outside the font, it contains no marks and is not altered by text output calls in either OPAQUE or TRANSPARENT mode. The designer may set this member to zero.

tmAveCharWidth
Specifies the average width of characters in the font (generally defined as the width of the letter *x*). This value does not include overhang required for bold or italic characters.

tmMaxCharWidth
Specifies the width of the widest character in the font.

tmWeight
Specifies the weight of the font.

tmOverhang
Specifies the extra width per string that may be added to some synthesized fonts. When synthesizing some attributes, such as bold or italic, graphics device interface (GDI) or a device may have to add width to a string on both a

per-character and per-string basis. For example, GDI makes a string bold by expanding the spacing of each character and overstriking by an offset value; it italicizes a font by shearing the string. In either case, there is an overhang past the basic string. For bold strings, the overhang is the distance by which the overstrike is offset. For italic strings, the overhang is the amount the top of the font is sheared past the bottom of the font.

The **tmOverhang** member enables the application to determine how much of the character width returned by a **GetTextExtentPoint** function call on a single character is the actual character width and how much is the per-string extra width. The actual width is the extent minus the overhang.

tmDigitizedAspectX
Specifies the horizontal aspect of the device for which the font was designed.

tmDigitizedAspectY
Specifies the vertical aspect of the device for which the font was designed. The ratio of the **tmDigitizedAspectX** and **tmDigitizedAspectY** members is the aspect ratio of the device for which the font was designed.

tmFirstChar
Specifies the value of the first character defined in the font.

tmLastChar
Specifies the value of the last character defined in the font.

tmDefaultChar
Specifies the value of the character to be substituted for characters not in the font.

tmBreakChar
Specifies the value of the character that will be used to define word breaks for text justification.

tmItalic
Specifies an italic font if it is nonzero.

tmUnderlined
Specifies an underlined font if it is nonzero.

tmStruckOut
Specifies a strikeout font if it is nonzero.

tmPitchAndFamily
Specifies the pitch and family of the selected font. The low-order bit specifies the pitch of the font. If it is 1, the font is variable pitch. If it is 0, the font is fixed pitch.

The four high-order bits designate the font family. The **tmPitchAndFamily** member can be combined with the hexadecimal value 0xF0 by using the bitwise AND operator and can then be compared with the font family names for an identical match. For information about the font families, see the description of the **LOGFONT** structure.

tmCharSet
Specifies the character set of the font.

See Also   **GetTextMetrics, LOGFONT**

TIME_ZONE_INFORMATION

New

```
typedef struct _TIME_ZONE_INFORMATION { /* tzi */
    LONG       Bias;
    WCHAR      StandardName[ 32 ];
    SYSTEMTIME StandardDate;
    LONG       StandardBias;
    WCHAR      DaylightName[ 32 ];
    SYSTEMTIME DaylightDate;
    LONG       DaylightBias;
} TIME_ZONE_INFORMATION;
```

The **TIME_ZONE_INFORMATION** structure specifies information specific to the time zone.

Members   **Bias**
Specifies the current bias, in minutes, for local time translation on this computer. The bias is the difference, in minutes, between Universal Time Convention (UTC) time and local time. All translations between UTC time and local time are based on the following formula:

```
UTC = local time + bias
```

This member is required.

StandardName
Specifies a null-terminated string associated with standard time on this operating system. For example, this parameter could contain "EST" to indicate Eastern Standard Time. This string is not used by the operating system, so anything stored there by using the **SetTimeZoneInformation** function is returned unchanged by the **GetTimeZoneInformation** function. This string can be empty.

StandardDate
Specifies a **SYSTEMTIME** structure that contains a date and UTC time when the transition from daylight time to standard time occurs on this operating system. If this date is not specified, the **wMonth** member in the **SYSTEMTIME** structure must be zero. If this date is specified, the **DaylightDate** value in the **TIME_ZONE_INFORMATION** structure must also be specified. Local time translations done during the standard-time range are relative to the supplied **StandardBias** value.

This member supports two date formats. Absolute format specifies an exact date and time when standard time begins. In this form, the **wYear**, **wMonth**, **wDay**, **wHour**, **wMinute**, **wSecond**, and **wMilliseconds** members of the **SYSTEMTIME** structure are used to specify an exact date.

Day-in-month format is specified by setting the **wYear** member to zero, setting the **wDayOfWeek** member to an appropriate weekday, and using a **wDay** value in the range 1 through 5 to select the correct day in the month. Using this notation, the first Sunday in April can be specified, as can the last Thursday in October (5 is equal to "the last").

StandardBias

Specifies a bias value to be used during local time translations that occur during standard time. This member is ignored if a value for the **StandardDate** member is not supplied.

This value is added to the value of the **Bias** member to form the bias used during standard time. In most time zones, the value of this member is zero.

DaylightName

Specifies a null-terminated string associated with daylight time on this operating system. For example, this parameter could contain "PDT" to indicate Pacific Daylight Time. This string is not used by the operating system, so anything stored there by using the **SetTimeZoneInformation** function is returned unchanged by the **GetTimeZoneInformation** function. This string can be empty.

DaylightDate

Specifies a **SYSTEMTIME** structure that contains a date and UTC time when the transition from standard time to daylight time occurs on this operating system. If this date is not specified, the **wMonth** member in the **SYSTEMTIME** structure must be zero. If this date is specified, the **StandardDate** value in the **TIME_ZONE_INFORMATION** structure must also be specified. Local time translations during the daylight-time range are relative to the supplied **DaylightBias** value. This member supports the absolute and day-in-month time formats described for the **StandardDate** member.

DaylightBias

Specifies a bias value to be used during local time translations that occur during daylight time. This member is ignored if a value for the **DaylightDate** member is not supplied.

This value is added to the value of the **Bias** member to form the bias used during daylight time. In most time zones, the value of this member is –60.

See Also   **GetTimeZoneInformation**, **SetTimeZoneInformation**

TIMECAPS

```
typedef struct timecaps_tag {
    UINT  wPeriodMin;
    UINT  wPeriodMax;
} TIMECAPS;
```

The **TIMECAPS** structure contains information about the resolution of the timer.

Members

wPeriodMin
Minimum period supported by the timer, in milliseconds.

wPeriodMax
Maximum period supported by the timer, in milliseconds.

See Also

timeGetDevCaps

TOKEN_CONTROL

New

```
typedef struct _TOKEN_CONTROL { /* tc */
    LUID TokenId;
    LUID AuthenticationId;
    LUID ModifiedId;
    TOKEN_SOURCE TokenSource;
} TOKEN_CONTROL ;
```

The **TOKEN_CONTROL** structure contains information that identifies an access token.

Members

TokenId
Specifies a locally unique identifier (LUID) identifying this instance of the token object.

AuthenticationId
Specifies an LUID assigned to the session this token represents. There can be many tokens representing a single logon session.

ModifiedId
Specifies an LUID that changes each time the token is modified. An application can use this value as a test of whether a security context has changed since it was last used.

TokenSource
Specifies a **TOKEN_SOURCE** structure identifying the agency that issued the token. This information is used in audit logging.

See Also   **LUID, TOKEN_DEFAULT_DACL, TOKEN_GROUPS, TOKEN_INFORMATION_CLASS, TOKEN_OWNER, TOKEN_PRIMARY_GROUP, TOKEN_PRIVILEGES, TOKEN_SOURCE, TOKEN_STATISTICS, TOKEN_TYPE, TOKEN_USER**

TOKEN_DEFAULT_DACL   `New`

```
typedef struct _TOKEN_DEFAULT_DACL {   /* tdd */
    PACL DefaultDacl;
} TOKEN_DEFAULT_DACL;
```

The **TOKEN_DEFAULT_DACL** structure specifies a discretionary access-control list (ACL).

Members   **DefaultDacl**
Points to an **ACL** structure assigned by default to any objects created by the user represented by the access token.

Comments   The **GetTokenInformation** function retrieves the default discretionary ACL for an access token, in the form of a **TOKEN_DEFAULT_DACL** structure. This structure is also used with the **SetTokenInformation** function to set the default discretionary ACL.

See Also   **GetTokenInformation, SetTokenInformation, ACL, TOKEN_CONTROL, TOKEN_GROUPS, TOKEN_INFORMATION_CLASS, TOKEN_OWNER, TOKEN_PRIMARY_GROUP, TOKEN_PRIVILEGES, TOKEN_SOURCE, TOKEN_STATISTICS, TOKEN_TYPE, TOKEN_USER**

TOKEN_GROUPS   `New`

```
typedef struct _TOKEN_GROUPS { /* tg */
    DWORD GroupCount;
    SID_AND_ATTRIBUTES Groups[ANYSIZE_ARRAY];
} TOKEN_GROUPS;
```

The **TOKEN_GROUPS** structure contains information about a set of groups in an access token.

Members   **GroupCount**
Specifies the number of groups in the access token.

Groups

Specifies an array of **SID_AND_ATTRIBUTES** structures containing a token's group security identifiers (SIDs) and corresponding attributes.

The following attributes can be used with this parameter:

Value	Meaning
SE_GROUP_MANDATORY	The group cannot be disabled.
SE_GROUP_ENABLED_BY_DEFAULT	The group is enabled by default.
SE_GROUP_ENABLED	The group is enabled.
SE_GROUP_OWNER	The user is the owner of the group or the SID can be assigned as the owner of the token or objects.
SE_GROUP_LOGON_ID	The group is a logon identifier.

See Also   **AdjustTokenGroups, SID_AND_ATTRIBUTES, TOKEN_CONTROL, TOKEN_DEFAULT_DACL, TOKEN_INFORMATION_CLASS, TOKEN_OWNER, TOKEN_PRIMARY_GROUP, TOKEN_PRIVILEGES, TOKEN_SOURCE, TOKEN_STATISTICS, TOKEN_TYPE, TOKEN_USER**

TOKEN_INFORMATION_CLASS

New

```
typedef enum tagTOKEN_INFORMATION_CLASS { /* tic */
    TokenUser = 1,
    TokenGroups,
    TokenPrivileges,
    TokenOwner,
    TokenPrimaryGroup,
    TokenDefaultDacl,
    TokenSource,
    TokenType,
    TokenImpersonationLevel,
    TokenStatistics
} TOKEN_INFORMATION_CLASS;
```

The **TOKEN_INFORMATION_CLASS** enumerated type is used to indicate the type of information being assigned to or retrieved from an access token.

See Also   **GetTokenInformation, SetTokenInformation, TOKEN_CONTROL, TOKEN_DEFAULT_DACL, TOKEN_GROUPS, TOKEN_OWNER, TOKEN_PRIMARY_GROUP, TOKEN_PRIVILEGES, TOKEN_SOURCE, TOKEN_STATISTICS, TOKEN_TYPE, TOKEN_USER**

TOKEN_OWNER

`New`

```
typedef struct _TOKEN_OWNER { /* to */
    PSID Owner;
} TOKEN_OWNER;
```

The **TOKEN_OWNER** structure contains information about the owner of an access token.

Members   **Owner**

Points to an **SID** structure representing a user who will become the owner of any objects created by a process using this access token. The security identifier (SID) must be one of the user or group SIDs already in the token.

See Also   **GetTokenInformation, SetTokenInformation, SID TOKEN_CONTROL, TOKEN_DEFAULT_DACL, TOKEN_GROUPS, TOKEN_INFORMATION_CLASS, TOKEN_PRIMARY_GROUP, TOKEN_PRIVILEGES, TOKEN_SOURCE, TOKEN_STATISTICS, TOKEN_TYPE, TOKEN_USER**

TOKEN_PRIMARY_GROUP

`New`

```
typedef struct _TOKEN_PRIMARY_GROUP { /* tpg */
    PSID PrimaryGroup;
} TOKEN_PRIMARY_GROUP;
```

The **TOKEN_PRIMARY_GROUP** structure specifies a group security identifier (SID) for an access token.

Members   **PrimaryGroup**

Points to an **SID** structure representing a group that will become the primary group of any objects created by a process using this access token. The security identifier (SID) must be one of the group SIDs already in the token.

See Also   **GetTokenInformation, SetTokenInformation, SID TOKEN_CONTROL, TOKEN_DEFAULT_DACL, TOKEN_GROUPS, TOKEN_INFORMATION_CLASS, TOKEN_OWNER, TOKEN_PRIVILEGES, TOKEN_SOURCE, TOKEN_STATISTICS, TOKEN_TYPE, TOKEN_USER**

TOKEN_PRIVILEGES

```
typedef struct _TOKEN_PRIVILEGES { /* tp */
    DWORD PrivilegeCount;
    LUID_AND_ATTRIBUTES Privileges[ANYSIZE_ARRAY];
} TOKEN_PRIVILEGES;
```

The **TOKEN_PRIVILEGES** structure contains information about the set of privileges for an access token.

Members

PrivilegeCount
Specifies the number of privileges in the token.

Privileges
Specifies an array of **LUID_AND_ATTRIBUTES** structures describing the token's privileges.

The following attributes can be used with this parameter:

Attribute	Description
SE_PRIVILEGE_ENABLED_BY_DEFAULT	
	The privilege is enabled by default.
SE_PRIVILEGE_ENABLED	
	The privilege is enabled.
SE_PRIVILEGE_USED_FOR_ACCESS	
	The privilege was used to gain access to an object or service. This flag is used to identify the relevant privileges in a set passed by a client application that may contain unnecessary privileges.

See Also

AdjustTokenPrivileges, **GetTokenInformation**, **PrivilegeCheck**, **PrivilegedServiceAuditAlarm**, **SetTokenInformation**, **LUID_AND_ATTRIBUTES**, **PRIVILEGE_SET**, **TOKEN_CONTROL**, **TOKEN_DEFAULT_DACL**, **TOKEN_GROUPS**, **TOKEN_INFORMATION_CLASS**, **TOKEN_OWNER**, **TOKEN_PRIMARY_GROUP**, **TOKEN_SOURCE**, **TOKEN_STATISTICS**, **TOKEN_TYPE**, **TOKEN_USER**

TOKEN_SOURCE

```
typedef struct _TOKEN_SOURCE { /* ts */
    CHAR SourceName[8];
    LUID SourceIdentifier;
} TOKEN_SOURCE;
```

The **TOKEN_SOURCE** structure identifies the source of an access token.

Members

SourceName

Specifies an eight-byte character string used to identify the source of an access token. This is used to distinguish between such sources as Session Manager, LAN Manager, and RPC Server. A string, rather than a constant, is used to identify the source so users and developers can make extensions to the system, such as by adding other networks, that act as the source of access tokens.

SourceIdentifier

Specifies a locally unique identifier (LUID) provided by the source component named by the **SourceName** member. This value aids the source component in relating context blocks, such as session-control structures, to the token. This value is typically, but not necessarily, an LUID.

See Also

GetTokenInformation, LUID, TOKEN_CONTROL, TOKEN_DEFAULT_DACL, TOKEN_GROUPS, TOKEN_INFORMATION_CLASS, TOKEN_OWNER, TOKEN_PRIMARY_GROUP, TOKEN_PRIVILEGES, TOKEN_STATISTICS, TOKEN_TYPE, TOKEN_USER

TOKEN_STATISTICS

```
typedef struct _TOKEN_STATISTICS { /* tst */
    LUID   TokenId;
    LUID   AuthenticationId;
    LARGE_INTEGER ExpirationTime;
    TOKEN_TYPE    TokenType;
    SECURITY_IMPERSONATION_LEVEL ImpersonationLevel;
    DWORD DynamicCharged;
    DWORD DynamicAvailable;
    DWORD GroupCount;
    DWORD PrivilegeCount;
    LUID  ModifiedId;
} TOKEN_STATISTICS;
```

The **TOKEN_STATISTICS** structure contains information about an access token. An application can retrieve this information by calling the **GetTokenInformation** function.

Members

TokenId
Specifies a locally unique identifier (LUID) that identifies this instance of the token object.

AuthenticationId
Specifies an LUID assigned to the session this token represents. There can may be many tokens representing a single logon session.

ExpirationTime
Specifies the time at which this token expires. Expiration times for access tokens are not supported in the current version of Windows NT.

TokenType
Specifies a **TOKEN_TYPE** enumerated type indicating whether the token is a primary or impersonation token.

ImpersonationLevel
Specifies a **SECURITY_IMPERSONATION_LEVEL** enumerated type indicating the impersonation level of the token. This member is valid only if the **TokenType** is TokenImpersonation.

DynamicCharged
Specifies the amount, in bytes, of memory allocated for storing default protection and a primary group identifier.

DynamicAvailable
Specifies the portion of memory allocated for storing default protection and a primary group identifier not already in use. This value is returned as a count of free bytes.

GroupCount
Specifies the number of supplemental group security identifiers (SIDs) included in the token.

PrivilegeCount
Specifies the number of privileges included in the token.

ModifiedId
Specifies an LUID that changes each time the token is modified. An application can use this value as a test of whether a security context has changed since it was last used.

See Also

GetTokenInformation, LUID, SECURITY_IMPERSONATION_LEVEL, TOKEN_CONTROL, TOKEN_DEFAULT_DACL, TOKEN_GROUPS, TOKEN_INFORMATION_CLASS, TOKEN_OWNER, TOKEN_PRIMARY_GROUP, TOKEN_PRIVILEGES, TOKEN_SOURCE, TOKEN_TYPE, TOKEN_USER

TOKEN_TYPE

`New`

```
typedef enum tagTOKEN_TYPE { /* tt */
    TokenPrimary = 1,
    TokenImpersonation
} TOKEN_TYPE;
```

The **TOKEN_TYPE** enumerated type differentiates between a primary and impersonation token.

See Also   **GetTokenInformation**, **TOKEN_CONTROL**, **TOKEN_DEFAULT_DACL**, **TOKEN_GROUPS**, **TOKEN_INFORMATION_CLASS**, **TOKEN_OWNER**, **TOKEN_PRIMARY_GROUP**, **TOKEN_PRIVILEGES**, **TOKEN_SOURCE**, **TOKEN_STATISTICS**, **TOKEN_USER**

TOKEN_USER

`New`

```
typedef struct _TOKEN_USER { /* tu */
    SID_AND_ATTRIBUTES User;
} TOKEN_USER;
```

The **TOKEN_USER** structure identifies the user associated with an access token.

Members   **User**
Specifies an **SID_AND_ATTRIBUTES** structure representing the user associated with the access token. There are currently no attributes defined for user security identifiers (SIDs).

See Also   **GetTokenInformation**, **SID_AND_ATTRIBUTES**, **TOKEN_CONTROL**, **TOKEN_DEFAULT_DACL**, **TOKEN_GROUPS**, **TOKEN_INFORMATION_CLASS**, **TOKEN_OWNER**, **TOKEN_PRIMARY_GROUP**, **TOKEN_PRIVILEGES**, **TOKEN_SOURCE**, **TOKEN_STATISTICS**, **TOKEN_TYPE**

TTPOLYCURVE

```
typedef struct tagTTPOLYCURVE { /* ttpc */
    WORD    wType;
    WORD    cpfx;
    POINTFX apfx[1];
} TTPOLYCURVE;
```

The **TTPOLYCURVE** structure contains information about a curve in the outline of a TrueType ® character.

Members

wType

Specifies the type of curve described by the structure. This member can be one of the following values:

Value	Meaning
TT_PRIM_LINE	Curve is a polyline.
TT_PRIM_QSPLINE	Curve is a Bézier spline.

cpfx

Specifies the number of **POINTFX** structures in the array.

apfx

Specifies an array of **POINTFX** structures that define the polyline or Bézier spline.

Comments

When an application calls the **GetGlyphOutline** function, a glyph outline for a TrueType character is returned in a **TTPOLYGONHEADER** structure, followed by as many **TTPOLYCURVE** structures as are required to describe the glyph. All points are returned as **POINTFX** structures and represent absolute positions, not relative moves. The starting point given by the **pfxStart** member of the **TTPOLYGONHEADER** structure is the point at which the outline for a contour begins. The **TTPOLYCURVE** structures that follow can be either polyline records or spline records.

Polyline records are a series of points; lines drawn between the points describe the outline of the character. Spline records represent the quadratic curves (that is, quadratic b-splines) used by TrueType.

See Also

POINTFX, TTPOLYGONHEADER

TTPOLYGONHEADER

```
typedef struct tagTTPOLYGONHEADER { /* ttph */
    DWORD    cb;
    DWORD    dwType;
    POINTFX  pfxStart;
} TTPOLYGONHEADER;
```

The **TTPOLYGONHEADER** structure specifies the starting position and type of a contour in a TrueType ® character outline.

Members   **cb**
Specifies the number of bytes required by the **TTPOLYGONHEADER** structure and **TTPOLYCURVE** structure or structures required to describe the contour of the character.

dwType
Specifies the type of character outline returned. Currently, this value must be TT_POLYGON_TYPE.

pfxStart
Specifies the starting point of the contour in the character outline.

Comments   Each **TTPOLYGONHEADER** structure is followed by one or more **TTPOLYCURVE** structures.

See Also   **POINTFX, TTPOLYCURVE**

ULARGE_INTEGER   New

```
typedef struct _ULARGE_INTEGER { /* uli */
    DWORD LowPart;
    DWORD HighPart;
} ULARGE_INTEGER;
```

The **ULARGE_INTEGER** structure is used to specify a 64-bit unsigned integer value.

Members   **LowPart**
Specifies the low-order 32 bits.

HighPart
Specifies the high-order 32 bits.

See Also   **LARGE_INTEGER**

UNLOAD_DLL_DEBUG_INFO

```
typedef struct _UNLOAD_DLL_DEBUG_INFO { /* uddi */
    LPVOID lpBaseOfDll;
} UNLOAD_DLL_DEBUG_INFO;
```

The **UNLOAD_DLL_DEBUG_INFO** structure contains information about a dynamic-link library (DLL) that has just been unloaded.

Members   **lpBaseOfDll**
　　　　　　　　Points to the base address of the DLL in the address space of the process unloading the DLL.

See Also   **DEBUG_EVENT**

Var

```
Var {
    WCHAR szKey[];
    BYTE  Padding[];
    Var   Value[];
};
```

The **Var** structure depicts the organization of data in a file-version resource. This structure is not a true C data structure because it contains variable-length members. This structure was created solely to depict the organization of data in a version resource and does not appear in any of the header files shipped with the Microsoft ® Win32 ™ Software Development Kit (SDK).

The **Var** structure contains version information not dependent on a particular language and code page.

Members   **szKey**
　　　　　　　　Specifies an arbitrary 7-bit ASCII English string. The **szKey** member can be the following value:

Value	Meaning
Translation	**Value** contains an array of doubleword values indicating the language and code-page combinations supported by this file. The high-order word of each doubleword contains a Microsoft language identifier and the low-order word contains the IBM ® code-page number. Either high-order or low-order word may be zero, indicating that the file is language or code-page independent. If this block is omitted, the file will be interpreted as language and code-page independent.

Padding

Contains as many zero bytes as necessary to align the **Value** member on a 32-bit boundary.

Value

Specifies a list of zero or more **Var** structures.

Comments   The **Children** member of the **VS_VERSION_INFO** structure may contain zero or more **Var** structures.

See Also   **VarFileInfo**, **VS_VERSION_INFO**

VarFileInfo

```
VarFileInfo {
    WCHAR szKey[];
    BYTE  Padding[];
    Var   Children[];
};
```

The **VarFileInfo** structure depicts the organization of data in a file-version resource. This structure is not a true C data structure because it contains variable-length members. This structure was created solely to depict the organization of data in a version resource and does not appear in any of the header files shipped with the Microsoft Win32 Software Development Kit (SDK).

The **VarFileInfo** structure contains version information not dependent on a particular language and code page.

Members   **szKey**

Contains "VarFileInfo".

Padding

Contains as many zero bytes as necessary to align the **Children** member on a 32-bit boundary.

Children
Specifies a list of zero or more **Var** structures.

Comments   The **Children** member of the **VS_VERSION_INFO** structure may contain zero or more **VarFileInfo** structures.

See Also   **Var, VS_VERSION_INFO**

VERIFY_INFORMATION

New

```
typedef struct _VERIFY_INFORMATION {
   LARGE_INTEGER  StartingOffset;
   DWORD  Length;
} VERIFY_INFORMATION ;
```

The **VERIFY_INFORMATION** structure provides information used to logically format a disk extent.

Members   **StartingOffset**
Specifies the starting offset of the disk extent.

Length
Length, in bytes, of the disk extent.

Comments   The **DeviceIoControl** function uses a **VERIFY_INFORMATION** structure as input to an **IOCTL_DISK_VERIFY** device i/o operation.

See Also   **DeviceIoControl, IOCTL_DISK_VERIFY**

VS_FIXEDFILEINFO

```
typedef struct tagVS_FIXEDFILEINFO {   /* vsffi */
    DWORD dwSignature;
    DWORD dwStrucVersion;
    DWORD dwFileVersionMS;
    DWORD dwFileVersionLS;
    DWORD dwProductVersionMS;
    DWORD dwProductVersionLS;
    DWORD dwFileFlagsMask;
    DWORD dwFileFlags;
    DWORD dwFileOS;
    DWORD dwFileType;
    DWORD dwFileSubtype;
    DWORD dwFileDateMS;
```

```
    DWORD dwFileDateLS;
} VS_FIXEDFILEINFO;
```

The **VS_FIXEDFILEINFO** structure contains version information about a file. This information is language and code-page independent.

Members

dwSignature

Contains the value 0xFEEFO4BD. This is used with the **szKey** member of **VS_VERSION_INFO** data when searching a file for the **VS_FIXEDFILEINFO** structure.

dwStrucVersion

Specifies the binary version number of this structure. The high-order word of this member contains the major version number, and the low-order word contains the minor version number. This value must be greater than 0x00000029.

dwFileVersionMS

Specifies the most significant 32 bits of the file's binary version number. This member is used with **dwFileVersionLS** to form a 64-bit value used for numeric comparisons.

dwFileVersionLS

Specifies the least significant 32 bits of the file's binary version number. This member is used with **dwFileVersionMS** to form a 64-bit value used for numeric comparisons.

dwProductVersionMS

Specifies the most significant 32 bits of the binary version number of the product with which this file was distributed. This member is used with **dwProductVersionLS** to form a 64-bit value used for numeric comparisons.

dwProductVersionLS

Specifies the least significant 32 bits of the binary version number of the product with which this file was distributed. This member is used with **dwProductVersionMS** to form a 64-bit value used for numeric comparisons.

dwFileFlagsMask

Contains a bitmask that specifies the valid bits in **dwFileFlags**. A bit is valid only if it was defined when the file was created.

dwFileFlags

Contains a bitmask that specifies the Boolean attributes of the file. This member can include one or more of the following values:

Flag	Description
VS_FF_DEBUG	The file contains debugging information or is compiled with debugging features enabled.

VS_FF_INFOINFERRED	The file's version structure was created dynamically; therefore, some of the members in this structure may be empty or incorrect. This flag should never be set in a file's **VS_VERSION_INFO** data.
VS_FF_PATCHED	The file has been modified and is not identical to the original shipping file of the same version number.
VS_FF_PRERELEASE	The file is a development version, not a commercially released product.
VS_FF_PRIVATEBUILD	The file was not built using standard release procedures. If this flag is set, the **StringFileInfo** structure should contain a PrivateBuild entry.
VS_FF_SPECIALBUILD	The file was built by the original company using standard release procedures but is a variation of the normal file of the same version number. If this flag is set, the **StringFileInfo** structure should contain a SpecialBuild entry.

dwFileOS

Specifies the operating system for which this file was designed. This member can be one of the following values:

Flag	Description
VOS_UNKNOWN	The operating system for which the file was designed is unknown to Windows.
VOS_DOS	The file was designed for MS-DOS.
VOS_OS216	The file was designed for 16-bit OS/2.
VOS_OS232	The file was designed for 32-bit OS/2.
VOS_NT	The file was designed for Windows NT.
VOS_WINDOWS16	The file was designed for 16-bit Windows.
VOS_PM16	The file was designed for 16-bit Presentation Manager.
VOS_PM32	The file was designed for 32-bit Presentation Manager.
VOS_WINDOWS32	The file was designed for the Win32 API.

An application can combine these values to indicate that the file was designed for one operating system running on another. The following **dwFileOS** values are examples of this, but are not a complete list:

Flag	Description
VOS_DOS_WINDOWS16	The file was designed for 16-bit Windows running on MS-DOS.
VOS_DOS_WINDOWS32	The file was designed for the Win32 API running on MS-DOS.
VOS_OS216_PM16	The file was designed for 16-bit Presentation Manager running on 16-bit OS/2.

VOS_OS232_PM32	The file was designed for 32-bit Presentation Manager running on 32-bit OS/2.
VOS_NT_WINDOWS32	The file was designed for the Win32 API running on Windows NT.

dwFileType

Specifies the general type of file. This member can be one of the following values:

Flag	Description
VFT_UNKNOWN	The file type is unknown to Windows.
VFT_APP	The file contains an application.
VFT_DLL	The file contains a dynamic-link library (DLL).
VFT_DRV	The file contains a device driver. If **dwFileType** is VFT_DRV, **dwFileSubtype** contains a more specific description of the driver.
VFT_FONT	The file contains a font. If **dwFileType** is VFT_FONT, **dwFileSubtype** contains a more specific description of the font file.
VFT_VXD	The file contains a virtual device.
VFT_STATIC_LIB	The file contains a static-link library.

All other values are reserved for future use by Microsoft.

dwFileSubtype

Specifies the function of the file. The possible values depend on the value of **dwFileType**. For all values of **dwFileType** not described in the following list, **dwFileSubtype** is zero.

If **dwFileType** is VFT_DRV, **dwFileSubtype** can be one of the following values:

Flag	Description
VFT2_UNKNOWN	The driver type is unknown by Windows.
VFT2_DRV_PRINTER	The file contains a printer driver.
VFT2_DRV_KEYBOARD	The file contains a keyboard driver.
VFT2_DRV_LANGUAGE	The file contains a language driver.
VFT2_DRV_DISPLAY	The file contains a display driver.
VFT2_DRV_MOUSE	The file contains a mouse driver.
VFT2_DRV_NETWORK	The file contains a network driver.
VFT2_DRV_SYSTEM	The file contains a system driver.
VFT2_DRV_INSTALLABLE	The file contains an installable driver.
VFT2_DRV_SOUND	The file contains a sound driver.

If **dwFileType** is VFT_FONT, **dwFileSubtype** can be one of the following values:

Flag	Description
VFT2_UNKNOWN	The font type is unknown by Windows.
VFT2_FONT_RASTER	The file contains a raster font.
VFT2_FONT_VECTOR	The file contains a vector font.
VFT2_FONT_TRUETYPE	The file contains a TrueType font.

If **dwFileType** is VFT_VXD, **dwFileSubtype** contains the virtual device identifier included in the virtual device control block.

All **dwFileSubtype** values not listed here are reserved for future use by Microsoft.

dwFileDateMS
Specifies the most significant 32 bits of the file's 64-bit binary creation date and time stamp.

dwFileDateLS
Specifies the least significant 32 bits of the file's 64-bit binary creation date and time stamp.

Comments   The **Value** member of the **VS_VERSION_INFO** data is a **VS_FIXEDFILEINFO** structure.

See Also   **StringFileInfo**, **VS_VERSION_INFO**

VS_VERSION_INFO

```
VS_VERSION_INFO {
    WORD  wLength;
    WORD  wValueLength;
    WORD  bText;
    WCHAR szKey[];
    BYTE  Padding1[];
    VS_FIXEDFILEINFO Value;
    BYTE  Padding2[];
    BYTE  Children[];
};
```

The **VS_VERSION_INFO** structure depicts the organization of data in a file-version resource. This structure is not a true C data structure because it contains variable-length members. This structure was created solely to depict the organization of data in a version resource and does not appear in any of the header files shipped with the Microsoft ® Win32 ™ Software Development Kit (SDK).

Members

wLength

Specifies the length of the **VS_VERSION_INFO** structure. This length does not include any padding that aligns the subsequent version structure on a 32-bit boundary.

wValueLength

Specifies the length of the **Value** member. This value is zero if there is no **Value** member associated with the current version structure.

bText

Specifies the type of data in the version resource. This member is 1 if the version resource contains text data and 0 if the version resource contains binary data.

szKey

Contains "VS_VERSION_INFO".

Padding1

Contains as many zero bytes as necessary to align the **Value** member on a 32-bit boundary.

Value

Contains a **VS_FIXEDFILEINFO** structure that specifies arbitrary data associated with this structure. The **wValueLength** member specifies the length of this member; if **wValueLength** is zero, this member does not exist.

Padding2

Contains as many zero bytes as necessary to align the **Children** member on a 32-bit boundary. These bytes are not included in **wValueLength**.

Children

Specifies a list of zero or more **StringFileInfo** or **VarFileInfo** structures (or both) that are children of the current version structure.

Comments

The **VS_VERSION_INFO** structure is the root structure that contains all other file information structures.

See Also

StringFileInfo, VarFileInfo, VS_FIXEDFILEINFO

WAVEFORMAT

```
typedef struct waveformat_tag {
    WORD   wFormatTag;
    WORD   nChannels;
    DWORD  nSamplesPerSec;
    DWORD  nAvgBytesPerSec;
    WORD   nBlockAlign;
} WAVEFORMAT;
```

The **WAVEFORMAT** structure describes the format of waveform data. Only format information common to all waveform data formats is included in this structure. For formats that require additional information, this structure is included as a member in another structure, along with the additional information.

Members

wFormatTag

Specifies the format type. The currently defined waveform format type is WAVE_FORMAT_PCM, which specifies that the waveform data is pulse code modulated (PCM).

nChannels

Specifies the number of channels in the waveform data. Monaural data uses one channel and stereo data uses two channels.

nSamplesPerSec

Specifies the sample rate, in samples per second.

nAvgBytesPerSec

Specifies the required average data-transfer rate, in bytes per second.

nBlockAlign

Specifies the block alignment, in bytes. The block alignment is the minimum atomic unit of data.

Comments

For PCM data, the block alignment is the number of bytes used by a single sample, including data for both channels, if the data is stereo. For example, the block alignment for 16-bit stereo PCM is 4 bytes (2 channels, 2 bytes per sample).

See Also

PCMWAVEFORMAT

WAVEHDR

```
typedef struct wavehdr_tag {
    LPSTR   lpData;
    DWORD   dwBufferLength;
    DWORD   dwBytesRecorded;
    DWORD   dwUser;
    DWORD   dwFlags;
    DWORD   dwLoops;
    struct wavehdr_tag *lpNext;
    DWORD   reserved;
} WAVEHDR;
```

The **WAVEHDR** structure defines the header used to identify a waveform data buffer.

Members

lpData

Points to the waveform data buffer.

dwBufferLength
Specifies the length of the data buffer.

dwBytesRecorded
Specifies the amount of data in the buffer, if the header is used in input.

dwUser
Specifies 32 bits of user data.

dwFlags
Specifies flags that provide information about the data buffer. This member can be one or more of the following values:

Value	Meaning
WHDR_DONE	Device driver is finished with the data buffer and is returning it to the application. This flag is set by the device driver.
WHDR_BEGINLOOP	Buffer is the first buffer in a loop. This flag is used only with output data buffers.
WHDR_ENDLOOP	Buffer is the last buffer in a loop. This flag is used only with output data buffers.
WHDR_PREPARED	Data buffer has been prepared by using the **waveInPrepareHeader** or **waveOutPrepareHeader** function. This flag is set by Windows.

dwLoops
Specifies the number of times to play the loop. This parameter is used only with output data buffers.

lpNext
Reserved; do not use.

reserved
Reserved; do not use.

Comments   Use the WHDR_BEGINLOOP and WHDR_ENDLOOP flags in the **dwFlags** member to specify the beginning and ending data blocks for looping. To loop on a single block, specify both flags for the same block. Use the **dwLoops** member in the **WAVEHDR** structure of the first block in the loop to specify the number of times to play the loop.

WAVEINCAPS

```
typedef struct waveincaps_tag {
    WORD  wMid;
    WORD  wPid;
    VERSION  vDriverVersion;
    TCHAR  szPname[MAXPNAMELEN];
    DWORD  dwFormats;
    WORD  wChannels;
} WAVEINCAPS;
```

The **WAVEINCAPS** structure describes the capabilities of a waveform input device.

Members

wMid

Specifies a manufacturer identifier for the device driver for the waveform input device. Manufacturer identifiers are defined in Appendix D, "Manufacturer and Product Identifiers" in the *Microsoft Win32 Programmer's Reference, Volume 2*.

wPid

Specifies a product identifier for the waveform input device. Product identifiers are defined in Appendix D, "Manufacturer and Product Identifiers" in the *Microsoft Win32 Programmer's Reference, Volume 2*.

vDriverVersion

Specifies the version number of the device driver for the waveform input device. The high-order byte is the major version number, and the low-order byte is the minor version number.

szPname

Specifies the product name in a null-terminated string.

dwFormats

Specifies the standard formats supported. This member can be a combination of the following values:

Value	Meaning
WAVE_FORMAT_1M08	11.025 kHz, monaural, 8-bit
WAVE_FORMAT_1S08	11.025 kHz, stereo, 8-bit
WAVE_FORMAT_1M16	11.025 kHz, monaural, 16-bit
WAVE_FORMAT_1S16	11.025 kHz, stereo, 16-bit
WAVE_FORMAT_2M08	22.05 kHz, monaural, 8-bit
WAVE_FORMAT_2S08	22.05 kHz, stereo, 8-bit
WAVE_FORMAT_2M16	22.05 kHz, monaural, 16-bit

WAVE_FORMAT_2S16	22.05 kHz, stereo, 16-bit
WAVE_FORMAT_4M08	44.1 kHz, monaural, 8-bit
WAVE_FORMAT_4S08	44.1 kHz, stereo, 8-bit
WAVE_FORMAT_4M16	44.1 kHz, monaural, 16-bit
WAVE_FORMAT_4S16	44.1 kHz, stereo, 16-bit

wChannels
Specifies whether the device supports monaural (1) or stereo (2) input.

See Also   **waveInGetDevCaps**

WAVEOUTCAPS   `Unicode`

```
typedef struct waveoutcaps_tag {
    WORD     wMid;
    WORD     wPid;
    MMVERSION  vDriverVersion;
    TCHAR    szPname[MAXPNAMELEN];
    DWORD    dwFormats;
    WORD     wChannels;
    DWORD    dwSupport;
} WAVEOUTCAPS;
```

The **WAVEOUTCAPS** structure describes the capabilities of a waveform output device.

Members   **wMid**
Specifies a manufacturer identifier for the device driver for the waveform output device. Manufacturer identifiers are defined in Appendix D, "Manufacturer and Product Identifiers" in the *Microsoft Win32 Programmer's Reference, Volume 2.*

wPid
Specifies a product identifier for the waveform output device. Product identifiers are defined in Appendix D, "Manufacturer and Product Identifiers" in the *Microsoft Win32 Programmer's Reference, Volume 2.*

vDriverVersion
Specifies the version number of the device driver for the waveform output device. The high-order byte is the major version number, and the low-order byte is the minor version number.

szPname
Specifies the product name in a null-terminated string.

dwFormats

Specifies the standard formats supported. This member can be a combination of the following values:

Value	Meaning
WAVE_FORMAT_1M08	11.025 kHz, monaural, 8-bit
WAVE_FORMAT_1S08	11.025 kHz, stereo, 8-bit
WAVE_FORMAT_1M16	11.025 kHz, monaural, 16-bit
WAVE_FORMAT_1S16	11.025 kHz, stereo, 16-bit
WAVE_FORMAT_2M08	22.05 kHz, monaural, 8-bit
WAVE_FORMAT_2S08	22.05 kHz, stereo, 8-bit
WAVE_FORMAT_2M16	22.05 kHz, monaural, 16-bit
WAVE_FORMAT_2S16	22.05 kHz, stereo, 16-bit
WAVE_FORMAT_4M08	44.1 kHz, monaural, 8-bit
WAVE_FORMAT_4S08	44.1 kHz, stereo, 8-bit
WAVE_FORMAT_4M16	44.1 kHz, monaural, 16-bit
WAVE_FORMAT_4S16	44.1 kHz, stereo, 16-bit

wChannels

Specifies whether the device supports monaural (1) or stereo (2) output.

dwSupport

Specifies optional functionality supported by the device. This member can be one or more of the following values:

Value	Meaning
WAVECAPS_PITCH	Supports pitch control.
WAVECAPS_PLAYBACKRATE	Supports playback rate control.
WAVECAPS_VOLUME	Supports volume control.
WAVECAPS_LRVOLUME	Supports separate left and right volume control.

Comments

If a device supports volume changes, the WAVECAPS_VOLUME flag is set for the **dwSupport** member. If a device supports separate volume changes on the left and right channels, both the WAVECAPS_VOLUME and the WAVECAPS_LRVOLUME flags are set for this member.

See Also

waveOutGetDevCaps

WIN32_FIND_DATA

```
typedef struct _WIN32_FIND_DATA { /* wfd */
    DWORD    dwFileAttributes;
    FILETIME ftCreationTime;
    FILETIME ftLastAccessTime;
    FILETIME ftLastWriteTime;
    DWORD    nFileSizeHigh;
    DWORD    nFileSizeLow;
    DWORD    dwReserved0;
    DWORD    dwReserved1;
    CHAR     cFileName[ MAX_PATH ];
    CHAR     cAlternateFileName[ 14 ];
} WIN32_FIND_DATA;
```

The **WIN32_FIND_DATA** structure describes a file found by the **FindFirstFile** or **FindNextFile** function.

Members

dwFileAttributes

Specifies the file attributes of the file found.

This flag can be one or more of the following values:

Value	Meaning
FILE_ATTRIBUTE_ARCHIVE	The file is an archive file. Applications use this flag to mark files for backup or removal.
FILE_ATTRIBUTE_DIRECTORY	The file is a directory.
FILE_ATTRIBUTE_HIDDEN	The file is hidden. It is not included in an ordinary directory listing.
FILE_ATTRIBUTE_NORMAL	The file has no other attributes set. This attribute is valid only if used alone.
FILE_ATTRIBUTE_READONLY	The file is a read-only file. Applications can read the file but cannot write to it or delete it.
FILE_ATTRIBUTE_SYSTEM	The file is part of or is used exclusively by the operating system.
FILE_ATTRIBUTE_TEMPORARY	

The file is a temporary file. Applications can write to the file only if absolutely necessary. Most of the file's data remains in memory without being flushed to the media because the file will soon be deleted.

FILE_ATTRIBUTE_ATOMIC_WRITE

The file is an atomic write file. Applications write to the file using atomic write semantics. If any write operation flushes data to the medium, all write operations up to that point are also flushed, as well as any file system structures. This ensures that the data is retrievable at a later time.

FILE_ATTRIBUTE_XACTION_WRITE

Reserved for future use. Do not specify.

ftCreationTime
Specifies the time the file was created. A value of 0,0 indicates that the file system containing the file does not support this time field.

ftLastAccessTime
Specifies the time that the file was last accessed. A value of 0,0 indicates that the file system containing the file does not support this time field.

ftLastWriteTime
Specifies the time that the file was last written to. All file systems support this time field.

nFileSizeHigh
Specifies the high-order word of the file size, in bytes.

nFileSizeLow
Specifies the low-order word of the file size, in bytes.

cFileName
Specifies a null-terminated string that is the name of the file.

cAlternateFileName
Specifies a null-terminated string that is an alternative name of the file, in the 8.3 (filename.ext) format.

WINDOW_BUFFER_SIZE_RECORD

```
typedef struct _WINDOW_BUFFER_SIZE_RECORD { /* wbsr */
    COORD dwSize;
} WINDOW_BUFFER_SIZE_RECORD;
```

The **WINDOW_BUFFER_SIZE_RECORD** structure is used in a console **INPUT_RECORD** structure to report changes in the size of the screen buffer.

Members	dwSize
	Specifies the new size of the screen buffer, in character cell columns and rows.
Comments	Buffer size events are placed in the input buffer when the console is in window-aware mode (ENABLE_WINDOW_INPUT).
See Also	**INPUT_RECORD**, **ReadConsoleInput**

WINDOWPLACEMENT

```
typedef struct tagWINDOWPLACEMENT {      /* wndpl */
    UINT  length;
    UINT  flags;
    UINT  showCmd;
    POINT ptMinPosition;
    POINT ptMaxPosition;
    RECT  rcNormalPosition;
} WINDOWPLACEMENT;
```

The **WINDOWPLACEMENT** structure contains information about the placement of a window on the screen.

Members

length

Specifies the length, in bytes, of the structure.

flags

Specifies flags that control the position of the minimized window and the method by which the window is restored. This member can be one or both of the following values:

Value	Meaning
WPF_SETMINPOSITION	
	Specifies that the coordinates of the minimized window may be specified. This flag must be specified if the coordinates are set in the **ptMinPosition** member.
WPF_RESTORETOMAXIMIZED	
	Specifies that the restored window will be maximized, regardless of whether it was maximized before it was minimized. This setting is only valid the next time the window is restored. It does not change the default restoration behavior. This flag is only valid when the SW_SHOWMINIMIZED value is specified for the **showCmd** member.

showCmd

Specifies the current show state of the window. This member can be one of the following values:

Value	Meaning
SW_HIDE	Hides the window and activates another window.
SW_MINIMIZE	Minimizes the specified window and activates the top-level window in the system's list.
SW_RESTORE	Activates and displays a window. If the window is minimized or maximized, Windows restores it to its original size and position (same as SW_SHOWNORMAL).
SW_SHOW	Activates a window and displays it in its current size and position.
SW_SHOWMAXIMIZED	Activates a window and displays it as a maximized window.
SW_SHOWMINIMIZED	Activates a window and displays it as an icon.
SW_SHOWMINNOACTIVE	Displays a window as an icon. The active window remains active.
SW_SHOWNA	Displays a window in its current state. The active window remains active.
SW_SHOWNOACTIVATE	Displays a window in its most recent size and position. The active window remains active.
SW_SHOWNORMAL	Activates and displays a window. If the window is minimized or maximized, Windows restores it to its original size and position (same as SW_RESTORE).

ptMinPosition

Specifies the coordinates of the window's top-left corner when the window is minimized.

ptMaxPosition

Specifies the coordinates of the window's top-left corner when the window is maximized.

rcNormalPosition

Specifies the window's coordinates when the window is in the restored position.

See Also **ShowWindow**, **POINT**, **RECT**

WINDOWPOS

```
typedef struct tagWINDOWPOS { /* wp */
    HWND hwnd;
    HWND hwndInsertAfter;
    int  x;
    int  y;
    int  cx;
    int  cy;
    UINT flags;
} WINDOWPOS;
```

The **WINDOWPOS** structure contains information about the size and position of a window.

Members

hwnd
Identifies the window.

hwndInsertAfter
Identifies the window behind which this window is placed.

x
Specifies the position of the left edge of the window.

y
Specifies the position of the right edge of the window.

cx
Specifies the window width, in pixels.

cy
Specifies the window height, in pixels.

flags
Specifies the window position. This member can be one of the following values:

Value	Meaning
SWP_DRAWFRAME	Draws a frame (defined in the window's class description) around the window. The window receives a WM_NCCALCSIZE message.
SWP_HIDEWINDOW	Hides the window.
SWP_NOACTIVATE	Does not activate the window.
SWP_NOCOPYBITS	Discards the entire contents of the client area. If this flag is not specified, the valid contents of the client area are saved and copied back into the client area after the window has been sized or repositioned.

SWP_NOMOVE	Retains the current position (ignores the x and y parameters).
SWP_NOOWNERZORDER	Does not change the owner window's position in the Z order.
SWP_NOSIZE	Retains the current size (ignores the cx and cy parameters).
SWP_NOREDRAW	Does not redraw changes.
SWP_NOREPOSITION	Same as the SWP_NOOWNERZORDER flag.
SWP_NOZORDER	Retains the current Z order (ignores the **hwndInsertAfter** member).
SWP_SHOWWINDOW	Displays the window.

See Also   **EndDeferWindowPos, SetWindowPos**

WNDCLASS

`Unicode`

```
typedef struct tagWNDCLASS {    /* wc */
    UINT    style;
    WNDPROC lpfnWndProc;
    int     cbClsExtra;
    int     cbWndExtra;
    HANDLE  hInstance;
    HICON   hIcon;
    HCURSOR hCursor;
    HBRUSH  hbrBackground;
    LPCTSTR lpszMenuName;
    LPCTSTR lpszClassName;
} WNDCLASS;
```

The **WNDCLASS** structure contains the window class attributes that are registered by the **RegisterClass** function.

Members   **style**
Specifies the class style. These styles can be combined by using the bitwise OR (|) operator. This member can be any combination of the following values:

Value	Action
CS_BYTEALIGNCLIENT	Aligns the window's client area on the byte boundary (in the x direction) to enhance performance during drawing operations. This style affects the width of the window and its horizontal position on the display.

CS_BYTEALIGNWINDOW	Aligns a window on a byte boundary (in the x direction) to enhance performance during operations that involve moving or sizing the window. This style affects the width of the window and its horizontal position on the display.
CS_CLASSDC	Allocates one device context (DC) to be shared by all windows in the class. Because window classes are process specific, it is possible for multiple threads of a multithreaded application to create a window of the same class. It is also possible for the threads to attempt to use the DC simultaneously. When this happens, the operating system allows only one of the threads to successfully finish its drawing operation.
CS_DBLCLKS	Sends double-click messages to the window procedure when the user double-clicks the mouse while the cursor is within a window belonging to the class.
CS_GLOBALCLASS	Allows an application to create a window of the class regardless of the value of the *hInstance* parameter passed to the **CreateWindow** or **CreateWindowEx** function. If you do not specify this style, the *hInstance* parameter passed to the **CreateWindow** (or **CreateWindowEx**) function must be the same as the *hInstance* parameter passed to the **RegisterClass** function.
	You can create a global class by creating the window class in a dynamic-link library (DLL) and listing the name of the DLL in the registration database under the following keys:
	HKEY_LOCAL_MACHINE\Software\Micros oft\Windows NT\ CurrentVersion\Windows\APPINIT_DLLS
	Whenever a process starts, the operating system loads the specified DLLs in the context of the newly started process before calling the **main** function in that process. The DLL must register the class during its initialization procedure and must specify the CS_GLOBALCLASS style.
CS_HREDRAW	Redraws the entire window if a movement or size adjustment changes the width of the client area.
CS_NOCLOSE	Disables the Close command on the System menu.
CS_OWNDC	Allocates a unique device context for each window in the class.

CS_PARENTDC	Gives the parent window's device context to the child windows. Specifying CS_PARENTDC enhances an application's performance. When an application calls the **GetDC** function, passing the handle of a window that belongs to a class with the CS_PARENTDC style, the operating system searches for a device context that has been precalculated for the window's parent window. If all child windows of a particular parent window specify this style, the system need not recalculate a device context for any of the child windows.
CS_SAVEBITS	Saves, as a bitmap, the portion of the screen image obscured by a window. Windows uses the saved bitmap to re-create the screen image when the window is removed. Windows displays the bitmap at its original location and does not send WM_PAINT messages to windows obscured by the window if the memory used by the bitmap has not been discarded and if other screen actions have not invalidated the stored image. This style is useful for small windows that are displayed briefly and then removed before other screen activity takes place (for example, menus or dialog boxes). This style increases the time required to display the window, because the operating system must first allocate memory to store the bitmap.
CS_VREDRAW	Redraws the entire window if a movement or size adjustment changes the height of the client area.

lpfnWndProc

Points to the window procedure. For more information, see the description of the **WindowProc** callback function.

cbClsExtra

Specifies the number of extra bytes to allocate following the window-class structure. The operating system initializes the bytes to zero.

cbWndExtra

Specifies the number of extra bytes to allocate following the window instance. The operating system initializes the bytes to zero. If an application uses the **WNDCLASS** structure to register a dialog box created by using the **CLASS** directive in the resource file, it must set this member to DLGWINDOWEXTRA.

hInstance

Identifies the instance that the window procedure of this class is within.

hIcon

Identifies the class icon. This member must be a handle of an icon resource. If this member is NULL, an application must draw an icon whenever the user minimizes the application's window.

hCursor

Identifies the class cursor. This member must be a handle of a cursor resource. If this member is NULL, an application must explicitly set the cursor shape whenever the mouse moves into the application's window.

hbrBackground

Identifies the class background brush. This member can be a handle to the physical brush to be used for painting the background, or it can be a color value. A color value must be one of the standard system colors listed below, and the value 1 must be added to the chosen color; for example, COLOR_BACKGROUND + 1 specifies the system background color. If a color value is given, you must convert it to one of the following **HBRUSH** types:

COLOR_ACTIVEBORDER
COLOR_ACTIVECAPTION
COLOR_APPWORKSPACE
COLOR_BACKGROUND
COLOR_BTNFACE
COLOR_BTNSHADOW
COLOR_BTNTEXT
COLOR_CAPTIONTEXT
COLOR_GRAYTEXT
COLOR_HIGHLIGHT
COLOR_HIGHLIGHTTEXT
COLOR_INACTIVEBORDER
COLOR_INACTIVECAPTION
COLOR_MENU
COLOR_MENUTEXT
COLOR_SCROLLBAR
COLOR_WINDOW
COLOR_WINDOWFRAME
COLOR_WINDOWTEXT

The operating system automatically deletes class background brushes when the class is freed. An application should not delete these brushes, because a class may be used by multiple instances of an application.

When this member is NULL, an application must paint its own background whenever it is requested to paint in its client area. To determine whether the background must be painted, an application can either process the WM_ERASEBKGND message or test the **fErase** member of the **PAINTSTRUCT** structure filled by the **BeginPaint** function.

lpszMenuName

Points to a null-terminated character string that specifies the resource name of the class menu, as the name appears in the resource file. If you use an integer to identify the menu, use the **MAKEINTRESOURCE** macro. If this member is NULL, windows belonging to this class have no default menu.

lpszClassName

Points to a null-terminated string or is an atom that identifies a string. If this parameter is an atom, it must be a global atom created by a previous call to the **GlobalAddAtom** function. The atom, a 16-bit value, must be in the low-order word of **lpszClassName**; the high-order word must be zero.

The **lpszClassName** string or atom specifies the window class name.

See Also   **GlobalAddAtom**, **PAINTSTRUCT**, **WindowProc**

XFORM

New

```
typedef struct  tagXFORM {  /* xfrm */
    FLOAT eM11;
    FLOAT eM12;
    FLOAT eM21;
    FLOAT eM22;
    FLOAT eDx;
    FLOAT eDy;
} XFORM;
```

The **XFORM** structure specifies a world-space to page-space transformation.

Members   **eM11**

Specifies the following:

Operation	Meaning
Scaling	Horizontal scaling component
Rotation	Cosine of rotation angle
Reflection	Horizontal component

eM12

Specifies the following:

Operation	Meaning
Shear	Horizontal proportionality constant
Rotation	Sine of the rotation angle

eM21

Specifies the following:

Operation	Meaning
Shear	Vertical proportionality constant
Rotation	Negative sine of the rotation angle

eM22

Specifies the following:

Operation	Meaning
Scaling	Vertical scaling component
Rotation	Cosine of rotation angle
Reflection	Vertical reflection component

eDx

Specifies the horizontal translation component.

eDy

Specifies the vertical translation component.

The following list describes how the members are used for each operation:

Operation	eM11	eM12	eM21	eM22
Rotation	Cosine	Sine	Negative sine	Cosine
Scaling	Horizontal scaling component	Nothing	Nothing	Vertical Scaling Component
Shear	Nothing	Horizontal Proportionality Constant	Vertical Proportionality Constant	Nothing
Reflection	Horizontal Reflection Component	Nothing	Nothing	Vertical Reflection Component

See Also

ExtCreateRegion, GetWorldTransform, ModifyWorldTransform, PlayEnhMetaFile, SetWorldTransform

C H A P T E R   4

Macros

GetBValue

BYTE GetBValue(*rgb*)
DWORD *rgb*;   /* 32-bit RGB value */

The **GetBValue** macro retrieves an intensity value for the blue component of a 32-bit red, green, blue (RGB) value.

Parameters   *rgb*
            Specifies an RGB color value.

Return Value   The return value is the intensity of the blue component of the specified RGB color.

Comments   The intensity value is in the range 0 through 255.

The **GetBValue** macro is defined as follows:

```
#define GetBValue(rgb)        ((BYTE)((rgb)>>16))
```

See Also   **GetGValue, GetRValue, PALETTEINDEX, PALETTERGB, RGB**

GetGValue

BYTE GetGValue(*rgb*)
DWORD *rgb*;   /* 32-bit RGB value */

The **GetGValue** macro retrieves an intensity value for the green component of a 32-bit red, green, blue (RGB) value.

Parameters   *rgb*
            Specifies an RGB color value.

Return Value   The return value is the intensity of the green component of the specified RGB color. .

Comments   The intensity value is in the range 0 through 255.

The **GetGValue** macro is defined as follows:

```
#define GetGValue(rgb)        ((BYTE)(((WORD)(rgb)) >> 8))
```

See Also   GetBValue, GetRValue, PALETTEINDEX, PALETTERGB, RGB

GetRValue

BYTE GetRValue(*rgb*)
DWORD *rgb*;   /* 32-bit RGB value */

The **GetRValue** macro retrieves an intensity value for the red component of a 32-bit red, green, blue (RGB) value.

Parameters   *rgb*
                     Specifies an RGB color value.

Return Value   The return value is the intensity of the red component of the specified RGB color.

Comments   The intensity value is in the range 0 through 255.

The **GetRValue** macro is defined as follows:

```
#define GetRValue(rgb)    ((BYTE)(rgb))
```

See Also   GetBValue, GetGValue, PALETTEINDEX, PALETTERGB, RGB

HIBYTE

BYTE HIBYTE(*wValue*)
WORD *wValue*;   /* value from which high-order byte is retrieved   */

The **HIBYTE** macro retrieves the high-order byte from the given 16-bit value.

Parameters   *wValue*
                     Specifies the value to be converted.

Return Value   The return value is the high-order byte of the specified value.

Comments   The **HIBYTE** macro is defined as follows:

```
#define HIBYTE(w)  ((BYTE)(((WORD)(w) >> 8) & 0xFF))
```

See Also   **HIWORD, LOBYTE**

HIWORD

WORD HIWORD(*dwValue*)
DWORD *dwValue*;   /* value from which high-order word is retrieved   */

The **HIWORD** macro retrieves the high-order word from the given 32-bit value.

Parameters   *dwValue*
                        Specifies the value to be converted.

Return Value   The return value is the high-order word of the specified value.

Comments   The **HIWORD** macro is defined as follows:

```
#define HIWORD(l)  ((WORD)(((DWORD)(l) >> 16) & 0xFFFF))
```

See Also   **HIBYTE, LOWORD**

LANGIDFROMLCID

New

WORD LANGIDFROMLCID(*lcid*)
LCID *lcid*;   /* locale identifier */

The **LANGIDFROMLCID** macro retrieves a language identifier from a locale identifier.

Parameters   *lcid*
                        Specifies the locale identifier. This parameter may have been created by using the **MAKELCID** macro.

Return Value   The return value is a language identifier.

Comments   The **LANGIDFROMLCID** macro is defined as follows:

```
#define LANGIDFROMLCID(lcid)  ((WORD) (lcid))
```

See Also   **MAKELANGID, MAKELCID, PRIMARYLANGID, SUBLANGID**

LOBYTE

BYTE LOBYTE(*wValue*)
WORD *wValue*;   /* value from which low-order byte is retrieved   */

The **LOBYTE** macro retrieves the low-order byte from the given 16-bit value.

Parameters   *wValue*
                            Specifies the value to be converted.

Return Value   The return value is the low-order byte of the specified value.

Comments   The **LOBYTE** macro is defined as follows:

```
#define LOBYTE(w)  ((BYTE)(w))
```

See Also   **HIBYTE, LOWORD**

LOWORD

WORD LOWORD(*dwValue*)
DWORD *dwValue*;   /* value from which low-order word is retrieved   */

The **LOWORD** macro retrieves the low-order word from the given 32-bit value.

Parameters   *dwValue*
                            Specifies the value to be converted.

Return Value   The return value is the low-order word of the specified value.

Comments   The **LOWORD** macro is defined as follows:

```
#define LOWORD(1)  ((WORD)(1))
```

See Also   **HIWORD, LOBYTE**

MAKEINTATOM

LPTSTR MAKEINTATOM(*wInteger*)
WORD *wInteger*;   /* integer to make into atom   */

The **MAKEINTATOM** macro creates an integer atom that represents a character string of decimal digits.

Integer atoms created by this macro can be added to an atom table by using the **AddAtom** or **GlobalAddAtom** function.

Parameters   *wInteger*
Specifies the numeric value to be made into an integer atom.

Return Value   The return value is a pointer to the atom created for the given integer.

Comments   Although the return value of the **MAKEINTATOM** macro is cast as an **LPTSTR** value, it cannot be used as a string pointer except when it is passed to atom-management functions that require an **LPTSTR** argument.

The **DeleteAtom** and **GlobalDeleteAtom** functions always succeed for integer atoms, even though they do nothing. The string returned by the **GetAtomName** and **GlobalGetAtomName** functions for an integer atom is a null-terminated string in which the first character is a pound sign (#) and the remaining characters are the decimal digits used in the **MAKEINTATOM** macro.

The **MAKEINTATOM** macro is defined as follows:

```
#define MAKEINTATOM(i)   (LPTSTR)((DWORD)((WORD)(i)))
```

See Also   **AddAtom, DeleteAtom, GetAtomName, GlobalAddAtom, GlobalDeleteAtom, GlobalGetAtomName**

MAKEINTRESOURCE

LPTSTR MAKEINTRESOURCE(*wInteger*)
WORD *wInteger*;   /* integer to convert */

The **MAKEINTRESOURCE** macro converts an integer value to a resource type compatible with Windows resource-management functions. This macro is used in place of a string containing the name of the resource.

Parameters	*wInteger* Specifies the integer value to be converted.
Return Value	The return value is the specified value in the low-order word and zero in the high-order word.
Comments	The return value should be passed only to the Windows resource-management functions, as the *lpType* parameter.

The **MAKEINTRESOURCE** macro is defined as follows:

```
#define MAKEINTRESOURCE(i)  (LPTSTR)((DWORD)((WORD)(i)))
```

MAKELANGID   New

WORD MAKELANGID(*usPrimaryLanguage*, *usSubLanguage*)
USHORT *usPrimaryLanguage*;   /* primary language identifier   */
USHORT *usSubLanguage*;   /* sublanguage identifier   */

The **MAKELANGID** macro creates a language identifier from a primary language identifier and a sublanguage identifier.

Parameters   *usPrimaryLanguage*
Specifies the primary language identifier. This parameter can be one of the following values:

LANG_ALBANIAN	LANG_ITALIAN
LANG_ARABIC	LANG_JAPANESE
LANG_BAHASA	LANG_KOREAN
LANG_BULGARIAN	LANG_NEUTRAL
LANG_CATALAN	LANG_NORWEGIAN
LANG_CHINESE	LANG_POLISH
LANG_CZECH	LANG_PORTUGUESE
LANG_DANISH	LANG_RHAETO_ROMAN
LANG_DUTCH	LANG_ROMANIAN
LANG_ENGLISH	LANG_RUSSIAN
LANG_FINNISH	LANG_SERBO_CROATIAN
LANG_FRENCH	LANG_SLOVAK
LANG_GERMAN	LANG_SPANISH
LANG_GREEK	LANG_SWEDISH

LANG_HEBREW   LANG_THAI

LANG_HUNGARIAN   LANG_TURKISH

LANG_ICELANDIC   LANG_URDU

usSubLanguage

Specifies the sublanguage identifier. This parameter can be one of the following values:

SUBLANG_CHINESE_SIMPLIFIED   SUBLANG_GERMAN_SWISS

SUBLANG_CHINESE_TRADITIONAL   SUBLANG_ITALIAN

SUBLANG_DEFAULT   SUBLANG_ITALIAN_SWISS

SUBLANG_DUTCH   SUBLANG_NEUTRAL

SUBLANG_DUTCH_BELGIAN   SUBLANG_NORWEGIAN_BOKMÅL

SUBLANG_ENGLISH_AUS   SUBLANG_NORWEGIAN_NYNORSK

SUBLANG_ENGLISH_CAN   SUBLANG_PORTUGUESE

SUBLANG_ENGLISH_UK   SUBLANG_PORTUGUESE_BRAZILIAN

SUBLANG_ENGLISH_US   SUBLANG_SERBO_CROATIAN_CYRILLIC

SUBLANG_FRENCH   SUBLANG_SERBO_CROATIAN_LATIN

SUBLANG_FRENCH_BELGIAN   SUBLANG_SPANISH

SUBLANG_FRENCH_CANADIAN   SUBLANG_SPANISH_MEXICAN

SUBLANG_FRENCH_SWISS   SUBLANG_SPANISH_MODERN

SUBLANG_GERMAN

Return Value

The return value is a language identifier that can be used with the **FindResourceEx** and **EnumResLangProc** functions.

Comments

The following two combinations of *usPrimaryLanguage* and *usSubLanguage* have special meaning:

Primary language ID	Sublanguage ID	Meaning
LANG_NEUTRAL	SUBLANG_NEUTRAL	Language neutral
LANG_NEUTRAL	SUBLANG_DEFAULT	Process default language

The **MAKELANGID** macro is defined as follows:

```
#define MAKELANGID(p, s) ((((USHORT)(s)) << 10) | (USHORT)(p))
```

See Also

LANGIDFROMLCID, MAKELCID, PRIMARYLANGID, SUBLANGID

MAKELCID

DWORD MAKELCID(*wLanguageID*)
WORD *wLanguageID*;   /* language identifier */

The **MAKELCID** macro creates a locale identifier from a language identifier.

Parameters   *wLanguageID*
Specifies the language identifier. This parameter is a combination of a primary language identifier and a sublanguage identifier and is usually created by using the **MAKELANGID** macro.

Return Value   The return value is a locale identifier.

Comments   The **MAKELCID** macro is defined as follows:

```
#define MAKELCID(lgid) \
    ((DWORD) (((WORD) (lgid)) | (((DWORD) ((WORD) (0))) << 16)))
```

See Also   **LANGIDFROMLCID, MAKELANGID**

MAKELONG

DWORD MAKELONG(*wLow*, *wHigh*)
WORD *wLow*;   /* low-order word of long value   */
WORD *wHigh*;   /* high-order word of long value   */

The **MAKELONG** macro creates an unsigned 32-bit value by concatenating two given 16-bit values.

Parameters   *wLow*
Specifies the low-order word of the new long value.

wHigh
Specifies the high-order word of the new long value.

Return Value   The return value is an unsigned 32-bit value.

Comments   The **MAKELONG** macro is defined as follows:

```
#define MAKELONG(a, b) \
    ((LONG)(((WORD)(a)) | ((DWORD)((WORD)(b))) << 16))
```

MAKELPARAM

LPARAM MAKELPARAM(*wLow*, *wHigh*)
WORD *wLow*;   /* low-order word   */
WORD *wHigh*;   /* high-order word   */

The **MAKELPARAM** macro creates an unsigned 32-bit value for use as an *lParam* parameter in a message. The macro concatenates two given 16-bit values.

Parameters   *wLow*
                        Specifies the low-order word of the new long value.

                        wHigh
                        Specifies the high-order word of the new long value.

Return Value   The return value is an unsigned 32-bit value.

Comments   The **MAKELPARAM** macro is defined as follows:

```
#define MAKELPARAM(1, h)   ((LPARAM)MAKELONG(1, h))
```

See Also   **MAKELONG, MAKELRESULT, MAKEWPARAM**

MAKELRESULT

LRESULT MAKELRESULT(*wLow*, *wHigh*)
WORD *wLow*;   /* low-order word   */
WORD *wHigh*;   /* high-order word   */

The **MAKELRESULT** macro creates an unsigned 32-bit value for use as a return value from a window procedure. The macro concatenates two given 16-bit values.

Parameters   *wLow*
                        Specifies the low-order word of the new long value.

                        wHigh
                        Specifies the high-order word of the new long value.

Return Value   The return value is an unsigned 32-bit value.

Comments   The **MAKELRESULT** macro is defined as follows:

```
#define MAKELRESULT(1, h)   ((LRESULT)MAKELONG(1, h))
```

See Also   MAKELONG, MAKELPARAM, MAKEWPARAM

MAKEPOINTS

New

POINTS MAKEPOINTS(*dwValue*)
DWORD *dwValue*;   /* coordinates of a point   */

The **MAKEPOINTS** macro converts a value that contains the x- and y-coordinates of a point into a **POINTS** structure.

Parameters   *dwValue*
Specifies the coordinates of a point. The x-coordinate is in the low-order word, and the y-coordinate is in the high-order word.

Return Value   The return value is a pointer to a **POINTS** structure.

Comments   The **MAKEPOINTS** macro is defined as follows:

```
#define MAKEPOINTS(1)  (*((POINTS FAR *)&(1)))
```

The **POINTS** structure has the following form:

```
typedef struct tagPOINTS { /* pts */
    SHORT x;
    SHORT y;
} POINTS;
```

For a full description of this structure, see Chapter 3, "Structures."

See Also   **GetMessagePos**

MAKEWORD

WORD MAKEWORD(*bLow*, *bHigh*)
BYTE *bLow*;   /* low-order byte of short value   */
BYTE *bHigh*;   /* high-order byte of short value   */

The **MAKEWORD** macro creates an unsigned 16-bit integer by concatenating two given unsigned character values.

Parameters

bLow

Specifies the low-order byte of the new short value.

bHigh

Specifies the high-order byte of the new short value.

Return Value

The return value is an unsigned 16-bit integer value.

Comments

The **MAKEWORD** macro is defined as follows:

```
#define MAKEWORD(a, b) \
    ((WORD)(((BYTE)(a)) | ((WORD)((BYTE)(b))) << 8))
```

MAKEWPARAM

LPARAM MAKEWPARAM(*wLow*, *wHigh*)
WORD *wLow*;   /* low-order word   */
WORD *wHigh*;   /* high-order word   */

The **MAKEWPARAM** macro creates an unsigned 32-bit value for use as a *wParam* parameter in a message. The macro concatenates two given 16-bit values.

Parameters

wLow

Specifies the low-order word of the new long value.

wHigh

Specifies the high-order word of the new long value.

Return Value

The return value is an unsigned 32-bit value.

Comments

The **MAKEWPARAM** macro is defined as follows:

```
#define MAKEWPARAM(1, h)    ((LPARAM)MAKELONG(1, h))
```

See Also

MAKELONG, MAKELPARAM, MAKELRESULT

max

max(*value1*, *value2*)

The **max** macro compares two values and returns the larger one. The data type can be any numeric data type, signed or unsigned. The data type of the arguments and the return value is the same.

Parameters

value1
Specifies the first of two values.

value2
Specifies the second of two values.

Return Value

The return value is the greater of the two specified values.

Comments

The **max** macro is defined as follows:

```
#define max(a, b)  (((a) > (b)) ? (a) : (b))
```

See Also

min

min

min(*value1*, *value2*)

The **min** macro compares two values and returns the smaller one. The data type can be any numeric data type, signed or unsigned. The data type of the arguments and the return value is the same.

Parameters

value1
Specifies the first of two values.

value2
Specifies the second of two values.

Return Value

The return value is the smaller of the two specified values.

Comments

The **min** macro is defined as follows:

```
#define min(a, b)  (((a) < (b)) ? (a) : (b))
```

See Also

max

PALETTEINDEX

COLORREF PALETTEINDEX(*wPaletteIndex*)
WORD *wPaletteIndex*;   /* index to palette entry */

The **PALETTEINDEX** macro accepts an index to a logical-color palette entry and returns a palette-entry specifier consisting of a 32-bit **COLORREF** value that specifies the color associated with the given index. An application using a logical color palette can pass this specifier, instead of an explicit red, green, blue (RGB) value, to graphics device interface (GDI) functions that expect a color. This allows the function to use the color in the specified palette entry.

Parameters   *wPaletteIndex*
                     Specifies an index to the palette entry containing the color to be used for a graphics operation.

Return Value   The return value is a logical-palette index specifier.

Comments   The **PALETTEINDEX** macro is defined as follows:

```
#define PALETTEINDEX(i) /
     ((COLORREF)(0x01000000 | (DWORD)(WORD)(i)))
```

See Also   **PALETTERGB, RGB**

PALETTERGB

COLORREF PALETTERGB(*bRed, bGreen, bBlue*)
BYTE *bRed*;   /* red component of palette-relative RGB   */
BYTE *bGreen*;   /* green component of palette-relative RGB   */
BYTE *bBlue*;   /* blue component of palette-relative RGB   */

The **PALETTERGB** macro accepts three values that represent the relative intensities of red, green, and blue and returns a palette-relative red, green, blue (RGB) specifier consisting of 2 in the high-order byte and an RGB value in the three low-order bytes. An application using a color palette can pass this specifier, instead of an explicit RGB value, to functions that expect a color.

Parameters   *bRed*
                     Specifies the intensity of the red color field.

bGreen
> Specifies the intensity of the green color field.

bBlue
> Specifies the intensity of the blue color field.

Return Value   The return value is a palette-relative RGB specifier. For output devices that support logical palettes, Windows matches a palette-relative RGB value to the nearest color in the logical palette of the device context as though the application had specified an index to that palette entry. If an output device does not support a system palette, Windows uses the palette-relative RGB as though it were a conventional RGB doubleword returned by the **RGB** macro.

Comments   The **PALETTERGB** macro is defined as follows:

```
#define PALETTERGB(r, g, b)  (0x02000000 | RGB(r,g,b))
```

See Also   **PALETTEINDEX, RGB**

POINTSTOPOINT

New

POINTSTOPOINT(*pt, pts*)
POINT *pt*;   /* POINT structure   */
POINTS *pts*;   /* POINTS structure   */

The **POINTSTOPOINT** macro copies the contents of a **POINTS** structure into a **POINT** structure.

Parameters   *pt*
> Specifies the **POINT** structure to receive the contents of the **POINTS** structure. The **POINT** structure has the following form:

```
typedef struct tagPOINT { /* pt */
    LONG x;
    LONG y;
} POINT;
```

> For more information about this structure, see Chapter 3, "Structures."

pts
> Specifies the **POINTS** structure to copy. The **POINTS** structure has the following form:

```
typedef struct tagPOINTS { /* pts */
    SHORT x;
    SHORT y;
} POINTS;
```

Comments   For more information about this structure, see Chapter 3, "Structures."
The **POINTSTOPOINT** macro is defined as follows:

```
#define POINTSTOPOINT(pt,pts) {(pt).x = (SHORT)LOWORD(pts); \
                               (pt).y = (SHORT)HIWORD(pts);}
```

See Also   **MAKEPOINTS, POINTTOPOINTS**

POINTTOPOINTS

POINTS POINTTOPOINTS(*pt*)
POINT *pt*;   /* coordinates of a point */

The **POINTTOPOINTS** macro converts a **POINT** structure to a **POINTS** structure.

Parameters   *pt*

Specifies the **POINT** structure to convert. The **POINT** structure has the following form:

```
typedef struct tagPOINT { /* pt */
    LONG x;
    LONG y;
} POINT;
```

For more information about this structure, see Chapter 3, "Structures."

Return Value   The return value is a **POINTS** structure.

Comments   The **POINTTOPOINTS** macro is defined as follows:

```
#define POINTTOPOINTS(pt) \
    (MAKELONG((short)((pt).x), (short)((pt).y)))
```

See Also   **MAKEPOINTS, POINTSTOPOINT**

PRIMARYLANGID

New

BYTE PRIMARYLANGID (*usLanguageID*)
USHORT *usLanguageID*;   /* language identifier */

The **PRIMARYLANGID** macro extracts a primary language identifier from a language identifier.

Parameters

wLanguageID
　　Specifies the language identifier. This value is a combination of a primary language identifier and a sublanguage identifier and is usually created by using the **MAKELANGID** macro.

Return Value

The return value is one of the following primary language identifiers:

LANG_ALBANIAN	LANG_ITALIAN
LANG_ARABIC	LANG_JAPANESE
LANG_BAHASA	LANG_KOREAN
LANG_BULGARIAN	LANG_NEUTRAL
LANG_CATALAN	LANG_NORWEGIAN
LANG_CHINESE	LANG_POLISH
LANG_CZECH	LANG_PORTUGUESE
LANG_DANISH	LANG_RHAETO_ROMAN
LANG_DUTCH	LANG_ROMANIAN
LANG_ENGLISH	LANG_RUSSIAN
LANG_FINNISH	LANG_SERBO_CROATIAN
LANG_FRENCH	LANG_SLOVAK
LANG_GERMAN	LANG_SPANISH
LANG_GREEK	LANG_SWEDISH
LANG_HEBREW	LANG_THAI
LANG_HUNGARIAN	LANG_TURKISH
LANG_ICELANDIC	LANG_URDU

Comments

The **PRIMARYLANGID** macro is defined as follows:

```
#define PRIMARYLANGID(lgid)  ((USHORT)(lgid) & 0x3FF)
```

See Also

LANGIDFROMLCID, MAKELANGID, SUBLANGID

RGB

COLORREF RGB(*bRed*, *bGreen*, *bBlue*)
BYTE *bRed*;   /* red component of color   */
BYTE *bGreen*;   /* green component of color   */
BYTE *bBlue*;   /* blue component of color   */

The **RGB** macro selects a red, green, blue (RGB) color based on the arguments supplied and the color capabilities of the output device.

Parameters

cRed
   Specifies the intensity of the red color.

cGreen
   Specifies the intensity of the green color.

cBlue
   Specifies the intensity of the blue color.

Return Value   The return value is the resultant RGB color.

Comments   The intensity for each argument is in the range 0 through 255. If all three intensities are zero, the result is black. If all three intensities are 255, the result is white.

For information about using color values in a color palette, see the descriptions of the **PALETTEINDEX** and **PALETTERGB** macros.

The **RGB** macro is defined as   s:

```
#define RGB(r, g ,b)  ((DW     .(BYTE)(r) | \
    ((WORD)(g) << 8)) | \
    (((DWORD`  `TE)(b))       ʋ)))
```

See Also   **PALETTEINDE**ʌ   **ʃTERGB**

SUBLANGID

BYTE SUBLANGID(*usLanguageID*)
USHORT *usLanguageID*;   /* language identifier */

The **SUBLANGID** macro extracts a sublanguage identifier from a language identifier.

Parameters	*usLanguageID*
	Specifies the language identifier. This value is a combination of a primary language identifier and a sublanguage identifier and is usually created by using the **MAKELANGID** macro.

Return Value   The return value is one of the following sublanguage identifiers:

SUBLANG_CHINESE_SIMPLIFIED	SUBLANG_GERMAN_SWISS
SUBLANG_CHINESE_TRADITIONAL	SUBLANG_ITALIAN
SUBLANG_DEFAULT	SUBLANG_ITALIAN_SWISS
SUBLANG_DUTCH	SUBLANG_NEUTRAL
SUBLANG_DUTCH_BELGIAN	SUBLANG_NORWEGIAN_BOKMÅL
SUBLANG_ENGLISH_AUS	SUBLANG_NORWEGIAN_NYNORSK
SUBLANG_ENGLISH_CAN	SUBLANG_PORTUGUESE
SUBLANG_ENGLISH_UK	SUBLANG_PORTUGUESE_BRAZILIAN
SUBLANG_ENGLISH_US	SUBLANG_SERBO_CROATIAN_CYRILLIC
SUBLANG_FRENCH	SUBLANG_SERBO_CROATIAN_LATIN
SUBLANG_FRENCH_BELGIAN	SUBLANG_SPANISH
SUBLANG_FRENCH_CANADIAN	SUBLANG_SPANISH_MEXICAN
SUBLANG_FRENCH_SWISS	SUBLANG_SPANISH_MODERN
SUBLANG_GERMAN	

Comments   The **SUBLANGID** macro is defined as follows:

```
#define SUBLANGID(lgid) ((USHORT)(lgid) >> 10)
```

See Also   **LANGIDFROMLCID, MAKELANGID, PRIMARYLANGID**

TEXT

New

TEXT(*string*)
LPTSTR *string*;   /* address of ANSI or Unicode string */

The **TEXT** macro identifies a string as Unicode™ when the UNICODE compile flag is used or as an ANSI string when UNICODE is not defined.

Parameters	*string*
	Specifies the string to be interpreted as either Unicode or ANSI.
Comments	The **TEXT** macro is defined as follows:

```
#define TEXT(quote) L##quote
```

CHAPTER 5

Dynamic Data Exchange Transactions

XTYP_ADVDATA

XTYP_ADVDATA

A dynamic data exchange (DDE) client callback function receives the XTYP_ADVDATA transaction after establishing an advise loop with a server. This transaction informs the client that the value of the data item has changed.

Parameters

uFmt
Specifies the format atom of the data sent from the server.

hconv
Identifies the conversation.

hsz1
Identifies the topic name.

hsz2
Identifies the item name.

hdata
Identifies the data associated with the topic name and item name pair. This parameter is NULL if the client specified the XTYPF_NODATA flag when it requested the advise loop.

dwData1
Not used.

dwData2
Not used.

Return Value

A DDE callback function should return DDE_FACK if it processes this transaction, DDE_FBUSY if it is too busy to process this transaction, or DDE_FNOTPROCESSED if it rejects this transaction.

Comments

An application must not free the data handle obtained during this transaction. An application must, however, copy the data associated with the data handle if the application must process the data after the callback function returns. An application can use the **DdeGetData** function to copy the data.

See Also

DdeClientTransaction, **DdePostAdvise**

XTYP_ADVREQ

XTYP_ADVREQ

The system sends the XTYP_ADVREQ transaction to a server after the server calls the **DdePostAdvise** function. This transaction informs the server that an advise transaction is outstanding on the specified topic name and item name pair and that data corresponding to the topic name and item name pair has changed.

Parameters   *uFmt*
Specifies the format in which the data should be submitted to the client.

hconv
Identifies the conversation.

hsz1
Identifies the topic name.

hsz2
Identifies the item name that has changed.

hdata
Not used.

dwData1
Specifies the count, in the low-order word, of XTYP_ADVREQ transactions that remain to be processed, on the same topic, item, and format name set, within the context of the current call to the **DdePostAdvise** function. The count is zero if the current XTYP_ADVREQ transaction is the last one. A server can use this count to determine whether to create an HDATA_APPOWNED data handle for the advise data.

The low-order word is set to CADV_LATEACK if the Dynamic Data Exchange Management Library (DDEML) issued the XTYP_ADVREQ transaction because of a late-arriving DDE_ACK message from a client being outrun by the server.

The high-order word is not used.

dwData2
Not used.

Return Value   The server should first call the **DdeCreateDataHandle** function to create a data handle that identifies the changed data and then return the handle. The server should return NULL if it is unable to complete the transaction.

Comments   A server cannot block this transaction type; the CBR_BLOCK return code is ignored.

See Also   **DdeCreateDataHandle, DdeInitialize, DdePostAdvise**

XTYP_ADVSTOP

XTYP_ADVSTOP

A dynamic data exchange (DDE) server callback function receives the XTYP_ADVSTOP transaction when a client specifies XTYP_ADVSTOP as the *uType* parameter of the **DdeClientTransaction** function. A client uses this transaction to end an advise loop with a server.

Parameters   *uFmt*
Specifies the data format associated with the advise loop being ended.

hconv
Identifies the conversation.

hsz1
Identifies the topic name.

hsz2
Identifies the item name.

hdata
Not used.

dwData1
Not used.

dwData2
Not used.

Comments   This transaction is filtered if the server application specified the CBF_FAIL_ADVISES flag in the **DdeInitialize** function.

See Also   **DdeClientTransaction**, **DdeInitialize**, **DdePostAdvise**

XTYP_ADVSTART

XTYP_ADVSTART

A dynamic data exchange (DDE) server callback function receives the XTYP_ADVSTART transaction when a client specifies XTYP_ADVSTART as the *uType* parameter of the **DdeClientTransaction** function. A client uses this transaction to establish an advise loop with a server.

Parameters   *uFmt*
Specifies the data format requested by the client.

hconv
> Identifies the conversation.

hsz1
> Identifies the topic name.

hsz2
> Identifies the item name.

hdata
> Not used.

dwData1
> Not used.

dwData2
> Not used.

Return Value   A server callback function should return TRUE to allow an advise loop on the specified topic name and item name pair, or FALSE to deny the advise loop. If the callback function returns TRUE, any subsequent calls to the **DdePostAdvise** function by the server on the same topic name and item name pair causes the system to send XTYP_ADVREQ transactions to the server.

Comments   If a client requests an advise loop on a topic, item, and format name set for an advise loop that is already established, the Dynamic Data Exchange Management Library (DDEML) does not create a duplicate advise loop but instead alters the advise loop flags (XTYPF_ACKREQ and XTYPF_NODATA) to match the latest request.

This transaction is filtered if the server application specified the CBF_FAIL_ADVISES flag in the **DdeInitialize** function.

See Also   **DdeClientTransaction**, **DdeInitialize**, **DdePostAdvise**,

---

XTYP_CONNECT

```
XTYP_CONNECT
```

A dynamic data exchange (DDE) server callback function receives the XTYP_CONNECT transaction when a client specifies a service name that the server supports, and a topic name that is not NULL, in a call to the **DdeConnect** function.

Parameters   *uFmt*
> Not used.

hconv
> Not used.

hsz1
> Identifies the topic name.

hsz2
> Identifies the service name.

hdata
> Not used.

dwData1
> Points to a **CONVCONTEXT** data structure that contains context information for the conversation. If the client is not a Dynamic Data Exchange Management Library (DDEML) application, this parameter is set to 0.

dwData2
> Specifies whether the client is the same application instance as the server. If the parameter is 1, the client is the same instance. If the parameter is 0, the client is a different instance.

Return Value   A server callback function should return TRUE to allow the client to establish a conversation on the specified service name and topic name pair, or FALSE to deny the conversation. If the callback function returns TRUE and a conversation is successfully established, the system passes the conversation handle to the server by issuing an XTYP_CONNECT_CONFIRM transaction to the server's callback function (unless the server specified the CBF_SKIP_CONNECT_CONFIRMS flag in the **DdeInitialize** function).

Comments   This transaction is filtered if the server application specified the CBF_FAIL_CONNECTIONS flag in the **DdeInitialize** function.

A server cannot block this transaction type; the CBR_BLOCK return code is ignored.

See Also   **DdeConnect**, **DdeInitialize**

XTYP_CONNECT_CONFIRM

XTYP_CONNECT_CONFIRM

A dynamic data exchange (DDE) server callback function receives the XTYP_CONNECT_CONFIRM transaction to confirm that a conversation has been established with a client and to provide the server with the conversation handle. The system sends this transaction as a result of a previous XTYP_CONNECT or XTYP_WILDCONNECT transaction.

Parameters

uFmt

Not used.

hconv

Identifies the new conversation.

hsz1

Identifies the topic name on which the conversation has been established.

hsz2

Identifies the service name on which the conversation has been established.

hdata

Not used.

dwData1

Not used.

dwData2

Specifies whether the client is the same application instance as the server. If the parameter is 1, the client is the same instance. If the parameter is 0, the client is a different instance.

Comments

This transaction is filtered if the server application specified the CBF_SKIP_CONNECT_CONFIRMS flag in the **DdeInitialize** function.

A server cannot block this transaction type; the CBR_BLOCK return code is ignored.

See Also

DdeConnect, DdeConnectList, DdeInitialize

XTYP_DISCONNECT

XTYP_DISCONNECT

An application's dynamic data exchange (DDE) callback function receives the XTYP_DISCONNECT transaction when the application's partner in a conversation uses the **DdeDisconnect** function to terminate the conversation.

Parameters

uFmt

Not used.

hconv

Identifies that the conversation was terminated.

hsz1

Not used.

hsz2

Not used.

hdata
　　Not used.

dwData1
　　Not used.

dwData2
　　Specifies whether the partners in the conversation are the same application instance. If the parameter is 1, the partners are the same instance. If the parameter is 0, the partners are different instances.

Comments   This transaction is filtered if the application specified the CBF_SKIP_DISCONNECTS flag in the **DdeInitialize** function.

The application can obtain the status of the terminated conversation by calling the **DdeQueryConvInfo** function while processing this transaction. The conversation handle becomes invalid after the callback function returns.

An application cannot block this transaction type; the CBR_BLOCK return code is ignored.

See Also   **DdeDisconnect**, **DdeQueryConvInfo**

XTYP_ERROR

XTYP_ERROR

A dynamic data exchange (DDE) callback function receives the XTYP_ERROR transaction when a critical error occurs.

Parameters   *uFmt*
　　Not used.

hconv
　　Identifies the conversation associated with the error. This parameter is NULL if the error is not associated with a conversation.

hsz1
　　Not used.

hsz2
　　Not used.

hdata
　　Not used.

dwData1
　　Specifies the error code in the low-order word. Currently, only the following error code is supported:

Error Code	Description
DMLERR_LOW_MEMORY	Memory is low—advise, poke, or execute data may be lost, or the system may fail.

dwData2
> Not used.

Comments   An application cannot block this transaction type; the CBR_BLOCK return code is ignored. The DDEML attempts to free memory by removing noncritical resources. An application that has blocked conversations should unblock them.

XTYP_EXECUTE

XTYP_EXECUTE

A dynamic data exchange (DDE) server callback function receives the XTYP_EXECUTE transaction when a client specifies XTYP_EXECUTE as the *uType* parameter of the **DdeClientTransaction** function. A client uses this transaction to send a command string to the server.

Parameters   *uFmt*
> Not used.

hconv
> Identifies the conversation.

hsz1
> Identifies the topic name.

hsz2
> Not used.

hdata
> Identifies the command string.

dwData1
> Not used.

dwData2
> Not used.

Return Value   A server callback function should return DDE_FACK if it processes this transaction, DDE_FBUSY if it is too busy to process this transaction, or DDE_FNOTPROCESSED if it rejects this transaction.

Comments   This transaction is filtered if the server application specified the CBF_FAIL_EXECUTES flag in the **DdeInitialize** function.

An application must free the data handle obtained during this transaction. An application must, however, copy the command string associated with the data handle if the application must process the string after the callback function returns. An application can use the **DdeGetData** function to copy the data.

Because most client applications expect a server application to perform an XTYP_EXECUTE transaction synchonrously, a server should attempt to perform all processing of the XTYP_EXECUTE transaction either from within the DDE callback function or by returning CBR_BLOCK. If the *hdata* parameter is a command that instructs the server to terminate, the server should do so after processing the XTYP_EXECUTE transaction.

See Also   **DdeClientTransaction**, **DdeInitialize**

XTYP_MONITOR

XTYP_MONITOR

The dynamic data exchange (DDE) callback function of a DDE debugging application receives the XTYP_MONITOR transaction whenever a DDE event occurs in the system. To receive this transaction, an application must specify the APPCLASS_MONITOR flag when it calls the **DdeInitialize** function.

Parameters   *uFmt*
    Not used.

hconv
    Not used.

hsz1
    Not used.

hsz2
    Not used.

hdata
    Identifies a DDE object that contains information about the DDE event. The application should use the **DdeAccessData** function to obtain a pointer to the object.

dwData1
    Not used.

dwData2
    Identifies the DDE event. This parameter may be one of the following values:

Value	Meaning
MF_CALLBACKS	The system sent a transaction to a DDE callback function. The DDE object contains a **MONCBSTRUCT** structure that provides information about the transaction.
MF_CONV	A DDE conversation was established or terminated. The DDE object contains a **MONCONVSTRUCT** structure that provides information about the conversation.
MF_ERRORS	A DDE error occurred. The DDE object contains a **MONERRSTRUCT** structure that provides information about the error.
MF_HSZ_INFO	A DDE application created, freed, or incremented the usage count of a string handle; or a string handle was freed as a result of a call to the **DdeUninitialize** function. The DDE object contains a **MONHSZSTRUCT** structure that provides information about the string handle.
MF_LINKS	A DDE application started or stopped an advise loop. The DDE object contains a **MONLINKSTRUCT** structure that provides information about the advise loop.
MF_POSTMSGS	The system or an application posted a DDE message. The DDE object contains a **MONMSGSTRUCT** structure that provides information about the message.
MF_SENDMSGS	The system or an application sent a DDE message. The DDE object contains a **MONMSGSTRUCT** structure that provides information about the message.

Return Value   The callback function should return 0 if it processes this transaction.

See Also   **DdeAccessData, DdeInitialize**

XTYP_POKE

XTYP_POKE

A dynamic data exchange (DDE) server callback function receives the XTYP_POKE transaction when a client specifies XTYP_POKE as the *uType* parameter of the **DdeClientTransaction** function. A client uses this transaction to send unsolicited data to the server.

Parameters   *uFmt*
    Specifies the format of the data sent from the server.

hconv
    Identifies the conversation.

hsz1
> Identifies the topic name.

hsz2
> Identifies the item name.

hdata
> Identifies the data that the client is sending to the server.

dwData1
> Not used.

dwData2
> Not used.

Return Value   A server callback function should return DDE_FACK if it processes this transaction, DDE_FBUSY if it is too busy to process this transaction, or DDE_FNOTPROCESSED if it rejects this transaction.

Comments   This transaction is filtered if the server application specified the CBF_FAIL_POKES flag in the **DdeInitialize** function.

See Also   **DdeClientTransaction**, **DdeInitialize**

XTYP_REGISTER

XTYP_REGISTER

A dynamic data exchange (DDE) callback function receives the XTYP_REGISTER transaction type whenever a Dynamic Data Exchange Library (DDEML) server application uses the **DdeNameService** function to register a service name, or whenever a non-DDEML application that supports the System topic is started.

Parameters   *uFmt*
> Not used.

hconv
> Not used.

hsz1
> Identifies the base service name being registered.

hsz2
> Identifies the instance-specific service name being registered.

hdata
> Not used.

dwData1
  Not used.

dwData2
  Not used.

Comments This transaction is filtered if the application specified the
CBF_SKIP_REGISTRATIONS flag in the **DdeInitialize** function.

A application cannot block this transaction type; the CBR_BLOCK return code is
ignored.

An application should use the *hsz1* parameter to add the service name to the list of
servers available to the user. An application should use the *hsz2* parameter to
identify which application instance has started.

See Also **DdeInitialize**, **DdeNameService**

XTYP_REQUEST

XTYP_REQUEST

A dynamic data exchange (DDE) server callback function receives the
XTYP_REQUEST transaction when a client specifies XTYP_REQUEST as the
uType parameter of the **DdeClientTransaction** function. A client uses this
transaction to request data from a server.

Parameters *uFmt*
  Specifies the format in which the server should submit data to the client.

hconv
  Identifies the conversation.

hsz1
  Identifies the topic name.

hsz2
  Identifies the item name.

hdata
  Not used.

dwData1
  Not used.

dwData2
  Not used.

Return Value The server should call the **DdeCreateDataHandle** function to create a data
handle that identifies the data and then return the handle. The server should return

NULL if it is unable to complete the transaction. If the server returns NULL, the client will receive a DDE_FNOTPROCESSED acknowledgment flag.

Comments

This transaction is filtered if the server application specified the CBF_FAIL_REQUESTS flag in the **DdeInitialize** function.

If responding to this transaction requires lengthy processing, the server can return CBR_BLOCK to suspend future transactions on the current conversation and then process the transaction asynchronously. When the server has finished and the data is ready to pass to the client, the server can call the **DdeEnableCallback** function to resume the conversation.

See Also

DdeClientTransaction, **DdeCreateDataHandle**, **DdeEnableCallback**, **DdeInitialize**

XTYP_UNREGISTER

XTYP_UNREGISTER

A dynamic data exchange (DDE) callback function receives the XTYP_UNREGISTER transaction whenever a Dynamic Data Exchange Management Library (DDEML) server application uses the **DdeNameService** function to unregister a service name, or whenever a non-DDEML application that supports the System topic is terminated.

Parameters

uFmt
Not used.

hconv
Not used.

hsz1
Identifies the base service name being unregistered.

hsz2
Identifies the instance-specific service name being unregistered.

hdata
Not used.

dwData1
Not used.

dwData2
Not used.

Comments

This transaction is filtered if the application specified the CBF_SKIP_REGISTRATIONS flag in the **DdeInitialize** function.

A application cannot block this transaction type; the CBR_BLOCK return code is ignored.

An application should use the *hsz1* parameter to remove the service name from the list of servers available to the user. An application should use the *hsz2* parameter to identify which application instance has terminated.

See Also   **DdeInitialize**, **DdeNameService**

XTYP_WILDCONNECT

XTYP_WILDCONNECT

A dynamic data exchange (DDE) server callback function receives the XTYP_WILDCONNECT transaction when a client specifies a NULL service name, a NULL topic name, or both, in a call to the **DdeConnect** or **DdeWildConnect** function. This transaction allows a client to establish a conversation on each of the server's service name and topic name pairs that match the specified service and topic name.

Parameters   *uFmt*
    Not used.

hconv
    Not used.

hsz1
    Identifies the topic name. If this parameter is NULL, the client is requesting a conversation on all topic names that the server supports.

hsz2
    Identifies the service name. If this parameter is NULL, the client is requesting a conversation on all service names that the server supports.

hdata
    Not used.

dwData1
    Points to a **CONVCONTEXT** data structure that contains context information for the conversation. If the client is not a Dynamic Data Exchange Management Library (DDEML) application, this parameter is set to 0.

dwData2
    Specifies whether the client is the same application instance as the server. If the parameter is 1, the client is same instance. If the parameter is 0, the client is a different instance.

Return Value   The server should return a data handle that identifies an array of **HSZPAIR** structures. The array should contain one structure for each service name and topic name pair that matches the service name and topic name pair requested by the client. The array must be terminated by a NULL string handle. The system sends the XTYP_CONNECT_CONFIRM transaction to the server to confirm each conversation and to pass the conversation handles to the server. The server will not receive these confirmations if it specified the CBF_SKIP_CONNECT_CONFIRMS flag in the **DdeInitialize** function.

The server should return NULL to refuse the XTYP_WILDCONNECT transaction.

Comments   This transaction is filtered if the server application specified the CBF_FAIL_CONNECTIONS flag in the **DdeInitialize** function.

A server cannot block this transaction type; the CBR_BLOCK return code is ignored.

See Also   **DdeConnect, DdeInitialize**

XTYP_XACT_COMPLETE

XTYP_XACT_COMPLETE

A dynamic data exchange (DDE) client callback function receives the XTYP_XACT_COMPLETE transaction when an asynchronous transaction, initiated by a call to the **DdeClientTransaction** function, has completed.

Parameters   *uFmt*

Specifies the format of the data associated with the completed transaction (if applicable), or NULL if no data was exchanged during the transaction.

hconv

Identifies the conversation.

hsz1

Identifies the topic name involved in the completed transaction.

hsz2

Identifies the item name involved in the completed transaction.

hdata

Identifies the data involved in the completed transaction, if applicable. If the transaction was successful but involved no data, this parameter will be TRUE. This parameter will be NULL if the transaction was unsuccessful.

dwData1
　　Contains the transaction identifier of the completed transaction.

dwData2
　　Contains any applicable DDE_ status flags in the low word. This provides
　　support for applications dependent on DDE_APPSTATUS bits. It is
　　recommended that applications no longer use these bits—future versions of
　　the Dynamic Data Exchange Management Library (DDEML) may not support
　　them.

Comments　　An application must not free the data handle obtained during this transaction. An
application must, however, copy the data associated with the data handle if the
application must process the data after the callback function returns. An
application can use the **DdeGetData** function to copy the data.

See Also　　**DdeClientTransaction**

Solid Programming Advice

Code Complete
Steve McConnell

This practical handbook of software construction covers the art and science of construction. Examples are provided in C, Pascal, Basic, Fortran, and Ada—but the focus is on programming techniques. Topics include planning up front, applying good design techniques to construction, using data effectively, reviewing for errors, managing construction activities, and relating personal character to superior software.

880 pages, softcover $35.00 ($44.95 Canada)   ISBN 1-55615-484-4

Microsoft® Visual C++™ Run-Time Library Reference
Microsoft Corporation

This official run-time library reference provides detailed information on more than 550 ready-to-use functions and macros designed for use in C and C++ programs and is an up-to-date complement to the Visual C++ online reference. The book provides a superb introduction to using the run-time library and to the library's variables and types. It also covers the important details for each function in the run-time library: syntax, meaning of each argument, include files, return value, cross-references to related functions, and compatibility notes. Covers version 1.0 of the Standard and Professional Editions of Visual C++.

704 pages, softcover $35.00 ($44.95 Canada)   ISBN 1-55615-559-X

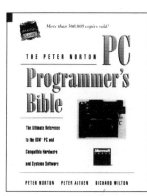

The Peter Norton PC Programmer's Bible
Peter Norton, Peter Aitken, and Richard Wilton
"Admirably explains the inner workings with no loss of detail."
Computer Book Review

This is *the* ultimate reference to the IBM PC and compatible hardware and systems software. This new edition of *The Peter Norton Programmer's Guide to the IBM PC & PS/2* is packed with unmatched, authoritative programming advice, solid technical data, and key information. This book is designed to teach programmers the fundamental concepts of PC hardware, MS-DOS system calls (current through version 6.0), essential ROM BIOS services, and graphical programming with Windows, Windows NT, and OS/2.

608 pages, softcover $29.95 ($39.95 Canada)   ISBN 1-55615-555-7

In-depth References

The Windows™ Interface: An Application Design Guide
Microsoft Corporation

The Microsoft guidelines for creating well-designed, visually and functionally consistent user interfaces—an essential reference for all programmers and designers working in Windows. Software includes a Visual Design Guide, an Interactive Style Guide, and Cursors and Buttons.

248 pages, softcover with two 1.44-MB 3.5" disks
$39.95 ($54.95 Canada)   ISBN 1-55615-439-9

The Microsoft® Windows™ 3.1 Developer's Workshop
Dr. John Butler, Bob Chiverton, John Clark Craig,
William S. Hall, Ray Patch, and Alok Sinha

This is a winning collection of articles on significant Windows 3.1 programming issues—from the best programming minds in the business. The book covers internationalizing software for Windows ■ programming Windows for Pen Computing ■ the GDI device transform ■ NetBIOS programming ■ developing virtual device drivers ■ Visual Basic as a professional tool. The accompanying disk contains all the source code and executable (EXE) files in the book.

350 pages, with one 1.44-MB 3.5" disk
$34.95 ($47.95 Canada)   ISBN 1-55615-480-1

Object Linking and Embedding Programmer's Reference
Microsoft Corporation

Object Linking and Embedding (OLE) is a powerful way to extend the functionality of your applications. This *Programmer's Reference*, critical to programmers in developing Windows-based applications, is both a tutorial and the application programming interface reference for OLE. The first half of the book lays the foundation for programming with OLE, describing the creation of OLE client and server applications. The second half offers a comprehensive and detailed reference to such topics as callback functions and data structures, DLL functions, the registration database, and error codes.

448 pages $27.95 ($37.95 Canada)   ISBN 1-55615-539-5

Register Today!

Return the
Microsoft® Win32™ Progammer's Reference
registration card for:

✔ a Microsoft Press catalog

✔ exclusive offers on specially
   priced books

Please mail the competed form to:
Microsoft Press Registration
Win32 References
P.O. Box 3019
Bothell, WA 98041-9910

or by fax to:
Microsoft Press
Attn: Marketing Dept.
Fax # 206-936-7329

Microsoft® Win32™ Programmer's References

This is the official documentation for the Microsoft Win32 Software Development Kit (SDK).
It's the resource material that you'll need to turn to during the design and development of a
Win32-based application. The *Programmer's References* contain overview material on systems, services,
Window management, and the Graphics Device Interface, as well as the alphabetical Application
Programming Interface (API) references and information about messages, structures, and data types.

Microsoft® Win32™ Programmer's Reference, Vol. 1
Window Management and Graphics Device Interface
836 pages, softcover $20.00 ($26.95 Canada) ISBN 1-55615-515-8

Microsoft® Win32™ Programmer's Reference, Vol. 2
System Services, Multimedia, Extensions, and Application Notes
960 pages, softcover $20.00 ($26.95 Canada) ISBN 1-55615-516-6

Microsoft® Win32™ Programmer's Reference, Vol. 3
Functions (A-G)
1000 pages, softcover $20.00 ($26.95 Canada) ISBN 1-55615-517-4

Microsoft® Win32™ Programmer's Reference, Vol. 4
Functions (H-Z)
1000 pages, softcover $20.00 ($26.95 Canada) ISBN 1-55615-518-2

Microsoft® Win32™ Programmer's Reference, Vol. 5
Messages, Structures, and Macros
704 pages, softcover $20.00 ($26.95 Canada) ISBN 1-55615-519-0